Lonely Planet

D0173647

EUROPE

TOP SIGHTS, AUTHENTIC EXPERIENCES

Alexis Averbuck, Anthony Ham, Catherine Le Nevez,
Andy Symington, Nicola Williams
Mark Baker, Oliver Berry, Cristian Bonetto, Kerry
Christiani, Belinda Dixon, Peter Dragicevich, Steve
Fallon, Emilie Filou, Damian Harper, Virginia Maxwell,
Christopher Pitts, Kevin Raub, Brendan Sainsbury,
Andrea Schulte-Peevers, Neil Wilson

Contents

Park Güell (p201), Barcelona
VLADITTO / SHUTTERSTOCK ©

Plan Your Trip
Europe's Top 27

London, Great Britain

Truly one of the world's greatest cities

London (p49) is mercurial and endlessly fascinating; you could spend a lifetime getting to know it, then realise it's gone and changed again. Stretching back from the mighty River Thames, its lush parks and historic districts are crammed with extraordinary sights: royal palaces, towering cathedrals and remarkable museums and galleries. Add the pick of the world's theatres, restaurants, sports venues and shops, and you'll be very reluctant to leave. From left: Tower Bridge (p70); afternoon tea

1

Venice, Italy

Magical city seemingly floating on water

A sunny winter's day, with far fewer tourists around, is the perfect time to lap up Venice's unique and magical atmosphere (p379). Ditch your map and wander the shadowy back lanes of Dorsoduro while imagining secret assignations and whispered conspiracies at every turn. Then visit two of Venice's top galleries, the Gallerie dell'Accademia and the Peggy Guggenheim Collection, which houses works by many of the giants of 20th-century art. From top: Palazzo Ducale (p386); Rio Marin Canal

LAPAS7 · SHUTTERSTOCK ©

Paris, France

Up close with an architectural icon

Designed as a temporary exhibit for the 1889 Exposition Universelle (World Fair), Paris' elegant art nouveau Eiffel Tower (pictured, p252) has become the defining fixture of the skyline. Its recent 1st-floor refit adds two glitzy glass pavilions housing interactive exhibits; outside, peer d-o-w-n through the glass floor to the ground below. Visit at dusk for the best day and night views of the City of Light (p249) and make a toast at the sparkling champagne bar.

Rome, Italy

Classical ruins mixed with contemporary style

From the crumbling Colosseum to the ancient Forum (pictured, p346) and the Appian Way, few sights are more evocative than the ruins of ancient Rome (p327). Two thousand years ago this city was the centre of the greatest empire of the ancient world, where gladiators battled and emperors lived in unimaginable luxury. Nowadays it's a haunting spot: as you walk the cobbled paths, you can almost sense the ghosts in the air.

Berlin, Germany

Catch the ever-changing zeitgeist

More than 25 years since the fall of the Berlin Wall, it's hard to believe that this most cosmopolitan of cities (p431) once marked the frontier of the Cold War. But reminders of Berlin's divided past still remain: whether you're passing the Brandenburg Gate, gazing at graffiti at the East Side Gallery (pictured, p435) or soaking up the history at Checkpoint Charlie, it's an essential part of understanding what makes Germany's capital.

Dubrovnik, Croatia

Spectacular walled city

Dubrovnik's main claim to fame are its historic ramparts, considered among the finest in the world, which surround luminous marble streets and finely ornamented buildings (p481). Built between the 13th and 16th centuries, the walls are still remarkably intact today, and the vistas over the terracotta rooftops and the Adriatic Sea are sublime, especially at dusk, when the fading light makes the hues dramatic and the panoramas unforgettable.

ALEKSANDARGEORGIEV / GETTY IMAGES ©

Prague, Czech Republic

An architectural central European jewel

The capital of the Czech Republic is one of Europe's most alluring and dynamic places (p535). For all its modern verve, some parts of the city have hardly changed since medieval times – cobbled cul-de-sacs twist through the Old Town, framed by teetering townhouses, baroque buildings and graceful bridges. And if castles are your thing, Prague Castle is an absolute beauty: a 1000-year-old fortress covering around 7 hectares – the world's largest.

Above: Church of Our Lady Before Týn (p548) looming over Old Town Square (p545)

7

Vienna, Austria

Grand heart of a former empire

The monumentally graceful Hofburg whisks you back to the age of empires in Vienna (p577) as you marvel at the treasury's imperial crowns, the equine ballet of the Spanish Riding School and the chandelier-lit apartments fit for Empress Elisabeth. The palace, a legacy of the 640-year Habsburg era, is rivalled in grandeur only by the 1441-room Schloss Schönbrunn, a Unesco World Heritage Site, and the baroque Schloss Belvedere (pictured, p590), both set in exquisite gardens.

UHRYN ARYSA / SHUTTERSTOCK ©

ELENA ELIACHEVITCH /
GETTY IMAGES ©

9

Amsterdam, Netherlands

World Heritage–listed canals and gabled buildings

To say Amsterdammers (p307) love the water is an understatement. Stroll next to the canals and check out some of the thousands of houseboats (pictured left). Or better still, go for a ride. From boat level you'll see a whole new set of architectural details, such as the ornamentation bedecking the bridges. And when you pass the canalside cafe terraces, mark the location for a later return.

Budapest, Hungary

Beautiful Hungarian capital straddling the Danube

Along both sides of the romantic Danube River, with the Buda Hills to the west and the start of the Great Plain to the east, Budapest (p559) is perhaps the most beautiful city in Eastern Europe. Parks brim with attractions, the architecture is second to none, museums are filled with treasures, pleasure boats sail up and down the scenic Danube Bend, Turkish-era thermal baths belch steam and its nightlife throbs till dawn most nights. Clockwise from top: Royal Palace (p562); Parliament (p570); Gellért Baths (p565)

ORBON ALIJA / GETTY IMAGES ©

Barcelona, Spain

The genius of a visionary architect

Barcelona (p181) is famous for its Modernista architecture, much of which was designed by Antoni Gaudí. His masterwork is the mighty cathedral La Sagrada Família (pictured, p184), which remains a work in progress close to a century after its creator's death. It's a bizarre combination of crazy and classic: Gothic touches intersect with eccentric experiments and improbable angles. No one is entirely sure when it will be finished, but even half completed it's a modern-day wonder.

STARCEVIC / GETTY IMAGES ©

Lisbon, Portugal

Soulful city armed with Gothic grit

Alfama, with its labyrinthine alleyways, hidden courtyards and curving, shadow-filled lanes, is a magical place to lose all sense of direction and delve into Lisbon's soul (p229). On the journey, you'll pass breadbox-sized grocers, brilliantly tiled buildings and views of steeply pitched rooftops leading down to the glittering Tejo. Pause at cosy taverns filled with easygoing chatter, with the scent of chargrilled sardines and the mournful rhythms of fado drifting in the breeze. Above: A Lisbon tram (p234)

SUSANNE POMMER / SHUTTERSTOCK ®

Scottish Highlands

Scenic grandeur and echoes of the past

Breathtaking views abound in the Highlands (p91). From the regal charm of Royal Deeside, via the brooding majesty of Glen Coe, to the mysterious waters of sweeping Loch Ness, these are landscapes that inspire awe. The region is scattered with fairy-tale castles and the hiking is suitably glorious. Add the nooks of warm Highland hospitality found in classic rural pubs and romantic hotels, and you have an unforgettable corner of the country. Above: Urquhart Castle (p98)

RODRIGO GARRIDO / SHUTTERSTOCK ®

Dublin, Ireland

Pints of Guinness and literary connections

Whether you're wandering around the leafy Georgian terraces of St Stephen's Green or getting acquainted with the past at Kilmainham Gaol (pictured, p117), in Dublin (p109) you're never far from a literary or historic sight. And then there are the city's pubs: there are few better places to down a pint than Dublin, and you can even make a pilgrimage to the original Guinness brewery on the city's outskirts. Either way, you'll surely make a few Irish friends along the way.

CATARI▄ BELOVA / SHUTTERSTOCK ®

KARL ALLGAEUER / SHUTTERSTOCK ®

Florence & Tuscany, Italy

LEFT: PETER ZELEI IMAGES / GETTY IMAGES ®

Italy's most romanticised region

The gently rolling hills of Tuscany (p397), bathed in golden light and dotted with vineyards, sum up Italy's attractions in a nutshell. Here picture-perfect hilltop towns vie with magnificent scenery and some of Italy's best food and wine. And there's Florence, home to what Unesco describes as 'the greatest concentration of universally renowned works of art in the world'. It's a city packed with blockbuster museums, elegant churches and flawless Renaissance streetscapes. Clockwise from top: Duomo (p400); Tuscan salami; a Tuscan vineyard

EDELLA / GETTY IMAGES ©

Ruins of Pompeii, Italy

Ancient city destroyed and preserved by Vesuvius

Frozen in its death throes, the sprawling, time-warped ruins of Pompeii (p370) hurtle you 2000 years into the past. Wander through chariot-grooved Roman streets, lavishly frescoed villas and bathhouses, food stores and markets, theatres and even an ancient brothel. Then, in the eerie stillness, with your eye on ominous Mt Vesuvius, ponder the town's final hours when the skies grew dark and heavy with volcanic ashes.

LUCVI / SHUTTERSTOCK ©

Andalucía, Spain

Vibrant cities studded with glorious architecture

Andalucía (p213), ancient al-Andalus, is awash with glorious architecture that dates back to the eight centuries of Moorish rule that ended in 1492. Granada, Córdoba and Seville are the high points of a journey of extraordinary riches. In Granada, the palace complex of the Alhambra, in particular, is close to perfection, and perhaps the most refined example of Islamic art anywhere in the world. Put simply, this is Spain's most beautiful monument. Above: The skyline of Seville (p224) as seen from the top of the Space Metropol Parasol. Architect: Jürgen Mayer

BRIAN PUDSLEY / SHUTTERSTOCK ©

Reykjavík, Iceland

The world's most northerly capital

Most Icelanders live in Reykjavík (p163) and even on the shortest visit you'll be struck by how quirky and creative the population is. Despite being on the northern margin of Europe, the locals have crafted a town packed with captivating art, rich cuisine and an epic music scene. Learn about a history stretching back to the Vikings and use the city as a base for trips to Iceland's amazing natural wonders. Above: Harpa (p172), designed by Henning Larsen Architects and Olafur Eliasson

ALEXDRIM / SHUTTERSTOCK ©

Copenhagen, Denmark

Coolest kid on the Nordic block

Scandivania is all about paired-back contemporary style – something that the Danish capital (p129) has in spades. Home to a thriving design scene, Copenhagen sports Michelin-starred restaurants, hipster cafes and bars, and swoon-worthy boutiques around every corner. Add in top-class museums and galleries and a thousand-year-old harbour town area with handsome historic architecture and you have the perfect Scandi city. Above: Nyhavn (p136)

VENTDUSUD / SHUTTERSTOCK ©

Provence, France

Gallic charm in the south of France

For many people, the pastoral landscapes of Provence (p289) are a French fantasy come true. Provence seems to sum up everything enviable about the French lifestyle: fantastic food, hilltop villages, legendary wines, bustling markets and a balmy climate. For decades, it's been a hot spot for holidaymakers and second-homers, inspired by the vision of the rustic good life in Peter Mayle's classic 1989 travelogue, *A Year in Provence*. Above: A lavender field in Provence

JANOKA82 / GETTY IMAGES ©

Swiss Alps, Switzerland

Hike, ski and admire these postcard-perfect peaks

The stirring ramparts of the Swiss Alps (p467) grace chocolate-bar wrappers and evoke stereotypical Heidi scenes, but nothing prepares you for their allure up close. Its most famous summit, the Matterhorn (pictured, p470), is a mesmerising peak that looms above the timber-chalet-filled Swiss village of Zermatt. Gaze at it from a tranquil cafe, hike in its shadow along the tangle of alpine paths above town, with cowbells clinking in the distance, or pause on a ski slope and admire its craggy, chiselled outline.

İstanbul, Turkey

Where Europe meets Asia and the Middle East

Serving stints as the capital of the Byzantine and Ottoman Empires and an ancient crossroads of civilisations, İstanbul (p517) is one of the world's great cities. The historical highlights cluster in Sultanahmet – the Aya Sofya (pictured, p520), Blue Mosque, Topkapı Palace and Grand Bazaar.

LEFT: MATTEO COLOMBO / GETTY IMAGES ©

Athens, Greece

Monument-strewn capital of Ancient Greece

Greece has ancient monuments at seemingly every turn, but it's in Athens (p497) where the greatest and most iconic still stand. High on a rocky outcrop overlooking the city, the Acropolis (pictured left, p500) epitomises the glory of ancient Greece with its graceful Parthenon and 17,000-seat Theatre of Dionysos (pictured right, p503). Other impressive ruins littering this vibrant city include the Temple of Olympian Zeus and two *agoras* (marketplaces; one Greek, one Roman) mingling with first-rate museums.

YURY DMITRIENKO / SHUTTERSTOCK ©

Schloss Neuschwanstein, Germany

Fairy-tale castle in a fairy-tale setting

Rising from Alpine foothills in the heart of Bavaria, the 19th-century Schloss Neuschwanstein (p462) seems to spring from a child's imagination of the perfect castle. Its pencil-thin turrets, vertiginous walls and glorious setting make it one of Europe's most recognisable structures, the prototype for many a Disney castle.

ANASTASIOS71 / SHUTTERSTOCK ©

CHANTAL / GETTY IMAGES ©

Greek Islands, Greece

Whitewashed Mediterranean villages above a turquoise sea

Wherever you land, the Greek Islands (p512) grab your attention and don't let go. Take Santorini, where the submerged caldera, surrounded by lava-layered cliffs topped by villages of white and blue, is one of nature's great wonders, best experienced by a walk along the clifftops from the main town of Fira to the northern village of Oia. The precariousness and impermanence of the place is breathtaking. Sunsets are epic. From left: Mykonos (p515); Oia (p514)

Ring of Kerry, Ireland

Wild and medieval Irish road trip

There's nowhere quite like Ireland, and the Ring of Kerry (p126), a 179km route through the Iveragh Peninsula, captures all the essential elements of Irish charm on one memorable circuit. Wild and craggy landscapes frame isolated beaches, evocative ruined fortresses stand sentinel over similarly wild Atlantic seas, and windswept mountains watch over villages and islands that could be nowhere else on earth but here.

Oslo, Norway

Scandinavia's gateway to the fjords

Norway's capital may lack the historic architectural grandeur of other Scandi cities, but Oslo (p145) is doing everything it can to claim the prize of Europe's capital of contemporary style. The Opera House evokes an iceberg in a fjord, public art is a national pastime, and the city's extraordinary museums span the Viking age to modern Norway. So impressive are the results, that Oslo has become so much more than a mere stopover on the road to the fjords. Oslo Opera House (p148). Architects: Snøhetta

Plan Your Trip
Need to Know

When to Go

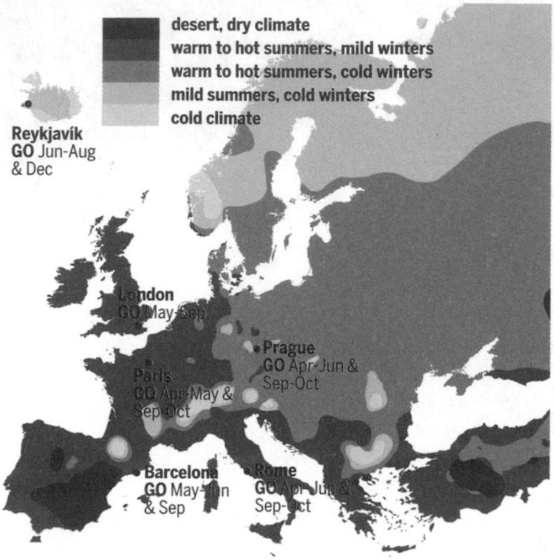

desert, dry climate
warm to hot summers, mild winters
warm to hot summers, cold winters
mild summers, cold winters
cold climate

Reykjavík
GO Jun–Aug
& Dec

London
GO May–Sep

Prague
GO Apr–Jun &
Sep–Oct

Paris
GO Apr–May &
Sep–Oct

Barcelona
GO May–Jun
& Sep

Rome
GO Apr–Jun &
Sep–Oct

High Season (Jun–Aug)

○ Everyone comes to Europe and all of Europe hits the road.

○ Hotel prices and temperatures are at their highest.

○ Expect all the major attractions to be nightmarishly busy.

Shoulder (Apr–May & Sep–Oct)

○ Crowds and prices drop, except in still-busy Italy.

○ Temperatures are comfortable but it can be hot in southern Europe.

○ Overall these are the best months to travel in Europe.

Low Season (Nov–Mar)

○ Outside ski resorts, hotels drop their prices or close down.

○ The weather can be cold and days short, especially in northern Europe.

○ Some places, such as resort towns, are like ghost towns.

Currency

Euro (€), pound (£), Croatian Kuna (KN), Czech crown (Koruna česká; Kč), Danish krone (Dkr), Hungarian Forint (Ft), Icelandic króna (kr), Norwegian krone (kr), Swiss franc (Sfr), Türk Lirası (Turkish lira; ₺)

Languages

Croatian, Czech, Danish, Dutch, English, French, German, Greek, Hungarian, Icelandic, Italian, Norwegian, Portuguese, Spanish, Turkish

Visas

EU citizens don't need visas for other EU countries. Australians, Canadians, New Zealanders and Americans don't need visas for visits of fewer than 90 days.

Money

ATMs are common; credit and debit cards are widely accepted.

Mobile Phones

If your mobile phone is European, it's often perfectly feasible to use it on roaming throughout the continent. If you're coming from outside Europe, it's usually worth buying a prepaid local SIM in one European country.

Useful Websites

The Man in Seat Sixty-One (www.seat61. com) Encyclopedic site dedicated to train travel plus plenty of other tips.

Hidden Europe (www.hiddeneurope.co.uk) Fascinating magazine and online dispatches from all the continent's corners.

Couchsurfing (www.couchsurfing.org) Find a free bed and make friends in any European country.

VisitEurope (www.visiteurope.com) With information about travel in 33 member countries.

Spotted by Locals (www.spottedbylocals. com) Insider tips for cities across Europe.

Lonely Planet (www.lonelyplanet.com/ europe) Destination information, hotel bookings, traveller forum and more.

Where to Stay

Europe offers the fullest possible range of accommodation for all budgets. Book up to two months in advance for a July visit or for ski resorts over Christmas and New Year.

Hotels Range from the local pub to restored castles.

B&Bs Small, family-run houses generally provide good value.

Hostels Enormous variety from backpacker palaces to real dumps.

Homestays and farmstays A great way to really find out how locals live.

Arriving in Europe

Schiphol Airport (Amsterdam) Trains to the centre (20 minutes).

Heathrow Airport (London) Trains (15 minutes) and tube (one hour) to the centre.

Aéroport de Charles de Gaulle (Paris) Many buses (one hour) and trains (30 minutes) to the centre.

Frankfurt Airport Trains (15 minutes) to the centre.

Leonardo da Vinci Airport (Rome) Buses (one hour) and trains (30 minutes) to the centre.

Barajas Airport (Madrid) Buses (40 minutes) and metro (15 minutes) to the centre.

Getting Around

In most European countries, the train is the best option for internal transport.

Train Europe's train network is fast and efficient but rarely a bargain unless you book well in advance or use a rail pass wisely.

Bus Usually taken for short trips in remoter areas, though long-distance intercity buses can be cheap.

Car You can hire a car or drive your own through Europe. Roads are excellent but petrol is expensive.

Ferry Boats connect Britain and Ireland with mainland Europe; Scandinavia to the Baltic countries and Germany; and Italy to the Balkans and Greece.

Air Speed things up by flying from one end of the continent to the other.

Bicycle Slow things down on a two-wheeler; a great way to get around just about anywhere.

For more on **getting around**, see p630 ➡

Plan Your Trip
Daily Costs

London, United Kingdom

Budget: Less than £85 (€95)

Dorm bed; market-stall lunch or supermarket sandwich; free museum entry; standby theatre tickets; daily bicycle hire

Midrange: £85–200 (€95–223)

Double room; two-course dinner with wine; temporary exhibitions; standard theatre tickets

Top end: More than £200 (€223)

Four-star or boutique hotel room; three-course dinner with wine in top restaurant; black-cab trip; top theatre tickets

Reykjavík, Iceland

Budget: Less than 25,000kr (€180)

Dorm bed or camping; grill-bar grub or soup lunch; museum entry; Golden Circle bus pass

Midrange: 25,000–41,000kr (€180–300)

Guesthouse double room; cafe meal; pool entry; small-vehicle rental

Top end: More than 41,000kr (€300)

Boutique double room; meal in top restaurant; spa day pass; 4WD rental

Barcelona, Spain

Budget: Less than €60

Dorm bed; set lunch; hourly bicycle hire

Midrange: €60–200

Standard double room; two-course dinner with wine; walking and guided tours

Top end: More than €200

Double room in boutique or luxury hotel; three-course meal at top restaurant; concert tickets

Reykjavík ICELAND

NORTHERN IRELAND

IRELAND

WALES

ENGLAND

North Sea

DENMARK

NETHERLANDS

London

BELGIUM

English Channel

NORTH ATLANTIC OCEAN

Bay of Biscay

FRANCE

SWITZERLAND

PORTUGAL

SPAIN

Barcelona

Mediterranean Sea

Budapest, Hungary

Budget: Less than 15,000Ft (€45)

Dorm bed; meal at self-service restaurant; three-day transport pass

Midrange: 15,000–35,000Ft (€45–110)

Single/double private room; two-course meal with drink; cocktails

Top end: More than 35,000Ft (€110)

Double room in superior hotel; dinner for two with wine at good restaurant; all-inclusive spa ticket

Rome, Italy

Budget: Less than €110

Dorm bed or double room in budget hotel; pizza and beer

Midrange: €110–250

Double room in hotel; local restaurant meal; admission to Vatican Museums; Roma Pass (72-hour card covering museum entry and public transport)

Top end: More than €250

Double room in a four- or five-star hotel; top restaurant dinner; opera/concert ticket; taxi ride

Athens, Greece

Budget: Less than €130

Dorm bed or double room in pension house; souvlaki or pitta; ouzo with snack; museum/site entry; 90-minute transit tickets

Midrange: €130–250

Double room in midrange hotel; traditional taverna meal; cocktails; taxi across town

Top end: More than €250

Double room in top hotel; trendy restaurant meal; Acropolis tour guide

RUSSIA

SWEDEN

BELARUS

POLAND

GERMANY

UKRAINE

CZECH
REPUBLIC   SLOVAKIA

MOLDOVA

Budapest ◉

AUSTRIA

HUNGARY

SLOVENIA   ROMANIA

CROATIA

SERBIA

BOSNIA
HERZEGOVINA   BULGARIA

ITALY   MONTENEGRO   KOSOVO

NORTH
MACEDONIA

◉
Rome   ALBANIA

GREECE   *Aegean
Sea*

Athens ◉

Plan Your Trip
Hotspots for...

NOPPASIN WONGCHUM / SHUTTERSTOCK ©

History

Europe's epic history is writ large across the continent with headline sights that bring it vividly to life – from majestic ruins to grand palaces and parliaments.

Rome
History reverberates all over the Eternal City, from the Colosseum to the Vatican.

Birth of an Empire
Romulus supposedly founded Rome in Palatino (p352).

London
Indomitable London has seen it all, from the Romans and the Great Fire to the Blitz and the Swinging Sixties.

Royal History
Monarchs were crowned in Westminster Abbey (p52).

Berlin
Reminders of the German capital's glorious and troubled past await you around every corner.

WWII Icon
Brandenburger Tor (p444) is a symbol of Cold War division.

CGE2010 / SHUTTERSTOCK ©

The Great Outdoors

From magnificent mountains and rolling hills covered in flowers and vines to sandy-beach coasts with vistas of charming islands, Europe's landscapes are a visual treat.

Switzerland
Switzerland's majestic landscapes soaring to the heights of the Alps will make your knees go weak.

Alpine Vistas
Marvel at the iconic Matterhorn (p470) from Zermatt.

Dubrovnik
An ancient walled town overlooks sapphire waters speckled with countless forested islands.

Coastal Enclaves
Admire the Adriatic from the walls of Dubrovnik (p484).

Scottish Highlands
Big skies, sweeping landscapes, mysterious lochs (lakes) and spectacular wildlife.

Big Skies
The Highlands' city Inverness (p100) is on River Ness.

Arts & Architecture

World-class museums and galleries, thriving theatres and concert halls, ancient castles and ornate public buildings: Europe's cultural treasures are guaranteed to excite and delight.

EVGENII IAROSHEVSKII / SHUTTERSTOCK ©

Florence
Florence is home to a magnificent array of Renaissance art and architecture.

Renaissance Treasures
Swoon over the art at Galleria degli Uffizi (p412).

Vienna
Grand imperial palaces, revered opera houses and superb art museums can be found in Vienna.

Empire of Art
Kunsthistorisches Museum (p582) brims with treasures.

Amsterdam
Ground zero for European art during the Golden Age, fostering the likes of Rembrandt and Vermeer.

Golden Age
Rijksmuseum (p314) is the city's premier art trove.

Food & Drink

Europe's culinary diversity and quality is almost unrivalled; whether you like Michelin-starred restaurants or casual cafes, you'll be treated to delicious local produce.

BONCHAN / GETTY IMAGES ©

Paris
Food is not fuel here – it's a religion and the reason you get up in the morning.

Artistic Food
Enjoy art-like masterpieces at Bouillon Racine (p282).

Barcelona
This Catalan city has a celebrated food scene fuelled by world-class chefs and imaginative recipes.

Avant Garde
Expect the unexpected at Disfrutar (p209).

Copenhagen
One of the hottest culinary destinations, with more Michelin stars than any other Scandinavian city.

New Nordic
Geranium (p141) transforms local ingredients into art.

Plan Your Trip
Essential Europe

Activities

Europe is just one big playground for lovers of the great outdoors. Hiking and biking trails criss-cross mountains, hills, fields, forests and coastlines. Among the huge range of activities you can take part in are fishing, horse riding, skiing, climbing, kayaking and sailing. And if outdoor pursuits are not your thing, then Europe's urban centres are well set up for those interested in learning to cook a local dish, learn a new language or follow a guided specialist tour.

Shopping

You've no doubt heard about the European Union's 'single market'. The reality is infinitely better: a multiplicity of markets and other varied retail options are to be found from the highlands of Scotland to the streets of Lisbon. Be it in the grand department stores and fashion houses of Paris, London and Rome, the craft stalls

and artist ateliers of Venice or Prague or farmers' markets everywhere, there are a million and one ways to find that perfect souvenir to bring home.

Entertainment

When it comes to mass entertainment, Europe practically wrote the book. Rome's Colosseum may no longer be a functioning arena, but there are countless other giant stadiums and storied venues across the continent. The sheer range of performing arts is impressive, spanning classical music to grunge rock, Shakespeare to contemporary dance. Europeans also love their sporting events, with soccer being a major preoccupation.

Eating

Europe's delicious cuisine reflects the multitude of different countries and regions spread across the continent. The Mediterranean diet is listed as an

GOSKOVA TATIANA / SHUTTERSTOCK ©

'Intangible Cultural Heritage' by Unesco and has a number of variants, including Italian, Spanish and Greek. French food is practically a religion. Nordic food is the trendy new upstart of the culinary world. The UK excels in cosmopolitan Asian flavours and has invented its own brand of spicy Anglo-Indian cuisine. Wherever you go in Europe, eating is not just a pleasure, but a valuable insight into the local history and culture.

Drinking & Nightlife

Whatever your tipple or taste in nightlife, Europe is sure to deliver. Whether you're pounding the streets of Reykjavík, Paris or Barcelona, you're sure to find pumping dance clubs with cutting edge DJs and designer cocktail bars, as well as cosy pubs and third-wave coffee shops. Slip into a local pub in Scotland to sample Highland whiskies, or a bar in Prague to sip on craft beers. And let's not even start

★ Best Restaurants

Dinner by Heston Blumenthal (p86)
Bouillon Racine (p282)
Cafe Jacques (p454)
Disfrutar (p209)
Bonci Pizzarium (p363)

on the wonderful wines of France, Spain and Italy – vineyard visits could keep you occupied the whole trip.

From left: Covent Garden, London (p49); Spanish tapas

Plan Your Trip
Month by Month

RANIERI PIEPER / SHUTTERSTOCK ©

February

Carnival, in all its manic glory, sweeps the Catholic regions. Cold temperatures are forgotten amid masquerades, street festivals and general bacchanalia.

✿ Carnevale, Italy

In the period before Ash Wednesday, Venice goes mad for masks (www.venice-carnival-italy.com). Costume balls, many with traditions centuries old, enliven the social calendar in this storied old city.

March

Spring arrives in southern Europe. It's colder further north, though days are often bright.

✿ St Patrick's Day, Ireland

Parades and celebrations with friends and family are held on 17 March across Ireland to honour the country's beloved patron saint.

☆ Budapest Spring Festival, Hungary

This two-week festival in March/April is one of Europe's top classical-music events (www.springfestival.hu). Concerts are held in a number of beautiful venues, including stunning churches, the opera house and the national theatre.

April

Spring arrives with a burst of colour, from the glorious bulb fields of Holland to the blooming orchards of Spain.

✿ Settimana Santa, Italy

Italy celebrates Holy Week with processions and passion plays. By Holy Thursday Rome is thronged with the faithful as hundreds of thousands converge on the Vatican and St Peter's Basilica.

VIGEN M / SHUTTERSTOCK ©

☃ Koninginnedag (Queen's Day), Netherlands

The nationwide celebration on 27 April is especially fervent in Amsterdam, awash with orange costumes and wigs, beer, dope, temporary roller coasters, clogs and general craziness.

May

May is usually sunny and warm and full of things to do – an excellent time to visit.

♟ Beer Festival, Czech Republic

This Prague beer festival (www.ceskypivni festival.cz) offers lots of food, music and – most importantly – around 70 beers from around the country from mid- to late May.

June

The sun has broken through the clouds and the weather is generally gorgeous across the continent.

★ Best Festivals

Carnevale (Venice), February

St Patrick's Day, March

Bastille Day, July

Notting Hill Carnival, August

Festes de la Mercè, October

☃ Karneval der Kulturen, Germany

This joyous street carnival (www. karneval-berlin.de) celebrates Berlin's multicultural tapestry with parties, global nosh and a fun parade of flamboyantly costumed dancers, DJs, artists and musicians.

☃ Festa de Santo António, Portugal

Feasting, drinking and dancing in Lisbon's Alfama in honour of St Anthony (12 to 13 June) top the even grander three-week

From left: St Patrick's Day celebrations in Dublin (p109); Carnevale, Venice (p379)

Festas de Lisboa (http://festasdelisboa.com), which feature processions and dozens of street parties.

July

One of the busiest months for travel across the continent with outdoor cafes, beer gardens and beach clubs all hopping.

⚔ Sanfermines (Running of the Bulls), Spain

Fiesta de San Fermín (Sanfermines) is the week-long nonstop Pamplona festival with the daily *encierro* (running of the bulls) as its centrepiece (www.bullrunpamplona.com). The antibullfighting event, the Running of the Nudes (www.runningofthenudes.com), takes place two days earlier.

⚔ Bastille Day, France

Fireworks, balls, processions, and – of course – good food and wine, for France's national day on 14 July, celebrated in every French town and city.

August

Everybody's going someplace as half of Europe shuts down to enjoy the traditional holiday month with the other half.

⚔ Amsterdam Gay Pride, Netherlands

Held at the beginning of August, this is one of Europe's best LGBT events (www.amsterdamgaypride.nl). It's more about freedom and diversity than protest.

⚔ Notting Hill Carnival, Britain

Europe's largest – and London's most vibrant – outdoor carnival is a two-day event where London's Caribbean community shows the city how to party (www.thelondonnottinghillcarnival.com).

☆ Sziget Music Festival, Hungary

A week-long, great-value world-music festival (www.sziget.hu) held all over Budapest. Sziget features bands from around the world playing at more than 60 venues.

September

Maybe the best time to visit: the weather's still good and the crowds have thinned.

☆ Venice International Film Festival, Italy

Italy's top film fest is a celebration of mainstream and indie moviemaking (www.labiennale.org). The judging here is seen as an early indication of what to look for at the next year's Oscars.

⚔ Festes de la Mercè, Spain

Barcelona's biggest celebration (around 24 September) has four days of concerts, dancing, *castellers* (human-castle builders), fireworks and *correfocs* – a parade of fireworks-spitting dragons and devils.

November

Leaves have fallen and snow is about to fall in much of Europe. Even in the temperate zones around the Med it can get chilly, rainy and blustery.

⚔ Guy Fawkes Night, Britain

Bonfires and fireworks erupt across Britain on 5 November, recalling the foiling of a plot to blow up the Houses of Parliament in the 1600s. Go to high ground in London to see glowing explosions erupt everywhere.

☆ Iceland Airwaves, Iceland

Roll on up to Reykjavík for Iceland Airwaves, a great music festival featuring both Icelandic and international acts (www.icelandairwaves.is).

December

Despite freezing temperatures this is a magical time to visit, with Christmas markets and decorations brightening Europe's dark streets. Prices remain surprisingly low provided you avoid Christmas and New Year's Eve.

⚔ Natale, Italy

Churches set up an intricate crib or a *presepe* (nativity scene) in the lead-up to Christmas. Some are quite famous, most are works of art, and many date back hundreds of years and are venerated for their spiritual ties.

Plan Your Trip
Get Inspired

GIORGIOGALANO / GETTY IMAGES ©

Read

Neither Here Nor There: Travels in Europe Bill Bryson retraces a youthful European backpacking trip with hilarious observations.

Europe: A History Professor Norman Davies' sweeping overview of European history.

In Europe: Travels through the Twentieth Century Fascinating account of journalist Geert Mak's travels.

Fifty Years of Europe: An Album A lifetime of travel around the continent, distilled by British travel writer Jan Morris.

The Imperfectionists Tom Rachman's novel charts the fortunes of an English-language newspaper based in Rome.

Watch

The Third Man (1949) Classic tale of wartime espionage in old Vienna, starring Orson Welles and that zither theme.

Notting Hill (1999) Superstar Julia Roberts falls for bookstore owner Hugh Grant in this London-based romcom.

Amélie (2001) Endearing tale following the quirky adventures of Parisian do-gooder Amélie Poulain and her gnome.

Vicky Cristina Barcelona (2008) Woody Allen–directed drama about the amorous adventures of two young American women in Spain.

Victoria (2016) Thriller set on the streets of Berlin that plays out in one continuous 138-minute camera shot.

Listen

The Original Three Tenors: 20th Anniversary Edition Operatic classics courtesy of Pavarotti, Carreras and Domingo.

The Best of Edith Piaf The sound of France, including a selection of the Little Sparrow's greatest hits.

Chambao Feel-good flamenco fused with electronica from Spain's deep south.

London Calling A post-punk classic from The Clash that incorporates a host of musical influences.

Fado Tradicional A return to basics from Mariza, a top contemporary exponent of Portugal's fado style of music.

Above: Portobello Road (p84), Notting Hill, London

Plan Your Trip
Five-Day Itineraries

Iberian Excursion

For a short European break, with a bright burst of sunshine whatever the time of year, Portugal and Spain can't be beat. This quartet of destinations also provides wonderful art, architecture and delicious food.

Barcelona (p181) Ramble along La Rambla, get lost in the medieval streets of the Barri Gòtic, and marvel at La Sagrada Família.

Lisbon (p229) Spend two days exploring this enchanting city from the cobbled lanes of Alfama to seaside Belem.
✈ 2 hrs to Seville

Seville (p224) Spend a day enjoying the superb Islamic architecture, enjoying the rich tapas culture and taking in some live flamenco.
🚌 4 hrs to Granada

Granada (p220) Devote a day to the fabled La Alhambra and the atmospheric Albayzin, stopping in tapas bars and tea houses along the way. ✈ 1½ hrs to Barcelona

Eastern Europe to Berlin

Known as the grim, grey 'Eastern Bloc' until the early 1990s, today this half of Europe is one of the continent's most dynamic and fascinating to visit. The four cities on this itinerary each have a distinct character and charm.

Berlin (p431) Enjoy diversity, alternative culture and the frisson of recent history in Germany's once-divided capital. **4**

Prague (p535) Wander this romantic city for a day, ending up on the iconic Charles Bridge at dusk. 🚌 5 hrs to Berlin **3**

Budapest (p559) Spend a day in Hungary's capital with its architectural gems and soothing thermal baths. **1**
🚌 2¾ hrs to Vienna

Vienna (p577) Allow two days for Austria's capital; it's packed with palaces, museums and splendid art galleries. 🚌 4 hrs to Prague **2**

3

4

FROM LEFT: ILHAN EROGLU / 500PX © ELXENEIZE / SHUTTERSTOCK ©

Plan Your Trip
Five-Day Itineraries

Italy & the Adriatic Coast

This whistle-stop itinerary gives a taste of the glories of Italy starting in its ancient capital Rome. Next, the Renaissance crucible of Florence and the floating wonder of Venice, before heading down the Adriatic Coast to historic Dubrovnik in Croatia.

Venice (p379) Hop in a gondola and sail the canals – before the day is out you'll be in love with Venice.
✈ 1½ hrs to Dubrovnik

Florence (p397) You'll need to move at a pace to cram in the art and architecture of this Renaissance beauty in a day. 🚆 2 hrs to Venice

Rome (p327) Allow a couple of days in the Eternal City, home to the Vatican and Colosseum.
🚌 1½ hrs to Florence

Dubrovnik (p481) One of the world's most magnificent walled cities has a pedestrian-only old town and sublime sea views.

Canals & Castles

Copenhagen (p129) Home to the Tivoli Gardens, palaces, the nonconformist enclave of Christiania and the Little Mermaid.
✈ 1 hr to Berlin

With only five days, you'll need to fly most of the way between Amsterdam's World Heritage–listed canals and the Schloss Neuschwanstein, a classic European castle. Make stops for an injection of Nordic cool in Copenhagen and nightclubbing in Berlin.

Berlin (p431) With no curfew, Berlin parties through the night. Start the evening off in Prater, a historic beer garden. ✈ 1 hr to Munich

Amsterdam (p307) Rent a bike to cycle around this city beside canals, stopping off at art museums and coffeeshops.
✈ 1½ hrs to Copenhagen

Schloss Neuschwanstein (p462) Ludwig II's fantasy castle, two hours southwest of Munich, was a model for the one in Disney's *Sleeping Beauty*.

FROM LEFT: PHOTOSMATIC / SHUTTERSTOCK ©, POCHOLO CALAPRE / SHUTTERSTOCK © (SCULPTOR: EDVARD ERIKSEN)

Plan Your Trip
10-Day Itinerary

Iceland to Ireland

This 1500km journey around northern Europe is one of the continent's most scenic, from the bubbling hot springs outside Reykjavík to the gentle Georgian architecture of Dublin, via the grand Scottish Highlands and the history, culture and fashion of London.

Reykjavík (p163) Allot two days for the city's excellent museums, shops and cafes, as well as its vibrant nightlife.
✈ 4 hrs to London

Inverness (p100) This is your three-day base for explorations around the splendid Scottish Highlands.
✈ 1¼ hrs to Dublin

Dublin (p109) Encounter the Dublin of James Joyce as you meander between the literary haunts, museums and pubs of Ireland's capital.

London (p49) You'll be amazed how much of London you can pack into three days if you try.
✈ 1½ hrs to Inverness

Plan Your Trip
10-Day Itinerary

Southern Mediterranean

Hire a car in Avignon, a great base for touring the hilltop villages and Roman ruins of France's beautiful Provence. Devote a day to driving the cliffside roads of the Cote d'Azur towards Italy – one of the world's great drives.

1

Avignon (p298) A couple of days is sufficient to see the sights in and around this ancient fortress town.
🚗 7¾ hrs to Siena

(1)

Florence (p397) Take in the city's Renaissance splendour from the cupola of its landmark Duomo.
🚌 1½ hrs to Rome

Siena (p422) Spend a day exploring one of Italy's most enchanting medieval settlements.
🚌 1 hr to Florence

Rome (p327) Linger on the Spanish steps, beside the Trevi Fountain and in the Piazza Navona.
🚌 2¾ hrs to Pompeii

3
2

4

5

Pompeii (p370) The Unesco-listed ruins provide a remarkable model of a working Roman city, including baths, taverns and a brothel.

2

5

Plan Your Trip
Two-Week Itinerary

Classic Europe

Eight countries in 14 days may sound like squeezing too much in, but Europe's extensive network of budget flights and trains makes this itinerary easy. It's a great introduction to the continent's infinite variety of cultures and terrain.

London (p49) Spend a couple of days in this endlessly intriguing city, one of history's great survivors.
🚄 2¼ hrs to Paris

Paris (p249) Swoon for two days over the beautiful boulevards and romantic alleys of the City of Light.
🚄 3½ hrs to Amsterdam

Zermatt (p474) Spend a day gawping in awe at the Matterhorn, the Alps' most famous peak.
🚄 4 hrs to Geneva, then 1 hr to Barcelona

Barcelona (p181) Wrap up your tour on the balmy shores of the Mediterranean in a city that's both a visual treat and a foodie heaven.

①

Amsterdam (p307) Chill out for a day cruising the canals and art galleries and enjoying the liberal atmosphere. ✈ 1½ hrs to Prague

Prague (p535) Devote a day to the town's two big attractions – the castle and the Old Town Square. 🚆 4½ hrs to Vienna

4

5

Vienna (p577) Allow two days for the grandeur of the former capital of the Austro-Hungarian empire. ✈ 1 hr to Venice

6

Venice (p379) Surrender to the haunting beauty of La Serenissima's watery world of piazza, domes, canals and bridges. 🚆 6 hrs to Zermatt

6

8

Plan Your Trip
Family Travel

MIHASTOCK / SHUTTERSTOCK ©

Getting Around

In general, Europe is an incredibly family-friendly place to travel, but distances can be long, so it's a good idea to break up the trip with things to see and do en route.

Traffic is at its worst during holiday seasons, especially between June and August, and journey times are likely to be much longer during this period.

Trains can be a great option for family travel – kids will have more space to move around, and you can pack books, puzzles and computer games to keep them entertained.

Children and young people qualify for cheap travel on most public transport in Europe (usually around 50% of the adult fare). Look out for railcards and passes that open up extra discounts – many cities offer passes that combine entry to sights and attractions with travel on public transport.

Sights & Attractions

Most attractions offer discounted entry for children (generally for 12 years and under, although this varies). If you can, try to mix up educational activities with fun excursions they're guaranteed to enjoy – balance that visit to the Tate Modern or the Louvre with a trip to the London Aquarium or a day at Disneyland Paris, for example. The number-one rule is to avoid packing too much in – you'll get tired, the kids will get irritable and tantrums are sure to follow. Plan carefully and you'll enjoy your time much more.

Hotels & Restaurants

It's always worth asking in advance whether hotels are happy to accept kids. Many are fully geared for family travel, with children's activities, child-minding services and the like, but others may impose a minimum age limit to deter guests with kids. Family-friendly hotels will usually be able to offer

GEORGE SANDU / SHUTTERSTOCK ©

a large room with two or three beds to accommodate families, or at least neighbouring rooms with an adjoining door. Dining out en famille is generally great fun, but again, it's always worth checking to see whether kids are welcome – generally the posher or more prestigious the establishment, the less kid friendly they're likely to be. Many restaurants offer cheaper children's menus, usually based around simple staples such as steak, pasta, burgers and chicken. Most will also offer smaller portions of adult meals. If your kids are fussy, buying your own ingredients at a local market can encourage them to experiment – they can choose their own food while simultaneously practising the local lingo.

Need to Know

Changing facilities Found at most supermarkets and major attractions.

Cots and high chairs Available in many restaurants and hotels, but ask ahead.

★ Best Cities for Kids

Paris (p249)

London (p49)

Barcelona (p181)

Copenhagen (p129)

Vienna (p577)

Health Generally good, but pack your own first-aid kit to avoid language difficulties.

Kids' menus Widely available.

Nappies (diapers) Sold everywhere, including pharmacies and supermarkets.

Strollers It's easiest to bring your own.

Transport Children usually qualify for discounts; young kids often travel free.

From left: Children in a lavender field in Provence (p289); Carousel in Tivoli Gardens (p132), Copenhagen

LONDON,
GREAT BRITAIN

London, Great Britain

One of the world's most visited cities, London has something for everyone: from history and culture to fine food and good times. Britain may have voted for Brexit (although the majority of Londoners didn't), but for now London remains one of the world's most cosmopolitan cities, and diversity infuses daily life, food, music and fashion. It even penetrates intrinsically British institutions; the British Museum and Victoria & Albert Museum have collections as varied as they are magnificent, while the flavours at centuries-old Borough Market run the full global gourmet spectrum.

Two Days in London

First stop, **Westminster Abbey** (p52) for an easy intro to the city's (and nation's) history and then to **Buckingham Palace** (p62). Walk up the Mall to **Trafalgar Square** (p75) for its architectural grandeur and photo-op views of **Big Ben** (p74) down Whitehall. Art lovers will make a beeline for the **National Gallery** (p74).

On day two, visit the **British Museum** (p58) and **Tate Modern** (p77), followed by **Tate Britain** (p75) and dinner at **Claridge's Foyer & Reading Room** (p86).

Four Days in London

Have a royally good time checking out the Crown Jewels at the **Tower of London** (p66), followed by some retail therapy at **Leadenhall Market** (p71) and a visit to **St Paul's Cathedral** (p75).

Dedicate the fourth day to the **V&A** (p80), **Natural History Museum** (p80) and **Hyde Park** (p80). End the day with a show at **Royal Albert Hall** (p88).

After London catch the Eurostar to Paris (p249) or Amsterdam (p307).

Previous page: Tower Bridge (p70)
ANDREW THOMAS / GETTY IMAGES ©

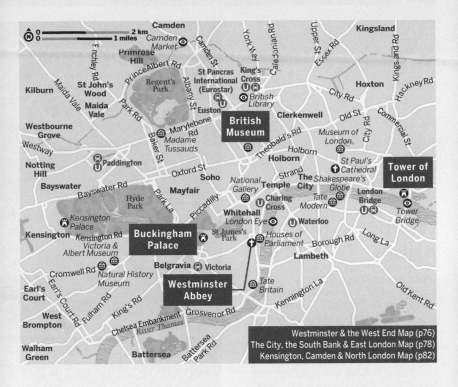

Westminster & the West End Map (p76)
The City, the South Bank & East London Map (p78)
Kensington, Camden & North London Map (p82)

Arriving in London

Heathrow Airport Trains, the tube and buses to London cost £5.10–27, taxis £48–90. From 2020, express trains will run along the Elizabeth Line (Crossrail),

Gatwick Airport Trains to London (4.30am–1.35am) cost £10–20; hourly buses to London 24/7 from £8; taxis £100.

Stansted Airport Trains to London (5.30am–12.30am) cost £17; 24/7 buses to London from £10; taxis £130.

St Pancras International Train Station In central London (for Eurostar train arrivals from Europe); connected by many Underground lines to other parts of the city.

Where to Stay

Hanging your hat in London can be painfully expensive and you'll need to book well in advance. Decent hostels are easy to find, but aren't as cheap as you might hope for. Hotels range from no-frills chains through to ultra-ritzy establishments, such as the Ritz itself. B&Bs are often better value and more atmospheric than hotels.

For information on what each London neighbourhood has to offer, see the table on p89.

Westminster Abbey

Westminster Abbey is such an important commemoration site that it's hard to overstate its symbolic value or imagine its equivalent anywhere else in the world. With a couple of exceptions, every English sovereign has been crowned here since William the Conqueror in 1066; many were married here and a total of 17 are buried here.

Great For...

🛈 Need to Know

Map p76; 📞020-7222 5152; www.west minster-abbey.org; 20 Dean's Yard, SW1; adult/child £22/9; 🕒9.30am-3.30pm Mon, Tue, Thu & Fri, to 6pm Wed, to 3pm Sat May-Aug, to 1pm Sat Sep-Apr; Ⓤ Westminster

★ **Top Tip**

The Abbey gets incredibly busy, even at opening, so come armed with patience.

There is an extraordinary amount to see at the Abbey. The interior is chock-a-block with ornate chapels, elaborate tombs of monarchs and grandiose monuments to sundry luminaries throughout the ages. First and foremost, however, it is a sacred place of worship.

A Regal History

Though a mixture of architectural styles, the Abbey is considered the finest example of Early English Gothic. The original church was built in the 11th century by King Edward the Confessor (later a saint), who is buried in an elaborate tomb behind the High Altar. King Henry III (r 1216–72) began work on the new building but didn't complete it; the Gothic nave was finished by King Richard II in 1388. Henry VII's huge and magnificent Lady Chapel was added in 1516.

The Abbey was initially a monastery for a dozen Benedictine monks, and many of the building's features attest to this collegial past, including the octagonal Chapter House, the Quire and the College Garden. In the 1530s, King Henry VIII separated the church in England from Rome and dissolved the monasteries. The king became head of the Church of England and the Abbey acquired its 'royal peculiar' status, meaning it is administered directly by the Crown and exempt from any ecclesiastical jurisdiction.

North Transept, Sanctuary & Quire

Entrance to the Abbey is via the Great North Door. The North Transept is often referred to as Statesmen's Aisle: politicians and eminent public figures are commemorated by large marble statues and imposing marble plaques.

At the heart of the Abbey is the beautifully tiled **sanctuary** (or sacrarium), a stage for coronations, royal weddings and funerals. George Gilbert Scott designed the ornate **high altar** in 1873. In front of the altar is the **Cosmati marble pavement** dating back to 1268. It has intricate designs of small pieces of marble inlaid into plain marble, which predicts the end of the world in AD 19,693! At the entrance to the lovely **Chapel of St John the Baptist** is a sublime Virgin and Child bathed in candlelight.

The **Quire**, a magnificent structure of gold, blue and red Victorian Gothic by Edward Blore, dates back to the mid-19th century. It sits where the original choir for the monks' worship would have been, but bears no resemblance to the original. Nowadays, the Quire is still used for singing, but its regular occupants are the Westminster Choir – 22 boys and 12 'lay vicars' (men) who sing the daily services.

Chapels & Chair

The sanctuary is surrounded by chapels. **Henry VII's Lady Chapel**, in the eastern-most part of the Abbey, is the most spectacular, with its fan vaulting on the ceiling, colourful banners of the Order of the Bath and dramatic oak stalls. Behind the chapel's altar is the elaborate sarcophagus of Henry VII and his queen, Elizabeth of York.

Beyond the chapel's altar is the **Royal Air Force Chapel**, with a stained-glass window commemorating the force's finest hour, the Battle of Britain (1940), and the 1500 RAF pilots who died. A stone plaque on the floor marks the spot where Oliver Cromwell's body lay for two years (1658) until the Restoration, when it was disinterred, hanged and beheaded. Two bodies, believed to be those of the child princes allegedly murdered in the Tower of London in 1483, were buried here almost two centuries later in 1674.

There are two small chapels either side of Lady Chapel with the tombs of famous monarchs: on the left (north) is where **Elizabeth I** and her half-sister **Mary I** (aka Bloody Mary) rest. On the right (south) is the tomb of **Mary Queen of Scots**, beheaded on the orders of her cousin Elizabeth.

☑ **Don't Miss**

Poet's Corner, the Coronation Chair, the 14th-century cloisters, the oldest door in the UK, a 900-year-old garden, the royal sarcophagi and much, much more.

JULIAN ELLIOTT PHOTOGRAPHY / GETTY IMAGES ©

✗ **Take a Break**

The only option for food inside the Abbey complex is **Cellarium** (Map p76; ☏020-7222 0516; www.benugo.com/restaurants/cellarium-cafe-terrace; mains £9.50-13.50; ⊗8am-6pm Mon, Tue, Thu & Fri, to 8pm Wed, 9am-5pm Sat, 10am-4pm Sun; ☏; ⓤWestminster), which was part of the original 14th-century Benedictine monastery.

The vestibule of the Lady Chapel is the usual place for the rather ordinary-looking **Coronation Chair**, upon which every monarch since the early 14th century has been crowned.

Shrine of St Edward the Confessor

The most sacred spot in the Abbey lies behind the high altar; access is generally restricted to protect the 13th-century flooring. St Edward was the founder of the Abbey and the original building was consecrated a few weeks before his death. His tomb was slightly altered after the original was destroyed during the Reformation, but still contains Edward's remains – the only complete saint's body in Britain. Ninety-minute **verger-led tours** (£5 plus admission) of the Abbey include a visit to the shrine.

South Transept & Nave

The south transept contains **Poets' Corner**, where many of England's finest writers are buried and/or commemorated by monuments or memorials.

In the nave's north aisle is **Scientists' Corner**, where you will find **Sir Isaac Newton's tomb**. Newton lies alongside fellow greats, including Charles Darwin and Stephen Hawking; the latter's ashes were placed here in 2018. Just ahead of it is the north aisle of the Quire, known as **Musicians' Aisle**, where baroque composer Henry Purcell is buried, as well as more modern music makers such as Benjamin Britten and Edward Elgar.

The two towers above the west door are the ones through which you exit. These were designed by Nicholas Hawksmoor and completed in 1745. Just above the door, perched in 15th-century niches, are the additions to the Abbey unveiled in 1998: 10 stone statues of international 20th-century martyrs who died for their Christian faith. These include US pacifist Dr Martin Luther King, the Polish priest St Maximilian Kolbe, who was murdered by the Nazis at Auschwitz, and Wang Zhiming, publicly executed during the Chinese Cultural Revolution.

Outer Buildings & Gardens

The oldest part of the cloister is the **East Cloister** (or East Walk), dating to the 13th century. Off the cloister is the octagonal **Chapter House**, with one of Europe's best-preserved medieval tile floors and religious murals on the walls. It was used as a meeting place by the House of Commons in the second half of the 14th century. To the right of the entrance to Chapter House is what is claimed to be the **oldest door in Britain** – it's been there for 950 years.

The adjacent **Pyx Chamber** is one of the few remaining relics of the original Abbey, including the 10th-century **Altar of St Dunstan**. The chamber contains the pyx, a chest with standard gold and silver pieces for testing coinage weights in a ceremony called the Trial of the Pyx, which nowadays

Stained-glass window in Chapter House

takes place in Goldsmiths' Hall in the City of London.

To reach the 900-year-old **College Garden** (Map p76; ☎020-7222 5152; www.westminster-abbey.org; off Great College St, SW1; ⏱10am-4pm Tue-Thu; Ⓤ Westminster) **FREE**, enter Dean's Yard and the Little Cloisters off Great College St.

Queen's Diamond Jubilee Galleries

Opened in 2018, the **Queen's Diamond Jubilee Galleries** (an additional £5) are a new museum and gallery space located in the medieval triforium, the arched gallery above the nave. Among its exhibits are the death masks and wax effigies of generations of royalty, armour and stained glass. Highlights are the graffiti-inscribed chair used for the coronation of Mary II, the beautifully illustrated manuscripts

of the Litlyngton Missal from 1380 and the 13th-century Westminster Retable, England's oldest surviving altarpiece.

Rising above the bustle of the Abbey below, these galleries are much quieter and less visited than the central nave and very much worth the extra ticket price, as they boast the best views of the Abbey.

☑ **Don't Miss**

Views from Queen's Diamond Jubilee Galleries are the best in the building.

★ **Top Tip**

Crowds are almost as solid as the Abbey's stonework, so buy tickets online in advance (which also nets a slight discount) or get in the queue first thing in the morning.

BPPERRY / GETTY IMAGES ©

JAROSLAV MORAVCIK / SHUTTERSTOCK ©

British Museum

Britain's most visited attraction – founded in 1753 when royal physician Hans Sloane sold his 'cabinet of curiosities' – is an exhaustive and exhilarating stampede through millennia of human civilisation.

The British Museum offers a stupendous selection of tours, many of them free. There are 14 free 30-minute Eye-opener tours of individual galleries per day. The museum also has free daily gallery talks, a highlights tour (£14, 11.30am and 2pm Friday, Saturday and Sunday) and free 20-minute spotlight tours on Friday evenings. Audio and family guides (adult/child £7/6) in 10 languages are available from the desk in the Great Court.

Great For...

☑ Don't Miss

The Rosetta Stone, the Mummy of Katebet and the marble Parthenon Sculptures.

Great Court

Past the entry hall is the gasp-worthy **Great Court**, covered with a spectacular glass-and-steel roof designed by architect Norman Foster in 2000. In its centre is the **Reading Room**, currently closed, which was once part of the British Library and frequented by the big brains of history, from Mahatma Gandhi to Karl Marx.

Ancient Egypt collection

ℹ️ Need to Know

Map p76; 📞020-7323 8000; www.britishmuseum.org; Great Russell St, WC1; ⊙10am-5.30pm Sat-Thu, to 8.30pm Fri; Ⓤ Tottenham Court Rd or Russell Sq **FREE**

✗ Take a Break

Just around the corner from the museum in a quiet, picturesque square is one of London's most atmospheric pubs, the **Queen's Larder** (Map p82; 📞020-7837 5627; www.queenslarder.co.uk; 1 Queen Sq, WC1; ⊙11.30am-11pm Mon-Fri, noon-11pm Sat, noon-10.30pm Sun; Ⓤ Russell Sq).

★ Top Tip

The museum is huge, so pick your interests and consider the free tours.

Ancient Egypt, Middle East & Greece

The star of the show here is the Ancient Egypt collection. It comprises sculptures, fine jewellery, papyrus texts, coffins and mummies, including the beautiful and intriguing **Mummy of Katebet** (room 63). The most prized item in the collection (and the most popular postcard in the shop) is the **Rosetta Stone** (room 4), the key to deciphering Egyptian hieroglyphics. In the same gallery is the enormous bust of the pharaoh **Ramesses the Great** (room 4).

Assyrian treasures from ancient Mesopotamia include the 16-tonne **Winged Bulls from Khorsabad** (room 10), the heaviest object in the museum. Behind it are the exquisite **Lion Hunt Reliefs from Nineveh** (room 10) from the 7th century BC, which influenced Greek sculpture. Such antiquities

are all the more significant after the Islamic State's bulldozing of Nimrud in 2015.

A major highlight of the museum is the **Parthenon sculptures** (room 18). The marble frieze is thought to be the Great Panathenaea, a blow-out version of an annual festival in honour of Athena.

Roman & Medieval Britain

Also on Level 3 are finds from Britain and Europe (rooms 40 to 51). Many go back to Roman times, when the empire spread across much of the continent, including the **Mildenhall Treasure** (room 49), a collection of almost three dozen pieces of 4th-century-AD Roman silverware unearthed in Suffolk in the east of England, which display both pagan and early Christian motifs.

Lindow Man (room 50) is the well-preserved remains of a 1st-century man discovered in a bog near Manchester in northern England in 1984. Equally fascinating are artefacts from the **Sutton Hoo Ship Burial** (room 41), an elaborate 7th-century Anglo-Saxon burial site from Suffolk.

Perennial favourites are the lovely **Lewis Chessmen** (room 40), some 82 12th-century game pieces carved from walrus tusk and whale teeth that were found on a remote Scottish island in the early 19th century. They served as models for the game of Wizard Chess in the first Harry Potter film.

Enlightenment Galleries

Formerly known as the King's Library, this stunning neoclassical space (room 1) just off the Great Court was built between 1823 and 1827 and was the first part of the new museum building as it is seen today. Through a fascinating collection of artefacts, the collection traces how such disciplines as biology, archaeology, linguis-

tics and geography emerged during the Enlightenment of the 18th century.

What's Nearby?

Sir John Soane's Museum   Museum
(Map p76; ☏020-7405 2107; www.soane.org; 13 Lincoln's Inn Fields, WC2; ☻10am-5pm Wed-Sun; ⓊHolborn) FREE This little museum is one of the most atmospheric and fascinating in London. The building is the beautiful, bewitching home of architect Sir John Soane (1753–1837), which he left brimming with surprising personal effects and curiosities; the museum represents his exquisite and eccentric taste.

Soane, a country bricklayer's son, is most famous for designing the Bank of England.

The heritage-listed house is largely as it was when Soane died and is itself a main part of the attraction. It has a canopy dome that brings light right down to the crypt, a

Russell Square

colonnade filled with statuary and a picture gallery where paintings are stowed behind each other on folding wooden panes. This is where Soane's choicest artwork is displayed, including *Riva degli Schiavoni, looking West* by Canaletto, architectural drawings by Christopher Wren and Robert Adam, and the original *Rake's Progress*, William Hogarth's set of satirical cartoons of late-18th-century London low life. Among Soane's more unusual acquisitions are an Egyptian hieroglyphic sarcophagus, a mock-up of a monk's cell and slaves' chains.

> ★ **Top Tip**
>
> Check out the outstanding *A History of the World in 100 Objects* radio series (www.bbc.co.uk/podcasts/series/ahow), which retraces two million years of history through 100 objects from the museum's collections.

CHRISPICTURES / SHUTTERSTOCK ©

Charles Dickens Museum   Museum

(Map p82; ☎020-7405 2127; www.dickens museum.com; 48-49 Doughty St, WC1; adult/child £9.50/4.50; ☺10am-5pm Tue-Sun; ⓤRussell Sq or Chancery Lane) The prolific writer Charles Dickens lived with his growing family in this handsome four-storey Georgian terraced house for a mere 2½ years (1837–39), but this is where his work really flourished, as he completed *The Pickwick Papers*, *Nicholas Nickleby* and *Oliver Twist* here. Each of the dozen rooms, some restored to their original condition, contains various memorabilia, including the study where you'll find the desk at which Dickens wrote *Great Expectations*.

The Squares of Bloomsbury   Squares

The Bloomsbury Group, they used to say, lived in squares, moved in circles and loved in triangles. **Russell Square** (Map p82; ⓤRussell Sq) sits at the very heart of the district. Originally laid out in 1800, a striking facelift at the start of the new millennium spruced it up and gave the square a 10m-high fountain. The centre of literary Bloomsbury was **Gordon Square** (Map p82; ⓤRussell Sq or Euston Sq), where some of the buildings are marked with blue plaques. Lovely **Bedford Square** (Map p76; ⓤTottenham Court Rd) is the only completely Georgian square still surviving in Bloomsbury.

Tavistock Square (Map p82; ⓤRussell Sq or Euston Sq), the 'square of peace', has a statue of Mahatma Gandhi, a memorial to wartime conscientious objectors and a cherry tree recalling the WWII bombings of Hiroshima and Nagasaki.

Many writers and artists made their home in Gordon Square, including Bertrand Russell (No 57), Lytton Strachey (No 51) and Vanessa and Clive Bell, Maynard Keynes and the Woolf family (No 46). Strachey, Dora Carrington and Lydia Lopokova (the future wife of Maynard Keynes) all took turns living at No 41.

> ★ **Did You Know?**
>
> Charles Dickens only spent 2½ years in the house that is now the Charles Dickens Museum, but it was here that he wrote many of his most famous works.

DAVID STEELE / SHUTTERSTOCK ©

Buckingham Palace

The palace has been the Royal Family's London lodgings since 1837, when Queen Victoria moved in from Kensington Palace as St James's Palace was deemed too old-fashioned.

Great For...

☑ Don't Miss

Peering through the gates, going on a tour of the interior (summer only) or catching the Changing of the Guard.

The State Rooms are only open in August and September, when Her Majesty is holidaying in Scotland. The Queen's Gallery and the Royal Mews are open year-round, however.

State Rooms

The tour starts in the **Grand Hall** at the foot of the monumental **Grand Staircase**, commissioned by King George IV in 1828. It takes in architect John Nash's Italianate **Green Drawing Room**, the **State Dining Room** (all red damask and Regency furnishings), the **Blue Drawing Room** (which has a gorgeous fluted ceiling by Nash) and the **White Drawing Room**, where foreign ambassadors are received.

Admission includes entry to a themed special exhibition (royal couture during the Queen's reign, growing up at the palace

Changing of the Guard

❶ Need to Know

Map p76; ☎0303 123 7300; www.rct.uk/
visit/the-state-rooms-buckingham-palace;
Buckingham Palace Rd, SW1; adult/child/
under 5yr £25/14/free, incl Royal Mews &
Queen's Gallery £45/24.50/free; ◷9.30am–
7pm mid-Jul–Aug, to 6pm Sep; Ⓤ Green Park
or St James's Park

✕ Take a Break

During the summer months, you can
enjoy light refreshments in the **Garden
Café** on the Palace's West Terrace.

★ Top Tip

Come early for front-row views of the
Changing of the Guard.

etc) in the enormous **Ballroom**, built
between 1853 and 1855, and these displays
are often the main reason for a visit. The
Throne Room is rather anticlimactic, with
his-and-her pink chairs monogrammed 'ER'
and 'P'.

Picture Gallery & Garden

The most interesting part of the tour is
the 47m-long Picture Gallery, featuring
splendid works by such artists as Van
Dyck, Rembrandt, Canaletto, Poussin,
Claude Lorrain, Rubens, Canova and
Vermeer.

Wandering the 18 hectares of gardens
is another highlight – as well as admiring
some of the 350 or so species of flowers
and plants and listening to the many birds,
you'll get beautiful views of the palace and
a peek of its famous lake.

Changing of the Guard

At 11am, weather permitting, Sunday,
Monday, Wednesday and Friday (daily
in June and July), the old guard (Foot
Guards of the Household Regiment)
comes off duty to be replaced by the new
guard on the forecourt of Buckingham
Palace.

Crowds come to **watch** (Map p76; www.
royal.uk/changing-guard; ◷11am Sun, Mon,
Wed, Fri Aug–May, 11am daily Jun & Jul) FREE
the carefully choreographed marching
and shouting of the guards in their bright-
red uniforms and bearskin hats. It lasts
about 45 minutes and is very popular, so
arrive early if you want to get a good spot.

Queen's Gallery

Since the reign of King Charles I, the Royal
Family has amassed a priceless collection
of paintings, sculpture, ceramics, furniture
and jewellery. The small **Queen's Gallery**

(Map p76; www.rct.uk/visit/the-queens-gallery-buckingham-palace; South Wing; adult/child £12/6, incl Royal Mews £20.70/11.20; ⊙10am-5.30pm, from 9.30am mid-Jul–Sep) showcases some of the palace's treasures on a rotating basis.

Originally on the site of the gallery, in the South Wing of Buckingham Palace, was a conservatory designed by Welsh architect John Nash. It was converted into a chapel for Queen Victoria in 1843, destroyed in a 1940 air raid and reopened as a gallery in 1962. A £20-million renovation for Queen Elizabeth II's Golden Jubilee in 2002 added three times more display space.

Royal Mews

Southwest of the palace, the **Royal Mews** (Map p76; www.rct.uk/visit/royalmews; Buckingham Palace Rd, SW1; adult/child £12/6.80, with Queen's Gallery £20.70/11.20; ⊙10am-5pm Apr-Oct, to 4pm Mon-Sat Feb, Mar & Nov; Ⓤ Victoria) started life as a falconry but is now a working stable looking after the Royal Family's immaculately groomed horses, along with the opulent vehicles the monarch uses for transport. The Queen is well known for her passion for horses; she names every steed that resides at the mews.

Highlights include the enormous and opulent Gold State Coach of 1762, which has been used for every coronation since that of King George IV in 1821; the 2014 Diamond Jubilee State Coach (the newest in the fleet); and the stunning 1820s stables where you might spot some of the Windsor Greys or Cleveland Bays.

State Dining Room (p62)

What's Nearby?

St James's Park Park

(Map p76; www.royalparks.org.uk/parks/
st-jamess-park; The Mall, SW1; ☺5am-mid-
night; ⓤSt James's Park or Green Park) At 23
hectares, St James's is the second-small-
est of the eight royal parks after **Green
Park** (Map p76; www.royalparks.org.uk/parks/
green-park; ☺5am-midnight; ⓤGreen Park).
But what it lacks in size it makes up for
in grooming, as it is the most manicured
green space in London. It has brilliant views
of the London Eye, Westminster, St James's
Palace, Carlton House Terrace and Horse
Guards Parade; the picture-perfect sight

★ **Did You Know?**

The State Rooms represent a mere 19 of
the palace's 775 rooms.

UKARTPICS / ALAMY STOCK PHOTO ©

of Buckingham Palace from the **Blue
Bridge** spanning the central lake is the best
you'll find.

Royal Academy of Arts Gallery

(Map p76; ☎020-7300 8000; www.royal
academy.org.uk; Burlington House, Piccadilly, W1;
☺10am-6pm Sat-Thu, to 10pm Fri; ⓤGreen Park)
FREE Britain's oldest society devoted to fine
arts was founded in 1768 and moved here
to Burlington House a century later. For its
250th birthday in 2018, the RA gave itself
a £56-million makeover, opening up 70%
more public space. It also made it free to
visit its historic collection, which includes
drawings, paintings, architectural designs,
photographs and sculptures by past and
present Royal Academicians, such as
Joshua Reynolds, John Constable, Thomas
Gainsborough, JMW Turner, David Hockney
and Norman Foster.

Horse Guards Parade Historic Site

(Map p76; off Whitehall, SW1; ⓤWestminster or
Charing Cross) In a more accessible version
of Buckingham Palace's Changing of the
Guard (p63), the horse-mounted troops
of the Household Cavalry swap soldiers
here at 11am from Monday to Saturday
and at 10am on Sunday. A slightly less
ceremonial version takes place at 4pm
when the dismounted guards are changed.
On the Queen's official birthday in June, the
Trooping the Colour (www.household
division.org.uk/trooping-the-colour; Horse
Guards Parade, SW1; ☺Jun; ⓤWestminster or
Charing Cross) takes place here.

★ **Local Knowledge**

At the centre of Royal Family life is the
Music Room, where four royal babies
have been christened – the Prince of
Wales (Prince Charles), the Princess
Royal (Princess Anne), the Duke of
York (Prince Andrew) and the Duke
of Cambridge (Prince William) – with
water brought from the River Jordan.

Tower of London as seen from the River Thames

ENTRY TO THE TRAITORS GATE

Tower of London

With a history as bleak as it is fascinating, the Tower of London is now one of the city's top attractions, thanks in part to the Crown Jewels.

Great For...

☑ Don't Miss

The colourful Yeoman Warders (or Beefeaters), the spectacular Crown Jewels, the soothsaying ravens and armour fit for a king.

Begun during the reign of William the Conqueror (1066–87), the Tower is in fact a castle containing 22 towers.

Tower Green

The buildings to the west and the south of this verdant patch have always accommodated Tower officials. Indeed, the current constable has a flat in Queen's House built in 1540. But what looks at first glance like a peaceful, almost village-like slice of the Tower's inner ward is actually one of its bloodiest.

Scaffold Site & Beauchamp Tower

Those 'lucky' enough to meet their fate here (rather than suffering the embarrassment of execution on Tower Hill, observed by tens of thousands of jeering and cheering onlookers) numbered but a handful and included two of Henry VIII's wives (and alleged adulterers), Anne Boleyn and Catherine Howard; 16-year-

Yeomen Warders

WILL RODRIGUES / SHUTTERSTOCK ©

ℹ️ Need to Know

Map p78; 📞020-3166 6000; www.hrp.org.
uk/tower-of-london; Petty Wales, EC3; adult/
child £26.80/12.70, audio guide £4; 🕘9am-
4.30pm Tue-Sat, from 10am Sun & Mon;
Ⓤ Tower Hill

✕ Take a Break

The **Wine Library** (Map p78; 📞020-7481
0415; www.winelibrary.co.uk; 43 Trinity Sq,
EC3; buffet £18; 🕘buffet 11.30am-3pm Mon-
Fri, 11am-5pm Sat, shop 10am-6pm Mon, to
8pm Tue-Fri, 11am-5pm Sat; Ⓤ Tower Hill) is
a great place for a light but boozy lunch
opposite the Tower.

★ Top Tip

Book online for cheaper rates for the
Tower.

old Lady Jane Grey, who fell foul of Henry's
daughter Mary I by attempting to have her-
self crowned queen; and Robert Devereux,
Earl of Essex, once a favourite of Elizabeth I.

Just west of the scaffold site is brick-
faced Beauchamp Tower, where high-
ranking prisoners left behind unhappy
inscriptions and other graffiti.

Chapel Royal of St Peter ad Vincula

Just north of the scaffold site is the
16th-century Chapel Royal of St Peter ad
Vincula (St Peter in Chains), a rare example
of ecclesiastical Tudor architecture. The
church can be visited on a Yeoman Warder
tour, or during the first and last hour of
normal opening times.

Crown Jewels

To the east of the Chapel Royal and north
of the White Tower is **Waterloo Barracks**,
the home of the Crown Jewels, which are, in
a very real sense, priceless. Visitors to the
barracks file past film clips of the jewels and
their role through history (including fascinating footage of Queen Elizabeth II's coronation in 1953) before reaching the vault itself.

Once inside you'll be dazzled by lavishly
bejewelled sceptres, orbs and crowns. Two
moving walkways take you past eight crowns
and other coronation regalia, including the
platinum crown of the late Queen Mother,
Elizabeth, which is set with the 106-carat
Koh-i-Nûr (Persian for 'Mountain of Light')
diamond, and the State Sceptre with Cross
topped with the 530-carat First Star of Africa
(or Cullinan I) diamond. Photography is
prohibited, so if you want a second (or third)
peek, double back to the beginning of the
walkways. A bit further on, exhibited on its
own, is the centrepiece: the Imperial State
Crown, set with 2868 diamonds (including

the 317-carat Second Star of Africa, or Cullinan II), sapphires, emeralds, rubies and pearls. It's worn by the Queen at the State Opening of Parliament in May/June.

White Tower

Built in stone as a fortress in 1078, this was the original 'Tower' of London – its current name came after Henry III whitewashed it in the 13th century. Standing just 30m high, it's not exactly a skyscraper by modern standards, but in the Middle Ages it would have dwarfed the wooden huts surrounding the castle walls and intimidated the peasantry.

Most of its interior is given over to a **Royal Armouries** collection of cannon, guns, and suits of mail and armour for men and horses. Among the most remarkable exhibits on the entrance floor are Henry VIII's two suits of armour, one made for him when he was a dashing 24-year-old and the other when he was a bloated 50-year-old with a waist measuring 129cm. You won't miss the oversize codpiece. Also here is the fabulous **Line of Kings**, a late-17th-century parade of carved wooden horses and heads of historic kings. On the 1st floor, check out the 2m suit of armour once thought to have been made for the giant-like John of Gaunt and, alongside it, a tiny child's suit of armour designed for James I's young son, the future Charles I. Up on the 2nd floor you'll find the block and axe used to execute Simon Fraser at the last public execution on Tower Hill in 1747.

Medieval Palace & the Bloody Tower

The Medieval Palace is composed of three towers: St Thomas's, Wakefield and Langthorn. Inside **St Thomas's Tower**

Edward I's bedchamber in St Thomas's Tower

(1279) you can look at what the hall and bed-chamber of Edward I might once have been like. Here, archaeologists have peeled back the layers of newer buildings to find what went before. Opposite St Thomas's Tower is **Wakefield Tower**, built by Edward's father, Henry III, between 1220 and 1240. Its upper floor is entered from St Thomas's Tower and has been even more enticingly furnished with a replica throne and other decor to give an impression of how it might have looked as an anteroom in a medieval palace. During the 15th-century Wars of the Roses between the Houses of York and Lancaster, King Henry

★ **Local Knowledge**

Those beheaded on the scaffold outside the Chapel Royal of St Peter ad Vincula – notably Anne Boleyn, Catherine Howard and Lady Jane Grey – were reburied in the chapel in the 19th century.

VI was murdered as (it is said) he knelt in prayer in this tower. A plaque on the chapel floor commemorates this Lancastrian king. The **Langthorn Tower**, residence of medieval queens, is to the east.

Below St Thomas's Tower along Water Lane is the famous **Traitors' Gate**, the portal through which prisoners transported by boat entered the Tower. Opposite Traitors' Gate is the huge portcullis of the Bloody Tower, taking its nickname from the 'princes in the Tower' – Edward V and his younger brother, Richard – who were held here 'for their own safety' and later murdered to annul their claims to the throne. An exhibition inside looks at the life and times of Elizabethan adventurer Sir Walter Raleigh, who was imprisoned here three times by the capricious Elizabeth I and her successor James I.

East Wall Walk

The huge inner wall of the Tower was added to the fortress in 1220 by Henry III to improve the castle's defences. It is 36m wide and is dotted with towers along its length. The East Wall Walk allows you to climb up and tour its eastern edge, beginning in the 13th-century **Salt Tower**, probably used to store saltpetre for gunpowder. The walk also takes in **Broad Arrow Tower** and **Constable Tower**, each containing small exhibits. It ends at the **Martin Tower**, which houses an exhibition about the original coronation regalia. Here you can see some of the older crowns, with their precious stones removed. It was from this tower that Colonel Thomas Blood attempted to steal the Crown Jewels in 1671 disguised as a clergyman. He was caught but – surprisingly – Charles II gave him a full pardon.

Yeoman Warders

A true icon of the Tower, the Yeoman Warders have been guarding the fortress since the 15th century. There can be up to 40 and, in order to qualify for the job, they

GOGA18128 / SHUTTERSTOCK ©

★ **Did You Know?**

Over the years, the tower has served as a palace, an observatory, an armoury, a mint and even a zoo.

must have served a minimum of 22 years in any branch of the British Armed Forces. In 2007 the first woman was appointed to the post. While officially they guard the Tower, their main role these days is as tour guides. Free 45-minute-long tours leave from the bridge near the main entrance every 30 minutes until 3.30pm (2.30pm in winter).

What's Nearby?

Tower Bridge
Bridge

(Map p78; ☎020-7403 3761; www.towerbridge. org.uk; Tower Bridge, SE1; ☺24hr; ⓤTower Hill) One of London's most recognisable sights, familiar from dozens of movies, Tower Bridge doesn't disappoint in real life. Its neo-Gothic towers and sky-blue suspension struts add extraordinary elegance to what is a supremely functional structure. London was a thriving port in 1894 when it was built as a much-needed crossing point in the east, equipped with a then-revolutionary steam-driven bascule (counterbalance) mechanism that could raise the roadway to make way for oncoming ships in just three minutes.

A lift leads up from the northern tower to the **Tower Bridge Exhibition** (Map p78; ☎020-7403 3761; www.towerbridge.org.uk; Tower Bridge, SE1; adult/child £9.80/4.20, incl the Monument £12/5.50; ☺10am-5.30pm Apr-Sep, 9.30am-5pm Oct-Mar; ⓤTower Hill), where the story of building the bridge is recounted. Tower Bridge was designed by architect Horace Jones, who was also responsible for Smithfield and Leadenhall markets, and completed by engineer John Wolfe Barry.

The bridge is still operational, although these days it's electrically powered and rises mainly for pleasure craft. It does so around 1000 times a year and as often as 10 times a day in summer; check the Exhibition website for times to see it in action.

Monument
Monument

(Map p78; ☎020-7621 0285; www.the monument.org.uk; Fish St Hill, EC3; adult/child £5/2.50, incl Tower Bridge Exhibition £12/5.50; ☺9.30am-5.30pm Apr-Sep, to 5pm Oct-Mar; ⓤMonument) Sir Christopher Wren's 1677 column, known simply as the Monument, is a memorial to the Great Fire of London of 1666,

whose impact on the city's history cannot be overstated. An immense Doric column made of Portland stone, the Monument is 4.5m wide and 60.6m tall – the exact distance it stands from the bakery in Pudding Lane where the fire is thought to have started.

Although Lilliputian by today's standards, the Monument towered over London when it was built. Climbing up the column's 311 spiral steps still rewards you with great views, due as much to its central location as to its height.

It's topped with a gilded bronze urn of flames that some think resembles a big gold pincushion. An earlier Wren design had in its place a phoenix rising from the ashes, while another substituted that for a large statue of Charles II, before the current appearance was selected. If you're wondering about the chiselled-out section of the Latin inscription on the side, text erroneously blaming Catholics for the fire was erased in 1830.

Leadenhall Market

Leadenhall Market Market

(Map p78; www.leadenhallmarket.co.uk; Whittington Ave, EC3; ☺public areas 24hr, Ⓤ Bank)
The Romans had their Forum on this site, but this covered shopping strip off Gracechurch St harks back to the Victorian era, with cobblestones underfoot and late-19th-century ironwork linking its shops and bars. The market appears as Diagon Alley in *Harry Potter and the Philosopher's Stone*, while the optician's shop with a blue door on Bull's Head Passage was used as the entrance to the Leaky Cauldron in *Harry Potter and the Goblet of Fire*.

30 St Mary Axe Notable Building

(Map p78; www.thegherkinlondon.com; 30 St Mary Axe, EC3; Ⓤ Aldgate) Nicknamed 'the Gherkin' for its distinctive shape and emerald hue, 30 St Mary Axe remains the City's most intriguing skyscraper, despite the best efforts of the engineering individualism that now surrounds it. It was built in 2003 by award-winning architect Norman Foster, with a futuristic exterior that has become an emblem of modern London – as recognisable as Big Ben. While the building is generally only open to those working in it, **HELIX**, a 39th-floor restaurant with panoramic views, is open to everyone (booking essential).

★ **Local Knowledge**

Common ravens, which once feasted on the corpses of beheaded traitors, have been here for centuries. Nowadays, they feed on raw beef and biscuits.

★ **Did You Know?**

Yeoman Warders are nicknamed Beefeaters. It's thought to be due to the rations of beef – then a luxury food – given to them in the past.

PHILIP BIRD LRPS CPAGB / SHUTTERSTOCK ©

A Northern Point of View

This walk takes in North London's most interesting locales, including celebrity-infested Primrose Hill and chaotic Camden Town, home to loud guitar bands and the last of London's cartoon punks.

Start Chalk Farm tube station
Distance 2.5 miles
Duration Two hours

Classic Photo: London's skyline from atop Primrose Hill

2 In **Primrose Hill**, walk to the top of the park where you'll find a classic view of central London's skyline.

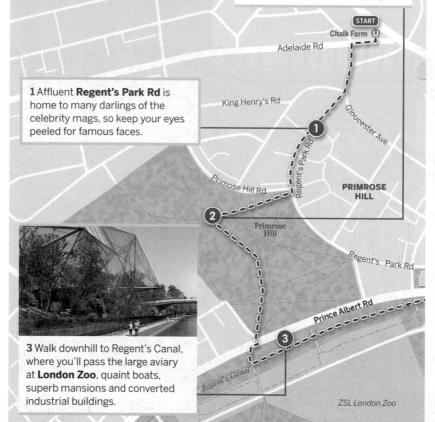

START
Chalk Farm Ⓤ

Adelaide Rd

1 Affluent **Regent's Park Rd** is home to many darlings of the celebrity mags, so keep your eyes peeled for famous faces.

King Henry's Rd

Gloucester Ave

❶

Regent's Park Rd

Primrose Hill Rd

PRIMROSE HILL

❷

Primrose Hill

Regent's Park Rd

Prince Albert Rd

❸

3 Walk downhill to Regent's Canal, where you'll pass the large aviary at **London Zoo**, quaint boats, superb mansions and converted industrial buildings.

Regent's Canal

ZSL London Zoo

0
400 m

0
0.2 miles

4 At **Camden Lock** turn left into buzzing Lock Market, with its original fashion, ethnic art and food stalls.

5 Exit onto **Camden High St** and turn right onto bar-lined Inverness St, which hosts its own little market.

Chalk Farm Rd

Camden Lock Pl

Camden High St

CAMDEN TOWN

Regent's Canal

Jamestown Rd

Princess Rd

Gloucester Ave

Gloucester Cres

Inverness St

Oval Rd

Parkway

6 At **Gloucester Cres** turn left and walk past the glorious Georgian townhouses.

Take a Break... Enjoy excellent fresh fish and seaweed-salted chips at Hook Camden Town (p83).

FINISH

Delancey St

Mornington Tce

Regent's Park

Albany St

7 Head towards Delancey St and make a beeline for the **Edinboro Castle** (Map p82; www.edinborocastle pub.co.uk; 57 Mornington Tce, NW1; ⊘noon-11pm Mon-Sat, to 10.30pm Sun; Ⓤ Camden Town), where this walk ends with a well-deserved drink!

◉ SIGHTS

◉ The West End

National Gallery   Gallery

(Map p76; 📞020-7747 2885; www.national
gallery.org.uk; Trafalgar Sq, WC2; ⏱10am-6pm
Sat-Thu, to 9pm Fri; Ⓤ Charing Cross) **FREE** With
more than 2300 European masterpieces in
its collection, this is one of the world's great
galleries, with seminal works from the 13th
to the mid-20th century, including masterpieces by Leonardo da Vinci, Michelangelo,
Titian, Vincent van Gogh and Auguste
Renoir. Many visitors flock to the eastern
rooms on the main floor (1700–1930),
where works by British artists such as
Thomas Gainsborough, John Constable
and JMW Turner, and Impressionist and
post-Impressionist masterpieces by Van
Gogh, Renoir and Claude Monet await.

National Portrait Gallery   Gallery

(Map p76; 📞020-7306 0055; www.npg.org.uk;
St Martin's Pl, WC2; ⏱10am-6pm Sat-Thu, to
9pm Fri; Ⓤ Charing Cross or Leicester Sq) **FREE**
What makes the National Portrait Gallery
so compelling is its familiarity; in many
cases, you'll have heard of the subject
(royals, scientists, politicians, celebrities)
or the artist (Andy Warhol, Annie Leibovitz,
Lucian Freud) but not necessarily recognise
the face. Highlights include the famous
'Chandos portrait', thought to be of William
Shakespeare (room 4), the first artwork the
gallery acquired (in 1856), and a touching
sketch of novelist Jane Austen by her sister
(room 18).

Houses of Parliament   Historic Building

(Map p76; 📞tours 020-7219 4114; www.
parliament.uk; Parliament Sq, SW1; guided tour
adult/child/under 5yr £28/12/free, audio guide
tour £20.50/8.50/free; Ⓤ Westminster) A visit
here is a journey to the heart of UK democracy. The Houses of Parliament are officially called the Palace of Westminster, and
its oldest part is 11th-century **Westminster
Hall**, one of only a few sections that survived a catastrophic 1834 fire. The rest is
mostly a neo-Gothic confection built over
36 years from 1840. The palace's most
famous feature is its clock tower, Elizabeth
Tower – but better known as **Big Ben** (Map
p76; www.parliament.uk/visiting/visiting-and-

National Gallery at Trafalgar Square

CLAUDIO DIVIZIA / SHUTTERSTOCK ©

tours/tours-of-parliament/bigben; Bridge St; [U]Westminster) – covered in scaffolding until restoration works are finished in 2021.

Trafalgar Square
Square

(Map p76; [U]Charing Cross or Embankment) Opened to the public in 1844, Trafalgar Sq is the true centre of London, where rallies and marches take place, tens of thousands of revellers usher in the New Year and locals congregate for anything from communal open-air cinema and Christmas celebrations to political protests. It is dominated by the 52m-high **Nelson's Column**, guarded by four **bronze lion statues**, and ringed by many splendid buildings, including the National Gallery and the church of **St Martin-in-the-Fields** (Map p76; ✆020-7766 1100; www.stmartin-in-the-fields.org; Trafalgar Sq, WC2; ⊗8.30am-6pm Mon-Fri, 9am-6pm Sat & Sun; [U]Charing Cross).

Churchill War Rooms
Museum

(Map p76; ✆020-7416 5000; www.iwm.org.uk/visits/churchill-war-rooms; Clive Steps, King Charles St, SW1; adult/child £21/10.50; ⊗9.30am-6pm; [U]Westminster) Former Prime Minister Winston Churchill helped coordinate the Allied resistance against Nazi Germany on a Bakelite telephone from this underground complex during WWII. The Cabinet War Rooms remain much as they were when the lights were switched off in 1945, capturing the drama and dogged spirit of the time, while the modern multimedia Churchill Museum affords intriguing insights into the life and times of the resolute, cigar-smoking wartime leader.

Tate Britain
Gallery

(Map p76; ✆020-7887 8888; www.tate.org.uk/visit/tate-britain; Millbank, SW1; ⊗10am-6pm; [U]Pimlico) **FREE** On the site of the former Millbank Penitentiary, the older and more venerable of the two Tate siblings opened in 1892 and celebrates British art from 1500 to the present, including pieces from William Blake, William Hogarth, Thomas Gainsborough and John Constable, as well as vibrant modern and contemporary pieces from Lucian Freud, Barbara

🛍 Camden Market

Although – or perhaps because – it stopped being cutting-edge several thousand cheap leather jackets ago, **Camden Market** (Map p82; www.camdenmarket.com; Camden High St, NW1; ⊗10am-late; [U]Camden Town or Chalk Farm) attracts millions of visitors each year and is one of London's most popular attractions. What started out as a collection of attractive craft stalls beside Camden Lock on the Regent's Canal now extends most of the way from Camden Town tube station to Chalk Farm tube station.

IVAN / GETTY IMAGES ©

Hepworth, Francis Bacon and Henry Moore. The stars of the show are, undoubtedly, the light-infused visions of JMW Turner in the Clore Gallery.

◎ The City
St Paul's Cathedral
Cathedral

(Map p78; ✆020-7246 8357; www.stpauls.co.uk; St Paul's Churchyard, EC4; adult/child £18/8; ⊗8.30am-4.30pm Mon-Sat; [U]St Paul's) Towering over diminutive Ludgate Hill in a superb position that's been a place of Christian worship for over 1400 years (and pagan before that), St Paul's is one of London's most magnificent buildings. For Londoners, the vast dome is a symbol of resilience and pride, standing tall for more than 300 years. Viewing Sir Christopher Wren's masterpiece from the inside and climbing to the top for sweeping views of the capital is a celestial experience.

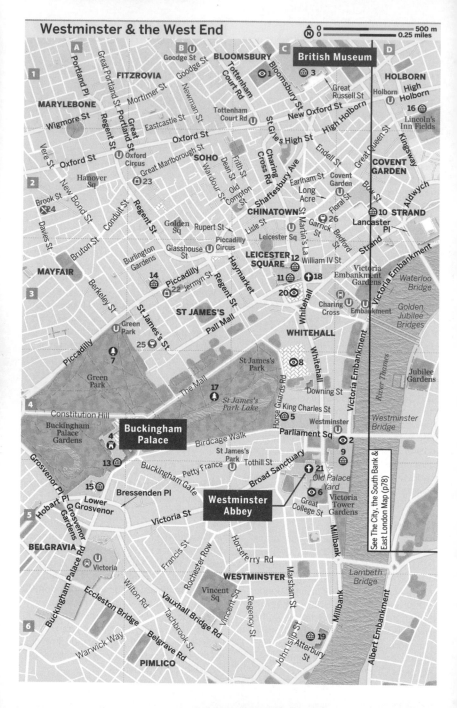

Westminster & the West End

N 0 / 0 — 500 m / 0.25 miles

British Museum

Buckingham Palace

Westminster Abbey

MARYLEBONE

FITZROVIA

BLOOMSBURY

HOLBORN

SOHO

COVENT GARDEN

CHINATOWN

MAYFAIR

LEICESTER SQUARE

STRAND

ST JAMES'S

WHITEHALL

BELGRAVIA

WESTMINSTER

PIMLICO

Green Park

St James's Park

St James's Park Lake

Green Park

Buckingham Palace Gardens

Victoria Embankment Gardens

Victoria Tower Gardens

Waterloo Bridge

Golden Jubilee Bridges

Jubilee Gardens

River Thames

Westminster Bridge

Lambeth Bridge

See The City, the South Bank & East London Map (p78)

Westminster & the West End

Museum of London   Museum

(Map p78; 📞020-7001 9844; www.museumof
london.org.uk; 150 London Wall, EC2; ⊙10am-
6pm; Ⓤ Barbican) **FREE** Set aside two hours
to romp through 450,000 years of London
history at this entertaining and educational
museum, one of the capital's finest. It exhibits everything from a mammoth's jaw found
in Ilford to Oliver Cromwell's death mask
via the desperate scrawls of convicts on a
cell from Wellclose Prison. Interactive displays and reconstructed scenes transport
visitors from Roman Londinium and Saxon
Ludenwic right up to the 21st-century
metropolis. Free themed tours offered daily;
times displayed by the entrance.

◎ The South Bank

Tate Modern   Gallery

(Map p78; 📞020-7887 8888; www.tate.org.uk;
Bankside, SE1; ⊙10am-6pm Sun-Thu, to 10pm Fri &
Sat; 🚇; Ⓤ Blackfriars, Southwark or London Bridge)
FREE One of London's most amazing attractions, this outstanding modern- and contemporary-art gallery is housed in the creatively
revamped Bankside Power Station south of
the **Millennium Bridge** (Map p78; Ⓤ St Paul's
or Blackfriars). A spellbinding synthesis of
modern art and capacious industrial brick
design, Tate Modern has been extraordinarily
successful in bringing challenging work to the
masses, both through its free permanent collection and fee-paying big-name temporary
exhibitions. The stunning **Blavatnik Building**
opened in 2016, increasing the available
exhibition space by 60%.

London Eye   Viewpoint

(Map p78; www.londoneye.com; near County Hall;
adult/child £28/23; ⊙11am-6pm Sep-May, 10am-
8.30pm Jun-Aug; Ⓤ Waterloo or Westminster)
Standing 135m high in a fairly flat city, the
London Eye affords views 25 miles in every
direction, weather permitting. Interactive
tablets provide great information (in six
languages) about landmarks as they appear
in the skyline. Each rotation – or 'flight' –
takes a gracefully slow 30 minutes. At peak
times (July, August and school holidays) it
can feel like you'll spend more time in the
queue than in the capsule; book premium
fast-track tickets to jump the line.

Borough Market   Market

(Map p78; www.boroughmarket.org.uk; 8 Southwark St, SE1; ⊙full market 10am-5pm Wed & Thu,
10am-6pm Fri, 8am-5pm Sat; Ⓤ London Bridge)
Located in this spot in some form or another
since at least the 13th century (and possibly
since 1014), this fantastic market is a sight in
its own right. Expect it to be crowded – even
on days with limited traders (Monday and
Tuesday) it always seems to be overflowing
with food lovers, wide-eyed visitors and
Londoners in search of inspiration for their

The City, the South Bank & East London

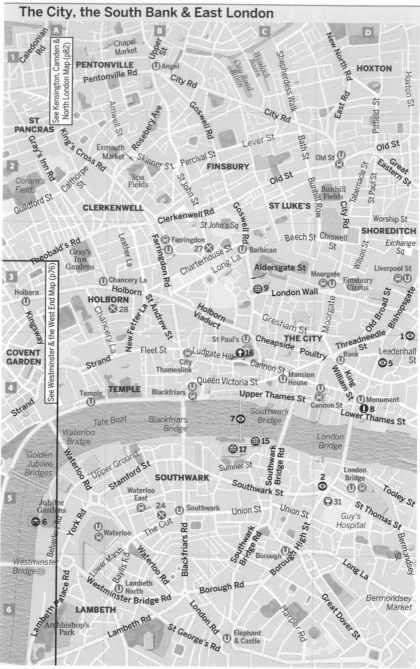

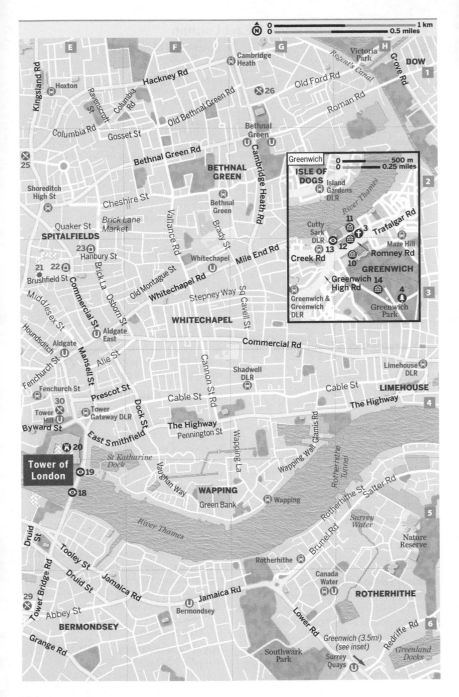

The City, the South Bank & East London

meals. The market specialises in high-end fresh products; there are also plenty of take-away stalls and lots of dessert options.

◎ Kensington & Hyde Park

Hyde Park　Park
(Map p82; www.royalparks.org.uk/parks/hyde-park; ☉5am-midnight; Ⓤ Marble Arch, Hyde Park Corner, Knightsbridge or Queensway) Hyde Park is central London's largest green space, expropriated from the church in 1536 by Henry VIII and turned into a hunting ground and later a venue for duels, executions and horse racing. The 1851 Great Exhibition was held here, and during WWII the park became an enormous potato field. These days, it's a place to stroll and picnic, boat on the **Serpentine lake** (Map p82; ☏020-7262 1330; Ⓤ Lancaster Gate or Knightsbridge), or to catch a summer concert or outdoor film during the warmer months.

Natural History Museum　Museum
(Map p82; www.nhm.ac.uk; Cromwell Rd, SW7; ☉10am-5.50pm; ⛪; Ⓤ South Kensington) FREE This colossal and magnificent-looking building is infused with the irrepressible Victorian spirit of collecting, cataloguing and interpreting the natural world. The **Dinosaurs Gallery** (Blue Zone) is a must

for children, who gawp at the animatronic T-rex, fossils and excellent displays. Adults will love the intriguing Treasures exhibition in the **Cadogan Gallery** (Green Zone), which houses a host of unrelated objects, from a chunk of moon rock to a dodo skeleton, each telling its own unique story.

Victoria & Albert Museum　Museum
(V&A; Map p82; ☏020-7942 2000; www.vam.ac.uk; Cromwell Rd, SW7; ☉10am-5.45pm Sat-Thu, to 10pm Fri; Ⓤ South Kensington) FREE The Museum of Manufactures, as the V&A was known when it opened in 1852, was part of Prince Albert's legacy to the nation in the aftermath of the successful Great Exhibition of 1851. It houses the world's largest collection of decorative arts, from Asian ceramics to Middle Eastern rugs, Chinese paintings, Western furniture, fashion from all ages and modern-day domestic appliances. The (ticketed) temporary exhibitions are another highlight, covering anything from David Bowie retrospectives to designer Alexander McQueen, special materials and trends.

◎ Greenwich

Royal Observatory　Historic Building
(Map p78; ☏020-8312 6565; www.rmg.co.uk/royal-observatory; Greenwich Park, Blackheath

Ave, SE10; adult/child £10/6.50, incl Cutty Sark £20/11.50; ⊙10am-5pm Sep-Jun, to 6pm Jul & Aug; Ⓤ Greenwich or Cutty Sark) Rising like a beacon of time atop **Greenwich Park** (Map p78; www.royalparks.org.uk; King George St, SE10; ⊙6am-around sunset; Ⓤ Greenwich, Maze Hill or Cutty Sark), the Royal Observatory is home to the **prime meridian** (longitude 0° 0' 0''). Tickets include access to the Christopher Wren–designed **Flamsteed House** (named for the first Royal Astronomer) and the **Meridian Courtyard**, where you can stand with your feet straddling the eastern and western hemispheres. You can also see the Great Equatorial Telescope (1893) inside the onion-domed observatory and explore space and time in the **Weller Astronomy Galleries**.

Old Royal Naval College
Historic Building

(Map p78; www.ornc.org; 2 Cutty Sark Gardens, SE10; ⊙10am-5pm, grounds 8am-11pm; Ⓤ Cutty Sark) FREE Sir Christopher Wren's baroque masterpiece in Greenwich and indeed Britain's largest ensemble of baroque architecture, the Old Royal Naval College contains the neoclassical **Chapel of St Peter and St Paul** (Map p78; www.ornc.org/chapel; SE10; ⊙10am-5pm; Ⓤ Cutty Sark) and the extraordinary **Painted Hall** (Map p78; ☎020-8269 4799; www.ornc.org; Old Royal Naval College, SE10; adult/child £12/free; ⊙10am-5pm; Ⓤ Cutty Sark) FREE. The entire Old Royal Naval College, including the chapel, the **visitor centre** (Map p78; www.ornc.org/visitor-centre; Pepys Bldg, King William Walk, SE10; ⊙10am-5pm; Ⓤ Cutty Sark) FREE, and the grounds, can be visited for free. Volunteers lead free 45-minute tours throughout the day from the visitor centre.

National Maritime Museum
Museum

(Map p78; ☎020-8312 6565; www.rmg.co.uk/national-maritime-museum; Romney Rd, SE10; ⊙10am-5pm; Ⓤ Cutty Sark) FREE Narrating the long, briny and eventful history of seafaring Britain, this excellent museum's exhibits are arranged thematically, with highlights including *Miss Britain III* (the first boat to top 100mph on open water) from 1933, the

19m-long golden state barge built in 1732 for Frederick, Prince of Wales, the huge ship's propeller and the colourful figureheads installed on the ground floor. Families will love these, as well as the ship simulator and the 'All Hands' children's gallery on the 2nd floor.

⊙ Kew & Hampton Court

Hampton Court Palace
Palace

(www.hrp.org.uk/hamptoncourtpalace; Hampton Court Palace, KT8; adult/child/family £22.70/11.35/40.40; ⊙10am-4.30pm Nov-Mar, to 6pm Apr-Oct; ⊕ Hampton Court Palace, ⒭ Hampton Court) Built by Cardinal Thomas Wolsey in 1515 but coaxed from him by Henry VIII just before Wolsey (as chancellor) fell from favour, Hampton Court Palace is England's largest and grandest Tudor structure. It was already one of Europe's most beautiful palaces when, in the 17th century, Christopher Wren designed an extension. The result is a beautiful blend of Tudor and 'restrained baroque' architecture. You could easily spend a day exploring the palace and its 24 hectares of riverside gardens, including a 300-year-old **maze** (adult/child/family £4.40/2.70/12.80; ⊙10am-5.15pm Apr-Oct, to 3.45pm Nov-Mar; ⊕ Hampton Court Palace, ⒭ Hampton Court).

Kew Gardens
Gardens

(Royal Botanic Gardens, Kew; www.kew.org; Kew Rd, TW9; adult/child £13.50/4.50; ⊙10am-6pm Sep, to 5pm Oct, to 3pm Nov-Jan, closes later Feb-Aug; ⊕ Kew Pier, ⒭ Kew Bridge, Ⓤ Kew Gardens) In 1759 botanists began rummaging around the world for specimens to plant in the 3-hectare Royal Botanic Gardens at Kew. They never stopped collecting, and the gardens, which have bloomed to 121 hectares, provide the most comprehensive botanical collection on earth (including the world's largest collection of orchids). A Unesco World Heritage Site, the gardens can easily devour a day's exploration; for those pressed for time, the **Kew Explorer** (☎020-8332 5648; www.kew.org/kew-gardens/whats-on/kew-explorer-land-train; Kew Gardens, TW9; adult/child £5/2; ⒭ Kew Gardens, Ⓤ Kew Gardens) hop-on/hop-off road train takes in the main sights.

Kensington, Camden & North London

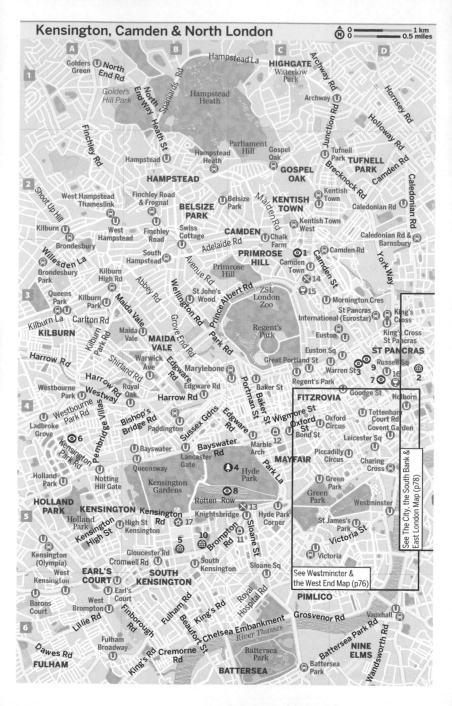

See The City, the South Bank & East London Map (p78)

See Westminster & the West End Map (p76)

Kensington, Camden & North London

⊙ TOURS

Guide London   Tours
(Association of Professional Tourist Guides;
📞020-7611 2545; www.guidelondon.org.uk; half-/
full day £165/270) Hire a prestigious Blue
Badge Tourist Guide, know-it-all guides who
have studied for two years and passed a
dozen written and practical exams to do
their job. They can tell you stories behind
the sights that you'd only hear from them
or whisk you on a themed tour (eg royalty,
the Beatles, parks, shopping). Go by car,
public transport, bike or on foot.

Hidden London   Tours
(📞020-7565 7298; www.ltmuseum.co.uk/
whats-on/hidden-london; tours £35-85) Get
under the skin of London on an incredible
insider-access tour run by the **London
Transport Museum** (Map p76; 📞020 7379
6344; www.ltmuseum.co.uk; Covent Garden
Piazza, WC2; adult/child £17.50/free; ☺10am-
6pm; 👪; Ⓤ Covent Garden). Excursions take
you to the depths of the city's abandoned
tube stations, which have been film sets for
a number of flicks including *Skyfall* and *V
for Vendetta*, and to the heights of London's
first skyscraper at 55 Broadway, Transport
for London's art-deco HQ.

Shoreditch Street Art Tours   Walking
(Map p78; 📞07834 088533; www.shoreditch
streetarttours.co.uk; tours start at Goat Statue,
Brushfield St, E1; adult/child under 16 £15/10;
☺tours usually 10am or 1.30pm Fri-Sun; Ⓤ Liver-

pool St) The walls of Brick Lane and Shoreditch are an ever-changing open-air gallery
of street art, moonlighting as the canvas for
legends such as Banksy and Eine as well
as more obscure artists. Passionate guide
Dave, who was bored of his job in the City,
once spent his lunch breaks roaming these
streets, but he now helps translate the
stunning pieces to a rapt audience.

🛍 SHOPPING

Fortnum & Mason   Department Store
(Map p76; 📞020-7734 8040; www.fortnum
andmason.com; 181 Piccadilly, W1; ☺10am-9pm
Mon-Sat, 11.30am-6pm Sun; Ⓤ Green Park or
Piccadilly Circus) With its classic eau-de-Nil
(pale green) colour scheme, the 'Queen's
grocery store' established in 1707 refuses
to yield to modern times. Its staff – men
and women – still wear old-fashioned
tailcoats, and its glamorous food hall is
supplied with hampers, marmalade and
speciality teas. Stop for a spot of afternoon
tea at the Diamond Jubilee Tea Salon,
visited by Queen Elizabeth II in 2012.

Liberty   Department Store
(Map p76; 📞020-7734 1234; www.liberty
london.com; Regent St, entrance on Great Marlborough St, W1; ☺10am-8pm Mon-Sat, 11.30am-
6pm Sun; ☏; Ⓤ Oxford Circus) One of London's
most recognisable shops, Liberty department store has a white-and-wood-beam
Tudor Revival facade that lures shoppers

London Markets

Perhaps the biggest draw for visitors is the capital's famed markets. These treasure troves of small designers, unique jewellery pieces, original framed photographs and posters, colourful vintage pieces and bric-a-brac, are the antidote to impersonal, carbon-copy shopping centres.

The most popular markets are Camden (p75), **Old Spitalfields** (Map p78; www.oldspitalfieldsmarket.com; Commercial St, E1; ⊗10am-8pm Mon-Fri, to 6pm Sat, to 5pm Sun; ⓤLiverpool St, Shoreditch High St or Aldgate East) and **Portobello Road** (Map p82; www.porto bellomarket.org; Portobello Rd, W10; ⊗8am-6.30pm Mon-Wed, Fri & Sat, to 1pm Thu; ⓤNotting Hill Gate or Ladbroke Grove), which operate most days, but there are dozens of others, such as Brick Lane's excellent **Sunday Upmarket** (Map p78; ☎020-7770 6028; www.sundayupmarket.co.uk; Old Truman Brewery, 91 Brick Lane, E1; ⊗11am-6pm Sat, 10am-5pm Sun; ⓤShoreditch High St), which only pop up on the weekend. Camden and Old Spitalfields are both mainly covered, but even the outdoor markets are busy, rain or shine.

Old Spitalfields Market
GRAPHICAL_BANK / SHUTTERSTOCK ©

in to browse luxury contemporary fashion, homewares, cosmetics and accessories, all at sky-high prices. Liberty is known for its fabrics and has a full haberdashery department; a classic London gift or souvenir is a Liberty fabric print, especially in the form of a scarf.

Selfridges Department Store

(Map p82; ☎0800 123 400; www.selfridges.com; 400 Oxford St, W1; ⊗9am-10pm Mon-Sat, 11.30am-6pm Sun; ⓤBond St) Set in a grandiose column-flanked Grade II–listed structure, Selfridges has been innovating since its doors opened in 1909. Its wacky, ever-changing window displays draw a crowd of its own, especially at Christmas. Inside, an unparalleled food hall, sprawling cosmetics stations and the usual department-store essentials are topped by a rooftop restaurant with delicious city views.

Harrods Department Store

(Map p82; ☎020-7730 1234; www.harrods.com; 87-135 Brompton Rd, SW1; ⊗10am-9pm Mon-Sat, 11.30am-6pm Sun; ⓤKnightsbridge) Garish and stylish in equal measure, perennially crowded Harrods is an obligatory stop for visitors, from the cash-strapped to the big spenders. The stock is astonishing, as are many of the price tags. High on kitsch, the 'Egyptian Elevator' resembles something out of an Indiana Jones epic, while the memorial fountain to Dodi and Di (lower ground floor) merely adds surrealism.

⊗ EATING

Once the butt of many a culinary joke, London has transformed itself over the last few decades and today is a global dining destination. World-famous chefs can be found at the helm of several top-tier restaurants, but it is the sheer diversity on offer that is head-spinning: from Afghan to Zambian, London delivers an A to Z of world cuisine.

Hook Camden Town Fish & Chips £

(Map p82; www.hookrestaurants.com; 63-65 Parkway, NW1; mains £8-12; ⊗hours vary, usually noon 3pm & 5.30-9pm/10pm most days; ⓐ; ⓤCamden Town) ✹ In addition to working entirely with sustainable small fisheries and local suppliers, Hook makes all its sauces on-site and wraps its fish in recycled materials, supplying diners with extraordinarily fine-tasting morsels. Totally fresh, the fish arrives in panko breadcrumbs or tempura batter, with seaweed salted chips. Wash it down with craft beer, wines and cocktails.

Watch House
Cafe £

(Map p78; 020 7407 6431; www.thewatch house.com; 199 Bermondsey St, SE1; mains from £4.95; 7am-6pm Mon-Fri, 8am-6pm Sat & Sun; ; Borough or London Bridge) Saying that the Watch House nails the sandwich wouldn't really do justice to this tip-top cafe: the sandwiches really are delicious. There is also great coffee and treats for the sweet-toothed. The small but lovely setting is a renovated 19th-century watch-house from where guards watched over the next-door cemetery. No bathroom.

St John
British ££

(Map p78; 020-7251 0848; www.stjohn restaurant.com; 26 St John St, EC1; mains £15.80-28; noon-3pm & 6-11pm Mon-Fri, 6-11pm Sat, 12.30-4pm Sun; Farringdon) Around the corner from London's last remaining meat market, St John is the standard-bearer for nose-to-tail cuisine, which makes use of every part of the animal. With whitewashed brick walls, high ceilings and simple wooden furniture, it's surely one of the most humble Michelin-starred restaurants anywhere. The menu changes daily but is likely to include the signature roast bone marrow and parsley salad.

Anchor & Hope
Gastropub ££

(Map p78; 020-7928 9898; www.anchorand hopepub.co.uk; 36 The Cut, SE1; mains £12-20; 5-11pm Mon, 11am-11pm Tue-Sat, 12.30-3.15pm Sun; Southwark) The Anchor & Hope is a quintessential gastropub: elegant but not formal, serving utterly delicious European fare with a British twist. The menu changes daily, but could include grilled sole served with spinach, or roast rabbit with green beans in a mustard and bacon sauce. Bookings taken for Sunday lunch only.

Corner Room
Modern British ££

(Map p78; 020-7871 0460; www.townhallhotel. com; Patriot Sq, E2; mains £13-14, 2-/3-course lunch £19/23; noon-4pm Mon-Fri, noon-2.30pm Sat & Sun, 6-9.45pm Sun-Wed, 6-10.15pm Thu-Sat; Bethnal Green) Tucked away on the 1st floor of the Town Hall Hotel, this relaxed industrial-chic restaurant serves expertly crafted dishes with complex yet delicate flavours, highlighting the best of British seasonal produce, with a French touch.

Harrods

PITK / SHUTTERSTOCK ©

Foyer & Reading Room at Claridge's

Foyer & Reading Room at Claridge's
British £££

(Map p76; 020-7107 8886; www.claridges. co.uk; Brook St, W1; afternoon tea £65, with champagne £75-85; afternoon tea 2.45-5.30pm; ; Bond St) Extend that pinkie finger to partake in afternoon tea within the classic art deco foyer and Reading Room of the landmark hotel Claridge's, where the gentle clink of fine porcelain and champagne glasses could be a defining memory of your trip to London. The setting is gorgeous and the dress code is smart casual to befit the surroundings.

Vanilla Black
Vegetarian £££

(Map p78; 020-7242 2622; www.vanillablack. co.uk; 17-18 Took's Ct; 3-/4-course £31/41.50; noon-2.30pm & 6-10pm Mon-Sat; ; Chancery Lane) You'll need a reservation (and perhaps a compass) to dine at this vegetarian institution, located along an empty backstreet behind Chancery Lane. But your efforts will be rewarded with one of the finest dining experiences in the City. An ever-changing menu of imaginative, decon-structed dishes elevates vegetables from

sideshow to superstar; think vanilla-roasted celeriac profiteroles with dill and raisins.

Clove Club
Gastronomy £££

(Map p78; 020-7729 6496; www.thecloveclub. com; Shoreditch Town Hall, 380 Old St, EC1; lunch £65, dinner £95-145; noon-1.45pm Tue-Sat, 6-10.30pm Mon-Sat; ; Old St) From humble origins as a supper club in a London flat, the Clove Club has transformed into this impressive Michelin-starred restaurant, named one of the world's best in 2017. The menu is a mystery until dishes arrive at the table; expect intricately arranged plates with impeccably sourced ingredients from around the British Isles. Your wallet might feel empty, but you sure won't.

Dinner by Heston Blumenthal
Modern British £££

(Map p82; 020-7201 3833; www.dinnerby heston.com; Mandarin Oriental Hyde Park, 66 Knightsbridge, SW1; 3-course set lunch £45, mains £33-52; noon-2pm & 6-10.15pm Mon-Fri, noon-2.30pm & 6.30-10.30pm Sat & Sun; ; Knightsbridge) Sumptuously presented Dinner is a gastronomic tour de force, taking diners on a journey through British culinary history (with inventive modern inflections). Dishes carry historical dates to convey context, while the restaurant interior is a design triumph, from the glass-walled kitchen and its overhead clock mechanism to the large windows looking onto the park. Book ahead.

🍷 DRINKING & NIGHTLIFE

You need only glance at William Hogarth's *Gin Lane* prints from 1751 to realise that Londoners and alcohol have had more than a passing acquaintance. The metropolis offers a huge variety of venues to wet your whistle in – from cosy neighbourhood pubs to glitzy all-night clubs, and everything in between.

Lamb & Flag
Pub

(Map p76; ☎020-7497 9504; www.lambandflag coventgarden.co.uk; 33 Rose St, WC2; ⊙11am-11pm Mon-Sat, noon-10.30pm Sun; ⓊCovent Garden) Perpetually busy pint-sized Lamb & Flag is full of charm and history, and has been a public house since at least 1772. Rain or shine, you'll have to elbow your way through the merry crowd drinking outside to get to the bar. The main entrance is at the top of tiny, cobbled Rose St.

Dukes London
Cocktail Bar

(Map p76; ☎020-7491 4840; www.dukeshotel. com/dukes-bar; Dukes Hotel, 35 St James's Pl, SW1; ⊙2-11pm Mon-Sat, 4-10.30pm Sun; ⓪; ⓊGreen Park) Sip to-die-for martinis in a gentlemen's-club-like ambience at this classic bar where white-jacketed masters mix up perfect preparations. James Bond fans in particular should make a pilgrimage here: author Ian Fleming used to frequent the place, where he undoubtedly ordered his drinks 'shaken, not stirred'. Smokers can ease into the secluded Cognac and Cigar Garden to light up cigars purchased here.

George Inn
Pub

(NT; Map p78; ☎020-7407 2056; www.national trust.org.uk/george-inn; 77 Borough High St, SE1; ⊙11am-11pm Mon-Thu, to midnight Fri & Sat,

The Pub

The pub (public house) is at the heart of London life and is one of the capital's great social levellers. Virtually every Londoner has a 'local' and looking for your own is a fun part of any visit to the capital.

Pubs in the City and other central areas are mostly after-work drinking dens, busy from 5pm onwards with the post-work crowd during the week. But in more residential areas, pubs come into their own at weekends, when long lunches turn into sloshy afternoons and groups of friends settle in for the night. Many also run popular quizzes on weeknights. Other pubs entice punters through the doors with live music or comedy. Some have developed such a reputation for the quality of their food that they've been dubbed gastropubs.

You can order almost any beverage you like in a pub: beer, wine, soft drinks, spirits and sometimes hot drinks too. Some specialise in craft beer, offering drinks from local microbreweries, including real ale, fruit beers, organic ciders and other rarer beverages. Others, particularly the gastropubs, invest in a good wine list.

In winter, some pubs offer mulled wine; in summer the must-have drink is Pimm's and lemonade (if it's properly done it should have fresh mint leaves, citrus, strawberries and cucumber).

noon-10.30pm Sun; [U]London Bridge) This magnificent galleried coaching inn is the last of its kind in London. The present building, owned by the National Trust, dates from 1677 and is mentioned in Charles Dickens' *Little Dorrit*. The picnic benches in the huge cobbled courtyard fill up on balmy evenings (no reservations); otherwise you can find a spot in the labyrinth of dark rooms and corridors inside.

⊘ ENTERTAINMENT

Shakespeare's Globe   Theatre

(Map p78; ✆020-7401 9919; www.shakespeares globe.com; 21 New Globe Walk, SE1; seats £20-45, standing £5; [U]Blackfriars or London Bridge) If you love Shakespeare and the theatre, the **Globe** (Map p78; ✆020-7902 1500; tours adult/child £17/10; ⊙9am-5pm; ⊕) will knock your theatrical socks off. This authentic Shakespearean theatre is a wooden 'O' without a roof over the central stage area, and although there are covered wooden bench seats in tiers around the stage, many people (there's room for 700) do as 17th-century 'groundlings' did, and stand in front of the stage.

Royal Albert Hall   Concert Venue

(Map p82; ✆0845 401 5034; 020-7589 8212; www.royalalberthall.com; Kensington Gore, SW7; [U]South Kensington) This splendid Victorian concert hall hosts classical music, rock and other performances, but is famously the venue for the BBC-sponsored Proms. Booking is possible, but from mid-July to mid-September Promenaders queue for £5 standing tickets that go on sale one hour before curtain-up. Otherwise, the box office and prepaid-ticket collection counter are through door 12 (south side of the hall).

ⓘ INFORMATION

Visit London (www.visitlondon.com) can fill you in on everything from tourist attractions and events (Changing the Guard, Chinese New Year parade etc) to river trips and tours, accommodation, eating, theatre, shopping, children's activities and LGBT+ venues. Kiosks are dotted about the city and can provide maps and brochures; some branches book theatre tickets.

ⓘ GETTING THERE & AWAY

The city has five main airports: Heathrow, which is the largest, to the west; Gatwick to the south; Stansted to the northeast; Luton to the northwest; and London City in Docklands.

Most trans-Atlantic flights land at Heathrow (average flight time from the US East Coast is between 6½ and 7½ hours, 10 to 11 hours from the West Coast; slightly more on the return).

Visitors from Europe are more likely to arrive at Gatwick, Stansted or Luton (the last two are used exclusively by low-cost airlines such as easyJet and Ryanair). Most flights to Continental Europe last from one to three hours.

An increasingly popular form of transport is the Eurostar – the Channel Tunnel train – between London and Paris or Brussels. The journey takes 2¼ hours to Paris and less than two hours to Brussels. Travellers depart from and arrive in the centre of each city.

ⓘ GETTING AROUND

The cheapest way to get around London is with an Oyster Card or a UK contactless card (foreign cardholders should check for contactless charges first).

Tube (London Underground) The fastest and most efficient way of getting around town. First/last trains operate from around 5.30am to 12.30am and 24 hours on Friday and Saturday on five lines.

Train The DLR and Overground network are ideal for zooming across more distant parts of the city. Trains run from a number of stations to more distant destinations in and around London.

Bus The London bus network is very extensive and efficient; while bus lanes free up traffic, buses can still be slow going.

Taxis Black cabs are ubiquitous, but not cheap. Available around the clock.

Bicycle Santander Cycles are great for shorter journeys around central London.

Where to Stay

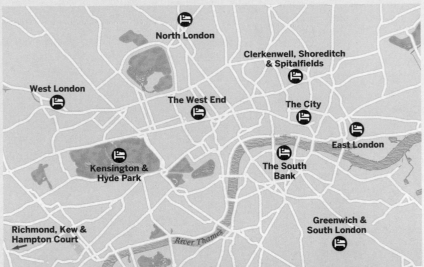

Neighbourhood	Atmosphere
West End	Close to main sights; great transport links; wide range of accommodation in all budgets; good restaurants. Busy tourist areas.
The City	Near St Paul's and Tower of London; good transport links; handy central location; quality hotels; some cheaper weekend rates. Very quiet at weekends; a business district so high prices during the week.
The South Bank	Near Tate Modern, London Eye and Southbank Centre; cheaper than West End; excellent pubs and views. Many chain hotels.
Kensington & Hyde Park	Excellent for South Kensington museums and shopping; great accommodation range; stylish area; good transport. Quite expensive; drinking and nightlife options limited.
Clerkenwell, Shoreditch & Spitalfields	Hip area with great bars and nightlife; excellent for boutique hotels. Few top sights.
East London	Markets, multicultural feel; great restaurants and traditional pubs. Limited sleeping options; some areas less safe at night.
North London	Leafy; vibrant nightlife; pockets of village charm; excellent boutique hotels and hostels; great gastropubs; quiet during the week.
West London	Good shopping, markets and pubs; excellent boutique hotels; good transport. Pricey; light on top sights.
Greenwich & South London	Great boutique options; leafy escapes; near top Greenwich sights. Sights spread out beyond Greenwich; transport limited.
Richmond, Kew & Hampton Court	Smart riverside hotels; semirural pockets; quiet; fantastic riverside pubs. Sights spread out; a long way from central London.

SCOTTISH HIGHLANDS, GREAT BRITAIN

Scottish Highlands, Great Britain

The hills, glens and wild coastline of Scotland's Highlands are the ultimate escape – one of the last corners of Europe where you can discover genuine solitude. Here the landscape is at its grandest, with soaring hills of rock and heather bounded by wooded glens and rushing waterfalls.

Aviemore, Glen Coe and Fort William draw hill walkers and climbers in summer, and skiers, snowboarders and ice climbers in winter. Inverness, the Highland capital, provides urban rest and relaxation, while nearby Loch Ness and its elusive monster add a hint of mystery.

Two Days in the Scottish Highlands

On day one, explore the sights east of Inverness, including **Culloden battlefield** (p102) and **Cawdor Castle** (p100). On day two it's time to go Loch Ness Monster–hunting on a **boat trip** (p98). Next up, tour iconic **Urquhart Castle** (p98), before exploring the loch's quieter eastern shore, including a meal at the lovely **Dores Inn** (p99).

Four Days in the Scottish Highlands

Spend day three exploring Inverness (p100) or take a dolphin-watching **tour** (p100). Finish up with a drive southwest to **Glen Coe**, stopping en route in Fort William to ride a **steam train** (p104) and tour a **distillery** (p95).

Finished with the highlands? Take a 13-hour overnight train to London (p49).

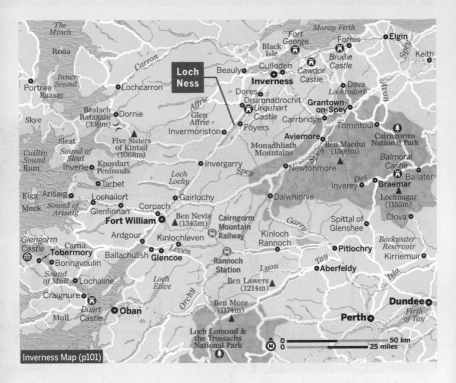

Inverness Map (p101)

Arriving in the Scottish Highlands

Air Inverness Airport at Dalcross has scheduled domestic and some international flights.

Bus There are regular bus services along the Great Glen between Inverness and Fort William.

Train Inverness is connected by train to Glasgow, Edinburgh and London.

Where to Stay

Inverness, Aviemore and Fort William are the main centres for accommodation, but most reasonably sized towns will also have a couple of hotels and a dozen or more B&Bs – many set in superb Victorian villas, farmhouses and manses (former church ministers' houses). Camping is a popular way to enjoy the great outdoors and there's no shortage of official campsites. Wild camping is also widely practised.

Edradour Distillery

On the Whisky Trail

Scotland's national drink – in Gaelic uisge bagh, meaning 'water of life' – has been distilled here for more than 500 years. Over 100 distilleries are still in business, producing hundreds of varieties of single malt, with new operations opening every year.

Great For...

☑ **Don't Miss**

Fèis Ìle (Islay Festival), which celebrates traditional Scottish music and whisky in May.

Whisky has been distilled in Scotland at least since the 15th century and probably much longer. Learning to distinguish the smoky, peaty whiskies of Islay from, say, the flowery, sherried malts of Speyside has become a hugely popular pastime.

Whisky Central

The Speyside region, around Dufftown and Glenlivet, is the epicentre of the whisky industry. More than 50 distilleries open their doors during the twice yearly **Spirit of Speyside Festival** (www.spiritofspeyside. com; ☉May & Sep), and many are open all year long.

Some pubs in the region have become known as whisky bars, because of their staggering range of single malt whiskies – the famous Quaich bar in the **Craigellachie Hotel** (☎01340-881204; www.craigellachie

GUEHOLLY / GETTY IMAGES ©

hotel.co.uk; Craigellachie; r from £150; P 🛜), established in 1894, offers more than 800 different varieties.

Visiting a Distillery

Many distilleries offer guided tours, rounded off with a tasting session. Trying local varieties is a great way to explore the whisky-making regions, but while visiting a distillery can be a memorable experience, only hardcore malt-hounds will want to go to more than one or two. The following are good options for a day trip from Inverness.

Edradour Distillery   Distillery

(☏01796-472095; www.edradour.co.uk; Moulin Rd; tour adult/child £10/5; ⊙10am-5pm Mon-Sat Apr-Oct, to 4.30pm Mon-Fri Nov-Mar; P🍴) This is proudly Scotland's smallest and most picturesque distillery and one of the best to visit: you can see the whole process, easily explained, in one building. It's 2.5 miles east of Pitlochry by car, along the Moulin road, or a pleasant 1-mile walk.

Blair Athol Distillery   Distillery

(☏01796-482003; www.malts.com; Perth Rd; standard tour £8; ⊙10am-5pm Apr-Oct, to 4pm Nov-Mar) Tours here focus on whisky making and the blending of this well-known dram. More detailed private tours give you greater insights and superior tastings.

Glenmorangie   Distillery

(☏01862-892477; www.glenmorangie.com; tours £7.50; ⊙tours 10am-4pm Jun-Aug, 10am-3pm Mon-Sat Apr-May & Sep-Oct, 10am & 2pm Mon-Fri Nov-Mar) Located on Tain's northern outskirts, Glenmorangie (emphasis on the second syllable) produces a fine lightish malt, subjected to a number of different cask finishes for variation. The tour is less in-depth than some but finishes with a free dram. There's a more comprehensive Signet tour (£35) and, for real whisky geeks, a full-day Heritage Tour (£130, April to October).

Nessie Sculpture, Fort Augustus

Loch Ness

Deep, dark and narrow, the bitterly cold waters of Loch Ness have long drawn waves of people hunting Nessie, the elusive Loch Ness Monster. Despite the crowds, it's still possible to find tranquillity and gorgeous views. Add a highly photogenic castle and some superb hiking and you have a loch with bags of appeal.

Great For...

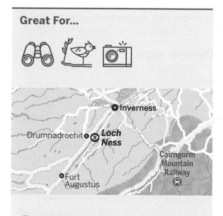

❶ Need to Know

A complete circuit of the loch is about 70 miles; travel anticlockwise for the best views.

★ **Top Tip**

Fancy a spot of Nessie hunting? Check out the latest at www.lochnesssightings. com.

Tales of the Loch Ness Monster truly took off in the 1930s, when reported sightings led to a press furore and a string of high-profile photographs. Reports have tailed off recently, but the bizarre mini-industry that's grown up around Nessie is a spectacle in itself.

Drumnadrochit

Seized by monster madness, its gift shops bulging with Nessie cuddly toys, Drumnadrochit is a hotbed of beastie fever, with Nessie attractions battling it out for the tourist dollar.

The **Loch Ness Centre & Exhibition** (☑01456-450573; www.lochness.com; adult/child £7.95/4.95; ⊗9.30am-6pm Jul & Aug, to 5pm Easter-Jun, Sep & Oct, 10am-4pm Nov-Easter; P⊌) adopts a scientific approach that allows you to weigh the evidence for yourself. Exhibits include those on hoaxes and optical illusions and some original equipment – sonar survey vessels, miniature submarines, cameras and sediment coring tools – used in various monster hunts, as well as original photographs and film footage of reported sightings.

If you want to head out yourself, **Nessie Hunter** (☑01456-450395; www.lochness-cruises.com; adult/child £16/10; ⊗Easter-Oct) offers one-hour monster-hunting cruises, complete with sonar and underwater cameras. Cruises depart from Drumnadrochit hourly (except 1pm) from 10am to 6pm daily.

Urquhart Castle

Commanding a superb location 1.5 miles east of Drumnadrochit, with outstanding views, **Urquhart Castle** (HES; ☑01456-

Urquhart Castle

450551; adult/child £9/5.40; ⊗9.30am-8pm Jun-Aug, to 6pm Apr, May & Sep, to 5pm Oct, to 4.30pm Nov-Mar; P) is a popular Nessie-hunting hotspot. A huge visitor centre (most of which is beneath ground level) includes a video theatre and displays of medieval items discovered in the castle.

The castle has been repeatedly sacked and rebuilt over the centuries; in 1692 it was blown up to prevent the Jacobites from using it. The five-storey tower house at the northern point is the most impressive remaining fragment and offers fine views across the water.

☑ Don't Miss

Climbing to the battlements of the iconic tower of Urquhart Castle, for grandstand views from the rocky head-land, up and down Loch Ness.

BUCCHI FRANCESCO / SHUTTERSTOCK ©

Loch Ness' East Side

While tour coaches pour down the west side of Loch Ness to the hotspots of Drumnadrochit and Urquhart Castle, the narrow B862 road along the eastern shore is relatively peaceful. It leads to the village of Foyers, where you can enjoy a pleasant hike to the Falls of Foyers.

It's also worth making the trip just for the **Dores Inn** (☑01463-751203; www.thedoresinn.co.uk; Dores; mains £10-27; ⊗pub 10am-11pm, food served noon-2pm & 6-9pm; P 🛜), a beautifully restored country pub adorned with recycled furniture, local landscape paintings and fresh flowers. The menu specialises in quality Scottish produce, from haggis, neeps (turnips) and tatties (potatoes), to steaks, scallops and seafood platters. The pub garden has stunning Loch Ness views and a dedicated monster-spotting vantage point.

Hiking at Loch Ness

The South Loch Ness Trail (www.visit invernesslochness.com) links a series of footpaths and minor roads along the less-frequented southern side of the loch. The 28 miles from Loch Tarff near Fort Augustus to Torbreck on the fringes of Inverness can be done on foot, by bike or on horseback.

The climb to the summit of Meallfuar-vonie (699m), on the northwestern shore of Loch Ness, makes an excellent short hill walk: the views along the Great Glen from the top are superb. It's a 6-mile round trip, so allow about three hours. Start from the car park at the end of the minor road lead-ing south from Drumnadrochit to Bunloit.

✕ Take a Break

Drumnadrochit has cafes and restau-rants aplenty, but they can get very busy. To avoid the crowds, head for the Dores Inn on the east side.

Inverness

Inverness has a great location astride the River Ness at the northern end of the Great Glen. In summer it overflows with visitors intent on monster hunting at nearby Loch Ness, but it's worth a visit in its own right for a stroll along the picturesque River Ness, a cruise on Loch Ness, and a meal in one of the city's excellent restaurants. The broad and shallow River Ness, famed for its salmon fishing, runs through the heart of the city.

◉ SIGHTS

Ness Islands   Park

The main attraction in Inverness is a leisurely stroll along the river to the Ness Islands. Planted with mature Scots pine, fir, beech and sycamore, and linked to the river banks and each other by elegant Victorian footbridges, the islands make an appealing picnic spot. They're a 20-minute walk south of the castle – head upstream on either side of the river (the start of the Great Glen Way) and return on the opposite bank.

Fort George   Fortress

(HES; ☑01667-462777; www.historic environment.scot; adult/child £9/5.40; ⊗9.30am-5.30pm Apr-Sep, 10am-4pm Oct-Mar; Ⓟ) One of the finest artillery fortifications in Europe, Fort George was established in 1748 in the aftermath of the Battle of Culloden, as a base for George II's army of occupation in the Highlands. By the time of its completion in 1769 it had cost the equivalent of around £1 billion in today's money. It still functions as a military barracks; public areas have exhibitions on 18th-century soldiery and the mile-plus walk around the ramparts offers fine views.

Given its size, you'll need at least two hours to do the place justice. The fort is off the A96 about 11 miles northeast of Inverness; there is no public transport.

Brodie Castle   Castle

(NTS; ☑01309-641371; www.nts.org.uk; Brodie; adult/child £11/6.50; ⊗10am-5pm Mar-Oct, 11am-3pm Nov & Dec; Ⓟ) Set in 70 hectares of parkland, Brodie Castle has a library with more than 6000 peeling, dusty volumes, wonderful clocks, a huge Victorian kitchen and a 17th-century dining room with wildly extravagant moulded plaster ceilings depicting mythological scenes. The Brodies have been living here since 1160, but the present structure dates mostly from 1567, with many additions over the years. The castle is 4 miles west of Forres.

Cawdor Castle   Castle

(☑01667-404615; www.cawdorcastle.com; Cawdor; adult/child £11.50/7.20; ⊗10am-5.30pm May-Sep; Ⓟ) This castle, 5 miles southwest of Nairn, was once the seat of the Thane of Cawdor, one of the titles bestowed on Shakespeare's *Macbeth*. The real Macbeth – an ancient Scottish king – couldn't have lived here though, since he died in 1057, 300 years before the castle was begun. Nevertheless the tour gives a fascinating insight into the lives of the Scottish aristocracy.

✪ ACTIVITIES

Dolphin Spirit   Wildlife Watching

(☑07544 800620; www.dolphinspirit.co.uk; Inverness Marina, Stadium Rd; adult/child £18.50/12; ⊗Easter-Oct) Four times a day in season, this outfit runs cruises from Inverness into the Moray Firth to spot the UK's largest pod of bottlenose dolphins – around 130 animals. The dolphins feed on salmon heading for the rivers at the head of the firth, and can often be seen leaping and bow-surfing.

Loch Ness by Jacobite   Boating

(☑01463-233999; www.jacobite.co.uk; Glenurquhart Rd; adult/child £23/15; ⊗Jun-Sep; ⛴) Boats depart from Tomnahurich Bridge twice daily for a three-hour cruise along the Caledonian Canal to Loch Ness and back, with a live commentary on local history and wildlife. Buy tickets at the tourist office (p102) and catch a free minibus to the boat. Other cruises and combined cruise

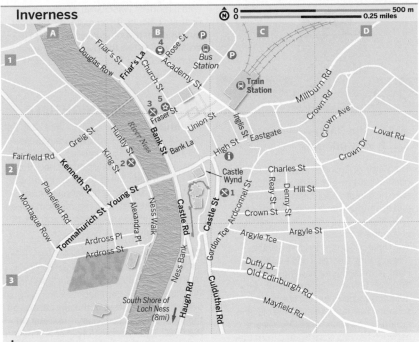

Inverness

🍴 Eating

🍷 Drinking & Nightlife

🎭 Entertainment

and coach tours, from one to 6½ hours, are also available, some year-round.

🍴 EATING

Café 1   Bistro ££

(☎01463-226200; www.cafe1.net; 75 Castle St; mains £12-28; ⊙noon-2.30pm & 5-9.30pm Mon-Fri, 12.30-3pm & 6-9.30pm Sat; 🖊🛗) ✎ Café 1 is a friendly, appealing bistro with candlelit tables amid elegant blond-wood and wrought-iron decor. There is an international menu based on quality Scottish produce, from Aberdeen Angus steaks to crisp pan-fried sea bass and meltingly tender pork belly. There's a separate vegan menu.

Kitchen Brasserie   Modern Scottish ££

(☎01463-259119; www.kitchenrestaurant.co.uk; 15 Huntly St; mains £11-22; ⊙noon-3pm & 5-10pm; 🛜🛗) This spectacular glass-fronted restaurant offers a great menu of top Scottish produce with a Mediterranean or Asian touch, and a view over the River Ness – try to get a table upstairs. Offers a great-value two-course lunch (£10; noon to 3pm) and early-bird menu (£14; 5pm to 7pm).

Mustard Seed   Bistro ££

(☎01463-220220; www.mustardseedrestaurant. co.uk; 16 Fraser St; mains £13-23; ⊙noon-3pm & 5.30-10pm) ✎ The menu at this bright and bustling bistro changes weekly, but focuses on Scottish and French cuisine

The Battle of Culloden

The Battle of Culloden in 1746 – the last pitched battle ever fought on British soil – saw the defeat of Bonnie Prince Charlie and the end of the Jacobite dream when 1200 Highlanders were slaughtered by government forces in a 68-minute rout. The Duke of Cumberland, son of the reigning King George II and leader of the Hanoverian army, earned the nickname 'Butcher' for his brutal treatment of the defeated Jacobite forces. The battle sounded the death knell for the old clan system, and the horrors of the Clearances, when tenants were evicted from their lands, soon followed. The sombre moor where the conflict took place has scarcely changed in the ensuing 260 years.

The impressive **Culloden Visitor Centre** (NTS; www.nts.org.uk/culloden; adult/child £11/9.50; ☉9am-7pm Jun-Aug, to 6pm Mar-May, Sep & Oct, 10am-4pm Nov-Feb; P) has everything you need to know about the Battle of Culloden in 1746, including the lead-up and the aftermath, with perspectives from both sides. An innovative film puts you on the battlefield in the middle of the mayhem, and a wealth of other audio presentations must have kept Inverness' entire acting community in business for weeks. The admission fee includes an audio guide for a self-guided tour of the battlefield itself.

Culloden is 6 miles east of Inverness. Bus 5 runs from Eastgate shopping centre in Inverness to Culloden battlefield (£3.15, 30 minutes, hourly except Sunday).

Culloden battlefield
ARGALIS / GETTY IMAGES ©

with a modern twist. Grab a table on the upstairs balcony if you can – it's the best outdoor lunch spot in Inverness, with a great view across the river. And a two-course lunch for £10 – yes, that's right – is hard to beat.

🍷 DRINKING & NIGHTLIFE

Phoenix   Pub

(☎01463-233685; www.phoenixalehouse.co.uk; 108 Academy St; ☉11am-1am Mon-Sat, noon-midnight Sun) Beautifully refurbished, this is the most traditional of the pubs in the city centre, with a mahogany horseshoe bar and several real ales on tap, including beers from the Cairngorm, Cromarty and Isle of Skye breweries.

Clachnaharry Inn   Pub

(☎01463-239806; www.clachnaharryinn.co.uk; 17-19 High St, Clachnaharry; ☉11am-11pm Mon-Thu, 11am-1am Fri & Sat, noon-11pm Sun; 🐾) Just over a mile northwest of the city centre, on the bank of the Caledonian Canal just off the A862, is this delightful old coaching inn (with beer garden out the back) serving an excellent range of real ales and good pub grub.

🎭 ENTERTAINMENT

Hootananny   Live Music

(☎01463-233651; www.hootanannyinverness. co.uk; 67 Church St; ☉noon-1am Mon-Thu, to 3am Fri & Sat, 4pm-midnight Sun) Hootananny is the city's best live-music venue, with traditional folk- and/or rock-music sessions nightly, including big-name bands from all over Scotland (and, indeed, the world). The bar is well stocked with a range of beers from the local Black Isle Brewery.

ℹ️ INFORMATION

Inverness Tourist Office (☎01463-252401; www.visithighlands.com; 36 High St; ☉9am-5pm Mon & Wed-Sat, from 10am Tue, 10am-3pm Sun, longer hours Mar-Oct; 🛜) **Accommodation**

booking service; also sells tickets for tours and cruises.

ℹ️ GETTING THERE & AWAY

AIR

Inverness Airport (INV; ☎01667-464000; www.invernessairport.co.uk) is at Dalcross, 10 miles east of the city, off the A96 towards Aberdeen. There are scheduled flights to Amsterdam, London, Manchester, Dublin, Orkney, Shetland and the Outer Hebrides, as well as other places in the UK.

Stagecoach (☎01463-233371; www.stagecoachbus.com) bus 11/11A runs from the airport to Inverness bus station (£4.40, 25 minutes, every 30 minutes).

BUS

Services depart from **Inverness bus station** (Margaret St). Most intercity routes are served by **Scottish Citylink** (☎0871 266 3333; www.citylink.co.uk) and Stagecoach. **National Express** (☎08717 818181; www.nationalexpress.com) has services to London (from £30, 13½ hours, one daily – more frequent services require changing at Glasgow).

Edinburgh £32.20, 3½ to 4½ hours, seven daily

Fort William £12.20, two hours, six daily

Glasgow £32.20, 3½ to 4½ hours, hourly

If you book far enough in advance, **Megabus** (☎0141-352 4444; www.megabus.com) offers fares from as little as £1 for buses from Inverness to Glasgow and Edinburgh, and £10 to London.

TRAIN

Edinburgh £40, 3½ hours, eight daily

Glasgow £40, 3½ hours, eight daily

Kyle of Lochalsh £20, 2½ hours, four daily Monday to Saturday, two Sunday; one of Britain's great scenic train journeys

London £180, eight to nine hours, one daily direct; others require a change at Edinburgh

Phoenix is the most traditional of the pubs in the city centre

Phoenix

ℹ️ GETTING AROUND

BICYCLE

Ticket to Ride (📞01463-419160; www.
tickettoridehighlands.co.uk; Bellfield Park; per
day from £30; ⏰9am-6pm Apr-Aug, Wed-Mon
Sep & Oct) Hires out mountain bikes, hybrids
and tandems; bikes can be dropped off in Fort
William. Will deliver bikes free to local hotels
and B&Bs.

BUS

City services and buses to places around
Inverness, including Nairn, Forres, the Culloden
battlefield, Beauly, Dingwall and Lairg, are
operated by Stagecoach (p103). An Inverness
Zone 2 Dayrider ticket costs £6.80 and gives
unlimited travel for a day on buses as far afield
as Culloden, Fortrose and Drumnadrochit.

CAR

Focus Vehicle Rental (📞01463-709517; www.
focusvehiclerental.co.uk; 6 Harbour Rd) The big
boys charge from around £55 to £75 per day,
but Focus has cheaper rates starting at £45
per day.

Fort William

◎ SIGHTS

Jacobite Steam Train Heritage Railway
(📞0844 850 4685; www.westcoastrailways.
co.uk; day return adult/child from £35/20;
⏰daily mid-Jun–Aug, Mon-Fri mid-May–mid-Jun,
Sep & Oct) The Jacobite Steam Train, hauled
by a former LNER K1 or LMS Class 5MT
locomotive, travels the scenic two-hour run
between Fort William and Mallaig. Classed
as one of the great railway journeys of
the world, the route crosses the historic
Glenfinnan Viaduct, made famous in the
Harry Potter films – the Jacobite's owners
supplied the steam locomotive and rolling
stock used in the film.

Trains depart from Fort William train station in the morning and return from Mallaig
in the afternoon. There's a brief stop at
Glenfinnan station, and you get 1½ hours
in Mallaig.

> *one of the great railway
> journeys of the world*

Jacobite Steam Train crossing the Glenfinnan Viaduct

SAMOT / SHUTTERSTOCK ©

West Highland Museum
Museum

(📞01397-702169; www.westhighlandmuseum.
org.uk; Cameron Sq; ⊙10am-5pm Mon-Sat May-
Sep, to 4pm Oct-Apr, 11am-3pm Sun Jul & Aug)
`FREE` This small but fascinating museum is
packed with all manner of Highland memorabilia. Look out for the secret portrait of
Bonnie Prince Charlie – after the Jacobite
rebellions, all things Highland were banned,
including pictures of the exiled leader; this
tiny painting looks like nothing more than a
smear of paint until viewed in a cylindrical
mirror, which reflects a credible likeness of
the prince.

🏃 ACTIVITIES

Nevis Range Downhill
& Witch's Trails
Mountain Biking

(📞01397-705825; www.nevisrange.co.uk/bike;
single/multitrip ticket £18.50/34.50; ⊙downhill
course 10.15am-3.45pm Apr-Oct, forest trails 24hr
year-round) Nevis Range **ski area** (📞01397-
705825; www.nevisrange.co.uk; day ticket per
adult/child £21/12; ⊙10am-6pm Jul & Aug, to 5pm
Apr-Jun, Sep & Oct, 9.30am-dusk Nov-Mar) has a
world championship downhill mountain-bike
trail – for experienced riders only; bikes are
carried up on the gondola cabin. There's
also a 4-mile XC red trail that begins at the
ski area's Snowgoose restaurant, and the
Witch's Trails – 25 miles of waymarked forest road and singletrack in the nearby forest,
including a 5-mile world championship loop.

Crannog Cruises
Wildlife

(📞01397-700714; www.crannog.net/cruises;
adult/child £15/7.50; ⊙11am, 1pm & 3pm
Easter-Oct) Operates 1½-hour wildlife cruises
on Loch Linnhe, visiting a seal colony and a
salmon farm.

🛍 SHOPPING

Highland Bookshop
Books

(www.highlandbookshop.com; 60 High St;
⊙9.30am-6pm Mon-Sat, 11am-4pm Sun) As well
as a good selection of fiction and children's
books, this shop stocks a superb range of
outdoor-related books and maps covering

🥾 Famous
Glen Coe

Scotland's most famous glen is also one
of its grandest and – in bad weather –
its grimmest. The approach to the glen
from the east is guarded by the rocky
pyramid of **Buachaille Etive Mor** –
the Great Shepherd of Etive – and the
lonely **Kings House Hotel** (closed for
renovation until 2019). After the Battle
of Culloden in 1745 it was used as a
Hanoverian garrison – hence the name.

The A82 road leads over the Pass
of Glencoe and into the narrow upper
glen. The southern side is dominated by
three massive, brooding spurs, known
as the **Three Sisters**, while the northern side is enclosed by the continuous
steep wall of the knife-edged **Aonach
Eagach** ridge, a classic mountaineering
challenge. The road threads its way past
deep gorges and crashing waterfalls to
the more pastoral lower reaches of the
glen around Loch Achtriochtan and the
only settlement here, **Glencoe village**.

Buachaille Etive Mor
ADRIAN PLUSKOTA / SHUTTERSTOCK ©

climbing, walking, cycling, canoeing and other
subjects. The upstairs lounge offers coffee
and tea, and hosts regular literary events.

🍴 EATING, DRINKING
& NIGHTLIFE

Crannog Seafood
Restaurant
Seafood ££

(📞01397-705589; www.crannog.net; Town Pier;
mains £15-24; ⊙noon-2.30pm & 6-9pm) 🍽

Climbing Ben Nevis

As the highest peak in the British Isles, Ben Nevis (1345m) attracts many would-be ascensionists who would not normally think of climbing a Scottish mountain. Although anyone who is reasonably fit should have no problem climbing Ben Nevis on a fine summer's day, an ascent should not be undertaken lightly; every year people have to be rescued from the mountain. You will need proper walking boots (the path is rough and stony, and there may be snow on the summit), warm clothing, waterproofs, a map and compass, and plenty of food and water. And don't forget to check the weather forecast (www.bennevisweather.co.uk).

There are three possible starting points for the tourist track ascent: **Achintee Farm**; the footbridge at **Glen Nevis SYHA** hostel; and, if you have a car, the car park at **Glen Nevis Visitor Centre** (☐01397-705922; www.bennevis weather.co.uk; ⊘8.30am-6pm Jul & Aug, 9am-5pm Apr-Jun, Sep & Oct, 9am-3pm Nov-Mar). The path climbs gradually to the shoulder at Lochan Meall an t-Suidhe (known as the Halfway Lochan), then zigzags steeply up beside the Red Burn to the summit plateau. The highest point is marked by a trig point on top of a huge cairn beside the ruins of the old observatory. The total distance to the summit and back is 8 miles; allow at least four or five hours to reach the top, and another 2½ to three hours for the descent.

The Crannog wins the prize for the best location in town – perched on the Town Pier, giving window-table diners an uninterrupted view down Loch Linnhe. Informal and unfussy, it specialises in fresh local fish – there are three or four daily fish specials plus the main menu – though there are lamb, venison and vegetarian dishes, too. Two-/three-course lunch costs £16/19.

Lime Tree   Scottish ££
(☐01397-701806; www.limetreefortwilliam.co.uk; Achintore Rd; mains £16-20; ⊘6.30-9.30pm; ℗ 🛜) 🍴 Fort William is not over-endowed with great places to eat, but the restaurant at this small hotel and art gallery has put the UK's Outdoor Capital on the gastronomic map. The chef turns out delicious dishes built around fresh Scottish produce, ranging from Loch Fyne oysters to Loch Awe trout and Ardnamurchan venison.

Grog & Gruel   Pub
(☐01397-705078; www.grogandgruel.co.uk; 66 High St; ⊘noon-midnight; 🛜) The Grog & Gruel is a traditional-style, wood-panelled pub with an excellent range of cask ales from regional Scottish and English microbreweries.

ℹ️ INFORMATION

Fort William Tourist Office (☐01397-701801; www.visithighlands.com; 15 High St; internet per 20min £1; ⊘9am-5pm Mon-Sat, 10am-3pm Sun, longer hours Jun-Aug; 🛜)

ℹ️ GETTING THERE & AWAY

BUS

Scottish Citylink (☐0871 266 3333; www.citylink.co.uk) buses link Fort William with other major towns and cities.

Edinburgh £37, 5¼ hours, four daily with a change at Glasgow; via Glencoe and Crianlarich

Glasgow £25, three hours, four daily

Inverness £12.20, two hours, six daily

Oban £9.40, 1½ hours, two daily

Crannog Seafood Restaurant (p105)

KEV GREGORY / SHUTTERSTOCK ©

CAR

Fort William is 146 miles from Edinburgh, 104 miles from Glasgow and 66 miles from Inverness. The tourist office has listings of car-hire companies.

Easydrive Car Hire (☎01397-701616; www.easy drivescotland.co.uk; North Rd; ☉8am-5.30pm Mon-Fri, to 5pm Sat, to 4pm Sun) Hires out small cars from £40/175 a day/week, including tax and unlimited mileage, but not Collision Damage Waiver (CDW).

TRAIN

The spectacular West Highland line runs from Glasgow to Mallaig via Fort William. The overnight **Caledonian Sleeper** (www.sleeper. scot) service connects Fort William and London Euston (from £135 sharing a twin-berth cabin, 13 hours).

Edinburgh £40, five hours; change at Glasgow's Queen St station, three daily, two on Sunday

Glasgow £30, 3¾ hours, three daily, two on Sunday

Mallaig £13, 1½ hours, four daily, three on Sunday

❶ GETTING AROUND

BICYCLE

Nevis Cycles (☎01397-705555; www.nevis cycles.com; cnr Montrose Ave & Locheil Rd, Inverlochy; per day from £25; ☉9am-5.30pm) Located a half-mile northeast of the town centre, this place rents everything from hybrid bikes and mountain bikes to full-suspension downhill racers. Bikes can be hired here and dropped off in Inverness.

BUS

A Zone 2 Dayrider ticket (£9.10) gives unlimited travel for one day on Stagecoach bus services in the Fort William area, as far as Glencoe and Fort Augustus. Buy from the bus driver.

DUBLIN,
IRELAND

Dublin, Ireland

A small capital with a huge reputation, Dublin's mix of heritage and hedonism will not disappoint. There are fascinating museums, mouthwatering restaurants and the best range of entertainment available anywhere in Ireland – and that's not even including the pub, the ubiquitous centre of the city's social life and an absolute must for any visitor. Dubliners at their ease are the greatest hosts of all, a charismatic bunch whose soul and sociability are so compelling and infectious that you mightn't ever want to leave.

Two Days in Dublin

Stroll through the grounds of **Trinity College** (p112), visiting the Long Room and the *Book of Kells,* before ambling up Grafton St to **St Stephen's Green** (p116). Then pick your heavyweight institution: the **National Museum of Ireland – Archaeology** (p117) (if only for the Ardagh Chalice and Tara Brooch) or the **National Gallery** (p117). On day two hit the medieval cathedrals of **St Patrick's** (p120) and **Christ Church** (p117) before pursuing pleasure at the **Guinness Storehouse** (p114).

Four Days in Dublin

After walking the length of **O'Connell St**, explore the collection of the **Dublin City Gallery – Hugh Lane** (p120), including Francis Bacon's reconstructed studio. Begin day four learning some Irish history at **Kilmainham Gaol** (p117). Then check out the fine collection at the **Irish Museum of Modern Art** (p120).

Next stop: Lisbon (p229) or the Scottish Highlands (p91).

Previous page: Temple Bar
CLAYTON HARRISON / SHUTTERSTOCK ©

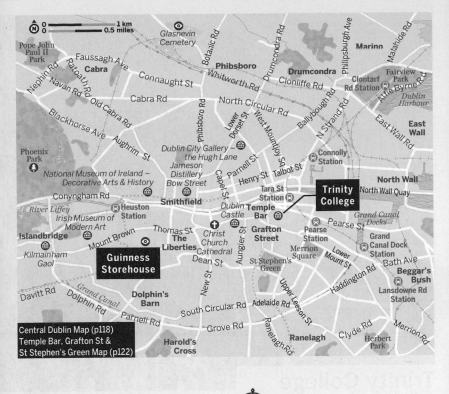

Central Dublin Map (p118)
Temple Bar, Grafton St &
St Stephen's Green Map (p122)

Arriving in Dublin

Dublin Airport Buses to the city centre run every 10 to 15 minutes between 6am and midnight; taxis (€25) take around 45 minutes.

Dublin Port terminal Buses (adult/child €3/1.50, 20 minutes) are timed to coincide with arrivals and departures.

Busáras All Bus Eireann services arrive at Busáras; private operators have arrival points in different parts of the city.

Heuston & Connolly Stations Main-line trains arrive at Heuston (for south and west of Dublin, including Wexford, Waterford, Cork, Limerick and Galway) or Connolly (for northwest and north of Dublin, including Sligo and Northern Ireland).

Where to Stay

There has only been a handful of hotel openings in Dublin in the last few years, which means that hotel prices in the city are higher than they were during the boom years of the Celtic Tiger.

There are good midrange options north of the Liffey, but the biggest spread of accommodation is south of the river.

For information on what each Dublin neighbourhood has to offer, see the table on p125.

CLU / GETTY IMAGES ©

Trinity College

This calm and cordial retreat from the bustle of contemporary Dublin is Ireland's most prestigious university, a collection of elegant Georgian and Victorian buildings, cobbled squares and manicured lawns that is among the most delightful places to wander.

The college was established by Elizabeth I in 1592 on land confiscated from an Augustinian priory in an effort to stop the brain drain of young Protestant Dubliners, who were skipping across to continental Europe for an education and getting 'infected with popery'. Trinity went on to become one of Europe's most outstanding universities, producing a host of notable graduates – how about Jonathan Swift, Oscar Wilde and Samuel Beckett at the same alumni dinner?

It remained completely Protestant until 1793, but even when the university relented and began to admit Catholics, the Catholic Church held firm; until 1970, any Catholic who enrolled here could consider themselves excommunicated.

The campus is a masterpiece of architecture and landscaping beautifully preserved in Georgian aspic. Most of the buildings and statues date from the 18th

Great For...

☑ Don't Miss

The Long Room, the *Book of Kells,* the Science Gallery and the Walking Tour.

Long Room, Old Library

❶ Need to Know

Map p122; 📞 01-896 1000; www.tcd.ie;
College Green; ⏱ 8am-10pm; 🚌 all city centre,
🚊 Westmoreland or Trinity FREE

✕ Take a Break

Fade Street Social (p121) is an excellent
lunch spot just a few blocks southwest.

★ Top Tip

A great way to see the grounds is on a
walking tour (Authenticity Tours; Map p122;
www.tcd.ie/visitors/tours; Trinity College;
tours €6, incl *Book of Kells* €15; ⏱ 9.30am-
3.40pm Mon-Sat, to 3.15pm Sun May-Sep,
fewer midweek tours Oct & Feb-Apr; 🚌 all city
centre, 🚊 College Green), which departs
from the College Green entrance.

and 19th centuries, each elegantly laid out
on a cobbled or grassy square. The newer
bits include the 1978 Arts & Social Science
Building, which backs on to Nassau St and
forms the alternative entrance to the college. Like the college's Berkeley Library, it
was designed by Paul Koralek; it houses the
Douglas Hyde Gallery of Modern Art.

To the south of Library Sq is the **Old
Library** (Map p122; www.tcd.ie; Library Sq; adult/
student/family €11/11/28, fast-track €14/11/28;
⏱ 8.30am-5pm Mon-Sat, from 9.30am Sun
May-Sep, 9.30am-5pm Mon-Sat, noon-4.30pm
Sun Oct-Apr; 🚌 all city centre, 🚊 Westmoreland
or Trinity), built in a severe style by Thomas
Burgh between 1712 and 1732. It is one of
five copyright libraries across Ireland and
the UK, which means it's entitled to a copy
of every book published in these islands –
around five million books, of which only a
fraction are stored here. You can visit the

library as part of a tour, taking in the Long
Room and the famous *Book of Kells*.

The **Book of Kells** is a breathtaking illuminated manuscript of the four Gospels of the
New Testament, created around AD 800 by
monks on the Scottish island of Iona. Trinity's
other great treasures are kept in the Old
Library's stunning 65m **Long Room**, which
houses about 200,000 of the library's oldest
volumes. Displays include a rare copy of the
Proclamation of the Irish Republic, which
was read out by Pádraig (Patrick) Pearse at
the beginning of the Easter Rising in 1916.

Also here is the so-called harp of Brian
Ború, which was definitely not in use when
the army of this early Irish hero defeated
the Danes at the Battle of Clontarf in 1014.
It does, however, date from around 1400,
making it one of the oldest harps in Ireland.
Your entry ticket also includes admission
to temporary exhibitions on display in the
East Pavilion.

STEFAN DZALEV / SHUTTERSTOCK ©

Guinness Storehouse

More than any beer produced anywhere in the world, Guinness is more than just a brand – for many devotees it's a substance with near-spiritual qualities. This beer lover's Disneyland is a multimedia homage to Ireland's most famous export.

Great For...

☑ Don't Miss

Enjoying the view from the Gravity Bar with your free pint of Guinness (price included with admission).

The mythology of Guinness is remarkably durable: it doesn't travel well; its distinctive flavour comes from Liffey water; it is good for you – not to mention the generally held belief that you will never understand the Irish until you develop a taste for the black stuff. All absolutely true, of course, so it should be no surprise that the Guinness Storehouse, in the heart of the St James's Gate Brewery, is the city's most visited tourist attraction, an all-singing, all-dancing extravaganza that combines sophisticated exhibits, spectacular design and a thick, creamy head of marketing hype.

Grain Storehouse & Brewery

The old grain storehouse, the only part of the massive, 26-hectare St James's Gate Brewery open to the public, is a suitable cathedral in which to worship the black

VANDERWOLF IMAGES / SHUTTERSTOCK ©

Guinness Storehouse ◉

Pim St

S Market St

Bellevue

❶ Need to Know

Map p118; www.guinness-storehouse.com; St James's Gate, South Market St; adult/child from €18.50/16, Connoisseur Experience €55; ⊙9.30am-7pm Sep-Jun, 9am to 8pm Jul & Aug; 🚌13, 21A, 40, 51B, 78, 78A, 123 from Fleet St, 🚆James's

✖ Take a Break

The 1837 Bar & Brasserie on the 5th floor of the building serves up straight-forward but delicious fare.

★ Top Tip

Aficionados can opt for the Connoisseur Experience, where you sample the four different kinds of Guinness while hearing their story from your designated bartender.

gold: shaped like a giant pint of Guinness, it rises seven impressive storeys high around a stunning central atrium. At the top is the head, represented by the Gravity Bar, with a panoramic view of Dublin.

Immediately below it is the brewery itself, founded in 1759 by Arthur Guinness who once employed over 5000 people; the gradual shift to greater automation has reduced the workforce to around 300.

The Perfect Pour

As you work your way to the top and your prize of arguably the nicest Guinness you could drink anywhere, you'll explore the various elements that made the beer the brand that it is and perhaps understand a little better the efforts made by the company to ensure its quasi-mythical status. From (the copy of) the original 9000-year lease (in a

glass box embedded in the ground floor) to the near-scientific lesson in how to pour the perfect pint, everything about this place is designed to make you understand that Guinness isn't like any other beer.

Arthur Guinness

One fun fact you will learn is that genius can be inadvertent: at some point in the 18th century, a London brewer accidentally burnt his hops while brewing ale, and so created the dark beer we know today. It came to be called 'porter' because the dark beer was very popular with London porters. In the 1770s, Arthur Guinness, who had until then only brewed ale, started brewing the dark stuff to get a jump on all other Irish brewers. By 1799 he decided to concentrate all his efforts on this single brew. He died four years later, aged 83, but the foundations for world domination were already in place.

⊙ SIGHTS

Chester Beatty Library   Museum

(Map p122; 📞01-407 0750; www.cbl.ie; Dublin Castle; ⊘10am-5pm Mon-Fri, from 11am Sat & Sun Mar-Oct, from 10am-5pm Tue-Fri, from 11am Sat & Sun Nov-Feb; 🚌all city centre) **FREE** This world-famous library in the grounds of Dublin Castle houses the collection of mining engineer Sir Alfred Chester Beatty (1875–1968), bequeathed to the Irish State on his death. Spread over two floors, the breathtaking collection includes more than 20,000 manuscripts, rare books, miniature paintings, clay tablets, costumes and other objects of artistic, historical and aesthetic importance. Free tours run at 1pm Wednesdays, 2pm Saturdays and 3pm Sundays. Entrance is free, but a donation of €5 is suggested.

Dublin Castle   Historic Building

(Map p122; 📞01-645 8813; www.dublincastle.ie; Dame St; guided tours adult/child €12/6, self-guided tours €8/4; ⊘9.45am-5.45pm, last admission 5.15pm; 🚌all city centre) **Despite its hotchpotch appearance, Dublin Castle was the stronghold of British power in Ireland for more than 700 years, beginning with the Anglo-Norman**

fortress commissioned by King John in 1204. Only the Record Tower (1258) survives from the original; most of what you see was built from the 18th century onwards – but its best bits are still impressive.

St Stephen's Green   Park

(Map p122; ⊘dawn-dusk; 🚌all city centre, 🚋St Stephen's Green) As you watch the assorted groups of friends, lovers and individuals splaying themselves across the nine elegantly landscaped hectares of Dublin's most popular green lung, St Stephen's Green, consider that those same hectares once formed a common for public whippings, burnings and hangings. These days, the harshest treatment you'll get is the warden chucking you out if you disturb the carefully tended flower beds.

Little Museum of Dublin   Museum

(Map p122; 📞01-661 1000; www.littlemuseum. ie; 15 St Stephen's Green N; adult/student €10/8; ⊘9.30am-5pm, to 8pm Thu, last admission 7pm; 🚌all city centre, 🚋St Stephen's Green) This award-winning museum tells the story of Dublin over the last century via memorabilia, photographs and artefacts donated by the

St Stephen's Green

ROLF G WACKENBERG / SHUTTERSTOCK ©

general public. The impressive collection, spread over the rooms of a handsome Georgian house, includes a lectern used by JFK on his 1963 visit to Ireland and an original copy of the fateful letter given to the Irish envoys to the treaty negotiations of 1921, whose contradictory instructions were at the heart of the split that resulted in the Civil War.

National Museum of Ireland – Archaeology   Museum

(Map p122; www.museum.ie; Kildare St; ⊙10am-5pm Tue-Sat, 1-5pm Sun; 🚌all city centre) **FREE** Established in 1877 as the primary repository of the nation's cultural and archaeological treasures, this is the country's most important museum. The original 1890 building is where you'll find stunning Celtic metalwork, Ireland's most famous crafted artefacts (the **Ardagh Chalice** and the **Tara Brooch**, from the 12th and 8th centuries respectively) and a collection of mummified bodies from the Iron Age, preserved to a disturbingly perfect degree by Ireland's peat bogs.

Christ Church Cathedral   Church

(Church of the Holy Trinity; Map p122; www.christchurchcathedral.ie; Christ Church Pl; adult/student/child €7/5.50/2.50, with Dublinia €15/12.50/7.50; ⊙9.30am-5pm Mon-Sat, 12.30-2.30pm Sun year-round, longer hours Mar-Oct; 🚌50, 50A, 56A from Aston Quay, 54, 54A from Burgh Quay) Its hilltop location and eye-catching flying buttresses make this the most photogenic of Dublin's cathedrals. It was founded in 1030 and rebuilt from 1172, mostly under the impetus of Richard de Clare, Earl of Pembroke (better known as Strongbow), the Anglo-Norman noble who invaded Ireland in 1170 and whose monument has pride of place inside.

Guided tours (Map p122; www.christchurch cathedral.ie; Christ Church Pl; €11; ⊙Hourly 11am-noon & 2-4pm Mon-Fri, 2-4pm Sat; 🚌50, 50A, 56A from Aston Quay, 54, 54A from Burgh Quay) include the belfry, where a campanologist explains the art of bell-ringing; you can even have a go.

National Gallery   Museum

(Map p118; www.nationalgallery.ie; W Merrion Sq; ⊙9.15am-5.30pm Tue-Wed, Fri & Sat, to 8.30pm

Gaelic Football & Hurling

Gaelic games are enmeshed in the fabric of Irish life and hold a unique place in the heart of its culture. Of the two main games, football is by far the most popular – and Dublin (www.dublingaa.ie) is currently the most dominant team in Ireland, winner of four consecutive All-Ireland Senior Championship titles between 2015 and 2018. They remain hot favourites to win their fifth in a row in 2019, which would give them seven titles since 2011.

The big event in both sports is the All-Ireland championship, a knockout contest that begins in April and ends on the first (for hurling) and third (for football) Sunday in September with the All-Ireland Final, played at a jam-packed **Croke Park** (Map p118; ☎01-819 2300; www.crokepark.ie; Clonliffe Rd; 🚌3, 11, 11A, 16, 16A, 123 from O'Connell St), which is also where the Dubs play all of their championship matches.

Hurling
SANDRA A. DUNLAP / SHUTTERSTOCK ©

Thu, 11am-5.30pm Sun-Mon; 🚌4, 7, 8, 39A, 46A from city centre) **FREE** A magnificent Caravaggio and a breathtaking collection of works by Jack B Yeats – William Butler's younger brother – are the main reasons to visit the National Gallery, but not the only ones. Its excellent collection is strong in Irish art, and there are also high-quality collections of every major European school of painting.

Kilmainham Gaol   Museum

(Map p118; ☎01-453 5984; www.kilmainham gaolmuseum.ie; Inchicore Rd; adult/child €9/5;

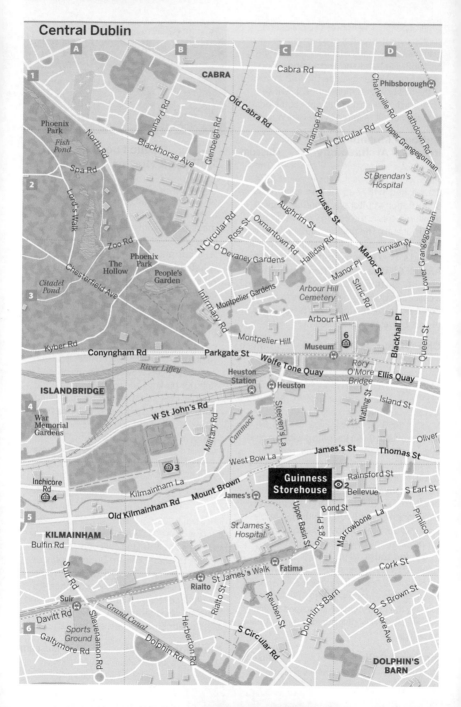

Central Dublin

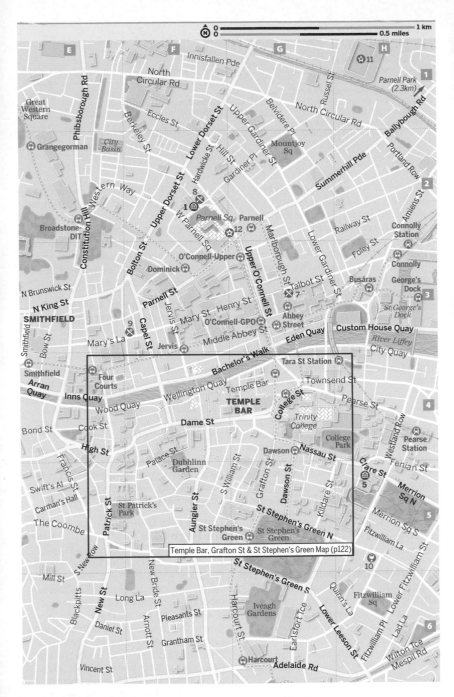

0
0

1 km
0.5 miles

E

F

G

H

Innisfallen Pde

11

1

North
Circular Rd

Parnell Park
(2.3km)

Phibsborough Rd

North Circular Rd

Ballybough Rd

Great
Western
Square

Eccles St

Berkeley St

Upper Dorset St

Upper Gardiner St

Belvidere Pl

Russel St

Portland Row

Grangegorman

City
Basin

Lower Dorset St

Hardwicke St

Hill St

Gardiner Pl

Mountjoy
Sq

Summerhill Pde

2

Western Way

8

1

Amiens St

Broadstone-
DIT

Constitution Hill

Bolton St

Upper Dorset St

W Parnell Sq

Parnell Sq

Parnell

12

Upper O'Connell St

Marlborough St

Lower Gardiner St

Railway St

Foley St

Connolly
Station

Connolly

George's
Dock

3

N Brunswick St

O'Connell-Upper

Dominick St

Talbot St

7

Busáras

St George's
Dock

N King St

SMITHFIELD

Parnell St

Jervis St

Capel St

Mary St

Henry St

O'Connell St

O'Connell-GPO

Abbey
Street

9

Mary's La

Bow St

Smithfield

Middle Abbey St

Jervis

Eden Quay

Custom House Quay

River Liffey

City Quay

Smithfield

Arran
Quay

Inns Quay

Bachelor's Walk

Tara St Station

Townsend St

4

Four
Courts

Wood Quay

Wellington Quay

Temple Bar

College St

Pearse St

Westland Row

Pearse
Station

Bond St

Cook St

Dame St

TEMPLE
BAR

Trinity
College

College
Park

High St

Palace St

Dubhlinn
Garden

Dawson

Nassau St

Clare St

5

Fenian St

Francis St

Swift's Al

Patrick St

St Patrick's
Park

S William St

Aungier St

Grafton St

Dawson St

Kildare St

Merrion
Sq N

5

Carman's Hall

The Coombe

St Stephen's
Green

St Stephen's Green N

St Stephen's
Green

Merrion Sq S

Merrion
Sq S

Fitzwilliam La

Temple Bar, Grafton St & St Stephen's Green Map (p122)

Mill St

S New Row

New St

New Bride St

St Stephen's Green S

Harcourt St

Iveagh
Gardens

Earlsfort Tce

Lower Leeson St

10

Fitzwilliam
Sq

Fitzwilliam Pl

Lower Fitzwilliam St

Lad La

6

Blackpitts

Long La

Pleasants St

Quinn's La

Wilton Tce

Mespil Rd

Daniel St

Arnott St

Grantham St

Harcourt St

Vincent St

Harcourt

Adelaide Rd

Central Dublin

⊙9am-7pm Jun-Aug, 9.30am-5.30pm Oct-Mar, 9am-6pm Apr, May & Sep; ☒69, 79 from Aston Quay, ☐13, 40 from O'Connell St) If you have *any* desire to understand Irish history – especially the long-running resistance to British rule – then a visit to this former prison is an absolute must. This threatening grey building, built in 1796, has played a role in virtually every act of Ireland's painful path to independence, and even today, despite closing in 1924, it still has the power to chill. Book online as far in advance as possible to get your preferred visiting time.

Irish Museum of Modern Art Museum
(IMMA; Map p118; www.imma.ie; Military Rd; ⊙11.30am-5.30pm Tue-Fri, from 10am Sat, from noon Sun, tours 1.15pm Wed, 2.30pm Sat & Sun; ☒51, 51D, 51X, 69, 78, 79 from Aston Quay, ☐Heuston) FREE Ireland's most important collection of modern and contemporary Irish and international art is housed in the elegant, airy expanse of the Royal Hospital Kilmainham, designed by Sir William Robinson and built between 1684 and 1687 as a retirement home for soldiers. It fulfilled this role until 1928, after which it languished for nearly 50 years until a 1980s restoration saw it come back to life as this wonderful repository of art.

St Patrick's Cathedral Cathedral
(Map p122; ☎01-453 9472; www.stpatricks cathedral.ie; St Patrick's Close; adult/student €8/7; ⊙9.30am-5pm Mon-Fri, 9am-6pm Sat, 9-10.30am, 12.30-2.30pm & 4.30-6pm Sun Mar-Oct, 9.30am-5pm Mon-Fri, 9am-5pm Sat, 9-10.30am & 12.30-2.30pm Sun Nov-Feb; ☒50, 50A, 56A from Aston Quay, 54, 54A from Burgh Quay) Ireland's largest church and the final resting place of Jona-

than Swift, St Patrick's stands on the spot where St Patrick himself reputedly baptised the local Celtic chieftains in the 5th century. Fiction or not, it's a sacred bit of turf upon which this cathedral was built between 1191 and 1270. The adjacent park was once an awful slum but is now a lovely garden to sit and catch some sunshine.

National Museum of Ireland – Decorative Arts & History Museum
(Map p118; www.museum.ie; Benburb St; ⊙10am-5pm Tue-Sat, 2-5pm Sun; ☐25, 66, 67, 90 from city centre, ☐Museum) FREE Once the world's largest military barracks, this splendid early neoclassical grey-stone building on the Liffey's northern banks was completed in 1704 according to the design of Thomas Burgh (he of Trinity College's Old Library). It is now home to the Decorative Arts & History collection of the National Museum of Ireland, with a range of superb permanent exhibits ranging from a history of the **Easter Rising** to the work of iconic Irish designer **Eileen Gray** (1878–1976).

Dublin City Gallery – the Hugh Lane Gallery
(Map p118; ☎01-222 5550; www.hughlane.ie; 22 N Parnell Sq; ⊙9.45am-6pm Tue-Thu, to 5pm Fri, 10am-5pm Sat, 11am-5pm Sun; ☐7, 11, 13, 16, 38, 40, 46A, 123 from city centre) FREE Whatever reputation Dublin has as a repository of world-class art has a lot to do with the simply stunning collection at this exquisite gallery, housed in the equally impressive Charlemont House, designed by William Chambers in 1763. Within its walls you'll find the best of contemporary Irish art,

a handful of Impressionist classics and Francis Bacon's relocated studio.

⊗ EATING

The choice of restaurants in Dublin has never been better. Every cuisine and every trend – from doughnuts on the run to kale with absolutely everything – is catered for, as the city seeks to satisfy the discerning taste buds of its diners.

Blazing Salads   Vegetarian €

(Map p122; ☑01-671 9552; www.blazingsalads. com; 42 Drury St; salads €5-10; ☺9am-6pm Mon-Sat; ☑; ☐all city centre) Organic breads (including many special diet varieties), Californian-style salads from a serve-yourself salad bar, smoothies and pizza slices can all be taken away from this delicious, vegetarian deli. It also runs wildly popular cooking classes, which you would be wise to book well in advance.

Oxmantown   Cafe €

(Map p118; www.oxmantown.com; 16 Mary's Abbey, City Markets; sandwiches €6.50; ☺8am-4pm Mon-Fri; ☐Four Courts, Jervis) Delicious breakfasts and excellent sandwiches make this cafe one of the standout places for day-time eating on the north side of the Liffey. Locally baked bread, coffee supplied by Cloud Picker (Dublin's only microroastery) and meats sourced from Irish farms are the ingredients, but it's the way it's all put together that makes it so worthwhile.

Fade Street Social   Modern Irish €€

(Map p122; ☑01-604 0066; www.fadestreet social.com; 4-6 Fade St; mains €20-36, tapas €6-17; ☺5-10.30pm Mon-Wed, 12.30-3pm & 5-10.30pm Thu, to 11pm Fri & Sat, to 10.30pm Sun; ☎; ☐all city centre) ✐ Two restaurants in one, courtesy of renowned chef Dylan McGrath: at the front, the buzzy tapas bar, which serves gourmet bites from a beautiful open kitchen. At the back, the more muted restaurant specialises in Irish cuts of meat – from veal to rabbit – served with home-grown, organic vegetables. There's a bar upstairs too. Reservations recommended.

Chapter One   Modern Irish €€€

(Map p118; ☑01-873 2266; www.chapterone restaurant.com; 18 N Parnell Sq; 2-course lunch €36.50, 4-course dinner €80; ☺12.30-2pm Fri, 5-10.30pm Tue-Sat; ☐3, 10, 11, 13, 16, 19, 22 from city centre) Flawless haute cuisine and a relaxed, welcoming atmosphere make this Michelin-starred restaurant in the basement of the Dublin Writers Museum our choice for the best dinner experience in town. The food is French-inspired contemporary Irish; the menus change regularly; and the service is top-notch. The three-course pretheatre menu (€44) is great if you're going to the **Gate** (Map p118; ☑01-874 4045; www.gate theatre.ie; 1 Cavendish Row; ☺performances 7.30pm Tue-Fri, 2.30pm & 7.30pm Sat; ☐all city centre) around the corner.

⊙ DRINKING & NIGHTLIFE

If there's one constant about life in Dublin, it's that Dubliners will always take a drink. Come hell or high water, the city's pubs will never be short of customers, and we suspect that exploring a variety of Dublin's legendary pubs and bars ranks pretty high on the list of reasons you're here.

Toner's   Pub

(Map p118; ☑01-676 3090; www.tonerspub.ie; 139 Lower Baggot St; ☺10.30am-11.30pm Mon-Thu, to 12.30am Fri & Sat, 11.30am-11.30pm Sun; ☐7, 46 from city centre) Toner's, with its stone floors and antique snugs, has changed little over the years and is the closest thing you'll get to a country pub in the heart of the city. Next door, Toner's Yard is a comfortable outside space. The shelves and drawers are reminders that it once doubled as a grocery shop.

Grogan's Castle Lounge   Pub

(Map p122; www.facebook.com/groganscastlel ounge; 15 S William St; ☺10.30am-11.30pm Mon-Thu, to 12.30am Fri & Sat, 12.30-11pm Sun; ☐all city centre) Known simply as Grogan's (after the original owner), this is a city-centre institution. It has long been a favourite haunt of Dublin's writers and painters, as well as others from the alternative bohemian set, who enjoy a fine Guinness while they wait

Temple Bar, Grafton St & St Stephen's Green

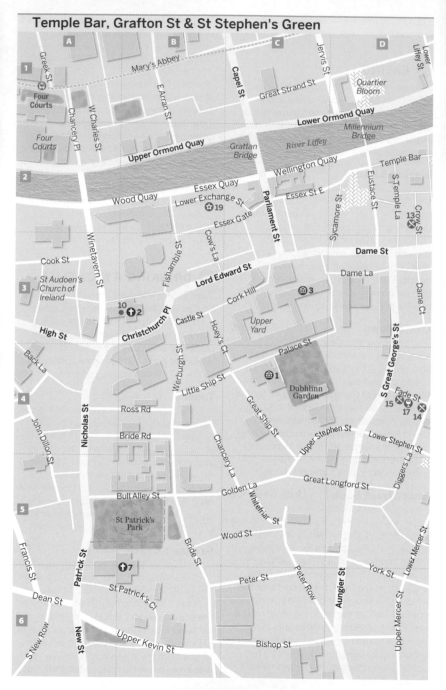

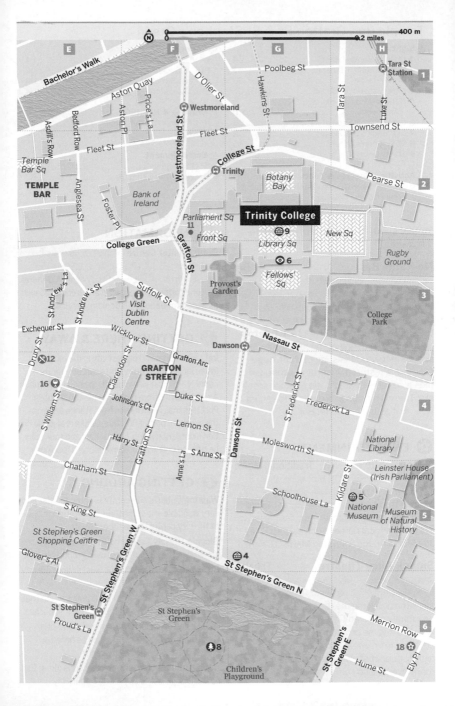

400 m
0.2 miles

E
Bachelor's Walk
Aston Quay
Price's La
Aston Pl
Bedford Row
Asdill's Row
Fleet St
Temple
Bar Sq
Anglesea St
Foster Pl
**TEMPLE
BAR**
Bank of
Ireland
College Green
Grafton St

F
D'Olier St
Westmoreland St
Fleet St
Westmoreland
Fleet St
College St
Trinity
Parliament Sq
11
Front Sq

G
Poolbeg St
Hawkins St
Botany
Bay
Trinity College
9
Library Sq
6
Fellows'
Sq
Provost's
Garden
New Sq

H
Tara St
Station
1
Tara St
Luke St
Townsend St
Pearse St
2
Rugby
Ground
College
Park
3

St Andrew's La
St Andrew's St
Suffolk St
Visit
Dublin
Centre
Exchequer St
Wicklow St
Drury St
12
16
S William St
Clarendon St
**GRAFTON
STREET**
Grafton Arc
Dawson
Duke St
Johnson's Ct
Lemon St
Grafton St
Harry St
S Anne St
Anne's La
Chatham St
S King St
St Stephen's Green
Shopping Centre
Glover's Al
St Stephen's
Green
Proud's La
St Stephen's Green W
Nassau St
Dawson St
Molesworth St
Schoolhouse La
4
St Stephen's Green N
St Stephen's
Green
8
Children's
Playground
St Stephen's Green E
S Frederick St
Frederick La
Kildare St
National
Library
Leinster House
(Irish Parliament)
4
5
National
Museum
Museum
of Natural
History
5
Merrion Row
18
Hume St
Ely Pl
6

Temple Bar, Grafton St & St Stephen's Green

for that inevitable moment when they're discovered.

No Name Bar
Bar

(Map p122; www.nonamebardublin.com; 3 Fade St; ◎1.30-11.30pm Mon-Wed, to 1am Thu, 12.30-2.30am Fri & Sat, noon-11pm Sun; ☐all city centre) A low-key entrance just next to the trendy French restaurant **L'Gueuleton** leads upstairs to one of the nicest bar spaces in town, consisting of three huge rooms in a restored Victorian townhouse plus a sizeable heated patio area for smokers. There's no sign or a name – folks just refer to it as the No Name Bar.

⊕ ENTERTAINMENT

O'Donoghue's
Traditional Music

(Map p122; ☑01-660 7194; www.odonoghues. ie; 15 Merrion Row; ◎from 7pm; ☐all city centre) There's traditional music nightly in the old bar of this famous boozer. Regular performers include local names such as Tom Foley, Joe McHugh, Joe Foley and Maria O'Connell.

Smock Alley Theatre
Theatre

(Map p122; ☑01-677 0014; www.smockalley.com; 6-7 Exchange St; ☐all city centre) One of the city's most diverse theatres is hidden in this beautifully restored 17th-century building. It boasts a diverse program of events (expect anything from opera to murder-mystery nights, puppet shows and Shakespeare) and many events also come with a dinner option.

ℹ INFORMATION

Dublin Visitor Centre (Map p122; www.visit dublin.com; 25 Suffolk St; ◎9am-5.30pm Mon-Sat, 10.30am-3pm Sun; ☐all city centre) General visitor information on Dublin and Ireland, as well as accommodation and booking service.

ℹ GETTING THERE & AWAY

Ireland's capital and biggest city is the most important point of entry and departure for the country – almost all airlines fly in and out of Dublin Airport. Ferries from the UK arrive at the Dublin Port terminal, while ferries from France arrive in the southern port of Rosslare. Dublin is also the nation's primary rail hub. Flights, cars and tours can be booked online at lonelyplanet.com/bookings.

ℹ GETTING AROUND

Walking Dublin's city centre is compact, flat and very walkable – it's less than 2km from one end of the city centre to the other.

Bicycle The city's rent-and-ride Dublinbikes scheme is the ideal way to cover ground quickly.

Bus Useful for getting to the west side of the city and the suburbs.

Luas A three-line light-rail transport system that links the city centre with the southern suburbs.

Taxi Easily recognised by light-green-and-blue 'Taxi' signs on the doors, they can be hailed or picked up at ranks in the city centre.

DART Suburban rail network that runs along the eastern edge of the city along Dublin Bay.

Neighbourhood	Atmosphere
Grafton Street & Around	Close to sights, nightlife and pretty much everything; a good choice of midrange and top-end hotels. Generally more expensive than elsewhere; not always good value for money and rooms tend to be smaller.
Merrion Square & Around	Lovely neighbourhood, elegant hotels and townhouse accommodation. Not a lot of choice; virtually no budget accommodation. Also relatively quiet after dark.
Temple Bar	In the heart of the action; close to everything, especially the party. Noisy and touristy; not especially good value for money; rooms are very small and often less than pristine.
Kilmainham & the Liberties	Close to the old city and the sights of west Dublin. An up-and-coming spot for great restaurants, too. If you want to hit the main city sights, you're facing a bit more of a walk in and out of town.
North of the Liffey	Good range of choices; within walking distance of sights and nightlife. Budget accommodation not always good quality; some locations not especially comfortable after dark.
Docklands & the Grand Canal	Excellent contemporary hotels with good service, including some top-end choices. Isolated neighbourhood that doesn't have a lot of life after dark; reliant on taxis or public transport to get to city centre.
The Southside	More bang for your buck; generally bigger rooms and properties with gardens. If not on the Luas line, bus transfers into town can take up valuable time.

Abbey Island, Derrynane National Historic Park

Ring of Kerry, Ireland

This 179km circuit of the Iveragh (pronounced eev-raa) Peninsula winds past pristine beaches, medieval ruins, mountains and loughs, with ever-changing views of the island-dotted Atlantic, particularly in the peninsula's spectacular southwest.

Great For...

Don't Miss

Watching the stars at night in this dark-sky reserve.

Killorglin

Kerry Bog Village Museum Museum

(www.kerrybogvillage.ie; Ballincleave, Glenbeigh; adult/child €6.50/4.50; ⊙9am-6pm; P) This museum re-creates a 19th-century bog village, typical of the small communities that carved out a precarious living in the harsh environment of Ireland's ubiquitous peat bogs. You'll see the thatched homes of the turf cutter, blacksmith, thatcher and labourer, as well as a dairy, and meet Kerry bog ponies (a native breed) and Irish wolfhounds. It's on the N70, 8.3km southwest of Killorglin near Glenbeigh; buy a ticket at the neighbouring Red Fox Inn if no one's at the gate.

Cahersiveen

Old Barracks Heritage Centre Museum

(☎066-401 0430; www.theoldbarracks cahersiveen.com; Bridge St; adult/child €4/2;

Stone hut on Skellig Michael

GAVIN QUIRKE / GETTY IMAGES ©

on trade with France and Spain. He was the uncle of Daniel O'Connell, the 19th-century campaigner for Catholic emancipation, who grew up here in his uncle's care and inherited the property in 1825, when it became his private retreat. The house is furnished with O'Connell memorabilia, including the impressive triumphal chariot in which he lapped Dublin after his release from prison in 1844.

Skellig Michael

Portmagee (an 80km drive west of Killarney) is the jumping-off point for an unforgettable experience: the Skellig Islands, two tiny rocks 12km off the coast. The vertiginous climb up uninhabited **Skellig Michael** inspires an awe that monks could have clung to life in the meagre beehive-shaped stone huts that cluster on the tiny patch of level land on top. Skellig Michael famously featured as Luke Skywalker's Jedi temple in *Star Wars: The Force Awakens* (2015) and *Star Wars: The Last Jedi* (2017), attracting a whole new audience to the island's dramatic beauty. From spring to late summer, weather permitting, boat trips run from Portmagee to Skellig Michael; the standard rate is around €80 per person, with boats departing in the morning and returning at 3pm. Advance booking is essential; there are a dozen boat operators, including **Skelligs Rock** (087 236 2344; www.skelligsrock.com; per person €100; ⊙mid-May–Sep).

⊙10am-5pm Mon-Sat, 11am-4pm Sun Mar-Nov; P) Established in response to the Fenian Rising of 1867, the Royal Irish Constabulary barracks at Cahersiveen were built in an eccentric Bavarian-Schloss style, complete with pointy turret and stepped gables. Burnt down in 1922 by anti-Treaty forces, the imposing building has been restored and now houses fascinating exhibitions on the Fenian Rising and the life and works of local hero Daniel O'Connell.

Caherdaniel

Derrynane National
Historic Park   Historic Site

(066-947 5113; www.derrynanehouse.ie; Derrynane; adult/child €5/3; ⊙10.30am-6pm mid-Mar–Sep, 10am-5pm Oct, to 4pm Sat & Sun Nov–early-Dec; P) Derrynane House was the home of Maurice 'Hunting Cap' O'Connell, a notorious local smuggler who grew rich

COPENHAGEN, DENMARK

Copenhagen, Denmark

Copenhagen is not only the coolest kid on the Nordic block, it also gets constantly ranked as the happiest city in the world. Ask a dozen locals why and they would probably all zone in on the hygge, which generally means coziness, but encompasses far more. It is this laidback contentment that helps give the Danish capital the X factor. The backdrop is pretty cool as well: its cobbled, bike-friendly streets are an enticing concoction of sherbet-hued town houses, craft studios and candlelit cafes. Add to this its compact size and it is possibly Europe's most seamless urban experience.

Two Days in Copenhagen

Get your bearings with a canal and harbour tour, wander **Nyhavn** (p136) then seek out a classic smørrebrød (Danish open sandwich), washed down with bracing akvavit (alcoholic spirit, commonly made with potatoes and spiced with caraway). Stroll through the Latin Quarter and the **Nationalmuseet** (p136) and while away the evening at **Tivoli Gardens** (p132).

On day two, walk in royal footsteps at **Rosenborg Slot** (p136) and **Kongens Have** (p137). Lunch at **Designmuseum Danmark** (p134) before exploring its extensive collection. Splurge on New Nordic cuisine at **Geranium** (p141).

Four Days in Copenhagen

If you have a third day, take a trip to **Louisiana** (p137), an easy train ride north of central Copenhagen. Back in the city, dine in Vesterbro's hip Kødbyen (the 'Meatpacking District'), an industrial area turned buzzing hub.

On day four, explore Statens Museum for Kunst and delve into Torvehallerne KBH, the city's celebrated food market.

Next up is Berlin (p431), a 7½-hour bus ride away.

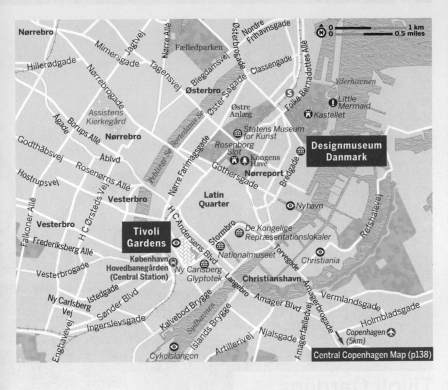

Central Copenhagen Map (p138)

Arriving in Copenhagen

Copenhagen Airport (p143) is Scandinavia's busiest hub, with direct flights to cities in Europe, North America and Asia, as well as a handful of Danish cities. The 24-hour metro (www.m.dk) runs every four to 20 minutes between the airport and the eastern side of the city centre. Trains (www.dsb.dk) to the city centre run around every 12 minutes and cost Dkr36. Taxis to the city centre take about 20 minutes and cost around Dkr300.

All long-distance trains arrive at and depart from **Københavns Hovedbanegård** (Central Station).

Where to Stay

Copenhagen's accommodation options span from higher-end Danish design establishments to excellent budget hotels and hostels, which are mainly centred on the western side of the Central Station. It's a good idea to reserve rooms in advance, especially hostels, during the busy summer season.

The **Copenhagen Visitors Centre** (p143) can book rooms in private homes. Depending on availability, it also books unfilled hotel rooms at discounted rates.

ANASTASIA PELIKH / SHUTTERSTOCK ©

Tivoli Gardens

The country's top-ranking tourist draw, tasteful Tivoli Gardens has been eliciting gleeful shrills since 1843. Whatever your idea of fun – hair-raising rides, twinkling pavilions, open-air stage shows or al-fresco pantomime and beer – this old-timer has you covered.

Great For...

☑ Don't Miss

The city views – taken at 70km/hr – from the Star Flyer, one of the world's tallest carousels.

Roller Coasters

The Rutschebanen is the best loved of Tivoli's roller coasters, rollicking its way through and around a faux 'mountain' and reaching speeds of 60km/h. Built in 1914, it claims to be the world's oldest operating wooden roller coaster. If you're after something a little more hardcore, the Dæmonen (Demon) is a 21st-century beast with faster speeds and a trio of hair-raising loops.

The Grounds

Beyond the carousels and side stalls is a Tivoli of landscaped gardens, tranquil nooks and eclectic architecture. Lower the adrenaline under beautiful old chestnut and elm trees, and amble around Tivoli Lake. Formed out of the old city moat, the lake is a top spot to snap pictures of Tivoli's commanding Chinese Tower, built in 1900.

❶ Need to Know

📞33 15 10 01; www.tivoligardens.com; Vesterbrogade 3; adult/child 3-7yr 120/50kr, Fri after 7pm 175/100kr; 🕙11am-11pm Sun-Thu, to midnight Fri & Sat early Apr-late Sep, reduced hours rest of year; 🚼; 🚌2A, 5C, 9A, 12, 14, 26, 33, 250S, Ⓜ København H, Ⓢ København H

✖ Take a Break

Jolly **Grøften** (📞33 75 06 75; www.groeften. dk; Tivoli Gardens, Vesterbrogade 3; smørrebrød 89-229kr, mains 179-425kr; 🕙noon-10pm Sun-Thu, to 11pm Fri & Sat early Apr-late Sep, reduced hours rest of year; 🛜; 🚌2A, 5C, 9A, 26, 250S, Ⓢ København H) is a local institution.

★ Top Tip

Amusement rides cost Dkr30 to Dkr90; consider purchasing a multiride ticket for Dkr230.

Illuminations & Fireworks

Throughout the summer season, Tivoli Lake wows the crowds with its nightly laser and water spectacular. The Saturday evening fireworks are a summer-season must, repeated again from 26 to 30 December for Tivoli's annual Fireworks Festival.

Live Performances

The indoor **Tivolis Koncertsal** (Concert Hall; https://www.tivoli.dk/da/haven+og+forlystelser/ spillesteder/koncertsalen; Tietgensgade 30; 🚌1A, 2A, 5C, 9A, 37, 250S, Ⓢ København H) hosts mainly classical music, with the odd musical and big-name pop or rock act. All tickets are sold at the **Tivoli Billetcenter** (Service Centre; 📞33 15 10 01; Vesterbrogade 3 (entrance from inside the Gardens); 🕙11am-11.30pm Sun-Thu, to 12.30am Fri & Sat during

Tivoli seasons; 🚌2A, 9A, 5C, 12, 14, 26, 66, 250S, Ⓢ København H) or online through the Tivoli website.

Pantomime Theatre

Each night during the summer this criminally charming theatre presents silent plays in the tradition of Italy's Commedia dell'Arte. Many of the performers also work at the esteemed Royal Ballet.

Christmas Market

From mid-November to early January, Tivoli hosts a large **market** (www.tivoligardens.com /en/saesoner/jul; 🚌1A, 2A, 9A, 5C, 14, 26, 37, 66, Ⓢ København H). Entertainment includes costumed staff and theatre shows. Fewer rides are operational but the *gløgg* (mulled wine) and *æbleskiver* (small doughnuts) are ample compensation.

Designmuseum Danmark

Don't know your Egg from your Swan? What about your PH4 from your PH5? For a crash course in Denmark's incredible design heritage, make an elegant beeline for Designmuseum Danmark, 250m north of Marmorkirken.

Housed in a converted 18th-century hospital, the museum is a must for fans of the applied arts and industrial design. Its booty includes Danish silver and porcelain, textiles and the iconic design pieces of modern innovators such as Kaare Klint, Poul Henningsen, Arne Jacobsen and Verner Panton.

20th Century Crafts & Design

The museum's main permanent exhibition explores 20th-century industrial design and crafts in the context of social, economic, technological and theoretical changes. The collection displays celebrated furniture and applied arts from both Denmark and abroad.

Great For...

☑ Don't Miss

The vintage poster collection, including the iconic 1959 'Wonderful Copenhagen' poster, depicting a duck and her little ones stopping traffic.

EVIKKA / SHUTTERSTOCK ©

ⓘ Need to Know

☑ 33 18 56 56; www.designmuseum.dk;
Bredgade 68; adult/child 115kr/free; ☉10am-
6pm Tue & Thu-Sun, to 9pm Wed; ♿; ☒1A,
Ⓜ Kongens Nytorv

✕ Take a Break

The museum's Klint Cafe, located just
off the lobby, serves Danish classics and
has a fine outdoor courtyard.

★ Top Tip

The museum shop is one of the city's
best places to pick up savvy gifts and
easy-to-carry souvenirs.

The Danish Chair

An ode to the humble chair and an exploration of what goes into making a 'good'
one, this permanent exhibition displays
more than 100 beautifully designed chairs,
including some international guests. Standing room only.

Porcelain

This detailed exhibition celebrates European porcelain and its journey from initial
attempts through to the current day.

Danish Design Now

Showcasing contemporary fashion,
furniture and products, this captivating
exhibition focuses on 21st-century Danish
design and innovation.

Fashion & Fabric

This permanent exhibition showcases
around 350 objects from the museum's
rich textile and fashion collections.
Spanning four centuries, the collection's
treasures include French and Italian silks,
ikat and batik weaving, and two extraordinary mid-20th-century tapestries
based on cartoons by Henri Matisse. As
you would expect, Danish textiles and
fashion feature prominently, including
Danish *hedebo* embroidery from the 18th
to 20th centuries, and Erik Mortensen's
collection of haute couture frocks from
French fashion houses Balmain and
Jean-Louis Scherrer.

◎ SIGHTS

One of the great things about Copenhagen is its size. Virtually all of Copenhagen's major sightseeing attractions are in or close to the medieval city centre. Only the perennially disappointing **Little Mermaid** (Den Lille Havfrue; Langelinie, Østerport; 🚃1A, 26, 🚢Nordre Toldbod) lies outside of the city proper, on the harbourfront.

Nyhavn   Canal
(Nyhavn; 🚃1A, 26, 66, 350S, Ⓜ️Kongens Nytorv) There are few nicer places to be on a sunny day than sitting at an outdoor table at a cafe on the quayside of the Nyhavn canal. The canal was built to connect Kongens Nytorv to the harbour and was long a haunt for sailors and writers, including Hans Christian Andersen. He wrote *The Tinderbox, Little Claus and Big Claus* and *The Princess and the Pea* while living at No 20, and also spent time living at Nos 18 and 67.

Nationalmuseet   Museum
(National Museum; ☎️33 13 44 11; https://en. natmus.dk; Ny Vestergade 10; adult/child 95kr/ free; ⊙10am-5pm Tue-Sun; 👶; 🚃1A, 2A, 9A, 12, 14, 26, 37, Ⓜ️Rådhuspladsen) For a crash course

in Danish history and culture, spend an afternoon at Denmark's National Museum. It has first claim on virtually every antiquity uncovered on Danish soil, including Stone Age tools, Viking weaponry, rune stones and medieval jewellery. Among the many highlights is a finely crafted 3500-year-old Sun Chariot, as well as bronze *lurs* (horns), some of which date back 3000 years and are still capable of blowing a tune.

Rosenborg Slot   Castle
(☎️33 15 32 86; www.kongernessamling.dk/en/ rosenborg; Øster Voldgade 4A; adult/child 110kr/ free; ⊙9am-6pm mid-Jun–mid-Sep, reduced hours rest of year; 🚃6A, 42, 184, 185, 350S, Ⓜ️Nørreport, Ⓢ️Nørreport) A 'once upon a time' combo of turrets, gables and moat, the early-17th-century Rosenborg Slot was built in Dutch Renaissance style between 1606 and 1633 by King Christian IV to serve as his summer home. Today the castle's 24 upper rooms are chronologically arranged, housing the furnishings and portraits of each monarch from Christian IV to Frederik VII. The pièce de résistance is the basement Treasury, home to the dazzling crown jewels, among them Christian IV's glorious

Rosenborg Slot

crown and Christian III's jewel-studded sword.

Statens Museum for Kunst Museum

(📞33 74 84 94; www.smk.dk; Sølvgade 48-50; adult/child 120kr/free; ⏱11am-5pm Tue & Thu-Sun, to 8pm Wed; 🚌6A, 26, 42, 184, 185) Denmark's National Gallery straddles two contrasting, interconnected buildings: a late-19th-century 'palazzo' and a sharply minimalist extension. The museum houses medieval and Renaissance works and impressive collections of Dutch and Flemish artists, including Rubens, Breughel and Rembrandt. It claims the world's finest collection of 19th-century Danish 'Golden Age' artists, among them Eckersberg and Hammershøi, foreign greats like Matisse and Picasso, and modern Danish heavyweights including Per Kirkeby.

Kongens Have Park

(King's Gardens; http://parkmuseerne.dk/kongens-have; Øster Voldgade; ⏱7am-10pm mid-Jun–mid-Aug, reduced hours rest of year; 🚼; 🚌26, ⓂNørreport, ⓈNørreport) **FREE** The oldest park in Copenhagen was laid out in the early 17th century by Christian IV, who used it as his vegetable patch. These days it has a little more to offer, including wonderfully romantic paths, a fragrant rose garden, some of the longest mixed borders in northern Europe and a marionette theatre with free performances from mid-July to mid-August (2pm and 3pm Tuesday to Sunday).

🌀 TOURS

You can't visit Copenhagen and not take a canal boat trip. Not only is it a fantastic way to view the city, but you see a side of it land-lubbers never experience. There are two outfits that operate guided canal tours during summer – **Canal Tours Copenhagen** (📞32 96 30 00; www.stromma.dk; Nyhavn; 1hr tour adult/child 85/43kr; ⏱9.30am-9pm late Jun–mid-Aug, reduced hours rest of year; 🚼; 🚌1A, 26, 66, 350S, ⓂKongens Nytorv) and **Netto-Bådene** (📞32 54 41 02; www.havnerundfart.dk; Holmens Bro; adult/child 40/15kr; ⏱tours 2-5 per hour, 10am-7pm Jul & Aug, reduced hours rest of year; 🚌1A, 2A, 9A, 26, 37, 66). Be aware that in

Louisiana Art Break

This extraordinary **museum** (📞49 19 07 19; www.louisiana.dk; Gammel Strandvej 13, Humlebæk; adult/student/child 125/110kr/free; ⏱11am-10pm Tue-Fri, to 6pm Sat & Sun; 🚌388, 🚆Humlebæk) of modern and contemporary art should be high on your 'to do' list even if you're not normally a gallery-goer. Along with its ever-changing, cutting-edge exhibitions, much of the thrill here is the glorious presentation. A maze-like web of halls and glass corridors weaves through rolling gardens in which magnificent trees, lawns, a lake and a beach view set off monumental abstract sculptures (Henry Moore, Jean Arp, Max Ernst, Barbara Hepworth etc), making them feel like discovered totems.

Louisiana is in the pretty town of Humlebæk, 30km north of Copenhagen.

The museum's facade
INOK CHOI / SHUTTERSTOCK ©

most boats you are totally exposed to the elements (which can be quite harsh in Copenhagen harbour, even during summer). Both operators offer tours in covered, heated boats from October to March.

Bike Copenhagen with Mike Cycling

(📞26 39 56 88; www.bikecopenhagenwithmike.dk; Sankt Peders Stræde 47; per person 300kr; 🚌5C, 6A) If you don't fancy walking, Bike Mike runs three-hour cycling tours of the city, departing Sankt Peders Stræde 47 in the city centre, just east of Ørstedsparken (which is southwest of Nørreport Station). The tour cost includes bike, helmet rental and Mike himself, a great character with

Central Copenhagen

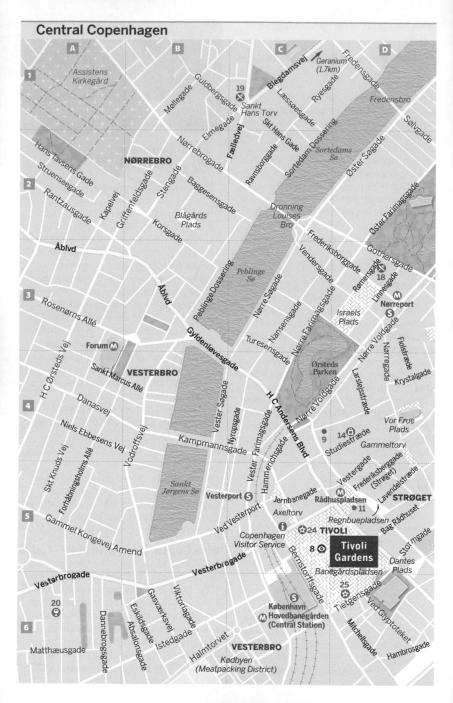

A **B** **C** **D**

1

Assistens Kirkegård

Guldbergsgade

Møllegade

Elmegade

Nørrebrogade

Blegdamsvej

Geranium (1.7km)

Fredensgade

19 Sankt Hans Torv

Skt Hans Gade

Læssøesgade

Ryesgade

Fredensbro

Sølvgade

Falledvej

Ravnsborggade

Sortedam Dossering

Sortedams Sø

Øster Søgade

NØRREBRO

Hans Tavsens Gade

Struenseegade

Rantzausgade

Kapelvej

Griffenfeldsgade

Stengade

Baggesensgade

Blågårds Plads

Korsgade

Dronning Louises Bro

Frederiksborggade

Vendersgade

Øster Farimagsgade

Gothersgade

2

Åblvd

Peblinge Dossering

Peblinge Sø

Nørre Søgade

Nansensgade

Nørre Farimagsgade

Rømersgade

18

Linnesgade

Nørreport

3

Rosenørns Allé

Åblvd

Gyldenløvesgade

Turesensgade

Israels Plads

Nørre Voldgade

Nørregade

Fiolstræde

Krystalgade

H C Ørsteds Vej

Forum

Sankt Marcus Allé

VESTERBRO

Danasvej

Vester Søgade

Nyropsgade

Ørsteds Parken

Nørre Voldgade

Larslejsstræde

Vor Frue Plads

4

Niels Ebbesens Vej

Vodroffsvej

Kampmannsgade

Vester Farimagsgade

H C Andersens Blvd

9

14

Studiestræde

Gammeltorv

Vestergade

Frederiksberggade (Strøget)

Lavendelstræde

STRØGET

Skt Knuds Vej

Forhåbningsholms Allé

Sankt Jørgens Sø

Vesterport

Hammerichsgade

Jernbanegade

Rådhuspladsen

11

Ved Vesterport

Axeltorv

Regnbuepladsen

Bag Rådhuset

Storm gade

5

Gammel Kongevej Amend

Copenhagen Visitor Service

24

TIVOLI

8

Tivoli Gardens

Banegårdspladsen

Dantes Plads

Vesterbrogade

Bernstorffsgade

25

Ved Glyptoteket

Vesterbrogade

20

Gasværksvej

Viktoriagade

Eskildsgade

Absalonsgade

Istedgade

Dannebrogsgade

Halmtorvet

VESTERBRO

Kødbyen (Meatpacking District)

København Hovedbanegården (Central Station)

Tietgensgade

Mitchellsgade

Hambrosgade

6

Matthæusgade

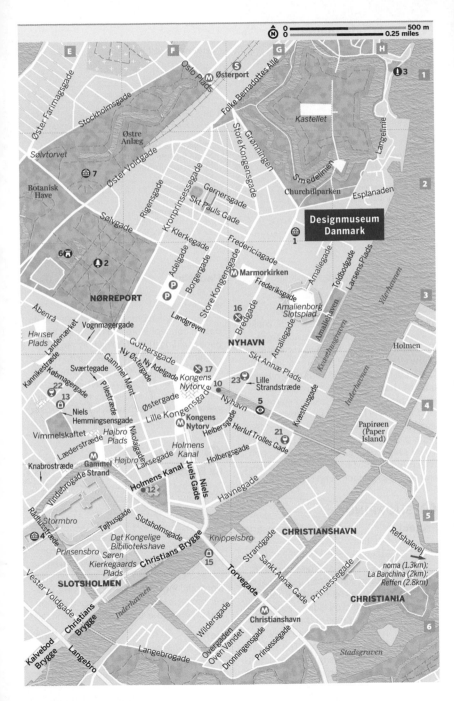

Ⓝ 0 ▭▭▭▭▭▭ 500 m
0 ▭▭▭▭▭▭ 0.25 miles

E **F** **G** **H**

Oslo Plads
Østerport **S**
❶3 **1**

Østre Faimagsgade
Stockholmsgade
Folke Bernadottes Allé
Grønningen
Store Kongensgade
Kastellet
Langelinie

Østre Anlæg
Smedelinien
Churchillparken
Esplanaden **2**

Sølvtorvet

🏛7
Øster Voldgade

Botanisk Have
Rigensgade
Kronprinsessegade
Gernersgade
Skt Pauls Gade
Designmuseum Danmark
🏛1

Sølvgade
Kr Klerkegade
Fredericiagade
Amaliegade
Toldbodgade
Larsens Plads
Yderhavnen **3**

6🏛 ❶2
Adelgade
Borgergade
Store Kongensgade
Marmorkirken Ⓜ
Frederiksgade
Amalienborg Slotsplad
Amaliehaven
Kvæsthusgraven

NØRREPORT
Ⓟ
Ⓟ
Landgreven
16
❌
Bredgade
NYHAVN
Inderhavnen
Holmen

Åbenrå
Vognmagergade
Guthersgade
Skt Annæ Plads

Hauser Plads
Landemærket
Ny Østergade
Ny Adelgade
Kongens Nytorv
17 ❌
23 ❷ Lille Strandstræde
Kvæsthusgade **4**

Kannikestræde
Sværtegade
Gammel Mont
Pilestræde
10
Nyhavn
5 ⊙
Papirøen (Paper Island)

Købmagergade
22
13
Niels Hemmingsensgade
Østergade
Lille Kongensgade
Kongens Nytorv Ⓜ
Heibersg
Herluf Trolles Gade
21 ⓐ

Vimmelskaftet
Højbro Plads
Nikolajgade
Holmens Kanal
Holbergsgade

Knabrostræde
Læderstræde
Gammel Strand Ⓜ
Højbro
Laksegade
Juels Gade
Niels Gade
Havnegade

Vindebrogade
12
Holmens Kanal **5**

Rådhus Stormbro
Tøjhusgade
Slotsholmsgade
Knippelsbro
CHRISTIANSHAVN
Refshalevej

🏛4
Prinsensbro
Det Kongelige Bibilotekshave
Christians Brygge
Strandgade
Sankt Annæ Gade
Prinsessegade
noma (1.3km);
La Banchina (2km);
Reffen (2.8km)

Søren Kierkegaards Plads
ⓐ 15
SLOTSHOLMEN
Torvegade
CHRISTIANIA

Vester Voldgade
Christians Brygge
Inderhavnen
Wildersgade
Overgaden Oven Vandet
Christianshavn Ⓜ **6**

Kalvebod Brygge
Langebro
Langebrogade
Dronningensgade
Prinsessegade
Stadsgraven

Central Copenhagen

deep, attention-grabbing knowledge of the city. Cash only.

Copenhagen Free Walking Tours
Walking

(www.copenhagenfreewalkingtours.dk) **FREE** This outfit runs free daily walking tours of the city. The three-hour Grand Tour of Copenhagen departs Rådhus (Town Hall) daily at 11am, with additional departures in the summer months, taking in famous landmarks and featuring interesting anecdotes. A 90-minute tour of Christianshavn departs daily at 3pm from Højbro Plads. There's also a 90-minute Classical Copenhagen Tour, departing Fridays, Saturdays and Sundays at noon. A tip is expected.

🛍 SHOPPING

Project 4
Fashion & Accessories

(📞81 92 50 80; https://project4.dk; Larsbjørnsstræde 19; ⊙11am-6pm Mon-Thu, to 7pm Fri, 10am-5pm Sat; 🚌5C, 6A, 14) Project 4 is the place to go to add some Scandi style to your wardrobe. This small boutique features a collection of handpicked ladies' fashion and accessories from a range of Danish brands such as Won Hundred, Rains and Arkk, as well as international designers. The shop is a treasure-trove of clothing, plus handcrafted jewellery, bags, eyewear and sneakers.

Paustian
Design

(📞39 16 65 65; www.paustian.com/en; Niels Hemmingsens Gade 24; ⊙10am-6pm Mon-Sat, 11am-5pm Sun) Danish brand Paustian opened its design concept store in a renovated historic bank building just off Strøget in late 2018. Admire the stylish furniture and home accessories in a sprawling showroom, which is as much an attraction itself. Features of the bank remain, including vaulted ceilings, golden columns, and bank vaults now used to display jewellery and special collections.

✪ EATING

La Banchina
Cafe €

(📞31 26 65 61; www.labanchina.dk; Refshalevej 141A; mains 70-90kr; ⊙8am-11pm Mon-Sun May-Sep, reduced hours rest of year; 🖉; 🚌9A, 🛥Refshaleøen) This tiny spot serves breakfast, lunch and dinner, cooked beautifully and served with little fanfare. The real magic is the setting, a small harbour cove with picnic tables and a wooden pier where summertime diners dip their feet while sipping vino, tucking into grub like tender barbecued salmon, and watching the sun sink over Copenhagen.

Reffen
Street Food €

(https://reffen.dk; Refshalevej 167a; meals from 80kr; ⊙noon-8pm Mon-Sun Apr-Sep, hours vary Oct-Mar; 🖉🚼🐾; 🚌9A, 🛥Refshaleøen) 🐾 This harbourside street-food market is a veritable village of converted shipping containers, peddling sustainable bites from across the globe. Multiculti options include organic polenta and pasta, dosas, burgers, sushi, satay skewers and Filipino BBQ. You'll also find a number of bars (open until 10pm or later Friday and Saturday). These include an outpost of Copenhagen's cult-status microbrewery Mikkeller.

Wulff & Konstali Cafe €€
(📞32 54 81 81; www.wogk.dk; Sankt Hans Torv 30, Nørrebro; set brunch 129-159kr; ☺7am-7pm Mon-Fri, to 6pm Sat & Sun; 🖋🚼; 🚌3A, 5C, 350S) 🍴 Wulff & Konstali offers up one of the best brunches in town – quite an accomplishment in this brunch-loving city. Choose a five- or seven-item spread, mixing and matching from offerings such as panini with mushroom, Parmesan and truffle, and chocolate waffle with sea-buckthorn cream. Accompany with fresh juices and smoothies for a delectable dining experience. Brunch 9am to 3pm daily.

AOC New Nordic €€€
(📞33 11 11 45; www.restaurantaoc.dk; Dronningens Tværgade 2; tasting menu 2000kr; ☺6.30-9:30pm Tue-Sat; 🖋; 🚌1A, 26, Ⓜ Kongens Nytorv) In the vaulted cellar of a 17th-century mansion, this intimate, two-starred Michelin standout thrills with evocative, often surprising Nordic flavour combinations, scents and textures. Here, sea scallops might conspire with fermented asparagus, while grilled cherries share the plate with smoked marrow and pigeon breast. AOC exclusively serves a tasting menu of ten-plus courses, and reservations should be made around a week in advance, especially for late-week dining.

noma New Nordic €€€
(www.noma.dk; Refshalevej 96; menu 2500kr, wine pairing 1550kr; ☺11:30am-close Tues-Sat; 🚌9A) Groundbreaking New Nordic restaurant noma re-opened in its new location in February 2018 after a one-year hiatus. A re-imagined menu presents dishes focusing on featured Nordic produce across three seasons: seafood, vegetables, and game and forest. The Scandi-style

minimalist interiors and tableware were designed from scratch for the new space. Reservations are essential.

Geist Danish €€€
(📞33 13 37 13; http://restaurantgeist.dk; Kongens Nytorv 8; plates 69-279kr; ☺12-3pm and 6pm-1am daily; 🚌1A, 26, Ⓜ Kongens Nytorv) Chic, monochromatic Geist is owned by celebrity chef Bo Bech, a man driven by experimentation. His long list of small plates pairs Nordic and non-Nordic ingredients in unexpected, often thrilling ways. Create your tasting menu from dishes like wafers of avocado with lightly salted caviar, turbot and fennel ravioli with gruyère, or out-of-the-box desserts like poached apple with mustard seed and sweet and sour mandarin.

Geranium New Nordic €€€
(📞69 96 00 20; www.geranium.dk; Per Henrik Lings Allé 4, Østerbro; tasting menu 2500kr, wine pairings 1400-4200kr, juice pairings 750kr; ☺noon-4pm & 6.30pm-midnight Wed-Sat; 🖋; 🚌1A, 14, Ⓜ Vibenshus Runddel) 🍴 On the 8th floor of Parken Stadium, Geranium is the only restaurant in town sporting three Michelin stars. At the helm is Bocuse d'Or prize-winning chef Rasmus Kofoed, who transforms local, organic ingredients into edible Nordic artworks like lobster paired with milk and the juice of fermented carrots and sea buckthorn, or cabbage sprouts and chicken served with quail egg, cep mushrooms and hay beer.

Selma New Nordic €€€
(http://selmacopenhagen.dk; Rømersgade 20; meals 200-345kr, tasting menus 335-485kr; ☺11.30am-3.30pm Sun-Tue, to 4pm Wed-Sat, 5.30pm-midnight Wed-Sat; 🖋; 🚌5C, 6A, Ⓜ Nørreport, Ⓢ Nørreport) Selma has taken the Copenhagen smørrebrød scene by storm with its innovative creations, with Danes happily baffled that a Swede (chef-owner Magnus Petersson) has such a handle on the Danish classic. His modern take on the traditional open-faced sandwiches includes a popular blackcurrant herring, which diners can pair with one of the 12 beers on tap, including from local brewer and Selma partners Mikkeller.

Copenhagen's Cykelslangen

Two of the Danes' greatest passions – design and cycling – meet in spectacular fashion with **Cykelslangen** (Cycle Snake). Designed by local architects Dissing + Weitling, the 235m-long cycling path evokes a slender orange ribbon, its gently curving form contrasting dramatically with the area's block-like architecture. The elevated path winds its way from Bryggebroen (Brygge Bridge) west to Fisketorvet Shopping Centre, weaving its way over the harbour and delivering a cycling experience that's nothing short of whimsical. To reach the path on public transport, catch bus 30 to Fisketorvet Shopping Centre. The best way to reach it, however, is on a bike, as Cykelslangen is only accessible to cyclists.

Cyclists on Bryggebroen
FRANCESCO DRAGONETTI / SHUTTERSTOCK ©

🍷 DRINKING & NIGHTLIFE

Copenhagen is packed with a diverse range of drinking options. Vibrant drinking areas include Kødbyen (the 'Meatpacking District') and Istedgade in Vesterbro; Ravnsborggade, Elmegade and Sankt Hans Torv in Nørrebro; and especially gay-friendly Studiestræde.

Den Vandrette   Wine Bar
(📞72 14 82 28; www.denvandrette.dk; Havnegade 53A; ⊗4-11pm Mon-Sat; 🚌66, 🚢Nyhavn) This is the harbourside wine bar for lauded wine wholesaler **Rosforth & Rosforth** (📞33 32 55 20; www.rosforth.dk; Knippelsbrogade 10; ⊗9am-5pm Mon-Fri, from noon Sat; 🚌2A, 9A, 37, 350S, MChristianshavn). The focus is on natural and

biodynamic drops, its short, sharply curated list of wines by the glass often including lesser-known blends like Terret Bourret–Vermentino. Guests are welcome to browse the cellar and pick their own bottle. Come summer, it has alfresco waterside tables and deckchairs for sun-kissed toasting.

Nebbiolo   Wine Bar
(📞60 10 11 09; http://nebbiolo-winebar.com; Store Strandstræde 18; ⊗3pm-midnight Sun-Thu, to 2am Fri & Sat; 🚇; 🚌1A, 66, MKongens Nytorv) Just off Nyhavn, this smart, contemporary wine bar and shop showcases wines from smaller, inspiring Italian vineyards. Wines by the glass are priced in one of three categories (75/100/125kr) and even those in the lowest price range are often wonderful.

Jane   Club
(www.thejane.dk; Gråbrødretorv 8; ⊗8pm-late Thu-Sat; 🚌5C, 6A, 14, 150S, 350S, MNørreport, SNørreport) With its plush armchairs, chesterfield sofas and soundtrack of jazz and blues, you'd be forgiven for thinking your name is Don Draper. But it probably isn't and you're definitely not on the set of *Mad Men*. You're at Jane, a hotspot, speakeasy-style bar with craft cocktails and a craftier bookshelf. As the night progresses, watch it open to reveal a hidden dance floor.

Ancestrale   Wine Bar
(📞60 40 74 14; http://ancestrale.dk; Oehlenschlægersgade 12, Vesterbro; ⊗4-11pm Mon-Thu, to midnight Fri & Sat) Ancestrale wine bar is tucked away on a quiet residential street just off Vesterbro's main strip. Featuring exposed brick, candlelight and good hospitality, Ancestrale is a perfect place to soak up some Danish hygge. Founded by alumni of acclaimed restaurants Noma, 108 and Radio, Ancestrale offers not only a nice range of wines, but also a selection of Nordic-inspired small plates.

ℹ️ INFORMATION

DISCOUNT CARDS

The **Copenhagen Card** (www.copenhagencard. com; adult/child 10-15yr 24hr 399/199kr, 48hr 569/289kr, 72hr 689/349kr, 120hr 899/449kr),

Plankton cake at noma (p141)

available at the Copenhagen Visitors Centre or online, gives you free access to 72 museums and attractions in the city and surrounding area, as well as free travel for all S-train, metro and bus journeys within the seven travel zones.

TOURIST INFORMATION

Copenhagen Visitors Centre (☏70 22 24 42; www.visitcopenhagen.com; Vesterbrogade 4A; ◷9am-8pm Mon-Fri, to 6pm Sat & Sun Jul & Aug, reduced hours rest of year; ☎; ▣2A, 5C, 6A, 12, 14, 26, Ⓜ København H, Ⓢ København H) Copenhagen's excellent and informative information centre has a superb cafe and lounge with free wi-fi; it also sells the Copenhagen Card.

ⓘ GETTING THERE & AWAY

AIR

Copenhagen Airport (☏32 31 32 31; www.cph. dk; Lufthavnsboulevarden, Kastrup; ⓂLufthavnen, Ⓢ Københavns Lufthavn)

BUS

Copenhagen is well connected to the rest of Europe by daily (or near-daily) buses. **Flixbus** (www.flixbus.dk) runs services throughout Europe, including into Sweden and Norway. Destinations, timetables and prices are all online. Flixbus has dynamic pricing, so it pays to book ahead, and the routes may use stops that are different to the main bus stations, so check your options.

TRAIN

DSB Billetsalg (DSB Ticket Office; ☏70 13 14 15; www.dsb.dk; Central Station, Bernstorffsgade 16-22; ◷7am-8.30pm Mon-Fri, 8am-6pm Sat & Sun; Ⓢ København H) is best for reservations and for purchasing international train tickets.

ⓘ GETTING AROUND

The best way to see Copenhagen is on foot. There are few main sights or shopping quarters more than a 20-minute walk from the city centre.

Copenhagen vies with Amsterdam as the world's most bike-friendly city. The superb, city-wide rental system is **Bycyklen** (City Bikes; www.bycyklen.dk; per hr 30kr). Visit the Bycyklen website for more information.

OSLO, NORWAY

Oslo, Norway

Surrounded by mountains and sea, compact, cultured and fun Oslo has a palpable sense of reinvention. Come to Oslo to pay homage to Edvard Munch and Henrik Ibsen, the city's two most famous sons, by all means, but don't leave without discovering its contemporary cultural life. Explore one of its many museums, get to know its booming contemporary-art scene, or marvel at the work of its starchitects.

Oslo's fast-growing skyline might be crowded with cranes, but this rapidly growing urban metropolis is also one of the world's greenest cities.

Two Days in Oslo

See Edvard Munch's *The Scream* at the **Nasjonalgalleriet** (p156). Visit the **Akershus Fortress** (p156), where you can wander for free and take in the view. Take the ferry from the nearby docks to the pretty Bygdøy peninsula, and see the **Vikingskipshuset** (p154).

Head to the island of Tjuvholmen and savour the contemporary-art collection of **Astrup Fearnley Museet** (p156) as well the amazing works of the surrounding **Tjuvholmen Sculpture Park** (p157).

Four Days in Oslo

Climb the roof of the spectacular **Oslo Opera House** (p148), take in the view and then go inside for a tour. Head to the **Munchmuseet** (p157), where you can explore the Oslo of the late 19th century through Munch's eyes.

Wander among the bold, sensuous statues of Gustav Vigeland in **Vigeland Sculpture Park** (p150), which fills the sprawling **Frognerparken** (p153).

Not done with the Nordic region? Head south to Copenhagen (p129) or west to Reykjavík (p163).

Previous page: Nationaltheatret (p161)
ANSHARPHOTO / SHUTTERSTOCK ©

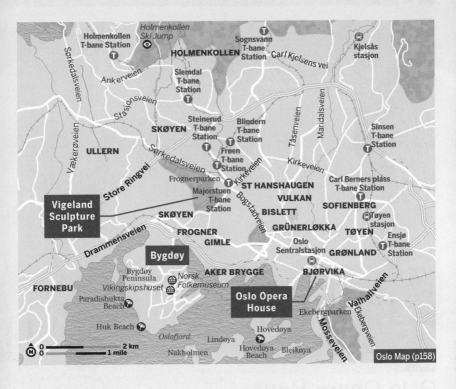

Oslo Map (p158)

Arriving in Oslo

Oslo Gardermoen International Airport Frequent Flytoget Airport Express trains connect the airport to the city centre (19 to 23 minutes, 190kr). Local train services are cheaper (23 minutes, 101kr). Buses (160kr) take 40 minutes. Taxis cost 789kr to 1311kr (30 minutes to one hour).

DFDS Seaways Port All ferries arriving from Denmark disembark here. Bus 60 stops nearby, or it's a short taxi ride from most hotels.

Oslo Central Station (Oslo S) All trains from Sweden arrive and depart from here.

Where to Stay

Aker Brygge & Bygdøy Scenic, central and close to all the major sites.

City Centre Close to everything. A wide variety to choose from.

Frogner & Western Oslo Serene and close to the city.

Grünerløkka & Vulkan Fantastic choice for experiencing local life; the city is an easy walk or short tram ride away.

Opera House & Bjørvika Great views, close to everything and increasingly scenic.

PLUSONE / SHUTTERSTOCK ©

Oslo Opera House

Oslo's eastern waterfront is undergoing rapid change. The stunning Opera House, an easy wander away from Central Station, is the main draw here, and is somewhere you'll probably want to linger.

Design Savvy

Oslo's waterfront renewal, the magnificent Opera House (2008), reminiscent of a glacier floating in the waters of the Oslofjord, is one of the most iconic buildings in Scandinavia. Conceived by Oslo architectural firm Snøhetta, its design is a thoughtful meditation on the notion of monumentality, the dignity of cultural production, Norway's unique place in the world and the conversation between public life and personal experience.

Resembling a glacier floating in the Bjørvika inlet, it's a fantastic place to visit, a truly engaging piece of Scandinavian design that is inclusive, sensual and fun, whether you're an opera fan or not. The architects imagined the site as one with huge metaphorical importance, conjuring the relationship between Oslo and the fjord, Norway and the world, performance and quotidian life, the artist and the audience. Unusually, the

Great For...

☑ Don't Miss

Architectural highlights like the roof 'carpet' and the foyer's 'wave wall.'

multilevel workshops and offices of the several hundred opera and ballet workers are an integral and visible part of the design.

The Roof

Both selfie-zone and joyful place to wander, sprawl, laugh or think, the roof is a broad, etched and variegated expanse of luminous marble known as the 'carpet' that consists of 36,000 blocks. It's a fantastically Norwegian expression of the notion of monumentality and of accessibility, its grandeur horizontal and all-encompassing rather than vertical. The roof is also an incredibly crafted piece of work, engaging in both its close detail as well as its sheer size.

The Interior

The main entrance is purposely small and unimposing, adding to the sense of vastness that greets you on entering the foyer (the windows alone are 15m high, flooding it with light). Aside from this large expanse of sky, the dominating feature of the foyer is the 'wave wall'. Made of a complex arrangement of golden oak cones, the wall curves up through the centre of the foyer and provides access to the upper levels of the building, while symbolically evoking a threshold. To fully appreciate the building's interior, join a **guided tour** (☎21 42 21 21; Kirsten Flagstads plass 1; adult/child 120/70kr; ☺English tours 1pm Sun-Fri, noon Sat, additional tours Jul & Aug; ⊤Sentralstasjonen).

Offshore

Floating just offshore is Monica Bonvicini's **She Lies**, a 3D interpretation of Caspar David Friedrich's 1823–24 painting *Das Eismeer* (The Sea of Ice). As the tides rush in and out of the harbour, the steel-and-glass sculpture spins and twists, creating a constantly changing perspective for the viewer.

Vigeland Sculpture Park

Gustav Vigeland is Norway's best-loved sculptor, and this collection of his work fills, and utterly transforms, the city's Frognerparken, with more than 200 granite, bronze and iron sculptures. This is the world's largest sculpture park dedicated to one artist, and the acres of figurative work are all in service to a circle-of-life theme.

Great For...

ⓘ Need to Know

Vigelandsparken; www.vigeland.museum.
no/no/vigelandsparken; Nobels gate 32;
🚇Vigelandsparken

★ **Top Tip**
Try to get to the park either early or late; tour buses dislodge crowds midmorning and midafternoon.

The Gate

The park's main entrance on Kirkeveien is marked with a grand granite and wrought-iron gate, or series of gates to be more precise, with curving railings on each side that meet copper-topped gatehouses. Despite their lovely organic geometry, they have an otherworldiness – perhaps in gentle preparation for the experience awaiting you within.

The Bridge

While not the park's most spectacular work (that would be the towering *Monolith*), the 100m-long bridge was the first part of the park to be open and its sculptures of children are its most enduring and endearing feature. It's here that you will find the much documented *Sinnataggen*, the little Angry Boy, a bronze of a child in the full throes of a tantrum. Below the bridge is a circular playground with eight bronze sculptures of small children, along with the unusual, rather jarring, science-fiction-like columns depicting humans in combat with large lizards.

The Fountain

Vigeland had long dreamed of a monumental fountain and its turn-of-the-century origins and Jugendstil influence are clear, although it was not until 1924 that this extraordinary work found its home. Its stylistic formality is highlighted by its bronze material and there's a rhythmic grace to the composition and siting. Twenty groups of trees shelter groups of human figures, depicting the journey from cradle to grave. The bronze reliefs which clad the outer side of the pool were not completed until 1947, after many changes. They too depict the eternal life cycle.

The *Fountain*

The Monolith

Flanked by steps lined with highly sensual couples in granite, the *Monolith* sits at the highest point of the park. Carved from a single enormous granite block, the tower rises more than 14m above its 3m plinth. The figures here clamber and climb over each other, and at the same time hold each other and will themselves ever upwards. After the emotionality of the bridge and the melancholy resignation of the fountain, it's a dynamic work of yearning and transcendence (if still an onslaught and not just a little bit creepy).

☑ Don't Miss

The most famous artworks: the *Monolith*, the *Fountain*, the *Bridge*, the *Wheel of Life*.

NEDOMACKI / GETTY IMAGES ©

The Wheel of Life & Other Sculptures

Furthest from the park's entrance is the *Wheel of Life*, first modelled in 1933–34. Its simple form of entwined human figures speaks to the entire theme of the park, that of neverending momentum where we both push eternally forward and cling to each other in support. It's also worth seeking out the group of figures known as the *Clan*. With its 21 entwined figures, it's the largest work besides the Monolith. Just inside the main entrance, back by the gate, you can see Vigeland himself, in a (self) portrait of the artist from 1942, tools to the ready and sporting his rustic sculpting uniform.

Around the Park

Near the southern entrance to Vigeland Park, charming **Oslo City Museum** (Oslo Bymuseet; ☑23 28 41 70; www.oslomuseum.no; Frognerveien 67; ☺11am-4pm Tue-Sun; ☒Solli) FREE is a lovely snapshot of traditional bourgeois Norwegian life of the era.

Surrounding the sculpture park, **Frognerparken** (☒Vigelandsparken) attracts westside locals with its broad lawns, ponds, stream and rows of shady trees for picnics, strolling or lounging on the grass. For a more in-depth look at Gustav Vigeland's work, **Vigeland Museum** (www.vigeland.museum.no; Nobelsgata 32; adult/child 60/30kr, with Oslo Pass free; ☺10am-5pm Tue-Sun May-Aug, noon-4pm Tue-Sun rest of year; ☒20, ☒12, ☒N12, ☒Borgen) is just opposite the southern entrance. There's also an **ice-skating rink** (☑910 05 955; www.frognerstadion.no; Middelthunsgate 26; adult/child 40/15kr; ☺11am-10pm Mon-Thu, to 9pm Fri, to 6pm Sat & Sun Dec-Mar; ☒Borgen) and a **swimming pool complex** (☑23 27 54 50; Middelthuns gate 28; adult/child 98/48kr; ☺7am-7.30pm Mon-Thu, to 8pm Fri-Sun Jun–mid-Aug; ☒Borgen).

✕ Take a Break

Well outside the park, **Lorry** (http://lorry.no; Parkveien 12; ☺11am-1am Mon, to 3.30am Tue-Sat, noon-1am Sun; ☒17B) is great for an atmospheric old-school beer and traditional Norwegian favourites.

TRABANTOS / SHUTTERSTOCK ©

A Day in Bygdøy

Best accessed by ferry, pretty, residential and rural-feeling Bygdøy is home to the city's most fascinating, and quintessentially Norwegian, museums. Enjoy summertime cafes and sublime views.

Great For...

☑ **Don't Miss**

Marvelling at the sheer beauty of the more-than-900-year-old Viking vessels at the Vikingskipshuset.

Vikingskipshuset

Around 1100 years ago, Vikings dragged up two longships from the shoreline and used them as the centrepiece for grand ceremonial burials, most likely for important chieftains or nobility. Along with the ships, they buried many items for the afterlife: food, drink, jewellery, furniture, carriages, weapons, and even a few dogs for companionship. Discovered in Oslofjord in the late 19th and early 20th centuries, the ships and their wares are beautifully restored **here** (Viking Ship Museum; ☎22 13 52 80; www.khm.uio.no; Huk Aveny 35; adult/child 100kr/free; ⊗9am-6pm May-Sep, 10am-4pm Oct-Apr; ☐30), offering an evocative, emotive insight into Viking life.

Polarship Fram Museum

This **museum** (Frammuseet; ☎23 28 29 50; www.frammuseum.no; Bygdøynesveien 39; adult/child 120/50kr, with Oslo Pass free; ⊗9am-6pm

Norsk Folkemuseum

Jun-Aug, 10am-6pm May & Sep, to 5pm Oct-Apr; 🚌30, ⛴Bygdøynes) is dedicated to one of the most enduring symbols of early polar exploration, the 39m schooner *Fram* (meaning 'Forward'). Wander the decks, peek inside the cramped bunk rooms and imagine life at sea and among the polar ice. Allow plenty of time, as there's an overwhelming volume of information to absorb, with detailed exhibits complete with maps, pictures and artefacts of various expeditions, from Nansen's attempt to ski across the North Pole to Amundsen's discovery of the Northwest Passage.

Norsk Folkemuseum

This folk **museum** (Norwegian Folk Museum; 📞22 12 37 00; www.norskfolkemuseum.no; Museumsveien 10; adult/child 160/40kr, with Oslo Pass free; ⊙10am-5pm May-Sep, 11am-4pm Sep-May; ⛴91, 🚌30) is Norway's largest open-air museum and one of Oslo's most popular at-

tractions. The museum includes more than 140 buildings, mostly from the 17th and 18th centuries, gathered from around the country, rebuilt and organised according to region of origin. Paths wind past old barns, elevated *stabbur* (raised storehouses) and rough-timbered farmhouses with sod roofs sprouting wildflowers. Little people will be entertained by the numerous farm animals, horse and cart rides, and other activities.

Kon-Tiki Museum

A favourite among children, this worthwhile **museum** (📞23 08 67 67; www.kon-tiki.no; Bygdøynesveien 36; adult/child 100/50kr, with Oslo Pass free; ⊙9.30am-6pm Jun-Aug, 10am-5pm Mar-May, Sep & Oct, 10am-4pm Nov-Feb; ⛴91, 🚌30) is dedicated to the balsa raft *Kon-Tiki*, which Norwegian explorer Thor Heyerdahl sailed from Peru to Polynesia in 1947. The museum also displays the totora-reed boat *Ra II*, built by Aymara people on the Bolivian island of Suriqui in Lake Titicaca. Heyerdahl used it to cross the Atlantic in 1970.

◉ SIGHTS

Akershus Festning   Fortress

(Akershus Fortress; www.akershusfestning.no; ⊘6am-9pm; ⛉Kontraskjæret) **FREE** When Oslo was named capital of Norway in 1299, King Håkon V ordered the construction of Akershus, strategically located on the eastern side of the harbour, to protect the city from external threats. Extended and modified over the centuries, it still dominates the Oslo harbourfront. The sprawling complex consists of a medieval castle, **Akershus Slott** (Akershus Castle; ☑22 41 25 21; www.nasjonalefestningsverk.no; Kongens gate; ⛉Kontraskjæret) (currently closed for renovations), a fortress and assorted other buildings, including still-active military installations.

Nasjonalgalleriet   Gallery

(National Gallery; ☑21 98 20 00; www.nasjonalmuseet.no; Universitetsgata 13; adult/child 120kr/free; ⊘10am-6pm Tue, Wed & Fri, to 7pm Thu, 11am-5pm Sat & Sun; ⛉Tullinløkka) The gallery houses the nation's largest collection of traditional and modern art, and many of Edvard Munch's best-known creations are on permanent display, including his most renowned piece, *The Scream*. But there's also a clutch of works by acclaimed European artists: Gauguin, Claudel, Picasso and El Greco, plus Manet, Degas, Renoir, Matisse, Cézanne and Monet are all in there. Nineteenth-century Norwegian artists have a strong showing too, including key figures such as JC Dahl and Christian Krohg.

Astrup Fearnley Museet   Gallery

(Astrup Fearnley Museum; ☑22 93 60 60; www.afmuseet.no; Strandpromenaden 2; adult/child 130kr/free; ⊘noon-5pm Tue, Wed & Fri, to 7pm Thu, 11am-5pm Sat & Sun year-round, plus noon-5pm Mon Jul & Aug; ⛉21, 54, ⛉Aker Brygge) This private contemporary-art museum resides in an arresting, silvered-wood building designed by Renzo Piano, with a sail-like glass roof that feels both maritime and at one with the Oslofjord landscape. The

> *Akershus Festning dominates the Oslo harbourfront*

Akershus Festning

PAULO MIGUEL COSTA / SHUTTERSTOCK ©

collection is rich in US work from the '80s (artists such as Jeff Koons, Tom Sachs, Cindy Sherman and Richard Prince are well represented), but boundary-pushing pieces by other key artists such as Sigmar Polke and Anselm Kiefer reflect a now-broader collecting brief.

Munchmuseet Gallery

(Munch Museum; ☑23 49 35 00; www.munch museet.no; Tøyengata 53; adult/child 120kr/free; ⊙10am-4pm, to 5pm mid-May–early Sep; ☐20, ⓣTøyen) This monographic museum dedicated to Norway's greatest artist, Edvard Munch (1863–1944), houses the largest collection of his work in the world: some 28,000 items, including 1100 paintings and 4500 watercolours, many of which were gifted to the city by Munch himself. Don't come looking for *The Scream,* though – it's at the Nasjonalgalleriet, along with a number of his other masterworks.

Tjuvholmen Sculpture Park Sculpture

(http://skulpturparken.webflow.io; Tjuvholmen; ⊙24hr; ☐Aker Brygge) **FREE** Like the Astrup Fearnley Museet that it surrounds, this sculpture park was designed by Renzo Piano and is also dedicated to international contemporary art. Don't miss (as if you could) Louise Bourgeois' magnificent and rather cheeky *Eyes* (1997), Ugo Rondinone's totemic and enchanting *Moonrise east. november* (2006) and Franz West's bright and tactile *Spalt* (2003). There are also works by Antony Gormley, Anish Kapoor, Ellsworth Kelly, and Peter Fischli and David Weiss.

🛍 SHOPPING

The city centre's Kirkegaten, Nedre Slottsgate and Prinsens gate are home to a well-considered collection of Scandinavian and international fashion and homewares shops, with Frogner and St Hanshaugen also having some good upmarket choices. Grünerløkka is great for unique buys, vintage items and Scandinavian fashion.

⛷ Holmenkollen Ski Jump

Watching over the city, and seemingly offering up the perpetual possibility of winter-sport fun, **Holmenkollen Ski Jump** (☑22 92 32 00; www.holmenkollen. com; Skiforeningen, Kongeveien 5; adult/child 140/70kr, with Oslo Pass free; ⊙9am-8pm Jun-Aug, 10am-5pm May & Sep, 10am-4pm rest of year; ⓣHolmen) is a beloved and historic Oslo landmark. Ski jumps have jutted from the mountain up here since 1892 and this, the most recent and most stunningly sculptural, was inaugurated in 2010. It's just 20 minutes from the centre.

NANISIMOVA / SHUTTERSTOCK ©

🍴 EATING

Vippa Street Food €

(☑91 72 80 43; www.vippa.no; Akershusstranda 25; dishes 65-160kr; ⊙noon-9pm Wed-Sat, to 8pm Sun) It's a little out of the way, but if you find yourself in the vicinity of Vippetangen quay, duck into this popular hangar-turned-street-food-hall for international flavours galore. Grab a bowl of what tickles your fancy from Thai to Syrian, Chinese to Eritrean, and pitch up at one of the communal benches for a chat with your table-mate.

Mathallen Oslo Food Hall €€

(☑40 00 12 09; www.mathallenoslo.no; Maridalsveien 17, Vulkan; ⊙10am-8pm Tue-Sat, 11am-6pm Sun; ☐54) Down by the river, this former industrial space is now a food hall dedicated to showcasing the very best

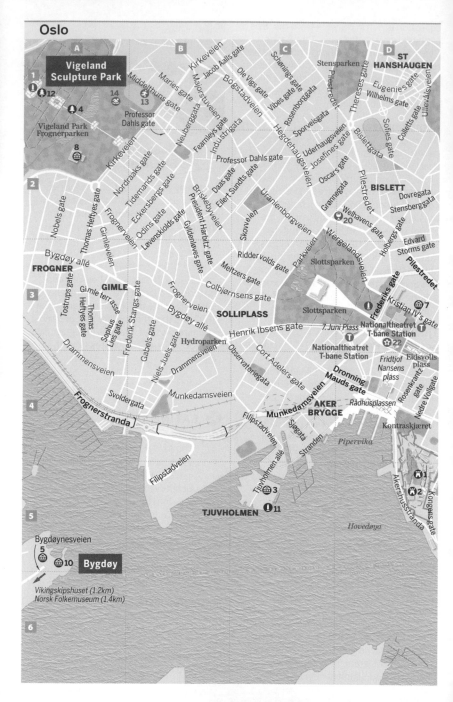

Oslo

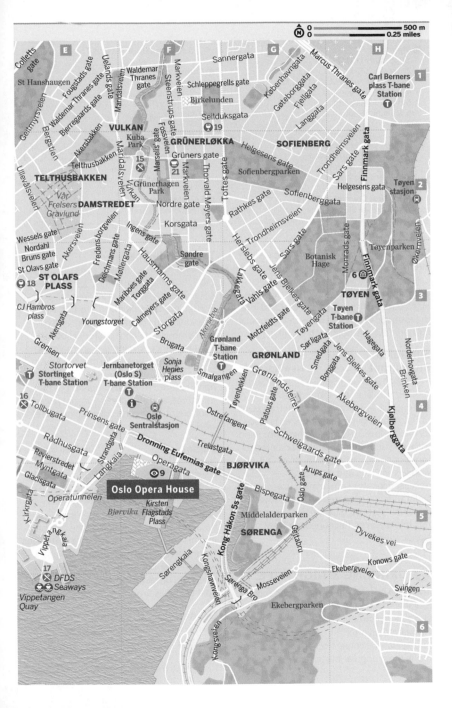

Oslo

Norwegian food, as well as some excellent international cuisines. Eating here is a casual affair – there are dozens of delis, cafes and miniature restaurants, and the place buzzes throughout the day and into the evening. Check the website for special culinary festivals held each month.

Sentralen Restaurant
New Nordic €€

(☑22 33 33 22; www.sentralen.no; Øvre Slottsgate 3; small plates 95-245kr; ⊙11am-10pm Mon-Fri, from noon Sat; ☒Øvre Slottsgate) One of Oslo's best dining experiences is also its most relaxed. A large dining room filled with old social-club chairs and painted in tones of deep, earthy green, draws city workers, visitors and natural-wine-obsessed locals in equal measure. Outstandingly prepared and presented, the small-plates concept makes it easy to sample across the appealing New Nordic menu.

🍷 DRINKING & NIGHTLIFE

The city's best neighbourhood bar scene is along Thorvald Meyers gate and the surrounding streets in Grünerløkka and the Torggata strip after the bridge across the Akerselva. The Youngstorget area has some of the most popular places close to the city centre.

Tim Wendelboe
Coffee

(☑944 31 627; www.timwendelboe.no; Grüners gate 1; ⊙8.30am-6pm Mon-Fri, 11am-5pm Sat & Sun; ☒Olaf Ryes plass) Tim Wendelboe is often credited with kick-starting the Scandinavian coffee revolution, and his eponymous cafe and roastery is both a local freelancers' hang-out and an international coffee-fiend pilgrimage site. All the beans are, of course, self-sourced and hand-roasted (the roaster is part of the furniture), and all coffees – from an iced pour-over to a regular cappuccino – are world class.

Fuglen
Cocktail Bar, Cafe

(www.fuglen.com; Universitetsgaten 2, enter on Pilestredet; ⊙7.30am-10pm Mon & Tue, to 1am Wed & Thu, to 3am Fri, 11am-3am Sat, 11am-6pm Sun; ☒33) Fuglen and its crew of merry entrepreneurs are part of Oslo's dour-to-dreamily-cool reinvention. Since overhauling this cafe, they've launched a coffee and Norwegian design mini-empire in Japan, while in their home city they continue to roast and brew, as well as mix some of the best cocktails around.

Grünerløkka Brygghus
Pub

(www.brygghus.no; Thorvald Meyers gate 30b; ⊙4-11pm Mon-Wed, 4pm-1am Thu, 3pm-3.30am Fri, noon-3.30am Sat, noon-11pm Sun; ☒Olaf Ryes plass) This atmospheric and amiable alehouse and microbrewery does a range of house brews from pilsners to *Weissbiers*, and also serves up some intriguing ales from guest breweries. Stomach liners – burgers, bangers and mash, and fish and chips – can be ordered at the bar. Streetside benches are at a premium but worth trying to snare.

⭐ ENTERTAINMENT

Oslo Opera House   Opera

(Den Norske Opera & Ballett; 🗹21 42 21 21; www.operaen.no; Kirsten Flagstads Plass 1; tickets 100-795kr; ⓉSentralstasjonen) Apart from being one of Norway's most impressive examples of contemporary architecture (p148), Oslo Opera House is also the venue for world-class opera and ballet performances.

Nationaltheatret   Theatre

(National Theatre; 🗹22 00 14 00; www.national theatret.no; Stortingsgata; ☺box office 11am-6.30pm Mon-Sat; 🚇Nationaltheatret) Designed in lavish fashion by Oslo's Henrik Bull, Norway's showcase theatre was constructed specifically as a venue to honour plays by Norwegian playwright Henrik Ibsen, whose works have been performed here since 1899.

ℹ️ INFORMATION

Oslo Visitor Centre (🗹23 10 62 00; www.visitoslo.com; Jernbanetorget 1; ☺9am-6pm; 🚇; 🚇Jernbanetorget, 🚇Jernbanetorget, 🚆Oslo S) Accessible from inside the main train station and from Jernbanetorget. Sells transport tickets as well as the useful **Oslo Pass** (www.visitoslo.com/en/activities-and-attractions/oslo-pass) and can help with booking activities.

ℹ️ GETTING THERE & AWAY

AIR

Oslo Gardermoen International Airport (www.avinor.no/en/airport/oslo-airport), the city's main airport, is 50km north of the city. Oslo Gardermoen International Airport is linked to the city by high-speed trains, as well as buses and taxis.

A handful of budget carriers operate a few flights from **Torp International Airport** (www.trop.no) in Sandefjord, some 123km southwest of Oslo. The **Torp-Expressen** (www.torp ekspressen.no; 1-way/return adult 290/530kr, child 150/300kr) bus runs from Torp airport to the Galleri Oslo bus terminal in about 95 minutes.

BOAT

Ferries operated by **DFDS Seaways** (www.dfds seaways.com; 🚌60) connect Oslo daily with Denmark from the **Vippetangen Quay** off Skippergata. Bus 60 stops within a couple of minutes' walk of the terminal.

ℹ️ GETTING AROUND

City-wide public transport is covered off by the **Ruter** (www.ruter.no) ticketing system; schedules and route maps are available online or at the **Ruter Customer Service Centre.** (Trafikanten; 🗹177; www.ruter.no; Jernbanetorget; ☺7am-8pm Mon-Fri, 8am-6pm Sat & Sun)

Tram Oslo's tram (*trikk*) network covers much of the city centre; services run until 1am.

T-bane The five-line Tunnelbane (T-bane) underground system is fast. Services stop just after midnight.

Bus Has extensive coverage over the whole city.

Ruter (www.ruter.no) tickets for trips in zone 1 (covering most of the city centre) cost adult/child 35/18kr in advance.

○ One-day (adult/child 105/53kr) and seven-day (adult/child 249/125kr) tickets are also available.

○ Children aged four to 16 and seniors over 67 years of age pay half price.

○ It's possible to buy tickets on board buses and ferries (with cash) for 20kr more than the standard fare, but not on trams, or the T-bane.

REYKJAVÍK, ICELAND

In This Chapter

Reykjavík, Iceland

Reykjavík is loaded with captivating art, rich cuisine and quirky, creative people. The music scene is epic, with excellent festivals, creative DJs gigging and any number of home-grown bands.

Even if you come for a short visit, be sure to take a trip to the countryside. Reykjavík and its people are best understood by experiencing the raw and gorgeous land they anchor. The majority of Icelanders live in the capital, but their spirits also roam free across the land. Absorb what you see, hear, taste and smell – it's all part of Iceland's rich heritage.

Two Days in Reykjavík

Spend your first morning exploring historic **Old Reykjavík** (p173) and your afternoon wandering up arty **Skólavörðustígur**, shopping and sightseeing. Head to **Laugavegur** for dinner, drinks and late-night dancing.

On your second day, catch a **whale-watching cruise** (p176) or explore the **Old Harbour** (p173) and its museums in the morning. While away the afternoon at **Laugardalur** (p173) and your evening at a top Icelandic restaurant (p177).

Four Days in Reykjavík

On your third day, rent a bike at the Old Harbour and ferry out to historic **Viðey** (p178). Come back in time for last-minute shopping around **Laugavegur** and **Skólavörðustígur**. Sample the area's seafood before catching a show, an Icelandic movie or some live music.

On your final day take a trip to the **Golden Circle** (p170). If you haven't the time to visit the **Blue Lagoon** (p168) coming or going from the airport, go late in the evening, after the crowds have dwindled.

After Reykjavík, catch a three-hour flight to London (p49) or Dublin (p109).

Previous page: Panoramic view of Reykjavík
OLGA_GAVRILOVA / GETTY IMAGES ©

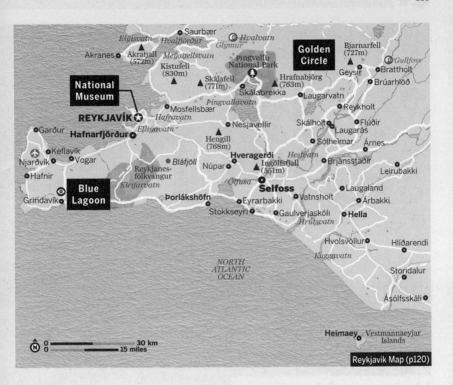

Arriving in Reykjavík

Keflavík International Airport

Iceland's primary international airport is 48km west of Reykjavík. Flybus, Airport Express and Airport Direct provide excellent bus links to the city (from 2700kr one way).

Reykjavík Domestic Airport Only a 2km walk into town.

Where to Stay

Reykjavík has loads of accommodation choices, with hostels, midrange guesthouses (often with shared bathrooms, kitchen and lounge) and business-class hotels galore, but top-end boutique hotels and apartments seem to be opening daily. Reservations are essential from June through August and prices are high. Plan for hostels, camping or short-term apartment rentals to save money.

Domestic life exhibit

VLADIMIR KOROSTYSHEVSKIY / SHUTTERSTOCK ©

National Museum

Iceland's premier museum is packed with artefacts and interesting displays. Exhibits give an excellent overview of the country's history and culture, and the audio guide adds loads of detail.

The superb National Museum beautifully displays Icelandic artefacts from settlement to the modern age, providing a meaningful overview of Iceland's history and culture. Brilliantly curated exhibits lead you through the struggle to settle and organise the forbidding island, the radical changes wrought by the advent of Christianity, the lean times of domination by foreign powers and Iceland's eventual independence.

Great For...

☑ **Don't Miss**

The gaming pieces made from cod ear bones, and the wooden doll that doubled as a kitchen utensil.

Settlement Era Finds

The premier section of the museum describes the Settlement Era – including how the chieftains ruled and the introduction of Christianity – and features swords, meticulously carved **drinking horns**, and **silver hoards**. A powerful **bronze figure of Thor** is thought to date to about 1000. The priceless 13th-century **Valþjófsstaðir church door** is

Modern era exhibit

JONATHAN SMITH / LONELY PLANET ©

❶ Need to Know

Þjóðminjasafn Íslands; ☏530 2200; www.
nationalmuseum.is; Suðurgata 41; adult/child
2000kr/free; ☉10am-5pm May–mid-Sep,
closed Mon mid-Sep–Apr; ☐1, 3, 6, 12, 14

✕ Take a Break

The ground-floor **Museum Café**
(snacks 750-1900kr; ☉9am-5pm Mon-Fri,
10am-5pm Sat & Sun; ☜) offers a welcome respite.

★ Top Tip

Entry also covers admission to the
fantastic **Culture House** (Þjóðmennin-
garhúsið; ☏530 2210; www.culturehouse.is;
Hverfisgata 15; ☉10am-5pm May–mid-Sep,
closed Mon mid-Sep–Apr).

carved with the story of a knight, his faithful
lion and a passel of dragons.

Domestic Life

Exhibits explain how the chieftains ruled
and how people survived on little, lighting
their dark homes and fashioning bog iron.
There's everything from the remains of
early *skyr* (yoghurt-like dessert) production
to intricate pendants and brooches. Look
for the Viking-era **hnefatafl game set** (a
bit like chess); this artefact's discovery in a
grave in Baldursheimar led to the founding
of the museum.

Viking Graves

Encased in the floor, you'll find Viking-era
graves with their precious burial goods:
horse bones, a sword, pins, a ladle, a comb.
One of the tombs containing an eight-
month-old infant is the only one of its kind
ever found.

Ecclesiastical Artefacts

The section of the museum that details
the introduction of Christianity is chock-
a-block with rare art and artefacts such as
the Valþjófsstaðir church door.

The Modern Era

Upstairs, collections span from 1600 to
today and give a clear sense of how Iceland
struggled under foreign rule, finally gained
independence and went on to modernise.
Look for the **papers and belongings of
Jón Sigurðsson**, the architect of Iceland's
independence.

Free Tours

Free English tours run at 11am on Wednesdays, Saturdays and Sundays from May to
mid-September.

NARONGSAK NAGADHANA / SHUTTERSTOCK ©

Blue Lagoon

In a magnificent black-lava field, this scenic spa is fed water from the futuristic Svartsengi geothermal plant. With its silver towers, roiling clouds of steam and people daubed in white silica mud, it's an other-worldly place.

Great For...

☑ **Don't Miss**

A bike or quad-bike tour in the lava fields.

A Good Soak

Before your dip, don't forget to practise standard Iceland pool etiquette: thorough naked prepool showering.

The superheated spa water (70% sea water, 30% fresh water) is rich in blue-green algae, mineral salts and fine silica mud, which condition and exfoliate the skin – sounds like advertising speak, but you really do come out as soft as a baby's bum. The water is hottest near the vents where it emerges, and the surface is several degrees warmer than the bottom. You can hire bathing suits.

Explore the Complex

The lagoon has been developed for visitors with an enormous, modern complex of changing rooms (with 700 lockers!), restaurants and a gift shop. It is also land-scaped with hot-pots, steam rooms, sauna,

ℹ️ Need to Know

Bláa Lónið; ☑420 8800; www.bluelagoon.com; Nordurljosavegur 9; adult/child from 7000kr/free, premium entry from 9600kr/free; ⊘7am–midnight Jul–mid-Aug, to 11pm late May–Jun, 8am–10pm Jan–late May & mid-Aug–Sep, to 9pm Oct-Dec

✕ Take a Break

Try on-site **Blue Café** (snacks 850kr, sandwiches 1200kr, cold meal trays 2200kr; reduced hours mid-Aug–May; 📶) or **LAVA Restaurant** (mains lunch/dinner 4500/5900kr, tasting menu 10,300kr; ⊘11.30am-9.30pm Jun-Aug, to 8.30pm Sep–May; 📶).

★ Top Tip

Avoid summertime between 10am and 2pm – go early or after 7pm.

---

a silica-mask station, a bar and a piping-hot waterfall that delivers a powerful hydraulic massage. A VIP section has its own interior wading space, lounge and viewing platform.

Massage

For extra relaxation, lie on a floating mattress and have a massage therapist knead your knots. Book spa treatments well in advance; look online for packages and winter rates.

Guided Tours

In addition to the spa opportunities at the Blue Lagoon, you can combine your visit with package tours, or hook up with nearby **ATV Adventures** (4x4 Adventures Iceland; ☑857 3001; www.4x4adventuresiceland.is; Tangasund; 1hr ATV tour 13,000kr, 2-3hr bike tour 10,900kr, bike rental 4/24hr 4900/6900kr) for quad-bike or cycling tours, or bicycle rental.

The company can pick you up and drop you off at the lagoon.

Planning Your Visit

Many day trips from Reykjavík tie in a visit to the lagoon, which is 47km southwest of the city. It's also seamless to visit on your journey to/from Keflavík International Airport (there's a luggage check in the car park (kr550 per bag, per day).

You should book ahead or risk being turned away. On a tour, always determine whether your ticket for the lagoon is included or if you need to book it separately.

Reykjavík Excursions (Kynnisferðir; ☑580 5400; www.re.is; BSÍ Bus Terminal, Vatnsmýrarvegur 10; tours 8000-47,300kr) and **Bustravel** (☑511 2600; www.bustravel.is; Golden Circle per half-/full day from 6750/10,000kr) connect the lagoon with Reykjavík and the airport (23km).

ELKENEIZE / SHUTTERSTOCK ©

Golden Circle

Diving in glacial waters, walking the Mid-Atlantic Ridge canyon, absorbing the grandeur of the first-ever parliamentary site and watching the earth belch boiling water 40m high – the Golden Circle has it all.

Great For...

☑ Don't Miss

The Sigríður memorial near the foot of the stairs from the Gullfoss visitors centre.

The Golden Circle offers you the opportunity to see a meeting point of the continental plates and the site of the ancient Icelandic parliament (Þingvellir), a spouting hot spring (Geysir) and a roaring waterfall (Gullfoss), all in one doable-in-a-day loop.

Travelling under your own steam allows you to visit at off-hours and explore exciting attractions further afield. Almost every tour company in the Reykjavík area offers a Golden Circle excursion, often combinable with virtually any activity from quad-biking to caving and rafting.

If you're planning to spend the night in the relatively small region, **Laugarvatn** is a good base with excellent dining options.

Þingvellir National Park

This **national park** (www.thingvellir.is; Rte 36/Þingvallavegur; parking 300-500kr), 40km

Þingvellir National Park

northeast of central Reykjavík, is Iceland's most important historical site and a place of vivid beauty. The Vikings established the world's first democratic parliament, the **Alþingi** (via Rte 36 & Rte 362), here in AD 930. The meetings were conducted outdoors and, as with many Saga sites, there are only the stone foundations of ancient **encampments**. The site has a superb natural setting with rivers and waterfalls in an immense, fissured rift valley, caused by the meeting of the North American and Eurasian **tectonic plates** (via Rte 35 & Rte 361; parking 300kr).

Geysir

One of Iceland's most famous attractions, **Geysir** (Biskupstungnabraut) **FREE** (*gay*-zeer; literally 'gusher') is the original hot-water spout after which all others are named. Earthquakes can stimulate activity, though eruptions are rare. Luckily for visitors, the very reliable **Strokkur** geyser sits alongside. You rarely have to wait more than five to 10 minutes for it to shoot an impressive 15m to 30m plume before vanishing down its enormous hole. Stand downwind only if you want a shower.

The geothermal area containing Geysir and Strokkur was free to enter at the time of writing, though there is discussion of instituting a fee.

Gullfoss

Iceland's most famous waterfall, **Gullfoss** (Golden Falls; www.gullfoss.is; Rte 35/Kjalvegur) **FREE** is a spectacular double cascade. It drops 32m, kicking up tiered walls of spray before thundering away down a narrow ravine. On sunny days the mist creates shimmering rainbows, and it's also magical in winter when the falls glitter with ice.

A tarmac path suitable for wheelchairs leads from the tourist information centre to a lookout over the falls, and stairs continue down to the edge. There is also an access road down to the falls.

◎ SIGHTS

◎ Laugavegur & Skólavörðustígur

This district is Reykjavík's liveliest. While it's justifiably well known for its shops and pubs, it's also home to some of the city's top restaurants, local music venues and the city's top art-house cinema.

Hallgrímskirkja   Church

(⟟510 1000; www.hallgrimskirkja.is; Skólavörðustígur; tower adult/child 1000/100kr; ⊙9am-9pm May-Sep, to 5pm Oct-Apr) Reykjavík's immense white-concrete church (1945–86), star of a thousand postcards, dominates the skyline and is visible from up to 20km away. An elevator trip up the 74.5m-high tower reveals an unmissable view of the city. In contrast to the high drama outside, the Lutheran church's interior is quite plain. The most eye-catching feature is the vast 5275-pipe organ installed in 1992. The church's size and radical design caused controversy, and its architect, Guðjón Samúelsson (1887–1950), never saw its completion.

Harpa   Arts Centre

(⟟box office 528 5050; www.harpa.is; Austurbakki 2; ⊙8am-midnight, box office noon-6pm) With its ever-changing facets glistening on the water's edge, Reykjavík's sparkling Harpa concert hall and cultural centre is a beauty to behold. In addition to a season of top-notch shows (some free), the shimmering interior with harbour vistas is worth stopping in for, or take a highly recommended, 30-minute guided tour (1500kr); these run two to three times daily year-round, with up to eight daily tours between mid-June and mid-August.

National Gallery of Iceland   Museum

(Listasafn Íslands; ⟟515 9600; www.listasafn. is; Fríkirkjuvegur 7; adult/child 1800kr/free; ⊙10am-5pm daily mid-May–mid-Sep, 11am-5pm Tue-Sun mid-Sep–mid-May) This pretty stack of marble atriums and spacious galleries overlooking Tjörnin offers ever-changing exhibits drawn from a 10,000-piece collection. The museum can only exhibit a small sample at any one time; shows range from 19th- and 20th-century paintings by Iceland's favourite artists (including Jóhannes

Hallgrímskirkja

Kjarval and Nína Sæmundsson) to sculptures by Sigurjón Ólafsson and others.

Icelandic Phallological Museum   Museum

(Hið Íslenzka Reðasafn; ☑561 6663; www.phallus. is; Laugavegur 116; adult/child 1500kr/free; ◷10am-6pm, from 9am Jun-Aug) Oh, the jokes are endless here... This unique museum houses a huge collection of penises, and it's actually very well done. From pickled pickles to petrified wood, there are 286 different members on display, representing all Icelandic mammals and beyond. Featured items include contributions from sperm whales and a polar bear, minuscule mouse bits, silver castings of each member of the Icelandic handball team and a single human sample – from deceased mountaineer Páll Arason.

◉ Old Harbour

The **Old Harbour** (Geirsgata; ☐1, 3, 6, 11, 12, 13, 14) has blossomed into a hotspot for tourists, with museums and excellent restaurants. Whale-watching and puffin-viewing trips depart from the pier.

Saga Museum   Museum

(☑511 1517; www.sagamuseum.is; Grandagarður 2; adult/child 2200/800kr; ◷10am-6pm; ☐14) The endearingly bloodthirsty Saga Museum is where Icelandic history is brought to life by eerie silicon models and a multilanguage soundtrack featuring the thud of axes and hair-raising screams. Don't be surprised if you see some of the characters wandering around town, as moulds were taken from Reykjavík residents (the owner's daughters are the Irish princess and the little slave gnawing a fish).

Reykjavík Maritime Museum   Museum

(Sjóminjasafnið í Reykjavík; ☑411 6300; www. maritimemuseum.is; Grandagarður 8; adult/child 1650kr/free, Óðinn & museum 2600kr; ◷10am-5pm, Óðinn tours at 11am, 1pm, 2pm & 3pm; ☗; ☐14) The crucial role fishing plays in Iceland's economy is celebrated through the imaginative displays in this former fish-freezing plant. The new exhibition **Fish & folk** evokes 150 years of the industry, using artefacts,

🍃🌊 Laugardalur: Hot-Springs Valley

Encompassing a verdant stretch of land 4km east of the city centre, **Laugardalur** (☐2, 5, 14, 15, 17) was once the main source of Reykjavík's hot-water supply: it translates as 'Hot-Springs Valley', and in the park's centre you'll find relics from the old wash house. The park is a favourite with locals for its huge **swimming complex** (☑411 5100; www.reykjavik. is/stadir/laugardalslaug; Sundlaugavegur 30a, Laugardalur; adult/child 950/150kr, suit/towel rental 850/570kr; ◷6.30am-10pm Mon-Fri, 8am-10pm Sat & Sun; ☗; ☐12, 14), fed by the geothermal spring, alongside a spa, a skating rink, botanical gardens, sporting and concert arenas, and a kids' zoo and entertainment park.

sepia photos and interactive games to chart a course from the row boats of the late 1800s to the trawlers of the 21st century. Make time for one of the daily guided tours of the former coastguard ship Óðinn (1300kr).

◉ Old Reykjavík

Old Reykjavík forms the heart of the capital and the focal point of many historic walking tours.

Settlement Exhibition   Museum

(Landnámssýningin; ☑411 6370; www.reykjavik museum.is; Aðalstræti 16; adult/child 1650kr/free; ◷9am-6pm) This fascinating archaeological ruin-museum is based around a 10th-century Viking longhouse unearthed here from 2001 to 2002 and other Settlement-Era finds from

Reykjavík

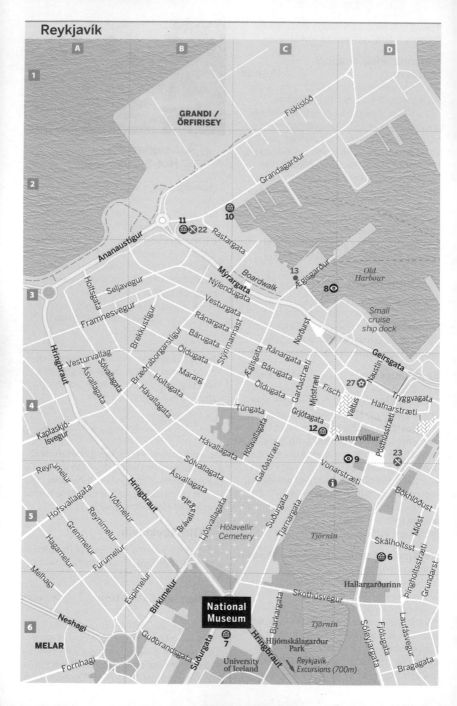

A B C D

1

2

3

4

5

6

GRANDI / ÖRFIRISEY

Fiskislóð

Grandagarður

MELAR

Neshagi

Fornhagi

Melhagi

Hagamelur

Reynimelur

Grenimelur

Furumelur

Hofsvallagata

Víðimelur

Reynimelur

Kaplaskjólsvegur

Hringbraut

Vesturvallagata

Ásvallagata

Sólvallagata

Brædraborgarstígur

Brekkustígur

Holtsgata

Framnesvegur

Seljavegur

Holtsgata

Ananaustigur

Mýrargata

Nýlendugata

Vesturgata

Ránargata

Bárugata

Öldugata

Marargata

Hávallagata

Túngata

Hávallagata

Sólvallagata

Ásvallagata

Ljósvallagata

Bárugata

Espimelur

Birkimelur

Guðbrandsgata

Suðurgata

Stýrimannast.

Ægisgata

Öldugata

Ránargata

Bárugata

Garðastræti

Hólavallagata

Garðastræti

Hólavellir Cemetery

Suðurgata

Tjarnargata

Mjóstræti

Grjótagata

Vonarstræti

Norðurst.

Fisch

Veltus.

Naustin

Geirsgata

Tryggvagata

Hafnarstræti

Pósthússtræti

Austurvöllur

Boardwalk

Rastargata

Ægisgarður

Old Harbour

Small cruise ship dock

13

8 ◎

11 🏛️❌**22**

🏛️ **10**

27 ✿

12 🏛️

◎**9**

ⓘ

23 ❌

Bókhlöðust.

Miðst.

Skálholtsst.

Pingholtsstræti

Grundarst.

Tjörnin

6 🏛️

Hallargarðurinn

Skothúsvegur

Bjarkargata

National Museum

🏛️ **7**

Hljómskálagarður Park

Hringbraut

Tjörnin

Laufásvegur

Sóleyjargata

Fjólugata

Bragagata

University of Iceland

Reykjavík Excursions (700m)

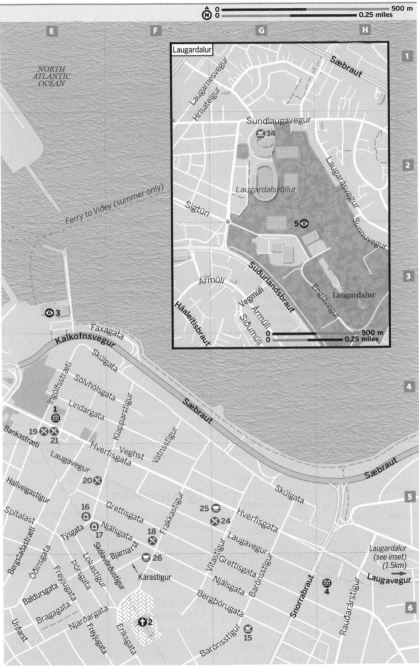

Reykjavík

central Reykjavík. It imaginatively combines technological wizardry and archaeology to give a glimpse into early Icelandic life. Don't miss the fragment of **boundary wall** at the back of the museum that is older still (and the oldest human-made structure in Reykjavík). Among the captivating high-tech displays, a wrap-around panorama shows how things would have looked at the time of the longhouse.

🏃 ACTIVITIES

Elding Adventures at Sea   Wildlife
(⌖519 5000; www.whalewatching.is; Ægisgarður 5; adult/child 11,000/5500kr; ⊗harbour kiosk 8am-9pm; 🚌14) ⚓ The city's most established and ecofriendly whale-watching tours feature a whale exhibition set in a converted fishing vessel; refreshments are sold on board. Elding also offers angling trips (adult/child 14,900/7450kr), puffin-watching trips (adult/child from 6500/3250kr) and combo tours. It also runs the ferry to Viðey (p178). Pick-up available.

Creative Iceland   Arts & Crafts
(⌖615 3500; www.creativeiceland.is) Get involved with knitting (19,500kr), cooking (24,900kr), graphic design, arts, crafts,

music...you name it. This service hooks you up with local creative people offering workshops in their specialities.

Sundhöllin   Geothermal Pool
(Sundhöll Reykjavíkur; ⌖411 5350; www.reykjavik.is/stadir/sundholl-reykjavikur; Barónsstígur 16; adult/child 950/150kr; ⊗6.30am-10pm Mon-Fri, from 8am Sat & Sun; ♿) Our top pick for a Reykjavík city-centre swim. Sundhöllin reopened in 2017 after a year-long revamp that added an entire outdoor area with hot tubs, sauna and a swimming pool. The original indoor pool remains open, as well as the secret upstairs hot tub with excellent city views.

🔒 SHOPPING

Laugavegur and Skólavörðustígur are the central streets of Reykjavík's shopping scene. You'll find them lined with everything from stereotypical souvenir shops to design shops and galleries selling beautiful handmade Icelandic arts and crafts.

Handknitting Association of Iceland   Clothing
(Handprjónasamband Íslands; ⌖552 1890; www.handknit.is; Skólavörðustígur 19; ⊗9am-10pm Mon-Fri, to 6pm Sat, 10am-6pm Sun) Traditional

handmade hats, socks and sweaters are sold at this knitting collective. You can also buy yarn, needles and knitting patterns and do it yourself. The association's smaller branch sells made-up items only.

Skúmaskot   Arts & Crafts
(☑663 1013; www.facebook.com/skumaskot.art. design; Skólavörðustígur 21a; ☺10am-6pm Mon-Fri, to 5pm Sat, noon-4pm Sun) Local designers create unique handmade porcelain items, women's and kids' clothing, paintings and cards. It's in a large renovated gallery that beautifully showcases the creative Icelandic crafts.

✪ EATING

Brauð & Co   Bakery €
(www.braudogco.is; Frakkastígur 16; ☺6am-6pm Mon-Fri, to 5pm Sat & Sun) Head for the building smothered in rainbow spray paint then queue for the locals' tip for the best *snúður* (cinnamon buns) in town – watch Viking hipsters make them while you wait.

Gló   Organic, Vegetarian €
(☑553 1111; www.glo.is; Laugavegur 20b; mains 1000-2400kr; ☺11.30am-10pm; 🛜🌱🍴) Join the cool cats in this airy upstairs restaurant serving fresh daily specials loaded with Asian-influenced herbs and spices. Though not exclusively vegetarian, it's a wonderland of raw and organic foods, with a broad bar of elaborate salads, from root veggies to Greek.

Messinn   Seafood €€
(☑546 0095; www.messinn.com; Lækjargata 6b; lunch mains 1850-2200kr, dinner mains 2700-4200kr; ☺11.30am-3pm & 5-10pm; 🛜) Make a beeline to Messinn for the best seafood that Reykjavík has to offer. The speciality here is the amazing pan-fried dishes: your pick of fish is served up in a sizzling cast-iron skillet, accompanied by buttery potatoes and salad. The mood is upbeat and comfortable and the staff friendly.

Matur og Drykkur   Icelandic €€
(☑571 8877; www.maturogdrykkur.is; Grandagarður 2; lunch/dinner mains from

1900/3400kr, tasting menu 10,000kr; ☺11.30am-3pm & 6-10pm, closed Sun lunch; 🍴; 🖥14) One of Reykjavík's top high-concept restaurants, Matur og Drykkur means 'Food and Drink', and you'll surely be plied with the best of both. This brainchild of brilliant chef Gísli Matthías Auðunsson, who also owns the excellent **Slippurinn** (☑481 1515; www.slippurinn.com; Strandvegur 76; lunch 2400-7200kr, dinner mains 3700-4900kr, set menu 6400-9900kr; ☺noon-2.30pm & 5-10pm early May–mid-Sep; 🛜), creates inventive versions of traditional Icelandic fare. Book ahead in high season and for dinner.

Nostra   New Nordic €€€
(☑519 3535; www.nostrarestaurant.is; Laugavegur 59; 4/6/8 courses 8900/11,900/13,900kr; ☺5.30-10pm Tue-Sat; 🍴) Fine-dining Nostra is where fresh, local ingredients – à la New Nordic Cuisine – are turned into French-inspired multicourse tasting menus, including those for vegans, vegetarians and pescatarians. Nostra refers to its menus as 'experiences' and with their intense flavours and picture-perfect presentation, it's not wrong.

Dill   Icelandic €€€
(☑552 1522; www.dillrestaurant.is; Hverfisgata 12; 5/7 courses 11,900/13,900kr; ☺6-10pm Wed-Sat) Exquisite New Nordic cuisine is the major drawcard at Reykjavík's elegant Michelin-starred bistro. Skilled chefs use a small number of ingredients to create highly complex dishes in a parade of courses. The owners are friends with Copenhagen's famous Noma clan and take Icelandic cuisine to similarly heady heights. It's hugely popular; book well in advance.

🍷 DRINKING & NIGHTLIFE

Reykjavík Roasters   Cafe
(☑517 5535; www.reykjavikroasters.is; Kárastígur 1; ☺7am-6pm Mon-Fri, 8am-5pm Sat & Sun) These folks take their caffeine seriously. The tiny hipster joint is easily spotted on warm days by its smattering of wooden tables on a small square. Swig a perfect latte and savour a flaky croissant and the scent of roasting coffee beans.

 Day Trip to Viðey

On fine-weather days, the tiny uninhabited island of Viðey (www.videy.com) makes a wonderful day trip. Just 1km north of Reykjavík's Sundahöfn Harbour, it feels a world away. Well-preserved historic buildings, surprising modern art, an abandoned village and great birdwatching add to its remote spell.

There are usually free guided walks in summer. Check online for the current schedule.

Viðey Ferry (☑533 5055; www.videy.com; Skarfabakki; return adult/child 1500/750kr; ☺from Skarfabakki hourly 10.15am-5.15pm mid-May–Sep, 1.15-4.30pm Sat & Sun Oct–mid-May) takes five minutes from Skarfabakki, 4.5km east of the city centre.

OLANA22 / SHUTTERSTOCK ©

Mikkeller & Friends — Craft Beer

(☑437 0203; www.mikkeller.dk; Hverfisgata 12; ☺5pm-1am Sun-Thu, 2pm-1am Fri & Sat; ☎) Climb to the top floor of the building shared with excellent pizzeria **Hverfisgata 12** (☑437 0203; www.hverfisgata12.is; Hverfisgata 12; pizzas 2450-3450kr; ☺5-10.30pm Mon-Fri, 11.30am-10.30pm Sat & Sun; ☑) to find a Danish craft-beer pub with 20 taps serving Mikkeller's own offerings and local Icelandic brews. Then enjoy the cool, colourful, laid-back vibe.

Kaffi Vínyl — Cafe

(☑537 1332; www.facebook.com/kaffivinyl; Hverfisgata 76; ☺8am-11pm Sun-Thu, to 1am Fri & Sat; ☎) 'Vegan is the new black' reads the neon sign, vinyl discs spin on the decks and a cool crowd tucks into meat-free noodles, burgers and pasta (mains from 1400kr). Happy hour lasts from 4pm to 7pm here – an ideal time to try an Icelandic beer or a vegan whiskey sour.

☺ ENTERTAINMENT

Húrra — Live Music

(www.facebook.com/hurra.is; Tryggvagata 22; ☺6pm-1am Mon-Thu, to 4.30am Fri & Sat, to 11.30pm Sun; ☎) Dark and raw, this large bar opens up its back room to create a much-loved concert venue, with a wide range of live music or DJs most nights. It's one of the best places in town to close out the evening. There's a range of beers on tap and happy hour runs till 9pm.

☺ INFORMATION

Main Tourist Office (Upplýsingamiðstöð Ferðamanna; ☑411 6040; www.visitreykjavik. is; Ráðhús, Tjarnargata 11; ☺8am-8pm; ☎) Friendly staff and mountains of free brochures, plus maps, Reykjavík City Card and Strætó city bus tickets. Books accommodation, tours and activities.

☺ GETTING THERE & AWAY

Iceland has become very accessible in recent years, with more flights from more destinations in Europe and North America.

☺ GETTING AROUND

Bus Excellent coverage in the city centre and environs; runs 7am until 11pm or midnight daily (from 11am on Sunday). A limited night-bus service runs until 4.30am on Friday and Saturday. **Strætó** (☑540 2700; www.straeto.is) operates regular buses around Reykjavík. The fare is 460kr; you can buy tickets at the bus terminal, pay on board (though no change is given) or by using the Strætó app. One-/three-day passes cost (1700/4000kr).

Taxi Prices are high. Flagfall starts at around 700kr. Tipping is not required.

Where to Stay

Demand always outstrips supply in Reykjavík. Try to book your accommodation three to six months ahead. Some of the best deals are holiday rentals.

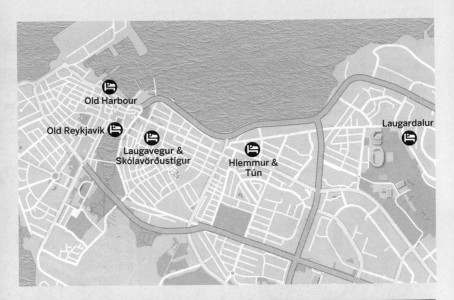

Neighbourhood	Atmosphere
Old Reykjavík	Central, easy with higher-end options. Can be crowded, busier and expensive.
Old Harbour	Less busy once back from the harbour. Guesthouses and hostels are more affordable, but it is slightly less central.
Laugavegur & Skólavörðustígur	Perfect for shopping and partying. Good range of options with certain quiet pockets. It's touristy on the main streets.
Hlemmur & Tún	Loads of high-rise hotels are popping up here. The areas are on the bland side and a bit far from the city centre.
Laugardalur	Near a large park and swimming complex. New high-rise hotels. Further from the city centre.

BARCELONA, SPAIN

Barcelona, Spain

Barcelona is a mix of sunny Mediterranean charm and European urban style. The city bursts with art and architecture, Catalan cooking is among the country's best, summer-sun seekers fill the beaches in and beyond the city, and bars and clubs heave year-round.

The city began as a middle-ranking Roman town, of which vestiges can be seen today, and its old centre has one of the greatest concentrations of Gothic architecture in Europe. Beyond this core are some of the world's more bizarre buildings: surreal spectacles, capped by Gaudí's La Sagrada Família.

Two Days in Barcelona

Start with the Barri Gòtic. After a stroll along **La Rambla** (p193), admire **La Catedral** (p200) and the **Museu d'Història de Barcelona** (p200) on historic **Plaça del Rei** (p201), then visit the **Basílica de Santa Maria del Mar** (p201), and the nearby **Museu Picasso** (p204). On day two, experience **Park Güell** (p201) and **La Sagrada Família** (p184).

Four Days in Barcelona

Start the third day with more Gaudí, visiting **Casa Batlló** (p205) and **La Pedrera** (p205), followed by beachside relaxation and seafood in **Barceloneta** (p204). Day four should be dedicated to **Montjuïc** (p196), with its museums, galleries, fortress, gardens and Olympic stadium.

Looking for more Spain? Fly, drive or catch a train to Andalucía (p213).

Arriving in Barcelona

El Prat airport has myriad flights. Frequent Aerobúses make the 35-minute run into town (€5.90) from 5.35am to 1am. Taxis cost around €25.

Barcelona Sants, near the centre of town, is the long-distance train station. It's connected to the metro.

Estació del Nord is the long-haul bus station in L'Eixample, about 1.5km northeast of Plaça de Catalunya. It's a short walk from the Arc de Triomf metro station.

Where to Stay

Barcelona has some fabulous accommodation, but never arrive in town without a reservation. Designer digs are something of a Barcelona specialty, with midrange and top-end travellers particularly well served. Apartments are also widespread and a fine alternative to hotels. Prices in Barcelona are generally higher than elsewhere in the country.

Passion Facade detail (p187)

La Sagrada Família

If you have time for only one sightseeing outing, this is it. La Sagrada Família inspires awe by its sheer verticality, inspiring use of light and Gaudí's offbeat design elements.

In the manner of the medieval cathedrals La Sagrada Família emulates, it's still under construction after more than 100 years. When completed (the latest target is 2026), the highest tower will be more than half as high again as those that stand today.

A Holy Mission

The Temple Expiatori de la Sagrada Família (Expiatory Temple of the Holy Family) was Antoni Gaudí's all-consuming obsession. Given the commission by a conservative society that wished to build a temple as atonement for the city's sins of modernity, Gaudí saw its completion as his holy mission. As funds dried up, he contributed his own, and in the last years of his life he was never shy of pleading with anyone he thought a likely donor.

Great For...

☑ **Don't Miss**

The apse, the extraordinary pillars and the stained glass.

Nativity Facade (p186) from Plaça de Gaudí

REB US / SHUTTERSTOCK ©

ⓘ Need to Know

Map p206; 📞93 208 04 14; www.sagrada familia.org; Carrer de la Marina; adult/child €15/free; ⊘9am-8pm Apr-Sep, to 7pm Mar & Oct, to 6pm Nov-Feb; Ⓜ Sagrada Família

✕ Take a Break

Across the square, **Michael Collins** (Map p206; 📞93 459 19 64; www.michael collinspubs.com; Plaça de la Sagrada Família 4; ⊘1pm-2.30am Sun-Thu, to 3am Fri & Sat; 📶; Ⓜ Sagrada Família) is good for a beer.

★ Top Tip

It's strongly advised to book all tickets online, allowing you to skip what can be very lengthy queues.

Gaudí devised a temple 95m long and 60m wide, able to seat 13,000 people, with a central tower 170m high above the transept (representing Christ) and another 17 of 100m or more. The 12 along the three façades represent the Apostles, while the remaining five represent the Virgin Mary and the four evangelists. With his characteristic dislike for straight lines (there were none in nature, he said), Gaudí gave his towers swelling outlines inspired by the weird peaks of the holy mountain Montserrat outside Barcelona, and encrusted them with a tangle of sculpture that seems an outgrowth of the stone.

At Gaudí's death, only the crypt, the apse walls, one portal and one tower had been finished. Three more towers were added by 1930, completing the northeast (Nativity) facade. In 1936 anarchists burned and smashed the interior, including workshops, plans and models. Work began again in 1952, but controversy has always clouded progress. Opponents of the continuation of the project claim that the computer models based on what little of Gaudí's plans survived the anarchists' ire have led to the creation of a monster that has little to do with Gaudí's plans and style. It is a debate that appears to have little hope of resolution. Like or hate what is being done, the fascination it awakens is undeniable.

Even as debate rages about when the building will be complete, some of the oldest parts of the church, especially the apse, have required restoration work.

The Interior & the Apse

Inside, work on roofing over the church was completed in 2010. The roof is held up by a forest of extraordinary angled pillars.

As the pillars soar toward the ceiling, they sprout a web of supporting branches, creating the effect of a forest canopy. The tree image is in no way fortuitous – Gaudí envisaged such an effect. Everything was thought through, including the shape and placement of windows to create the mottled effect one would see with sunlight pouring through the branches of a thick forest. The pillars are of four different types of stone. They vary in colour and load-bearing strength, from the soft Montjuïc stone pillars along the lateral aisles through to granite, dark grey basalt and finally burgundy-tinged Iranian porphyry for the key columns at the intersection of the nave and transept. The stained glass, divided in shades of red, blue, green and ochre, creates a hypnotic, magical atmosphere when the sun hits the windows.

Tribunes built high above the aisles can host two choirs: the main tribune up to 1300 people and the children's tribune up to 300.

Nativity Facade

The Nativity Facade is the artistic pinnacle of the building, mostly created under Gaudí's personal supervision. You can climb high up inside some of the four towers by a combination of lifts and narrow spiral staircases – a vertiginous experience. Do not climb the stairs if you have cardiac or respiratory problems. The towers are destined to hold tubular bells capable of playing complex music at great volume. Their upper parts are decorated with mosaics spelling out 'Sanctus, Sanctus, Sanctus, Hosanna in Excelsis, Amen, Alleluia'. Asked why he lavished so much care on the tops

Nativity Facade detail

of the spires, which no one would see from close up, Gaudí answered: 'The angels will see them.'

Three sections of the portal represent, from left to right, Hope, Charity and Faith. Among the forest of sculpture on the Charity portal you can see, low down, the manger surrounded by an ox, an ass, the shepherds and kings, and angel musicians. Some 30 different species of plant from around Catalonia are reproduced here, and the faces of the many figures are taken from plaster casts done of local people and the occasional one made from corpses in the local morgue.

PECOLD / SHUTTERSTOCK ©

Directly above the blue stained-glass window is the archangel Gabriel's Annunciation to Mary. At the top is a green cypress tree, a refuge in a storm for the white doves of peace dotted over it. The mosaic work at the pinnacle of the towers is made from Murano glass, from Venice.

To the right of the facade is the curious Claustre del Roser, a Gothic-style mini-cloister tacked on to the outside of the church (rather than the classic square enclosure of the great Gothic church monasteries). Once inside, look back to the intricately decorated entrance. On the lower right-hand side you'll notice the sculpture of a reptilian devil handing a terrorist a bomb. Barcelona was regularly rocked by political violence, and bombings were frequent in the decades prior to the civil war. The sculpture is one of several on the 'temptations of men and women'.

Passion Facade

The southwestern Passion Facade, on the theme of Christ's last days and death, was built between 1954 and 1978 based on surviving drawings by Gaudí, with four towers and a large, sculpture-bedecked portal. Sculptor Josep Subirachs worked on its decoration from 1986 to 2006. He did not attempt to imitate Gaudí, instead producing angular, controversial images of his own. The main series of sculptures, on three levels, are in an S-shaped sequence, starting with the Last Supper at the bottom left and ending with Christ's burial at the top right.

To the right, in front of the Passion Facade, the Escoles de Gaudí is one of his simpler gems. Gaudí built this as a children's school, creating an original, undulating roof of brick that continues to charm architects to this day. Inside is a re-creation of Gaudí's modest office as it was when he died, and explanations of the geometric patterns and plans at the heart of his building techniques.

A Hidden Portrait

Careful observation of the Passion Facade will reveal a special tribute from sculptor Josep Subirachs to Gaudí. The central sculptural group (below Christ crucified) shows, from right to left, Christ bearing his cross, Veronica displaying the cloth with Christ's bloody image, a pair of soldiers and, watching it all, a man called the evangelist. Subirachs used a rare photo of Gaudí, taken a couple of years before his death, as the model for the evangelist's face.

Glory Facade

The Glory Facade is under construction and will, like the others, be crowned by four towers – the total of 12 representing the Twelve Apostles. Gaudí wanted it to be the most magnificent facade of the church. Inside will be the narthex, a kind of foyer made up of 16 'lanterns', a series of hyperboloid forms topped by cones. Further decoration will make the whole building a microcosmic symbol of the Christian church, with Christ represented by a massive 170m central tower above the transept, and the five remaining planned towers symbolising the Virgin Mary and the four evangelists.

Museu Gaudí

Open the same times as the church, the Museu Gaudí, below ground level, includes interesting material on Gaudí's life and other works, as well as models and photos of La Sagrada Família. You can see a good example of his plumb-line models that showed him the stresses and strains he could get away with in construction. A side hall towards the eastern end of the museum leads to a viewing point above the simple crypt in which the genius is buried. The crypt, where Masses are now held, can also be visited from the Carrer de Mallorca side of the church.

What's Nearby?

Església de les Saleses   Church

(Map p206; ☑93 458 76 67; Passeig de Sant Joan 90; ⊙10am-1pm & 5-7pm Mon-Sat, 10am-2pm Sun; Ⓜ Verdaguer) A singular neo-Gothic effort, this church is interesting because it was designed by Joan Martorell i Montells (1833–1906), Gaudí's architecture professor. Raised in 1878–85 with an adjacent convent (badly damaged in the civil war and now a school), his use of brick, mosaics and sober stained glass offers hints of what was to come with Modernisme.

Recinte Modernista de Sant Pau   Architecture

(☑93 553 78 01; www.santpaubarcelona.org; Carrer de Sant Antoni Maria Claret 167; adult/child €14/free; ⊙9.30am-7pm Mon-Sat, to 3pm Sun Apr-Oct, 9.30am-5.30pm Mon-Sat, to

Recinte Modernista de Sant Pau

3pm Sun Nov-Mar; MSant Pau/Dos de Maig) Domènech i Montaner outdid himself as architect and philanthropist with the Modernista Hospital de la Santa Creu i de Sant Pau, redubbed in 2014 the 'Recinte Modernista'. It was long considered one of the city's most important hospitals and only recently repurposed, its various spaces becoming cultural centres, offices and something of a monument. The complex, including 16 pavilions, is lavishly decorated and each pavilion is unique. Together with the Palau de la Música Catalana it is a World Heritage Site.

Museu del Disseny de Barcelona   Museum

(☎93 256 68 00; www.museudeldisseny.cat; Plaça de les Glòries Catalanes 37; permanent/ temporary exhibitions adult €6/3, child €4/2, combination tickets adult/child €6/4, free from 3pm Sun & 1st Sun of the month; ☺10am-8pm Tue-Sun; MGlòries) Barcelona's design museum lies inside a new monolithic building with geometric facades and a rather brutalist appearance – which has earned the nickname *la grapadora* (the stapler) by locals. Architecture aside, the museum houses a dazzling collection of ceramics, decorative arts and textiles, and is a must for anyone interested in the design world.

★ **Did You Know?**

Pope Benedict XVI consecrated the church in a huge ceremony in November 2010.

★ **Top Tip**

Guided tours (€24) last 50 minutes. Alternatively, take an audio tour (€7), for which you need ID.

La Sagrada Família

A TIMELINE

1882 Construction begins on a neo-Gothic church designed by Francisco de Paula del Villar y Lozano.

1883 Antoni Gaudí takes over as chief architect and plans a far more ambitious church to hold 13,000 faithful.

1926 Gaudí dies; work continues under Domènec Sugrañes i Gras. Much of the **apse ❶** and **Nativity Facade ❷** is complete.

1930 Bell towers ❸ of the Nativity Facade completed.

1936 Construction interrupted by Spanish Civil War; anarchists destroy Gaudí's plans.

1939–40 Architect Francesc de Paula Quintana i Vidal restores the crypt and meticulously reassembles many of Gaudí's lost models, some of which can be seen in the **museum ❹**.

1976 Passion Facade ❺ completed.

1986–2006 Sculptor Josep Subirachs adds sculptural details to the Passion Facade including the panels telling the story of Christ's last days, amid much criticism for employing a style far removed from what was thought typical of Gaudí.

2000 Central nave vault ❻ completed.

2010 Church completely roofed over; Pope Benedict XVI consecrates the church; work begins on a high-speed rail tunnel that will pass beneath the church's **Glory Facade ❼**.

2026 Projected completion date.

TOP TIPS

➡ The best light through the stained-glass windows of the Passion Facade bursts into the heart of the church in the late afternoon.

➡ Visit at opening time on weekdays to avoid the worst of the crowds.

➡ Head up the Nativity Facade bell towers for the views, as long queues generally await at the Passion Facade towers.

KIEVVICTORY / SHUTTERSTOCK ©

Spiral Staircase

Nativity Facade
Gaudí used plaster casts of local people and even of the occasional corpse from the local morgue as models for the portraits in the Nativity scene.

Central Nave Vault
30m wide, with lateral naves of 7.5m bringing the total width to 60m. The central dome reaches 65m in height.

❶

Apse
Built just after the crypt in mostly neo-Gothic style, it is capped by pinnacles that show a hint of the genius that Gaudí would later deploy in the rest of the church.

Bell Towers

The towers of the three facades will represent the Twelve Apostles. Eight are completed. Lifts whisk visitors up one tower of the Nativity and Passion Facades (the latter gets longer queues) for fine views.

NIKADA / GETTY IMAGES ©

Completed Church

Along with the Glory Facade and its four towers, six other towers remain to be completed. They will represent the four evangelists, the Virgin Mary and, soaring above them all over the transept, a 170m colossus symbolising Christ.

③

②

⑥

Glory Facade

This will be the most fanciful facade of all, with a narthex boasting 16 hyperboloid lanterns topped by cones that will look something like an organ made of melting ice cream.

⑦

Museu Gaudí

Jammed with old photos, drawings and restored plaster models that bring Gaudí's ambitions to life, the museum also houses an extraordinarily complex plumb-line device he used to calculate his constructions.

⑤

④

Escoles de Gaudí

Crypt

The first completed part of the church, the crypt is in largely neo-Gothic style and lies under the transept. Gaudí's burial place here can be seen from the Museu Gaudí.

Passion Facade

See the story of Christ's last days from Last Supper to burial in an S-shaped sequence from bottom to top of the facade. Check out the cryptogram in which the numbers always add up to 33, Christ's age at his death.

YURY DMITRIENKO / SHUTTERSTOCK ©

BRZOZOWSKA / GETTY IMAGES ©

La Rambla

Barcelona's most famous street is both tourist magnet and window into Catalan culture, with arts centres, theatres and intriguing architecture. The middle is a broad pedestrian boulevard, crowded daily with a wide cross-section of society. A stroll here is pure sensory overload, with souvenir hawkers, buskers, pavement artists and living statues part of the ever-changing street scene.

Great For...

☑ Don't Miss

Strolling the whole Rambla from end to end, keeping an eye on the architecture alongside.

History

La Rambla takes its name from a seasonal stream (derived from the Arabic word for sand, *raml*) that once ran here. From the early Middle Ages, it was better known as the Cagalell (Stream of Shit) and lay outside the city walls until the 14th century. Monastic buildings were then built and, subsequently, mansions of the well-to-do from the 16th to the early 19th centuries. Unofficially, La Rambla is divided into five sections, which explains why many know it as Las Ramblas.

La Rambla de Canaletes

The section of La Rambla north of Plaça de Catalunya is named after the **Font de Canaletes** (Map p202; La Rambla; Ⓜ Catalunya), an inconspicuous turn-of-the-20th-century drinking fountain, the water of which supposedly emerges from what were

❶ Need to Know

Map p202; Ⓜ Catalunya, Liceu, Drassanes
The stroll, from Plaça de Catalunya to
Plaça del Portal de la Pau, is 1.5km.

★ Local Knowledge

While there are some decent eateries
in the vicinity, the vast majority of cafes
and restaurants along La Rambla are
expensive, mediocre tourist traps.

★ Top Tip

La Rambla is at its best first thing in
the morning, before the cruise ships
disgorge their passengers.

once known as the springs of Canaletes. It
used to be said that *barcelonins* 'drank the
waters of Les Canaletes'. Nowadays people
claim that anyone who drinks from the
fountain will return to Barcelona, which is
not such a bad prospect. Delirious football
fans gather here to celebrate whenever the
city's principal team, FC Barcelona, wins a
cup or league title.

La Rambla dels Estudis

La Rambla dels Estudis, from Carrer de
la Canuda running south to Carrer de la
Portaferrissa, was formerly home to a twit-
tering bird market, which closed in 2010
after 150 years in operation.

Església de Betlem

Just north of Carrer del Carme, this
church (Map p202; ☎ 93 318 38 23; www.

mdbetlem.net; Carrer d'en Xuclà 2; ⊙ 8.30am-
1.30pm & 6-9pm; Ⓜ Liceu) was constructed
in baroque style for the Jesuits in the late
17th and early 18th centuries to replace
an earlier church destroyed by fire in 1671.
Fire was a bit of a theme for this site: the
church was once considered the most
splendid of Barcelona's few baroque
offerings, but leftist arsonists torched it
in 1936.

Palau Moja

Looming over the eastern side of La
Rambla, **Palau Moja** (Map p202; ☎ 93
316 27 40; https://palaumoja.com; Carrer de
Portaferrissa 1; ⊙ 10am-9pm, cafe 9.30am-
midnight Mon-Fri, 11am-midnight Sat & Sun;
Ⓜ Liceu) **FREE** is a neoclassical building
dating from the second half of the 18th
century. Its clean, classical lines are best
appreciated from across La Rambla.
Unfortunately, interior access is limited, as
it houses mostly government offices.

La Rambla de Sant Josep

From Carrer de la Portaferrissa to Plaça de la Boqueria, what is officially called La Rambla de Sant Josep (named after a now nonexistent monastery) is lined with flower stalls, which give it the alternative name La Rambla de les Flors.

Palau de la Virreina

The **Palau de la Virreina** (Map p202; La Rambla 99; M Liceu) is a grand 18th-century rococo mansion (with some neoclassical elements) that houses a municipal arts/ entertainment information and ticket office run by the Ajuntament (town hall). Built by Manuel d'Amat i de Junyent, the corrupt Viceroy of Peru (a Spanish colony that included the silver mines of Potosí), it is a rare example of such a postbaroque

building in Barcelona. It's home to the **Centre de la Imatge** (Map p202; ☎93 316 10 00; http://ajuntament.barcelona.cat/lavir-reina; Palau de la Virreina; ⊕11am-8pm Tue-Sun; M Liceu) FREE, which has rotating photo-graphy exhibits.

Mosaïc de Miró

At Plaça de la Boqueria, where four side streets meet just north of Liceu metro station, you can walk all over a Miró – the colourful **mosaic** (Map p202; Plaça de la Boqueria; M Liceu) in the pavement, with one tile signed by the artist. Miró chose this site as it's near the house where he was born on the Passatge del Crèdit. The mosaic's bold colours and vivid swirling forms are instantly recognisable to Miró fans, though plenty of tourists stroll right over it without realising.

Pla de l'Os Mosaic by Joan Miró

La Rambla dels Caputxins

La Rambla dels Caputxins, named after a former monastery, runs from Plaça de la Boqueria to Carrer dels Escudellers. The latter street is named after the potters' guild, founded in the 13th century, the members of which lived and worked here. On the western side of La Rambla is the **Gran Teatre del Liceu** (Map p202; ☎93 485 99 14; www.liceubarcelona.cat; La Rambla 51-59; tours adult/concession/under 7yr 30min €6/5/free, 45min €9/7.50/free; ⊙30min tours 1pm Mon-Sat, 45min tours hourly 2-5pm Mon-Fri, from 11am Sat; ⓂLiceu); to the southeast is

ANSHARPHOTO / SHUTTERSTOCK ©

the entrance to the palm-shaded Plaça Reial. Below this point La Rambla gets seedier, with the occasional strip club and peep show.

La Rambla de Santa Mònica

The final stretch of La Rambla widens out to approach the Mirador de Colom overlooking Port Vell. La Rambla here is named after the Convent de Santa Mònica, which once stood on the western flank of the street and has since been converted into a cultural centre.

What's Nearby?

Basílica de Santa Maria del Pi   Church

(Map p202; ☎93 318 47 43; www.basilicadelpi.cat; Plaça del Pi; adult/concession/child under 8yr €4.50/3.50/free; ⊙10am-6pm; ⓂLiceu) This striking 14th-century church is a classic of Catalan Gothic, with an imposing facade, a wide interior and a single nave. The simple decor in the main sanctuary contrasts with the gilded chapels and exquisite stained-glass windows that bathe the interior in ethereal light. The beautiful rose window above its entrance is one of the world's largest. Occasional concerts are staged here (classical guitar, choral groups and chamber orchestras).

Plaça Reial   Square

(Map p202; ⓂLiceu) One of the most photogenic squares in Barcelona, the Plaça Reial is a delightful retreat from the traffic and pedestrian mobs on the nearby Rambla. Numerous eateries, bars and nightspots lie beneath the arcades of 19th-century neoclassical buildings, with a buzz of activity at all hours.

FEEL GOOD STUDIO / SHUTTERSTOCK ©

Montjuïc

The Montjuïc hillside, crowned by a castle and gardens, overlooks the port with some of the city's finest art collections: the Museu Nacional d'Art de Catalunya, the Fundació Joan Miró and CaixaForum.

Museu Nacional d'Art de Catalunya

From across the city, the bombastic neo-baroque silhouette of the **Museu Nacional d'Art de Catalunya** (MNAC; Map p208; ☑936 22 03 76; www.museunacional.cat; Mirador del Palau Nacional; adult/child €12/free, after 3pm Sat & 1st Sun of month free, rooftop viewpoint only €2; ☉10am-8pm Tue-Sat, to 3pm Sun May-Sep, to 6pm Tue-Sat, to 3pm Sun Oct-Apr; ☐55, Ⓜ Espanya) can be seen on the slopes of Montjuïc. Built for the 1929 World Exhibition and restored in 2005, it houses a vast collection of mostly Catalan art, from the early Middle Ages to the early 20th century. The highlight is the collection of extraordinary Romanesque frescoes. Rescued from neglected country churches across northern Catalonia, the collection consists of 21 frescoes, woodcarvings and painted altar frontals.

Great For...

☑ **Don't Miss**

The Romanesque frescoes in the Museu Nacional d'Art de Catalunya.

❶ Need to Know

The metro stops at the foot of Montjuïc; buses and funiculars go all the way.

✕ Take a Break

Montjuïc eateries tend to be over-priced. The gardens surrounding Fundació Joan Miró museum are perfect for a picnic.

★ Top Tip

Ride the Transbordador Aeri from Barceloneta for a bird's-eye approach to Montjuïc.

Fundació Joan Miró

Joan Miró, the city's best-known 20th-century artistic progeny, bequeathed the **Fundació Joan Miró** (Map p208; ☎93 443 94 70; www.fmirobcn.org; Parc de Montjuïc; adult/child €12/free; ☺10am-8pm Tue, Wed, Fri & Sat, to 9pm Thu, to 3pm Sun Apr-Oct, 10am-6pm Tue, Wed & Fri, to 9pm Thu, to 8pm Sat, to 3pm Sun Nov-Mar; ☐55, 150, ☐Paral·lel) to his hometown in 1971. Its light-filled buildings, designed by close friend and architect Josep Lluís Sert (who also built Miró's Mallorca studios), are crammed with seminal works, from Miró's earliest timid sketches to paintings from his last years. Highlights include **Sala Joan Prats**, with works from the early years until 1919; **Sala Pilar Juncosa**, which covers his surrealist years (1932–55); and Rooms 18 and 19, which contain masterworks from his later years (1956–83).

CaixaForum

The Caixa building society prides itself on its involvement in (and ownership of) art, in particular all that is contemporary. **Caixa-Forum** (Map p208; ☎93 476 86 00; www.caixa forum.es; Avinguda de Francesc Ferrer i Guàrdia 6-8; adult/child €4/free, 1st Sun of month free; ☺10am-8pm; MEspanya) hosts part of the bank's extensive collection from around the globe. The setting is a completely renovated former factory, the Fàbrica Casaramona, an outstanding Modernista brick structure designed by Puig i Cadafalch. On occasion portions of La Caixa's own collection goes on display, but more often than not major international exhibitions are the key draw.

Castell de Montjuïc

This forbidding castle dominates the south-eastern heights of Montjuïc and enjoys commanding views over the Mediterranean. It dates, in its present form, from the late 17th and 18th centuries. For most of its dark history, it has been used to watch over the city and as a political prison and killing ground.

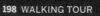

Hidden Treasures in the Barri Gòtic

This scenic walk through the Barri Gòtic will take you back in time, from the early days of Roman-era Barcino through to the medieval era.

Start La Catedral
Distance 1.5km
Duration 1½ hours

Classic Photo: La Catedral

1 Before entering the cathedral, look at three Picasso friezes on the building facing the square. Next, wander through magnificent **La Catedral** (p200).

2 Pass through the city gates; turn right into **Plaça de Sant Felip Neri**. The shrapnel-scarred church was damaged by pro-Francoist bombers in 1939.

3 Head west to the looming 14th-century **Basílica de Santa Maria del Pi** (p195), famed for its magnificent rose window.

4 Follow the curving road to pretty **Plaça Reial** (p195). Flanking the fountain are Gaudí-designed lamp posts.

C d'en Roca
C del Petritxol
Plaça del Pi
Plaça de St Josep Oriol
La Rambla de Sant Josep
3 Plaça de Sant Josep Oriol
La Rambla
C de la Boqueria
C d'en Quintana
Plaça de la Boqueria
Ⓜ Liceu
C de n'Arcs
C de Sant Pau
La Rambla dels Caputxins
C de la Unió

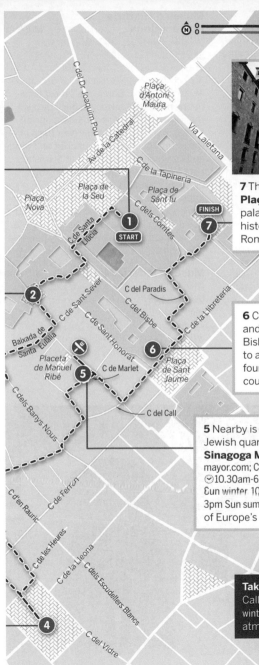

7 The final stop is picturesque **Plaça del Rei** (p201). The former palace today houses an interesting history museum, with significant Roman ruins.

6 Cross Plaça de Sant Jaume and turn left after Carrer del Bisbe. You'll pass the entrance to a ruined **Roman Temple**, with four columns hidden in a small courtyard.

5 Nearby is El Call, the medieval Jewish quarter. Here you'll find **Sinagoga Major** (www.sinagoga mayor.com; Carrer de Marlet 5; ⊘10.30am-6.30pm Mon-Fri, to 3pm Sun winter 10.30am-6.30pm Mon-Fri, to 3pm Sun summer; ⓂLiceu) **FREE**, one of Europe's oldest synagogues.

Take a Break... In the heart of the Call, **Alcoba Azul** (⊘6pm-2.30am winter, noon-2am summer) is an atmospheric tapas bar.

◉ SIGHTS

◉ La Rambla & Barri Gòtic

La Catedral · Cathedral

(Map p202; ☑93 342 82 62; www.catedralbcn.
org; Plaça de la Seu; donation €7 or choir €3, roof
€3; ☉worshipping 8.30am-12.30pm & 5.45-
7.30pm Mon-Fri, 8.30am-12.30pm & 5.15-8pm
Sat, 8.30am-1.45pm & 5.15-8pm Sun, tourist
visits 12.30-7.45pm Mon-Fri, 12.30-5.30pm Sat,
2-5.30pm Sun; Ⓜ Jaume I) Barcelona's central
place of worship presents a magnificent
image. The richly decorated main facade,
dotted with gargoyles and the kinds of stone
intricacies you would expect of northern
European Gothic, sets it quite apart from
other churches in Barcelona. The facade was
actually added in 1870, although the rest
of the building was built between 1298 and
1460. Its other facades are sparse in decoration, and the octagonal, flat-roofed towers
are a clear reminder that, even here, Catalan
Gothic architectural principles prevailed.

> *Palau Güell is a magnificent
> example of early Gaudí*

Museu d'Història de Barcelona · Museum

(MUHBA; Map p202; ☑93 256 21 00; www.
museuhistoria.bcn.cat; Plaça del Rei; adult/
concession/child €7/5/free, 3-8pm Sun & 1st Sun
of month free; ☉10am-7pm Tue-Sat, to 8pm Sun;
Ⓜ Jaume I) One of Barcelona's most fascinating museums takes you back through
the centuries to the very foundations of
Roman Barcino. You'll stroll over ruins of
the old streets, sewers, laundries and wine-
and fish-making factories that flourished
here following the town's founding by
Emperor Augustus around 10 BC. Equally
impressive is the building itself, which was
once part of the Palau Reial Major (Grand
Royal Palace) on Plaça del Rei, among the
key locations of medieval princely power in
Barcelona.

Museu Frederic Marès · Museum

(Map p202; ☑93 256 35 00; www.museumares.
bcn.cat; Plaça de Sant Iu 5; adult/concession/
child €4.20/2.40/free, 3-8pm Sun & 1st Sun of
month free; ☉10am-7pm Tue-Sat, 11am-8pm Sun;
Ⓜ Jaume I) One of the wildest collections
of historical curios lies inside this vast

Palau Güell

medieval complex, once part of the royal palace of the counts of Barcelona. A rather worn coat of arms on the wall indicates that it was also, for a while, the seat of the Spanish Inquisition in Barcelona. Frederic Marès i Deulovol (1893–1991) was a rich sculptor, traveller and obsessive collector, and displays of religious art and vast varieties of antique *objets* litter the museum.

Plaça del Rei Square

(King's Square; Map p202; MJaume I) Plaça del Rei is a picturesque plaza where Fernando and Isabel are thought to have received Columbus following his first New World voyage. It is the courtyard of the former Palau Reial Major. The palace today houses a superb history museum, with significant Roman ruins underground.

◉ El Raval

MACBA Arts Centre

(Museu d'Art Contemporani de Barcelona; ☑93 412 08 10; www.macba.cat; Plaça dels Àngels 1; adult/concession/child under 14yr €10/8/free, 4-8pm Sat free; ⊗11am-7.30pm Mon & Wed-Fri, 10am-8pm Sat, 10am-3pm Sun & holidays; MUniversitat) Designed by Richard Meier and opened in 1995, MACBA has become the city's foremost contemporary art centre, with captivating exhibitions for the serious art lover. The permanent collection is on the ground floor and dedicates itself to Spanish and Catalan art from the second half of the 20th century, with works by Antoni Tàpies, Joan Brossa and Miquel Barceló, among others; international artists, such as Paul Klee, Bruce Nauman and John Cage, are also represented.

Palau Güell Palace

(Map p202; ☑93 472 57 75; www.palauguell.cat; Carrer Nou de la Rambla 3-5; adult/concession/child under 10yr incl audio guide €12/9/free, 1st Sun of month free; ⊗10am-8pm Tue-Sun Apr-Oct, to 5.30pm Nov-Mar; MDrassanes) Palau Güell is a magnificent example of the early days of Gaudí's fevered architectural imagination. The extraordinary neo-Gothic mansion, one of the few major buildings of that

🐦 Park Güell

North of Gràcia, Unesco-listed **Park Güell** (☑93 409 18 31; www.parkguell.cat; Carrer d'Olot 7; adult/child €8.50/6; ⊗8am-9.30pm May-Aug, to 8.30pm Apr, Sep & Oct, to 6.15pm Nov–mid-Feb, to 7pm mid-Feb–Mar; ☐24, 92, MLesseps, Vallcarca) is where architect Antoni Gaudí turned his hand to landscape gardening. It's a strange, enchanting place where his passion for natural forms really took flight and the artificial almost seems more natural than the natural.

The park is extremely popular, and access to the central area is limited to a certain number of people every half-hour – book ahead online (and you'll also save on the admission fee). The rest of the park is free and can be visited without booking.

era raised in Ciutat Vella (Old City), gives an insight into its maker's prodigious genius.

◉ La Ribera

Basílica de Santa Maria del Mar Church

(Map p202; ☑93 310 23 90; www.santamaria delmarbarcelona.org; Plaça de Santa Maria; guided tour €10; ⊗9am-8.30pm Mon-Sat, 10am-8pm Sun, tours 1-5pm; MJaume I) At the southwestern end of Passeig del Born stands the apse of Barcelona's finest Catalan Gothic church, Santa Maria del Mar (Our Lady of the Sea). Built in the 14th century with record-breaking alacrity for

Central Barcelona

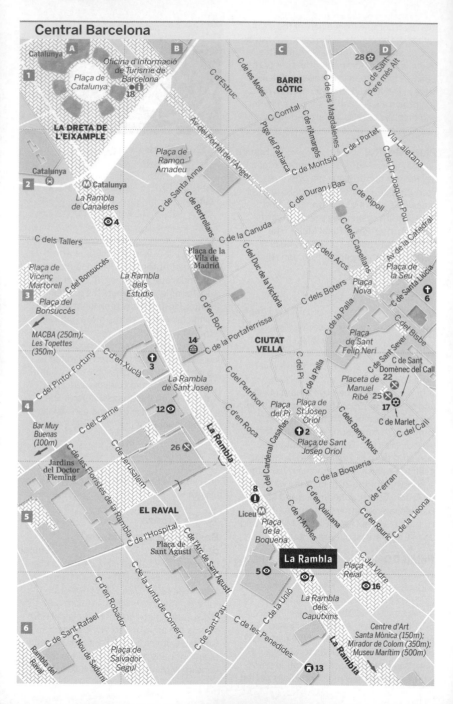

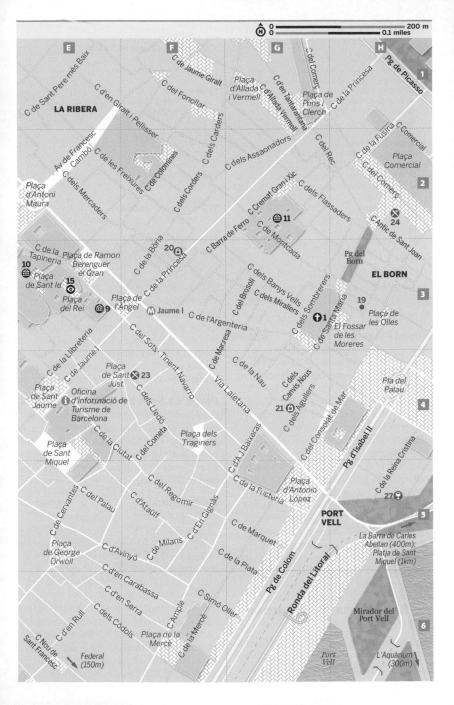

E
F
G
H

Pg de Picasso

1

C de Jaume Giralt

C de Sant Pere més Baix

C del Comerç

Plaça d'Allada i Vermell

C d'en Tantarantana

C d'Allada Vermell

Plaça de Pons i Clerch

C de la Princesa

LA RIBERA

C d'en Giralt i Pellisser

C del Fonollar

C dels Assaonadors

C de la Fusina

C Comercial

Av de Francesc Cambó

C de les Freixures

C Colomines

C dels Carders

C dels Corders

C del Rec

Plaça Comercial

C del Comerç

2

Plaça d'Antoni Maura

C dels Mercaders

C Cremat Gran i Xic

C dels Flassaders

C Antic de Sant Joan

24

C de la Tapineria

C de la Bòria

C Barra de Ferro

C de Montcada

11

Pg del Born

EL BORN

10

Plaça de Ramon Berenguer el Gran

20

C de la Princesa

C dels Banys Vells

C dels Sombrerers

19

Plaça de Sant Iu

15

C dels Brosoli

C dels Mirallers

C de Santa Maria

Plaça de les Olles

3

Plaça del Rei

9

Plaça de l'Angel

Jaume I

C de l'Argenteria

1

El Fossar de les Moreres

C de la Llibreteria

C del Sots-Tinent Navarro

C de Marresa

C dels Canvis Nous

Pla del Palau

4

C de Jaume I

Plaça de Sant Just

23

C de la Nau

Via Laietana

C dels Agullers

21

Plaça de Sant Jaume

Oficina d'Informació de Turisme de Barcelona

C dels Lledó

C del Consolat de Mar

Pg d'Isabel II

C de la Reina Cristina

Plaça de Sant Miquel

C de la Ciutat

C del Cometa

Plaça dels Traginers

C d'A J Baixeras

27

Plaça de George Orwell

C de Cervantes

C del Palau

C d'Ataülf

C del Regomir

C d'En Gignàs

C de la Fusteria

Plaça d'Antonio López

PORT VELL

5

La Barra de Carles Abellán (400m); Platja de Sant Miquel (1km)

C d'Avinyó

C de Milans

C de Marquet

C de la Plata

C d'en Carabassa

Pg de Colom

C d'en Serra

C dels Còdols

C Simó Oller

C Ample

C de la Mercè

Ronda del Litoral

Mirador del Port Vell

6

C Nou de Sant Francesc

C d'en Rull

Plaça de la Mercè

Federal (150m)

Port Vell

L'Aquàrium (300m)

Central Barcelona

the time (it took just 54 years), the church is remarkable for its architectural harmony and simplicity.

Museu Picasso
Museum

(Map p202; ☑93 256 30 00; www.museupicasso. bcn.cat; Carrer de Montcada 15-23; adult/concession/under 16yr permanent collection & temporary exhibit €14/7.50/free, 6-9.30pm Thu & 1st Sun of month free; ⊙9am-7pm Tue, Wed & Fri-Sun, to 9.30pm Thu; MJaume I) The setting alone, in five contiguous medieval stone mansions, makes the Museu Picasso unique (and worth the queues). The pretty courtyards, galleries and staircases preserved in the first three of these buildings are as delightful as the collection inside. While the collection concentrates on Pablo Picasso's formative years – potentially disappointing for those hoping for a feast of his better-known later works – there is enough material from subsequent periods to give you a thorough impression of the artist's versatility and genius.

◉ Barceloneta, the Waterfront & El Poblenou

Museu Marítim
Museum

(☑93 342 99 20; www.mmb.cat; Avinguda de les Drassanes; adult/child €10/5, free from 3pm Sun; ⊙10am-8pm; MDrassanes) The city's maritime museum occupies Gothic shipyards – a remarkable relic from Barcelona's days as the seat of a seafaring empire. Highlights include a full-scale 1970s replica of Don Juan of Austria's 16th-century flagship, fishing vessels, antique navigation charts and dioramas of the Barcelona waterfront.

Platja de Sant Miquel
Beach

(www.barcelona.cat; MBarceloneta) Taking its name from the 18th-century church in nearby Barceloneta, this stretch of sand fills with beachgoers when warm days arrive. Given its proximity to the old city, the crowds are thicker here than at beaches further out.

L'Aquàrium
Aquarium

(☑93 221 74 74; www.aquariumbcn.com; Moll d'Espanya; adult/child €20/15, dive from €150; ⊙10am-9.30pm Jul & Aug, shorter hours Sep-Jun; MDrassanes) It's hard not to shudder at the sight of a shark gliding above you, displaying its toothy, wide-mouthed grin. But this, the 80m shark tunnel, is the highlight of one of Europe's largest aquariums. It has the world's best Mediterranean collection and plenty of colourful fish from as far off as the Red Sea, the Caribbean and the Great Barrier Reef. All up, some 11,000 creatures of 450 species reside here.

◉ L'Eixample

Casa Batlló   Architecture

(Map p206; ☑93 216 03 06; www.casabatllo.es;
Passeig de Gràcia 43; adult/child €28.50/25.50;
⊙9am-9pm, last admission 8pm; MPasseig
de Gràcia) One of the strangest residential
buildings in Europe, this is Gaudí at his
hallucinatory best. The facade, sprinkled
with bits of blue, mauve and green tiles and
studded with wave-shaped window frames
and balconies, rises to an uneven blue-tiled
roof with a solitary tower.

La Pedrera   Architecture

(Casa Milà; Map p206; ☑93 214 25 76; www.
lapedrera.com; Passeig de Gràcia 92; adult/
child €25/14; ⊙9am-8.30pm & 9-11pm Mar-Oct,
9am-6.30pm & 7-9pm Nov-Feb; MDiagonal) This
madcap Gaudí masterpiece was built in
1905–10 as a combined apartment and office block. Formally called Casa Milà, after
the businessman who commissioned it, it
is better known as La Pedrera (the Quarry)
because of its uneven grey stone facade,
which ripples around the corner of Carrer
de Provença.

⊕ TOURS

Barcelona Walking Tours   Walking

(Map p202; ☑93 285 38 32; www.barcelona
turisme.com; Plaça de Catalunya 17; MCatalunya)
The Oficina d'Informació de Turisme de
Barcelona (p210) organises several one- to
two-hour guided walking tours (available in English) exploring the Barri Gòtic
(adult/child €16/free), Picasso's footsteps
(€22/7) and Modernisme (€16/free).
A two-hour gourmet food tour (€22/7)
includes tastings. Various street-art walking
and cycling tours (from €21) also take
place. There is a 10% discount on most
tours if you book online.

Bike Tours Barcelona   Cycling

(Map p202; ☑93 268 21 05; www.biketours
barcelona.com; Carrer de l'Esparteria 3; per person
€25; ⊙10am-7pm; MJaume I) One of the oldest
bike-tour operators in the city, they offer
daily three-hour bicycle tours of the Barri

Gòtic, the waterfront, La Sagrada Família
and other Gaudí landmarks. Tours depart
from the tourist office on Plaça de Sant
Jaume; check the website for departure
times, and for details of vineyard tours. Bike
rental (from €5 per hour) is also available.

🛍 SHOPPING

Les Topettes   Cosmetics

(☑93 500 55 64; www.lestopettes.com; Carrer de
Joaquín Costa 33; ⊙11am-2pm & 4-9pm Tue-Sat,
4-9pm Mon; MUniversitat) The items in this
chic little temple to soap and perfume have
been picked for their designs as much as
for the products themselves. You'll find
gorgeously packaged scents, candles and
unguents from Diptyque, Cowshed and
L'Artisan Parfumeur, among others.

Joan Múrria   Food & Drinks

(☑93 215 57 89; www.murria.cat; Carrer de
Roger de Llúria 85; ⊙10am-8.30pm Tue-Fri,
10am-2pm & 5-8.30pm Sat; MGirona) Ramon
Casas designed the 1898 Modernista
shopfront advertisements featured at this
culinary temple of speciality food goods
from around Catalonia and beyond. Artisan
cheeses, Iberian hams, caviar, canned
delicacies, smoked fish, cavas and wines,
coffee and loose-leaf teas are among the
treats in store.

Colmillo
de Morsa   Fashion & Accessories

(☑645 206 365; www.colmillodemorsa.com;
Carrer de Vic 15; ⊙11am-2.30pm & 4.30-7pm
Mon-Fri, 11am 3pm Sat; ℝFGC Gràcia) Design
team Javier Blanco and Elisabet Vallecillo,
who have made waves at Madrid's Cibeles
Fashion Week and Paris' fashion fair Who's
Next, showcase their Barcelona-made
women's fashion here at their flagship
boutique. They've also opened the floor to
promote other up-and-coming local labels.

El Rei de la Màgia   Magic

(☑93 319 39 20; www.elreydelamagia.com; Carrer
de la Princesa 11; ⊙10.30am-7.30pm Mon-Fri,
10.30am-2pm & 4-7.30pm Sat; MJaume I) For
more than 100 years, the owners have been

La Sagrada & L'Eixample

⊙ Sights
1 Casa Batlló	C3
2 Església de les Saleses	D2
3 La Pedrera	B3
4 La Sagrada Família	D1

⊞ Shopping
5 Colmillo de Morsa	A2
6 Joan Múrria	C3

⊗ Eating
7 Lasarte	B3
8 Tapas 24	C3

⊖ Drinking & Nightlife
9 Les Gens Que J'Aime	C3
10 Michael Collins Pub	D1

keeping locals both astounded and amused. Should you decide to stay in Barcelona and make a living as a magician, this is the place to buy levitation brooms, glasses of disappearing milk and decks of magic cards.

Vila Viniteca   Wine

(☏90 232 77 77; www.vilaviniteca.es; Carrer dels Agullers 7; ⊗8.30am-8.30pm Mon-Sat; ⓜJaume I) One of the best wine stores in Barcelona (and there are a few...), Vila Viniteca has been searching out the best local and imported wines since 1932. On a couple of November evenings it organises what has become an almost riotous wine-tasting event in Carrer dels Agullers and surrounding lanes, at which cellars from around Spain present their young new wines.

⊗ EATING

Traditional Catalan recipes showcase the great produce of the Mediterranean: fish, prawns, cuttlefish, clams, pork, rabbit, game, first-rate olive oil, peppers and loads of garlic. Classic dishes also feature unusual pairings (seafood with meat, fruit with fowl): cuttlefish with chickpeas, cured pork with caviar, rabbit with prawns, goose with pears.

✪ La Rambla & Barri Gòtic

Federal   Cafe €

(📞93 280 81 71; www.federalcafe.es; Passatge de la Pau 11; mains €7-10; ◷9am-midnight Mon-Thu, to 1am Fri & Sat, to 5.30pm Sun; 🛜; MDrassanes) Don't be intimidated by the industrial chic, the sea of open MacBooks or the stack of design mags – this branch of the Poble Sec Federal mothership is incredibly welcoming, with healthy, good-value food. Set in a lovely, quiet square, it's best known for its Australian-inspired brunches such as baked eggs with feta and chorizo, avocado toast and French toast with berry compote.

Cafè de l'Acadèmia   Catalan €€

(Map p202; 📞93 319 82 53; Carrer dels Lledó 1; mains €8-20; ◷1-3.30pm & 8-11.30pm Mon-Fri; 🛜; MJaume I) Expect a mix of traditional Catalan dishes with the occasional creative twist. At lunchtime, local city hall workers pounce on the *menú del día* (€16). In the evening it is rather more romantic, as low lighting emphasises the intimacy of the beamed ceiling and stone walls. On warm days you can also dine in the pretty square at the front.

La Vinateria del Call   Spanish €€

(Map p202; 📞93 302 60 92; www.lavinateria delcall.com; Carrer Salomó Ben Adret 9; raciones €7-12; ◷7.30pm-1am; 🛜; MJaume I) In a magical setting in the former Jewish quarter, this tiny jewel-box of a wine bar serves up tasty Iberian dishes including Galician octopus, cider-cooked chorizo and the Catalan *escalivada* (roasted peppers, aubergine and onions) with anchovies. Portions are small and made for sharing, and there are over 160 varieties of wine to choose from.

✪ El Raval

Bar Muy Buenas   Catalan €

(📞93 807 28 57; http://muybuenas.cat; Carrer del Carme 63; mains €9-15; ◷1-3.30pm & 8-11pm Sun-Thu, 1-4pm & 8-11.30pm Fri & Sat; MLiceu) Modernista classic Muy Buenas has been a bar since 1928, and wears its past proudly with stunning and sinuous original woodwork, etched-glass windows and a marble bar. Though the cocktails are impressive, these days it's more restaurant than bar, expertly turning out traditional Catalan dishes such as *esqueixada* (salad of shredded salted cod) and *fricandó* (pork and vegetable stew).

Pinotxo Bar   Tapas €€

(Map p202; 📞93 317 17 31; www.pinotxobar. com; Mercat de la Boqueria, La Rambla 89; mains €9-17; ◷6.30am-4pm Mon-Sat; MLiceu) Pinotxo is arguably La Boqueria's, and even Barcelona's, best tapas bar. The ever-charming owner, Juanito, might serve up chickpeas with pine nuts and raisins, a soft mix of potato and spinach sprinkled with salt, soft baby squid with cannellini beans, or a quivering cube of caramel-sweet pork belly.

✪ La Ribera

Casa Delfín   Catalan €€

(Map p202; 📞93 319 50 88; www.casadelfin restaurant.com; Passeig del Born 36; mains €12-18; ◷noon-midnight Sun-Thu, to 1am Fri & Sat; 🛜; MJaume I) One of Barcelona's culinary delights, Casa Delfín is everything you dream of when you think of Catalan (and Mediterranean) cooking. Start with salt-strewn *Padrón* peppers, moving on to plump anchovies from L'Escala in the Costa Brava, then tackle *suquet de los pescadores* (traditional Catalan fish stew; €14.50, minimum two people).

✪ Barceloneta, the Waterfront & El Poblenou

Can Recasens   Catalan €€

(📞93 300 81 23; www.facebook.com/can recasens; Rambla del Poblenou 102; mains €8-21; ◷restaurant 8pm-1am; delicatessen 9.30am-1.30pm & 5pm-1am Mon-Fri, 9.30am-2pm & 5pm-1am Sat; MPoblenou) One of El Poblenou's most romantic settings, Can Recasens hides a warren of warmly lit rooms full of oil paintings, flickering candles, fairy lights and baskets of fruit. The food is outstanding, with a mix of salads, smoked meats,

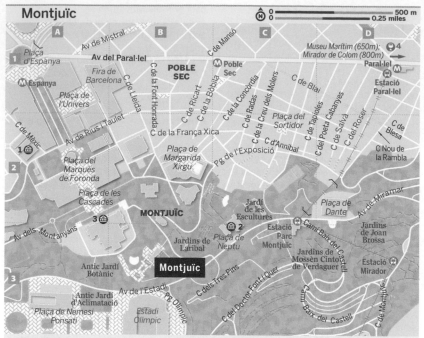

Montjuïc

fondues, and open sandwiches topped with delicacies like wild mushrooms and Brie, *escalivada* (grilled vegetables) and Gruyère, and spicy chorizo.

There's live jazz every second Wednesday.

La Barra de Carles Abellan   Seafood €€€

(☏93 760 51 29; www.carlesabellan.com/mis-restaurantes/la-barra; Passeig de Joan de Borbó 19; tapas €5-18, mains €22-36; ⏰1.30-4pm & 8-11pm Tue-Sat, 1.30-4pm Sun; Ⓜ Barceloneta) Catalan chef Carles Abellán's stunning glass-encased, glossy-tiled restaurant celebrates seafood in tapas such as pickled octopus and fried oyster with salmon roe. Even more show-stopping are the mains: grilled razor clams with *ponzu* citrus sauce, squid filled with spicy poached egg yolk,

and stir-fried sea cucumber. Most seats are at long, communal counter-style tables, making it great for solo diners.

🔵 L'Eixample

Tapas 24   Tapas €

(Map p206; ☏93 488 09 77; www.carlesabellan.com; Carrer de la Diputació 269; tapas €4-12; ⏰9am-midnight; 🛜; Ⓜ Passeig de Gràcia) Hotshot chef Carles Abellán runs this basement tapas haven known for its gourmet versions of old faves. Highlights include the *bikini* (toasted ham and cheese sandwich – here the ham is cured and the truffle makes all the difference) and zesty *boquerones al limón* (lemon-marinated anchovies). You can't book, and service can be slow, but it's worth the wait.

Lasarte Modern European €€€

(☏93 445 32 42; www.restaurantlasarte.com; Carrer de Mallorca 259; mains €52-70; ☉1.30-3pm & 8.30-10pm Tue-Sat; MDiagonal) One of the preeminent restaurants in Barcelona – and the city's first to gain three Michelin stars – Lasarte is overseen by lauded chef Martín Berasategui. From Duroc pig's trotters with quince to squid tartare with kaffir consommé, this is seriously sophisticated stuff, served in an ultra-contemporary dining room by waiting staff who could put the most overawed diners at ease.

Disfrutar Modern European €€€

(☏93 348 68 96; www.disfrutarbarcelona.com; Carrer de Villarroel 163; tasting menus €150-190; ☉1-2.30pm & 8-9.30pm Mon-Fri; MHospital Clínic) Disfrutar ('Enjoy' in Catalan and Spanish) is among the city's finest restaurants, with two Michelin stars. Run by alumni of Ferran Adrià's game-changing (now closed) El Bulli restaurant, nothing is as it seems, such as black and green olives that are actually chocolate ganache with orange-blossom water.

🍷 DRINKING & NIGHTLIFE

Perikete Wine Bar

(Map p202; ☏93 024 22 29; www.gruporeini.net/perikete; Carrer de Llauder 6; ☉11am-1am; MBarceloneta) Since opening in 2017, this fabulous wine bar has been jam-packed with locals. Hams hang from the ceilings, barrels of vermouth sit above the bar and wine bottles cram every available shelf space – over 200 varieties are available by the glass or bottle, accompanied by 50-plus tapas dishes. In the evening, the action spills into the street.

La Confitería Bar

(Map p208; ☏93 140 54 35; http://confiteria.cat; Carrer de Sant Pau 128; ☉7pm-2am Mon-Thu, 6pm-3am Fri & Sat, 5pm-2am Sun; 🛜; MParal·lel) This is a trip into the 19th century. Until the 1980s it was a confectioner's shop, and although the original cabinets are now lined with booze, the look of the place barely changed with its conversion. The back room is similarly evocative, and the vibe these days is lively cocktail bar.

Les Gens Que J'Aime Bar

(Map p206; ☏93 215 68 79; www.facebook.com/lesgensquejaime.pub; Carrer de València 286; ☉6pm-2.30am Sun-Thu, 7pm-3am Fri & Sat; MPasseig de Gràcia) Atmospheric and intimate, this basement relic of the 1960s follows a deceptively simple formula: chilled jazz music in the background, minimal lighting from an assortment of flea-market lamps and a cosy, cramped scattering of red-velvet-backed lounges around tiny dark tables.

⭐ ENTERTAINMENT

Palau de la Música Catalana Classical Music

(☏93 295 72 00; www.palaumusica.cat; Carrer de Palau de la Música 4-6; tickets from €18; ☉box office 9.30am-9pm Mon-Sat, 10am-3pm Sun; MUrquinaona) A feast for the eyes, this Modernista confection is also the city's most traditional venue for classical and choral music, although it has a wide-ranging program, including flamenco, pop and – particularly – jazz. Just being in the building is an experience. In the foyer, its tiled pillars all a-glitter, you can sip a preconcert tipple.

Camp Nou Football

(☏902 189900; www.fcbarcelona.com; Carrer d'Arístides Maillol; MPalau Reial) The massive stadium of Camp Nou ('New Field' in Catalan) is home to the legendary Futbol Club Barcelona. Attending a game amid the roar of the crowds is an unforgettable experience; the season runs from August to May. Alternatively, get a taste of all the excitement at the interactive **Barça Stadium Tour & Museum** (☏902 189900; www.fcbarcelona.com; Gate 9, Avinguda de Joan XXIII; adult/child self-guided tour €29.50/23.50, guided tour €50/35; ☉9.30am-7.30pm mid-Apr–mid-Oct, 10am-6.30pm Mon-Sat, to 2.30pm Sun mid-Oct–mid-Apr; MPalau Reial).

 Shopping Strips

Avinguda del Portal de l'Àngel This broad pedestrian avenue is lined with high-street chains, shoe shops, bookshops and more.

Avinguda Diagonal This boulevard is loaded with international fashion names and design boutiques.

Carrer d'Avinyó A dynamic young fashion street.

Carrer del Petritxol Best for chocolate shops and art.

Passeig de Gràcia This is the premier shopping boulevard, home to big-name international brands.

Passeig de Gràcia
IVAN MARC / SHUTTERSTOCK ©

ℹ INFORMATION

Several tourist offices operate in Barcelona. Information booths operate at Estació del Nord bus station and at Portal de la Pau, at the foot of the Mirador de Colom at the port end of La Rambla.

Plaça de Catalunya (Map p202; 📞93 285 38 34; www.barcelonaturisme.com; Plaça de Catalunya 17-S, underground; ⏰8.30am-9pm; Ⓜ Catalunya)

Plaça Sant Jaume (Map p202; 📞93 285 38 34; www.barcelonaturisme.com; Plaça Catalunya 17; ⏰8.30am-9pm; Ⓜ Catalunya)

Estació Sants (📞93 285 38 34; www.barcelonaturisme.com; Barcelona Sants; ⏰8.30am-8.30pm; 🚉Sants Estació)

El Prat Airport (📞93 378 81 49; www.barcelonaturisme.com; ⏰8.30am-8.30pm)

ℹ GETTING THERE & AWAY

El Prat Airport (📞91 321 10 00; www.aena.es; 📶) has service across Spain and worldwide.

Barcelona is well connected by bus to other parts of Spain, as well as to major European cities. Long-distance buses leave from **Estació del Nord** (📞93 706 53 66; www.barcelonanord.cat; Carrer d'Ali Bei 80; Ⓜ Arc de Triomf).

Highspeed trains serve Barcelona from Madrid and France. The main train station is **Barcelona Sants** (📞912 432343; www.adif.es; Plaça dels Països Catalans; Ⓜ Sants Estació), located 2.5km west of La Rambla.

ℹ GETTING AROUND

Transports Metropolitans de Barcelona (TMB; 📞93 298 70 00; www.tmb.cat) operates local buses, the metro etc.

Metro The most convenient transport option. Runs 5am to midnight Sunday to Thursday, till 2am on Friday and 24 hours on Saturday. Targeta T-10 (10-ride pass; €10.20) is the best value; otherwise, it's €2.20 per ride.

Bus A hop-on, hop-off Bus Turístic, departing from Plaça de Catalunya, is handy for those wanting to see the city's highlights in one or two days.

Taxi You can hail taxis on the street (try La Rambla, Via Laietana, Plaça de Catalunya and Passeig de Gràcia) or at taxi stands. Or call **Fonotaxi** (📞93 300 11 00; www.fonotaxi.net).

Where to Stay

Barcelona has a wide range of sleeping options, from cheap hostels in the old quarter to luxury hotels overlooking the waterfront. Small-scale apartment rentals around the city are a good-value choice.

Neighbourhood	Atmosphere
La Rambla & Barri Gòtic	Great location, close to major sights, with good nightlife and dining options. This is the perfect area for exploring on foot. It can be very touristy and noisy.
El Raval	This central option, with good local nightlife and access to sights, has a bohemian vibe with few tourists. However, it can be noisy, seedy and run-down in parts.
La Ribera	Great restaurant scene and neighbourhood exploring, La Ribera is central and close to top sights. It can be noisy, overcrowded and touristy.
Barceloneta & the Waterfront	Excellent seafood restaurants, with an easygoing local vibe and handy to the promenade and beaches, but it has few sleeping options.
La Sagrada Família & L'Eixample	Offering a wide range of options for all budgets, it is close to Modernista sights, good restaurants and nightlife, and is a prime neighbourhood for the LGBT scene (in the 'Gaixample'). Can be very noisy with lots of traffic though, and it's a little far from the old city.

ANDALUCÍA, SPAIN

Andalucía, Spain

The scent of orange blossom, the swish of a flamenco dress, the first glimpse of the Alhambra: memories of Andalucía linger. Immortalised in operas and vividly depicted in 19th-century art and literature, Andalucía often acts as a synonym for Spain as a whole, a spirited and passionate place where the atmosphere sneaks up and envelops you when you least expect it – perhaps as you're crammed into a buzzing tapas bar sipping one of the superb local sherries.

Start at Andalucía's two great cities, Granada and Seville. Both are filled with magnificent architectural and cultural treasures and are unmissable.

Two Days in Andalucía

Granada's extraordinary **Alhambra** (p216) can easily fill two days. Fully exploring this hilltop Moorish citadel with its extraordinary gardens and views is not an experience you should rush. However venturing elsewhere in this beautiful, inviting city will let you see sites like the **Mirador San Nicolás** (p220) and **Basílica San Juan de Dios** (p220). Later bar-hop around the city enjoying free tapas.

Four Days in Andalucía

In Seville, marvel at the mind-blowing Mudéjar decor and gardens of the **Real Alcázar** (p225) royal palace complex. Then pay homage to architectural and artistic treasures at the **Catedral** (p224), the world's largest Gothic cathedral, then surveying sensational views from its belltower, the **Giralda**. Contemplate artistic masterpieces from Seville's Golden Age at the **Hospital de los Venerables Sacerdotes** (p225). Later, stroll medieval streets cafe-hopping.

Next stop: Andalucía is pleasantly situated between Barcelona (p181) and Lisbon (p229).

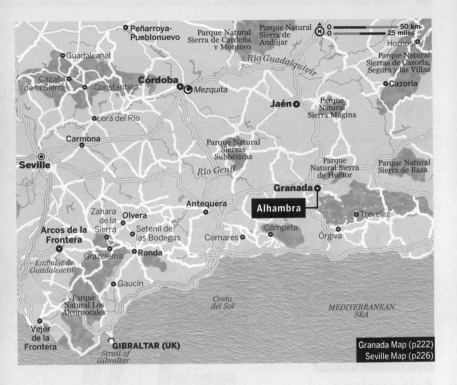

Granada Map (p222)
Seville Map (p226)

Arriving in Andalucía

Seville's airport has regional connections from Europe. Seville and Granada are both connected to Madrid by high-speed trains. Regional train and bus service connects towns and cities across Andalucía as well as with the rest of Spain. Your own vehicle is useful for exploring backroads and hilltop villages, but for the most important places, public transport will serve you well.

Where to Stay

Granada has plenty of hotels and hostels, many in the compact area around the cathedral. Some of the prettiest lodgings are in the hilly Albayzín district.

Seville has a good selection of places to stay in the three most atmospheric areas: Barrio de Santa Cruz (walkable from Prado de San Sebastián bus station), El Arenal and El Centro (both nearer Plaza de Armas bus station).

Alcazaba

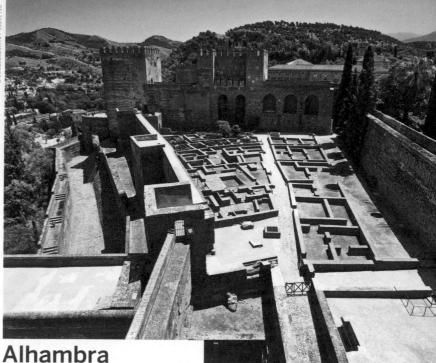

DELTAOFF / SHUTTERSTOCK ©

Alhambra

The Alhambra is part palace, part fort, part World Heritage Site and part lesson in medieval architecture. It is unlikely that, as a historical monument, it will ever be surpassed.

Great For...

☑ Don't Miss

Patio de los Leones, the Alhambra's centrepiece and gateway to the inner sanctum.

Palacios Nazaríes

The central palace complex, the **Palacios Nazaríes** (Nasrid Palaces), is the pinnacle of the Alhambra's design. Highlights include the Patio de Arrayanes where rooms look onto the rectangular pool edged in myrtles, and the **Salón de los Embajadores**, where the marvellous domed marquetry ceiling uses more than 8000 cedar pieces to create its intricate star pattern representing the seven heavens.

The adjacent **Patio de los Leones** (Courtyard of the Lions), built in the second half of the 14th century, has a fountain that channelled water through the mouths of 12 marble lions as its centrepiece. The stucco work hits its apex here, with almost lacelike detail. On the patio's northern side is the **Sala de Dos Hermanas** (Hall of Two Sisters) whose dizzying ceiling is a fantastic *muqarnas* dome with

Courtyard of Generalife

DAVID IONUT / SHUTTERSTOCK ©

ⓘ Need to Know

🖉958 02 79 71, tickets 858 95 36 16; www. alhambra-patronato.es; adult/12-15yr/under 12yr €14/8/free, Generalife & Alcazaba adult/ under 12yr €7/free; ⊗8.30am-8pm Apr–mid-Oct, to 6pm mid-Oct–Mar, night visits 10-11.30pm Tue & Sat Apr–mid-Oct, 8-9.30pm Fri & Sat mid-Oct–Mar

✖ Take a Break

Bring a picnic and behave like royalty by relaxing in the Generalife gardens.

★ Top Tip

Reserve tickets in advance at https:// tickets.alhambra-patronato.es/en/

some 5000 tiny cells. A reflecting pool and terraced garden front the small Palacio del Partal (Palace of the Portico), the oldest surviving palace in the Alhambra, from the time of Mohammed III (r 1302–09).

Generalife

From the Arabic *jinan al-'arif* (the over-seer's gardens), the Generalife is a soothing arrangement of pathways, patios, pools, fountains, tall trees and, in season, flowers. At the north end is the emirs' **summer palace**, a whitewashed structure on the hillside facing the Alhambra. The courtyards here are particularly graceful; in the second courtyard, the trunk of a 700-year-old cypress tree suggests what delicate shade once graced the patio. Climb the steps out-side the courtyard to the Escalera del Agua, a delightful bit of garden engineering, where water flows along a shaded staircase.

Alcazaba & Christian Buildings

The western end of the Alhambra grounds are the remnants of the Alcazaba, chiefly its ramparts and several towers including the Torre de la Vela (Watchtower), with a narrow staircase leading to the top terrace where the cross and banners of the Recon-quista were raised in January 1492.

By the Palacios Nazaríes, the hulking Renaissance-era Palacio de Carlos V, built in 1527 after the Reconquista, clashes spectacularly with its surroundings. Inside, the **Museo de la Alhambra** (🖉958 91 80 29; www.alhambra.org/en/museum-alhambra.html; EU/non-EU citizens free/€1.50; ⊗8.30am-8pm Wed-Sat, to 2.30pm Sun & Tue mid-Mar–mid-Oct, 8.30am-6pm Wed-Sat, to 2.30pm Sun & Tue mid-Oct–mid-Mar) has a collection of Alhambra artefacts and the **Museo de Bellas Artes** (Fine Arts Museum; 🖉958 56 35 08; EU/non-EU citizens free/€1.50; ⊗9am-3.30pm Tues-Sun mid-Jun–mid-Sep, 9am-7.30pm Tue-Sat mid-Mar–mid-Jun & mid-Sep–mid-Oct, to 6pm mid-Oct–Mid-Mar, 9am-3.30pm Sun) displays paintings and sculptures from Granada's Christian history.

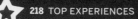

A sherry and cured meats board in Jerez de la Frontera

QIN XIE / SHUTTERSTOCK ©

Sherry Tasting & Tapas

In the sun-dappled vineyards of western Andalucía, sherry, an often-misunderstood fortified wine, is enjoying a renaissance; you can dig deeper with tours, tastings, sherry-pairing menus and more. Savour its oakiness in the Sherry Triangle towns of Jerez de la Frontera, El Puerto de Santa María and Sanlúcar de Barrameda.

Great For...

☑ Don't Miss

Jerez de la Frontera's **Fiestas de la Vendimia** (⊘Sep) and Sanlúcar de Barrameda's **Feria de la Manzanilla** (⊘late May/early Jun).

Tasting Sherry

Fortified white wine has been produced since Phoenician times, enjoyed by everyone from Christopher Columbus to Francis Drake. A distinctly Spanish product, sherry is a result of aging and the mixing of various wines. Its popularity has waxed and waned but is again on the upswing as quality products replace plonk best left for guzzling or cooking.

The main distinctions in sherry are *fino*, very dry and straw coloured, and *oloroso* (sweet and dark, with a strong bouquet). Important variations include the *amontillado*, a moderately dry *fino* with a nutty flavour and a higher alcohol content; cream sherry, an *oloroso* combined with a sweet wine; and *manzanilla*, a *fino* produced in Sanlúcar de Barrameda, with a delicate flavour that comes from sea breezes.

Tapas

EDWARDOLIVE / GETTY IMAGES ©

Jerez de la Frontera

Jerez is a vibrant modern city and Andalucía's sherry capital. On its winding streets, traditional, early-20th-century *tabancos* (humble taverns serving sherry from the barrel) have burst back into life, reinvigorated under keen new ownership. Jerez (the word even means 'sherry') also has around 20 sherry bodegas. Most require bookings for visits; the **tourist office** (📞956 33 88 74; www.turismojerez.com; Plaza del Arenal; ⊘9am-3pm & 5-6.30pm Mon-Fri, 9.30am-2.30pm Sat & Sun) has details.

El Puerto de Santa María

With its abundance of sandy blonde beaches and smattering of architectural heirlooms, El Puerto is southern Andalucía in microcosm. **Bodegas Osborne** (📞956 86 91 00; www.bodegas-osborne.com; Calle los Moros 7; tours from €12, tastings €8-30), with its famous bull logo (a highly recognisable symbol of Spain), was founded and retains its headquarters here, as do half a dozen other sherry bodegas.

Sanlúcar de Barrameda

Sanlúcar cooks up some of the region's best seafood on a hallowed waterside strip called Bajo de Guía. The town's seaside location results in the much-admired one-of-a-kind *manzanilla*.

Founded in 1821, **Bodegas Barbadillo** (📞956 38 55 21; www.barbadillo.com; Calle Sevilla 6; tours €10; ⊘tours noon & 1pm Tue-Sun, in English 11am Tue-Sun, open Mon Jul & Aug, closed Sun Nov-Mar) was the first family to bottle *manzanilla*. Tours end with a four-wine tasting.

Granada

Drawn by the allure of the Alhambra, many visitors head to Granada unsure of what to expect. What they find is a gritty, compelling city where serene Islamic architecture and Arab-flavoured street life go hand in hand with monumental churches, old-school tapas bars and counterculture graffiti art.

The city, sprawled at the foot of the Sierra Nevada, was the last stronghold of the Spanish Moors; their legacy lies all around.

There's also an energy to Granada's streets, packed as they are with bars, student dives, bohemian cafes and intimate flamenco clubs, and it's this as much as the more traditional sights that leaves a lasting impression.

◎ SIGHTS

Basílica San Juan de Dios   Basilica
(www.sjdgranada.es; Calle San Juan de Dios 19; €4; ☉10am-1pm & 4-7pm Mon-Sat, 4-7pm Sun) Head to this historic basilica, built between 1737 and 1759, for a blinding display of opulent baroque decor. Barely a square inch of its interior lacks embellishment, most of it in gleaming gold and silver. Frescos by Diego Sánchez Sarabia and the Neapolitan painter Corrado Giaquinto adorn the ceilings and side chapels, while up above, the basilica's dome soars to a height of 50m. The highlight, however, is the extraordinary gold altarpiece in the Capilla Mayor (main chapel).

Mirador San Nicolás   Viewpoint
(Plaza de San Nicolás) This is the place for those classic sunset shots of the Alhambra sprawled along a wooded hilltop with the dark Sierra Nevada mountains looming in the background. It's a well-known spot, accessible via Callejón de San Cecilio, so expect crowds of camera-toting tourists, students and buskers. It's also a haunt of pickpockets and bag-snatchers, so keep your wits about you as you enjoy the views.

Capilla Real   Historic Building
(Royal Chapel; ☎958 22 78 48; www.capillareal granada.com; Calle Oficios; adult/concession/child €5/3.50/free; ☉10.15am-6.30pm Mon-Sat,

Capilla Real

11am-6pm Sun) The Royal Chapel is the last resting place of Spain's Reyes Católicos (Catholic Monarchs), Isabel I de Castilla (1451–1504) and Fernando II de Aragón (1452–1516), who commissioned the elaborate Isabelline-Gothic-style mausoleum that was to house them. It wasn't completed until 1517, hence their interment in the Alhambra's **Convento de San Francisco** until 1521.

Their monumental marble tombs (and those of their heirs) lie in the chancel behind a gilded wrought-iron screen created by Bartolomé de Jaén in 1520.

Catedral de Granada
Cathedral

(📞958 22 29 59; http://catedraldegranada.com; Plaza de las Pasiegas; adult/reduced €5/3.50; ⏰10am-6.30pm Mon-Sat, 3-5.45pm Sun) From street level it's difficult to appreciate the immensity of Granada's cavernous cathedral. It's too boxed in by other buildings to stand out, but it's nonetheless a monumental work of architecture. Built atop the city's former mosque, it was originally intended to be Gothic in appearance, but over the two centuries of its construction (1523–1704) it underwent major modifications. Most notably, architect Diego de Siloé changed its layout to a Renaissance style, and Alonso Cano added a magnificent 17th-century baroque facade.

🟢 ACTIVITIES

Play Granada
Cultural

(📞958 16 36 84; www.playgranada.com; Calle Santa Ana 2; tours from €20) On foot, by electric bike, on a Segway – this outfit offers a choice of tours, taking in the city and its historic quarters, as well as packages for the Alhambra (p216). Reckon on €29 for a two-hour 8km Segway ride, and from €49 for a guided tour of the Alhambra.

🟢 EATING

Bodegas Castañeda
Tapas €

(📞958 21 54 64; Calle Almireceros 1; tapas €2-5; ⏰11.30am-4.30pm & 7.30pm-1am Mon-Thu, to

📷 Andalucía's White Towns

Choosing your favourite *pueblo blanco* (white town) is like choosing your favourite Beatles album: they're all so damned good, it's impossible to decide. Most people hunt down the classic calling cards: a thrillingly sited location and an evocative old town.

Arcos de la Frontera The quintessential Cádiz white town, with castle, church and centuries-old houses clinging to a crag.

Vejer de la Frontera Cavernous restaurants, ornate tiled fountains, esoteric festivals, luxury boutique hotels and a magical timelessness.

Zahara de la Sierra Wander sunbleached, bougainvillea-wrapped streets below a crag-top Moorish castle, in prime Cádiz province mountain-hiking country.

Segura de la Sierra Steeply stacked Jaén province village with medieval castle amid the mountains of Andalucía's largest protected area.

Cómpeta One of Málaga province's most popular whitewashed hill towns, with good walking and excellent restaurants.

Zahara de la Sierra

2am Fri-Sun) Eating becomes a contact sport at this traditional tapas bar where crowds of hungry punters jostle for food under hanging hams. Don't expect any experimental nonsense here, just classic tapas (and *raciones*) served lightning fast, with booze poured from big wall-mounted casks.

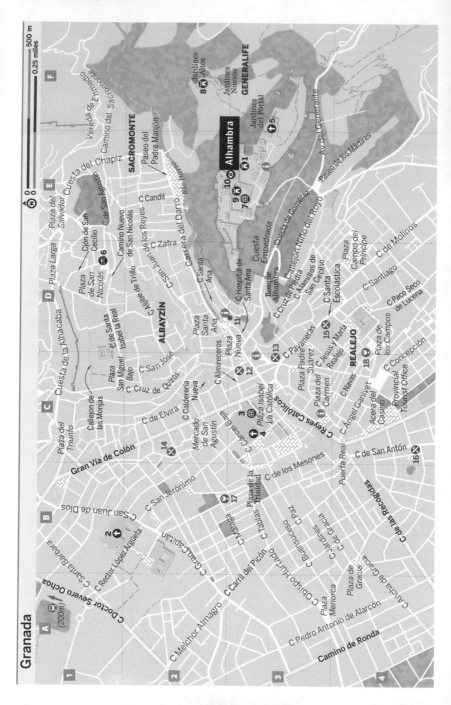

Granada

GENERALIFE

SACROMONTE

Alhambra

ALBAYZÍN

REALEJO

Granada

Hicuri Art Restaurant   Vegan €

(☎858 98 74 73; www.restaurantehicuriartvegan. com; Plaza de los Girones 3; mains €8-12, menú del día €14; ⊙noon-11pm Mon-Sat; 🖉) Granada's leading graffiti artist, El Niño de las Pinturas, has been let loose inside Hicuri, creating a psychedelic backdrop to the vegan food served at this friendly, laid-back restaurant. Zingy salads, tofu, and curried seitan provide welcome alternatives to the traditional meat dishes that dominate so many city menus.

Carmela Restaurante   Spanish €€

(☎958 22 57 94; www.restaurantecarmela. com; Calle Colcha 13; tapas €7, mains €9-20; ⊙8am-midnight, kitchen noon-midnight) Traditional tapas updated for the 21st century are the star turn at this smart all-day cafe-restaurant at the jaws of the Realejo quarter. Bag a table in the cool brick-lined interior or on the outdoor terrace and bite into croquettes with black pudding and caramelised onion, or tuna *tataki* with soy reduction.

El Bar de Fede   International €€

(☎958 28 88 14; www.elbardefede.com; Calle Marqués de Falces 1; raciones €11-21; ⊙9am-2am) The 'Fede' in the name refers to hometown poet Federico García Lorca, whose free spirit seems to hang over this hip, gay-friendly bar. It's a good-looking spot with patterned wallpaper and high tables set around a ceramic-tiled island, and the food is a joy. Standouts include chicken pâté served with orange sauce and heavenly melt-in-your mouth grilled squid.

La Fábula Restaurante   Gastronomy €€€

(☎958 25 01 50; www.restaurantelafabula.com; Calle de San Antón 28; mains €23.50-34, tasting menus €75-90; ⊙2-3.30pm & 8.30-10.30pm Tue-Sat) It's hard to avoid the pun: Fábula is pretty fabulous. A formal fine-dining restaurant set in the refined confines of the Hotel Villa Oniria, it's the domain of chef Ismael Delgado López whose artfully composed plates of contemporary Spanish cuisine will impress. Be sure to book.

🍷 DRINKING & NIGHTLIFE

Botánico   Bar

(☎958 27 15 98; www.botanicocafe.es; Calle Málaga 3; ⊙1pm-1am Mon-Thu, to 2am Fri & Sat, to 6pm Sun) Dudes with designer beards, students finishing off their Lorca dissertations, and bohemians with arty inclinations hang out at Botánico, a casual eatery by day, a cafe at *merienda* (afternoon snack) time (5pm to 7pm), and a buzzing bar come the evening.

Taberna La Tana   Wine Bar

(☎958 22 52 48; Placeta del Agua 3; ⊙12.30-4pm & 8.30pm-midnight) With bottles stacked to the rafters, hanging strings of garlic, and a small wood-and-brick interior, friendly La Tana is a model wine bar. It specialises in Spanish wines, which it backs up with some beautifully paired tapas. Ask the bartender about the 'wines of the month' and state your preference – a *suave* (smooth) red, or something more *fuerte* (strong).

Unmissable Córdoba

One of the world's great works of Islamic architecture, Córdoba's magnificent **mosque** (Mosque; ☑957 47 05 12; www.mezquita-catedraldecordoba.es; Calle Cardenal Herrero; adult/child aged 10-14/child under 10 €10/5/free; ☺10am-7pm Mon-Sat, 8.30-11.30am & 3-7pm Sun Mar-Oct, 8.30am-6pm Mon-Sat, 8.30-11.30am & 3-6pm Sun Nov-Feb, Mass 9.30am Mon-Sat, noon & 1.30pm Sun) is a grand symbol of the time when Islamic Spain was at its cultural and political peak, and Córdoba, its capital, was western Europe's largest, most cultured city. In the Mezquita's interior, mesmerising rows of horseshoe arches stretch away in every direction. The most intricate surround the gold-mosaic-decorated portal of the *mihrab* (prayer niche). While most Córdoba visitors rightly make a beeline for the Mezquita, you'll find the old city that grew up around it just as fascinating.

High-speed AVE trains link Córdoba to Seville in a little over an hour.

Mosque interior
EMPERORCOSAR / SHUTTERSTOCK ©

❶ INFORMATION

Information is available at various offices in town:

Alhambra Tourist Information Point (☑958 02 79 71; www.granadatur.com; Calle Real de la Alhambra Granada, Alhambra; ☺8.30am-8.30pm) Up in the Alhambra.

Municipal Tourist Office (☑958 24 82 80; www.granadatur.com; Plaza del Carmen 9; ☺9am-6pm Mon-Sat, to 2pm Sun) The official city tourist office.

Regional Tourist Office (☑958 57 52 02; www.andalucia.org; Calle Santa Ana 2; ☺9am-7.30pm Mon-Fri, 9.30am-3pm Sat & Sun) For information on the whole Andalucía region.

this.is:granada (☑958 21 02 39; www.thisisgranada.com; Plaza de Cuchilleros; ☺9.30am-2pm & 4-7pm Mon-Sat, to 6pm Sun) An agency selling tickets for flamenco shows, city tours and buses.

❶ GETTING THERE & AWAY

Granada Airport (Aeropuerto Federico García Lorca; ☑913 211 000; www.aena.es) is 17km west of the city. There are limited flights to Spanish and and European cities.

The **train station** (☑902 240 202; Avenida de Andaluces) is 1.5km northwest of the centre. Service includes Barcelona (7¾ hours), Madrid (four hours) and Seville (3¼ hours).

❶ GETTING AROUND

Opened in 2017, Granada's metro – in fact more a light rail link as all but a 3km stretch is overground – runs between Albolote in the north and Armilla in the southwest. Buses cover the city. Transit tickets cost €1.40.

Seville

◎ SIGHTS

Catedral de Sevilla & Giralda   Cathedral

(☑902 09 96 92; www.catedraldesevilla.es; Av de la Constitución; adult/child €9/free, incl rooftop guided tour €15; ☺11am-3.30pm Mon, to 5pm Tue-Sat, 2.30-6pm Sun) Seville's immense cathedral is awe-inspiring in its scale and majesty. The world's largest Gothic cathedral, it was built between 1434 and 1517 over the remains of what had previously been the city's main mosque. Highlights include the Giralda, the mighty bell tower, which incorporates the mosque's original minaret, the monumental tomb of Christopher Columbus, and the Capilla Mayor with an astonishing gold altarpiece.

Real Alcázar

Note that children must be aged 11 years and over to access the rooftop tours. Audio guides cost €3.

Real Alcázar
Palace

(📞954 50 23 24; www.alcazarsevilla.org; Patio de Banderas; adult/concession/child €11.50/2/free; ⏰9.30am-7pm Apr-Sep, to 5pm Oct-Mar) A magnificent marriage of Christian and Mudéjar architecture, Seville's Unesco-listed palace complex is a breathtaking spectacle. The site, which was originally developed as a fort in 913, has been revamped many times over the 11 centuries of its existence, most spectacularly in the 14th century when King Pedro added the sumptuous Palacio de Don Pedro, still today the Alcázar's crown jewel. More recently, the Alcázar featured as a location for the *Game of Thrones* TV series.

Hospital de los Venerables Sacerdotes
Museum

(📞954 56 26 96; www.focus.abengoa.es; Plaza de los Venerables 8; adult/child €10/5, 1st Thu of month free; ⏰10am-2pm Thu-Sun) This gem of a museum, housed in a former hospice

for ageing priests, is one of Seville's most rewarding. The artistic highlight is the Focus-Abengoa Foundation's collection of 17th-century paintings in the Centro Velázquez. It's not a big collection, but each work is a masterpiece of its genre – highlights include Diego Velázquez' *Santa Rufina*, his *Inmaculada Concepción*, and a sharply vivid portrait of *Santa Catalina* by Bartolomé Murillo.

Museo del Baile Flamenco
Museum

(📞954 34 03 11; www.museodelbaileflamenco. com; Calle Manuel Rojas Marcos 3; adult/ reduced €10/8; ⏰10am-7pm) The brainchild of *sevillana* flamenco dancer Cristina Hoyos, this museum showcases the dance with interactive displays, paintings and photos of revered erstwhile (and contemporary) performers, and a display of period dresses. Even better are the fantastic nightly performances (at 5pm, 7pm and 8.45pm; €22) staged both in the courtyard and the more intimate basement space (€30 including one drink). Combined museum and flamenco show tickets (€26) are a good option.

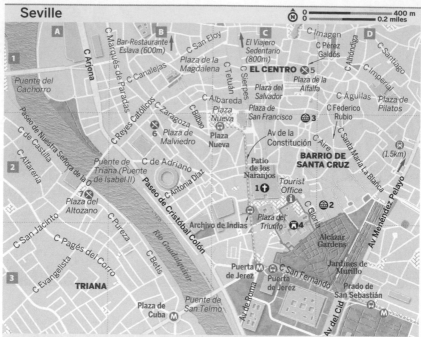

Seville

⊙ Sights
1 Catedral de Sevilla & Giralda	C2
2 Hospital de los Venerables Sacerdotes	D2
3 Museo del Baile Flamenco	C2
4 Real Alcázar	C3

⊗ Eating
5 Fargo	C1
6 La Brunilda	B2
7 Manu Jara Dulcería	A2

🟢 TOURS

Pancho Tours
Tours

(☑664 642 904; www.panchotours.com) FREE
Runs excellent free tours, although you're
welcome to tip the hard-working guide
who'll furnish you with an encyclopedia's
worth of anecdotes, stories, myths and
theories about Seville's fascinating past.
Tours kick off daily, normally at 11am –
check the website for exact details. Pancho
also offers bike tours (€25), skip-the-line
cathedral and Alcázar visits (from €12.50)
and nightlife tours (€10 to €15).

⊗ EATING & DRINKING

Manu Jara Dulcería
Pastries €

(☑675 873 674; Calle Pureza 5; pastries
€1.60-3.50; ☺10am-2pm & 4.30-8.30pm
Mon-Fri, 10am-8.30pm Sat-Sun) This exquisite
patisserie has heavenly cakes laid out in
a traditional wood-and-tile interior. Try
the creamy *milhojas (mille feuille,* aka
vanilla slice) with chantilly cream. There's
another branch in Nervión by the Sevilla FC
stadium, as well as a Bocasú stall in nearby
Triana Market.

La Brunilda
Tapas €

(☑954 22 04 81; www.labrunildatapas.com; Calle Galera 5; tapas €3.20-7.50; ☺1-4pm & 8.30-11.30pm Tue-Sat, 1-4pm Sun) A regular fixture on lists of Seville's best tapas joints, this backstreet Arenal bar is at the forefront of the city's new wave of gourmet eateries. The look is modern casual with big blue doors, brick arches and plain wooden tables, and the food is imaginative and good looking. The word is out, though, so arrive promptly or expect to queue.

Fargo
Andalucian €€

(☑955 27 65 52; www.facebook.com/fargobio; Calle Pérez Galdós 20; tapas €6-9, mains €15-21; ☺12.30-3pm & 7.30-11pm; ☑🐾) Excellent restaurant in the Alfalfa serving locally sourced, almost exclusively organic food, with a pleasantly different vibe: relaxed decor, low lighting and soft music create a calm ambience. Standouts are the salads, fresh juices, and ceviche using fish from Parque Nacional de Doñana. Plenty of vegetarian and vegan options, as well as natural (sulphate-free) wines; at the back, there's a children's area.

Bar-Restaurante Eslava
Fusion, Andalucian €€

(☑954 90 65 68; www.espacioeslava.com; Calle Eslava 3; tapas €2.90-4.50, restaurant mains €16.50-26; ☺bar 12.30-midnight Tue-Sat, restaurant 1.30-4pm & 8.30-midnight Tue-Sat) A hit with locals and savvy visitors, much-lauded Eslava shirks the traditional tilework and bullfighting posters of tapas-bar lore in favour of a simple blue space and a menu of creative contemporary dishes. Standouts include slow-cooked egg served on a mushroom cake, and memorable pork ribs in a honey and rosemary glaze. Expect crowds and a buzzing atmosphere.

El Viajero Sedentario
Cafe

(☑677 53 55 12; Alameda de Hércules 77; ☺9am-2pm & 6pm-2am) With its bright murals, shady courtyard and tiny book-stacked interior, this boho book cafe is a lovely place to hang out. From breakfast to the early hours people stop by, and it's not uncommon to find people dancing to low-key jazz tunes on sultry summer nights.

❶ INFORMATION

Tourist information is readily available at official tourist offices throughout the city.

Airport Tourist Office (☑954 78 20 35; www.andalucia.org; ☺9am-7.30pm Mon-Fri, 9.30am-3pm Sat & Sun)

Tourist Office (☑954 78 75 78; www.turismosevilla.org; Plaza del Triunfo 1; ☺9am-7.30pm Mon-Fri, 9.30am-7.30pm Sat & Sun)

Train Station Tourist Office (www.andalucia.org; Estación Santa Justa; ☺9am-7.30pm Mon-Fri, 9.30am-3pm Sat & Sun)

❶ GETTING THERE & AWAY

Seville Airport (Aeropuerto de Sevilla; ☑902 44 90 00; www.aena.es; A4, Km 532), 7km east of the city, has flights to/from Spanish cities and destinations across Europe. The **EA Bus** (☑955 01 00 10; www.tussam.es; one way/return €4/6) connects the airport to the city centre.

Frequent high-speed AVE trains serve Madrid (2½ hours). Other trains serve Barcelona (5½ hours) and Seville (3¼ hours).

❶ GETTING AROUND

Central Seville is relatively compact and best explored on foot. Getting around by bike is also an option – the city is flat and bike lanes are ubiquitous. Buses are also useful for getting around the main visitor areas. Driving is not recommended in the city centre.

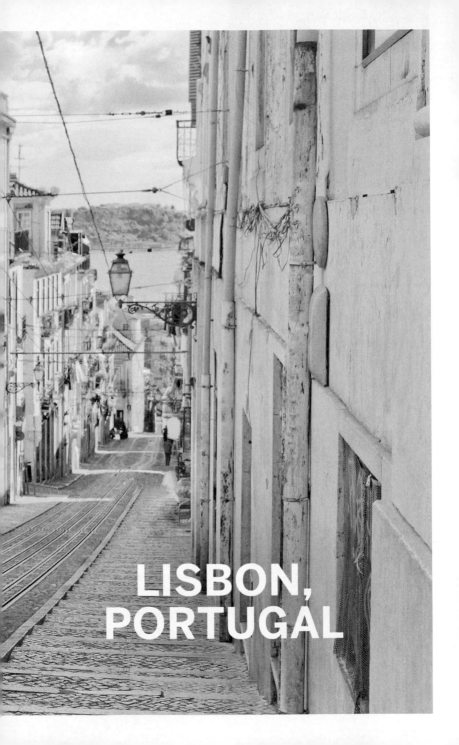

LISBON,
PORTUGAL

Lisbon, Portugal

Spread across steep hillsides that overlook the Rio Tejo, Lisbon has captivated visitors for centuries. Windswept vistas reveal the city in all its beauty: Roman and Moorish ruins, white-domed cathedrals, grand plazas and a labyrinth of narrow cobblestone lanes to lose oneself in. As yellow trams clatter through tree-lined streets, lisboêtas stroll through lamp-lit old quarters. Gossip is exchanged over wine at tiny restaurants while fado performers sing their hearts out. In nearby hoods, Lisbon reveals her youthful alter ego at bohemian bars and late-night street parties.

Two Days in Lisbon

Explore Lisbon's old town – **the Alfama** – on day one, perhaps taking a ride on old **tram 28E** part of the way. Round off with a **fado performance** in the evening. On day two explore **Belém** and the fantastical **Mosteiro dos Jerónimos** (p232). In the evening sample some of Lisbon's famous nightlife.

Four Days in Lisbon

On day three hit the museums – Lisbon has plenty dedicated to a range of subjects, but one highlight is the **Museu Nacional do Azulejo** (p238) packed with traditional tiles. On day four seek out a picnic lunch at the **Mercado da Ribeira** (p244) and laze away the day lusting over bird's-eye city views from **Miradouro da Graça** (p239) and chilling in the park below.

Finished in Lisbon? Fly to Copenhagen (p129) or Prague (p535).

Parque das Nações

Aeroporto de Lisboa

Av Infante Dom Henrique

Alameda dos Oceanos

Av Marechal Craveiro Lopes

Av General Norton de Matos

Av Lusiada

Campo Grande

Av das Forças Armadas

Av da República

Unidos da América

Av Almirante Gago Coutinho

Gomes da Costa

Av do Santo Condestável

Est de Chelas

Sete Rios

Av de Berna

Av Joao XXI

Av Calouste Gulbenkian

Saldanha

Parque Eduardo VII

Estefânia

Av Almirante Reis

Xabregas

Museu Nacional do Azulejo

Av Mouzinho de Albuquerque

Parque Florestal de Monsanto

Av da Ponte

Av Duarte Pacheco

Rato

R da Palma

Estrada do Alvito

Mosteiro dos Jerónimos

Estrela

Av Infante Santo

Cç do Combro

Bairro Alto

Av da Liberdade

R de Aurea

Alfama

Baixa

Av Infante Dom Henrique

Av de Ceuta

Lapa

Av 24 de Julho

Restelo

Alcântara

Ajuda

Museu Nacional dos Coches

Av da Índia

Belém

Museu Coleção Berardo

Ponte 25 de Abril

Rio Tejo

Central Lisbon Map (p240)

0 — 2 km
0 — 1 mile

Arriving in Lisbon

Aeroporto de Lisboa Convenient metro access to downtown from Aeroporto station; change at Alameda (green line) for Rossio and Baixa. Pay around €16 for the 15-minute taxi ride into town.

Sete Rios bus station Main long-distance bus terminal, adjacent to both Jardim Zoológico metro station and Sete Rios train station.

Gare do Oriente Lisbon's largest train station and bus terminal (services north and on to Spain), with metro station linking both to the rest of the city.

Where to Stay

Lisbon has an array of boutique hotels, upmarket hostels and both modern and old-fashioned guesthouses. Be sure to book ahead for high season (July to September). A word to those with weak knees and/or heavy bags: many guesthouses lack lifts, meaning you'll have to haul your luggage up three flights or more. If this disconcerts, be sure to book a place with a lift. Rates do not include a €2 per person per night tourist tax.

CHRIS-MUELLER / GETTY IMAGES ©

Mosteiro dos Jerónimos

One of Lisbon's top attractions is this Unesco-listed monastery in riverside Belém. With its intricately carved church and honey-stone cloisters guarded for centuries by menacing gargoyles and other fantastical stone beasts, it is one of the finest examples of the elaborate Manueline style.

Great For...

☑ Don't Miss

The rows of seats in the church are Portugal's first Renaissance woodcarvings.

The Monastery's Story

Belém's undisputed heart-stealer is the stuff of pure fantasy; a fusion of Diogo de Boitaca's creative vision and the spice-and-pepper dosh of Manuel I, who commissioned it to trumpet Vasco da Gama's discovery of a sea route to India in 1498. The building embodies the golden age of Portuguese discoveries and was funded using the profits from the spices Vasco da Gama brought back from the subcontinent. Building began in 1502 but was not completed for almost a century. Wrought for the glory of God, Jerónimos was once populated by monks of the Order of St Jerome, whose spiritual job for four centuries was to comfort sailors and pray for the king's soul. The monastery withstood the 1755 earthquake but fell into disrepair when the order was dissolved

Facade detail

GORAN BOGICEVIC / SHUTTERSTOCK ©

Jardim do Ultramar

Mosteiro dos Jerónimos ◎

Belém Train Station ◉

Av da Índia

Rio Tejo

ⓘ Need to Know

www.mosteirojeronimos.pt; Praça do Império; adult/child €10/5, free Sun until 2pm for Portuguese citizens/residents only; ◷10am-6.30pm Tue-Sun Jun-Sep, to 5.30pm Oct-May

✗ Take a Break

Grab a *pastel de Belém* (custard tart) at Antiga Confeitaria de Belém (p243) to enjoy in the gardens opposite.

★ Top Tip

Save a few euros by buying a combined ticket with the Museu Nacional de Arqueologia for €12, or enter free with the Lisboa Card.

in 1833. It was later used as a school and orphanage until about 1940. In 2007 the now much-discussed Treaty of Lisbon was signed here.

Vasco da Gama

Born in Alentejo in the 1460s, Vasco da Gama was the first European explorer to reach India by ship. This was a key moment in Portuguese history as it opened up trading links to Asia and established Portugal's maritime empire, the wealth from which made the country into a world superpower. Da Gama died from malaria on his third voyage to India in 1524.

The Church

Entering the church through the western portal, you'll notice tree-trunk-like columns that seem to grow into the ceiling, which is

itself a spiderweb of stone. Windows cast a soft golden light over the church. Superstar Vasco da Gama is interred in the lower chancel, just left of the entrance, opposite venerated 16th-century poet Luís Vaz de Camões. From the upper choir, there's a superb view of the church.

The Cloisters

There's nothing like the moment you walk into the honey-stone Manueline cloisters, dripping with organic detail in their delicately scalloped arches, twisting auger-shell turrets and columns intertwined with leaves, vines and knots. It will simply wow. Keep an eye out for symbols of the age such as the armillary sphere and the cross of the Military Order, plus gargoyles and fantastical beasties on the upper balustrade.

FARBREGAS HARELUYA / SHUTTERSTOCK ©

Lisbon's Trams

Quintessentially Lisbon, a ride on one of the city's typical yellow trams should be on your to-do list. Tram 28E climbs through the Moorish time capsule of Alfama – the city's most atmospheric neighbourhood stitched from labyrinthine lanes and rust-shaded rooftops – and rewards visitors with a fun and different perspective on urban life.

Great For

☑ Don't Miss

In addition to tram 28E, two other useful other city-centre tram routes are 15E and 18E.

Lisbon's Old Trams

Lisbon's old yellow streetcars are a nostalgic throwback to the early days of urban public transport and would have long since been pensioned off to a transport museum in most other European countries. They have survived largely because they were specially designed for a specific task – to trundle up and down central Lisbon's steep gradients (just like their San Francisco cousins) and would be much too expensive to replace. These roller-coaster vintage trams have been shaking, rattling and rolling around the city since 1901 (they were horse-pulled before that) and are called *remodelados* (remodelled). The name comes from the fact the cars were slightly upgraded in the 1990s to include such luxuries as late-20th-century brakes. There were once 27 lines in the city, but the construction of the metro put the

system into decline. Today there are only five lines left – *remodelados* run on all of them.

Tram Stops & Fares

Lisbon's tram stops are marked by a small yellow *paragem* (stop) sign strung from a lamp post or overhead wires. You'll pay more for a tram ride if you buy your ticket on board rather than purchasing a prepaid card. On-board one-way prices are €3, but a day pass costs just €6.40 and is valid on all of the city's public transport for 24 hours.

Tram 28E

The famous tram 28E, Lisbon's longest tram route, is extremely popular with tourists as it heads through Baixa, Graça, Alfama and Estrela, climbing the steep hill from Baixa to the castle and Alfama as well as three of the city's seven other hills en route. There are 34 stops between Campo Ourique in the west of the city centre to Martim Monique; the most interesting section is between Estrela and Graça. Trams depart every 11 minutes, though the last leaves fairly early (before 10pm). The experience on the museum-piece tram can be uncomfortable for some, with varnished wooden benches, steps and crowds of tourists getting in each other's way. But it's worth it for the ride – there's no cheaper way to see the city.

With groups of tourists crammed into a small space, sadly tram 28E is a happy hunting ground for pickpockets. Take the usual precautions to avoid being parted from your possessions.

Other Tram Routes

Two other useful routes are tram 15E, which runs from Praça da Figueira and Praça do Comércio via Alcântara to Belém, and tram 18E, running from Praça do Comércio via Alcântara to Ajuda. Tram 15E features space-age articulated trams with on-board machines for buying tickets and passes. Tram stops are marked by a small yellow *paragem* (stop) sign hanging from lamp posts or overhead wires.

Funiculars

Funiculars generally have somewhat shorter hours of operation. The **Ascensor da Bica** runs up Rua da Bica de Duarte Belo to Calçada do Combro; **Ascensor da Glória** runs from Praça dos Restauradores to Rua São Pedro de Alcântara; and **Ascensor da Lavra** goes from Largo da Anunciada near Av da Liberdade to Rua Câmara Pestana in Lavra.

Palácio Nacional da Pena

LEOKS / SHUTTERSTOCK ©

Day Trip: Sintra

A memorable side trip from Lisbon, Sintra is like a page torn from a fairy tale with its rippling mountains, dewy forests, exotic gardens and lush bevy of glittering palaces. Its Unesco World Heritage–listed centre, Sintra-Vila, is dotted with pastel-hued manors folded into luxuriant hills that roll down to the blue Atlantic.

Great For...

☑ Don't Miss

The extraordinary palace kitchens and banquet halls at Palácio Nacional de Sintra.

Palácio Nacional de Sintra

The star of Sintra-Vila is this **palace** (www.parquesdesintra.pt; Largo Rainha Dona Amélia; adult/child €10/8.50; ⊘9.30am-7pm), with its iconic twin conical chimneys and lavish, whimsical interior, which is a mix of Moorish and Manueline styles. It has arabesque courtyards, barley-twist columns and 15th- and 16th-century geometric *azulejos* (hand-painted tiles) – among Portugal's oldest.

Quinta da Regaleira

This magical **villa and gardens** (www.regaleira.pt; Rua Barbosa du Bocage; adult/child €6/4, tours €12/8; ⊘9.30am-7pm Apr-Sep, to 5pm Oct-Mar) is a neo-Manueline extravaganza, dreamed up by Italian opera-set designer, Luigi Manini, under the orders of Brazilian coffee tycoon, António Carvalho Monteiro, aka 'Monteiro dos Milhões' (Moneybags Monteiro). The

Parque da Pena

ADWO / SHUTTERSTOCK ©

villa is surprisingly homely inside, despite its ferociously carved fireplaces, frescos and Venetian-glass mosaics. Keep an eye out for mythological and Knights Templar symbols.

Palácio Nacional da Pena

Rising from a thickly wooded peak and often enshrouded in swirling mist, **Palácio Nacional da Pena** (www.parquesdesintra. pt; combined ticket with Parque da Pena adult/child €14/12.50; ☺9.45am-7pm) is a wacky confection of onion domes, Moorish keyhole gates, writhing stone snakes and crenellated towers in pinks and lemons. It is considered the greatest expression of 19th-century romanticism in Portugal.

Castelo dos Mouros

Soaring 412m above sea level, this mist-enshrouded ruined **castle** (www.parquesde

sintra.pt; adult/child €8/6.50; ☺9.30am-8pm) looms high above the surrounding forest. When the clouds peel away, the vistas over Sintra's palace-dotted hill and dale, across to the glittering Atlantic are – like the climb – breathtaking. The 10th-century Moorish castle's dizzying ramparts stretch across the mountain ridges and past moss-clad boulders the size of small buses.

Tickets and info are available at the entrance (open 10am to 6pm).

Parque da Pena

Nearly topped by King Ferdinand II's whimsical Palácio Nacional da Pena (only Cruz Alta, at 529m, is higher), these romantic **gardens** (☎219 237 300; www.parquesde sintra.pt; adult/child €7.50/6.50, combined ticket with Palácio Nacional da Pena €14/12.50; ☺9.30am-8pm) are filled with tropical plants, huge redwoods and fern trees, camellias, rhododendrons and lakes (note the castle-shaped duck houses for web-footed royalty!). Save by buying a combined ticket if you want to visit Palácio Nacional da Pena, too.

◎ SIGHTS

Castelo de São Jorge   Castle

(www.castelodesaojorge.pt; adult/student/
child €8.50/4/free; ◷9am-9pm Mar-Oct, to
6pm Nov-Feb) Towering dramatically above
Lisbon, the mid-11th-century hilltop fortifications of Castelo de São Jorge sneak into
almost every snapshot. Roam its snaking
ramparts and pine-shaded courtyards
for superlative views over the city's red
rooftops to the river. Three guided tours
daily (in Portuguese, English and Spanish)
at 10.30am, 1pm and 4pm are included
in the admission price (additional tours
available).

Convento do Carmo & Museu Arqueológico   Ruins

(www.museuarqueologicodocarmo.pt; Largo do
Carmo; adult/child €4/free; ◷10am-7pm Mon-
Sat Jun-Sep, to 6pm Oct-May) Soaring above
Lisbon, the skeletal Convento do Carmo was

> *Castelo de São Jorge sneaks into almost every snapshot*

all but devoured by the 1755 earthquake and
that's precisely what makes it so captivating. Its shattered pillars and wishbone-like
arches are completely exposed to the
elements. The Museu Arqueológico shelters
archaeological treasures, such as 4th-
century sarcophagi, griffin-covered column
fragments, 16th-century *azulejo* (hand-
painted tile) panels and two gruesome
16th-century Peruvian mummies.

Museu Nacional do Azulejo   Museum

(☎218 100 340; www.museudoazulejo.pt;
Rua Madre de Deus 4; adult/child €5/free;
◷10am-6pm Tue-Sun) Housed in a sublime
16th-century convent, Lisbon's Museu
Nacional do Azulejo covers the entire
azulejo (hand-painted tile) spectrum. Star
exhibits feature a 36m-long panel depicting
pre-earthquake Lisbon, a Manueline
cloister with web-like vaulting and exquisite
blue-and-white *azulejos,* and a gold-
smothered baroque chapel.

Sé de Lisboa   Cathedral

(Largo de Sé; ◷9am-7pm Tue-Sat, to 5pm Sun &
Mon) FREE The fortress-like Sé de Lisboa is

Castelo de São Jorge

one of Lisbon's icons. It was built in 1150 on the site of a mosque soon after Christians recaptured the city from the Moors. It was sensitively restored in the 1930s. Despite the masses outside, the rib-vaulted interior, lit by a rose window, is calm. Stroll around the cathedral to spy leering gargoyles above the orange trees.

Museu do Fado
Museum

(www.museudofado.pt; Largo do Chafariz de Dentro; adult/child €5/3; ⊘10am-6pm Tue-Sun) Fado (traditional Portuguese melancholic song) was born in Alfama. Immerse yourself in its bittersweet symphonies at Museu do Fado. This engaging museum traces fado's history from its working-class roots to international stardom.

Igreja & Museu São Roque
Church, Museum

(www.museu-saoroque.com; Largo Trindade Coelho; church free, museum adult/child €2.50/free, 10am-2pm Sun free; ⊘2-7pm Mon, 10am-7pm Tue, Wed & Fri-Sun, 10am-8pm Thu, shorter hours in winter) The plain facade of 16th-century Jesuit Igreja de São Roque belies its dazzling interior of gold, marble and Florentine *azulejos* – bankrolled by Brazilian riches. Its star attraction is **Capela de São João Baptista**, a lavish confection of amethyst, alabaster, lapis lazuli and Carrara marble. The **museum** adjoining the church is packed with elaborate sacred art and holy relics.

Praça do Comércio
Plaza

(Terreiro do Paço; Praça do Comércio) With its grand 18th-century arcades, lemon-meringue facades and mosaic cobbles, the riverfront Praça do Comércio is a square to out-pomp them all. Everyone arriving by boat used to disembark here, and it still feels like the gateway to Lisbon, thronging with activity and rattling trams.

Museu Nacional dos Coches
Museum

(www.museudoscoches.pt; Av da Índia 136; €8, combined ticket with Antigo Picadeiro Real €10, free Sun to 2pm for Portuguese citizens/residents only; ⊘10am-6pm Tue-Sun) Cinderella

🔭 Bird's-Eye City Views

Hitch a ride on vintage Ascensor da Glória from Praça dos Restauradores or puff your way up steep Calçada da Glória to **Miradouro de São Pedro de Alcântara** (Rua São Pedro de Alcântara; ⊘viewpoint 24hr, kiosk 10am-midnight Sun-Wed, to 2am Thu-Sat), a terrific hilltop viewpoint, clad with fountains, Greek busts and open-air kiosk selling wine, beer and snacks.

Miradouro da Graça (Largo da Graça) is a much-loved summertime hangout with incredible castle and hillside views, and one of the best sunset shows in town.

Torre de Belém (www.torrebelem.pt; Av de Brasília; adult/child €6/3, free Sun until 2pm for Portuguese citizens/residents only; ⊘10am-6.30pm Tue-Sun May-Sep, to 5.30pm Oct-Apr) is the spot to get up high in Belém: scale the tower at this Unesco World Heritage–listed fortress for sublime views.

The view from Miradouro da Graça
STEFANO_VALERI / SHUTTERSTOCK ©

wannabes delight in Portugal's most visited museum, which dazzles with its world-class collection of 70 17th- to 19th-century coaches in an ultramodern (and some might say inappropriately contrasting) space that debuted in 2015. Don't miss Pope Clement XI's stunning ride, the scarlet-and-gold *Coach of the Oceans,* or the old royal riding school, **Antigo Picadeiro Real** (Old Royal Riding School; www.museudoscoches.pt; Praça Afonso de Albuquerque; €4, combined ticket with Museu Nacional

Central Lisbon

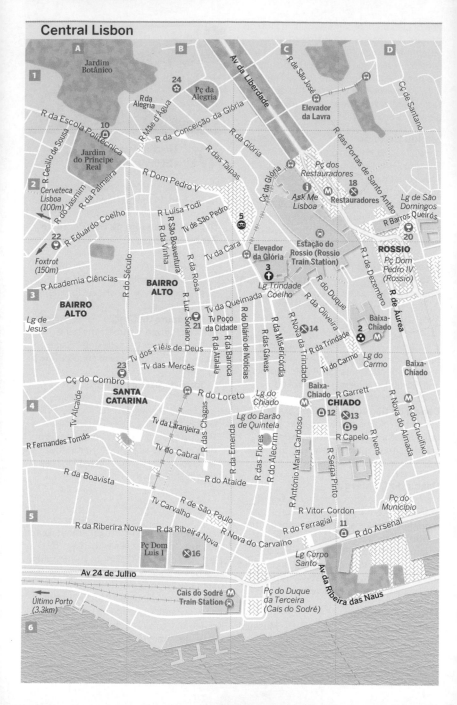

Jardim Botânico

24

Pç da Alegria

Av da Liberdade

R de São José

Cç de Santano

R da Alegria

R da Escola Politécnica

R Cecílio de Sousa

R Mãe d'Água

R da Conceição da Glória

R da Glória

Elevador da Lavra

R das Portas de Santo Antão

10

Jardim do Príncipe Real

R do Jasmim

R da Palmeira

R Dom Pedro V

R das Taipas

Cç da Glória

Pç dos Restauradores

18

Lg de São Domingos

Cerveteca Lisboa (100m)

R Luísa Todi

R de São Pedro

Tv de São Pedro

5

Ask Me Lisboa

Restauradores

R Barros Queirós

22

R Eduardo Coelho

R da Boaventura

R da Vinha

Tv da Cara

Elevador da Glória

Estação do Rossio (Rossio Train Station)

ROSSIO

20

Foxtrot (150m)

R Academia Ciências

R do Século

BAIRRO ALTO

R da Rosa

R Luz Soriano

3

Lg Trindade Coelho

R do Duque

Pç Dom Pedro IV (Rossio)

R de Áurea

BAIRRO ALTO

Tv da Queimada

R da Oliveira

Lg de Jesus

21

Tv Poço da Cidade

R do Diário de Notícias

R da Barroca

R da Atalaia

R das Gáveas

R da Misericórdia

R Nova da Trindade

14

R da Trindade

Baixa-Chiado

2

Baixa-Chiado

23

Tv dos Fiéis de Deus

Tv das Mercês

Tv do Carmo

Lg do Carmo

Baixa-Chiado

Cç do Combro

SANTA CATARINA

R do Loreto

Lg do Chiado

Baixa-Chiado

R Garrett

CHIADO

12

13

R Nova do Almada

Tv Alcaide

Tv da Laranjeira

R das Chagas

Lg do Barão de Quintela

9

R Capelo

R Ivens

Baixa-Chiado

R Fernandes Tomás

Tv do Cabral

R da Emenda

R das Flores

R do Alecrim

R António Maria Cardoso

R Serpa Pinto

Pç do Município

R da Boavista

R do Ataíde

R Vitor Cordon

Tv Carvalho

R de São Paulo

11

R do Ferragial

R do Arsenal

R da Ribeira Nova

R da Ribeira Nova

R Nova do Carvalho

Lg Corpo Santo

Pç Dom Luís I

16

Av da Ribeira das Naus

Av 24 de Julho

Último Porto (3.3km)

Cais do Sodré Train Station

Pç do Duque da Terceira (Cais do Sodré)

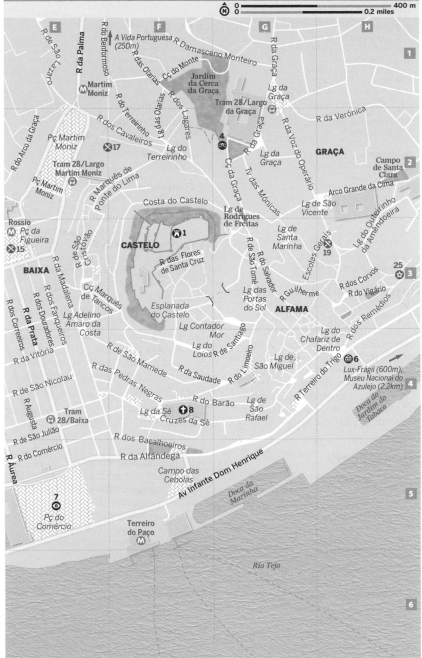

N 0 — 400 m
0 — 0.2 miles

R de São Lázaro
R da Palma
R do Benformoso
A Vida Portuguesa (250m)
R das Olarias
R Damasceno Monteiro
Cç do Monte
R da Graça

Jardim da Cerca da Graça
Tram 28/Largo da Graça
Lg da Graça
R da Verónica

Martim Moniz Ⓜ
R do Terreirinho
R dos Cavaleiros
R dos Lagares
Olarias
R da Voz do Operário

Pç Martim Moniz
Ⓧ17
Lg do Terreirinho
4
Lg da Graça
GRAÇA

Tram 28/Largo Martim Moniz
R Marquês de Ponte do Lima
Cç da Graça
Tv das Mónicas

Pç Martim Moniz
Costa do Castelo
Lg de Rodrigues de Freitas
Lg de São Vicente
Campo de Santa Clara

Rossio Ⓜ
Pç da Figueira
Ⓧ15
R São Cristóvão
①1
Lg de Santa Marinha
Arco Grande da Cima
Lg do Outeirinho da Amendoeira

BAIXA
CASTELO
R das Flores de Santa Cruz
Escolas Gerais
19Ⓧ
25Ⓧ

R da Madalena
R dos Fanqueiros
R dos Douradores
R dos Correeiros
R da Prata
Cç Marquês de Tancos
R de São Tomé
R do Salvador
R Guilherme
ALFAMA
R dos Corvos
R do Vigário
R dos Remédios

Esplanada do Castelo
Lg das Portas do Sol

R da Vitória
R de São Nicolau
Cç Adelino Amaro da Costa
Lg Contador Mor
Lg do Chafariz de Dentro
6⊕
Lux-Frágil (600m); Museu Nacional do Azulejo (2.2km)

R Augusta
R de São Mamede
R das Pedras Negras
Lg do Loios
R de Santiago
Lg de São Miguel
R Terreiro do Trigo
Doca do Jardim do Tabaco

Tram 28/Baixa Ⓗ
R da Saudade
R do Limoeiro
Lg de São Rafael
R de São Julião
R do Barão
Lg da Sé
①8
Cruzes da Sé
Lg de São Rafael

R Áurea
R do Comércio
R dos Bacalhoeiros
R da Alfândega
Campo das Cebolas
Av Infante Dom Henrique
Doca da Marinha

7
◎
Pç do Comércio
Terreiro do Paço Ⓜ

Rio Tejo

Central Lisbon

dos Coches €10, free Sun to 2pm for Portuguese citizens/residents only; ⏰10am-6pm Tue-Sun), across the street.

Museu Coleção Berardo   Museum

(www.museuberardo.pt; Praça do Império; adult/student/child under 6yr €5/2.50/free, free Sat; ⏰10am-7pm) Culture fiends can get their contemporary-art fix at Museu Coleção Berardo, the star of the Centro Cultural de Belém. The ultrawhite, minimalist gallery displays billionaire José Berardo's eye-popping collection of abstract, surreal and pop art, including Hockney, Lichten-stein, Warhol and Pollock originals.

🛍 SHOPPING

A Vida Portuguesa   Gifts & Souvenirs

(www.avidaportuguesa.com; Rua Anchieta 11; ⏰10am-8pm Mon-Sat, from 11am Sun) A flash-back to the late 19th century with its high ceilings and polished cabinets, this former warehouse and perfume factory lures nostalgics with its all-Portuguese products, from retro-wrapped Tricona sardines to Claus Porto soaps, and heart-embellished Viana do Castelo embroideries to Bordalo Pinheiro porcelain swallows. There's also a location in **Intendente** (www.avidaportuguesa.com; Largo do Intendente 23; ⏰10.30am-7.30pm).

Loja das Conservas   Food

(www.facebook.com/lojadasconservas; Rua do Arsenal 130; ⏰10am-8pm Mon-Sat, from noon Sun) What appears to be a gallery is on closer inspection a fascinating temple to tinned fish (or *conservas* as the Portuguese say) – the result of an industry on its death-bed revived by a savvy marketing about-face and new generations of hipsters. The retro-wrapped tins, displayed along with the history of each canning factory, are artworks.

Loja do Burel   Clothing

(www.burelfactory.com; Rua Serpa Pinto 15B; ⏰10am-8pm Mon-Sat, 11am-7pm Sun) Once a clothing staple of Serra da Estrela mountain-dwelling shepherds, Burel, a Portuguese black wool, was all but left to disappear until this company single-handedly resurrected the industry, giving it a stylish makeover fit for 21st-century fashion. The colourful blankets, hand-bags, jackets, hats and other home decor items aren't like anything anyone has back home.

Embaixada   Shopping Centre

(www.embaixadalx.pt; Praça do Príncipe Real 26; ⏰noon-8pm Mon-Fri, 11am-7pm Sat & Sun, restaurants to 2am) Take an exquisite 19th-century neo-Moorish palace and fill it with fashion, design and concept stores on the cutting-edge of cool and you have one of Lisbon's most exciting new shopping experiences: Embaixada. Centred on a grand sweeping staircase and courtyard are boutiques selling everything from vintage records to organic cosmetics, eco-homewares, contemporary Portuguese ceramics and catwalk styles.

❌ EATING

Antiga Confeitaria de Belém
Pastries €

(Pastéis de Belém; www.pasteisdebelem.pt; Rua de Belém 84-92; pastries from €1.10; ⊙8am-11pm Oct-Jun, to midnight Jul-Sep) Since 1837 this patisserie has been transporting locals to sugar-coated nirvana with heavenly *pastéis de Belém*. The crisp pastry nests are filled with custard cream, baked at 200°C for that perfect golden crust, then lightly dusted with cinnamon. Admire *azulejos* in the vaulted rooms or devour a still-warm tart at the counter and try to guess the secret ingredient.

Casa Bota Feijão
Portuguese €

(☑218 532 489; www.restaurantebotafeijao.pt; Rua Conselheiro Lopo Vaz 5; half/whole portions €8.50/12; ⊙8am-8pm Mon-Fri) Don't be fooled by the nondescript decor and railroad-track views – when a tucked-away place is this crowded with locals at lunchtime midweek, it must be doing something right. Everyone's here for one thing and one thing only: Bairrada-style *leitão* – suckling pig spit-roasted on an open fire until juicy and meltingly tender, doused in a beautiful peppery garlic sauce.

Ti-Natércia
Portuguese €

(☑218 862 133; Rua Escola Gerais 54; mains €5.50-12; ⊙7pm-midnight Tue-Fri, noon-3pm & 7pm midnight Sat) 'Aunt' Natércia and her downright delicious Portuguese home cooking is a tough ticket: there are but a mere six tables and they fill up fast. She'll talk your ear off (and doesn't mince words – some have been rubbed the wrong way; vegetarians in particular should avoid) while you devour her excellent take on

the classics. Reservations are essential (cash only).

Pinóquio
Portuguese €€

(☑213 465 106; www.restaurantepinoquio.pt; Praça dos Restauradores 79; mains €17-26; ⊙noon-midnight; 🐦) Bustling Pinóquio is easy to miss as it's tucked into a *praça* corner partially obstructed by a souvenir kiosk. Dressed in white tablecloths against pea-green walls, it's distinctly old school, with indomitable waiters slinging a stunning slew of classic dishes: *arroz de pato* (duck rice), seafood *feijoada*, *arroz de bacalhau* (codfish rice), and pork chops with almonds and coriander.

O Zé da Mouraria
Portuguese €€

(☑218 865 436; Rua João do Outeiro 24; mains for 2 €16.50-33.50; ⊙noon-4pm Mon-Sat; 🐦) Don't be fooled by the saloon-like doors, there's a typical Portuguese *tasca* (tavern) inside: homey local cuisine, blue-and-white-tiled walls, chequered tablecloths – and it's one of Lisbon's best. The house-baked cod loaded with chickpeas, onions, garlic and olive oil is rightfully popular, and daily specials (duck rice on Wednesday!) make return trips tempting. Service is a lost cause, however.

Último Porto
Seafood €€

(☑308 808 939; Estação Marítima da Rocha do Conde de Óbidos; mains €8.50-17; ⊙8am-4.30pm Mon-Sat) An absolute local's secret for a reason, this top seafooder takes an act of God to find. Hidden among the shipping-container cranes of the Port of Lisbon, fantastically simple grilled fish paired with top Alentejan and Douro wines draw locals in droves. With shipping containers and departmental port buildings framing the ambience, María do Céu oversees a parking-lot-style grill.

Bairro de Avillez
Portuguese €€

(☑215 830 290; www.bairrodoavillez.pt; Rua Nova da Trindade 18; small plates €2-16.50; mains €7-18.50; ⊙noon-midnight; 🐦) Step into the latest culinary dream by Portugal's most famous chef – Michelin-starred maestro José Avillez – who has set up

The casual space exudes understated style amid the original stone flooring and gorgeous hardwood tables, but it's Pessoa's outrageously good nouveau Portuguese cuisine that draws the foodie flock from far and wide.

🍽️ A Market Lunch

Doing trade in fresh fruit and veg, fish and flowers since 1892, domed market hall **Mercado da Ribeira** (www.timeout market.com; Av 24 de Julho; ⊗10am-midnight Sun-Wed, to 2am Thu-Sat, traditional market 6am-2pm Mon-Sat; 🛜) is a gourmet food court and chaotic culinary microcosm: Garrafeira Nacional wines, Café de São Bento steaks, Manteigaria Silva cold cuts and Michelin-star chef creations from Henrique Sá Pessoa. Browse in the morning followed by lunch at a kiosk here. In Baixa, tented market-cum-glorious food court **Mercado da Baixa** (www.adbaixapombalina.pt/mercado-da-baixa; Praça da Figueira; ⊗10am-10pm Fri-Sun last weekend of month), c 1855, is the foodie hot spot to drool over cheese, wine, smoked sausages and other gourmet goodies, and to eat, drink and lunch.

Diners at Mercado da Ribeira
RADU BERCAN / SHUTTERSTOCK ©

his gastronomic dream destination as a 'neighbourhood' featuring several dining environments, including everything from a traditional tavern to an avant-garde gourmet cabaret.

Alma · Modern Portuguese €€€

(📞213 470 650; www.almalisboa.pt; Rua Anchieta 15; mains €32-36, tasting menus €110-120; ⊗noon-3pm & 7-11pm Tue-Sun; 🛜) Two-Michelin-starred Henrique Sá Pessoa's flagship Alma is one of Portugal's destination restaurants and, in our humble opinion, Lisbon's best gourmet dining experience.

Feitoria · Modern Portuguese €€€

(📞210 400 208; www.restaurantefeitoria.com; Altis Belém Hotel, Doca do Bom Sucesso; mains €39-40, tasting menus €85-135, with wine €130-195; ⊗7.30-10pm Mon-Sat; 🛜) A defining dining experience awaits at chef João Rodrigues' slick, contemporary, Michelin-starred restaurant overlooking the riverfront. Rich textures and clean, bright flavours dominate throughout three tasting menus, which showcase Portugal's rich and vibrant bounty. Pigeon with wild mushrooms, foie gras and truffles, Algarve scarlet shrimp and Iberian pork neck progressively exhilarate with every bite.

🍸 DRINKING & NIGHTLIFE

Park · Bar

(www.facebook.com/parklisboaofficial; Calçada do Combro 58; ⊗1pm-2am Tue-Sat, to 8pm Sun; 🛜) If only all multistorey car parks were like this... Take the lift to the 5th floor, and head up and around to the top, which has been transformed into one of Lisbon's hippest rooftop bars, with sweeping views reaching right down to the Rio Tejo and over the bell towers of Igreja de Santa Catarina.

BA Wine Bar do Bairro Alto · Wine Bar

(📞213 461 182; bawinebar@gmail.com; Rua da Rosa 107; ⊗6-11pm Tue-Sun; 🛜) Reserve ahead unless you want to get shut out of Bairro Alto's best wine bar, where the genuinely welcoming staff will offer you three fantastic tasting choices based on your wine proclivities (wines from €5; tasting boards for one/four €13/47). The cheeses (from small artisanal producers) and charcuterie (melt-in-your-mouth black-pork *presuntos*) are not to be missed, either. Reservations are essential.

Cinco Lounge
Lounge

(www.cincolounge.com; Rua Ruben António Leitão 17; ⏰9pm-2am) Take an award-winning London-born mixologist, Dave Palethorpe, add a candlelit, turquoise-kissed setting and give it a funky twist – *et voilà* – you have Cinco Lounge. Come here to converse, sip legendary cocktails (€7.50 to €15) or join a cocktail-mixing workshop. Cash only.

Foxtrot
Bar

(www.barfoxtrot.com; Tv Santa Teresa 28; ⏰6pm-2am Mon-Thu, to 3am Fri & Sat, 8pm-2am Sun; 🛜) A cuckoo-clock doorbell announces new arrivals to this dark, decadent slither of art-nouveau glamour, in the bar business since 1978. Foxtrot keeps the mood mellow with jazzy beats and excruciatingly attentive mixology detailed on a tracing-paper menu (cocktails €7 to €15). It's a wonderfully moody spot for a drink.

Cerveteca Lisboa
Craft Beer

(www.cervetecalisboa.com; Praça das Flores 62; ⏰3.30pm-1am Sun-Thu, to 2am Fri & Sat; 🛜) Lisbon's best craft-beer bar is a boozy godsend: 14 oft-changing taps (including two hand pumps) focusing on local and Northern European artisanal brews, including numerous local microbreweries. Not only will hopheads rejoice at IPAs from Lisbon including standouts such as Dois Corvos and 8ª Colina, but having choice alone inspires cartwheels. *Adeus*, tasteless lagers!

A Ginjinha
Bar

(Largo de São Domingos 8; ⏰9am-10pm) Hipsters, old men in flat caps, office workers and tourists all meet at this microscopic *ginjinha* (cherry liqueur) bar for that moment of cherry-licking, pip-spitting pleasure (€1.40 a shot).

Lux-Frágil
Club

(www.luxfragil.com; Av Infante D Henrique, Armazém A, Cais de Pedra; ⏰11pm-6am Thu-Sat) Lisbon's ice-cool, must-see club, glammy Lux hosts big-name DJs spinning

> *Hipsters, old men in flat caps, office workers and tourists all meet at this ginjinha bar*

A Ginjinha

SARIONUNES / SHUTTERSTOCK ©

★ **Top Five Places to Eat**

Alma (p244)

Mercado da Ribeira (p244)

Pinóquio (p243)

O Zé da Mouraria (p243)

Antiga Confeitaria de Belém (p243)

From left: *Pastéis de Nata* (Portuguese egg tarts); O Zé da Mouraria (p243); Foxtrot (p245)

electro and house. It was started by late Lisbon nightlife impresario Marcel Reis and is part-owned by John Malkovich. Grab a spot on the terrace to see the sun rise over the Rio Tejo, or chill like a king or queen on the throne-like giant interior chairs.

😊 ENTERTAINMENT

Hot Clube de Portugal   Jazz

(📞213 460 305; www.hcp.pt; Praça da Alegria 48; ⏱10pm-2am Tue-Sat) As hot as its name suggests, this small, poster-plastered cellar (and newly added garden) has staged top-drawer jazz acts since the 1940s. It's considered one of Europe's best.

Mesa de Frades   Live Music

(📞917 029 436; www.facebook.com/mesade fradeslisboa; Rua dos Remédios 139A; prix-fixe shows €50; ⏱8pm-2.30am Mon-Sat) A magical place to hear fado, tiny Mesa de Frades used to be a chapel. It's tiled with

exquisite *azulejos* and has just a handful of tables, including a dark and sexy mezzanine level. Shows begin at around 10.30pm.

ℹ️ INFORMATION

Ask Me Lisboa (📞213 463 314; www.askme lisboa.com; Praça dos Restauradores, Palácio Foz; ⏱9am-8pm) Lisbon's largest and most helpful tourist office faces Praça dos Restauradores inside the Palácio Foz. Has maps and information, and books accommodation and rental cars.

ℹ️ GETTING THERE & AWAY

AIR

Situated around 6km north of the centre, the ultramodern **Aeroporto de Lisboa** (Lisbon Airport; 📞218 413 500; www.ana.pt/pt/lis/home; Alameda das Comunidades Portuguesas) oper-

ates direct flights to major international hubs including London, New York, Paris and Frankfurt. Low-cost carriers (Norwegian, easyJet, Ryanair, Transavia, Blue Air and Wizz Air) leave from the less efficient Terminal 2 – you'll need to factor in extra time for the shuttle ride if arriving at the airport on the metro.

BUS

Lisbon's main long-distance bus terminal is **Terminal Rodoviário de Sete Rios** (Praça General Humberto Delgado, Rua das Laranjeiras), adjacent to both Jardim Zoológico metro station and Sete Rios train station.

TRAIN

Lisbon is linked by train to other major cities. Check the website of **Comboios de Portugal** (☑707 210 220; www.cp.pt) for schedules – cheaper promo fares are often available online.

ⓘ GETTING AROUND

Lisboa Move-me (www.move-me.mobi; iOS/Android) and **Lisboa Viagem by Transporlis** (Android) are city-transportation apps for real-time routes and arrival/departure times.

Metro Lisbon's subway is the quickest way around; useful for Gare do Oriente and Parque das Nações. Runs from 6.30am to 1am.

Tram The best way to get up into hilltop neighbourhoods (Alfama, Castelo, Graça) and western neighbourhoods (Estrela, Campo de Ourique). Runs from 5am/6am to about 10pm/11pm.

Bus Particularly good for reaching Príncipe Real.

Paris, France

The enchanting French capital is awash with iconic landmarks, world-class museums and galleries safeguarding one of the world's finest art repositories. Cream-stone Haussmann townhouses, dove-grey mansard rooftops, lamp-lit bridges and fountain-clad parks are other integral elements of the city fabric. Dining is a quintessential part of the Parisian experience – whether it be in traditional bistros, Michelin-starred restaurants, boulangeries (bakeries) or street markets. But against this cinematic backdrop, Paris' real magic lies in the unexpected: hidden parks, small unsung museums and sun-spangled cafe pavement terraces.

Two Days in Paris

Start early with the **Louvre** (p256) or the **Eiffel Tower** (p252). Afterwards, head to the Champs-Élysées to shop and climb the **Arc de Triomphe** (p278). On day two take a boat cruise along the Seine and visit **Musée d'Orsay** (p279) and the impossibly romantic **Musée Rodin** (p279); or trade both for a **Versailles** (p266) day trip. Make soulful St-Germain your dinner date.

Four Days in Paris

Devote day three to exploring Montmartre. On day four, begin with a top sight you missed on day one. Picnic in a Parisian park and spend the afternoon scouting out treasures at the **St-Ouen flea market** (p281) or checking out famous graves in **Cimetière du Père Lachaise** (p279). By night, take in a performance at **Opéra Bastille** (p285) or **Philharmonie de Paris** (p286) and bar crawl in Le Marais.

Not finished with France? Head south to Provence (p289).

St-Germain & Les Invalides Map (p274)
Les Halles, Le Marais & the Islands Map (p276)
Western Paris, Champs-Élysées,
Latin Quarter Map (p280)

Arriving in Paris

Charles de Gaulle Airport Trains (RER), buses and night buses to the city centre €6 to €18; taxi €50 to €55.

Orly Airport Trains (Orlyval then RER), buses and night buses to the city centre €8.70 to €13.25; T7 tram to Villejuif-Louis Aragon, then metro to centre (€3.80); a taxi costs from €30 to €35.

Gare du Nord train station Within central Paris; served by metro (€1.90).

Where to Stay

Paris has a wealth of accommodation for all budgets, but it's often *complet* (full) well in advance. Reservations are recommended year-round and are essential during the warmer months (April to October) and all public and school holidays.

Parisian hotel rooms tend to be small by international standards.

Breakfast is rarely included in hotel rates.

RCLASSENLAYOUTS / GETTY IMAGES ©

Eiffel Tower

Paris today is unimaginable without its signature spire. Originally constructed as a temporary 1889 Exposition Universelle exhibit, it went on to become the defining fixture of the city's skyline.

Great For...

☑ Don't Miss

The view of the tower in lights – each night, every hour on the hour, the entire tower sparkles for five minutes with 20,000 6-watt lights. For the best view of the light show, head across the Seine to the Jardins du Trocadéro.

Named after its designer, Gustave Eiffel, the Tour Eiffel was built for the 1889 Exposition Universelle (World Fair). It took 300 workers, 2.5 million rivets and two years of non-stop labour to assemble. Upon completion the tower became the tallest human-made structure in the world (324m or 1063ft) – a record held until the completion of the Chrysler Building in New York (1930). This symbol of the modern age faced massive opposition from Paris' artistic and literary elite, and the 'metal asparagus', as some Parisians derided it, was originally slated to be torn down in 1909. It was spared only because it proved an ideal platform for the transmitting antennas needed for the new-fangled science of radio-telegraphy.

Tickets & Queues

Buy tickets in advance online to avoid monumental queues. Print your ticket or show

Parc du Champ de Mars, as seen from the Eiffel Tower

❶ Need to Know

Map p274; 📞08 92 70 12 39; www.toureiffel.
paris; Champ de Mars, 5 av Anatole France, 7e;
adult/child lift to top €25/12.50, lift to 2nd fl
€16/8, stairs to 2nd fl €10/5; ⏲lifts & stairs
9am-12.45am mid-Jun–Aug, lifts 9.30am-
11.45pm, stairs 9.30am-6.30pm Sep–mid-Jun;
Ⓜ Bir Hakeim or RER Champ de Mars–Tour Eiffel

✕ Take a Break

At the tower's restaurants, Macaroon
Bar or top-floor Bar à Champagne.

★ Top Tip

Head here at dusk for the best daytime
vistas and glittering night-time city views.

1st Floor

Of the tower's three floors, the 1st (57m)
has the most space, but the least impressive views. The glass-enclosed **Pavillon
Ferrié** houses an immersion film along
with a small cafe and souvenir shop, while
the outer walkway features a discovery
circuit to help visitors learn more about
the tower's ingenious design. Check out
the sections of glass flooring that proffer a
dizzying view of the ant like people walking
on the ground far below.

This level also hosts the casual brasserie
restaurant, **58 Tour Eiffel** (Map p274; 📞08
25 56 66 62; www.restaurants-toureiffel.com;
menus lunch €41, dinner €86-125; ⏲11.30am-
3.30pm & 6.30-11pm; 📷🕁).

Not all lifts stop at the 1st floor (check
before ascending), but it's an easy walk
down from the 2nd floor should you accidentally end up one floor too high.

2nd Floor

Views from the 2nd floor (115m) are the
best – impressively high, but still close

it on a smartphone screen. If you can't
reserve your tickets ahead of time, expect
waits of well over an hour in high season.

Stair tickets can't be reserved online.
They are sold at the south pillar, where the
staircase can also be accessed: the climb
consists of 360 steps to the 1st floor and
another 360 steps to the 2nd floor.

Ascend as far as the 2nd floor (either
on foot or by lift), from where it is lift-only
to the top floor. Pushchairs must be
folded in lifts and you are not allowed
to take bags or backpacks larger than
aeroplane-cabin size.

Despite the new 2.5m-high bulletproof
glass wall around the tower, the base is
still free to visit after passing through the
security checks. Along with a renovated
2nd floor, it's part of a 15-year, €300 million
modernisation project.

enough to see the details of the city below. Telescopes and panoramic maps placed around the tower pinpoint locations in Paris and beyond. Story windows give an overview of the lifts' mechanics, and the vision well allows you to gaze through glass panels to the ground. Also up here are toilets, a souvenir shop and gastronomic restaurant **Le Jules Verne** (Map p274).

Top Floor

Views from the wind-buffeted top floor (276m) stretch up to 60km on a clear day, though at this height the panoramas are more sweeping than detailed. Celebrate your ascent with a glass of bubbly (€13 to €22) from the Bar à Champagne (open 11am to 10.30pm, to midnight in July and August). Afterwards peep into Gustave Eiffel's restored top-level office where lifelike wax models of Eiffel and his daughter Claire greet Thomas Edison.

To access the top floor, take a separate lift on the 2nd floor (closed during heavy winds).

What's Nearby?

Parc du Champ de Mars   Park
(Map p274; Champ de Mars, 7e; ⊙24hr; MÉcole Militaire or RER Champ de Mars–Tour Eiffel) Running southeast from the Eiffel Tower, the grassy Champ de Mars – an ideal summer picnic spot – was originally used as a parade ground for the cadets of the 18th-century **École Militaire**, the vast French-classical building at the southeastern end of the park, which counts Napoléon Bonaparte among its graduates. The steel-and-etched-glass **Wall for Peace Memorial** (Map p274; http://wallforpeace.org; MÉcole Militaire or RER Champ de Mars–Tour Eiffel), erected in 2000, is by Clara Halter.

Bar à Champagne, on the Tower's top floor

Musée du Quai Branly – Jacques Chirac   Museum

(Map p274; ☑01 56 61 70 00; www.quaibranly.fr; 37 quai Branly, 7e; adult/child €10/free; ⊘11am-7pm Tue, Wed & Sun, 11am-9pm Thu-Sat, plus 11am-7pm Mon during school holidays; Ⓜ Alma Marceau or RER Pont de l'Alma) A tribute to the diversity of human culture, Musée du Quai Branly inspires travellers, armchair anthropologists, and anyone who appreciates the beauty of traditional craftsmanship, through an overview of indigenous and folk art. Spanning four main sections – Oceania, Asia, Africa and the Americas – an impressive array of masks, carvings, weapons,

---

★ Did You Know?

Slapping a fresh coat of paint on the tower is no easy feat. It takes a 25-person team 18 months to apply the 60 tonnes of paint, redone every seven years.

PIO3 / SHUTTERSTOCK ©

jewellery and more makes up the body of the rich collection, displayed in a refreshingly unique interior without rooms or high walls. Look out for excellent temporary exhibitions and performances.

Musée Guimet des Arts Asiatiques   Gallery

(Map p274; ☑01 56 52 54 33; www.guimet.fr; 6 place d'Iéna, 16e; adult/child €8.50/free; ⊘10am-6pm Wed-Mon; Ⓜ Iéna) France's foremost Asian art museum has a superb collection of sculptures, paintings and religious articles that originated in the vast stretch of land between Afghanistan and Japan. Observe the gradual transmission of both Buddhism and artistic styles along the Silk Road in pieces ranging from 1st-century Gandhara Buddhas from Afghanistan and Pakistan to later Central Asian, Chinese and Japanese Buddhist sculptures and art. Part of the collection is housed in the nearby **Galeries du Panthéon Bouddhique** (Map p274; www.guimet.fr; 19 av d'Iéna, 16e; incl in Musée Guimet admission; ⊘10am-6pm Wed-Mon, garden during special events; Ⓜ Iéna) with a **Japanese garden**.

Palais de Tokyo   Gallery

(Map p274; ☑01 81 97 35 88; www.palaisdetokyo. com; 13 av du Président Wilson, 16e; adult/child €12/free; ⊘noon-midnight Wed-Mon; Ⓜ Iéna) The Tokyo Palace, created for the 1937 Exposition Internationale des Arts et Techniques dans la Vie Moderne (International Exposition of Art and Technology in Modern Life), has no permanent collection. Instead, its shell-like interior of concrete and steel is a stark backdrop to interactive contemporary-art exhibitions and installations. Its bookshop is fabulous for art and design magazines, and its eating and drinking options are magic.

Musée Marmottan Monet   Gallery

(☑01 44 96 50 33; www.marmottan.fr; 2 rue Louis Boilly, 16e; adult/child €12/8.50; ⊘10am-6pm Tue, Wed & Fri-Sun, to 9pm Thu; Ⓜ La Muette) This museum showcases the world's largest collection of works – about 100 – by impressionist painter Claude Monet (1840–1926). Some of the masterpieces to look out for include La Barque (1887), Cathédrale de Rouen (1892), Londres, le Parlement (1901) and the various Nymphéas.

ALEXANDRA LANDE / SHUTTERSTOCK ©

The Louvre

The Mona Lisa and the Venus de Milo are just two of the priceless treasures resplendently housed inside the fortress turned royal palace turned France's first national museum: Paris' pièce de résistance that no first-time visitor to the city can (or should) resist.

Few art galleries are as prized or as daunting as the Musée du Louvre – one of the world's largest and most diverse museums. The museum showcases 35,000 works of art; it would take nine months to glance at every piece, so planning your visit is essential.

Works of art from Europe form the permanent exhibition, alongside priceless collections of Mesopotamian, Egyptian, Greek, Roman and Islamic art and antiquities – a fascinating presentation of the evolution of Western art up through the mid-19th century.

Visiting

You need to queue twice to get in: once for security and then again to buy tickets. The longest queues are outside the Grande Pyramide; use the Carrousel du Louvre entrance (99 rue de Rivoli or direct from the metro).

Great For...

☑ Don't Miss

Self-guided thematic trails, from the art of eating to love, downloadable from the website.

Room 700, Denon Wing

❶ Need to Know

Map p274; ☑ 01 40 20 53 17; www.louvre.fr; rue de Rivoli & quai des Tuileries, 1er; adult/child €15/free, 6-9.45pm 1st Sat of month free; ⏰ 9am-6pm Mon, Thu, Sat & Sun, to 9.45pm Wed, Fri & 1st Sat of month; Ⓜ Palais Royal–Musée du Louvre

✖ Take a Break

Grab a sandwich from Hall Napoléon beneath Pei's Grande Pyramide to eat in the Jardin des Tuileries (p275).

★ Top Tip

Tickets are valid for the whole day, so you can come and go.

Palais du Louvre

The Louvre today rambles over four floors and through three wings: the **Sully Wing** creates the four sides of the Cour Carrée (literally 'Square Courtyard') at the eastern end of the complex; the **Denon Wing** stretches 800m along the Seine to the south; and the northern **Richelieu Wing** skirts rue de Rivoli. The building started life as a fortress built by Philippe-Auguste in the 12th century – medieval remnants are still visible on the Lower Ground Floor (Sully). In the 16th century it became a royal residence, and after the Revolution, in 1793, it was turned into a national museum. At the time, its booty was no more than 2500 paintings and objets d'art.

Over the centuries French governments amassed the paintings, sculptures and artefacts displayed today. The 'Grand Louvre' project, inaugurated by the late President Mitterrand in 1989, doubled the museum's exhibition space, and both new and renovated galleries have since

A Paris Museum Pass or Paris City Passport gives you priority; buying tickets in advance (on the Louvre website; €2 surcharge) also helps expedite the process.

You can rent a Nintendo 3DS multimedia guide (€5; ID required). More formal, English-language **guided tours** (Map p274; ☑ 01 40 20 52 63; adult/child €12/7; ⏰ 11am & 2pm daily except 1st Tue & Sun of month, plus 7pm Wed; Ⓜ Palais Royal–Musée du Louvre) depart from the Hall Napoléon. Reserve a spot up to 14 days in advance or sign up on arrival at the museum.

Check the 'Schedule of Room Closures' on the website to ensure you'll be able to see what you want to see. In 2018, two new rooms were opened to the public on the 2nd floor of the Richelieu Wing (displaying artworks stolen during the Nazi occupation of France and recovered postwar by the French government).

opened, including the state-of-the-art **Islamic art galleries** (Lower Ground Floor, Denon) in the stunningly restored Cour Visconti.

Priceless Antiquities

Whatever your plans are, don't rush by the Louvre's astonishing cache of treasures from antiquity: both Mesopotamia (ground floor, Richelieu) and Egypt (ground and 1st floors, Sully) are well represented, as seen in the *Code of Hammurabi* (Room 227, ground floor, Richelieu) and the *Seated Scribe* (Room 635, 1st floor, Sully). Room 324 (ground floor, Sully), otherwise known as Le Temple (Temple Room), holds impressive friezes, an enormous two-headed-bull column from the Darius Palace in ancient Iran and an enormous seated statue of Pharaoh Ramesses II.

Also worth a look are the mosaics and figurines from the Byzantine empire (lower ground floor, Denon), and the Greek statuary collection, culminating with the world's most famous armless duo, the *Venus de Milo* (Room 346, ground floor, Sully) and the *Winged Victory of Samothrace* (top of Daru staircase, 1st floor, Denon).

French & Italian Masterpieces

The 1st floor of the Denon Wing, where the *Mona Lisa* is found, is the most popular part of the Louvre. Rooms 700 to 702 are hung with monumental French paintings, many iconic: look for the *Consecration of the Emperor Napoleon I* (David), *The Raft of the Medusa* (Géricault) and *Grande Odalisque* (Ingres).

Room 706, with graceful frescoes by Botticelli, and the Grande Galerie (Rooms

Italian sculptures, Denon Wing

710, 712 and 716 – filled with classic works by Italian Renaissance masters such as Raphael, Titian, Uccello, Botticini – are must-visits. A crowd always fills Room 711 (Salle de La Joconde), which stars Da Vinci's *Mona Lisa* and, directly opposite, Paolo Veronese's superbly detailed *Wedding Feast at Cana*.

Mona Lisa

Easily the Louvre's most admired work (and the world's most famous painting) is Leonardo da Vinci's *La Joconde* (in French;

★ **Italian Sculptures**

On the ground floor of the Denon Wing, take time for the Italian sculptures, including Michelangelo's *The Dying Slave* and Canova's *Psyche and Cupid* (Room 403).

HERACLES KRITIKOS / SHUTTERSTOCK ©

La Gioconda in Italian), the lady with that enigmatic smile known as *Mona Lisa* (Room 711, 1st floor, Denon).

Mona (*monna* in Italian) is a contraction of *madonna*, and Gioconda is the feminine form of the surname Giocondo. Canadian scientists used infrared technology to peer through paint layers and confirm *Mona Lisa's* identity as Lisa Gherardini (1479–1542?), wife of Florentine merchant Francesco de Giocondo. Scientists also discovered that her dress was covered in a transparent gauze veil typically worn in early 16th-century Italy by pregnant women or new mothers; it's surmised that the work was painted to commemorate the birth of her second son around 1503, when she was aged about 24.

The Pyramid Inside & Out

Almost as stunning as the masterpieces inside is the 21m-high glass pyramid designed by Chinese-born American architect IM Pei that bedecks the main entrance to the Louvre. Beneath Pei's Grande Pyramide is the **Hall Napoléon**, the main entrance area, comprising an information booth, temporary exhibition hall, bookshop, souvenir store, cafe and auditoriums. To revel in another Pei pyramid of equally dramatic dimensions, head toward the **Carrousel du Louvre** (Map p274; www.carrouseldulouvre.com; 99 rue de Rivoli, 1er; ⊙10am-8pm Wed-Mon, 11am-7pm Tue; 🛜; Ⓜ Palais Royal–Musée du Louvre), a busy shopping mall – its centrepiece is Pei's **Pyramide Inversée** (inverted glass pyramid).

★ **Behind the Smile**

Recent tests done with 'emotion recognition' computer software suggest that the smile on 'Madame Lisa' is at least 83% happy. And one other point remains unequivocally certain: she was not the lover of Leonardo, who preferred his *Vitruvian Man* to his Mona.

The Louvre

A HALF-DAY TOUR

Successfully visiting the Louvre is a fine art. Its complex labyrinth of galleries and staircases spiralling across three wings and four floors renders discovery a snakes-and-ladders experience. Initiate yourself with this three-hour itinerary – a playful mix of *Mona Lisa*–obvious and up-to-the-minute unexpected.

Arriving in the newly renovated **❶ Cour Napoléon** beneath IM Pei's glass pyramid, pick up colour-coded floor plans at an information stand, then ride the escalator up to the Sully Wing and swap passport or credit card for a multimedia guide (there are limited descriptions in the galleries) at the wing entrance.

The Louvre is as much about spectacular architecture as masterful art. To appreciate this, zip up and down Sully's Escalier Henri II to admire **❷ Venus de Milo**, then up parallel Escalier Henri IV to the palatial displays in **❸ Cour Khorsabad**. Follow signs for the escalator up to the 1st floor and the opulent **❹ Napoléon III apartments**. Next traverse 25 consecutive galleries (thank you, floor plan!) to flip conventional contemplation on its head with Cy Twombly's **❺ The Ceiling**, and the hypnotic **❻ Winged Victory of Samothrace**, which brazenly insists on being admired from all angles. End with the impossibly famous **❼ Raft of the Medusa**, **❽ Mona Lisa** and **❾ Virgin & Child**.

TOP TIPS

➡ Don't even consider entering the Louvre's maze of galleries without a floor plan, free from the information desk in the Hall Napoléon.

➡ The Denon Wing is always packed; visit on late nights (Wednesday or Friday) or trade Denon in for the notably quieter Richelieu Wing.

➡ Tickets to the Louvre are valid for the whole day, meaning that you can nip out for lunch.

BRIAN KINNEY / SHUTTERSTOCK ©

Napoléon III Apartments
Rooms 544 & 547, 1st Floor, Richelieu
Napoléon III's gorgeous gilt apartments were built from 1854 to 1861, featuring an over-the-top decor of gold leaf, stucco and crystal chandeliers that reaches a dizzying climax in the Grand Salon and State Dining Room.

Jardin du Carrousel

Galerie du Carrousel Entrances

Porte des Lions

LOUVRE AUDITORIUM

Classical-music concerts are staged several times a week at the Louvre Auditorium (off the main entrance hall). Don't miss the Thursday lunchtime concerts featuring emerging composers and musicians. The season runs from September to April or May, depending on the concert series.

Mona Lisa
Room 711, 1st Floor, Denon
No smile is as enigmatic or bewitching as hers. Da Vinci's diminutive *La Joconde* hangs opposite the largest painting in the Louvre – sumptuous, fellow Italian Renaissance artwork *The Wedding at Cana*.

The Raft of the Medusa
Room 700, 1st Floor, Denon
Decipher the politics behind French romanticism in Théodore Géricault's *Raft of the Medusa*.

Cour Khorsabad
Ground Floor, Richelieu
Time travel with a pair of winged human-headed bulls to view some of the world's oldest Mesopotamian art. DETOUR» Night-lit statues in Cour Puget.

The Ceiling
Room 663, Sully
Admire the blue shock of Cy Twombly's 400-sq-metre contemporary ceiling fresco – the Louvre's latest, daring commission. DETOUR» *The Braque Ceiling*, Room 662.

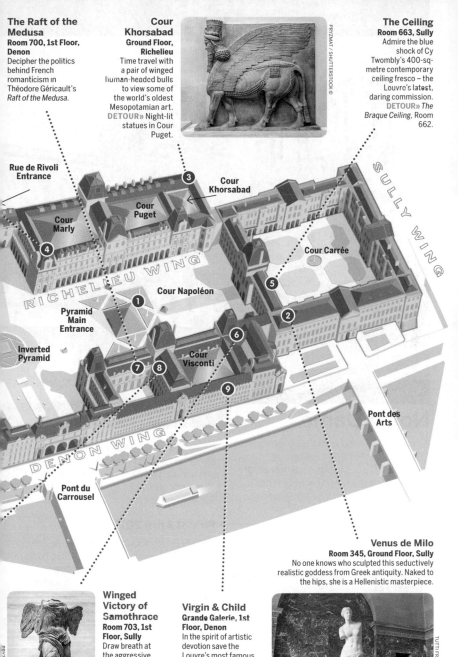

PRYZMAT / SHUTTERSTOCK ©

Rue de Rivoli Entrance

3 Cour Khorsabad

Cour Puget

Cour Marly

4

Cour Carrée

SULLY WING

RICHELIEU WING

Cour Napoléon

1

5

Pyramid Main Entrance

Inverted Pyramid

2

6

Cour Visconti

7 **8**

9

DENON WING

Pont des Arts

Pont du Carrousel

Venus de Milo
Room 345, Ground Floor, Sully
No one knows who sculpted this seductively realistic goddess from Greek antiquity. Naked to the hips, she is a Hellenistic masterpiece.

PRYZMAT / SHUTTERSTOCK ©

Winged Victory of Samothrace
Room 703, 1st Floor, Sully
Draw breath at the aggressive dynamism of this headless, handless Hellenistic goddess. DETOUR» The razzle-dazzle of the Apollo Gallery's crown jewels.

Virgin & Child
Grande Galerie, 1st Floor, Denon
In the spirit of artistic devotion save the Louvre's most famous gallery for last: a feast of Virgin-and-child paintings by Da Vinci, Raphael, Domenico Ghirlandaio, Giovanni Bellini and Francesco Botticini.

TUTTI FRUTTI / SHUTTERSTOCK ©

TATIANA DYUVBANOVA / SHUTTERSTOCK ©

Notre Dame

A vision of stained-glass rose windows, flying buttresses and frightening gargoyles, Paris' glorious cathedral, on the larger of the two inner-city islands, is the city's geographic and spiritual heart.

When you enter the cathedral its grand dimensions are immediately evident: the interior alone is 127m long, 48m wide and 35m high, and can accommodate some 6000 worshippers.

Fire of April 2019

A blaze broke out under the cathedral's roof on the evening of 15 April 2019. Though firefighters were able to control the fire and ultimately save the church, it suffered devastating damage.

The fire destroyed most of the roof and toppled its spire, a 19th-century addition. However, the oldest parts of the cathedral – notably the two bell towers, the rose windows and the west facade – were all saved.

At the time of the fire, Notre Dame was undergoing a planned restoration, and this spared several statues and other

Great For...

🛈 Notre Dame Closed

The cathedral suffered a devastating fire in 2019. Visitors will most likely not be able to enter Notre Dame for many years.

Notre Dame shortly after the April 2019 fire

ℹ Need to Know

Map p276; www.notredamedeparis.fr; 6 Parvis
Notre Dame – place Jean-Paul-II, 4e; ⊘closed
indefinitely; Ⓜ Cité

★ Top Tip

One of the best views of the cathedral's
forest of flying buttresses is from square
Jean XXIII, the little park behind the
cathedral.

---

artefacts, which had been taken off site to
be restored.

Despite the damage, the awesome exterior of the cathedral and its surrounding
squares are well worth a visit – for the sublime gothic architecture and the church's
historical and cultural significance.

Rebuilding Notre Dame

After the fire, French President Emmanuel
Macron said he'd like the cathedral to be
rebuilt by 2024, in time for the Olympic
Games, but others estimate that a full
restoration could take decades.

There is debate over the form that the
restoration should take: should it be restored
to its original era, to the 19th-century update
or something more modern still?

Though it will be a long while before visits
to the interior can resume, the cathedral's

significance has not dimmed. The gothic
structure stands strong and continues to
inspire awe and devotion more than 800
years after it was first built.

Architecture

Built on a site occupied by earlier churches
and, a millennium prior, a Gallo-Roman
temple, the construction of Notre Dame
was begun in 1163 and largely completed
by the early 14th century. The cathedral
was badly damaged during the Revolution,
prompting architect Eugène Emmanuel
Viollet-le-Duc to oversee extensive renovations between 1845 and 1864.

Notre Dame is known for its sublime balance, though if you look closely you'll see all
sorts of minor asymmetrical elements introduced to avoid monotony, in accordance
with standard Gothic practice. These include
the slightly different shapes of each of the
three main portals, whose statues were
once brightly coloured to make them more
effective as a *Biblia pauperum* – a 'Bible of
the poor' to help the illiterate faithful understand Old Testament stories, the Passion of
the Christ and the lives of the saints.

The grand dimensions of the cathedral are immediately evident: the interior

alone is 127m long, 48m wide and 35m high, and can accommodate some 6000 worshippers.

Rose Windows

A cathedral highlight, the three rose windows are Notre Dame's most spectacular feature. All three windows appear to have survived the 2019 fires, with no catastrophic damage.

Towers

Gargoyles grimace and grin on the rooftop Galerie des Chimères (Gargoyles Gallery), around the cathedral's bell towers. These grotesque statues divert rainwater from the roof to prevent masonry damage, with the water exiting through their elongated open mouths. They also, purportedly, ward off evil spirits. Although they appear medieval, they were installed by Eugène Viollet-le-Duc in the 19th century.

In the South Tower hangs Emmanuel, the cathedral's original 13-tonne bourdon bell (all of the cathedral's bells are named). During the night of 24 August 1944, when the Île de la Cité was retaken by French, Allied and Resistance troops, the tolling of the Emmanuel announced Paris' approaching liberation. Emmanuel's peal purity comes from the precious gems and jewels Parisian women threw into the pot when it was recast from copper and bronze in 1631.

As part of 2013's celebrations for Notre Dame's 850th anniversary since construction began, nine new bells were installed, replicating the original medieval chimes.

Point Zéro

Distances from Paris to every part of metropolitan France are measured from this bronze star, embedded in the paving stones of Place Jean-Paul II, the vast square in front of Notre Dame. When the sun floods onto the cathedral's exquisitely sculptured front facade, the square is packed, making it a challenge to locate the **Point Zéro des Routes de France** (Map p276; Parvis Notre Dame – place Jean-Paul II, 4e; Ⓜ Cité), emperor of the Franks, on horseback.

The south Rose Window

PHOTOFIRES / SHUTTERSTOCK ©

Day Trip: Château de Versailles

This monumental, 700-room palace and sprawling estate – with its gardens, fountains, ponds and canals – is a Unesco World Heritage–listed wonder situated an easy 40-minute train ride from central Paris.

Great For...

☑ Don't Miss

Summertime 'dancing water' displays set to music by baroque- and classical-era composers.

Amid magnificently landscaped formal gardens, this splendid and enormous palace was built in the mid-17th century during the reign of Louis XIV – the Roi Soleil (Sun King) – to project the absolute power of the French monarchy, which was then at the height of its glory. The château has undergone relatively few alterations since its construction, though almost all the interior furnishings disappeared during the Revolution and many of the rooms were rebuilt by Louis-Philippe (r 1830–48).

Some 30,000 workers and soldiers toiled on the structure, the bills for which all but emptied the kingdom's coffers. Work began in 1661 under the guidance of architect Louis Le Vau (Jules Hardouin-Mansart took over from Le Vau in the mid-1670s); painter and interior designer Charles Le Brun; and landscape artist André Le Nôtre,

The Hall of Mirrors

TAKASHI IMAGES / SHUTTERSTOCK ©

❶ Need to Know

☎ 01 30 83 78 00; www.chateauversailles.fr; place d'Armes; adult/child passport ticket incl estate-wide access €20/free, with musical events €27/free, palace €18/free except during musical events; ⏰ 9am-6.30pm Tue-Sun Apr-Oct, to 5.30pm Tue-Sun Nov-Mar; Ⓜ RER Versailles-Château–Rive Gauche

✕ Take a Break

Nearby rue de Satory is lined with restaurants and cafes.

★ Top Tip

Prepurchase tickets on the château's website or at Fnac (p287) branches and head straight to the entrance.

---

whose workers flattened hills, drained marshes and relocated forests as they laid out the seemingly endless **gardens** (www.chateauversailles.fr; place d'Armes; free except during musical events; ⏰ gardens 8am-8.30pm Apr-Oct, to 6pm Nov-Mar, park 7am-8.30pm Apr-Oct, 8am-6pm Nov-Mar), ponds and fountains.

Le Brun and his hundreds of artisans decorated every moulding, cornice, ceiling and door of the interior with the most luxurious and ostentatious of appointments: frescos, marble, gilt and woodcarvings, many with themes and symbols drawn from Greek and Roman mythology. The King's Suite of the Grands Appartements du Roi et de la Reine (King's and Queen's State Apartments) includes rooms dedicated to Hercules, Venus, Diana, Mars and Mercury. The opulence reaches its peak in the Galerie des Glaces (Hall of Mirrors), a

75m-long ballroom with 17 huge mirrors and an equal number of windows looking out over the gardens and the setting sun.

Guided Tours

To access areas that are otherwise off limits, prebook a 90-minute **guided tour** (☎ 01 30 83 77 88; www.chateauversailles.fr; Château de Versailles; tours €10, plus palace entry; ⏰ English-language tours 11am, 1.30pm & 3pm Tue-Sun) of the Private Apartments of Louis XV and Louis XVI and the Opera House or Royal Chapel.

Planning Your Visit

The château is situated in the leafy, bourgeois suburb of Versailles, about 22km southwest of central Paris. Take the frequent RER C5 (return €7.10) from Paris' Left Bank RER stations to Versailles-Château–Rive Gauche station.

Versailles

A DAY IN COURT

Visiting Versailles – even just the State Apartments – may seem overwhelming at first, but think of it as a house where people ate, drank, worked, slept and conspired and you'll be on the right path.

Some two decades into his long reign, Louis XIV began turning his father's hunting lodge into a palace large enough to house his entire court (to keep closer tabs on the 6000-strong army of courtiers). Sparing no expense, the Sun King employed the greatest artists and craftspeople of the day and by 1682 he'd created the most extravagant dormitory in history.

The royal schedule was as accurate and predictable as a Swiss watch. By following this itinerary of rooms you can recreate the king's day, starting with the ❶ **King's Bedchamber** and the ❷ **Queen's Bedchamber**, where the royal couple was roused at about the same time. The royal procession then leads through the ❸ **Hall of Mirrors** to the ❹ **Royal Chapel** for morning Mass and returns to the ❺ **Council Chamber** for late-morning meetings with ministers. After lunch the king might ride or hunt or visit the ❻ **King's Library**. Later he could join courtesans for an 'apartment evening' starting from the ❼ **Hercules Drawing Room** or play billiards in the ❽ **Diana Drawing Room** before supping at 10pm.

VERSAILLES BY NUMBERS

Rooms 700 (11 hectares of roof)

Windows 2153

Staircases 67

Gardens and parks 800 hectares

Trees 200,000

Fountains 50 (with 620 nozzles)

Paintings 6300 (measuring 11km laid end to end)

Statues and sculptures 2100

Objets d'art and furnishings 5000

Visitors 5.3 million per year

VICHIE81 / SHUTTERSTOCK ©

Queen's Bedchamber
Chambre de la Reine
The queen's life was on constant public display and even the births of her children were watched by crowds of spectators in her own bedchamber. DETOUR » The Guardroom, with a dozen armed men at the ready.

Guardroom

South Wing

LUNCH BREAK

Contemporary French cuisine at Alain Ducasse's restaurant Ore, or a picnic in the park.

Hercules Drawing Room
Salon d'Hercule
This salon, with its stunning ceiling fresco of the strong man, gave way to the State Apartments, which were open to courtiers three nights a week. DETOUR» Apollo Drawing Room, used for formal audiences and as a throne room.

T.W.VAN URK / SHUTTERSTOCK ©

Hall of Mirrors
Galerie des Glaces
The solid-silver candelabra and furnishings in this extravagant hall, devoted to Louis XIV's successes in war, were melted down in 1689 to pay for yet another conflict. DETOUR» The antithetical Peace Drawing Room, adjacent.

WALTER G / SHUTTERSTOCK ©

King's Bedchamber
Chambre du Roi
The king's daily life was anything but private and even his *lever* (rising) at 8am and *coucher* (retiring) at 11.30pm would be witnessed by up to 150 sycophantic courtiers.

Council Chamber
Cabinet du Conseil
This chamber, with carved medallions evoking the king's work, is where the monarch met his various ministers (state, finance, religion etc) depending on the days of the week.

Peace Drawing Room

② **③** **Hall of Mirrors**

① **⑤**

Apollo Drawing Room

Marble Courtyard

King's Library
Bibliothèque du Roi
The last resident, bibliophile Louis XVI, loved geography and his copy of *The Travels of James Cook* (in English, which he read fluently) is still on the shelf here.

⑥ **⑧**

Entrance

Entrance

North Wing

Diana Drawing Room
Salon de Diane
With walls and ceiling covered in frescoes devoted to the mythical huntress, this room contained a large billiard table reserved for Louis XIV, a keen player.

⑦

To Royal Opera

④

Royal Chapel
Chapelle Royale
This two-storey chapel (with gallery for the royals and important courtiers, and the ground floor for the B-list) was dedicated to St Louis, patron of French monarchs. DETOUR» The sumptuous Royal Opera.

COJATO / BUDGET TRAVEL ©

SAVVY SIGHTSEEING

Avoid Versailles on Monday (closed), Tuesday (Paris' museums close, so visitors flock here) and Sunday, the busiest day. Also, book tickets online so you don't have to queue.

Seine-Side Meander

The world's most romantic city has no shortage of beguiling spots, but the Seine and its surrounds are Paris at its most seductive. Descend the steps along the quays wherever possible to stroll along the water's edge.

Start Place de la Concorde
Distance 7km
Duration 3 hours

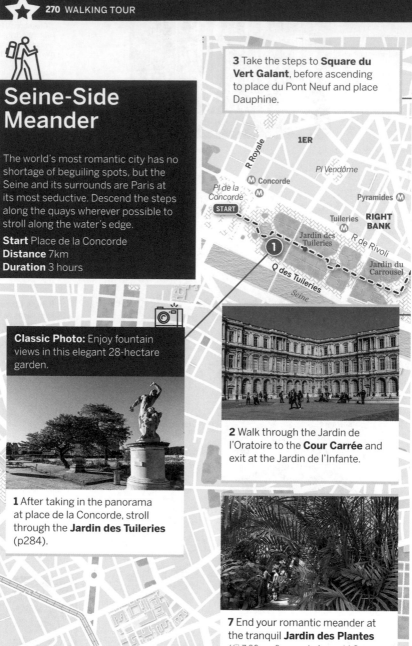

3 Take the steps to **Square du Vert Galant**, before ascending to place du Pont Neuf and place Dauphine.

R. Royale
1ER
Pl Vendôme
Ⓜ Concorde
Pl de la Concorde Ⓜ
Pyramides Ⓜ
START
Tuileries Ⓜ **RIGHT BANK**
Jardin des Tuileries
R de Rivoli
❶
Jardin du Carrousel
Q des Tuileries
Seine

Classic Photo: Enjoy fountain views in this elegant 28-hectare garden.

2 Walk through the Jardin de l'Oratoire to the **Cour Carrée** and exit at the Jardin de l'Infante.

1 After taking in the panorama at place de la Concorde, stroll through the **Jardin des Tuileries** (p284).

7 End your romantic meander at the tranquil **Jardin des Plantes** (⊙7.30am-8pm early Apr–mid-Sep, shorter hours rest of year). Cruise back along the Seine by Batobus.

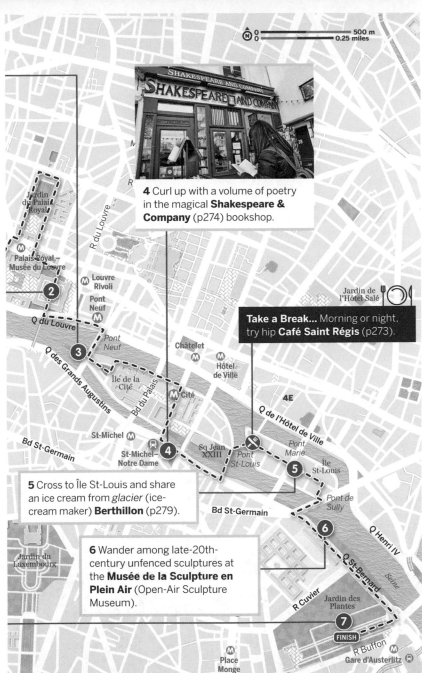

500 m
0.25 miles

Jardin du Palais Royal

Palais-Royal – Musée du Louvre

2

R du Louvre

Louvre Rivoli

Pont Neuf

Q du Louvre

Pont Neuf

3

Q des Grands Augustins

Île de la Cité

Bd du Palais

Cité

Châtelet

Hôtel de Ville

Jardin de l'Hôtel Salé

4 Curl up with a volume of poetry in the magical **Shakespeare & Company** (p274) bookshop.

Take a Break... Morning or night, try hip **Café Saint Régis** (p273).

4E

Q de l'Hôtel de Ville

St-Michel

Bd St-Germain

St-Michel– Notre Dame

4

Sq Jean XXIII

Pont St-Louis

Pont Marie

Île St-Louis

5

5 Cross to Île St-Louis and share an ice cream from *glacier* (ice-cream maker) **Berthillon** (p279).

Bd St-Germain

Pont de Sully

6

Q Henri IV

Q St-Bernard

Seine

Jardin du Luxembourg

6 Wander among late-20th-century unfenced sculptures at the **Musée de la Sculpture en Plein Air** (Open-Air Sculpture Museum).

R Cuvier

Jardin des Plantes

7

FINISH

R Buffon

Place Monge

Gare d'Austerlitz

⊙ SIGHTS
◉ Right Bank
Basilique du Sacré-Cœur   Basilica
(Map p276; ☎01 53 41 89 00; www.sacre-coeur-montmartre.com; Parvis du Sacré-Cœur, 18e; basilica free, dome adult/child €6/4, cash only; ⊗basilica 6am-10.30pm, dome 8.30am-8pm May-Sep, 9am-5pm Oct-Apr; ⓂAnvers or Abbesses) Begun in 1875 in the wake of the Franco-Prussian War and the chaos of the Paris Commune, Sacré-Cœur is a symbol of the former struggle between the conservative Catholic old guard and the secular, republican radicals. It was finally consecrated in 1919, standing in contrast to the bohemian lifestyle that surrounded it. The view over Paris from its parvis is breathtaking. Avoid walking up the steep hill by using a regular metro ticket aboard the **funicular** (www.ratp.fr; place St-Pierre, 18e; ⊗6am-12.45am; ⓂAnvers or Abbesses) to the **upper station** (www.ratp.fr; rue du Cardinal Dubois, 18e; ⊗6am-12.45am; ⓂAbbesses).

> *The view over Paris from Sacré-Cœur's parvis is breathtaking*

Basilique du Sacré-Cœur

Centre Pompidou   Museum
(Map p276; ☎01 44 78 12 33; www.centrepompidou.fr; place Georges Pompidou, 4e; museum, exhibitions & panorama adult/child €14/free, panorama only ticket €5/free; ⊗11am-9pm Wed-Mon, temporary exhibits to 11pm Thu; ⓂRambuteau) Renowned for its radical architectural statement, the 1977-opened Centre Pompidou brings together galleries and cutting-edge exhibitions, hands-on workshops, dance performances, cinemas and other entertainment venues, with street performers and fanciful fountains outside. The **Musée National d'Art Moderne**, France's national collection of art dating from 1905 onwards, is the main draw; a fraction of its 100,000-plus pieces – including Fauvist, cubist, surrealist, pop art and contemporary works – is on display. Don't miss the spectacular Parisian panorama from the rooftop.

Sainte-Chapelle   Chapel
(Map p276; ☎01 53 40 60 80, concerts 01 42 77 65 65; www.sainte-chapelle.fr; 8 bd du Palais, 1er; adult/child €10/free, joint ticket with Conciergerie €15/free; ⊗9am-7pm Apr-Sep, to 5pm

Oct-Mar; MCité) Try to save Sainte-Chapelle for a sunny day, when Paris' oldest, finest stained glass is at its dazzling best. Enshrined within the Palais de Justice (Law Courts), this gem-like Holy Chapel is Paris' most exquisite Gothic monument. It was completed in 1248, just six years after the first stone was laid, and was conceived by Louis IX to house his personal collection of holy relics, including the famous Holy Crown (eventually moved to Notre Dame).

Musée National Picasso — Museum

(Map p276; ☎01 85 56 00 36; www.musee picassoparis.fr; 5 rue de Thorigny, 3e; adult/child €12.50/free; ⊙10.30am-6pm Tue-Fri, from 9.30am Sat & Sun; MChemin Vert or St-Paul) One of Paris' most treasured art collections is showcased inside the mid-17th-century Hôtel Salé, an exquisite private mansion owned by the city since 1964. The Musée National Picasso is a staggering art museum devoted to Spanish artist Pablo Picasso (1881–1973), who spent much of his life living and working in Paris. The collection includes more than 5000 drawings, engravings, paintings, ceramic works and sculptures by the *grand maître* (great master), although they're not all displayed at the same time.

Arc de Triomphe — Landmark

(Map p274; www.paris-arc-de-triomphe.fr; place Charles de Gaulle, 8e; viewing platform adult/child €12/free; ⊙10am-11pm Apr-Sep, to 10.30pm Oct-Mar; MCharles de Gaulle–Étoile) If anything rivals the Eiffel Tower (p252) as the symbol of Paris, it's this magnificent 1836 monument to Napoléon's victory at Austerlitz (1805), which he commissioned the following year. The intricately sculpted triumphal arch stands sentinel in the centre of the Étoile (Star) roundabout. From the viewing platform on top of the arch (50m up via 284 steps and well worth the climb) you can see the dozen avenues.

If anything rivals the Eiffel Tower as the symbol of Paris, it's this magnificent 1836 monument to Napoléon's victory at Austerlitz (1805). For two weeks in April 2020, conceptual artist Christo – of Jeanne-Claude and Christo fame – will wrap the

🍵 Parisian Island Life

Paris' geographic and spiritual heart lies on its island twinset, and there is no finer spot for admiring Notre Dame or lapping up local life than on the pavement terrace at **Café Saint Régis** (Map p276; ☎01 43 54 59 41; www.cafesaintregis paris.com; 6 rue Jean du Bellay, 4e; breakfast & snacks €3.50-15.50; mains €18-33.50; ⊙6.30am-2am, kitchen 8am-midnight; 🛜; MPont Marie) on Île St-Louis. Waiters in long white aprons, a ceramic-tiled interior and retro vintage decor make it a hip hang-out for eating or drinking any time of day. Nearby, **Berthillon** (Map p276; www.berthillon.fr; 29-31 & 46 rue St-Louis en l'Île, 4e; 1/2/3/4 scoops takeaway €3/4.50/6/7.50; ⊙10am-8pm Wed-Sun, closed mid-Feb–early Mar & Aug; MPont Marie) is the capital's most-esteemed *glacier* (ice-cream maker), founded in 1954 and still run by the same family.

Café Saint Régis

arch in silvery-blue polypropylene fabric, tied by 7000m of red rope.

Palais Garnier — Historic Building

(Map p274; ☎08 92 89 90 90; www.operade paris.fr; cnr rues Scribe & Auber, 9e; self-guided tours adult/child €12/8, guided tours adult/child €15.50/8.50; ⊙self-guided tours 10am-5pm, English-language guided tours 11am & 2.30pm; MOpéra) The fabled 'phantom of the opera' lurked in this opulent opera house designed in 1860 by Charles Garnier (then an unknown 35-year-old architect). Reserve a spot on a 90-minute English-language

Western Paris, Champs-Élysées, St-Germain & Les Invalides

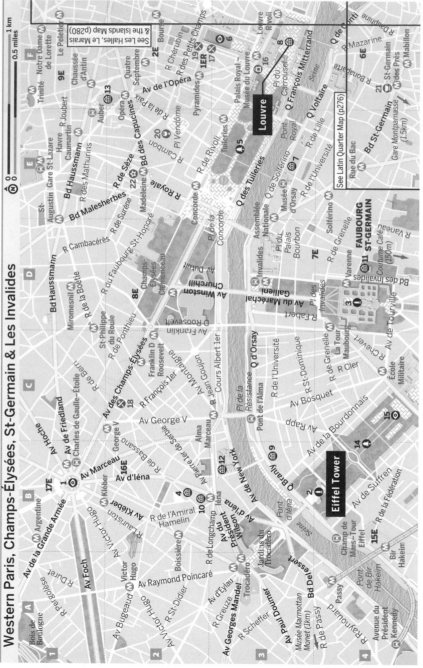

See Les Halles, Le Marais & the Islands Map (p280)

See Latin Quarter Map (p276)

Louvre

Eiffel Tower

FAUBOURG ST-GERMAIN

1 km
0.5 miles

Western Paris, Champs-Élysées, St-Germain & Les Invalides

guided tour, or visit on your own (audio-guides available; €5). Don't miss the Grand Staircase and gilded auditorium with red velvet seats, a massive chandelier and Marc Chagall's ceiling mural. Also worth a peek is the museum, with posters, costumes, backdrops, original scores and other memorabilia.

Cimetière du Père Lachaise Cemetery

(Map p276; ☎01 55 25 82 10; www.pere-lachaise. com; 16 rue du Repos & 8 bd de Ménilmontant, 20e; ◷8am-6pm Mon-Fri, from 8.30am Sat, from 9am Sun mid-Mar–Oct, shorter hours Nov–mid-Mar; Ⓜ Père Lachaise or Gambetta) Opened in 1804, Père Lachaise is today the world's most visited cemetery. Its 70,000 ornate tombs of the rich and famous form a verdant, 44-hectare sculpture garden. The most visited are those of 1960s rock star Jim Morrison (division 6) and Oscar Wilde (division 89). Pick up cemetery maps at the **conservation office** (Bureaux de la Conservation; Map p276; ◷8.30am-12.30pm & 2-5pm Mon-Fri; Ⓜ Philippe Auguste, Père Lachaise) near the main bd de Ménilmontant entrance. Other notables buried here include composer Chopin, playwright Molière, poet Apollinaire, and writers Balzac, Proust, Stein and Colette.

Jardin des Tuileries Park

(Map p274; rue de Rivoli, 1er; ◷7am-9pm Apr-late Sep, 7.30am-7.30pm late Sep-Mar; Ⓜ Tuileries or Concorde) Filled with fountains, ponds and sculptures, the formal 28-hectare Tuileries Garden, which begins just west of the Jardin du Carrousel, was laid out in its present form in 1664 by André Le Nôtre, architect of the gardens at Versailles. The Tuileries soon became the most fashionable spot in Paris for parading about in one's finery. It now forms part of the Banks of the Seine Unesco World Heritage Site.

Canal St-Martin Canal

(Map p276; 10e; Ⓜ République, Jaurès, Jacques Bonsergent) The tranquil, 4.5km-long Canal St-Martin was inaugurated in 1825 to provide a shipping link between the Seine and Paris' northeastern suburbs. Emerging from below ground near place de la République, its towpaths take you past locks, bridges and local neighbourhoods. Come for a romantic stroll, cycle, picnic or dusk-time drink. From the iron footbridge by the intersection of rue de la Grange aux Belles and quai de Jemmapes, watch the vintage road bridge swing open to let canal boats pass.

Les Halles, Le Marais & the Islands

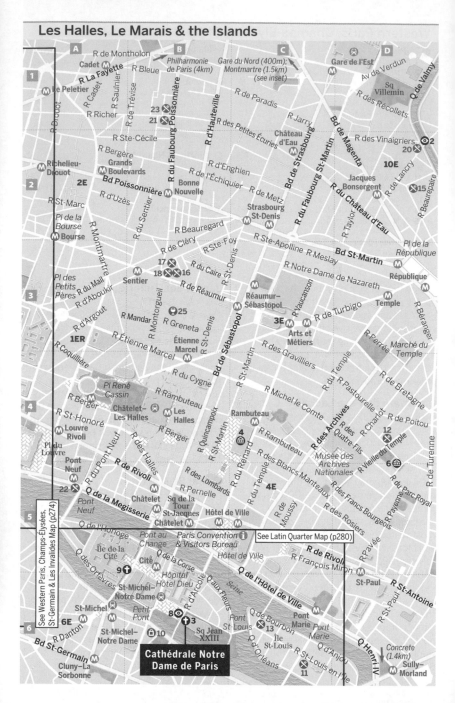

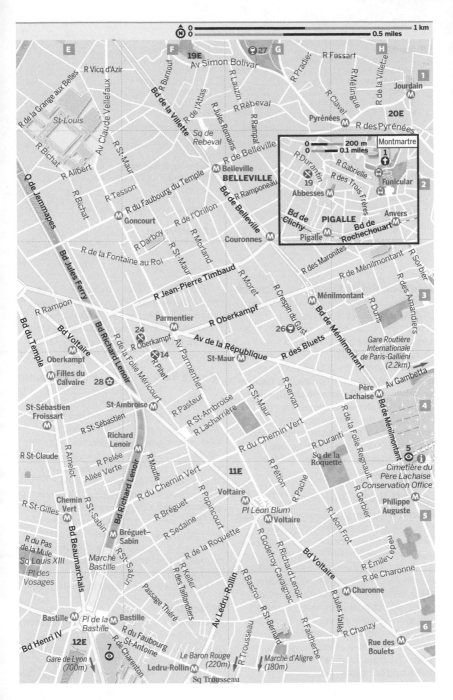

Les Halles, Le Marais & the Islands

◎ Sights
1	Basilique du Sacré-Cœur	H2
2	Canal St-Martin	D2
3	Cathédrale Notre Dame de Paris	B6
4	Centre Pompidou	C4
5	Cimetière du Père Lachaise	H4
6	Musée National Picasso	D4
7	Opéra Bastille	E6
8	Point Zéro des Routes de France	B6
9	Sainte-Chapelle	B5

⊕ Shopping
10	Shakespeare & Company	B6

⊗ Eating
11	Berthillon	C6
12	Breizh Café	D4
13	Café Saint Régis	C6
14	Chambelland	F4
15	Du Pain et des Idées	D2

16	Frenchie	B3
17	Frenchie Bar à Vins	B3
18	Frenchie to Go	B3
19	Le Grenier à Pain	G2
20	Le Verre Volé	D2
	L'Epicerie du Breizh Café	(see 12)
21	L'Office	B1
22	Maison Maison	A5
23	Richer	B1
24	The French Bastards	F3

◎ Drinking & Nightlife
25	Experimental Cocktail Club	B3
26	Le Perchoir	G3
27	Pavillon Puebla	G1
	Shakespeare & Company Café	(see 10)

◎ Entertainment
28	Le Bataclan	E4
	Opéra Bastille	(see 7)

Jardin du Palais Royal　　Gardens

(Map p274; www.domaine-palais-royal.fr; 2 place Colette, 1er; ☉8am-10.30pm Apr-Sep, to 8.30pm Oct-Mar; ⓜPalais Royal–Musée du Louvre) The Jardin du Palais Royal is a perfect spot to sit, contemplate and picnic between boxed hedges, or shop in the trio of beautiful arcades that frame the garden: the **Galerie de Valois** (east), **Galerie de Montpensier** (west) and **Galerie Beaujolais** (north). However, it's the southern end of the complex, polka-dotted with sculptor Daniel Buren's 260 black-and-white striped columns, that has become the garden's signature feature.

◎ Left Bank

Musée d'Orsay　　Museum

(Map p274; ☑01 40 49 48 14; www.musee-orsay.fr; 1 rue de la Légion d'Honneur, 7e; adult/child €14/free; ☉9.30am-6pm Tue, Wed & Fri-Sun, to 9.45pm Thu; ⓜAssemblée Nationale or RER Musée d'Orsay) This is the home of France's national collection from the impressionist, post-impressionist and art nouveau movements spanning from 1848 to 1914. The glorious former Gare d'Orsay train station – itself an art nouveau showpiece – displays a roll-call of masters and their world-famous works.

Top of every visitor's must-see list is the world's largest collection of impressionist and post-impressionist art. Allow ample time to swoon over masterpieces by Manet, Monet, Cézanne, Renoir, Degas, Pissarro and Van Gogh.

Musée Rodin　　Museum, Garden

(Map p274; ☑01 44 18 61 10; www.musee-rodin.fr; 79 rue de Varenne, 7e; adult/child €10/free, garden only €4/free; ☉10am-5.45pm Tue-Sun; ⓜVarenne or Invalides) Sculptor, painter, sketcher, engraver and collector Auguste Rodin donated his entire collection to the French state in 1908 on the proviso that it dedicate his former workshop and showroom, the beautiful 1730 Hôtel Biron, to displaying his works. They're now installed not only in the mansion itself, but also in its rose-filled garden – one of the most peaceful places in central Paris and a wonderful spot to contemplate his famous work The Thinker.

Purchase tickets online to avoid queuing.

Hôtel des Invalides　　Monument, Museum

(Map p274; www.musee-armee.fr; 129 rue de Grenelle, 7e; adult/child €12/free; ☉10am-6pm Apr-Oct, to 5pm Nov-Mar; ⓜVarenne or La Tour Maubourg) Flanked by the 500m-long

Esplanade des Invalides lawns, Hôtel des Invalides was built in the 1670s by Louis XIV to house 4000 *invalides* (disabled war vet erans). On 14 July 1789, a mob broke into the building and seized 32,000 rifles before heading on to the prison at Bastille and the start of the French Revolution.

Admission includes entry to all Hôtel des Invalides sights (temporary exhibitions cost extra). Hours for individual sites can vary – check the website for updates.

Panthéon   Mausoleum

(Map p280; ☑01 44 32 18 00; www.paris-pantheon.fr; place du Panthéon, 5e; adult/child €9/free; ☉10am-6.30pm Apr-Sep, to 6pm Oct-Mar; MMaubert-Mutualité or RER Luxembourg) The Panthéon's stately neoclassical dome is an icon of the Parisian skyline. Its vast interior is an architectural masterpiece: originally an abbey church dedicated to Ste Geneviève and now a mausoleum, it has served since 1791 as the resting place of some of France's greatest thinkers, including Voltaire, Rousseau, Braille and Hugo. A copy of Foucault's pendulum, first hung from the dome in 1851 to demonstrate the rotation of the earth, takes pride of place.

Les Catacombes   Cemetery

(☑01 43 22 47 63; www.catacombes.paris.fr; place Denfert-Rochereau, 14e; adult/child €13/ free, online booking incl audio guide €29/5; ☉10am-8.30pm Tue-Sun; MDenfert-Rochereau) These skull- and bone-lined underground tunnels are Paris' most macabre sight. In 1785 it was decided to rectify the hygiene problems of Paris' overflowing cemeteries by exhuming the bones and storing them in disused quarry tunnels, and the Catacombes were created in 1810. After descending 20m (via 131 narrow, dizzying spiral steps), you follow dark, subterranean passages to the ossuary (1.5km in all). Exit up 112 steps via a 'transition space' (with gift shop onto 21bis av René Coty, 14e.

Jardin du Luxembourg   Park

(Map p280; www.senat.fr/visite/jardin; 6e; ☉hours vary; MMabillon, St-Sulpice, Rennes, Notre Dame des Champs or RER Luxembourg)

This inner-city oasis of formal terraces, chestnut groves and lush lawns has a special place in Parisians' hearts. Napoléon dedicated the 23 gracefully laid-out hectares of the Luxembourg Gardens to the children of Paris, and many residents spent their childhood prodding 1920s wooden **sailboats** (sailboat rental per 30min €4; ☉11am-6pm Apr-Oct) with long sticks on the octagonal **Grand Bassin** pond, watching puppets perform puppet shows at the **Théâtre du Luxembourg** (☑01 43 29 50 97; www.marionnettesduluxembourg.fr; tickets €6.40; ☉Wed, Sat & Sun, daily during school holidays) and riding the *carrousel* (merry-go-round) or **ponies** (☑06 07 32 53 95; www.animaponey.com; 600m/900m pony ride €6/8.50; ☉3-6pm Wed, Sat, Sun & school holidays).

🛍 SHOPPING

La Grande Épicerie
de Paris   Food & Drinks

(www.lagrandeepicerie.com; 38 rue de Sèvres, 7e; ☉8.30am-9pm Mon-Sat, 10am-8pm Sun; MSèvres-Babylone) The magnificent food hall of department store **Le Bon Marché** (Map p280; ☑01 44 39 80 00; www.24sevres.com; 24 rue de Sèvres, 7e; ☉10am-8pm Mon-Wed, Fri & Sat, 10am-8.45pm Thu, 11am-7.45pm Sun; MSèvres-Babylone) sells 30,000 rare and/ or luxury gourmet products, including 60 different types of bread baked on-site and delicacies such as caviar ravioli. Its fantastical displays of chocolates, pastries, biscuits, cheeses, fresh fruit and vegetables and deli goods are a sight in themselves. Wine tastings regularly take place in the basement.

Shakespeare & Company   Books

(Map p276; ☑01 43 25 40 93; www.shakespeareandcompany.com; 37 rue de la Bûcherie, 5e; ☉10am-10pm; MSt-Michel) Enchanting nooks and crannies overflow with new and secondhand English-language books. The original shop (12 rue l'Odéon, 6e; closed by the Nazis in 1941) was run by Sylvia Beach and became the meeting point for Hemingway's 'Lost Generation'. Readings by emerging and illustrious authors regularly take place

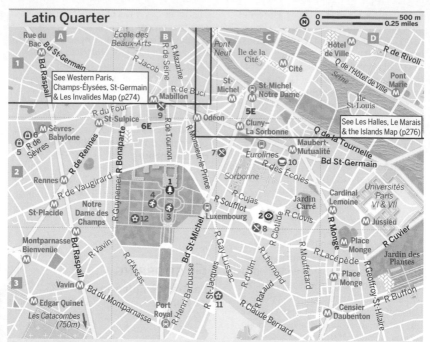

Latin Quarter

◉ Sights
1 Jardin du Luxembourg B2
2 Panthéon C2

✦ Activities, Courses & Tours
3 Grand Bassin Toy Sailboats B2
4 Pony Rides B2

🛍 Shopping
5 La Grande Épicerie de Paris A2
6 Le Bon Marché A2

✗ Eating
7 Bouillon Racine C2
8 Café de la Nouvelle Mairie C2
9 Huîtrerie Regis B1

🍷 Drinking & Nightlife
10 Nuage C2

✪ Entertainment
11 Café Universel C3
12 Théâtre du Luxembourg B2

and there's a wonderful **cafe** (Map p276; www.shakespeareandcompany.com; 2 rue St-Julien le Pauvre, 5e; ⏱9.30am-7pm Mon-Fri, to 8pm Sat & Sun; 🛜; Ⓜ St-Michel) 🗺 next door.

Marché aux Puces de St-Ouen
Market

(www.marcheauxpuces-saintouen.com; rue des Rosiers, St-Ouen; ⏱ Sat-Mon; Ⓜ Porte de Clignancourt) Spanning 9 hectares, this vast flea market was founded in 1870 and is said to be Europe's largest. Over 2000 stalls are grouped into 15 *marchés* (markets) selling everything from 17th-century furniture to 21st-century clothing. Each market has different opening hours – check the website for details. There are miles upon miles of 'freelance' stalls; come prepared to spend some time.

✗ EATING

✗ Right Bank

Le Verre Volé
Bistro €

(Map p276; 📞01 48 03 17 34; www.leverrevole.fr; 67 rue de Lancry, 10e; mains €11-22, sandwiches

€7.90; ⊘bistro 12.30-2.30pm & 7.30-11.30pm, wine bar 10am-?am; 🛜; Ⓜ Jacques Bonsergent) The tiny 'Stolen Glass' – a wine shop with a few tables – is one of Paris' most popular wine bar–restaurants, with outstanding natural and unfiltered wines and expert advice. Unpretentious, hearty *plats du jour* are excellent. Reserve in advance for meals, or stop by to pick up a gourmet sandwich (such as mustard-smoked burrata with garlic-pork sausage) and a bottle.

Richer   Bistro €

(Map p276; www.lericher.com; 2 rue Richer, 9e; mains €17-28; ⊘noon-2.30pm & 7.30-10.30pm; Ⓜ Poissonnière or Bonne Nouvelle) Run by the same team as across-the-street neighbour **L'Office** (Map p276; 📞 01 47 70 67 31; www. office-resto.com; 3 rue Richer, 9e; 2-/3-course lunch menus €22/27, mains €22-29; ⊘noon-2pm & 7.30-10.30pm Mon-Fri), Richer's pared-back, exposed-brick decor is a smart setting for genius creations including smoked-duck-breast ravioli in miso broth, and quince-and-lime cheesecake for dessert. It doesn't take reservations, but it serves snacks and Chinese tea, and has a full bar (open until midnight). Fantastic value.

Breizh Café   Crêpes €

(Map p276; 📞 01 42 72 13 77; www.breizhcafe.com; 109 rue Vieille du Temple, 3e; crêpes & galettes €6.80-18.80; ⊘10am-11pm; Ⓜ St-Sébastien–Froissart) Everything at the Breizh ('Breton' in Breton) is 100% authentic, including its organic-flour crêpes and *galettes* (savoury buckwheat crêpes) that top many Parisians' lists for the best in the city. Other specialities include Cancale oysters and 20 types of cider. Tables are limited and there's often a wait; book ahead or try its deli, **L'Épicerie** (Map p276; 📞 01 42 71 39 44; 111 rue Vieille du Temple, 3e; ⊘10am-10pm), next door.

Ladurée   Pastries €€

(Map p274; 📞 01 40 75 08 75; www.laduree.fr; 75 av des Champs-Élysées, 8e; pastries €2.60-13, mains €20-45, 2-/3-course lunch menu €35/42; ⊘7.30am-11.30pm Mon-Thu, 7.30am-12.30am Fri, 8.30am-12.30am Sat, 8.30am-11.30pm Sun; 🛜♿; Ⓜ George V) One of Paris' oldest

patisseries, Ladurée has been around since 1862 and first created the lighter-than-air, ganache-filled macaron in the 1930s. Its tearoom is the classiest spot to indulge on the Champs. Alternatively, pick up some pastries to go – from croissants to its trademark macarons, it's all quite heavenly.

Maison Maison   Mediterranean €€

(Map p276; 📞 09 67 82 07 32; www.restaurant-maisonmaison.com; 63 Parc Rives de Seine, 1er; 2-/3-course lunch menu €20/25, small plates €7-16; ⊘kitchen 7-10pm Mon, noon-3pm & 7-10pm Tue-Sun, bar to 2am; Ⓜ Pont Neuf) Halfway down the stairs by Pont Neuf is this wonderfully secret space beneath the *bouquinistes* (used-book sellers), where you can watch the *bateaux-mouches* (river-cruise boats) float by as you dine on creations such as beetroot and pink-grapefruit-cured bonito or gnocchi with white asparagus and broccoli pesto. In nice weather, cocktails at the glorious riverside terrace are not to be missed.

Frenchie   Bistro €€€

(Map p276; 📞 01 40 39 96 19; www.frenchie-ruedunil.com; 5 rue du Nil, 2e; 3-course lunch menu €48, 5-course dinner menu €65, with wine €175; ⊘6.30-10pm Mon-Wed, noon-2.30pm & 6.30-10pm Thu & Fri; Ⓜ Sentier) Tucked down an inconspicuous alley, this tiny bistro with wooden tables and old stone walls is always packed and for good reason: French chef Gregory Marchand's modern, market-driven dishes prepared with unpretentious flair have earned him a Michelin star. Reserve well in advance or arrive early and pray for a cancellation (it does happen). Alternatively, head to neighbouring **Frenchie Bar à Vins** (Map p276; www.frenchie-bav.com; 6 rue du Nil, 2e; dishes €8-28; ⊘6.30-11pm).

No reservations at Frenchie Bar à Vins – write your name on the sheet of paper strung outside and wait for your name to be called.

During the day, swing by its adjacent deli-style takeaway outlet **Frenchie to Go** (Map p276; 📞 01 40 26 23 43; www.frenchie-ftg. com; 9 rue du Nil, 2e; dishes €11-21; ⊘8.30am-5pm; 🛜).

Verjus — Modern American €€€

(Map p274; ☎01 42 97 54 40; www.verjusparis.com; 52 rue de Richelieu, 1er; menu €78, with wine €133; ⊗7-11pm Mon-Fri; Ⓜ Bourse, Pyramides) Opened by American duo Braden Perkins and Laura Adrian, Verjus was born out of their former clandestine supper club, the Hidden Kitchen. The restaurant builds on that tradition, offering a chance to sample some excellent, creative cuisine in a casual space. The tasting menu is a series of small plates, using ingredients sourced straight from producers. Reserve well in advance.

If you're just after an aperitif or a prelude to dinner, the downstairs **Verjus Bar à Vins** (Map p274; 47 rue de Montpensier, 1er; ⊗6-11pm Mon-Fri) serves a handful of charcuterie and cheese plates. For lunch or a more casual dinner, don't miss nearby **Ellsworth** (Map p274; ☎01 42 60 59 66; www.ellsworthparis.com; 34 rue de Richelieu, 1er; 2-/3-course lunch menu €24/30, small dinner plates €12-20; ⊗12.15-2.15pm & 7-10.30pm Tue-Fri, 7-10.30pm Sat; Ⓜ Pyramides), Verjus' sister restaurant.

🞊 Left Bank

Café de la Nouvelle Mairie — Cafe €

(Map p280; ☎01 44 07 04 41; 19 rue des Fossés St-Jacques, 5e; mains €11-17; ⊗8am-12.30am Mon-Fri, kitchen noon-2.30pm & 8-10.30pm Mon-Thu, 8-10pm Fri; Ⓜ Cardinal Lemoine) Shhhh... just around the corner from the Panthéon (p279) but hidden away on a small, fountained square, this hybrid cafe-restaurant and wine bar is a tip-top neighbourhood secret, serving natural wines and delicious seasonal bistro fare, from oysters and ribs (à la française) to grilled lamb sausage over lentils. It takes reservations for dinner but not lunch – arrive early.

Bouillon Racine — Brasserie €€

(Map p280; ☎01 44 32 15 60; www.bouillonracine.fr; 3 rue Racine, 6e; 2-course weekday lunch menu €17.50, 3-course menu €35, mains €17-24.50; ⊗noon-11pm; 👬; Ⓜ Cluny–La Sorbonne) Inconspicuously situated in a quiet street, this heritage-listed art nouveau 'soup kitchen', with mirrored walls, floral motifs and ceramic tiling, was built in 1906 to feed market workers. Despite the magnificent interior, the food – inspired by

BRIAN KINNEY / SHUTTERSTOCK ©

age-old recipes – is no afterthought and superbly executed (stuffed, spit-roasted suckling pig, pork shank in Rodenbach red beer, scallops and shrimps with lobster coulis).

Huîtrerie Regis   Seafood €€

(Map p280; www.huitrerie-regis.com; 3 rue de Montfaucon, 6e; dozen oysters from €26; ⊙noon-2.30pm & 6.30-10.30pm Mon-Fri, noon-10.45pm Sat, noon-10pm Sun; Ⓜ Mabillon) Hip, trendy, tiny and white, this is the spot for slurping oysters on crisp winter days – inside or on the tiny pavement terrace sporting sage-green Fermob chairs. Oysters arrive live from the Bassin de Marennes-Oléron and come only by the dozen. Wash them down with a glass of chilled Muscadet. No reservations, so arrive early.

🅾 DRINKING & NIGHTLIFE

Bar Hemingway   Cocktail Bar

(Map p274; www.ritzparis.com; Hôtel Ritz Paris, 15 place Vendôme, 1er; ⊙6pm-2am; 🕿; Ⓜ Opéra) Black-and-white photos and memorabilia (hunting trophies, old typewriters and framed handwritten letters by the great writer) fill this snug bar inside the Ritz. Head bartender Colin Peter Field mixes monumental cocktails, including three different Bloody Marys made with juice from freshly squeezed seasonal tomatoes. Legend has it that Hemingway himself, wielding a machine gun, helped liberate the bar during WWII.

Le Baron Rouge   Wine Bar

(www.lebaronrouge.net; 1 rue Théophile Roussel, 12e; ⊙5-10pm Mon, 10am-2pm & 5-10pm Tue-Fri, 10am-10pm Sat, 10am-4pm Sun; Ⓜ Ledru-Rollin) Just about the ultimate Parisian wine-bar experience, this wonderfully unpretentious local meeting place, where everyone is welcome, has barrels stacked against the bottle-lined walls and serves cheese, charcuterie and oysters in season. It's especially busy on Sunday after the Marché d'Aligre wraps up. For a small deposit, you can fill up 1L bottles straight from the barrel for less than €5.

★ Top Five Museums

Musée du Louvre (p256)

Musée d'Orsay (p278)

Centre Pompidou (p272)

Musée Rodin (p278)

Musée National Picasso (p273)

From left: Naopleon III apartments, Louvre (p256); *The Thinker*, Musée Rodin (p278); Musée d'Orsay (p278)

Best Boulangeries

Du Pain et des Idées (Map p276; www.dupainetdesidees.com; 34 rue Yves Toudic, 10e; breads €1.20-7, pastries €2.50-6.50; ☺6.45am-8pm Mon-Fri, closed Aug; MJacques Bonsergent) Traditional bakery with dazzling 1889 interior.

The French Bastards (Map p276; 61 rue Oberkampf, 11e; pastries €1.50-5.50, sandwiches €7.50-9; ☺7am-8.30pm Mon-Wed & Fri, 8am-8pm Sat, 8am-6pm Sun; MParmentier) Fantastic pastries and sandwiches near Canal St-Martin.

Le Grenier à Pain (Map p276; www.legrenierapain.com; 38 rue des Abbesses, 18e; pastries €1.10-4.50; ☺7.30am-8pm Thu-Mon; MAbbesses) Perfect Montmartre picnic stop.

Chambelland (Map p276; ☏01 43 55 07 30; www.chambelland.com; 14 rue Ternaux, 11e; lunch menus €10-12, pastries €2.50-5.50; ☺8am-8pm Tue-Sat, to 6pm Sun; MParmentier) A 100%-gluten-free bakery.

Du Pain et des Idées
GORODISSKIJ / SHUTTERSTOCK ©

Coutume Café   Coffee
(☏01 45 51 50 47; www.coutumecafe.com; 47 rue de Babylone, 7e; ☺8.30am-5.30pm Mon-Fri, 9am-6pm Sat & Sun; ☎; MSt-François Xavier) ⚑ The Parisian coffee revolution is thanks in no small part to Coutume, artisanal roaster of premium beans for scores of establishments around town. Its flagship cafe – a light-filled, post-industrial space – is ground zero for innovative preparation methods including cold extraction and siphon brews. Couple some of Paris' finest coffee with tasty, seasonal cuisine and the place is always packed out.

Les Deux Magots   Cafe
(Map p274; ☏01 45 48 55 25; www.lesdeux magots.fr; 6 place St-Germain des Prés, 6e; ☺7.30am-1am; MSt-Germain des Prés) If ever there was a cafe that summed up St-Germain des Prés' early-20th-century literary scene, it's this former hang-out of anyone who was anyone. You'll spend substantially more here to sip un café (€4.80) in a wicker chair on the pavement terrace shaded by dark-green awnings and geraniums spilling from window boxes, but it's an undeniable piece of Parisian history.

Le Perchoir   Rooftop Bar
(Map p276; ☏01 48 06 18 48; www.leperchoir.tv; 14 rue Crespin du Gast, 11e; ☺6pm-2am Tue-Sat; ☎; MMénilmontant) Sunset is the best time to head up to this 7th-floor bar for a drink overlooking Paris' rooftops, where DJs spin on Saturday nights. Greenery provides shade in summer; in winter it's covered by a sail-like canopy and warmed by fires burning in metal drums. It's accessed off an inner courtyard via a lift (or a spiralling staircase).

Experimental Cocktail Club   Cocktail Bar
(ECC; Map p276; www.experimentalcocktail club.fr; 37 rue St-Sauveur, 2e; ☺7pm-2am; MRéaumur Sébastopol) With a black curtain façade, this retro-chic speakeasy – with sister bars in London, Ibiza, New York and, bien sûr, Paris – is a sophisticated flashback to those années folles (crazy years) of Prohibition New York. Cocktails are individual and fabulous, and DJs keep the party going until dawn at weekends. It's not a large space, however, and fills to capacity quickly.

Pavillon Puebla   Beer Garden
(www.leperchoir.tv; Parc des Buttes Chaumont, 39 av Simon Bolivar, 19e; ☺6pm-2am Wed-Fri, from noon Sat, noon-10pm Sun; ☎; MButtes Chaumont) Strung with fairy lights, this rustic ivy-draped cottage's two rambling terraces in the Parc des Buttes Chaumont

evoke a *guinguette* (old-fashioned outdoor tavern/dance venue), with a 21st-century vibe provided by its Moroccan decor, contemporary furniture, and DJ beats from Thursdays to Saturdays. Alongside mostly French wines and craft beers, cocktails include its signature Spritz du Pavillon (Aperol, Prosecco and soda).

Nuage   Cafe
(Map p280; ☎09 82 39 80 69; www.nuagecafe.fr; 14 rue des Carmes, 5e; per hr/day €5/25; ⊗9am-7pm Mon-Fri, 11am-8pm Sat & Sun; 🛜; Ⓜ Maubert-Mutualité) One of a crop of co-working cafes to mushroom in Paris, Nuage (Cloud) lures a loyal following of nomadic digital creatives with its cosy, home-like spaces in an old church (and subsequent school where Cyrano de Bergerac apparently studied). Payment is by the hour or day, craft coffee is by Parisian roaster Coutume and gourmet snacks stave off hunger pangs.

Concrete   Club
(www.concreteparis.fr; 69 Port de la Rapée, 12e; ⊗from 10pm Thu-Mon; Ⓜ Gare de Lyon) Moored by Gare de Lyon on a barge on the Seine, this wild-child club with two dance floors is famed for introducing an 'after-hours' element to Paris' somewhat staid clubbing scene, with the country's first 24-hour licence. Watch for world-class electro DJ appearances and all-weekend events on social media.

⭐ ENTERTAINMENT

Opéra Bastille   Opera
(Map p276; ☎international calls 01 71 25 24 23, within France 08 92 89 90 90; www.operade paris.fr; 2-6 place de la Bastille, 12e; ⊗box office 11.30am-6.30pm Mon-Sat, 1hr prior to performances Sun; Ⓜ Bastille) Paris' premier opera hall, Opéra Bastille's 2745-seat main auditorium also stages ballet and classical concerts. Online tickets go on sale up to three weeks before telephone or box-office sales (from noon on Wednesdays; online flash sales offer significant discounts). Standing-only tickets (*places débouts;* €5) are available 90 minutes before performances. French-language

A coffee and croissant at a Paris cafe

STRINGER / STRINGER / GETTY IMAGES ©

Sting performing at Le Bataclan

90-minute **guided tours** (Map p276; ☑within France 08 92 89 90 90; www.operade paris.fr; 2-6 place de la Bastille, 12e; tours adult/child €17/12; ☺tours Sep–mid-Jul; Ⓜ Bastille) take you backstage.

Philharmonie de Paris   Concert Venue
(☑01 44 84 44 84; www.philharmoniedeparis.fr; 221 av Jean Jaurès, 19e; ☺box office noon-6pm Tue-Fri, from 10am Sat & Sun, plus concerts; Ⓜ Porte de Pantin) Major complex the Cité de la Musique – Philharmonie de Paris hosts an eclectic range of concerts, from classical to North African and Japanese, in the Philharmonie building's Grande Salle Pierre Boulez, with an audience capacity of 2400 to 3600. The adjacent Cité de la Musique's Salle des Concerts has a capacity of 900 to 1600.

Café Universel   Jazz, Blues
(Map p280; ☑01 43 25 74 20; www.facebook. com/cafeuniversel.paris05; 267 rue St-Jacques, 5e; ☺concerts from 8.30pm Tue-Sat, cafe 8.30am-3pm Mon, 8.30am-1am Tue-Fri, 4.30pm-1am Sat, 1.30pm-1am Sun; ☎; Ⓜ Censier Daubenton or RER Port Royal) Café Universel hosts a brilliant array of live concerts with

everything from bebop and Latin sounds to vocal jazz sessions. Plenty of freedom is given to young producers and artists, and its convivial, relaxed atmosphere attracts a mix of students and jazz lovers. Concerts are free, but you should tip the artists when they pass the hat around.

Le Bataclan   Live Music
(Map p276; ☑01 43 14 00 30; www.bataclan.fr; 50 bd Voltaire, 11e; Ⓜ Oberkampf, Filles du Calvaire) Built in 1864, intimate concert, theatre and dance hall Le Bataclan was Maurice Chevalier's debut venue in 1910. The 1497-capacity venue reopened with a concert by Sting on 12 November 2016, almost a year to the day following the tragic 13 November 2015 terrorist attacks that took place here, and once again hosts French and international rock and pop legends.

ℹ INFORMATION
Paris Convention & Visitors Bureau (Paris Office de Tourisme; Map p276; ☑01 49 52 42 63; www.parisinfo.com; 29 rue de Rivoli, 4e; ☺9am-7pm May-Oct, 10am-7pm Nov-Apr; ☎; Ⓜ Hôtel de

Ville) Paris' main tourist office is at the Hôtel de Ville. It sells tickets for tours and several attractions, plus museum and transport passes.

ℹ GETTING THERE & AWAY

AIR

Paris is a major air-transport hub serviced by virtually all major airlines, with three airports.

Aéroport de Charles de Gaulle (CDG; ☎01 70 36 39 50; www.parisaeroport.fr) Major international airport, also known as 'Roissy', 28km northeast of central Paris.

Aéroport d'Orly (ORY; ☎01 70 36 39 50; www. parisaeroport.fr) Located 19km south of central Paris but not as frequently used by international airlines as CDG.

Aéroport de Beauvais (BVA; ☎08 92 68 20 66; www.aeroportbeauvais.com) Served by a few low-cost flights, 75km north of Paris.

BUS

Eurolines (Map p280; ☎08 92 89 90 91; www. eurolines.fr; 55 rue St-Jacques, 5e; ⊙10am-1pm & 2-6pm Mon-Fri; Ⓜ Cluny–La Sorbonne) connects all major European capitals to Paris' international bus terminal, **Gare Routière Internationale de Paris-Galliéni** (28 av du Général de Gaulle, Bagnolet; Ⓜ Galliéni). The terminal is in the eastern suburb of Bagnolet; it's about a 15-minute metro ride to the more central République station.

Major European bus company FlixBus (www. flixbus.com) uses western **Parking Pershing** (16-24 bd Pershing, 17e; Ⓜ Porte Maillot).

TRAIN

Paris has six major train stations serving both national and international destinations. For mainline train information, check SNCF (www. sncf-voyages.com).

ℹ GETTING AROUND

Walking is a pleasure in Paris, and the city also has one of the most efficient and inexpensive

Buying Tickets

The most convenient place to purchase concert, theatre and other cultural and sporting-event tickets is from electronics and entertainment megashop **Fnac** (☎08 92 68 36 22; www.fnactickets.com) or by phone or online. On the day of performance, theatre, opera and ballet tickets are sold for half price (plus €3 commission) at the central **Kiosque Théâtre Madeleine** (Map p274; www. kiosqueculture.com; opposite 15 place de la Madeleine, 8e; ⊙12.30-2.30pm & 3-7.30pm Tue-Sat, 12.30-3.45pm Sun Sep-Jun, closed Sun Jul & Aug; Ⓜ Madeleine).

Fnac
MIKEDOTTA / SHUTTERSTOCK ©

public-transport systems in the world, which makes getting around a breeze.

Metro & RER The fastest way to get around. Metros run from about 5.30am and finish around 1.15am (around 2.15am on Friday and Saturday nights), depending on the line. RER commuter trains operate from around 5.30am to 1.20am daily.

Bicycle Virtually free pick-up, drop-off Vélib' bikes have docking stations across the city; electric bikes are also available.

Bus Good for parents with prams/strollers and people with limited mobility.

Boat The Batobus is a handy hop-on, hop-off service stopping at nine key destinations along the Seine.

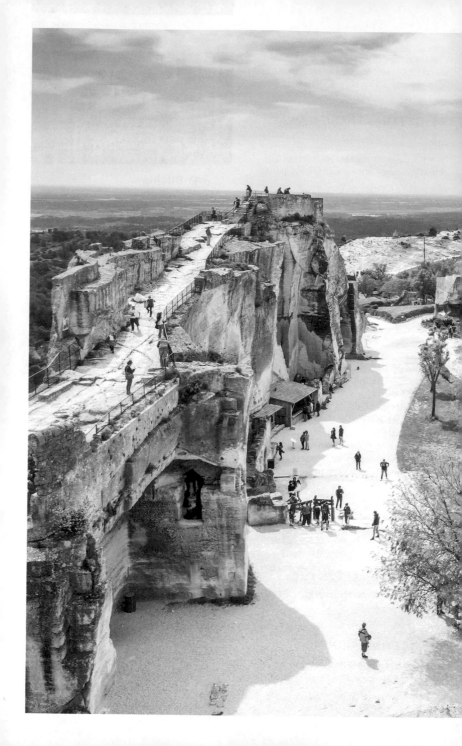

PROVENCE, FRANCE

Provence, France

Travelling in this sun-blessed part of southern France means touring scenic backroads strewn with stunning landscapes: lavender fields, olive groves, deep gorges and eagle-pecked mountains. Factor in prehistoric sites, magnificent Roman relics, medieval abbeys and elegant churches, and Provence becomes a living history book. Then there's the low-key village ambling, wine tasting and mellow alfresco lunching for hours on end. The region is prime cycling and hiking territory, with mountains of unique spots to explore, Roussillon's fiery-red ochre quarries and the shimmering white stone-capped summit of Provence's highest peak included.

Two Days in Provence

Spend day one in **Avignon** (p298), exploring the old town and the **Palais des Papes** (p298), and perhaps trying some local wine. On day two, make a day trip to either **Les Baux-de-Provence** (p294) for hilltop-village meandering or to the **Pont du Gard** (p296) for Roman history and memorable canoeing action on the River Gard.

Four Days in Provence

Day three, hop between hilltop villages – don't miss a red-rock hike in **Roussillon** (p295) or wine tasting and truffles in **Ménerbes** (p295). Aim to make it to **Gordes** (p294) for sunset. Devote the fourth day to exploring the breathtaking **Gorges du Verdon** (p304) or communing with Provence's highest peak, **Mont Ventoux** (p303).

Finished in Provence? Catch a train to Barcelona (p181) or fly to London (p49).

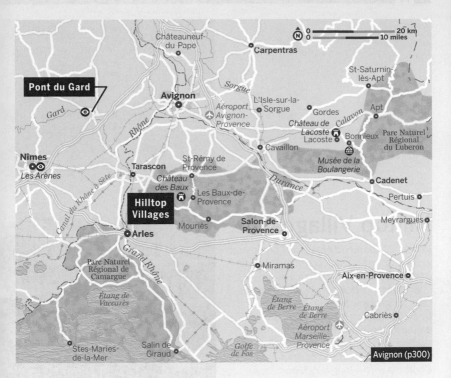

Avignon (p300)

Arriving in Provence

Aéroport Marseille-Provence (MRS; ☎08 20 81 14 14; www.marseille.aeroport. fr) Buses to Aix-en-Provence every 20 minutes. Direct trains to destinations including Marseille, Arles and Avignon.

Aéroport Avignon-Provence (p302) Bus 30 (www.tcra.fr; €1.40; 35 minutes) to the post office and LER bus 22 (www. info-ler.fr; €1.50) to Avignon bus station and TGV station. Taxis about €35 to €40.

Where to Stay

Provence has a huge variety of accommodation, embracing everything from super-luxury hotels to treehouses or cosy cottages overlooking vines and lavender fields. In summer, prices skyrocket and rooms are scarce. Avignon is an excellent base for Pont du Gard (a 30-minute drive); Moustiers Ste-Marie is a key stop for Gorge du Verdon explorers; Apt and its rural surrounds are perfect for touring the Luberon's hilltop villages. Find accommodation listings at **Avignon & Provence** (www. avignon-et-provence.com).

Les Baux-de-Provence (p294)

Hilltop Villages

Impossibly perched on a rocky peak, gloriously lost in back country, fortified or château-topped: Provence's impressive portfolio of villages perchés calls for go-slow touring – on foot, by bicycle or car. Most villages are medieval, built from golden stone and riddled with cobbled lanes, flower-filled alleys and fountain-pierced squares. Combine with a long lazy lunch for a perfect day.

Great For...

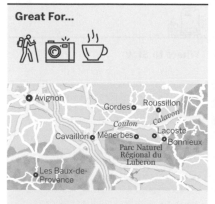

ℹ Need to Know

Apt Tourist Office (☏ 04 90 74 03 18; www.luberon-apt.fr; 788 av Victor Hugo; ⊙ 9.30am-12.30pm & 2-6pm Mon-Sat, also 9.30am-12.30pm Sun Jul & Aug)

★ **Top Tip**
Visit early in the morning or just before sunset for the best light and fewer crowds.

Les Baux-de-Provence

Clinging precariously to an ancient limestone *baou* (Provençal for 'rocky spur'), this fortified hilltop village is one of the most visited in France. It's easy to understand its popularity: narrow cobbled streets wend car-free past ancient houses, up to the splendid **Château des Baux** (📞04 90 49 20 02; www.chateau-baux-provence.com; adult/child Apr-Sep €10/8, Oct-Mar €8/6; ⊙9am-8pm Jul & Aug, to 7pm Apr-Jun & Sep, reduced hours Oct-Mar), whose dramatic maze-like ruins date to the 10th century. The clifftop castle was largely destroyed in 1633, during the reign of Louis XIII, and is a thrilling place to explore – climb crumbling towers for incredible views, descend into disused dungeons and flex your knightly prowess with giant medieval weapons dotting the open-air site. Medieval-themed entertainment abounds in summer.

Gordes

Like a giant wedding cake rising over the rivers Sorgue and Calavon, the tiered village of Gordes juts spectacularly out of the white-rock face of the Vaucluse plateau. Come sunset, the village glows gold.

From the central square, meander downhill along rue Baptist in Picca to **La Boulangerie de Mamie Jane** (📞04 90 72 09 34; rue Baptistin Picca; dishes €7-10; ⊙7am-6pm Thu-Tue winter, to 7pm Thu-Tue summer), a family-run bakery with outstanding bread, pastries, cakes and biscuits, including lavender-perfumed *navettes* and delicious peanut-and-almond brittle known as *écureuil* (from the French for squirrel).

Abbaye Notre-Dame de Sénanque

Roussillon

Dazzling Roussillon was once the centre of local ochre mining and is still unmistakably marked by its vivid crimson colour. Artist workshops lace its streets and the **Sentier des Ocres** (Ochre Trail; adult/child €3/free; ⊙9am-7.30pm Jul & Aug, shorter hours rest yr, closed Jan; 🖼) plunges intrigued visitors into a mini-desert landscape of chestnut groves, pines and sunset-coloured ochre formations. Information panels along the two circular trails (30 or 50 minutes) highlight flora to spot. Wear walking shoes and avoid white clothing!

☑ Don't Miss

Rows of summertime lavender in bloom at **Abbaye Notre-Dame de Sénanque** (www.senanque.fr), a supremely peaceful Cistercian abbey 4km northwest of Gordes.

PROCHASSON FRÉDÉRIC / SHUTTERSTOCK ©

Ménerbes

Hilltop Ménerbes gained fame as the home of expat British author Peter Mayles, whose book *A Year in Provence* recounts his renovation of a farmhouse just outside the village in the late 1980s. Opposite the village's 12th-century church, the **Maison de la Truffe et du Vin** (House of Truffle & Wine; 🖉04 90 72 38 37; www.vin-truffe-luberon. com; place de l'Horloge; ⊙10am-6pm Apr-Oct, 10am-5pm Thu-Sat Dec-Mar) represents 60 local *domaines* (wine-growing estates). April to October, there is free wine tasting and wine sales at bargain-basement prices. Winter brings black truffle workshops.

Lacoste

Lacoste has nothing to do with the designer brand – although it does have couturier connections. In 2001 designer Pierre Cardin purchased the 9th-century **Château de Lacoste**. The château was looted by revolutionaries in 1789, and the 45-room palace remained an eerie ruin until Cardin arrived. He created a 1000-seat theatre and opera stage adjacent, only open during July's month-long **Festival de Lacoste** (www.festivaldelacoste. com). Daytime visits are possible only by reservation.

Bonnieux

Settled by the Romans, Bonnieux is a medieval maze of alleyways and hidden staircases: from place de la Liberté, 86 steps lead to its 12th-century church. The **Musée de la Boulangerie** (🖉04 90 75 88 34; 12 rue de la République; adult/child €4/free; ⊙10.30am-1pm & 2.30-6pm Thu-Tu Apr-Oct), in an old 17th-century bakery building, explores bread-making history. Time your visit for the lively Friday market.

✗ Take a Break

The villages are the ideal place to try Provençal specialities like *aïoli* (a fish dish with garlicky mayo) and *daube provençale* (a rich stew).

CGL2010 / SHUTTERSTOCK ©

Pont du Gard

Southern France has some fine Roman sites, but nothing can top the Unesco World Heritage–listed Pont du Gard. Officially it's not in Provence at all (but rather in neighbouring Languedoc), but it's close enough to include in any Provence itinerary. Find the breathtaking three-tiered aqueduct 25km west of Avignon.

Great For...

☑ Don't Miss

With kids: fun, hands-on learning in the Ludo activity play area.

The extraordinary three-tiered Pont du Gard, 21km northeast of Nîmes, was once part of a 50km-long system of channels built around 19 BC to transport water from Uzès to Nîmes. The scale is huge: the bridge is 48.8m high, 275m long and graced with 52 precision-built arches. It was sturdy enough to carry up to 20,000 cubic metres of water per day.

Le Musée & Ludo

Each block was carved by hand and transported from nearby quarries – no mean feat, considering the largest blocks weighed over 5 tonnes. The height of the bridge descends by 2.5cm across its length, providing just enough gradient to keep the water flowing – an amazing demonstration of the precision of Roman engineering. At the visitor centre on the

❶ Need to Know

☑04 66 37 50 99; www.pontdugard.fr; adult/
child €9.50/free, top tier guided visit adult/
child €6/free; ☉9am-8pm Jul & Aug, to 7pm
Apr-Jun & Sep, to 6pm Oct, to 5pm Nov-Feb, to
5.50pm Mar

✕ Take a Break

Dine at outstanding neobistro **Le
Tracteur** (☑04 66 62 17 33; Bord Nègre,
Argilliers; set menu €27-33; ☉noon-2pm
Mon-Thu, noon-2pm & 7.30-9.30pm Fri) in
Argilliers, 6km northwest.

★ Top Tip

Evening is a good time to visit: admission is cheaper and the bridge is
stunningly illuminated after dark.

left, northern bank, there's an impressive,
high-tech **museum** featuring the bridge,
the aqueduct and the role of water in
Roman society. The **Ludo** play area helps
kids to learn in a fun, hands-on way.

Mémoires de Garrigue

You can walk across the tiers for panoramic
views over the Gard River, but the best perspective on the bridge is from downstream,
along the 1.4km Mémoires de Garrigue
walking trail. If you buy the **Pass Aqueduc**,
you can walk the bridge's topmost tier,
along which the water flowed (guided tour).

Canoeing on the Gard

Paddling beneath the Pont du Gard is
unforgettable. The best time is between
April and June. The Gard flows from the
Cévennes mountains all the way to the
aqueduct, passing through the dramatic
Gorges du Gardon en route. Hire companies are in Collias, 8km from the bridge, a
journey of about two hours by kayak.

What's Nearby?

Les Arènes   Roman Site

(☑04 66 21 82 56; www.arenes-nimes.com; place
des Arènes; adult/child incl audio guide €10/8;
☉9am-8pm Jul & Aug, to 7pm Jun, to 6.30pm Apr,
May & Sep, to 6pm Mar & Oct, 9.30am-5pm Jan,
Feb, Nov & Dec) Roman buffs can continue
to Nîmes, a city 30km southwest, heralded
as the 'Rome of France' thanks to its twin-
tiered amphitheatre dating from 100 BC. It
once seated 24,000 spectators and staged
gladiatorial contests and public executions,
and remains an impressive venue for gigs
and events. An audioguide provides context
as you explore the arena, seating areas,
stairwells and corridors (known to Romans
as *vomitories*).

Avignon

Attention, quiz fans: name the city where the pope lived during the early 14th century. Answered Rome? Bzzz: sorry, wrong answer. For 70-odd years of the early 1300s, the Provençal town of Avignon served as the centre of the Roman Catholic world, and though its stint as the seat of papal power only lasted a few decades, it's been left with an impressive legacy of ecclesiastical architecture, most notably the soaring, World Heritage–listed fortress-cum-palace known as the Palais des Papes.

Avignon is now best known for its annual arts festival, the largest in France, which draws thousands of visitors for several weeks in July. The rest of the year, it's a lovely city to explore, with boutique-lined streets, leafy squares and some excellent restaurants – as well as an impressive medieval wall that entirely encircles the old city.

◎ SIGHTS

Serial museum lovers will do well to invest in an Avignon City Pass (€21/28 for 24/48 hours) covering admission to all the key museums; buy it online in advance or at the tourist office (p302).

Palais des Papes   Palace

(Papal Palace; ☑tickets 04 32 74 32 74; www.palais-des-papes.com; place du Palais; adult/child €12/10, with Pont St-Bénézet €14.50/11.50; ☺9am-8pm Jul, to 8.30pm Aug, shorter hours Sep-Jun) The largest Gothic palace ever built, the Palais des Papes was erected by Pope Clement V, who abandoned Rome in 1309 as a result of violent disorder following his election. It served as the seat of papal power for seven decades, and its immense scale provides ample testament to the medieval might of the Roman Catholic church. Ringed by 3m-thick walls, its cavernous halls, chapels and antechambers are largely bare today, but an audioguide (€2) provides a useful backstory.

Pont St-Bénézet   Bridge

(☑tickets 04 32 74 32 74; bd de la Ligne; adult/child 24hr ticket €5/4, with Palais des Papes €14.50/11.50; ☺9am-8pm Jul, to 8.30pm

Palais des Papes

PAUL DANIELS / SHUTTERSTOCK ©

Aug, shorter hours Sep-Jun) Legend says Pastor Bénezet had three saintly visions urging him to build a bridge across the Rhône. Completed in 1185, the 900m-long bridge with 20 arches linked Avignon with Villeneuve-lès-Avignon. It was rebuilt several times before all but four of its spans were washed away in the 1600s.

If you don't want to pay to visit the bridge, admire it for free from Rocher des Doms park or Pont Édouard Daladier or on Île de la Barthelasse's chemin des Berges.

Musée du Petit Palais   Museum
(☑04 90 86 44 58; www.petit-palais.org; place du Palais; ⊙10am-1pm & 2-6pm Wed-Mon) **FREE** The archbishops' palace during the 14th and 15th centuries now houses outstanding collections of primitive, pre-Renaissance, 13th- to 16th-century Italian religious paintings by artists including Botticelli, Carpaccio and Giovanni di Paolo – the most famous is Botticelli's *La Vierge et l'Enfant* (1470).

Musée Angladon   Gallery
(☑04 90 82 29 03; www.angladon.com; 5 rue du Laboureur; adult/child €8/1.50; ⊙1-6pm Tue-Sun Apr-Sep, 1-6pm Tue-Sat Oct-Mar) Tiny Musée Angladon harbours an impressive collection of impressionist treasures, including works by Cézanne, Sisley, Manet and Degas – but the star piece is Van Gogh's *Wagons de chemin de fer à Arles (Railway Wagons;* 1888), the only painting by the artist on display in Provence. Impress your friends by pointing out that the 'earth' isn't actually paint, but bare canvas.

🟢 ACTIVITIES & TOURS
Le Carré du Palais   Wine Tasting
(☑04 65 00 01 01; www.carredupalais.fr; 1 place du Palais) The historic Hôtel Calvet de la Palun building in central Avignon is today a wine centre promoting and serving local Côtes du Rhône and Vallée du Rhône appellations. Its **École des Vin** (Wine School) runs two-hour, themed tasting workshops (€35) and three-wine

✳️ Festivals in Avignon

The three-week annual **Festival d'Avignon** (☑box office 04 90 14 14 14; www. festival-avignon.com; ⊙Jul) is one of the world's great performing-arts festivals. More than 40 international works of dance and drama play to 100,000-plus spectators at venues around town. Tickets don't go on sale until springtime, but hotels sell out by February. Paralleling the festival is the equally fabulous fringe event, **Festival Off** (www. avignonleoff.com; ⊙Jul), with eclectic experimental programming.

In season, from mid-August to mid-October, spectacular *son-et-lumière* show **Avignon Vibrations** (http://avignon-vibrations.com; adult/reduced €12/10; performances 9.30pm & 10.30pm Aug & Oct, 9.30pm Mon, Wed & Sun, 9.30pm & 10.30pm Fri & Sat Sep) transforms the ancient stone walls of Palais du Papes' main courtyard into a dazzling mirage of sound, light and fantastical digital imagery. Shows last 30 minutes.

Playbills for the Festival d'Avignon
PHOTOPROFI30 / SHUTTERSTOCK ©

tastings (€25) take place in the **Cave de Dégustation** (Tasting Cellar); both require advance reservations.

Avignon Wine Tour   Tours
(☑06 28 05 33 84; www.avignon-wine-tour.com; per person €95-130) Visit the region's vineyards with a knowledgeable guide, leaving you free to enjoy the wine.

Avignon

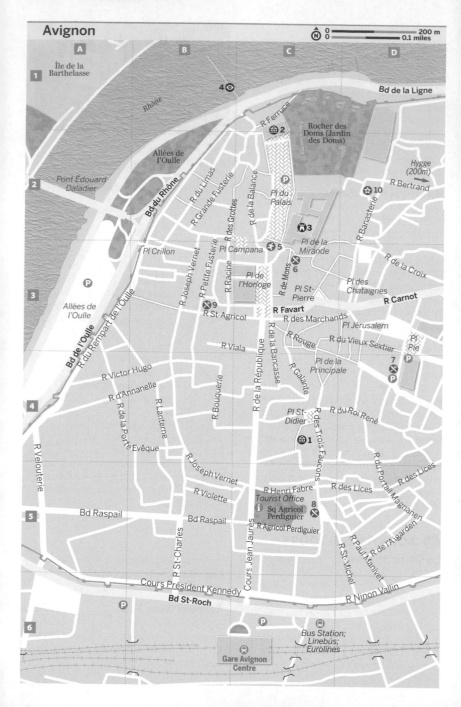

Île de la Barthelasse

Rhône

Bd de la Ligne

R Ferruce

Rocher des Doms (Jardin des Doms)

Allées de l'Oulle

Hygge (200m)

R Bertrand

Pont Édouard Daladier

Bd du Rhône

R du Limas

R Grande Fusterie

R des Grottes

R de la Balance

Pl du Palais

R Banasterie

Allées de l'Oulle

Pl Crillon

R Joseph Vernet

R Petite Fusterie

R Racine

Pl Campana

Pl du Palais

Pl de la Mirande

R de la Croix

Bd de l'Oulle

R du Rempart de l'Oulle

Pl de l'Horloge

R de Mons

Pl St-Pierre

Pl des Chataignes

R Carnot

R St-Agricol

R Favart

R des Marchands

Pl Jérusalem

R Viala

R de la Bancasse

R Rouge

R du Vieux Sextier

Pl de la Principale

Pl Pie

R Victor Hugo

R Galante

R d'Annanelle

R Bouquerie

R de la République

R de la Porte Evêque

R Lanterne

Pl St-Didier

R du Roi René

R Velouterie

R Joseph Vernet

R Violette

R des Trois Faucons

R des Lices

R du Portail Magnanen

Bd Raspail

R Henri Fabre

Tourist Office

Sq Agricol Perdiguier

R Agricol Perdiguier

Bd Raspail

R St-Charles

Cours Jean Jaurès

R Paul Manivet

R de l'Aigarden

R St-Michel

Cours Président Kennedy

R Ninon Vallin

Bd St-Roch

Bus Station; Linebús; Eurolines

Gare Avignon Centre

Avignon

🍴 EATING

Place de l'Horloge is crammed with touristy restaurants that don't offer the best cuisine or value in town. Delve instead into the pedestrian old city where ample pretty squares tempt: place des Châtaignes and place de la Principle are two particularly beautiful restaurant-clad squares.

Restaurants open seven days during the summer festival season, when reservations become essential.

Maison Violette   Bakery €

(📞06 59 44 62 94; www.facebook.com/maisonvioletteavignon/; 30 place des Corps Saints; ⊗7am-7.30pm Tue-Sat) We simply defy you not to walk into this bakery and not instantly be tempted by the stacks of baguettes, *ficelles* and *pains de campagne* loaded up on the counter, not to mention the orderly ranks of eclairs, *millefeuilles*, fruit tarts and cookies lined up irresistibly behind the glass. Go on, a little bit of what you fancy does you good, *non*?

Hygge   Cafe €

(📞04 65 81 06 87; https://hygge.bio/; 25 place des Carmes; 2-/3-course lunch €15.90/17.90; ⊗9am-4pm Mon-Sat) 🍴 Having worked at a smorgasbord of high-flying restaurants (including Copenhagen's Noma and Avignon's La Mirande), Jacques Pampiri opened his own place in Avignon, and it's a big hit with the locals. Hearty, wholesome organic food is dished up canteen-style to keep costs down, and the mix-and-match thrift-store decor is great fun. Arrive early for a prime table on the square.

Les Halles   Market €

(www.avignon-leshalles.com; place Pie; ⊗6am-1.30pm Tue-Fri, to 2pm Sat & Sun) Over 40 food stalls showcase seasonal Provençal ingredients. Cooking demonstrations are held at 11am Saturday. Outside on place Pie, admire Patrick Blanc's marvellous vegetal wall.

Restaurant L'Essentiel   French €€

(📞04 90 85 87 12; www.restaurantlessentiel.com; 2 rue Petite Fusterie; lunch/dinner menus €25/36-48; ⊗noon-2pm & 7-9.45pm Tue-Sat) Snug in an elegant, caramel-stone *hôtel particulier*, the Essential is one of the finest places to eat in town – inside or in the wonderful courtyard garden. Begin with courgette flowers poached in a crayfish-and-truffle sauce, then continue with rabbit stuffed with candied aubergine, perhaps.

Christian Etienne   French €€€

(📞04 84 88 51 27; www.christianetienne.fr; 10 rue de Mons; lunch/dinner menus €38-51/78-133; ⊗noon-1.30pm & 7.30-9pm Fri-Tue Aug-Jun, daily Jul) One of Avignon's top tables, this Michelin-starred restaurant occupies a 12th-century palace with a leafy outdoor terrace, adjacent to Palais des Papes. Chef Guilhem Sevin changes his elaborate menu each season, working with fresh local produce to create his refined Provençal cuisine.

🍷 DRINKING & NIGHTLIFE

Chic yet laid-back Avignon is awash with gorgeous, tree-shaded pedestrian squares buzzing with cafe life. Favourite options, loaded with pavement terraces and drinking opportunities, include place Crillon, place Pie, place de l'Horloge and place des Corps Saints.

 Rue des Teinturiers

Canalside rue des Teinturiers (literally 'street of dyers') is a picturesque pedestrian street known for its alternative vibe in Avignon's old dyers' district. A hive of industrial activity until the 19th century, populated by weavers and tapestry-makers, the street today is renowned for its bohemian bistros, cafes and gallery-workshops. Stone 'benches' in the shade of ancient plane trees make the perfect perch to ponder the irresistible trickle of the River Sorgue, safeguarded since the 16th century by Chapelle des Pénitents Gris.

TSTGRAPH / SHUTTERSTOCK ©

Students tend to favour the many bars dotted along the aptly named rue de la Verrerie (Glassware St).

La Manutention　　　　Arts Center
(☑04 90 86 86 77; 4 rue des Escaliers Ste-Anne; ☽noon-midnight) No address better reflects Avignon's artsy soul than this bistro-bar at cultural centre La Manutention. Its leafy terrace basks in the shade of Palais des Papes' stone walls and, inside, giant conservatory-style windows open onto the funky decor of pocket-sized bar Utopia. There's a cinema too.

ⓘ INFORMATION

Tourist Office (☑04 32 74 32 74; www. avignon-tourisme.com; 41 cours Jean Jaurès; ☽9am-6pm Mon-Sat, 10am-5pm Sun Apr-Oct,

shorter hours Nov-Mar) Offers guided walking tours and information on other tours and activities, including boat trips on the River Rhône and wine-tasting trips to nearby vineyards.

ⓘ GETTING THERE & AWAY

AIR

Aéroport Avignon-Provence (AVN; ☑04 90 81 51 51; www.avignon.aeroport.fr; Caumont) In Caumont, 8km southeast of Avignon. Direct flights to London, Birmingham and Southampton in the UK.

BUS

The **bus station** (bd St-Roch; ☽information window 8am-7pm Mon-Fri, to 1pm Sat) is next to the central train station. Tickets are sold on board. For schedules, see www.lepilote.com, www.info-ler.fr and www.vaucluse.fr. Long-haul companies **Linebús** (☑04 90 85 30 48; www. linebus.com) and **Eurolines** (☑04 90 85 27 60; www.eurolines.com) have offices at the far end of bus platforms and serve places such as Barcelona.

TRAIN

Avignon has two train stations: **Gare Avignon Centre** (42 bd St-Roch), on the southern edge of the walled town, and **Gare Avignon TGV** (Courtine), 4km southwest in Courtine. Local shuttle trains link the two every 15 to 20 minutes (€1.60, six minutes, 6am to 11pm). Note that there is no luggage storage at the train station.

ⓘ GETTING AROUND

BICYCLE

Vélopop (☑08 10 45 64 56; www.velopop.fr; per half-hour €0.50) Shared-bicycle service, with 17 stations around town. Membership per day/week is €1/5.

Provence Bike (☑04 90 27 92 61; www. provence-bike.com; 7 av St-Ruf; bicycles per day/week from €12/65, scooters €25/150; ☽9am-6.30pm Mon-Sat, plus 10am-1pm Sun Jul) Rents city bikes, mountain bikes, scooters and motorcycles.

CAR & MOTORCYCLE

Find car-hire agencies at both train stations (reserve ahead, especially in July). Narrow, one-way streets and impossible parking make driving within the ramparts difficult: park outside the walls. The city has 900 free spaces at **Parking de L'Ile Piot**, and 1150 at **Parking des Italiens**, both under surveillance and served by the free **TCRA shuttle bus** (Transports en Commun de la Région d'Avignon; ☏ 04 32 74 18 32; www.tcra.fr).

Mont Ventoux

Visible for miles around, Mont Ventoux (1912m) stands like a sentinel over northern Provence. From its summit, accessible by road between May and October, vistas extend to the Alps and, on a clear day, the Camargue. The white stone-capped peak is just over an hour's drive northeast from Avignon, making it a perfect day out.

Because of the mountain's dimensions, every European climate type is represented here, from Mediterranean on its lower southern reaches to Arctic on its exposed northern ridge. As you climb, temperatures can plummet by 20°C, and the fierce mistral wind blows 130 days a year, sometimes at speeds of 250km/h. Bring warm clothes and rain gear, even in summer. You can ascend by road year round, but you cannot traverse the summit from 15 November to 15 April.

The mountain's diverse fauna and flora have earned the mountain Unesco Biosphere Reserve status. Some species, including the rare snake eagle, are unique to the area.

Activities

Tourist offices in nearby **Malaucène** (http://villagemalaucene.free.fr), **Bédoin** (www.bedoin.org) and **Sault** (www. ventoux-sud.com) distribute free maps detailing cycling itineraries – graded easy to difficult – and highlighting artisanal farms en route. For more cycling trails, see www.lemontventoux.net. Cycle-hire outfits also offer electric bikes.

The road to the summit of Mont Ventoux

Gorges du Verdon

Ventoux Bike Park   Cycling

(☎04 90 61 84 55; www.facebook.com/Ventoux
BikePark; Chalet Reynard; half/full day €10/14;
⊙10am-5pm Sat & Sun, hours vary Mon-Fri)
Near the Mont Ventoux summit, at Chalet
Reynard, mountain bikers ascend via rope
tow (minimum age 10 years), then descend
ramps and jumps down three trails (5km in
total). In winter it's possible to mountain-
bike on snow. Bring a bike, helmet and
gloves or rent all gear at Chalet Reynard.
Call to check opening times, which are
highly weather dependent.

❶ GETTING THERE & AWAY

Getting up the mountain by public transport isn't
feasible – you'll need a car or, if you're feeling
fit, a bike.

Gorges du Verdon

For sheer, jaw-dropping drama, few sights
in France can match the epic Gorges du
Verdon. The 'Grand Canyon of Europe',
etched out over millions of years by the

Verdon River, slices a 25km swath through
Haute-Provence's limestone plateau all
the way to the foothills of the Alps. Key
bases from which to explore the gorges are
Moustiers Ste-Marie (west) and Castellane
(east).

◎ SIGHTS & ACTIVITIES

Castellane is the main water-sports base
(April to September); its **tourist office** (☎04
92 83 61 14; www.castellane-verdontourisme.
com; rue Nationale; ⊙9am-7.30pm daily Jul &
Aug, 9am-noon & 2-6pm Mon-Sat, 10am-1pm
Sun May-Jun & Sep, closed Sun rest of year) has
lists of local operators who can organise
rafting, canyoning, kayaking and hydrospeed
expeditions.

Route des Crêtes   Driving Tour

(D952 & D23; ⊙mid-Mar–mid-Nov) A 23km-
long loop with 14 lookouts along the
northern rim with drop-dead vistas of the
plunging Gorges du Verdon. En route the
most thrilling view is from **Belvédère de
l'Escalès** – one of the best places to spot
vultures overhead.

You'll see signs for the route as you drive through La Palud-sur-Verdon. Note that the road is generally closed outside April to October due to snowfall.

Verdon Nature — Walking

(☏06 82 23 21 71; www.verdon-nature.com; per person €25) Local man Laurent Pichard runs excellent guided walks into the gorges, including vulture-spotting trips, nature hikes and guided routes following several classic hiking paths. He also offers a sunset walk and a night sleeping under the stars including the gorges' highest summit, Le Grand Margès.

Sortie de Découverte des Vautours du Verdon — Wildlife Watching

(☏04 92 83 61 14; adult/child €10/6; ⊙9.30am & 6pm Tue, Wed & Fri mid-Jun–mid-Sep) Two-hour guided walks to spot and observe vultures in the Gorges du Verdon. Tours start and finish in the village of Rougon, 18km southwest of Castellane. Binoculars are provided. Book through Castellane tourist office.

Latitude Challenge — Adventure Sports

(☏04 91 09 04 10; www.latitude-challenge. fr; bungee jumps €130) Bungee jumps from Europe's highest bungee site, the 182m Pont de l'Artuby (Artuby Bridge). Also offers skydiving.

✖ EATING

Places to eat in the gorges themselves are limited, although there are a few tiny villages with seasonal restaurants and roadside snack bars dotted along the route. Given the eye-popping scenery, a picnic is always a grand idea – shopped for prior to departure at Avignon's Les Halles (p301). Or plan a meal in Moustiers Ste-Marie into your gorges day out: consider Mediterranean cuisine on a sun-dappled terrace at **La Ferme Ste-Cécile** (☏04 92 74 64 18; www. ferme-ste-cecile.com; D952; 2-/3-course menu €30/39; ⊙noon-2pm & 7.30-10pm Tue-Sat, noon-2pm Sun), or the Full Monty gastronomic dining experience with France's legendary

🍷 Châteauneuf-du-Pape

A mere 20-minute motor north of Avignon plunges you into the world of fine wines. Arguably the best known of the Rhône appellations, Châteauneuf-du-Pape vintages are prized by oenophiles the world over. As its name hints, the hilltop château after which the wine is named was originally built as a summer residence for Avignon's popes, but it's little more than a ruin now – plundered for stone after the Revolution, and bombed by Germany in WWII for good measure. Even so, the wrap-around views of the Rhône valley and surrounding vineyards are epic, stretching all the way to Mont Ventoux. In the village, the **tourist office** (☏04 90 83 71 08; www.ot-chateauneuf-du-pape.mobi; place du Portail; ⊙9.30am-6pm Mon-Sat, closed lunch & Wed Oct-May) has loads of advice on wine tasting and visiting local vineyards, including ones that offer English-language tours. It can also make appointments for you.

LUCENTIUS / GETTY IMAGES ©

chef supremo Alain Ducasse at Michelin-starred **La Bastide de Moustiers** (☏04 92 70 47 47; www.bastide-moustiers.com; chemin de Quinson; menus €60-90; ⊙12.30-1.30pm & 7.30-9pm, closed Oct-Feb).

ℹ️ GETTING THERE & AROUND

A car makes exploring the gorges much more fun, though if you're very fit, cycling is an option too. Bus services run to Castellane and Moustiers, but there's scant transport inside the gorges.

AMSTERDAM, NETHERLANDS

Amsterdam, Netherlands

Amsterdam works its fairy-tale magic in many ways: via the gabled, Golden Age buildings; glinting, boat-filled canals; and especially the cosy, centuries-old bruin cafés (traditional pubs), where candles burn low and beers froth high. Add in mega art museums and cool street markets, and it's easy to see why this atmospheric city is one of Europe's most popular getaways.

Two Days in Amsterdam

Ogle the masterpieces at the **Van Gogh Museum** (p310) and **Rijksmuseum** (p314) in the Old South and spend the afternoon in the city centre at the Begijnhof or Royal Palace. At night venture into the eye-popping Red Light District, then sip in a *bruin café* such as **In 't Aepjen** (p323).

Start the next day at the **Albert Cuypmarkt** (p318) then head to the Southern Canal Ring for a canal boat tour. At night party at hyperactive **Leidseplein** (p323).

Four Days in Amsterdam

On day three head to the haunting **Anne Frank Huis** (p312) and spend the evening in the Jordaan for dinner and canal-side drinks.

Begin your fourth day at **Museum het Rembrandthuis** (p314) or cycling around **Vondelpark** (p314), then mosey over to organic brewery **Brouwerij 't IJ** (p323), at the foot of a windmill.

After Amsterdam, hop on a train to Paris (p249), a mere 3¼ hours away, or fly just over an hour to Copenhagen (p129).

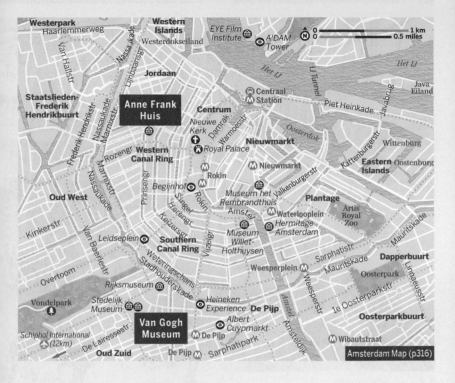

Arriving in Amsterdam

Schiphol Airport Trains to Centraal Station depart every 10 minutes or so from 6am to 12.30am. The trip takes 17 minutes and costs €5.20; taxis cost around €40.

Centraal Station Located in central Amsterdam. Most tram lines connect it to the rest of the city. Taxis queue near the front entrance.

Duivendrecht station Eurolines buses arrive here, south of the centre. Easy links to Centraal Station.

Where to Stay

Amsterdam has loads of accommodation in wild and wonderful spaces: inspired architects have breathed new life into old buildings, from converted schools and industrial lofts to entire rows of canal houses joined at the hip. Many lodgings overlook gorgeous waterways or courtyards.

Hostels are plentiful, with most geared to youthful party animals. Hotels typically are small and ramble over several floors in charming old buildings.

Reserve as far ahead as possible, especially for summer bookings and weekends any time.

ALEXANDER TOLSTYKH / SHUTTERSTOCK ©

Van Gogh Museum

The world's largest Van Gogh collection is a superb line-up of masterworks. Opened in 1973 to house the collection of Vincent's younger brother, Theo, the museum comprises some 200 paintings and 500 drawings by Vincent and his contemporaries.

Great For...

☑ Don't Miss

The Potato Eaters, The Yellow House, Wheatfield with Crows and *Sunflowers*.

Visit Planner

Allow at least a couple of hours to browse the galleries, spread across four floors. The multimedia audio guide (adult/child €5/3) is helpful, as is the family version aimed at those with children aged six to 12 years; reserve online when purchasing your ticket.

Potato Eaters

Van Gogh's earliest works – shadowy and crude – are from his time in the Dutch countryside and in Antwerp between 1883 and 1885. He was particularly obsessed with peasants. *The Potato Eaters* (1885) is his most famous painting from this period.

Bible & Skeleton

Still Life with Bible (1885) is another early work, and it shows Van Gogh's religious

ℹ️ Need to Know

☑020-570 52 00; www.vangoghmuseum.nl; Museumplein 6; adult/child €19/free, audioguide €5/3; ⊙9am-7pm Sun-Thu, to 9pm Fri & Sat late Jun-Aug, 9am-6pm Sat-Thu, to 9pm Fri Sep-late Oct & May-late Jun, 9am-5pm Sat-Thu, to 9pm Fri Nov-Mar; ⛭2/3/5/12 Van Baerlestraat

✕ Take a Break

Nibble on quiche and sip wine at the museum cafe; window tables overlook the Museumplein.

★ Top Tip

To cut queues, visit after 3pm or Friday evening when the museum is open late.

inclination. The burnt-out candle is said to represent the recent death of his father, who was a Protestant minister. *Skeleton with Burning Cigarette* (1886) was painted when Van Gogh was a student at Antwerp's Royal Academy of Fine Arts.

Shoes

Who'd have thought a pair of tatty old *Shoes* (1886) could be a masterpiece? Van Gogh bought the boots at a flea market then traipsed through mud until they were 'suitable' to paint.

Self-portraits

In 1886 Van Gogh moved to Paris, where his brother, Theo, was working as an art dealer. Vincent wanted to master the art of portraiture, but was too poor to pay for models. Several self-portraits resulted. You can see his palette begin to brighten as he comes under the influence of the Parisian Impressionists.

Sketchbooks & Letters

Intriguing displays enhance what's on the walls. For instance, you might see Van Gogh's actual sketchbook alongside an interactive kiosk that lets you page through a reproduction of it or listen to recordings of Van Gogh's diverse letters to and from his closest brother Theo, who championed his work. The museum has categorised all of Van Gogh's letters online at www. vangoghletters.org.

Other Artists

Thanks to Theo van Gogh's prescient collecting and that of the museum's curators, you'll also see works by Vincent's contemporaries, including Paul Gauguin, Claude Monet and Henri de Toulouse-Lautrec.

DUTCHMEN / SHUTTERSTOCK ©

Anne Frank Huis

It is one of the 20th century's most compelling stories: a young Jewish girl forced into hiding with her family and their friends to escape deportation by the Nazis. Walking through the book-case-door means stepping back into a time that seems both distant and tragically real.

Great For...

☑ Don't Miss

Details including Anne's red-plaid diary, WWII newsreels and a video of Anne's schoolmate Hanneli Goslar.

Background

It took the German army just five days to occupy all of the Netherlands, along with Belgium and much of France. Once Hitler's forces had swept across the country, many Jews – like Anne Frank and her family – went into hiding. Anne's diary describes how restrictions were gradually imposed on Dutch Jews: from being forbidden to ride streetcars to being forced to turn in their bicycles and not being allowed to visit Christian friends.

The Franks moved into the upper floors of the specially prepared rear of the building, with another couple, the Van Pels (called the Van Daans in Anne's diary), and their son Peter. Four months later Fritz Pfeffer (called Mr Dussel in the diary) joined the household. Here they survived until the Gestapo discovered them in August 1944.

Statue of Anne Frank. Sculptor: Mari Andriessen

❶ Need to Know

📞020-556 71 05; www.annefrank.
org; Prinsengracht 263-267; adult/child
€10.50/5.50; ⏰9am-10pm Apr-Oct, 9am-
7pm Sun-Fri, to 10pm Sat Nov-Mar; 🚊13/17
Westermarkt

✗ Take a Break

For pancakes and 18th-century atmosphere aplenty, stroll over to 't Smalle
(p323).

★ Top Tip

Tickets are not sold at the door. Buy
timed-entry tickets from two months in
advance online.

Ground Floor

After several renovations, the house itself
is now contained within a modern, square
shell that attempts to retain the original feel
of the building (it was used during WWII as
offices and a warehouse). Renovations in
2018 shifted the museum entrance around
the corner to Westermarkt 20.

Offices & Warehouse

The building originally held Otto Frank's
pectin (a substance used in jelly-making)
business. On the lower floors you'll see
the former offices of Victor Kugler, Otto's
business partner; and the desks of Miep
Gies, Bep Voskuijl and Jo Kleiman, all of
whom worked in the office and provided
food, clothing and other goods for the
household.

Secret Annexe

The upper floors in the *achterhuis* (rear
house) contain the Secret Annexe, where
the living quarters are preserved in powerful austerity. As you enter Anne's bedroom,
you can sense the remnants of a young
girl's dreams: view photos of Hollywood
stars and postcards of the Dutch royal
family pasted on the wall.

The Diary

More haunting exhibits and videos await
you in the front house – including Anne's
red-plaid diary in a glass case. View other
notebooks in which Anne wrote down
favourite quotes and penned short stories.
Watch the video of Anne's old schoolmate
Hanneli Goslar, who describes encountering Anne at Bergen-Belsen. Read heart-
breaking letters from Otto, the only Secret
Annexe occupant to survive the concentration camps.

⊙ SIGHTS

Rijksmuseum   Museum
(National Museum; ☑020-674 70 00; www.rijks
museum.nl; Museumstraat 1; adult/child €20/
free; ⊘9am-5pm; ⓐ2/5/12 Rijksmuseum) The
Rijksmuseum is among the world's finest
art museums, packing in works by local
heroes Rembrandt, Vermeer and Van Gogh
as well as other masterpieces in the 8000
works on display over 1.5km of galleries.
To avoid the biggest crowds, come before
10am or after 3pm. Start on the 2nd floor
in the Gallery of Honour with the astound-
ing Golden Age works. Prebooking tickets
online provides fast-track entry.

Museum het Rembrandthuis Museum
(Rembrandt House Museum; ☑020-520 04 00;
www.rembrandthuis.nl; Jodenbreestraat 4; adult/
child €14/5; ⊘10am-6pm; Ⓜ Waterlooplein) This
evocative museum is housed in Rembrandt's former home, where the master
painter spent his most successful years,
painting big commissions such as *The
Night Watch* and running the Netherlands'
largest painting studio. It wasn't to last,
however: his work fell out of fashion, he had

some expensive relationship problems and
bankruptcy came a-knocking. The inventory
drawn up when he had to leave the house is
the reason that curators have been able to
refurnish the house so faithfully.

Vondelpark   Park
(www.hetvondelpark.net; ⓐ12 Van Baerlstraat, 5
Museumplein) A private park for the wealthy
until 1953, Vondelpark now occupies a special place in Amsterdam's heart. It's a magical escape, but also supplies a busy social
scene, encompassing cycle ways, pristine
lawns, ponds with swans, quaint cafes, footbridges and winding footpaths. On a sunny
day, an open-air party atmosphere ensues
when tourists, lovers, cyclists, in-line skaters,
pram-pushing parents, cartwheeling children, football-kicking teenagers, spliff-
sharing friends and champagne-swilling
picnickers all come out to play.

Stedelijk Museum   Museum
(☑020-573 29 11; www.stedelijk.nl; Museumplein
10; adult/child €18.50/free; ⊘10am-6pm, to
10pm Fri; ⓐ2/3/5/12 Van Baerlestraat) This
fabulous museum houses the collection
amassed by postwar curator Willem

Vondelpark

Sandberg. The ground-floor Stedelijk Base exhibition displays a rotating selection of the amazing collection's highlights, featuring works by Picasso, Matisse, Mondrian, Van Gogh, Rothko, Jeff Koons, Yves Klein, Lichtenstein, Yayoi Kusama and more, plus an exuberant Karel Appel mural. The museum also hosts excellent temporary exhibitions. The free in-depth audioguide is fantastic and there are themed guided tours; book online. Unlike other museums in the area, you seldom have to queue.

Royal Palace — Palace

(Koninklijk Paleis; ☎020-522 61 61; www. paleisamsterdam.nl; Dam; adult/child €10/free; ☺10am-5pm; 🚊4/14/24 Dam) Opened as a town hall in 1655, this resplendent building became a palace in the 19th century. The interiors gleam, especially the marble work – at its best in a floor inlaid with maps of the world in the great *burgerzaal* (citizens' hall) at the heart of the building. Pick up a free audioguide at the desk when you enter; it explains everything you'll see in vivid detail. King Willem-Alexander uses the palace only for ceremonies; check for periodic closures.

A'DAM Tower — Notable Building

(www.adamlookout.com; Overhoeksplein 1; lookout adult/child/family €13.50/7.50/32, swing €5 extra; ☺lookout 10am-10pm, last admission 9pm; 🚊Buiksloterweg) The 22-storey A'DAM Tower used to be the Royal Dutch Shell oil company offices, but has had a makeover to become one of Amsterdam's biggest attractions. Take the trippy lift to the rooftop for awe-inspiring views in all directions, with a giant six-person swing that kicks out over the edge for those who have a head for heights (you're well secured and strapped in).

Hermitage Amsterdam — Museum

(☎020-530 87 55; www.hermitage.nl; Amstel 51; single exhibitions adult/child €18/free, all exhibitions adult/child €25/free; ☺10am-5pm; Ⓜ Waterlooplein, 🚊Waterlooplein) There have long been links between Russia and the Netherlands – Tsar Peter the Great learned shipbuilding here in 1697 – hence this branch of St Petersburg's State Hermitage Museum. Blockbuster temporary exhibi-

📷 On the Edge: NDSM-werf

Fifteen minutes upriver from the city centre **NDSM-werf** (www.ndsm.nl; NDSM-plein; 🚢NDSM-werf) is a derelict shipyard turned edgy arts community. It wafts a post-apocalyptic vibe: an old submarine slumps in the harbour, abandoned trams rust by the water's edge, and street art is splashed around on most surfaces. Young creatives hang out at the smattering of cool cafes. Hip businesses like MTV and Red Bull have their European headquarters here. The area is also a centre for underground culture and events, such as the **Over het IJ Festival**. A new street-art museum, billed as the world's largest, is due to open here in late 2019; check www.streetart.today for updates.

Old tram in NDSM-werf
UNIQUE VISION / SHUTTERSTOCK ©

tions show works from the Hermitage's vast treasure trove, while the permanent Portrait Gallery of the Golden Age has formal group portraits of the 17th-century Dutch A-list; the Outsider Gallery also has temporary shows. I Amsterdam and Museum cards allow free entrance or a discount, depending on the exhibition.

Museum Willet-Holthuysen — Museum

(☎020-523 18 70; www.willetholthuysen.nl; Herengracht 605; adult/child €12.50/free; ☺10am-5pm; 🚊4/14 Rembrandtplein) This exquisite canal house was built in 1687 for Amsterdam mayor Jacob Hop, then remodelled in 1739. It's named after Louisa Willet-Holthuysen, who inherited the house from her coal-and-glass-merchant father and lived a lavish,

Amsterdam

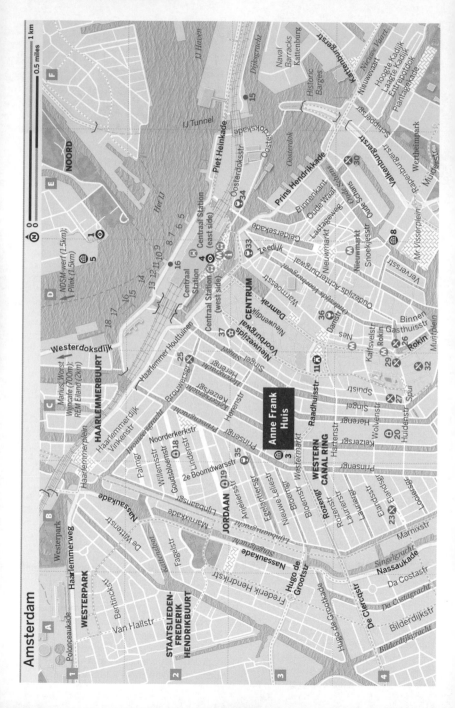

1 km
0.5 miles

NOORD

WESTERPARK

HAARLEMMERBUURT

JORDAAN

**STAATSLIEDEN-
FREDERIK
HENDRIKBUURT**

CENTRUM

**WESTERN
CANAL RING**

Anne Frank
Huis

Westerdoksdijk

Marius/Worst
Wijncafe (700m);
REM Eiland (2km)

NDSM-werf (1.5km);
Pllek (1.5km)

IJ Haven

IJ Tunnel

Het IJ

Piet Heinkade

Centraal Station
(east side)

Centraal Station
(west side)

Centraal
Station

Naval
Barracks
Kattenburg

Historic
Barges

Prins Hendrikkade

Valkenburgerstr

Kattenburgerstr

Nieuwevaart

Hoogte Kadijk
Laagte Kadijk
Entrepotdok
Plantagekade

Oosterdok

Oosterdokskade

Oosterdokstr

Binnenkant

Oude Waal

Lastageweg

Nieuwmarkt

Snoekjessstr

Mr Visserplein

Zeedijk

Geldersekade

Oudezijds Voorburgwal

Oudezijds Achterburgwal

Warmoesstr

Damrak

Nieuwendijk

Nieuwezijds Voorburgwal

Singel

Spuistr

Herengr

Keizersgr

Prinsengr

Brouwersgr

Haarlemmer Houttuinen

Westerdoksdijk

Haarlemmer Houttuinen

Marnixstr

Nassaukade

Singelgracht

Nassaukade

Lijnbaansgracht

Da Costastr

Da Costagracht

Bilderdijkstr

Bilderdijkgracht

De Clercqstr

Hugo de Grootkade

Hugo de Grootstr

Frederik Hendrikstr

Fagelstr

Kattensloot

De Wittenstr

Van Hallstr

Bentinckstr

Poloneaukade

Haarlemmerweg

Haarlemmerplein

Haarlemmerdijk

Vinkenstr

Palingstr

Willemsstr

Goudsbloemstr

2e Lindenstr

Noorderkerkstr

1e Lindenstr

2e Boomdwarsstr

Anjeliersstr

Egelantiersgr

Nieuwe Leliestr

Bloemgr

Rozengr

Laurierstr

Elandsgr

Looiersgr

Lauriergr

Rozenstr

Hartenstr

Raadhuisstr

Wolvenstr

Huidenstr

Spui

Singel

Herengr

Spuistr

Nes

Rokin

Rokin

Kalfsvelstr

Damstr

Binnen
Gasthuisstr

Binnen
Amstel

Muntplein

Reguliersgracht

Rapenburgerstr

Schippersgr

Wertheimpark

Muiderstr

Ververstr

Dam

Damrak

Singelgracht

Lindengracht

Egelantiersgracht

Bloemgracht

Prinsengracht

1 15

1 1

5

16

4

33

34

30

8

36

11

37

25

18

19

35

3

26

29

27

32

23

20

10 9 8 7 6 5

13 12 11 10 9

18 17 16 15 14

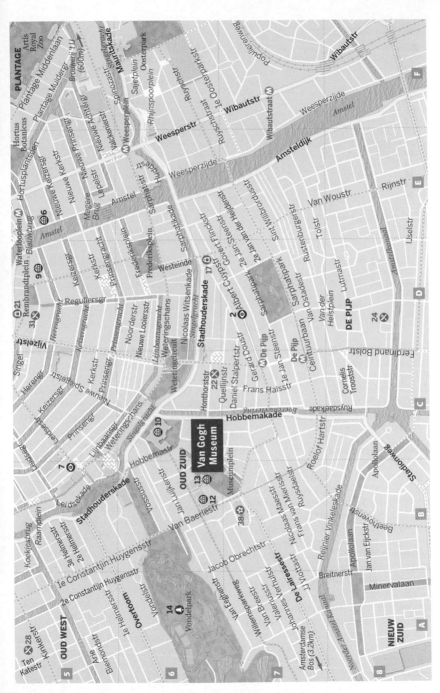

Amsterdam

bohemian life here with her husband. She bequeathed the property to the city in 1895. With displays including part of the family's 275-piece Meissen table service, and an immaculate French-style garden, the museum is a fascinating window into the world of the 19th-century super-rich.

Albert Cuypmarkt
Market

(www.albertcuyp-markt.amsterdam; Albert Cuypstraat, btwn Ferdinand Bolstraat & Van Woustraat; ☉9am-5pm Mon-Sat; Ⓜ De Pijp, ⛱24 Marie Heinekenplein) Some 260 stalls fill the Albert Cuypmarkt, Amsterdam's largest and busiest market. Vendors loudly tout their array of gadgets, homewares, and flowers, fruit, vegetables, herbs and spices. Many sell clothes and other goods, too, and they're often cheaper than anywhere else. Snack vendors tempt passers-by with raw-herring sandwiches, *frites* (fries), *poffertjes* (tiny Dutch pancakes dusted with icing sugar) and caramel syrup–filled *stroopwafels*. If you have room after all that, the surrounding area teems with cosy *cafés* (pubs) and restaurants.

EYE Film Institute
Museum, Cinema

(☏020-589 14 00; www.eyefilm.nl; IJpromenade 1; adult/child exhibitions €11/free, films €11/7.50; ☉10am-7pm exhibitions; ⛴Buiksloterweg) At this modernist architectural triumph that seems to balance on its edge on the banks of the IJ (also pronounced 'eye') River, the institute screens movies from the 40,000-title archive in four theatres, sometimes with live music. Exhibitions of costumes, digital art and other cinephile amusements run in conjunction with what's playing. A view-tastic bar-restaurant with a fabulously sunny terrace (when the sun makes an appearance) is a popular hang-out on this side of the river.

⊙ TOURS

Amsterdam has more canals than Venice and getting on the water is one of the best ways to feel the pulse of the city.

Rederji Lampedusa
Boating

(http://rederjilampedusa.nl; Dijksgracht 6; 2hr canal tour €19; ☉canal tours 11am & 1.30pm Sat May-Sep; ⛱26 Muziekgebouw) Take a two-hour canal-boat tour around Amsterdam harbour in former refugee boats, brought from Lampedusa by Dutch founder Tuen. The tours are full of heart and offer a fascinating insight, not only into stories of contemporary migration, but also about how immigration shaped Amsterdam's history – especially the canal tour. Departs from next to Mediamatic.

Wetlands Safari   Boating
(☑06 5355 2669; www.wetlandssafari.nl; incl transport & picnic adult/child €64/35; ☺9.30am Mon-Fri, 10am Sat & Sun early Apr-Sep; ☒2/4/11/12/13/14/17/24/26 Centraal Station) For a change from Amsterdam's canals, book a five-hour wetlands boat trip. Participants take a bus to just north of the centre, then canoe through boggy, froggy wetlands and on past windmills and 17th-century villages. Departure is from behind Centraal Station at the 'G' bus stop. Four-hour sunset tours (adult/child €54/33) depart at 5pm from early May to late August.

🅐 SHOPPING

The busiest shopping streets are Kalverstraat by the Dam and Leidsestraat, which leads into Leidseplein. Near Vondelpark, stylish fashion boutiques line Cornelis Schuytstraat and Willemsparkweg.

Moooi Gallery   Design
(☑020-528 77 60; www.moooi.com; Westerstraat 187; ☺10am-6pm Tue-Sat; ☒3/5 Marnixplein) Founded by Marcel Wanders, this galleryshop features Dutch design at its most over-the-top, from the life-size black horse lamp to the 'blow-away vase' (a whimsical twist on the classic Delft vase) and the 'killing of the piggy bank' ceramic pig (with a gold hammer).

Hutspot   Design
(www.hutspot.com; Van Woustraat 4; ☺10am-7pm Mon-Sat, noon-6pm Sun; 🛜; ☒4 Stadhouderskade) Named after the Dutch dish of boiled and mashed veggies, 'Hotchpotch' was founded with a mission to give young entrepreneurs the chance to sell their work. As a result, this concept store is an inspired mishmash of Dutch-designed furniture, furnishings, art, homewares and clothing as well as an in-house cafe, a barber, a photo booth and various pop-ups.

Negen Straatjes   Area
(Nine Streets; www.de9straatjes.nl; ☒2/11/12 Spui) In a city packed with countless shopping opportunities, each seemingly more alluring than the last, the Negen Straatjes represent the very densest concentration of consumer pleasures. These 'nine little streets' are indeed small, each just a block long. The shops are tiny too, and many are highly specialised. Eyeglasses? Cheese? Single-edition art books? Each has its own dedicated boutique.

Lindengracht Market   Market
(www.jordaanmarkten.nl; Lindengracht; ☺9am-4pm Sat; ☒3 Nieuwe Willemsstraat) Dating from 1895, Saturday's Lindengracht Market is a wonderfully local affair, with 232 stalls selling fresh produce, including fish and a magnificent array of cheese, as well as Dutch delicacies like *stroopwafels,* flowers, clothing and homewares. Arrive as early as possible to beat the crowds.

Vlieger   Stationery
(☑020-623 58 34; www.vliegerpapier.nl; Amstel 34; ☺noon-6pm Mon, from 9am Tue-Fri, 11am-5.30pm Sat; ☒4/14 Rembrandtplein) Love stationery and paper? Make a beeline for Vlieger. Since 1869, this two-storey shop has been supplying it all: Egyptian papyrus, beautiful handmade papers from Asia and Central America, papers inlaid with flower petals or bamboo, and paper textured like snakeskin.

🅧 EATING

Vleminckx   Fast Food €
(www.vleminckxdesausmeester.nl; Voetboogstraat 33; fries €3-5, sauces €0.70; ☺noon-7pm Mon, 11am-7pm Tue, Wed & Fri-Sun, 11am-8pm Thu; ☒2/11/12 Koningsplein) Frying up *frites* (fries) since 1887, Amsterdam's best *friterie* has been based at this hole-in-the-wall takeaway shack near the Spui since 1957.

Green City

Amsterdam's forest, **Amsterdamse Bos** (Amsterdam Forest; www.amsterdamsebos.nl; Bosbaanweg 5; ⊙24hr; Ⓜ Van Boshuizenstraat, ⓠ347, 357), is a vast swathe (roughly 1000 hectares) of almost countryside, 20 minutes by bike south of Vondelpark (p314). It was planted in 1934 in order to provide employment during the Great Depression. Its lakes, woods and meadows are crisscrossed by paths and dotted with cafes. You can rent bicycles, feed baby goats in spring, take a horse-riding lesson, boat the rural-feeling waterways, see a play at the open-air theatre and ascend to the treetops in the climbing park.

It's a glorious place to go with kids, though best if you explore by bike due to its size. There's a **bike rental kiosk** across from the forest entrance and a **visitor centre** with information. In the densest thickets you forget you're near a city at all (though you're right by Schiphol airport). A lot of locals use the park, but it rarely feels crowded.

Bridge in Amsterdamse Bos
MIRZA AHMAD / SHUTTERSTOCK ©

The standard order of perfectly cooked crispy, fluffy *frites* is smothered in mayonnaise, though its 28 sauces also include apple, green pepper, ketchup, peanut, sambal and mustard. Queues almost always stretch down the block, but they move fast.

Foodhallen   Food Hall €

(www.foodhallen.nl; De Hallen, Hannie Dankbaar Passage 3; dishes €3-20; ⊙11am-11.30pm Sun-Thu, to 1am Fri & Sat; ▣; ⓠ7/17 Ten Katestraat) This glorious international food hall in soaring ex-tram sheds has food stands surrounding an airy open-plan eating area. Some are offshoots of popular Amsterdam eateries and breweries. Look out for Viet View Vietnamese street food and Jabugo Iberico Bar ham, and the Beer Bar, serving real ale tipples from local heroes 2 Chefs and Oedipus.

Gartine   Cafe €

(☏020-320 41 32; www.gartine.nl; Taksteeg 7; dishes €6.50-15, high tea €18-25.50; ⊙10am-6pm Wed-Sat; ▣; Ⓜ Rokin, ⓠ4/14/24 Rokin) ✿ Gartine is magical, from its covert location in an alley off busy Kalverstraat to its mismatched antique tableware and its sublime breakfast pastries (including a dark-chocolate, honey and raspberry soufflé), sandwiches and salads (made from produce grown in its garden plot and eggs from its chickens). The sweet-and-savoury high tea, from 2pm to 5pm, is a treat.

De Laatste Kruimel   Cafe, Bakery €

(☏020-423 04 99; www.delaatstekruimel.nl; Langebrugsteeg 4; dishes €3-10.50; ⊙8am-8pm Mon-Sat, from 9am Sun; Ⓜ Rokin, ⓠ4/14/24 Rokin) Decorated with vintage finds from the Noordermarkt and wooden pallets upcycled as furniture, and opening to a tiny canal-side terrace, the 'Last Crumb' has glass display cases filled with pies, quiches, breads, cakes and lemon-and-poppy-seed scones. Grandmothers, children, couples on dates and just about everyone else crowd in for sweet treats and fantastic organic sandwiches.

Bakers & Roasters   Cafe €

(www.bakersandroasters.com; 1e Jacob van Campenstraat 54; dishes €9-16.50; ⊙8.30am-4pm; 🛜; ⓠ24 Marie Heinekenplein) Sumptuous brunch dishes served up at Brazilian-Kiwi-owned Bakers & Roasters include banana-nutbread French toast with homemade banana marmalade and crispy bacon; Navajo eggs with pulled pork, avocado, mango salsa and chipotle cream; and a smoked-salmon stack with poached eggs, potato cakes and hollandaise. Wash your choice down with a fiery Bloody Mary. Fantastic pies, cakes and slices, too.

Van Dobben
Dutch €

(☑020-624 42 00; www.eetsalonvandobben.
nl; Korte Reguliersdwarsstraat 5-9; dishes €3-8;
⊙10am-9pm Mon-Thu, to 2am Fri & Sat, 10.30am-
8pm Sun; ☐4/14 Rembrandtplein) Open since
the 1940s, Van Dobben has a cool diner
feel, with white tiles and a siren-red ceiling.
Traditional meaty Dutch fare is its forte:
low-priced, finely sliced roast-beef sandwiches with mustard are an old-fashioned
joy, or try the *pekelvlees* (akin to corned
beef) or *halfom* (if you're keen on *pekelvlees* mixed with liver).

Balthazar's Keuken
Mediterranean €€

(☑020-420 21 14; www.balthazarskeuken.nl;
Elandsgracht 108; 3-course menu €34.50; ⊙6-
10.30pm Tue-Sun; ☐5/7/19 Elandsgracht) In a
former blacksmith's forge, with a modern-
rustic look and an open kitchen, this is
consistently one of Amsterdam's top-rated
restaurants. Don't expect a wide-ranging
menu: the philosophy is basically 'whatever
we have on hand', which might mean sea
bass and crab gnocchi or rabbit with sauerkraut jelly and pear sauce, but it's invariably
delectable. Reservations recommended.

D'Vijff Vlieghen
Dutch €€

(☑020-530 40 60; www.vijffvlieghen.nl; Spuistraat 294-302; mains €19.50-26.50; ⊙6-10pm;
☐2/11/12 Spui) Spread across five 17th-
century canal houses, the 'Five Flies' is a
jewel. Old-wood dining rooms overflow with
character, featuring Delft-blue tiles and
original works by Rembrandt; chairs have
copper plates inscribed with the names
of famous guests (Walt Disney, Mick Jag-
ger...). Exquisite dishes range from smoked
goose breast with apple to roast veal and
turnips with Dutch crab mayonnaise.

De Belhamel
European €€

(☑020-622 10 95; www.belhamel.nl; Brouwers-
gracht 60; mains €24-26, 3-/4-course menus
€38/48; ⊙noon-4pm & 5.30-10pm; ☐18/21/22
Buiten Brouwersstraat) In warm weather the
canal-side tables here at the head of the
Herengracht are enchanting, and the richly
wallpapered art-nouveau interior set over two
levels provides the perfect backdrop for exquisitely presented dishes such as poached
sole with wild-spinach bisque, veal sweet-
breads with polenta and spring onion jus, or a
half lobster with velvety truffle mayonnaise.

Foodhallen

Marius
European €€€

(☏020-422 78 80; www.restaurantmarius.nl; Barentszstraat 173; 4-course menu €49; ⊗6.30-10pm Mon-Sat; ⛴3 Zoutkeetsgracht) Foodies swoon over pocket-sized Marius, tucked amid artists' studios in the Western Islands. Chef Kees Elfring shops at local markets, then creates his daily four-course, no-choice menu from what he finds. The result might be grilled prawns with fava-bean purée or beef rib with polenta and rata-touille. Marius also runs the fabulous wine and tapas bar **Worst Wijncafe** (☏020-625 61 67; www.deworst.nl; Barentszstraat 171; tapas €9-17, brunch mains €9-13; ⊗noon-midnight Mon-Sat, 10am-10pm Sun; ⛴3 Zoutkeetsgracht) next door.

Greetje
Dutch €€€

(☏020-779 74 50; www.restaurantgreetje.nl; Peperstraat 23-25; mains €24-29; ⊗6-10pm; ⛴22/48 Prins Hendrikkade) ✔ Greetje is Amsterdam's most creative Dutch restaurant, using the best seasonal produce to resurrect and re-create traditional Dutch recipes, like slow-cooked veal with Dutch brandy–marinated apricots, and suckling pork in apple syrup with Dutch mustard sauce. The tasting menu (€55) starts off with the Big Beginning, a selection of six starters served high-tea style.

Ciel Bleu
Gastronomy €€€

(☏020-678 74 50; www.cielbleu.nl; Hotel Okura Amsterdam, Ferdinand Bolstraat 333; tasting menus from €195; ⊗6.30-10pm Mon-Sat; ⛴4/12 Cornelius Troostplein) Mind-blowing, two-Michelin-star creations at this pinnacle of gastronomy change with the seasons; spring, for instance, might see scallops and oysters with vanilla sea salt and gin-and-tonic foam, king crab with salted lemon, beurre blanc ice cream and caviar, or salt-crusted pigeon with pomegranate jelly and pistachio dust. Also incomparable is the 23rd-floor setting with aerial views north across the city.

If your budget doesn't stretch to dining here, try the bar snacks at the adjacent **Twenty Third Bar** (www.okura.nl; Hotel Okura Amsterdam, Ferdinand Bolstraat 333; ⊗6pm-1am Sun-Thu, to 2am Fri & Sat; ⛴12 Cornelius Troostplein).

🍸 DRINKING & NIGHTLIFE

Bars, clubs and live-music venues fan out around nightlife hubs **Leidseplein** and **Rembrandtplein,** ensnared within the Southern Canal Ring.

In 't Aepjen   Brown Cafe

(Zeedijk 1; ⊗noon-1am Mon-Thu, to 3am Fri & Sat; ⛟2/4/11/12/13/14/17/24/26 Centraal Station) Candles burn even during the day in this 15th-century building – one of two remaining wooden buildings in the city – which has been a tavern since 1519: in the 16th and 17th centuries it served as an inn for sailors from the Far East, who often brought *aapjes* (monkeys) to trade for lodging. Vintage jazz on the stereo enhances the time-warp feel.

't Smalle   Brown Cafe

(www.t-smalle.nl; Egelantiersgracht 12; ⊗10am-1am Sun-Thu, to 2am Fri & Sat; ⛟13/17 Westermarkt) Dating back to 1786 as a *jenever* (Dutch gin) distillery and tasting house, and restored during the 1970s with antique porcelain beer pumps and lead-framed windows, locals' favourite 't Smalle is one of

Amsterdam's most charming *bruin cafés*. Dock your boat right by the pretty stone terrace, which is wonderfully convivial by day and impossibly romantic at night.

SkyLounge   Cocktail Bar

(☎020-530 08 75; www.skyloungeamsterdam. com; Oosterdoksstraat 4; ⊗11am-1am Sun-Tue, to 2am Wed & Thu, to 3am Fri & Sat; 📶; ⛟4/12/14/24/26 Centraal Station) With wow-factor views whatever the weather, this bar offers a 360-degree panorama of Amsterdam from the 11th floor of the DoubleTree Amsterdam Centraal Station hotel – and it just gets better when you head out to its vast SkyTerrace, with an outdoor bar. Toast the view with a huge range of cocktails, craft beers and spirits. DJs regularly hit the decks from 9pm.

Brouwerij 't IJ   Brewery

(www.brouwerijhetij.nl; Funenkade 7; ⊗brewery 2-8pm, English tour 3.30pm Fri-Sun; ⛟7 Hoogte Kadijk) 🍺 Can you get more Dutch than drinking a craft beer beneath the creaking sails of the 1725-built De Gooyer Windmill? This is Amsterdam's leading microbrewery, with delicious standard, seasonal and

★ Top Five Museums

Van Gogh Museum (p310)

Anne Frank Huis (p312)

Rijksmuseum (p314)

Museum het Rembrandthuis (p314)

Stedelijk Museum (p314)

From left: 't Smalle; a dessert at Ciel Bleu; *The Night Watch,* Rijksmuseum (p314)

Pllek

limited-edition brews; try the smooth, fruity 'tripel' Zatte, their first creation back in 1985. Enjoy yours in the tiled tasting room, lined by an amazing bottle collection, or the plane-tree-shaded terrace.

Wynand Fockink
Distillery

(☏020-639 26 95; www.wynand-fockink.nl; Pijlsteeg 31; tours €17.50; ⊗tasting tavern 2-9pm daily, tours 3pm, 4.30pm, 6pm & 7.30pm Sat & Sun; 🚊4/14/24 Dam) Dating from 1679, this small tasting house in an arcade behind NH Grand Hotel Krasnapolsky serves scores of *jenevers* (Dutch gins) and liqueurs. Although there's no seating, it's an intimate place to knock back a shot glass or two. At weekends, guides give 45-minute distillery tours (in English) that are followed by six tastings; reserve online.

Pllek
Bar

(www.pllek.nl; TT Neveritaweg 59; ⊗9.30am-1am Sun-Thu, to 3am Fri & Sat; 🚢NDSM-werf) Uber-cool Pllek is a Noord magnet, with hip things of all ages streaming over to hang out in its interior made of old shipping containers and lie out on its artificial sandy beach when the weather allows. It's a terrific spot for a waterfront beer or glass of wine.

✪ ENTERTAINMENT

Amsterdam supports a flourishing arts scene, with loads of big concert halls, theatres, cinemas, comedy clubs and other performance venues filled on a regular basis. Music fans are superbly catered for here, and there is a fervent subculture for just about every genre, especially jazz, classical, rock and avant-garde beats.

Concertgebouw
Classical Music

(Concert Hall; ☏020-671 83 45; www.concert gebouw.nl; Concertgebouwplein 10; ⊗box office 1-7pm Mon-Fri, from 10am Sat & Sun; 🚊3/5/12 Museumplein) The Concert Hall was built in 1888 by AL van Gendt, who managed to engineer its near-perfect acoustics. Bernard Haitink, former conductor of the Royal Concertgebouw Orchestra, remarked that the world-famous hall was the orchestra's best instrument. Free half-hour concerts take place Wednesdays at 12.30pm from

September to June; arrive early. Try the **Last Minute Ticket Shop** (www.lastminute ticketshop.nl; ⊘online ticket sales from 10am on day of performance) for half-price seats to selected performances.

Bitterzoet   Live Music

(☎020-421 23 18; www.bitterzoet.com; Spuistraat 2; ⊘8pm-late; 🚊2/11/12/5/13/17 Nieuwezijds Kolk) Always full, always changing, this venue with a capacity of just 350 people is one of the friendliest places in town, with a diverse crowd. Music (sometimes live, sometimes courtesy of a DJ) can be funk, roots, drum 'n' bass, Latin, Afro-beat, old-school jazz or hip-hop groove.

ℹ INFORMATION

I Amsterdam Visitor Centre (☎020-702 60 00; www.iamsterdam.com; Stationsplein 10; ⊘9am-6pm; 🚊2/4/11/12/13/14/17/24/26 Centraal Station) Located outside Centraal Station.

I Amsterdam Visitor Centre Schiphol (www.iamsterdam.com; ⊘7am-10pm) Inside Schiphol International Airport in the Arrivals 2 hall.

ℹ GETTING THERE & AWAY

Schiphol International Airport (AMS; www.schiphol.nl) is among Europe's busiest airports and has copious air links worldwide, including many on low-cost European airlines.

National and international trains arrive at **Centraal Station** (Stationsplein; 🚊2/4/11/12/13/14/17/24/26 Centraal Station). There are good links with several European cities. For information on international trains (including ICE), see NS International (www.nsinternational.nl).

Buses operated by Eurolines (www.eurolines.com) and FlixBus (www.flixbus.com) connect Amsterdam with all major European capitals and numerous smaller destinations.

ℹ GETTING AROUND

GVB passes in chip-card form are the most convenient option for public transport. Buy them at GVB ticket offices or visitor centres. Tickets

🍽 Jordaan Dining Up High

Though gentrified today, the Jordaan neighbourhood was once a rough, densely populated *volksbuurt* (district for the common people) until the mid-20th century. That history still shows amid the cosy pubs, galleries and markets now squashed into its grid of tiny lanes. For a bird's-eye view of the industrial docklands head to **REM Eiland** (☎020-688 55 01; www.remeiland.com; Haparandadam 45; mains lunch €8.50-13, dinner €18.50-29.50; ⊘kitchen noon-4pm & 5.30-10pm, bar to 11pm; 🚊48 Koivistokade), a fire-engine-red sea rig towering 22m above the IJ. Built in the 1960s as a pirate radio and TV broadcaster, it's a top-notch restaurant today, with dining rooms opening onto wrap-around platforms and an outdoor bar filling the rooftop ex-helipad.

REM Eiland
RAFAEL CROONEN / SHUTTERSTOCK ©

aren't sold on board. Always wave your card at the pink machine when entering and departing.

Walking Central Amsterdam is compact and very easy to cover by foot.

Bicycle This is the locals' main mode of getting around. Rental companies are all over town; bikes cost about €12 per day.

Tram Fast, frequent and ubiquitous, operating between 6am and 12.30am.

Bus and metro Primarily serve the outer districts; not much use in the city centre.

Ferry Free ferries depart for northern Amsterdam from docks behind Centraal Station.

Taxi Expensive and not very speedy given Amsterdam's maze of streets.

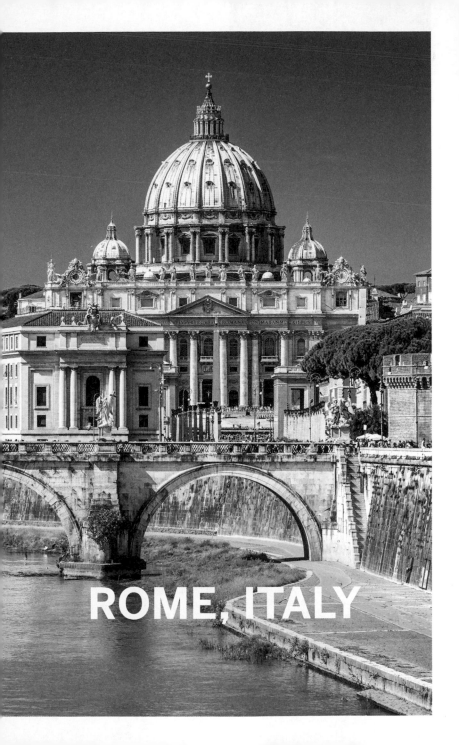

Rome, Italy

A heady mix of haunting ruins, breathtaking art, vibrant street life and incredible food, Italy's hot-blooded capital is one of the world's most romantic and inspiring cities. Ancient icons such as the Colosseum, Roman Forum and Pantheon recall the city's golden age as caput mundi (capital of the world), while monumental basilicas testify to the role that great popes have played in its history. And Rome's astonishing artistic heritage is almost unrivalled. A walk around the centre will have you encountering masterpieces by the giants of Western art: sculptures by Michelangelo, canvases by Caravaggio, frescoes by Raphael and fountains by Bernini.

Two Days in Rome

Start early at the **Colosseum** (p330), then visit the **Palatino** (p352) and **Roman Forum** (p346). Spend the afternoon in the *centro storico* (historic centre), exploring **Piazza Navona** (p353) and the **Pantheon** (p334). On day two, hit the **Vatican Museums** (p342) and **St Peter's Basilica** (p338). Afterwards, check out the **Spanish Steps** (p359) and **Trevi Fountain** (p358). Round the day off in the **Campo de' Fiori** (p355).

Four Days in Rome

Spend day three investigating **Villa Borghese** (p359) – make sure to book for the **Museo e Galleria Borghese** (p360). End the day with dinner in Trastevere. Next day, admire classical art at the **Capitoline Museums** (p352) before checking out the basilicas on the Esquiline.

Next up? Catch the train to Florence and Tuscany (p397) or step back in time at Pompeii (p370).

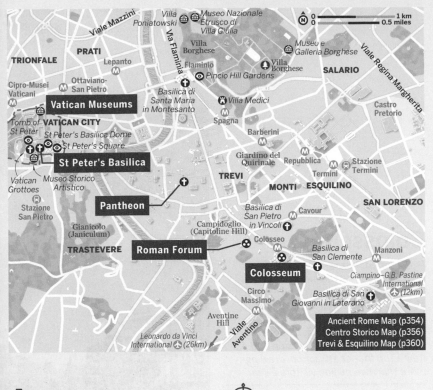

Arriving in Rome

Leonardo da Vinci (Fiumicino) Airport Half-hourly Leonardo Express trains run to Stazione Termini (€14, 30 minutes). A taxi to the centre is €48.

Ciampino Airport Buses to Stazione Termini 4am to 12.15am, €6; airport-to-hotel shuttles €25 per person; taxis €30.

Stazione Termini Rome's principal train station.

Where to Stay

Rome has many boutique-style guesthouses offering chic accommodation at midrange to top-end prices. Alternatively, try a *pensione* (a small family-run hotel with simple rooms, most with private bathroom). Some religious institutions also offer good-value rooms, though many have strict curfews and the rooms are no-frills.

For information on what each Roman neighbourhood has to offer, see the table on p369.

Colosseum

A monument to raw, merciless power, the Colosseum is the most thrilling of Rome's ancient sights. It was here that gladiators met in mortal combat and condemned prisoners fought off wild beasts in front of baying, bloodthirsty crowds. Two thousand years on and it's Italy's top tourist attraction, drawing more than five million visitors a year.

Great For...

❶ Need to Know

Colosseo; ☏06 3996 7700; www.parco colosseo.it; Piazza del Colosseo; adult/ reduced incl Roman Forum & Palatino €12/7.50, SUPER ticket €18/13.50; ⏱8.30am-1hr before sunset; Ⓜ Colosseo

★ Top Tip

Beat the queues by buying your ticket at the Palatino (Via di San Gregorio 30).

Built by Vespasian (r AD 69–79) in the grounds of Nero's vast Domus Aurea complex, the arena was inaugurated in AD 80, eight years after it had been commissioned. To mark the occasion, Vespasian's son and successor Titus (r AD 79–81) staged games that lasted 100 days and nights, during which 5000 animals were slaughtered. Trajan (r AD 98–117) later topped this, holding a marathon 117-day killing spree involving 9000 gladiators and 10,000 animals.

The 50,000-seat arena was originally known as the Flavian Amphitheatre, and although it was Rome's most fearsome arena it wasn't the biggest – the Circo Massimo could hold up to 250,000 people. The name Colosseum, when introduced in medieval times, was a reference not to its size but to the Colosso di Nerone, a giant statue of Nero that stood nearby.

With the fall of the Roman Empire in the 5th century, the Colosseum was abandoned and gradually became overgrown. In the Middle Ages it served as a fortress for two of the city's warrior families, the Frangipani and the Annibaldi. Later, during the Renaissance and baroque periods, it was plundered of its precious travertine, and the marble stripped from it was used to make huge palaces such as Palazzo Venezia, Palazzo Barberini and Palazzo Cancelleria.

More recently, pollution and vibrations caused by traffic and the metro have taken their toll, but a €25-million clean-up, the first in its 2000-year history, has once again revealed the creamy hues of the Colosseum walls.

Interior

Exterior

The outer walls have three levels of arches, framed by Ionic, Doric and Corinthian columns. These were originally covered in travertine, and marble statues filled the niches on the 2nd and 3rd storeys. The upper level, punctuated with windows and slender Corinthian pilasters, had supports for 240 masts that held up a huge canvas awning over the arena, shielding spectators from sun and rain. The 80 entrance arches, known as vomitoria, allowed the spectators to enter and be seated in a matter of minutes.

☑ Don't Miss

Visit the mysterious underground area (hypogeum) and/or upper floors (Belvedere). These cost €9 (or €15 for both) plus the normal Colosseum ticket.

ALENA STALMASHONAK / SHUTTERSTOCK ©

Arena

The arena originally had a wooden floor covered in sand to prevent the combatants from slipping and to soak up the blood. It could also be flooded for mock sea battles. Trapdoors led down to the hypogeum, a subterranean complex of corridors, cages and lifts beneath the arena floor.

The Seating

The *cavea*, for spectator seating, was divided into three tiers: magistrates and senior officials sat in the lowest tier, wealthy citizens in the middle, and the plebeians in the highest tier. Women (except for vestal virgins) were relegated to the cheapest sections at the top. As in modern stadiums, tickets were numbered and spectators assigned a seat in a specific sector. The podium, a broad terrace in front of the tiers of seats, was reserved for the emperor, senators and VIPs.

After a long period of closure, the top three rings, known collectively as the Belvedere, are now open and can be visited on guided tours.

Hypogeum

The hypogeum served as the stadium's backstage area. Sets for the various battle scenes were prepared here and hoisted up to the arena by a complicated system of pulleys. Caged animals were kept here and gladiators would gather here before showtime, having come in through an underground corridor from the nearby Ludus Magnus (gladiator school).

✖ Take a Break

Head up to Via Cavour where **Cavour 313** (Map p354; ☑06 678 54 96; www. cavour313.it; Via Cavour 313; ☑12.30-2.45pm daily & 6-11.30pm Mon-Thu, to midnight Fri & Sat, 7-11pm Sun, closed Aug; ⓂCavour) is a good bet for a glass of wine accompanied by platters of cheese and cured meats.

Pantheon

A striking 2000-year-old temple that's now a church, the Pantheon is Rome's best-preserved ancient monument and one of the most influential buildings in the Western world. Its greying, pockmarked exterior may look its age, but inside it's a different story. It's a unique and exhilarating experience to pass through the vast bronze doors and gaze up at the largest unreinforced concrete dome ever built.

Great For...

❶ Need to Know

Map p356; www.pantheonroma.com; Piazza della Rotonda; ☺8.30am-7.30pm Mon-Sat, 9am-6pm Sun; ☐Largo di Torre Argentina
FREE

In its current form the Pantheon dates to around AD 125. The original temple, built by Marcus Agrippa in 27 BC, burnt down in AD 80, and although it was rebuilt by Domitian, it was struck by lightning and destroyed for a second time in AD 110. The emperor Hadrian had it reconstructed between AD 118 and 125, and it's this version that you see today.

Hadrian's temple was dedicated to the classical gods – hence the name Pantheon, a derivation of the Greek words *pan* (all) and *theos* (god) – but in 608 it was consecrated as a Christian church. It's now officially known as the Basilica di Santa Maria ad Martyres.

Thanks to this consecration, it was spared the worst of the medieval plundering that reduced many of Rome's ancient buildings to near dereliction. But it didn't escape entirely unscathed – its gilded-bronze roof tiles were removed and bronze from the portico was used by Bernini for the *baldachino* at St Peter's Basilica.

Exterior

The dark-grey pitted exterior faces onto busy, cafe-lined Piazza della Rotonda. And while its facade is somewhat the worse for wear, it's still an imposing sight. The monumental entrance **portico** consists of 16 Corinthian columns, each 13m high and made of Egyptian granite, supporting a triangular **pediment**. Behind the columns, two 20-tonne **bronze doors** – 16th-century restorations of the original portal – give onto the central rotunda. Rivets and holes in the building's brickwork indicate where marble-veneer panels were originally placed.

Interior

Inscription

For centuries the inscription under the pediment – M:AGRIPPA.L.F.COS.TERTIUM.FECIT or 'Marcus Agrippa, son of Lucius, consul for the third time, built this' – led scholars to think that the current building was Agrippa's original temple. However, 19th-century excavations revealed traces of an earlier temple and historians realised that Hadrian had simply kept Agrippa's original inscription.

Interior

Although impressive from outside, it's only when you get inside that you can really appreciate the Pantheon's full size. With

> ☑ **Don't Miss**
>
> The 7m-high bronze doors, which provide a suitably grand entrance to your visit.

TFSTUDIO / SHUTTERSTOCK ©

light streaming in through the **oculus** (the 8.7m-diameter hole in the centre of the dome), the cylindrical marble-clad interior seems vast.

Opposite the entrance is the church's main **altar**, over which hangs a 7th-century icon of the *Madonna col Bambino* (Madonna and Child). To the left are the tombs of the artist Raphael, King Umberto I and Margherita of Savoy. Over on the opposite side of the rotunda is the tomb of King Vittorio Emanuele II.

Dome

The Pantheon's dome, considered to be the Romans' most important architectural achievement, was the largest dome in the world until Brunelleschi beat it with his Florentine cupola. Its harmonious appearance is due to a precisely calibrated symmetry – its diameter is exactly equal to the building's interior height of 43.3m. At its centre, the oculus, which symbolically connected the temple with the gods, plays a vital structural role by absorbing and redistributing the dome's huge tensile forces.

What's Nearby?

Basilica di Santa Maria Sopra Minerva
Basilica

(Map p356; www.santamariasopraminerva.it; Piazza della Minerva 42; ⊘6.55am-7pm Mon-Fri, 10am-12.30pm & 3.30-7pm Sat, 8.10am-12.30pm & 3.30-7pm Sun; ⬚Largo di Torre Argentina) Built on the site of three pagan temples, including one to the goddess Minerva, the Dominican Basilica di Santa Maria Sopra Minerva is Rome's only Gothic church. However, little remains of the original 13th-century structure and these days the main drawcard is a minor Michelangelo sculpture and the colourful, art-rich interior.

> ✗ **Take a Break**
>
> For an uplifting espresso, try the nearby **La Casa del Caffè Tazza d'Oro** (Map p356; ⬚06 678 97 92; www.tazzadorocoffeeshop.com; Via degli Orfani 84-86; ⊘7am-8pm Mon-Sat, 10.30am-7.30pm Sun; ⬚Via del Corso), one of Rome's finest coffee-houses.

PHANT / SHUTTERSTOCK ©

St Peter's Basilica

In this city of outstanding churches, none can hold a candle to St Peter's, Italy's largest, richest and most spectacular basilica.

The original church was commissioned by the emperor Constantine and built around 349 on the site where St Peter is said to have been buried between AD 64 and 67. But like many medieval churches, it eventually fell into disrepair. It wasn't until the mid-15th century that efforts were made to restore it, first by Pope Nicholas V and then, rather more successfully, by Julius II.

In 1506 construction began on a design by Bramante, but ground to a halt when the architect died in 1514. In 1547 Michelangelo stepped in to take on the project. He simplified Bramante's plans and drew up designs for what was to become his greatest architectural achievement: the dome. He didn't live to see it built, though, and it was left to Giacomo della Porta, Domenico Fontana and Carlo Maderno to complete the basilica, which was finally consecrated in 1626.

Great For...

☑ Don't Miss

Climbing the (numerous, steep and tiring, but worth it) steps of the dome for views over Rome.

Interior

WIDE PHOTO / SHUTTERSTOCK ©

❶ Need to Know

Basilica di San Pietro; ☑06 6988 3731; www.
vatican.va; St Peter's Sq; ⊙7am-7pm Apr-Sep,
to 6pm Oct-Mar; ⎁Piazza del Risorgimento,
Ⓜ Ottaviano-San Pietro FREE

✕ Take a Break

For a salad or tasty panino, try organic
takeaway **Fa-Bìo** (☑06 3974 6510; Via
Germanico 71; meals €5-7; ⊙10.30am-5.30pm
Mon-Fri, to 4pm Sat; ⎁Piazza del Risorgimento,
Ⓜ Ottaviano-San Pietro) 🍴, or join the fashionable locals at **Il Sorpasso** (☑06 8902
4554; www.sorpasso.info; Via Properzio 31-33;
meals €20-35; ⊙7.30am-1am Mon-Fri, 9am-
1am Sat; 🛜; ⎁Piazza del Risorgimento).

★ Top Tip

Strict dress codes are enforced, which
means no shorts, miniskirts or bare
shoulders.

Facade

Built between 1608 and 1612, Maderno's
immense facade is 48m high and 118.6m
wide. Eight 27m-high columns support
the upper attic on which 13 statues stand
representing Christ the Redeemer, St John
the Baptist and the 11 apostles. The central
balcony, the **Loggia della Benedizione**, is
where the pope stands to deliver his *Urbi et
Orbi* blessing at Christmas and Easter.

Interior

At the beginning of the right aisle is Michelangelo's hauntingly beautiful *Pietà*. Sculpted
when the artist was 25 (in 1499), it's the only
work he ever signed; his signature is etched
into the sash across the Madonna's breast.

On a pillar just beyond the *Pietà*, Carlo
Fontana's gilt and bronze **monument to
Queen Christina of Sweden** commemorates the far-from-holy Swedish monarch
who converted to Catholicism in 1655.

Moving on, you'll come to the **Cappella
di San Sebastiano**, home of Pope John
Paul II's tomb, and the **Cappella del
Santissimo Sacramento**, a sumptuously
decorated baroque chapel.

Dominating the centre of the basilica is
Bernini's 29m-high **baldachin**. Supported
by four spiral columns and made with
bronze taken from the Pantheon, it stands
over the **high altar**, which itself sits on the
site of St Peter's grave.

Above the baldachin, Michelangelo's
dome soars to a height of 119m. Based on
Brunelleschi's cupola in Florence, it's supported by four massive stone **piers** named
after the saints whose statues adorn
the Bernini-designed niches – Longinus,
Helena, Veronica and Andrew.

At the base of the **Pier of St Longinus** is Arnolfo di Cambio's much-loved 13th-century bronze **statue of St Peter**, whose right foot has been worn down by centuries of caresses.

Dominating the tribune behind the altar is Bernini's extraordinary **Cattedra di San Pietro**, centred on a wooden seat that was once thought to have been St Peter's but in fact dates to the 9th century.

To the right of the throne, Bernini's **monument to Urban VIII** depicts the pope flanked by the figures of Charity and Justice.

Near the head of the left aisle are the so-called **Stuart monuments**. On the right is the monument to Clementina Sobieska, wife of James Stuart, by Filippo Barigioni, and on the left is Canova's vaguely erotic monument to the last three members of the Stuart clan, the pretenders to the English throne who died in exile in Rome.

Dome

From the **dome** (St Peter's Sq; with/without lift €10/8; ⊙8am-6pm Apr-Sep, to 5pm Oct-Mar; ⊟Piazza del Risorgimento, ⓂOttaviano-San Pietro) entrance on the right of the basilica's main portico, you can walk the 551 steps to the top or take a small lift halfway and then follow on foot for the last 320 steps. Either way, it's a long, steep climb and not recommended for anyone who suffers from claustrophobia or vertigo. Make it to the top, though, and you're rewarded with stunning views.

Museo Storico Artistico

Accessed from the left nave, the **Museo Storico Artistico** (Tesoro, Treasury; 📞06 6988 1840; St Peter's Basilica, St Peter's Sq; €5 incl audioguide; ⊙9am-6.10pm Apr-Sep, to 5.10pm Oct-Mar, last entrance 30min before closing; ⊟Piazza del Risorgimento, ⓂOttaviano-San

St Peter's Square

Pietro) sparkles with sacred relics. Highlights include a tabernacle by Donatello and the 6th-century *Crux Vaticana* (Vatican Cross).

Vatican Grottoes

Extending beneath the basilica, the **Vatican Grottoes** (St Peter's Basilica, St Peter's Sq; ⊙8am-5pm Apr-Sep, to 4pm Oct-Mar; 🚇Piazza del Risorgimento, ⓂOttaviano-San Pietro) `FREE` contain the tombs and sarcophagi of numerous popes, as well as several columns from the original 4th-century basilica. The entrance is in the Pier of St Andrew.

★ Free Tours

Free, two-hour English-language tours usually start at 2.15pm Monday, Wednesday and Friday, from the Ufficio Pellegrini e Turisti (p367). No need to book, but check the website for dates.

St Peter's Tomb

Excavations beneath the basilica have uncovered part of the original church and what archaeologists believe is the **Tomb of St Peter** (🕿06 6988 5318; www.scavi.va; St Peter's Basilica, St Peter's Sq; €13; 🚇Piazza del Risorgimento, ⓂOttaviano-San Pietro).

The excavations can only be visited by guided tour. To book a spot (this must be done well in advance), check out the website of the **Ufficio Scavi** (Excavations Office; Fabbrica di San Pietro; 🕿06 6988 5318; www.scavi.va; €13; ⊙9am-6pm Mon-Fri, to 5pm Sat; 🚇Piazza del Risorgimento, ⓂOttaviano-San Pietro).

What's Nearby?

St Peter's Square   Piazza

(Piazza San Pietro; 🚇Piazza del Risorgimento, ⓂOttaviano-San Pietro) Overlooked by St Peter's Basilica (p338), the Vatican's central square was laid out between 1656 and 1667 to a design by Gian Lorenzo Bernini. Seen from above, it resembles a giant keyhole with two semicircular colonnades, each consisting of four rows of Doric columns, encircling a giant ellipse that straightens out to funnel believers into the basilica. The effect was deliberate – Bernini described the colonnades as representing 'the motherly arms of the church'.

Castel Sant'Angelo   Museum, Castle

(Map p356; 🕿06 681 91 11; www.castelsantangelo. beniculturali.it; Lungotevere Castello 50; adult/reduced €14/7, free 1st Sunday of the month Oct-Mar; ⊙9am-7.30pm, ticket office to 6.30pm; 🚇Piazza Pia) With its chunky round keep, this castle is an instantly recognisable landmark. Built as a mausoleum for the emperor Hadrian, it was converted into a papal fortress in the 6th century and named after an angelic vision that Pope Gregory the Great had in 590. Nowadays, it houses the **Museo Nazionale di Castel Sant'Angelo** and its eclectic collection of paintings, sculpture, military memorabilia and medieval firearms.

JEMINA VIRTANEN / EYEEM / GETTY IMAGES ©

★ Local Knowledge

Near the main entrance, a red floor disk marks the spot where Charlemagne and later Holy Roman Emperors were crowned by the pope.

Vatican Museums

Founded in the 16th century, the Vatican Museums boast one of the world's greatest art collections. Highlights include spectacular classical statuary, rooms frescoed by Raphael, and the Michelangelo-decorated Sistine Chapel.

Housing the museums are the lavishly decorated halls and galleries of the Palazzo Apostolico Vaticano. This vast 5.5-hectare complex consists of two palaces – the Vatican palace (nearer to St Peter's) and the Belvedere Palace – joined by two long galleries. Inside are three courtyards: the Cortile della Pigna, the Cortile della Biblioteca and, to the south, the Cortile del Belvedere. You'll never cover it all in one day, so it pays to be selective.

Great For...

☑ Don't Miss

The unforgettable Sistine Chapel and the Stanze di Raffaello (Raphael Rooms).

Pinacoteca

Often overlooked by visitors, the papal picture gallery contains Raphael's last work, *La Trasfigurazione* (Transfiguration; 1517–20), and paintings by Giotto, Fra Angelico, Filippo Lippi, Perugino, Titian, Guido Reni, Guercino, Pietro da Cortona, Caravaggio and Leonardo da Vinci, whose haunting *San Gerolamo* (St Jerome; c 1480) was never finished.

Museo Pio-Clementino

ⓘ Need to Know

Musei Vaticani; ☏06 6988 4676; www.musei
vaticani.va; Viale Vaticano; adult/reduced
€17/8; ⏱9am-6pm Mon-Sat, to 2pm last Sun
of month, last entry 2hr before close; ⊠Piazza
del Risorgimento, ⓂOttaviano-San Pietro

✕ Take a Break

Head to Bonci Pizzarium (p363), one of
Rome's best *pizza al taglio* (sliced pizza)
joints.

★ Top Tip

Avoid queues by booking online: at
http://biglietteriamusei.vatican.va/
musei/tickets/do (€4 fee; print voucher
and swap it for a ticket at the appointed
time at the entrance) or Ufficio Pellegrini e Turisti (p367).

Museo Chiaramonti & Braccio Nuovo

The Museo Chiaramonti is effectively the
long corridor that runs down the eastern
side of the Belvedere Palace. Its walls are
lined with thousands of statues and busts
representing everything from immortal
gods to playful cherubs and unattractive
Roman patricians. Near the end of the hall,
off to the right, is the Braccio Nuovo (New
Wing), which contains a famous statue of
the Nile as a reclining god covered by 16
babies.

Museo Pio-Clementino

This stunning museum contains some of
the Vatican Museums' finest classical statuary, including the peerless *Apollo Belvedere*
and the 1st-century *Laocoön,* both in the
Cortile Ottagono (Octagonal Courtyard).

Before you go into the courtyard, take a
moment to admire the 1st-century *Apoxyo-
menos,* one of the earliest known sculptures
to depict a figure with a raised arm.

Museo Gregoriano Egizio

Founded by Gregory XVI in 1839, this
museum contains pieces taken from Egypt
in Roman times. The collection is small, but
there are fascinating exhibits including the
Trono di Ramses II (part of a statue of the
seated king), vividly painted sarcophagi
dating from around 1000 BC, and some
macabre mummies.

Museo Gregoriano Etrusco

At the top of the 18th-century Simon-
etti staircase, the Museo Gregoriano
Etrusco contains artefacts unearthed in
the Etruscan tombs of northern Lazio, as
well as a superb collection of vases and

Roman antiquities. Of particular interest is the *Marte di Todi* (Mars of Todi), a black bronze of a warrior dating to the late 5th century BC.

Galleria delle Carte Geografiche & Sala Sobieski

The last of three galleries – the other two are the **Galleria dei Candelabri** (Gallery of the Candelabra) and the **Galleria degli Arazzi** (Tapestry Gallery) – this 120m-long corridor is hung with 40 huge topographical maps. These were created between 1580 and 1583 for Pope Gregory XIII based on drafts by Ignazio Danti, one of the leading cartographers of his day.

Beyond the gallery, the **Sala Sobieski** is named after an enormous 19th-century painting depicting the victory of the Polish king John III Sobieski over the Turks in 1683.

Stanze di Raffaello

These four frescoed chambers, currently undergoing partial restoration, were part of Pope Julius II's private apartments. Raphael himself painted the Stanza della Segnatura (1508–11) and the Stanza d'Eliodoro (1512–14), while the Stanza dell'Incendio (1514–17) and Sala di Costantino (1517–24) were decorated by students following his designs.

Sistine Chapel

The jewel in the Vatican's crown, the Sistine Chapel (Cappella Sistina) is home to two of the world's most famous works of art: Michelangelo's ceiling frescoes and his *Giudizio Universale* (Last Judgement).

The chapel was originally built for Pope Sixtus IV, after whom it's named, and was consecrated on 15 August 1483. However,

Marble scultpures in one of the Vatican museums

apart from the wall frescoes and floor, little remains of the original decor, which was sacrificed to make way for Michelangelo's two masterpieces. The first, the ceiling, was commissioned by Pope Julius II and painted between 1508 and 1512; the second, the spectacular *Giudizio Universale,* was painted between 1535 and 1541.

Michelangelo's ceiling design, which is best viewed from the chapel's main entrance in the far east wall, covers the entire 800-sq-m surface. With painted architectural features and a cast of colourful biblical characters, it's centred on nine panels depicting

★ Local Knowledge

Tuesdays and Thursdays are the quietest days to visit. Wednesday mornings are also good, and afternoons are better than mornings. Avoid Mondays, when many other museums are shut.

scenes from the Creation, the story of Adam and Eve, the Fall, and the plight of Noah.

As you look up from the east wall, the first panel is the *Drunkenness of Noah,* followed by *The Flood* and the *Sacrifice of Noah.* Next, *Original Sin and Banishment from the Garden of Eden* famously depicts Adam and Eve being sent packing after accepting the forbidden fruit from Satan, represented by a snake with the body of a woman coiled around a tree. The *Creation of Eve* is then followed by the *Creation of Adam.* This, one of the most famous images in Western art, shows a bearded God pointing his finger at Adam, thus bringing him to life. Completing the sequence are the *Separation of Land from Sea;* the *Creation of the Sun, Moon and Plants;* and the *Separation of Light from Darkness,* featuring a fearsome God reaching out to touch the sun. Set around the central panels are 20 athletic male nudes, known as *ignudi.*

Opposite, on the west wall is Michelangelo's mesmeric *Giudizio Universale,* showing Christ – in the centre near the top – passing sentence over the souls of the dead as they are torn from their graves to face him. The saved get to stay in heaven (in the upper right); the damned are sent down to face the demons in hell (in the bottom right).

The chapel's walls also boast superb frescoes. Painted between 1481 and 1482 by a crack team of Renaissance artists, including Botticelli, Ghirlandaio, Pinturicchio, Perugino and Luca Signorelli, they represent events in the lives of Moses (to the left looking at the *Giudizio Universale*) and Christ (to the right). Highlights include Botticelli's *Temptations of Christ* and Perugino's *Handing over of the Keys.*

As well as providing a showcase for priceless art, the Sistine Chapel serves an important religious function as the place where the conclave meets to elect a new pope.

★ Top Tip

Exhibits are simply labelled – consider an audioguide (€8) or *Guide to the Vatican Museums and City* (€13).

Roman Forum

The Roman Forum was ancient Rome's showpiece centre, a grandiose district of temples, basilicas and vibrant public spaces. Nowadays, it's a collection of impressive, if badly labelled, ruins that can leave you drained and confused. But if you can get your imagination going, there's something wonderfully compelling about walking in the footsteps of Julius Caesar and other legendary figures of Roman history.

Great For...

❶ Need to Know

Foro Romano; Map p354; ☎06 3996 7700; www.parcocolosseo.it; Largo della Salara Vecchia, Piazza di Santa Maria Nova; adult/reduced incl Colosseum & Palatino €12/7.50, SUPER ticket €18/13.50; ⏰8.30am-1hr before sunset; SUPER ticket sites Tue, Thu, Sat & afternoon Sun only; 🚍Via dei Fori Imperiali

★ **Top Tip**

Get grandstand views of the Roman Forum from the Palatino and Campidoglio.

Originally an Etruscan burial ground, the Forum was first developed in the 7th century BC, growing over time to become the social, political and commercial hub of the Roman Empire. In the Middle Ages it was reduced to pasture land and extensively plundered for its marble. The area was systematically excavated in the 18th and 19th centuries and work continues to this day.

Via Sacra Towards Campidoglio

Entering the Forum from Largo della Salara Vecchia, you'll see the **Tempio di Antonino e Faustina** (Map p354; Largo della Salara Vecchia, Roman Forum; 🚊Via dei Fori Imperiali) ahead to your left. Erected in AD 141, this was transformed into a church in the 8th century, the **Chiesa di San Lorenzo in Miranda** (Map p354; Largo della Salara Vecchia, Roman Forum; 🚊Via dei Fori Imperiali). To your

right is the 179 BC **Basilica Fulvia Aemilia** (Map p354; Largo della Salara Vecchia, Roman Forum; 🚊Via dei Fori Imperiali).

At the end of the path, you'll come to **Via Sacra** (Map p354; Largo della Salara Vecchia, Roman Forum; 🚊Via dei Fori Imperiali), the Forum's main thoroughfare, and the Tempio di Giulio Cesare, which stands on the spot where Julius Caesar was cremated.

Heading right brings you to the **Curia** (Map p354; Largo della Salara Vecchia, Roman Forum; 🚊Via dei Fori Imperiali), the original seat of the Roman Senate, though what you see today is a reconstruction of how it looked in the reign of Diocletian (r 284–305).

At the end of Via Sacra, the **Arco di Settimio Severo** (Arch of Septimius Severus; Map p354; Largo della Salara Vecchia, Roman Forum; 🚊Via dei Fori Imperiali) is dedicated to the eponymous emperor and his sons, Caracalla and Geta. Close by the **Colonna**

Basilica di Massenzio and Tempio di Romolo

di Foca (Column of Phocus; Map p354; Largo della Salara Vecchia, Roman Forum; 🚇Via dei Fori Imperiali) rises above what was once the Forum's main square, Piazza del Foro.

The eight granite columns that rise behind the Colonna are all that survive of the **Tempio di Saturno** (Temple of Saturn; Map p354; Largo della Salara Vecchia, Roman Forum; 🚇Via dei Fori Imperiali), an important temple that doubled as the state treasury.

Tempio di Castore e Polluce & Casa delle Vestali

From the path that runs parallel to Via Sacra, you'll pass the stubby ruins of the

☑ Don't Miss

The Basilica di Massenzio, to get some idea of the scale of ancient Rome's mammoth buildings.

STEFANO_VALERI / SHUTTERSTOCK ©

Basilica Giulia (Map p354; Largo della Salara Vecchia, Roman Forum; 🚇Via dei Fori Imperiali), which was begun by Caesar and finished by Augustus. At the end of the basilica, three columns remain from the 5th-century-BC **Tempio di Castore e Polluce** (Temple of Castor and Pollux; Map p354; Largo della Salara Vecchia, Roman Forum; 🚇Via dei Fori Imperiali) . Nearby, the 6th-century **Chiesa di Santa Maria Antiqua** (Map p354; Largo della Salara Vecchia, Roman Forum; SUPER ticket adult/reduced €18/13.50; ⊙9am-6.30pm Tue, Thu & Sat, from 2pm Sun summer, 9am-3.30pm Tue, Thu & Sat, from 2pm Sun winter; 🚇Via dei Fori Imperiali) is the oldest Christian church in the Forum.

Back towards Via Sacra is the **Casa delle Vestali** (House of the Vestal Virgins; Map p354; Largo della Salara Vecchia, Roman Forum; 🚇Via dei Fori Imperiali), currently off limits, home of the virgins who tended the flame in the adjoining **Tempio di Vesta** (Map p354; Largo della Salara Vecchia, Roman Forum; 🚇Via dei Fori Imperiali).

Via Sacra Towards the Colosseum

Heading up Via Sacra past the **Tempio di Romolo** (Temple of Romulus; Map p354; Largo della Salara Vecchia, Roman Forum; SUPER ticket adult/reduced €18/13.50; ⊙9am-6.30pm Tue, Thu & Sat, from 2pm Sun summer, 9am-3.30pm Tue, Thu & Sat, from 2pm Sun winter; 🚇Via dei Fori Imperiali), you'll come to the **Basilica di Massenzio** (Basilica di Costantino; Map p354; Piazza di Santa Maria Nova, Roman Forum; 🚇Via dei Fori Imperiali), the largest building on the forum.

Beyond the basilica, the **Arco di Tito** (Arch of Titus; Map p354; Piazza di Santa Maria Nova, Roman Forum; 🚇Via dei Fori Imperiali) was built in AD 81 to celebrate Vespasian and Titus' victories against rebels in Jerusalem.

✕ Take a Break

For a restorative coffee break, head up to the Campidoglio and the **Terrazza Caffarelli** (Caffetteria dei Musei Capitolini; Map p354; ☏06 6919 0564; Piazzale Caffarelli 4; ⊙9.30am-7pm; 🚇Piazza Venezia), the Capitoline Museums' panoramic rooftop cafe.

Centro Storico Piazzas

Rome's *centro storico* boasts some of the city's most celebrated piazzas, and several lovely but lesser-known squares. Each has its own character, but together they encapsulate much of the city's beauty, history and drama.

Start Piazza Colonna
Distance 1.5km
Duration 3½ hours

Classic Photo: Piazza della Rotonda with the Pantheon in the background.

4 It's a short walk along Via del Seminario to Piazza della Rotonda, where the **Pantheon** (p334) needs no introduction.

5 Piazza Navona (p353) is Rome's great showpiece square, where you can compare the two giants of Roman baroque – Gian Lorenzo Bernini and Francesco Borromini.

Take a Break... Those in the know head to **Forno di Campo de' Fiori** (Map p356; ☎ 06 6880 6662; www.forno campodefiori.com; Campo de' Fiori 22; pizza slices around €3; ⏰ 7.30am-2.30pm & 4.45-8pm Mon-Sat, closed Sat afternoon Jul & Aug; ☐ Corso Vittorio Emanuele II) for some of Rome's best *pizza bianca* (white pizza with olive oil and salt).

7 Just beyond the Campo, the more sober **Piazza Farnese** is overshadowed by the austere facade of the Renaissance **Palazzo Farnese** (p355).

1 Piazza Colonna is dominated by the 30m-high Colonna di Marco Aurelio and flanked by Palazzo Chigi, the official residence of the Italian PM.

2 Follow Via dei Bergamaschi to **Piazza di Pietra**, a refined space overlooked by the 2nd-century Tempio di Adriano.

3 Continue down Via de' Burro to **Piazza di Sant'Ignazio Loyola**, a small piazza with a church boasting celebrated *trompe l'œil* frescoes.

6 On the other side of Corso Vittorio Emanuele II, **Campo de' Fiori** (p355) hosts a noisy market and boisterous drinking scene.

1 VQE / SHUTTERSTOCK © 2 VALERIO ROSATI / ALAMY STOCK PHOTO © 4 WJAREK / 1 VQE / SHUTTERSTOCK © 6 PIT STOCK / SHUTTERSTOCK ©

◉ SIGHTS

◉ Ancient Rome

Palatino   Archaeological Site

(Palatine Hill; Map p354; ☎06 3996 7700; www.parcocolosseo.it; Via di San Gregorio 30, Piazza di Santa Maria Nova; adult/reduced incl Colosseum & Roman Forum €12/7.50, SUPER ticket €18/13.50; ⊘8.30am-1hr before sunset; some SUPER ticket sites Mon, Wed, Fri & morning Sun only; ⓂColosseo) Sandwiched between the Roman Forum and the Circo Massimo, the Palatino (Palatine Hill) is one of Rome's most spectacular sights, a beautiful, atmospheric area of towering pine trees, majestic ruins and unforgettable views. This is where Romulus supposedly founded the city in 753 BC and Rome's emperors lived in palatial luxury. Look out for the **stadio** (stadium; Map p354; Via di San Gregorio 30, Palatino; ⓂColosseo), the ruins of the **Domus Flavia** (imperial palace; Map p354; Via di San Gregorio 30, Palatino; ⓂColosseo), and grandstand views over the Roman Forum from the **Orti Farnesiani** (Map p354; Via di San Gregorio 30, Palatino; ⓂColosseo).

Capitoline Museums   Museum

(Musei Capitolini; Map p354; ☎06 06 08; www.museicapitolini.org; Piazza del Campidoglio 1; adult/reduced €11.50/9.50; ⊘9.30am-7.30pm, last admission 6.30pm; ☐Piazza Venezia) Dating from 1471, the Capitoline Museums are the world's oldest public museums. Their collection of classical sculpture is one of Italy's finest, boasting works such as the iconic *Lupa Capitolina* (Capitoline Wolf), a life-size bronze of a she-wolf suckling Romulus and Remus, and the *Galata morente* (Dying Gaul), a moving depiction of a dying warrior. There's also a formidable gallery with masterpieces by the likes of Titian, Tintoretto, Rubens and Caravaggio.

Ticket prices increase when there's a temporary exhibition on.

Vittoriano   Monument

(Victor Emanuel Monument; Map p354; Piazza Venezia; ⊘9.30am-5.30pm summer, to 4.30pm winter; ☐Piazza Venezia) **FREE** Love it or

Piazza Navona is central Rome's elegant showcase square

Piazza Navona

BELENOS / SHUTTERSTOCK ©

loathe it, as many Romans do, you can't ignore the Vittoriano (aka the Altare della Patria, Altar of the Fatherland), the colossal mountain of white marble that towers over Piazza Venezia. Built at the turn of the 20th century to honour Italy's first king, Vittorio Emanuele II – who's immortalised in its vast equestrian statue – it provides the dramatic setting for the **Tomb of the Unknown Soldier** and, inside, the small **Museo Centrale del Risorgimento** (Map p354; ☑06 679 35 98; www.risorgimento. it; Vittoriano, Piazza Venezia; adult/reduced €5/2.50; ⊙9.30am-6.30pm; ☐Piazza Venezia), documenting Italian unification.

Also inside is the **Complesso del Vittoriano** (Map p354; ☑06 871 51 11; www.ilvittoriano. com; Via di San Pietro in Carcere; admission variable; ⊙9.30am-7.30pm Mon-Thu, to 10pm Fri & Sat, to 8.30pm Sun; ☐Via dei Fori Imperiali), a gallery that regularly hosts major art exhibitions. But as impressive as any of the art on show are the glorious 360-degree views from the top of the monument. See for yourself by taking the panoramic **Roma dal Cielo** (Map p354; Vittoriano, Piazza Venezia; adult/reduced €10/5; ⊙9.30am-7.30pm, last admission 6.45pm; ☐Piazza Venezia) lift up to the Terrazza delle Quadrighe.

Bocca della Verità   Monument

(Mouth of Truth; Map p354; Piazza Bocca della Verità 18; voluntary donation; ⊙9.30am-5.50pm summer, to 4.50pm winter; ☐Piazza Bocca della Verità) A bearded face carved into a giant marble disc, the *Bocca della Verità* is one of Rome's most popular curiosities. Legend has it that if you put your hand in the mouth and tell a lie, the Bocca will slam shut and bite it off.

The mouth, which was originally part of a fountain, or possibly an ancient manhole cover, now lives in the portico of the **Chiesa di Santa Maria in Cosmedin**, a handsome medieval church.

◎ Centro Storico

Piazza Navona   Piazza

(Map p356; ☐Corso del Rinascimento) With its showy fountains, baroque *palazzi* and

👍 Rome for Free

Some of Rome's most famous sights are free, including all state museums and monuments on the first Sunday of the month, and all of Rome's churches. Vatican Museums (p342) are free on the last Sunday of the month.

Trevi Fountain (pictured, p358)
Spanish Steps (p359)
Pantheon (p334)
St Peter's Basilica (p338)

LEOKS / SHUTTERSTOCK ©

colourful cast of street artists, hawkers and tourists, Piazza Navona is central Rome's elegant showcase square. Built over the 1st-century **Stadio di Domiziano** (Domitian's Stadium; Map p356; ☑06 6880 5311; www.stadiodomiziano.com; Via di Tor Sanguigna 3; adult/reduced €8/6; ⊙10am-6.30pm Sun-Fri, to 7.30pm Sat), it was paved over in the 15th century and for almost 300 years hosted the city's main market. Its grand centrepiece is Bernini's **Fontana dei Quattro Fiumi** (Fountain of the Four Rivers; Map p356), a flamboyant fountain featuring an Egyptian obelisk and muscular personifications of the rivers Nile, Ganges, Danube and Plate.

Galleria Doria Pamphilj   Gallery

(Map p356; ☑06 679 73 23; www.doriapamphilj. it; Via del Corso 305; adult/reduced €12/8; ⊙9am-7pm, last entry 6pm; ☐Via del Corso) Hidden behind the grimy grey exterior of Palazzo Doria Pamphilj, this wonderful gallery boasts one of Rome's richest private art collections, with works by Raphael,

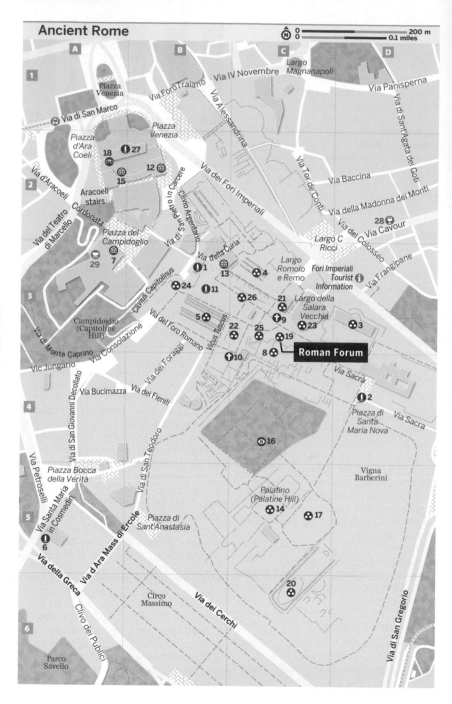

Ancient Rome

N 0 ————————————— 200 m
0 ————————————— 0.1 miles

Ancient Rome

Tintoretto, Titian, Caravaggio, Bernini and Velázquez, as well as several Flemish masters. Masterpieces abound, but the undisputed star is Velázquez' portrait of an implacable Pope Innocent X, who grumbled that the depiction was 'too real'. For a comparison, check out Gian Lorenzo Bernini's sculptural interpretation of the same subject.

Chiesa del Gesù   Church

(Map p356; ☑06 69 70 01; www.chiesadelgesu. org; Piazza del Gesù; ⊙6.45am-12.45pm & 4-7.30pm, St Ignatius rooms 4-6pm Mon-Sat, 10am noon Sun; ☐Largo di Torre Argentina) An imposing example of Counter-Reformation architecture, Rome's most important Jesuit church is a fabulous treasure trove of baroque art. Headline works include a swirling vault fresco by Giovanni Battista Gaulli (aka Il Baciccia) and Andrea del Pozzo's opulent tomb for Ignatius Loyola, the Spanish soldier and saint who founded the Jesuits in 1540. St Ignatius lived in the church from 1544 until his death in 1556 and you can visit his private rooms to the right of the main church.

Palazzo Farnese   Historic Building

(Map p356; www.inventerrome.com; Piazza Farnese; tours €9; ⊙guided tours 3pm, 4pm & 5pm Mon, Wed & Fri; ☐Corso Vittorio Emanuele II) Home to the French embassy, this towering Renaissance *palazzo*, one of Rome's

finest, was started in 1514 by Antonio da Sangallo the Younger, continued by Michelangelo and finished by Giacomo della Porta. Inside, it boasts frescoes by Annibale and Agostino Carracci that are said by some to rival Michelangelo's in the Sistine Chapel. The highlight, painted between 1597 and 1608, is the monumental ceiling fresco *Amori degli Dei* (The Loves of the Gods) in the Galleria dei Carracci.

Campo de' Fiori   Piazza

(Map p356; ☐Corso Vittorio Emanuele II) Colourful and always busy, *Il Campo* is a major focus of Roman life: by day it hosts one of the city's best-known markets; by night it heaves with tourists and young drinkers who spill out of its many bars and restaurants. For centuries the square was the site of public executions. It was here that philosopher Giordano Bruno was burned for heresy in 1600, now marked by a sinister statue of the hooded monk, created by Ettore Ferrari in 1889.

◎ Monti & Esquilino

Museo Nazionale Romano: Palazzo Massimo alle Terme   Museum

(Map p360; ☑06 3996 7700; www.coopculture. it; Largo di Villa Peretti 1; adult/reduced €10/5; ⊙9am-7.45pm Tue-Sun; Ⓜ Termini) One of Rome's preeminent museums, this treasure trove of classical art is a must-see

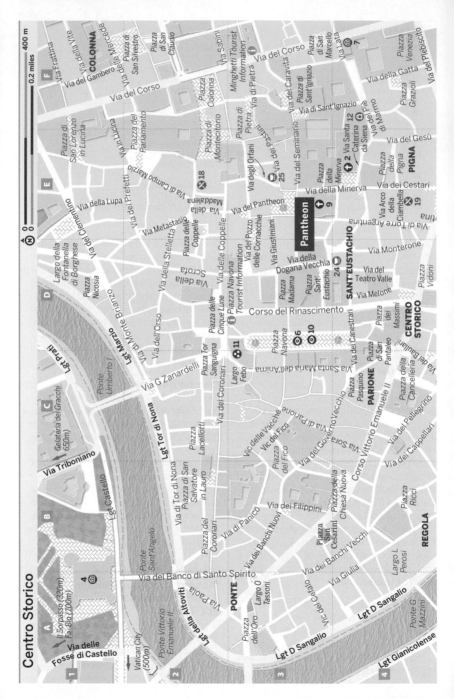

Centro Storico

Pantheon

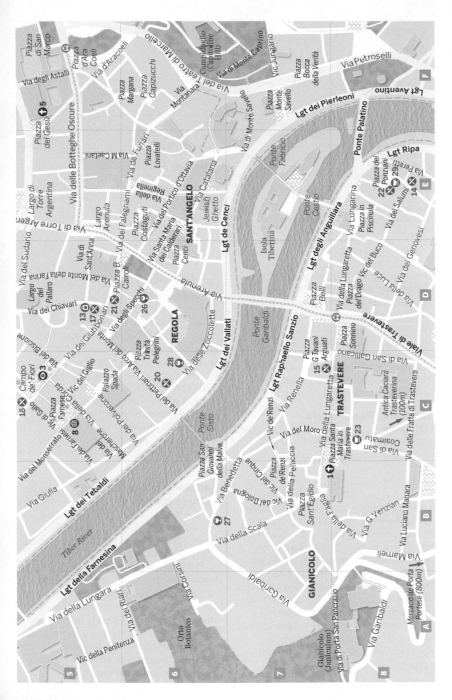

Piazza di San Marco

Piazza d'Ara Coeli

Via degli Astalli

Via d'Aracoeli

Via del Teatro di Marcello

Campidoglio (Capitoline Hill)

Via di Monte Caprino

Vic Jungario

Via Petroselli

Piazza Margana

Piazza Capizucchi

Piazza del Gesù 5

Piazza del Bottegle Oscure

Via M Caetani

Via Montanara

Via di Monte Savello

Piazza Monte Savello

Piazza Bocca della Verità

Lgt Aventino

Lgt dei Pierleoni

Ponte Palatino

Piazza Lovatelli

Via dei Funari

Lgt Ripa

Ponte Fabricio

Piazza dei Ponziani 22 29

Via Perefici 14

Via dei Salumi

Via della Reginella

Via del Portico d'Ottavia

Jewish Ghetto

SANTANGELO

Via Catalana

Ponte Cestio

Isola Tiberina

Lgt degli Anguillara

Via Lungarina

Piazza in Piscinula

Via dei Genovesi

Via di Torre Argen

Largo di Torre Argentina

Largo Arenula

Piazza Costaguti

Via dei Falegnami

Via Santa Maria dei Caldarari

Piazza Cenci

Lgt de Cenci

Via Arenula

Via della Lungaretta

Via della Luce

Via dei Buco

Via del Sudario

Via di Sant'Anna

Via B Piazza Cairoli

Piazza della Lungaretta

Vic Vic dell'Atleta

Piazza Belli

Piazza del Drago

Largo del Pallaro

Via del Monte della Farina

13 17

Via del Chiavari

21 26

REGOLA

Via degli Specchi

Via delle Zoccolette

Lgt dei Vallati

Ponte Garibaldi

Viale di Trastevere

Piazza Sonnino

Via del Biscione

Via dei Giubbonari

Via dell'Arco del Monte

Piazza Trinità Pelegrini

28

Via della Lungaretta

TRASTEVERE

Via di San Gallicano

Campo de' Fiori 3

16

Via del Gallo

Via dei Pettinari

20

Ponte Sisto

Lgt Raphaello Sanzio

Piazza G Tavani Arguati 15

Via della Lungaretta

Piazza Santa Maria in Trastevere 1

Antica Caciara Trasteverina (100m)

Via della Fratte di Trastevere

Piazza Farnese

Palazzo Spada

Via di Monserrato

Via della Polverione

8

Via della Mascherone

Via Giulia

Lgt dei Tebaldi

Piazza San Giovanni della Malva

Via Benedetta

Piazza de' Renzi

Vic de Renzi

Via del Moro

Via della Pelliccia

Via di San Cosimato 23

Via della Lungaretta

Lgt della Farnesina

Via della Lungara

Via Corsini

Vic del Bologna

Piazza della Cinque

Piazza Sant'Egidio

Via G Venzian

Via Luciano Manara

Tiber River

27

Via della Scala

GIANICOLO

Via della Fiaglia

Via Mameli

Via della Lungara

Via dei Riari

Via Garibaldi

Mercato de Porta Portese (800m)

Orto Botanico

Vic della Penitenza

Gianicolo (Janiculum)

Via di Porta San Pancrazio

Via Garibaldi

Centro Storico

when you're in the city. The ground and 1st floors are devoted to sculpture, with some breathtaking pieces – don't miss *The Boxer*, a 2nd-century-BC Greek bronze excavated on the Quirinale Hill in 1885, and the *Dying Niobid*, a 4th-century-BC Greek marble statue. But it's the magnificent and vibrantly coloured Villa Livia and Villa Farnesia frescoes on the 2nd floor that are the undisputed highlight.

Basilica di Santa Maria Maggiore   Basilica

(Map p360; ☏06 6988 6800; Piazza Santa Maria Maggiore; basilica free, adult/reduced museum €3/2, loggia €5; ⊙7am-6.45pm, loggia guided tours 9.30am-5.45pm; MTermini or Cavour) One of Rome's four patriarchal basilicas, this 5th-century church stands on Esquiline Hill's summit, on the spot where snow is said to have miraculously fallen in the summer of AD 358. Every year on 5 August the event is recreated during a light show in Piazza Santa Maria Maggiore. Much altered over the centuries, the basilica is an architectural hybrid with 14th-century Romanesque campanile, Renaissance coffered ceiling, 18th-century baroque facade, largely baroque interior and a series of glorious 5th-century mosaics.

⊙ Tridente & Trevi

Trevi Fountain   Fountain

(Fontana di Trevi; Map p360; Piazza di Trevi; MBarberini) The Fontana di Trevi, scene of movie star Anita Ekberg's late-night dip in *La Dolce Vita,* is a flamboyant baroque ensemble of mythical figures and wild horses taking up the entire side of the 17th-century Palazzo Poli. After a Fendi-sponsored restoration finished in 2015, the fountain gleams brighter than it has for years. The tradition is to toss a coin into the water, thus ensuring that you'll return to Rome – on average about €3000 is thrown in every day.

Gallerie Nazionali: Palazzo Barberini   Gallery

(Galleria Nazionale d'Arte Antica; Map p360; ☏06 481 45 91; www.barberinicorsini.org; Via delle Quattro Fontane 13; adult/reduced €12/6; ⊙8.30am-6pm Tue-Sun; MBarberini) Commissioned to celebrate the Barberini family's rise to papal power, this sumptuous baroque palace impresses even before you view its breathtaking art collection. Many high-profile architects worked on it, including rivals Bernini and Borromini; the former contributed a square staircase, the latter a helicoidal one. Amid the masterpieces on display, don't miss Filippo

Lippi's *Annunciazione* (*Annunciation*; 1440–45) and Pietro da Cortona's ceiling fresco *Il Trionfo della Divina Provvidenza* (*The Triumph of Divine Providence*; 1632–39).

Piazza di Spagna & the Spanish Steps
Piazza

(Map p360; Ⓜ Spagna) A magnet for visitors since the 18th century, the Spanish Steps (Scalinata della Trinità dei Monti) provide a perfect people-watching perch. The 135 gleaming steps rise from Piazza di Spagna to the landmark **Chiesa della Trinità dei Monti** (Map p360; ☑ 06 679 41 79; http://trinitadeimonti.net/it/chiesa/; Piazza Trinità dei Monti 3; ⊘ 10.15am-8pm Tue-Thu, noon-9pm Fri, 9.15am-8pm Sat, 9am-8pm Sun).

Piazza di Spagna was named after the Spanish Embassy to the Holy See, although the staircase, designed by the Italian Francesco de Sanctis, was built in 1725 with money bequeathed by a French diplomat.

Villa Medici
Palace

(☑ 06 676 13 11; www.villamedici.it; Viale Trinità dei Monti 1; guided tour adult/reduced €12/6; ⊘ 10am-7pm Tue-Sun; Ⓜ Spagna) Built for Cardinal Ricci da Montepulciano in 1540, this sumptuous Renaissance palace was purchased by Ferdinando de' Medici in 1576 and remained in Medici hands until 1801, when Napoleon acquired it for the French Academy. Guided tours (1½ hours) in multiple languages take in the sculpture-filled gardens and orchard, a garden studio exquisitely frescoed by Jacopo Zucchi in 1577 and the cardinal's private apartments. Note the pieces of ancient Roman sculpture from the Ara Pacis embedded in the villa's walls.

◉ Trastevere

Trastevere is one of central Rome's most vivacious neighbourhoods, a tightly packed warren of ochre *palazzi*, ivy-clad facades and photogenic lanes. Originally working class, it's now a trendy hang-out full of bars and restaurants.

Basilica di Santa Maria in Trastevere
Basilica

(Map p356; ☑ 06 581 48 02; Piazza Santa Maria in Trastevere; ⊘ 7.30am-9pm Sep-Jul, 8am-noon & 4-9pm Aug; ⒬ Viale di Trastevere, ⒬ Belli) Nestled in a quiet corner of Trastevere's focal square, this is said to be the oldest church dedicated to the Virgin Mary in Rome. In its original form, it dates to the early 3rd century, but a major 12th-century makeover saw the addition of a Romanesque bell tower and a glittering facade. The portico came later, added by Carlo Fontana in 1702. Inside, the 12th-century mosaics are the headline feature.

◉ San Giovanni & Testaccio

Basilica di San Giovanni in Laterano
Basilica

(☑ 06 6988 6493; Piazza di San Giovanni in Laterano 4; basilica free, cloister €5 incl Museo del Tesoro; ⊘ 7am-6.30pm, cloister 9am-6pm; Ⓜ San Giovanni) For a thousand years this monumental cathedral was the most important church in Christendom. Commissioned by the emperor Constantine and consecrated in AD 324, it was the first Christian basilica built in Rome and, until the late 14th century, was the pope's main place of worship. It's still Rome's official cathedral and the seat of the pope as the bishop of Rome.

Basilica di San Clemente
Basilica

(☑ 06 774 00 21; www.basilicasanclemente.com; Piazza di San Clemente; basilica free, excavations adult/reduced €10/5; ⊘ 9am-12.30pm & 3-6pm Mon-Sat, 12.15-6pm Sun; ⒬ Via Labicana) Nowhere better illustrates the various stages of Rome's turbulent past than this fascinating multilayered church. The ground-level 12th-century basilica sits atop a 4th-century church, which, in turn, stands over a 2nd-century pagan temple and a 1st-century Roman house. Beneath everything are foundations dating from the Roman Republic.

◉ Villa Borghese

Accessible from Piazzale Flaminio, Pincio Hill and the top of Via Vittorio Veneto, **Villa Borghese** (entrances at Piazzale San Paolo del

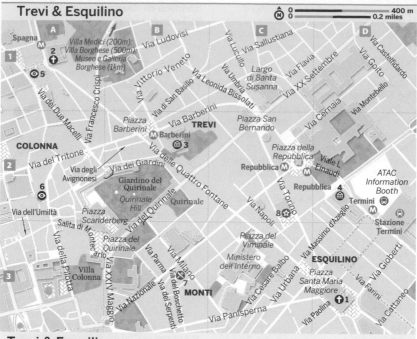

Trevi & Esquilino

Brasile, Piazzale Flaminio, Via Pinciana, Via Rai-
mondo, Largo Pablo Picasso; ⊙sunrise-sunset;
🚇Via Pinciana) is Rome's best-known park.

Museo e Galleria Borghese   Museum
(📞06 3 28 10; http://galleriaborghese.beni
culturali.it; Piazzale del Museo Borghese 5;
adult/child €15/8.50; ⊙9am-7pm Tue-Sun;
🚇Via Pinciana) If you only have time for
one art gallery in Rome, make it this one.
Housing what's often referred to as the
'queen of all private art collections', it
boasts paintings by Caravaggio, Raphael
and Titian, plus sensational sculptures
by Bernini. Highlights abound, but look

for Bernini's *Ratto di Proserpina* (Rape of
Proserpina) and Canova's *Venere vincitrice*
(Venus Victrix).

To limit numbers, visitors are admitted
at two-hourly intervals – you'll need to
book tickets well in advance and get an
entry time.

Museo Nazionale Etrusco
di Villa Giulia   Museum
(📞06 322 65 71; www.villagiulia.beniculturali.
it; Piazzale di Villa Giulia; adult/reduced €8/4;
⊙9am-8pm Tue-Sun; 🚇Via delle Belle Arti)
Pope Julius III's 16th-century villa provides
the often-overlooked but charming setting

for Italy's finest collection of Etruscan and pre-Roman treasures. Exhibits, many of which came from tombs in the surrounding Lazio region, range from bronze figurines and black *bucchero* tableware to temple decorations, terracotta vases and a dazzling display of sophisticated jewellery.

Must-sees include a polychrome terracotta statue of Apollo from a temple in Veio, and the 6th-century-BC *Sarcofago degli Sposi* (Sarcophagus of the Betrothed), found in 1881 in Cerveteri.

🔒 SHOPPING

What makes shopping in Rome fun is its legion of small, independent shops: family-run delis, small-label fashion boutiques, artisans' studios and neighbourhood markets.

Confetteria Moriondo & Gariglio
Chocolate

(Map p356; 📞06 699 08 56; Via del Piè di Marmo 21-22; �9am-7.30pm Mon-Sat; 🚌Via del Corso) Roman poet Trilussa was so smitten with this chocolate shop – established by the Torinese confectioners to the royal house of Savoy – that he was moved to mention it in verse. And we agree: it's a gem. Decorated like an elegant tearoom, it specialises in handmade chocolates and confections such as *marrons glacés*, many prepared according to original 19th-century recipes.

Antica Caciara Trasteverina
Food & Drinks

(📞06 581 28 15; www.facebook.com/antica caciaratrasteverina; Via di San Francesco a Ripa 140; �7.30am-8pm Mon-Sat; 🚌Viale di Trastevere, 🚋Trastevere/Mastai) The fresh ricotta is a prized possession at this century-old deli, and it's usually gone by lunchtime. If you're too late, take solace in the luscious *ricotta infornata* (oven-baked ricotta), wheels of famous, black-waxed *pecorino romano*, and garlands of *guanciale* (pig's jowl) ready for the perfect carbonara. The lovely, caring staff answer questions and

plastic-wrap cheese and hams for transport home.

Salumeria Roscioli
Food & Drinks

(Map p356; 📞06 687 52 87; www.salumeria roscioli.com; Via dei Giubbonari 21; �8.30am-8.30pm Mon-Sat; 🚌Via Arenula) Rome's most celebrated deli showcases a spectacular smorgasbord of prize products ranging from cured hams and cheeses to conserves, dried pastas, olive oils, aged balsamic vinegars and wines. Alongside celebrated Italian fare you'll also find top international foodstuffs such as French cheese, Iberian ham and Scottish salmon.

As well as buying, you can also dine here at the deli's excellent restaurant (p362).

Ibiz – Artigianato in Cuoio
Fashion & Accessories

(Map p356; 📞06 6830 7297; www.ibizroma.it; Via dei Chiavari 39; �10am-7.30pm Mon-Sat; 🚌Corso Vittorio Emanuele II) In her diminutive family workshop, Elisa Nepi and her team craft beautiful butter-soft leather wallets, bags, belts, keyrings and sandals, in elegant designs and myriad colours. You can pick up a belt for about €35, while for a shoulder bag you should bank on around €145.

Mercado de Porta Portese
Market

(Piazza Porta Portese; �6am-2pm Sun; 🚌Viale di Trastevere, 🚋Trastevere/Min P Istruzione) Head to this mammoth flea market to see Rome bargain-hunting. Thousands of stalls sell everything from rare books and fell-off-a-lorry bikes to Peruvian shawls and off-brand phones. It's crazily busy and a lot of fun. Keep your valuables safe and wear your haggling hat for the inevitable discovery of a treasure amid the dreck.

✖ EATING

The most atmospheric neighbourhoods to dine in are the *centro storico* and Trastevere. There are also excellent choices in Monti and Testaccio. Watch out for overpriced tourist traps around Termini and the Vatican.

ⓧ Centro Storico

Forno Roscioli   Bakery €

(Map p356; ☏06 686 40 45; www.anticoforno
roscioli.it; Via dei Chiavari 34; pizza slices from
€2, snacks €2.50; ⊘7am-8pm Mon-Sat, 8.30am-
7pm Sun; ⓡVia Arenula) This is one of Rome's
top bakeries, much loved by lunching locals
who crowd here for luscious sliced pizza,
prize pastries and hunger-sating *supplì*
(risotto balls). The pizza margherita is
superb, if messy to eat, and there's also a
counter serving hot pastas and vegetable
side dishes.

La Ciambella   Italian €€

(Map p356; ☏06 683 29 30; www.la-ciambella.
it; Via dell'Arco della Ciambella 20; meals
€35-45; ⊘noon-11pm Tue-Sun; ⓡLargo di
Torre Argentina) Near the Pantheon but as
yet largely undiscovered by the tourist
hordes, this friendly restaurant beats
much of the neighbourhood competition.
Its handsome, light-filled interior is set
over the ruins of the Terme di Agrippa,
visible through transparent floor panels,
setting an attractive stage for interesting,
imaginative food.

Pianostrada   Ristorante €€

(Map p356; ☏06 8957 2296; www.facebook.
com/pianostrada; Via delle Zoccolette 22; meals
€40-45; ⊘1-4pm & 7pm-midnight Tue-Fri,
10am-midnight Sat & Sun; ⓡVia Arenula) This
uberhip bistro-restaurant, in a white space
with vintage furnishings and a glorious
summer courtyard, is a must. Reserve
ahead, or settle for a stool at the bar and
enjoy views of the kitchen at work. The cuisine is creative, seasonal and veg-packed,
including gourmet open sandwiches and
sensational focaccia, as well as full-blown
mains.

Salumeria Roscioli   Ristorante €€€

(Map p356; ☏06 687 52 87; www.salumeria
roscioli.com; Via dei Giubbonari 21; meals €55;
⊘12.30-4pm & 7pm-midnight Mon-Sat; ⓡVia
Arenula) The name Roscioli has long been
a byword for foodie excellence in Rome,
and this deli-restaurant is the place to
experience it. Tables are set alongside the
counter, laden with mouth-watering Italian
and foreign delicacies, and in a small bottle-
lined space behind. The food, including
traditional Roman pastas, is top notch and

there are some truly outstanding wines. Reservations essential.

Vatican City, Borgo & Prati

Bonci Pizzarium Pizza €

(☎06 3974 5416; www.bonci.it; Via della Meloria 43; pizza slices €5; ☺11am-10pm Mon-Sat, from noon Sun; Ⓜ Cipro) Pizzarium, the take-away of Gabriele Bonci, Rome's acclaimed pizza emperor, serves Rome's best sliced pizza, bar none. Scissor-cut squares of soft, springy base are topped with original combinations of seasonal ingredients and served for immediate consumption. Often jammed, there are only a couple of benches and stools for the tourist hordes; head across to the plaza at the metro station for a seat.

Monti & Esquilino

La Barrique Italian €€

(Map p360; ☎06 4782 5953; www.facebook.com/la.barrique.94/; Via del Boschetto 41b; meals €40; ☺1-2.30pm & 7.30-11pm Mon-Fri, 7.30-11.30pm Sat; Ⓜ Cavour) This traditional *enoteca* is a classy yet casual place to linger over a meal. There's a large wine

list, mostly sourced from small producers, with lots of natural wines to choose from. A small menu of creative pastas and mains provide a great accompaniment – this is one of the best places to eat in Monti. Bookings recommended.

Trastevere

Trattoria Da Teo Trattoria €€

(Map p356; ☎06 581 83 55; www.facebook.com/Trattoria.da.teo; Piazza dei Ponziani 7; meals €35-45; ☺12.30-3pm & 7.30-11.30pm Mon-Sat; Ⓠ Viale di Trastevere, Ⓠ Belli) One of Rome's classic trattorias, Da Teo buzzes with locals digging into steaming platefuls of Roman standards, such as carbonara, *pasta cacio e pepe* (cheese-and-black-pepper pasta) and the most fabulous seasonal artichokes – both Jewish (deep-fried) and Roman-style (stuffed with parsley and garlic, and boiled). In keeping with hard-core trattoria tradition, Teo's homemade gnocchi is only served on Thursday. Reservations essential.

Da Enzo Trattoria €€

(Map p356; ☎06 581 22 60; www.daenzoal29.com; Via dei Vascellari 29; meals €30-35; ☺12.30-3pm & 7.30-11pm Mon-Sat; Ⓠ Lungotevere

★ **Top Five Art Collections**

St Peter's Basilica (p338)

Capitoline Museums (p352)

Museo Nazionale Romano: Palazzo Massimo alle Terme (p355)

Museo e Galleria Borghese (p360)

Galleria Doria Pamphilj (p353)

From left: Galleria Borghese (p360); Galleria Doria Pamphilj (p353); Palazzo Massimo alle Terme (p355)

ANNA PAKUTINA / SHUTTERSTOCK ©

ANNA PAKUTINA / SHUTTERSTOCK ©

 Rome's Best Gelato

Fior di Luna (Map p356; ☑06 6456 1314; http://fiordiluna.com; Via della Lungaretta 96; gelato from €2.50; ☺1-8pm Sun & Mon, 1-11pm Tue-Sat; ☐Belli, ☐Viale di Trastevere) Produced in small batches using natural, seasonal ingredients.

Gelateria dei Gracchi (☑06 321 66 68; www.gelateriadeigracchi.it; Via dei Gracchi 272; gelato from €2.50; ☺noon-12.30am; ☐Piazza Cola Di Rienzo) The flavours vary by day and season, but you're always assured of a top treat.

Neve di Latte (☑06 320 84 85; www. facebook.com/NevedilatteRomaFlaminio; Via Poletti 6; gelato €2.50-5; ☺noon-11pm Sun-Thu, to midnight Fri & Sat summer, noon-10pm winter; ☐Viale Tiziano) The classics, all prepared with high-quality seasonal ingredients.

Giolitti (Map p356; ☑06 699 12 43; www. giolitti.it; Via degli Uffici del Vicario 40; gelato €2.80-5; ☺7am-1am; ☐Via del Corso) Rome's most famous gelateria.

Ripa, ☐Belli) Vintage ochre walls, yellow-checked tablecloths and a traditional menu featuring all the Roman classics: what makes this tiny and staunchly traditional trattoria exceptional is its careful sourcing of local, quality products, many from nearby farms in Lazio. The seasonal, deep-fried Jewish artichokes and the *pasta cacio e pepe* (cheese-and-black-pepper pasta) are among the best in Rome.

🍽 San Giovanni & Testaccio

Flavio al Velavevodetto   Roman €€
(☑06 574 41 94; www.ristorantevelavevodetto. it; Via di Monte Testaccio 97-99; meals €30-35; ☺12.30-3pm & 7.45-11pm; ☐Via Galvani) The pick of Testaccio's trattorias, this casual spot is celebrated locally for its earthy, no-nonsense *cucina romana* (Roman cuisine). For a taste, start with *carciofo alla giudia* (deep-fried artichoke) before moving onto *rigatoni alla carbonara* (pasta tubes wrapped in a silky egg sauce spiked with morsels of cured pig's cheek) and finishing up with tiramisu.

🍷 DRINKING & NIGHTLIFE

Much of the drinking action is in the *centro storico*: Campo de' Fiori's scene is young and lively, while the area around Piazza Navona hosts a more upmarket scene. Over the river, Trastevere is another favoured spot with dozens of bars and pubs.

Rome's clubbing scene is centred on Testaccio and the Ostiense area.

Caffè Sant'Eustachio   Coffee
(Map p356; ☑06 6880 2048; www.santeustachio ilcaffe.it; Piazza Sant'Eustachio 82; ☺7.30am-1am Sun-Thu, to 1.30am Fri, to 2am Sat; ☐Corso del Rinascimento) Always busy, this workaday cafe near the Pantheon is reckoned by many to serve the best coffee in town. To make it, the bartenders sneakily beat the first drops of an espresso with several teaspoons of sugar to create a frothy paste to which they add the rest of the coffee. The result is superbly smooth.

Rimessa Roscioli   Wine Bar
(Map p356; ☑06 6880 3914; www.winetasting rome.com; Via del Conservatorio 58; ☺6.30-11.30pm Mon-Fri, noon-3pm & 6.30-11.30pm Sat & Sun; 🛜; ☐Lungotevere dei Tebaldi) An offshoot of the popular Roscioli empire, Rimessa is for wine lovers: labels from all over Italy and further afield crowd the shelves, while exquisite wine-tasting dinners (€33 to €65) unfold in both English

and Italian. Also available is a Tasting Bar option, where a sommelier crafts a tasting tailored to your budget and preferences.

Open Baladin   Craft Beer

(Map p356; ☑06 683 89 89; www.openbaladin roma.it; Via degli Specchi 6; ☺noon-2am; ☏; ☐Via Arenula) This modern pub near Campo de' Fiori has long been a leading light in Rome's craft-beer scene, and with more than 40 beers on tap and up to 100 bottled brews (many from Italian artisanal micro-breweries) it's a top place for a pint. As well as great beer, expect a laid-back vibe and a young, international crowd.

There's also a decent food menu with *panini*, burgers and daily specials.

Terra Satis   Cafe, Wine Bar

(Map p356; ☑06 9893 6909; Piazza dei Ponziani 1a; ☺7am-1am Mon-Thu, to 2am Fri & Sat; ☏; ☐Viale di Trastevere, ☐Belli) This hip neigh-bourhood cafe and wine bar in Trastevere has it all: newspapers, great coffee and charming bar staff, not to mention vintage furniture, comfy banquette seating and really good snacks. On warm days the

laid-back action spills out onto its bijou, vine-covered terrace on cobbled Piazza di Ponziani. Good wine and beer selection.

Bar San Calisto   Cafe

(Map p356; Piazza San Calisto 3-5; ☺6am-2am Mon-Sat; ☐Viale di Trastevere, ☐Viale di Trastevere) Head to 'Sanca' for its basic, stuck-in-time atmosphere, cheap prices and large terrace. It attracts everyone from intellectuals to people-watching idlers and foreign students. It's famous for its choco-late – come for hot chocolate with cream in winter and chocolate gelato in summer. Try the *sambuca con la mosca* ('with flies' – raw coffee beans). Expect occasional late-night jam sessions.

Pimm's Good   Bar

(Map p356; ☑06 9727 7979; www.pimmsgood. it; Via di Santa Dorotea 8; ☺10am-2am; ☏; ☐Piazza Trilussa) 'Anyone for Pimm's?' is the catchphrase of both the namesake fruity English liqueur and this eternally popular bar. It has a part-red-brick ceiling and does indeed serve Pimm's – the classic way or in a variety of cocktails. The lively bartenders

Open Baladin

Auditorium Parco della Musica. Architect: Renzo Piano Building Workshop

> *Auditorium Parco della Musica is the hub of Rome's thiriving cultural scene*

are serious mixologists and well-crafted cocktails are their thing. Look for the buzzing street-corner pavement terrace.

⭐ ENTERTAINMENT

Rome has a thriving cultural scene. Check what's on at www.060608.it, www.romeing.it and www.inromenow.com.

Auditorium Parco della Musica Concert Venue

(☎06 8024 1281; www.auditorium.com; Viale Pietro de Coubertin; 🚌Viale Tiziano) The hub of Rome's thriving cultural scene, the Auditorium is the capital's premier concert venue. Its three concert halls offer superb acoustics and, together with a 3000-seat open-air arena, stage everything from classical music concerts to jazz gigs, public lectures and film screenings.

The Auditorium is also home to Rome's world-class Orchestra dell'Accademia Nazionale di Santa Cecilia (www.santacecilia.it).

Teatro dell'Opera di Roma Opera

(Map p360; ☎06 48 16 01; www.operaroma.it; Piazza Beniamino Gigli 1; ⊙box office 10am-6pm Mon-Sat, 9am-1.30pm Sun; Ⓜ Repubblica) Rome's premier opera house boasts a dramatic red-and-gold interior, a Fascist 1920s exterior and an impressive history: it premiered both Puccini's *Tosca* and Mascagni's *Cavalleria rusticana*. Opera and ballet performances are staged between November and June.

ℹ️ INFORMATION

DANGERS & ANNOYANCES

Rome is not a dangerous city, but petty theft can be a problem. Watch out for pickpockets around the big tourist sites, at Stazione Termini and on crowded public transport – the 64 Vatican bus is notorious.

MEDICAL SERVICES

Policlinico Umberto I (☏06 4 99 71; www.
policlinicoumberto1.it; Viale del Policlinico 155;
Ⓜ Policlinico, Castro Pretorio) Rome's largest
hospital is located near Stazione Termini.

TOURIST INFORMATION

There are tourist information points at **Fiumicino** (Fiumicino Airport; International Arrivals,
Terminal 3; ⊗8am-8.45pm) and **Ciampino**
(Arrivals Hall; ⊗8.30am-6pm) airports, as well as
locations across the city. Each can provide city
maps and sell the Roma Pass.

Information points:

Pazza delle Cinque Lune (Map p356; Piazza
delle Cinque Lune; ⊗9.30am-7pm; 🚌Corso del
Rinascimento) Near Piazza Navona.

Stazione Termini (☏06 06 08; www.
turismoroma.it; Via Giovanni Giolitti 34; ⊗8am-
6.45pm; Ⓜ Termini) In the hall adjacent to
platform 24.

Imperial Forums (Map p354; Via dei Fori Imperiali; ⊗9.30am-7pm, to 8pm Jul & Aug; 🚌Via dei
Fori Imperiali)

Via Marco Minghetti (Map p356; ☏06 06
08; www.turismoroma.it; Via Marco Minghetti;
⊗9.30am-7pm; 🚌Via del Corso) Between Via del
Corso and the Trevi Fountain.

Castel Sant'Angelo (Map p356; www.
turismoroma.it; Piazza Pia; ⊗9.30am-7pm summer, 8.30am-6pm winter; 🚌Piazza Pia)

Trastevere (Map p356; www.turismoroma.
it; Piazza Sonnino; ⊗10.30am-8pm; 🚌Viale di
Trastevere, 🚋Belli)

For information about the Vatican, contact
the **Ufficio Pellegrini e Turisti** (☏06 6988 1662;
www.vatican.va; St Peter's Sq; ⊗8.30am-6.30pm
Mon-Sat; 🚌Piazza del Risorgimento, Ⓜ Ottaviano-
San Pietro).

Rome's official tourist website, Turismo Roma
(www.turismoroma.it), has comprehensive
information about sights, accommodation and
city transport, as well as itineraries and up-to-
date listings.

The **Comune di Roma** (☏06 06 08;
www.060608.it; ⊗9am-7pm) runs a free multilingual tourist information phone line providing

Sightseeing with Roma Pass

A cumulative sightseeing and transport card,
available online or from tourist information
points and participating museums, the
Roma Pass (www.roma pass.it) comes in two
forms:

72 hours (€38.50) Provides free admission
to two museums or sites, as well as reduced
entry to extra sites, unlimited city transport,
and discounted entry to other exhibitions
and events.

48 hours (€28) Gives free admission to
one museum or site, and then as per the
72-hour pass.

Roman tram
EGD / SHUTTERSTOCK ©

info on culture, shows, hotels, transport etc. Its
website is also an excellent resource.

❶ GETTING THERE & AWAY

AIR

Rome's main international airport, **Leonardo da
Vinci** (Leonardo da Vinci International Airport;
☏06 6 59 51; www.adr.it/fiumicino), aka Fiumicino, is 30km west of the city.

The much smaller **Ciampino Airport** (☏06 6
59 51; www.adr.it/ciampino), 15km southeast of
the city centre, is the hub for European low-cost
carrier Ryanair.

BOAT

The nearest port to Rome is at Civitavecchia,
about 80km north of town. Ferries sail here
from Barcelona and Tunis, as well as Sicily and

Sardinia. Check www.traghettiweb.it for route details, prices and bookings.

Half-hourly trains connect Civitavecchia and Termini (€5 to €16, 45 minutes to 1½ hours).

BUS

Long-distance national and international buses use **Autostazione Tibus** (Autostazione Tiburtina; ☎06 44 25 95; www.tibusroma.it; Largo Guido Mazzoni; Ⓜ Tiburtina). Get tickets at the bus station or at travel agencies.

CAR & MOTORCYCLE

Rome is circled by the Grande Raccordo Anulare (GRA), to which all autostrade (motorways) connect, including the main A1 north–south artery, and the A12, which runs to Civitavecchia and Fiumicino airport.

Car hire is available at the airport and Stazione Termini.

TRAIN

Rome's main station and principal transport hub is **Stazione Termini** (www.romatermini.com; Piazza dei Cinquecento; Ⓜ Termini). It has regular connections to other European countries, all major Italian cities and many smaller towns. **Left Luggage** (Stazione Termini; 1st 5hr €6, 6-12hr per hour €1, 13hr & over per hour €0.50; ⊙6am-11pm; Ⓜ Termini) is available by platform 24 on the Via Giolitti side of the station.

ⓘ GETTING AROUND

TO/FROM THE AIRPORTS

FIUMICINO

Leonardo Express trains to Stazione Termini 6.08am to 11.23pm, €14; slower FL1 trains to Trastevere, Ostiense and Tiburtina stations 5.57am to 10.42pm, €8; buses to Stazione Termini 6.05am to 12.40am, €6-6.90; airport-to-hotel shuttles from €22 per person; taxis €48 (fixed fare to within the Aurelian walls).

CIAMPINO

Buses to Stazione Termini 4am to 12.15am, €6; airport-to-hotel shuttles €25 per person; taxis €30 (fixed fare to within the Aurelian walls).

PUBLIC TRANSPORT

Rome's public transport system includes buses, trams, a metro and a suburban train network.

Tickets are valid on all forms of public transport, except for routes to Fiumicino airport. Buy tickets at tabaccherie, newsstands or from vending machines. They come in various forms:

BIT (€1.50) Valid for 100 minutes and one metro ride.

Roma 24h (€7) Valid for 24 hours.

Roma 48h (€12.50) Valid for 48 hours.

Roma 72h (€18) Valid for 72 hours.

BUS

○ Rome's public bus service is run by **ATAC** (☎06 5 70 03; www.atac.roma.it).

○ The main bus station is in front of Stazione Termini on Piazza dei Cinquecento, where there's an **information booth** (Map p360; Piazza dei Cinquecento; ⊙8am-8pm; Ⓜ Termini).

○ Other important hubs are at Largo di Torre Argentina and Piazza Venezia.

○ Buses generally run from about 5.30am until midnight, with limited services throughout the night.

METRO

○ Rome has two main metro lines, A (orange) and B (blue), which cross at Termini.

○ Trains run from 5.30am to 11.30pm (to 1.30am on Fridays and Saturdays).

TAXI

○ Official licensed taxis are white with a taxi sign on the roof and Roma Capitale written on the front door along with the taxi's licence number.

○ Always go with the metered fare, never an arranged price (the set fares to/from the airports are exceptions).

○ MyTaxi is a good app. It allows you to order a taxi without having to deal with potentially tricky language problems.

🛎 Where to Stay

Accommodation in Rome is expensive, and with the city busy year round, you'll want to book as far ahead as you can to secure the best deal and to enjoy top properties. In balmy months look for places with rooftop decks.

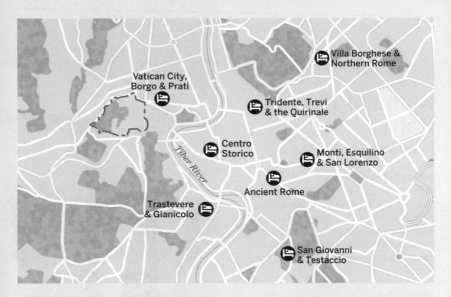

Neighbourhood	Atmosphere
Ancient Rome	Close to major sights such as the Colosseum and Roman Forum; quiet at night; not cheap; restaurants are touristy.
Centro Storico	Atmospheric area with everything on your doorstep – Pantheon, Piazza Navona, restaurants, bars, shops; most expensive part of town; can be noisy.
Tridente, Trevi & the Quirinale	Good for Spanish Steps, Trevi Fountain and designer shopping; excellent midrange to top-end options; good transport links.
Vatican City, Borgo & Prati	Near St Peter's Basilica; decent range of accommodation; some excellent shops and restaurants; on the metro; not much nightlife; sells out quickly for religious holidays.
Monti, Esquilino & San Lorenzo	Lots of budget accommodation around Stazione Termini; top eating in Monti and good nightlife in San Lorenzo; good transport links; some dodgy streets near Termini.
Trastevere & Gianicolo	Gorgeous, atmospheric area; party vibe with hundreds of bars, cafes and restaurants; expensive; noisy, particularly in summer.
San Giovanni & Testaccio	Authentic atmosphere with good eating and drinking options; Testaccio is a top food and nightlife district; not many big sights.
Villa Borghese & Northern Rome	Largely residential area good for the Auditorium and Stadio Olimpico; some top museums; generally quiet after dark.

Bronze statue in ancient Pompeii

Ruins of Pompeii, Italy

Around 30 minutes by train from Naples, you'll find Europe's most compelling archaeological site: the ruins of Pompeii. Sprawling and haunting, the site is a remarkably well-preserved slice of ancient life. Here you can walk down Roman streets and snoop around millennia-old houses, temples, shops, cafes, amphitheatres and even a brothel.

Great For...

ℹ Need to Know

081 857 53 47; www.pompeiisites.org; entrances at Porta Marina & Piazza Anfiteatro; adult/reduced €15/7.50, incl Oplontis & Boscoreale €18/9; ⊙9am-7.30pm Mon-Fri, from 8.30am Sat & Sun, last entry 6pm Apr-Oct, 9am-5.30pm Mon-Fri, from 8.30am Sat & Sun, last entry 3.30pm Nov-Mar

★ **Top Tip**

Buy your ticket online to avoid long queues, especially in high season.

Visiting the Site

Much of the site's value lies in the fact that the city wasn't blown away by Vesuvius in AD 79, but buried beneath a layer of lapilli (burning fragments of pumice stone). The remains first came to light in 1594, but systematic exploration didn't begin until 1748. Since then 44 of Pompeii's original 66 hectares have been excavated.

Remember that you'll need sustenance for your explorations. You'll find an on-site cafeteria at the ruins, and no shortage of touristy, mediocre eateries directly outside the site. The modern town is home to a few better-quality options, or bring your own snacks and beverages.

Before entering the site through **Porta Marina**, the gate that originally connected the town with the nearby harbour, note the **Terme Suburbane**. This 1st-century-BC bathhouse is famous for several erotic frescoes that scandalised the Vatican when they were revealed in 2001. It remains under long-term closure. Continue through the city walls to the main part of the site. The following are highlights to look out for.

Foro

A huge grassy rectangle flanked by limestone columns, the **foro** (Forum) was ancient Pompeii's main piazza, as well as the site of gladiatorial battles before the Anfiteatro was constructed. The buildings surrounding the forum are testament to its role as the city's hub of civic, commercial, political and religious activity. At its northern end are the remains of the **Tempio di Giove** (Temple of Jupiter; Capitolium), the heart of religious life in Pompeii.

Teatro Grande

Lupanare

Ancient Pompeii's only dedicated brothel, **Lupanare** is a tiny two-storey building with five rooms on each floor. Its collection of raunchy frescoes was a menu of sorts for clients. The walls in the rooms are carved with graffiti – including declarations of love and hope written by the brothel workers – in various languages.

Teatro Grande

The 2nd-century-BC **Teatro Grande** was a huge 5000-seat theatre carved into the lava mass on which Pompeii was originally built.

★ Top Tip

There are free lockers by the entrance to the ruins.

DIEGO FIORE / SHUTTERSTOCK ©

Anfiteatro

Gladiatorial battles thrilled up to 20,000 spectators at the grassy **anfiteatro** (Amphitheatre). Built in 70 BC, it's the oldest known Roman amphitheatre in existence.

Casa del Fauno

Covering an entire *insula* (city block) and boasting two atria at its front end (humbler homes had one), **Casa del Fauno** (House of the Faun), Pompeii's largest private house, is named after the delicate bronze statue in the *impluvium* (rain tank). It was here that early excavators found Pompeii's greatest mosaics, most of which are now in Naples' Museo Archeologico Nazionale. Valuable on-site survivors include a beautiful, geometrically patterned marble floor.

Villa dei Misteri

This restored, 90-room **villa** is one of the most complete structures left standing in Pompeii. The Dionysiac frieze, the most important fresco still on-site, spans the walls of the large dining room. One of the biggest and most arresting paintings from the ancient world, it depicts the initiation of a bride-to-be into the cult of Dionysus, the Greek god of wine.

A farm for much of its life, the villa's vino-making area is still visible at the northern end.

Follow Via Consolare northwest out of the town through **Porta Ercolano**. Continue past **Villa di Diomede** and you'll come to Villa dei Misteri.

✕ Take a Break

For a memorable bite in Pompeii town, head to Michelin-starred **President** (☎081 850 72 45; www.ristorantepresident.it; Piazza Schettini 12; meals €60, tasting menus €65-95; ⊗noon-3.30pm & 7pm-late Tue-Sun; ☒FS to Pompei, Circumvesuviana to Pompei Scavi–Villa dei Misteri).

Body Casts

One of the most haunting sights at Pompeii are the body casts in the **Granai del Foro** (Forum Granary). These were made in the late 19th century by pouring plaster into the hollows left by disintegrated bodies. Among the casts is a pregnant slave; the belt around her waist would have displayed the name of her owner.

Tours

You'll almost certainly be approached by a guide outside the ticket office. Authorised guides wear identification tags. Reputable tour operators include **Yellow Sudmarine** (📞329 1010328; www.yellowsudmarine.com; 2hr Pompeii guided tour €150, plus entrance fee) and **Walks of Italy** (www.walksofitaly.com; 3hr Pompeii guided tour per person €59), both of which also offer excursions to other areas of Campania.

Getting to Pompeii

To reach the *scavi* (ruins) by **Circumvesuviana** (📞800 211388; www.eavsrl.it) train (€2.80 from Naples, 36 minutes; €2.40 from Sorrento, 30 minutes), alight at Pompei Scavi–Villa dei Misteri station, located beside the main entrance at Porta Marina. Regional trains (www.trenitalia.com) stop at Pompei station in the centre of the modern town.

From mid-March to mid-October, tourist train *Campania Express* runs four times daily between Naples (Porta Nolana and Piazza Garibaldi Circumvesuviana stations) and Sorrento, stopping at Ercolano–Scavi, Torre Annunziata (Oplontis), Pompei Scavi–Villa dei Misteri, Castellammare and Vico Equense en route. One-day return tickets from Naples to Pompeii (€11, 29 minutes) or from Sorrento to Pompeii (€7, 24 minutes) can be purchased at the stations or online at **EAV** (📞800 211388; www.eavsrl.it).

What's Nearby?

Ruins of
Herculaneum   Archaeological Site

(📞081 777 70 08; http://ercolano.beniculturali.it; Corso Resina 187, Ercolano; adult/reduced €11/5.50; ⊗8.30am-7.30pm Apr-Oct, to 5pm Nov-Mar; 🅿; 🚈Circumvesuviana to Ercolano–Scavi)

Herculaneum harbours a wealth of archaeological finds, from ancient advertisements and stylish mosaics to carbonised furniture and terror-struck skeletons. Indeed, this superbly conserved Roman fishing town of 4000 inhabitants is easier to navigate than Pompeii, and can be explored with a map and highly recommended audio guide (€8).

MAV   Museum

(Museo Archeologico Virtuale; 📞081 777 68 43; www.museomav.com; Via IV Novembre 44; adult/reduced €10/8; ⊗9am-5.30pm daily Mar-May, 10am-6.30pm daily Jun-Sep, to 4pm Tue-Sun Oct-Feb; 👶; 🚈Circumvesuviana to Ercolano–Scavi)

Using computer-generated recreations, this 'virtual archaeological museum' brings ruins such as Pompeii's forum and Capri's Villa Jovis back to virtual life. Some of the

Mt Vesuvius

displays are in Italian only. The short documentary gives an overview of the history of Mt Vesuvius and its infamous eruption in AD 79 ... in rather lacklustre 3D. The museum is on the main street linking Ercolano–Scavi train station to the ruins of Herculaneum.

Mt Vesuvius
Volcano

(☑081 239 56 53; www.parconazionaledelvesuvio.it; crater adult/reduced €10/8; ☉crater 9am-6pm Jul & Aug, to 5pm Apr-Jun & Sep, to 4pm Mar & Oct, to 3pm Nov-Feb, ticket office closes 1hr before crater) Since exploding into history in AD 79, Vesuvius has blown its top more than 30 times. What redeems this slumbering menace is the spectacular panorama from its crater, which takes in Naples, its world-famous bay, and part of the Apennine Mountains. Vesuvius is the focal point of the **Parco Nazionale del Vesuvio** (Vesuvius National Park;

☑081 239 56 53; www.parconazionaledelvesuvio.it), with nine nature walks around the volcano – download a simple map from the park's website. **Horse Riding Tour Naples** (☑345 8560306; www.horseridingnaples.com; guided tour €60) also runs daily horse-riding tours.

The mountain is widely believed to have been higher than it currently stands, claiming a single summit rising to about 3000m rather than the 1281m of today. Its violent outburst in AD 79 not only drowned Pompeii in pumice and pushed the coastline back several kilometres but also destroyed much of the mountain top, creating a huge caldera and two new peaks. The most destructive explosion after that of AD 79 was in 1631, while the most recent was in 1944.

> ★ **Top Tip**
>
> Vesuvius can be reached by bus from Pompeii and Ercolano.

TATIANA DYUVBANOVA / SHUTTERSTOCK ©

Tragedy in Pompeii

24 AUGUST AD 79

8am Buildings including the **❶ Terme Suburbane** and the **❷ Foro** are still undergoing repair after an earthquake in AD 63 caused significant damage to the city. Despite violent earth tremors overnight, residents have little idea of the catastrophe that lies ahead.

Midday Peckish locals pour into the **❸ Thermopolium di Vetutius Placidus**. The lustful slip into the **❹ Lupanare**, and gladiators practise for the evening's planned games at the **❺ Anfiteatro**. A massive boom heralds the eruption. Shocked onlookers witness a dark cloud of volcanic matter shoot some 14km above the crater.

3pm–5pm Lapilli (burning pumice stone) rains down on Pompeii. Terrified locals begin to flee; others take shelter. Within two hours, the plume is 25km high and the sky has darkened. Roofs collapse under the weight of the debris, burying those inside.

25 AUGUST AD 79

Midnight Mudflows bury the town of Herculaneum. Lapilli and ash continue to rain down on Pompeii, bursting through buildings and suffocating those taking refuge within.

4am–8am Ash and gas avalanches hit Herculaneum. Subsequent surges smother Pompeii, killing all remaining residents, including those in the **❻ Orto dei Fuggiaschi**. The volcanic 'blanket' will safeguard frescoed treasures like the **❼ Casa del Menandro** and **❽ Villa dei Misteri** for almost two millennia.

TOP TIPS

➡ Visit in the afternoon.
➡ Allow three hours.
➡ Wear comfortable shoes and a hat.
➡ Bring drinking water.
➡ Don't use flash photography.

Villa dei Misteri
Home to the world-famous *Dionysiac Frieze* fresco. Other highlights at this villa include *trompe l'oeil* wall decorations in the *cubiculum* (bedroom) and Egyptian-themed artwork in the *tablinum* (reception).

Villa di Diomede

Casa del Poeta Tragico

Porta Ercolano

Casa del Fauno

Tempio di Apollo

Basilica

Porta Marina

❶

❷

❹

Terme del Foro

Macellum

Teatro Grande

Quadriportico dei Teatri

Porta di Stabia

Teatro Piccolo

❽

Foro
An ancient Times Square of sorts, the forum sits at the intersection of Pompeii's main streets and was closed to traffic in the 1st century AD. The plinths on the southern edge featured statues of the imperial family.

Lupanare

The prostitutes at this brothel were often slaves of Greek or Asian origin. Mattresses once covered the stone beds and the names engraved in the walls are possibly those of the workers and their clients.

PORJONICU STELIAN / SHUTTERSTOCK ©

Thermopolium di Vetutius Placidus

The counter at this ancient snack bar once held urns filled with hot food. The *lararium* (household shrine) on the back wall depicts Dionysus (the god of wine) and Mercury (the god of profit and commerce).

Casa dei Vettii

Porta del Vesuvio

Porta di Nola

Casa della Venere in Conchiglia

Porta di Sarno

③

⑦

Grande Palestra

⑤

Tempio di Iside

⑥

Orto dei Fuggiaschi

The Garden of the Fugitives showcases the plaster moulds of 13 locals seeking refuge during Vesuvius' eruption – the largest number of victims found in any one area. The huddled bodies make for a moving scene.

EDELLA / GETTY IMAGES ©

Casa del Menandro

This dwelling most likely belonged to the family of Poppaea Sabina, Nero's second wife. A room to the left of the atrium features Trojan War paintings and a polychrome mosaic of pygmies rowing down the Nile.

Anfiteatro

Magistrates, local senators and the games' sponsors and organisers enjoyed front-row seating at this veteran amphitheatre, home to gladiatorial battles and the odd riot. The parapet circling the stadium featured paintings of combat, victory celebrations and hunting scenes.

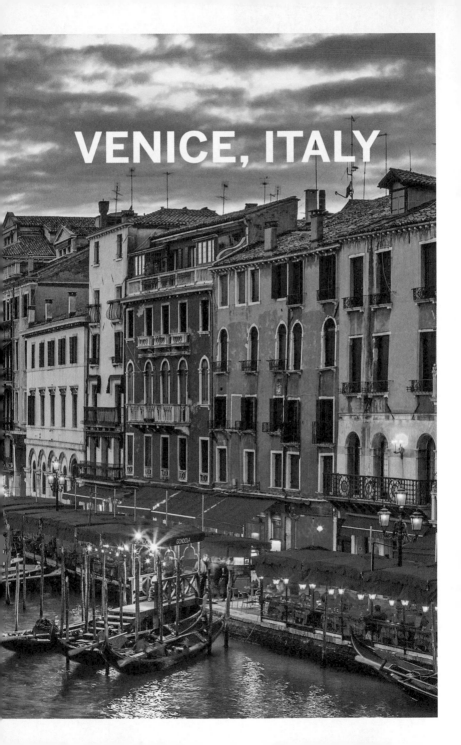

VENICE, ITALY

Venice, Italy

Imagine the audacity of deciding to build a city of marble palaces on a lagoon. Instead of surrendering to acque alte (high tides), Venetians flooded the world with vivid painting, baroque music, modern opera, spice-route cuisine, boho-chic fashions and a Grand Canal's worth of spritz: the signature prosecco and Aperol cocktail. At the end of Venice's signature waterway, the Palazzo Ducale and Basilica di San Marco add double exclamation points. Today, cutting-edge art mixes with this timeless beauty and a stroll down any backstreet yields one surprise after another. In a world of cookie-cutter culture, Venice's originality still stands out.

Two Days in Venice

Spend your first day in Venice cruising the Grand Canal, hopping on and off *vaporetti* as the mood takes you.

On the second day rise early to get to **Basilica di San Marco** (p384) and **Palazzo Ducale** (p386), then revive your spirits (but not your wallet!) at **Caffè Florian** (p394). Glimpse gorgeous **La Fenice** (p395), and make sure you don't leave Venice without indulging in an evening **gondola trip**.

Four Days in Venice

Explore **Ca' Rezzonico** (p390), then choose between the **Gallerie dell'Accademia** (p390) or the **Peggy Guggenheim** (p390) before finishing at the **Basilica di Santa Maria della Salute** (p390). On day four begin at the **Rialto Market** (p383), then wander to Gothic **I Frari** (p391). Once you're done admiring, slip into **Grancaffè Quadri** (p395) to to watch the sunset over the piazza.

After Venice hop on the train to Rome (p327) or get high in the Swiss Alps (p467).

Map legend labels:

Marco Polo Airport (8km); Treviso Airport (25km)

Sacca Serenella

Murano

Canale delle Sacche

Canale delle Navi

Canale delle Navi

Isola di San Michele

Cannaregio

Canale delle Fondamente Nuove

Laguna Veneta

Isola del Tronchetto

Stazione di Santa Lucia (Ferrovia)

Stazione Merci

Grand Canal

Santa Croce

Former Stazione Marittima (Merci)

San Polo

Rialto

Grand Canal

Santa Marta

Basilica di San Marco

San Marco

Castello

La Tana

Isola di San Pietro

Santa Marta

San Basilio Terminal

Gallerie dell'Accademia

San Marco

Palazzo Ducale

Arsenale

Canale di Fusina

Dorsoduro

Canale di San Marco

Sacca Fisola

Sacca Fisola

Canale della Giudecca

Sant'Elena

Isola di Sant'Elena

Giudecca

Isola della Giudecca

San Marco & San Polo Map (p392)

Arriving in Venice

Marco Polo airport Located on the mainland 12km from Venice. Alilaguna operates a ferry service (€15) to Venice from the airport ferry dock. Water taxis cost from €110. Buses (€8, every 15 minutes) connect with Piazzale Roma.

Stazione Santa Lucia Venice's train station. *Vaporetti* (small passenger boats) depart from Ferrovia (Station) docks.

Stazione Venezia Mestre The mainland train station; transfer here to Stazione Santa Lucia.

Where to Stay

With many Venetians opening their homes to visitors, here you can become a local overnight. Venice was once known for charmingly decrepit hotels where English poets quietly expired, but a bevy of design-literate boutique hotels are glamming up historic palaces. In peak seasons quality hotels fill up fast. In summer, many people decamp to the Lido where prices are more reasonable.

YASONYA / SHUTTERSTOCK ©

Grand Canal

Never was a thoroughfare so aptly named as the Grand Canal. Snaking through the heart of the city, Venice's signature waterway is flanked by a magnificent array of Gothic, Moorish, Renaissance and Rococo palaces.

Great For...

☑ Don't Miss

The Ponte di Rialto and iconic Basilica di Santa Maria della Salute.

For most people, a trip down the Canal starts near the train station and Ponte di Calatrava. Officially known as Ponte della Costituzione (Constitution Bridge), this contemporary bridge, designed by avant-garde Spanish architect Santiago Calatrava (2008), is one of the few modern structures in central Venice.

To the Rialto

Leaving the bridge in your wake, one of the first landmarks, on your left, is the arcaded Gothic facade of the **Ca' d'Oro** (☑041 522 23 49; www.cadoro.org; Calle di Ca' d'Oro 3932; adult/reduced €8.50/2; ⊗8.15am-2pm Mon, to 7.15pm Tue-Sun, 2nd fl 10am-6pm Tue-Sun; ☗Ca' d'Oro), a 15th-century palazzo, now an art museum.

Ponte di Rialto & Around

A short way on, the **Ponte di Rialto** (☗Rialto) is the oldest of the four bridges that cross the canal. Built in the late 16th

Ponte di Rialto and Grand Canal

Grand Canal ⦿

ⓘ Need to Know

Take *vaporetti* 1 or 2 from the Ferrovia; it takes 35 to 40 minutes to Piazza San Marco.

✕ Take a Break

Jump off at Rialto and search out **Cantina Do Spade** (p395) for a cosy drink.

★ Top Tip

Avoid the crowds and tour the canal in the early evening or at night.

cademia, a bridge whose simple design seems strangely out of place amid Venice's fairy-tale architecture. Nearby, the Gallerie dell'Accademia (p390) is Venice's premier art gallery and the Peggy Guggenheim (p390) impresses with its collection of celebrated modern paintings.

century to a monumental design by Antonio da Ponte, it links the *sestieri* of San Marco and San Polo, and is a popular vantage point for photographers. Nearby, local shoppers crowd the **Rialto Market** (p391) and **Pescaria fish market** (p391).

Palazzo Grassi

The clean, geometric form of **Palazzo Grassi** (☏041 200 10 57; www.palazzograssi. it; Campo San Samuele 3231; adult/reduced incl Punta della Dogana €18/15; ☉10am-7pm Wed-Mon mid-Mar–Nov; ⚓San Samuele) comes into view on the first bend after the Rialto. This noble 18th-century palace now provides the neoclassical setting for show-stopping contemporary art. Over the water, spy out the sumptuous Ca' Rezzonico (p390).

Ponte dell'Accademia & Around

A couple of ferry stops further down and you arrive at the wooden Ponte dell'Ac-

Basilica di Santa Maria della Salute

The imperious dome of the Basilica di Santa Maria della Salute (p390) has been overlooking the canal's entrance since the 17th century. Impressive both outside and in, the basilica harbours a number of important works by local painter Titian. Beyond the basilica, the **Punta della Dogana** (☏041 200 10 57; www.palazzograssi.it; Fondamenta Salute 2; adult/reduced €15/10, incl Palazzo Grassi €18/15; ☉10am-7pm Wed-Mon Apr-Nov; ⚓Salute) is a former customs warehouse now staging contemporary art exhibitions.

St Mark's & Palazzo Ducale

At the mouth of the canal, you can disembark for Piazza San Marco. Dominating the waterside here is Palazzo Ducale (p386), the historic residence of the Venetian Doges.

Basilica di San Marco from St Mark's Square

Basilica di San Marco

With its profusion of spires and domes, lavish marble-work and 8500 sq metres of luminous mosaics, the Basilica di San Marco, Venice's signature basilica, is an unforgettable sight.

Great For...

☑ Don't Miss

Loggia dei Cavalli, where reproductions of the four bronze horses gallop off the balcony over Piazza San Marco.

The basilica was founded in the 9th century to house the corpse of St Mark after wily Venetian merchants smuggled it out of Egypt in a barrel of pork fat. When the original burnt down in 932, Venice rebuilt the basilica in its own cosmopolitan image, with Byzantine domes, a Greek cross layout and walls clad in marbles from Syria, Egypt and Palestine.

Exterior & Portals

The front of St Mark's ripples and crests like a wave, its five niched portals capped with shimmering mosaics and frothy stonework arches. The oldest mosaic on the facade (1270) is in the lunette above the far-left portal, depicting St Mark's stolen body arriving at the basilica. The theme is echoed in three of the other lunettes, including one showing turbaned officials recoiling from the hamper of pork fat containing the sainted corpse.

Interior

VIACHESLAV LOPATIN / SHUTTERSTOCK ©

Piazza
San Marco

◉ **Basílica di
San Marco**

Piazzetta
San Marco

Canale di
San Marco

❶ Need to Know

St Mark's Basilica; ☑041 270 83 11; www.
basilicasanmarco.it; Piazza San Marco;
🕑9.30am-5pm Mon-Sat, 2-5pm Sun summer, to 4.30pm Sun winter; ⛴San Marco
FREE

✕ Take a Break

Treat yourself to a *bellini* at world-famous **Harry's Bar** (☑041 528 57 77;
www.cipriani.com; Calle Vallaresso 1323;
🕑10.30am-11pm; ⛴San Marco).

★ Top Tip

There's no charge to enter the church
and wander around the roped-off central circuit: dress modestly, with knees
and shoulders covered, and leave large
bags at nearby Ateneo San Basso Left
Luggage Office.

Mosaics

It's natural to blink upon your first glimpse
of the basilica's glittering ceiling mosaics,
many made with 24-carat gold leaf. Just
inside the vestibule are the basilica's oldest mosaics: Apostles with the Madonna,
standing sentry by the main door for
more than 950 years. Inside the church
proper, three golden domes vie for your
attention. The Pentecost Cupola shows
the Holy Spirit, represented by a dove,
shooting tongues of flame onto the heads
of the surrounding saints. In the central
13th-century Ascension Cupola, angels
swirl around the figure of Christ hovering
among the stars.

Pala d'Oro

Tucked behind the main altar (€2), this
stupendous golden screen is studded with

2000 emeralds, amethysts, sapphires,
rubies, pearls and other gemstones. But
the most priceless treasures here are
biblical figures in vibrant cloisonné, begun
in Constantinople in AD 976 and elaborated
by Venetian goldsmiths in 1209.

Tesoro & Museum

Holy bones and booty from the Crusades
fill the Tesoro (Treasury; €3); while ducal
treasures on show in the **museum** (☑041
2730 8311; www.basilicasanmarco.it; Basilica di
San Marco; adult/reduced €5/2.50; 🕑9.45am-
4.45pm; ⛴San Marco) would put a king's ransom to shame. A highlight is the Quadriga
of St Mark's, a group of four bronze horses
originally plundered from Constantinople
and later carted off to Paris by Napoleon
before being returned to the basilica and
installed in the 1st-floor gallery.

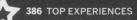

Sala del Maggior Consiglio

VIACHESLAV LOPATIN / SHUTTERSTOCK ©

Palazzo Ducale

Gothic Palazzo Ducale was the doge's official residence and the seat of the Venetian Republic's government (and location of its prisons) for over seven centuries.

Although the ducal palace probably moved to this site in the 10th century, the current complex only started to take shape in around 1340. In 1424, the wing facing Piazzetta San Marco was added and the palace assumed its final form, give or take a few major fires and refurbishments.

1st Floor

The doge's suite of private 1st-floor rooms is now used to house temporary art exhibitions, which are ticketed separately (around €10 extra). The doge lived like a caged lion in his gilded suite in the palace, which he could not leave without permission. The most intriguing room is the Sala dello Scudo (Shield Room), covered with world maps that reveal the extent of Venetian power (and the limits of its cartographers).

Great For...

☑ **Don't Miss**

The face of a grimacing man with his mouth agape at the top of the Scala d'Oro; this was a post box for secret accusations.

Exterior detail

TRO′ALO / SHUTTERSTOCK ©

Piazza San Marco · *Palazzo Ducale* · Piazzetta San Marco · Canale di San Marco

❶ Need to Know

Ducal Palace; ☏ 041 271 59 11; www.palazzo ducale.visitmuve.it; Piazzetta San Marco 1; adult/reduced incl Museo Correr €20/13, with Museum Pass free; ⊙ 8.30am-7pm summer, to 5.30pm winter; ☗ San Zaccaria

✕ Take a Break

Continue the rarefied vibe within the jewellery-box interior of Caffè Florian (p394).

★ Top Tip

Book tickets online, in advance to avoid queues. And turn up before 9am to avoid huge groups.

2nd Floor

Ascend Sansovino's 24-carat gilt stucco work Scala d'Oro (Golden Staircase) and emerge into 2nd-floor rooms covered with gorgeous propaganda. In the Palladio-designed Sala delle Quattro Porte (Hall of the Four Doors), ambassadors awaited ducal audiences under a lavish display of Venice's virtues by Giovanni Cambi, Titian and Tiepolo.

Few were granted an audience in the Palladio-designed Collegio (Council Room), where Veronese's 1575–78 *Virtues of the Republic* ceiling shows Venice as a bewitching blonde waving her sceptre like a wand over Justice and Peace. Father-son team Jacopo and Domenico Tintoretto attempt similar flattery, showing Venice keeping company with Apollo, Mars and Mercury in their *Triumph*

of Venice ceiling for the Sala del Senato (Senate Hall).

Government cover-ups were never so appealing as in the Sala Consiglio dei Dieci (Trial Chambers of the Council of Ten), where Venice's star chamber plotted under Veronese's *Juno Bestowing Her Gifts on Venice*. Arcing over the Sala della Bussola (Compass Room) is his *St Mark in Glory* ceiling.

Sala del Maggior Consiglio

The cavernous 1419 Sala del Maggior Consiglio (Grand Council Hall) provides the setting for Domenico Tintoretto's swirling *Paradise*, a work that's more politically correct than pretty: heaven is crammed with 500 prominent Venetians, including several Tintoretto patrons. Veronese's political posturing is more elegant in his oval *Apotheosis of Venice* ceiling, where gods marvel at Venice's coronation by angels, with foreign dignitaries and Venetian blondes rubbernecking on the balcony below.

Venice Gourmet Crawl

From market discoveries to delectable gelato, Venice is a gourmand's paradise waiting to be explored.

Start Rialto Market
Distance 2.9km
Duration 2 hours

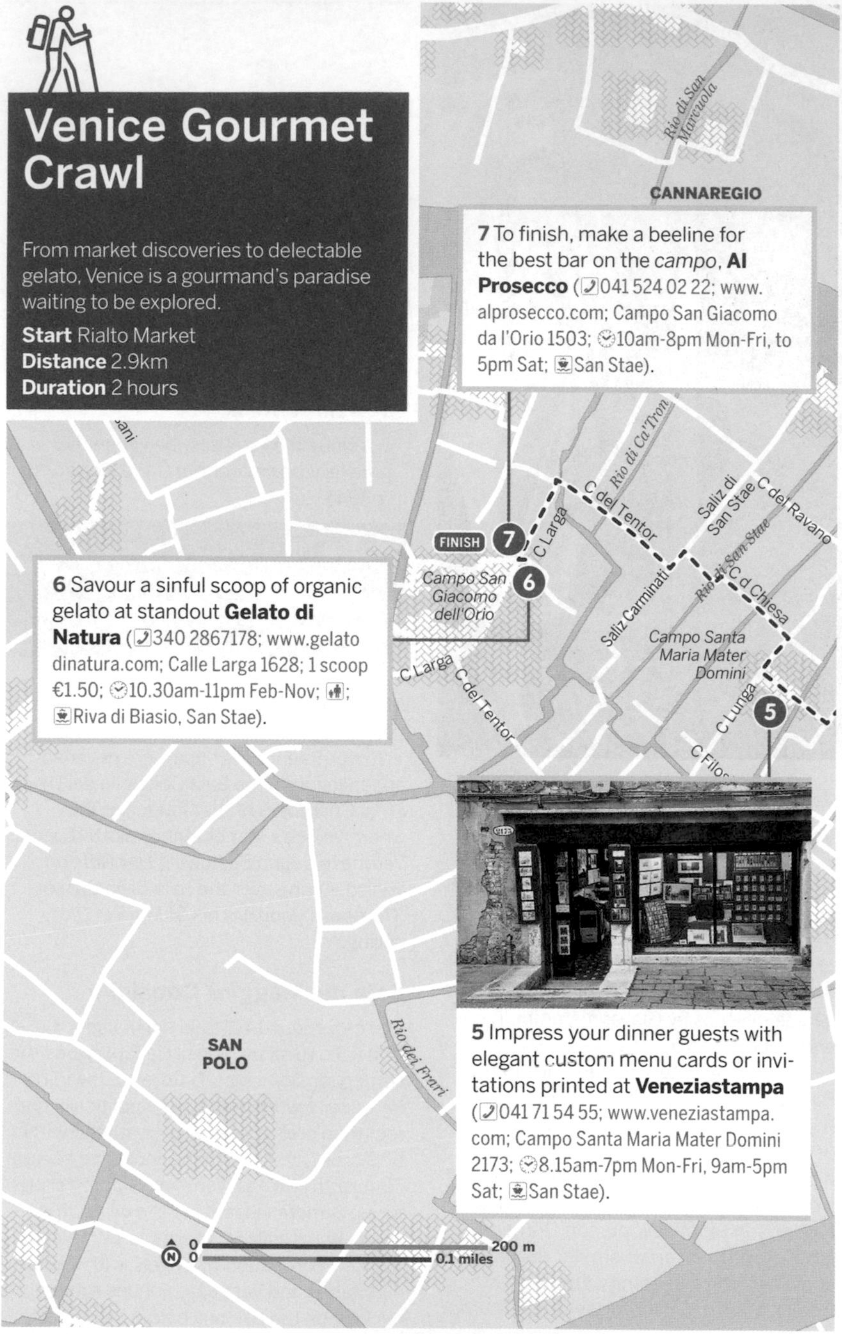

CANNAREGIO

7 To finish, make a beeline for the best bar on the *campo*, **Al Prosecco** (☏041 524 02 22; www.alprosecco.com; Campo San Giacomo da l'Orio 1503; ⊙10am-8pm Mon-Fri, to 5pm Sat; ☕San Stae).

6 Savour a sinful scoop of organic gelato at standout **Gelato di Natura** (☏340 2867178; www.gelato dinatura.com; Calle Larga 1628; 1 scoop €1.50; ⊙10.30am-11pm Feb-Nov; 🚼; ☕Riva di Biasio, San Stae).

5 Impress your dinner guests with elegant custom menu cards or invitations printed at **Veneziastampa** (☏041 71 54 55; www.veneziastampa.com; Campo Santa Maria Mater Domini 2173; ⊙8.15am-7pm Mon-Fri, 9am-5pm Sat; ☕San Stae).

FINISH **7**

Campo San Giacomo dell'Orio **6**

Campo Santa Maria Mater Domini **5**

SAN POLO

0 200 m
0 0.1 miles

Classic Photo: Colourful produce at the Rialto Market.

1 A trip through gourmet history starts at the city's main market, **Rialto Market** (p383), which has been whetting appetites for seven centuries.

2 At **Drogheria Mascari** (☎041 522 97 62; www.imascari.com; Ruga dei Spezieri 381; ☉8am-1pm & 4-7.30pm Mon, Tue & Thu-Sat, 8am-1pm Wed; 🚤Rialto Mercato) glimpse the fragrant spices and trade-route treasures that made Venice's fortune.

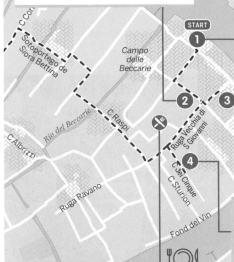

3 Casa del Parmigiano (☎041 520 65 25; www.aliani-casadelparmigiano. it; Campo Cesare Battisti già de la Bella Vienna 214; ☉8am-1.30pm Mon-Wed, to 7.30pm Thu-Sat; 🚤Rialto Mercato) is a historic deli laden with hard-to-find cheeses and mouthwatering cured meats.

4 Stop for an aromatic espresso at specialist coffee roaster **Caffè del Doge** (☎041 522 77 87; www. caffedeldoge.com; Calle dei Cinque 609; ☉7am-7pm; 🚤San Silvestro).

Take a Break... Duck into **All'Arco** (☎041 520 56 66; Calle de l'Ochialer 436; cicheti €2-2.50; ☉9am-2.30pm Mon-Sat; 🚤Rialto Mercato) for some of the city's best *cicheti* (Venetian tapas).

◎ SIGHTS

Gallerie dell'Accademia Gallery

(☏041 522 22 47; www.gallerieaccademia.
it; Campo de la Carità 1050; adult/reduced
€12/2; ⏱8.15am-2pm Mon, to 7.15pm Tue-Sun;
⛴Accademia) Venice's historic gallery traces
the development of Venetian art from the
14th to 19th centuries, with works by all of
the city's artistic superstars. The complex housing the collection maintained
its serene composure for centuries until
Napoleon installed his haul of art trophies
here in 1807 – looted from various religious
institutions around town.

Peggy Guggenheim
Collection Museum

(☏041 240 54 11; www.guggenheim-venice.it;
Calle San Cristoforo 701; adult/reduced €15/9;
⏱10am-6pm Wed-Mon; ⛴Accademia) After
losing her father on the *Titanic*, heiress
Peggy Guggenheim became one of the

great collectors of the 20th century. Her
palatial canalside home, Palazzo Venier dei
Leoni, showcases her stockpile of surrealist, futurist and abstract expressionist art,
with works by up to 200 artists, including
her ex-husband Max Ernst, Jackson Pollock
(among her many rumoured lovers), Pablo
Picasso and Salvador Dalí.

Ca' Rezzonico Museum

(Museum of 18th-Century Venice; ☏041 241 01
00; www.visitmuve.it; Fondamenta Rezzonico
3136; adult/reduced €10/7.50, or with Museum
Pass; ⏱10am-5pm Wed-Mon; ⛴Ca' Rezzonico)
Baroque dreams come true at this Bal-
dassare Longhena–designed Grand Canal
palazzo, where a marble staircase leads
to a vast gilded **ballroom** and sumptuous
salons filled with period furniture, paintings,
porcelain and mesmerising ceiling frescoes.

Basilica di Santa Maria
della Salute Basilica

(Our Lady of Health Basilica; www.basilicasalute
venezia.it; Campo de la Salute 1; sacristy adult/
reduced €4/2; ⏱9.30am-noon & 3-5.30pm;
⛴Salute) **FREE** Guarding the entrance to

> " *Baroque dreams come true at
> this Grand Canal palazzo* "

Ca' Rezzonico

ISOGOOD, PATRICK / SHUTTERSTOCK ©

the Grand Canal, this 17th-century domed church was commissioned by Venice's plague survivors as thanks for their salvation. Titian eluded the plague until age 94, leaving 12 key paintings in the basilica's art-slung sacristy.

Campanile
Tower

(www.basilicasanmarco.it; Piazza San Marco; adult/reduced €8/4; ☉8.30am-9pm summer, 9.30am-5.30pm winter, last entry 45min before closing; ⚑San Marco) Basilica di San Marco's 99m-tall bell tower has been rebuilt twice since its initial construction in AD 888. Galileo Galilei tested his telescope here in 1609 but modern-day visitors head to the top for 360-degree lagoon views.

Rialto Market
Market

(Rialto Mercato; ☏041 296 06 58; Campo de la Pescaria; ☉7am-2pm; ⚑Rialto Mercato) Venice's main market has been whetting appetites for seven centuries, with fruit and vegetable stands abutting the rather more pungent **Pescaria** (Fish Market; Campo de la Pescaria; ☉7am-2pm Tue-Sun; ⚑Rialto Mercato). To see it at its best, arrive in the morning along with the trolley-pushing shoppers and you'll be rewarded with pyramids of colourful seasonal produce like Sant'Erasmo *castraure* (baby artichokes), *radicchio trevisano* (bitter red chicory) and thick, succulent white asparagus. If you're in the market for picnic provisions, vendors may offer you samples.

I Frari
Basilica

(Basilica di Santa Maria Gloriosa dei Frari; ☏041 272 86 18; www.basilicadeifrari.it; Campo dei Frari 3072, San Polo; adult/reduced €3/1.50, with Chorus Pass free; ☉9am-6pm Mon-Sat, 1-6pm Sun; ⚑San Tomà) A soaring Gothic church, the Friary's assets include marquetry choir stalls, Canova's pyramid mausoleum, Bellini's achingly sweet *Madonna with Child* triptych in the sacristy, and Longhena's creepy Doge Pesaro funereal monument. Upstaging them all, however, is Titian's 1518 *Assunta* (Assumption) altarpiece, in which a radiant red-cloaked Madonna reaches heavenward, steps onto a cloud and es-

📷 Gondola Rides

Cheesy or the ultimate romance? You decide. Daytime rates for gondola rides cost up to €80 for 40 minutes (with a maximum of six passengers); from 7pm to 8am rides cost around €100 for 35 minutes. These rates don't include songs – which must be negotiated separately – or tips.

Gondolier
GIVAGA / GETTY IMAGES ©

capes this mortal coil. Titian himself – lost to the plague in 1576 at the age 94 – has his memorial here.

🔒 SHOPPING

Chiarastella Cattana
Homewares

(☏041 522 43 69; www.chiarastellacattana.com; Salizada San Samuele 3216; ☉11am-1pm & 3-7pm Mon-Sat; ⚑San Samuele) Transform any home with these locally woven, strikingly original Venetian linens. Whimsical cushions feature chubby purple rhinoceroses and grumpy scarlet elephants straight out of Pietro Longhi paintings, and hand-tasselled jacquard hand towels will dry your guests in style.

Vittorio Costantini
Glass

(☏041 522 22 65; www.vittoriocostantini.com; Calle del Fumo 5311; ☉9.30am-1pm & 2.15-5.30pm Mon-Fri; ⚑Fondamente Nove) Kids and adults alike are thrilled at the magical, miniature insects, butterflies, shells and birds that Vittorio Costantini fashions out of glass using a lampwork technique.

San Marco & San Polo

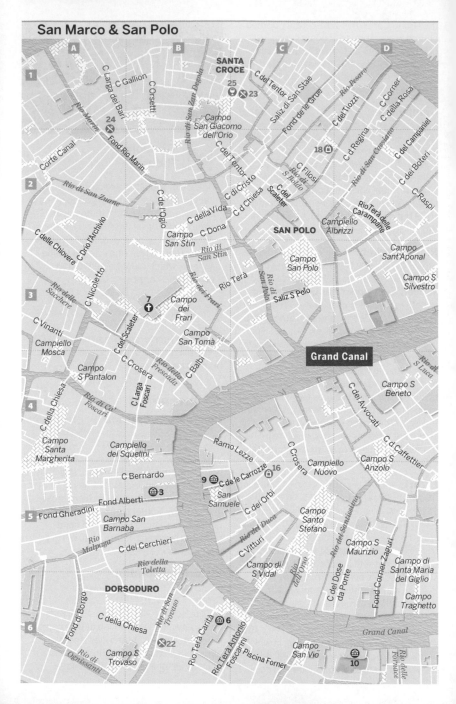

SANTA CROCE

SAN POLO

DORSODURO

Grand Canal

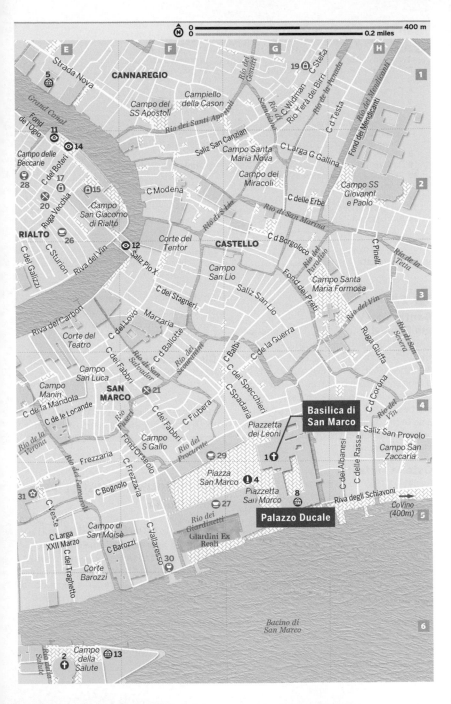

San Marco & San Polo

🍴 EATING

Cantine del Vino già Schiavi
Venetian €

(☎041 523 00 34; www.cantinaschiavi.com; Fondamenta Priuli 992; cicheti €1.50; ⊙8.30am-8.30pm Mon-Sat; 🚤Zattere) It may look like a wine shop and function as a bar, but this legendary canalside spot also serves the best *cicheti* (Venetian tapas) on this side of the Grand Canal. Choose from the impressive counter selection or ask for a filled-to-order roll.

Osteria Trefanti
Venetian €€

(☎041 520 17 89; www.osteriatrefanti.it; Fondamenta del Rio Marin o dei Garzoti 888; meals €40-45; ⊙noon-2.30pm & 7-10.30pm Tue-Sun; 🚊; 🚤Riva de Biasio) La Serenissima's spice trade lives on at simple, elegant Trefanti, where gnocchi might get an intriguing kick from cinnamon, and turbot is flavoured with almond and coconut. Seafood is the focus; try the 'doge's fettucine'. Book ahead.

CoVino
Venetian €€

(☎041 241 27 05; www.covinovenezia.com; Calle del Pestrin 3829; fixed-price menu lunch €27-36, dinner €40; ⊙12.45-2.30pm & 7pm-midnight Thu-Mon; 🚊; 🚤Arsenale) Tiny CoVino has only 14 seats but demonstrates bags of ambition with its inventive, seasonal menu inspired by the Venetian terroir.

Bistrot de Venise
Venetian €€€

(☎041 523 66 51; www.bistrotdevenise.com; Calle dei Fabbri 4685; meals €47-78; ⊙noon-3pm & 5pm-1am; 🚊; 🚤Rialto) Indulge in some culinary time travel in the red-and-gilt dining room at this fine-dining bistro reviving the recipes of Renaissance chef Bartolomeo Scappi.

🍷 DRINKING & NIGHTLIFE

Caffè Florian
Cafe

(☎041 520 56 41; www.caffeflorian.com; Piazza San Marco 57; ⊙9am-11pm; 🚤San Marco) The oldest still-operating cafe in Europe and one of the first to welcome women, Florian maintains rituals (if not prices) established in 1720: besuited waiters serve cappuccino on silver trays; lovers get cosy on plush banquettes; and the orchestra strikes up as the sunset illuminates San Marco's mosaics. Piazza seating during concerts costs €6 extra, but dreamy-eyed romantics will hardly notice.

Grancaffè Quadri   Cafe

(📞041 522 21 05; www.alajmo.it; Piazza San Marco 121; ⏱9am-midnight; 🚤San Marco) Powdered wigs seem appropriate inside this baroque bar-cafe that's been serving happy hours since 1638. During Carnevale, costumed Quadri revellers party like it's 1699. Grab a seat on the piazza to watch the best show in town: the sunset setting the basilica's golden mosaics ablaze.

Cantina Do Spade   Wine Bar

(📞041 521 05 83; www.cantinadospade.com; Sotoportego de le Do Spade 860; ⏱10am-3pm & 6-10pm Wed-Mon, 6-10pm Tue; 📶; 🚤Rialto Mercato) Famously mentioned in Casanova's memoirs, cosy 'Two Spades' was founded in 1488 and continues to keep Venice in good spirits with its bargain Tri-Veneto and Istrian wines and young, laid-back management. Come early for market-fresh *fritture* (fried battered seafood) and grilled squid, or linger longer with satisfying, sit-down dishes like *bigoli in salsa* (pasta in anchovy and onion sauce).

⊕ ENTERTAINMENT

Teatro La Fenice   Opera

(📞041 78 66 54; www.teatrolafenice.it; Campo San Fantin 1977; tickets €25-250; 🚤Giglio) One of Italy's top opera houses, La Fenice stages a rich roster of opera, ballet and classical music. The main opera season runs from January to July and September to October. The cheapest seats (€25) are in the boxes at the top: the view is extremely restricted, but you will get to hear the music, watch the orchestra, soak up the atmosphere and people-watch.

ⓘ INFORMATION

Vènezia Unica (📞041 24 24; www.veneziaunica.it) runs all tourist information services and offices in Venice. It provides information on sights, itineraries, day trips, transport, special events, shows and temporary exhibitions. Discount passes can be prebooked on its website.

ⓘ GETTING THERE & AWAY

AIR

Most flights to Venice fly in to **Marco Polo Airport** (📞flight information 041 260 92 60; www.veniceairport.it; Via Galileo Gallilei 30/1, Tessera), 12km outside Venice, east of Mestre. Ryanair and some other budget airlines also use **Treviso Airport** (📞0422 31 51 11; www.trevisoairport.it; Via Noalese 63), about 4km southwest of Treviso and a 26km, one-hour drive from Venice.

BOAT

Venice has regular ferry connections with Greece, Croatia and Slovenia.

CAR

To get to Venice by car or motorcycle, take the often-congested Trieste–Turin A4, which passes through Mestre. From Mestre, take the 'Venezia' exit. Once over Ponte della Libertà from Mestre, cars must be left at a car park in Piazzale Roma or on the Isola del Tronchetto, an artificial island located at the westernmost tip of Santa Croce. Be warned: you'll pay a hefty price in parking fees, and traffic backs up at weekends.

TRAIN

Direct intercity services operate out of Venice to most major Italian cities, as well as points in France, Germany, Austria, Switzerland, Slovenia and Croatia. The main station is Stazione Venezia Santa Lucia.

ⓘ GETTING AROUND

Traghetto Locals use this daytime public gondola service (€2) to cross the Grand Canal between bridges.

Vaporetto (small passenger ferry) Venice's main public transport. Single rides cost €7.50; for frequent use, get a timed pass for unlimited travel within a set period (1-/2-/3-/7-day passes cost €20/30/40/60). Tickets and passes are available dockside from ACTV ticket booths and ticket vending machines, or from tobacconists.

Water taxi Sleek teak boats offer taxi services for €15 plus €2 per minute, plus €5 for pre-booked services and extra for night-time, luggage and large groups.

FLORENCE & TUSCANY, ITALY

Florence & Tuscany, Italy

With its lyrical landscapes, world-class art and superb cucina contadina (food from the farmer's kitchen), Tuscany offers a splendid array of treats for travellers. No land is more caught up with the fruits of its fertile earth than Tuscany, a gourmet destination where locality, seasonality and sustainability are revered. And oh, the art! During the medieval and Renaissance periods, Tuscany's painters, sculptors and architects created world-class masterpieces. Nowhere is this more apparent than in magnificent Florence and in towns and cities like Siena, Arezzo and Montepulciano.

Two Days in Tuscany

Base yourself in Florence, and spend your first day exploring this illustrious city, including a visit to the **Duomo** (p400) and the **Galleria dell'Accademia** (p404). On day two, head to San Gimignano's famed **towers** (p406), or to **Arezzo** (p425) for churches, museums and, if the timing is right, antiques.

Four Days in Tuscany

With an additional two days, head to legendary **Siena** on day three, and over to Pisa and its famous **tower** (p409) on day four or to **Montepulciano** (p428) for hilltop wonders.

After leaving Tuscany, Rome (p327) and Venice (p379) are ideal next stops.

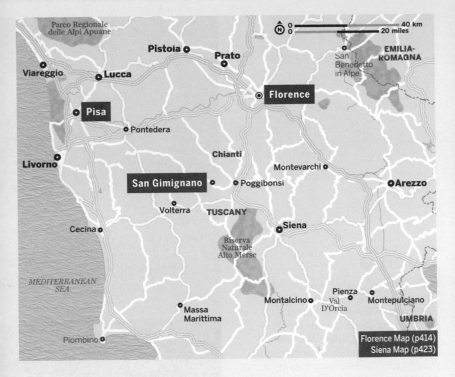

Arriving in Tuscany

Pisa International Airport Tuscany's principal international gateway; from here, buses run to Pisa, Florence and Siena. The automated, speedy PisaMover links the airport with Pisa Centrale train station.

Florence Airport This smaller airport serves flights from Italian and European destinations.

Stazione di Santa Maria Novella Florence's station is the region's biggest and busiest; it's served by regular fast trains on the main Rome–Milan line.

Where to Stay

In Florence, advance reservations are essential between Easter and September, while winter ushers in some great deals for visitors – room rates are practically halved. Elsewhere in Tuscany, an *agriturismo* (rural accommodation on a working farm, winery or agricultural domain) is an idyllic five-star way of experiencing country life. It's perfect for those with a car and usually highly practical for those travelling with children. Tuscany also abounds in historic palatial *palazzo* hotels.

A rooftop view of the Duomo

Duomo

Florence's Duomo is the city's most iconic landmark. Capped by Filippo Brunelleschi's red-tiled cupola, it's a staggering construction, and its breathtaking pink, white and green marble facade and graceful campanile (bell tower) dominate the medieval cityscape.

Great For...

❶ Need to Know

Cattedrale di Santa Maria del Fiore; ☑055 230 28 85; www.museumflorence.com; Piazza del Duomo; ☺10am-5pm Mon-Wed & Fri, to 4.30pm Thu & Sat, 1.30-4.45pm Sun FREE

★ **Top Tip**

Reservations are required to climb the dome. Book online or at the ticket office at Piazza San Giovanni 7, opposite the Baptistry's northern entrance.

Sienese architect Arnolfo di Cambio began work on the Duomo in 1296, but construction took almost 150 years and it wasn't consecrated until 1436.

Facade

The neo-Gothic facade was designed in the 19th century by architect Emilio de Fabris to replace the uncompleted original, torn down in the 16th century. The oldest and most clearly Gothic part of the cathedral is its south flank, pierced by the Porta dei Canonici (Canons' Door), a mid-14th-century High Gothic creation (you enter here to climb up inside the dome).

Dome

One of the finest masterpieces of the Renaissance, the **cupola** (Brunelleschi's Dome; adult/reduced incl baptistry, campanile, crypt & museum €18/3; ⊘8.30am-7pm Mon-Fri, to 5pm Sat, 1-4pm Sun) is a feat of engineering that cannot be fully appreciated without climbing its 463 interior stone steps. It was built between 1420 and 1436 to a design by Filippo Brunelleschi, and is a staggering 91m high and 45.5m wide.

Taking his inspiration from Rome's Pantheon, Brunelleschi arrived at an innovative engineering solution of a distinctive octagonal shape of inner and outer concentric domes resting on the drum of the cathedral rather than the roof itself, allowing artisans to build from the ground up without needing a wooden support frame. Over four million bricks were used in the construction, all of them laid in consecutive rings in horizontal courses using a vertical herringbone pattern.

Frescoes on the cupola

The climb up the spiral staircase is relatively steep. Be sure to pause when you reach the balustrade at the base of the dome, which gives an aerial view of the octagonal *coro* (choir) in the cathedral below and the seven round stained-glass windows (by Donatello, Andrea del Castagno, Paolo Uccello and Lorenzo Ghiberti) that pierce the octagonal drum.

Interior

After the visual wham-bam of the facade, the sparse decoration of the cathedral's vast interior, 155m long and 90m wide, comes as a surprise – most of its artistic treasures have been removed over the centuries

BLACKMAC / SHUTTERSTOCK ©

according to the vagaries of ecclesiastical fashion, and many are on show in the Grande Museo del Duomo (p412). The interior is also unexpectedly secular in places (a reflection of the sizeable chunk of the cathedral not paid for by the church): down the left aisle two immense frescoes of equestrian statues portray two *condottieri* (mercenaries) – on the left Niccolò da Tolentino by Andrea del Castagno (1456), and on the right Sir John Hawkwood (who fought in the service of Florence in the 14th century) by Uccello (1436).

Between the left (north) arm of the transept and the apse is the Sagrestia delle Messe (Mass Sacristy), its panelling a marvel of inlaid wood carved by Benedetto and Giuliano da Maiano. The fine bronze doors were executed by Luca della Robbia – his only known work in the material. Above the doorway is his glazed terracotta *Resurrezione* (Resurrection).

A stairway near the main entrance of the cathedral leads down to the Cripta Santa Reparata (crypt), where excavations between 1965 and 1974 unearthed parts of the 5th-century Chiesa di Santa Reparata that originally stood on the site.

Campanile

The 414-step climb up the cathedral's 85m-tall **campanile** (bell tower; adult/reduced incl baptistry, cupola, crypt & museum €18/3; ☺8.15am-7pm), begun by Giotto in 1334, rewards with a staggering city panorama. The first tier of bas-reliefs around the base of its elaborate Gothic facade are copies of those carved by Pisano depicting the Creation of Man and the *attività umane* (arts and industries). Those on the second tier depict the planets, the cardinal virtues, the arts and the seven sacraments. The sculpted Prophets and Sibyls in the upper-storey niches are copies of works by Donatello and others.

✖ **Take a Break**

Take time out over a taste of Tuscan wine at stylish **Coquinarius** (🖉055 230 21 53; www.coquinarius.com; Via delle Oche 11r; ☺12.30-3pm & 6.30-10.30pm Wed-Mon).

JOHN KELLERMAN / ALAMY STOCK PHOTO ©

Galleria dell'Accademia

A lengthy queue marks the door to the Galleria dell'Accademia, the late 18th-century gallery that's home to one of the Renaissance's most iconic master-pieces, Michelangelo's David.

Great For...

☑ Don't Miss

David – look for the two pale lines visible on his lower left arm where it was broken in 1527.

David

Fortunately, the world's most famous statue is worth the wait. Standing at over 5m tall and weighing in at 19 tonnes, it's a formidable sight. But it's not just its scale that impresses, it's also the subtle detail – the veins in David's sinewy arms, the muscles in his legs, the change in expression as you move around him. Carved from a single block of marble, Michelangelo's most famous work was also his most challenging – he didn't choose the marble himself, it was veined, and its larger-than-life dimensions were already decided.

When the statue of the boy-warrior, depicted for the first time as a man in the prime of life rather than a young boy, assumed its pedestal in front of Palazzo Vecchio on Piazza della Signoria in 1504, Florentines immediately adopted it as

Sculptures and paintings in the Galleria dell'Accademia

❶ Need to Know

☎055 238 86 09; www.galleriaaccademia firenze.beniculturali.it; Via Ricasoli 60; adult/ reduced €12/6; ◷8.15am-6.50pm Tue-Sun

✕ Take a Break

Grab a pizza slice at the much-loved Pugi (p419), a stone's throw from the Galleria.

★ Top Tip

Cut queuing time by booking tickets in advance at www.firenzemusei.it; the reservation fee is €4.

a powerful emblem of Florentine power, liberty and civic pride. It stayed in the piazza until 1873, when it was moved to its current purpose-built tribune in the Galleria.

Other Works

Michelangelo was also the master behind the unfinished *San Matteo* (St Matthew; 1504–08) and four *Prigioni* ('Prisoners' or 'Slaves'; 1521–30), also displayed in the gallery. The prisoners seem to be writhing and struggling to free themselves from the marble; they were meant for the tomb of Pope Julius II, itself never completed.

Adjacent rooms contain paintings by Andrea Orcagna, Taddeo Gaddi, Domenico Ghirlandaio, Filippino Lippi and Sandro Botticelli.

What's Nearby?

To the east of the Galleria, Giambologna's equestrian statue of Grand Duke Ferdinando I de' Medici lords it over **Piazza della Santissima Annunziata**, a majestic square dominated by the facades of the **Chiesa della Santissima Annunziata**, built in 1250, then rebuilt by Michelozzo et al in the mid-15th century, and the **Ospedale degli Innocenti** (Hospital of the Innocents), Europe's first orphanage founded in 1421. Look up to admire Brunelleschi's classically influenced portico, decorated by Andrea della Robbia (1435–1525) with terracotta medallions of babies in swaddling clothes.

About 200m southeast of the piazza is the **Museo Archeologico** (☎055 23 57; www.archeotoscana.beniculturali.it; Piazza della Santissima Annunziata 9b; adult/reduced €4/2, with Uffizi ticket free; ◷8.30am-7pm Tue-Fri, to 2pm Sat, Mon & 1st & 3rd Sun of month). Its rich collection of finds, including most of the Medici hoard of antiquities, plunges you deep into the past and offers an alternative to Renaissance splendour.

PQL89 / SHUTTERSTOCK ©

Towers of San Gimignano

A favourite of day trippers, San Gimignano lies deep in the Tuscan countryside northwest of Siena. Known as the 'medieval Manhattan', it features 15 11th-century towers that soar above its hilltop centro storico (historic centre).

Great For...

☑ Don't Miss

The town's **Galleria Continua** (☎0577 94 31 34; www.galleriacontinua.com; Via del Castello 11; ☺10am-1pm & 2-7pm) **FREE**, one of the best contemporary art galleries in Europe.

Originally an Etruscan village, the town was named after the bishop of Modena, San Gimignano, who is said to have saved it from Attila the Hun. It became a *comune* in 1199 and quickly flourished, thanks in no small part to its position on the Via Francigena. Up to 72 towers were built as the town's prosperous burghers sought to outdo their neighbours and flaunt their wealth.

Collegiata

San Gimignano's Romanesque cathedral, the **Collegiata** (Duomo; Basilica di Santa Maria Assunta; ☎0577 28 63 00; www.duomosan gimignano.it; Piazza del Duomo; adult/reduced €4/2; ☺10am-7pm Mon-Sat, 12.30-7pm Sun Apr-Oct, 10am-4.30pm Mon-Sat, 12.30-4.30pm Sun Nov-Mar, closed 2nd half Jan and 2nd half Nov), is named after the college of priests who originally managed it. Parts of the building were built in the second half of the 11th century,

but its remarkably vivid frescoes date from the 14th century.

Entry is via the side stairs and through a loggia that originally functioned as the baptistry. Once in the main space, face the altar and look to your left (north). On the wall are scenes from Genesis and the Old Testament by Bartolo di Fredi, dating from around 1367. On the right (south) wall are scenes from the New Testament by the workshop of Simone Martini, which were completed in 1336. On the inside of the front facade is Taddeo di Bartolo's striking depiction of the *Last Judgement* – on the upper-left side is a fresco depicting *Paradiso* (Heaven) and on the upper-right *Inferno* (Hell).

Palazzo Comunale

The 12th-century **Palazzo Comunale** (⌯0577 28 63 00; www.sangimignanomusei.it; Piazza del Duomo 2; combined Civic Museums ticket adult/reduced €9/7; ⊙10am-7pm Apr-Sep, 11am-5pm Oct-Mar) has always been the centre of local government – its Sala di Dante is where the great poet addressed the town's council in 1299, urging it to support the Guelph cause. The room (also known as the Sala del Consiglio) is home to Lippo Memmi's early 14th-century *Maestà*, which portrays the enthroned Virgin and Child surrounded by angels, saints and local dignitaries. Upstairs, the pinacoteca has a charming collection of paintings from the Sienese and Florentine schools of the 12th to 15th centuries.

In the Camera del Podestà is a meticulously restored cycle of frescoes by Memmo di Filippuccio, illustrating a moral history – the rewards of marriage are shown in the scenes of a husband and wife naked in a bath and in bed.

After you've enjoyed the art, be sure to climb the 218 steps of the palazzo's 54m-tall Torre Grossa for spectacular views of the town and surrounding countryside.

DELPIXART / GETTY IMAGES ©

Leaning Tower of Pisa

One of Italy's signature sights, Pisa's stunning Torre Pendente *(Leaning Tower) truly lives up to its name, leaning a startling 3.9 degrees off the vertical. Visit Pisa as a day trip from Florence or another charming Tuscan town.*

The 56m-high tower, officially the Duomo's *campanile* (bell tower), took almost 200 years to build, but was already leaning when it was unveiled in 1372. Over time, the tilt, caused by a layer of weak subsoil, steadily worsened until it was finally halted by a major stabilisation project in the 1990s.

Planning Your Visit

Access to the Leaning Tower is limited to 40 people at a time – children under eight are not allowed in and those aged eight to 10 years must hold an adult's hand.

Visits last 35 minutes and involve a steep climb up 251 occasionally slippery steps. All bags, handbags included, must be deposited at the free left-luggage desk next to the

Great For...

☑ Don't Miss

Planning an enchanting after-dark visit: if you're in Pisa from mid-June to late August, doors don't close till 10pm.

Leaning Tower next to the Duomo

ⓘ Need to Know

Torre Pendente; ☑050 83 50 11; www.
opapisa.it; Piazza dei Duomo; €18;
⊗8.30am-10pm mid-Jun-Aug, 9am-8pm
Apr-mid-Jun & Sep, to 7pm Oct & Mar, to 6pm
Nov-Feb

✕ Take a Break

For honest, unpretentious Tuscan cooking, go to old-timer **Ristorante Galileo**
(☑050 2 82 87; www.ristorantegalileo.com;
Via San Martino 6-8; meals €25-35; ⊗12.30-
2.30pm & 7.30-11pm).

★ Top Tip

With two million visitors every year,
crowds are the norm; November to
March queues are shorter.

central ticket office – cameras are about
the only thing you can take up.

Tower & Combo Tickets

Admissions to the Leaning Tower are
limited: book in advance online or grab the
first available slot as soon as you arrive.
Ticket desks are behind the tower and in
the Museo delle Sinopie. Ticket offices in
Pisa also sell combination tickets for other
city sights.

What's Nearby?

Pisa's medieval heart lies north of the
water; from **Piazza Cairoli**, with its evening
bevy of bars and gelato shops, meander
along **Via Cavour**. A daily fresh-produce
market fills **Piazza delle Vettovaglie**.

Duomo   Cathedral

(Duomo di Santa Maria Assunta; ☑050 83 50
11; www.opapisa.it; Piazza dei Duomo; ⊗10am-
8pm Apr-Oct, 10am-6pm or 7pm Nov-Feb) **FREE**
The Romanesque Duomo was begun in
1064 and consecrated in 1118. Admission is free, but you'll need an entrance
coupon from the ticket office or a ticket
from one of the other Piazza dei Miracoli
sights.

Battistero   Christian Site

(Battistero di San Giovanni; ☑050 83 50 11;
www.opapisa.it; Piazza dei Miracoli; €5, with
Camposanto & Museo €8; ⊗8am-8pm Apr-Oct,
9am-6pm or 7pm Nov-Mar) This unusual round
baptistry (1395) has one dome piled on top
of another, each roofed half in lead, half in
tiles, and topped by a gilt-bronze John the
Baptist.

Driving Tuscany

Taking in Tuscany's two great medieval rivals, Florence and Siena, Chianti's wine-rich hills, and the Unesco-listed Val d'Orcia, this drive offers artistic masterpieces, soul-stirring scenery and captivating Renaissance towns.

Start Florence
Distance 185km
Duration Four days

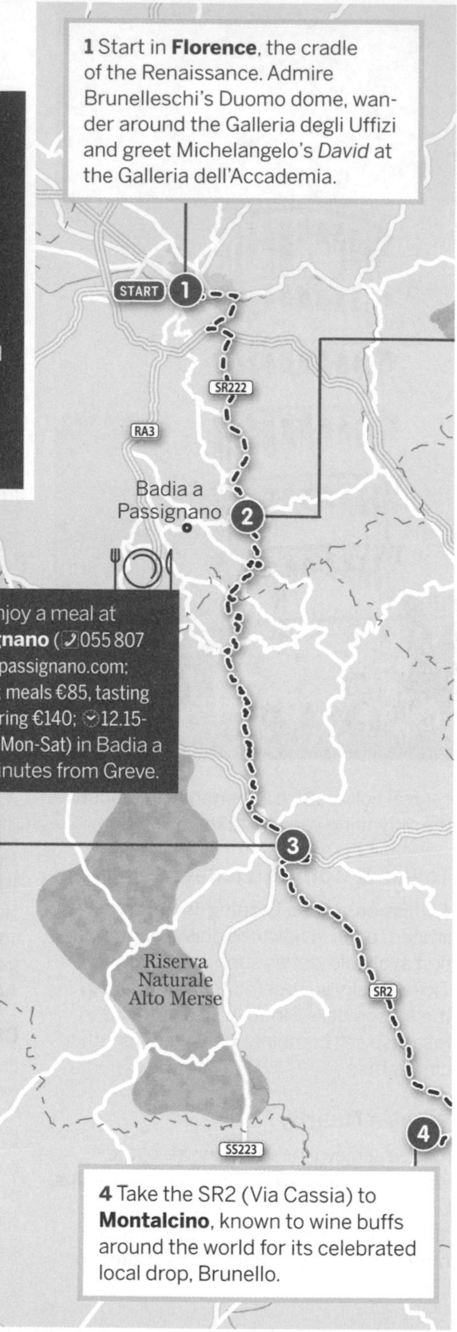

1 Start in **Florence**, the cradle of the Renaissance. Admire Brunelleschi's Duomo dome, wander around the Galleria degli Uffizi and greet Michelangelo's *David* at the Galleria dell'Accademia.

START **1**

SR222

RA3

Badia a Passignano **2**

Take a Break... Enjoy a meal at **Osteria di Passignano** (☎055 807 12 78; www.osteriadipassignano.com; Via di Passignano 33; meals €85, tasting menus €90, wine pairing €140; ☻12.15-2.15pm & 7.30-10pm Mon-Sat) in Badia a Passignano, 20 minutes from Greve.

3

Riserva Naturale Alto Merse

SR2

3 The medieval cityscape of **Siena** is captivating. Be inspired by the Duomo's intricate facade, bustling Piazza del Campo and fine art in the Museo Civico.

SS223

4

4 Take the SR2 (Via Cassia) to **Montalcino**, known to wine buffs around the world for its celebrated local drop, Brunello.

San
Godenzo

Parco Nazionale
delle Foreste
Casentinesi, Monte
Falterona e Campigna

Monte
Falterona

2 Pick up the SR222 (Via Chianti-giana) and head south to Chianti wine country. Stop off in the centuries-old wine centre of **Greve**, then continue south to Siena.

Classic Photo: The stunning Val d'Orcia offers views of undulating fields, stone farmhouses and rows of elegant cypresses.

5 Head east to the Val d'Orcia and pretty **Pienza**. Magnificent Renaissance buildings in and around Piazza Pio II went up in just four years in the 15th century and haven't changed since.

FINISH

SR2

6 Steeply stacked **Montepulciano** harbours a wealth of *palazzi* and fine buildings, plus views over the Val di Chiana and Val d'Orcia. Finish up with a glass or two of the local Vino Nobile.

Florence

⊙ SIGHTS

Florence's wealth of museums and galleries house many of the world's most exquisite examples of Renaissance art, and its architecture is unrivalled. Yet don't feel pressured to see everything: combine your personal pick of sights with ample meandering through the city's warren of narrow streets broken by cafe and *enoteca* (wine bar) stops.

Churches enforce a strict dress code for visitors: no shorts, sleeveless shirts or plunging necklines. Photography with no flash is allowed in museums, but leave the selfie stick at home – they are officially forbidden.

Galleria degli Uffizi   Gallery
(Uffizi Gallery; ☑055 29 48 83; www.uffizi.it; Piazzale degli Uffizi 6; adult/reduced Mar-Oct €20/10, Nov-Feb €12/6; ⊙8.15am-6.50pm Tue-Sun) Home to the world's greatest collection of Italian Renaissance art, Florence's premier gallery occupies the vast U-shaped Palazzo degli Uffizi (1560–80), built as government offices. The collection, bequeathed to the

city by the Medici family in 1743 on condition that it never leave Florence, contains some of Italy's best-known paintings, including a room full of Botticelli masterpieces.

A combined ticket (valid three days) with Palazzo Pitti, Giardino di Boboli and Museo Archeologico is available for €38/21 (€18/11 November to February).

Museo dell'Opera del Duomo   Museum
(Cathedral Museum; ☑055 230 28 85; www.museumflorence.com; Piazza del Duomo 9; adult/reduced incl cathedral bell tower, cupola, baptistry & crypt €15/3; ⊙9am-7pm) The awe-inspiring story of how the *duomo* and its cupola came to life is told in this well-executed museum. Among its sacred and liturgical treasures are the baptistry's original doors: the gloriously golden, 16m-tall gilded bronze *Porta del Paradiso* (Door of Paradise; 1425–52) designed by Ghiberti for the eastern entrance; the northern doors (1402–24), also by Ghiberti; and – from the end of 2019 – the spectacular *Porta Sud* (South Door; 1330-36) by Andrea Pisano, illustrating the story of John the Baptist.

Galleria degli Uffizi

Palazzo Vecchio Museum

(☑055 276 85 58; www.musefirenze.it; Piazza della Signoria; adult/reduced museum €12.50/10, tower €12.50/10, museum & tower €17.50/15, museum & archaeological tour €16/13.50, archaeological tour €4, combination ticket €19.50/17.50; ☺museum 9am-11pm Fri-Wed, to 2pm Thu summer, 9am-7pm Fri-Wed, to 2pm Thu summer, tower 9am-9pm Fri-Wed, to 2pm Thu summer, 10am-5pm Fri-Wed, to 2pm Thu winter) This fortress palace, with its crenellations and 94m-high tower, was designed by Arnolfo di Cambio between 1298 and 1314 for the *signoria* (city government). Today it is home to the mayor's office and the municipal council. From the top of the **Torre d'Arnolfo** (tower), you can revel in unforgettable views. Inside, Michelangelo's *Genio della Vittoria* (Genius of Victory) sculpture graces the Salone dei Cinquecento, a magnificent painted hall created for the city's 15th-century ruling Consiglio dei Cinquecento (Council of 500).

Battistero di San Giovanni Landmark

(Baptistry; ☑055 230 28 85; www.museum florence.com; Piazza di San Giovanni; adult/reduced incl campanile, cupola, crypt & museum €18/3; ☺8.15-10.15am & 11.15am-7.30pm Mon-Fri, 8.15am-6.30pm Sat, 8.15am-1.30pm Sun) This 11th-century baptistry – the oldest religious building on the vast cathedral square – is a Romanesque, octagonal-striped structure of white-and-green marble with three sets of doors conceived as panels illustrating the story of humanity and the Redemption. Most celebrated are Lorenzo Ghiberti's gilded bronze doors at the eastern entrance, the *Porta del Paradiso* (Gate of Paradise). What you see today are copies – the originals are in the Museo dell'Opera del Duomo. Buy tickets online or at the ticket office at Piazza di San Giovanni 7, opposite the main Baptistry entrance.

Piazza della Signoria Piazza

The hub of local life since the 13th century, Florentines flock here to meet friends and chat over early-evening *aperitivi* at historic cafes. Presiding over everything is Palazzo Vecchio, Florence's city hall, and the 14th-century **Loggia dei Lanzi** FREE, an

📷 Guided Tours of Florence

In a city with such an immense, and at times overwhelming, art heritage, guided tours can be an excellent means of navigating to the heart of the matter – particularly for first-time visitors who might be uncertain quite where to start. On a very practical level, signing up for a guided tour can also mean bypassing the headache of securing tickets in advance for popular museums like the Uffizi and Galleria dell'Accademia (p404), which get booked up quickly in high season.

Research carefully what sort of guided tour you are signing yourself up for. Some tours cater specifically to families; some are specialist tours for die-hard art connoisseurs; some, such as walking or cycling tours, might involve exerting more energy than you want to or are capable of. If you are taking a food tour, be sure to tell the tour company in advance if you have any food allergies.

open-air gallery showcasing Renaissance sculptures, including Giambologna's *Rape of the Sabine Women* (c 1583), Benvenuto Cellini's bronze *Perseus* (1554) and Agnolo Gaddi's *Seven Virtues* (1384–89).

Piazza della Repubblica Piazza

The site of a Roman forum and heart of medieval Florence, this busy civic space was created in the 1880s as part of a controversial plan of 'civic improvements' involving the demolition of the old market,

Florence

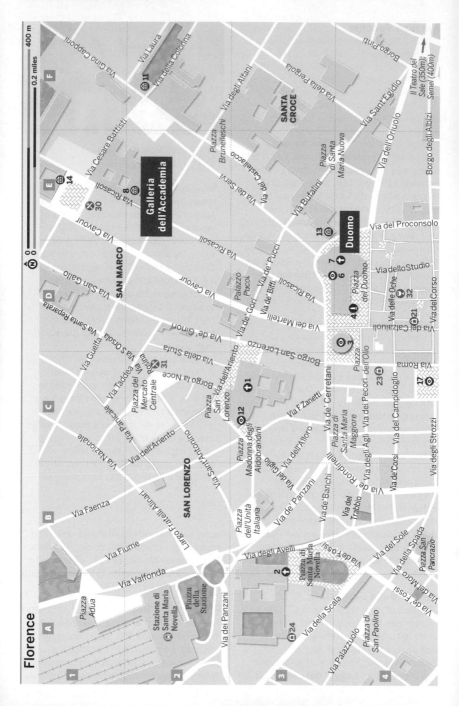

0 200 m
0 0.2 miles
400 m

Galleria dell'Accademia

Duomo

SAN MARCO

SANTA CROCE

SAN LORENZO

Il Teatro del Sale (350m);
Sennel (400m)

Stazione di Santa Maria Novella

Piazza Adua

Piazza della Stazione

Piazza di Santa Maria Novella

Piazza dell'Unità Italiana

Piazza Madonna degli Aldobrandini

Piazza San Lorenzo

Piazza del Mercato Centrale

Piazza di Santa Maria Maggiore

Piazza del Duomo

Piazza di Santa Maria Nuova

Piazza Brunelleschi

Piazza San Paolino

Piazza di San Paolino

Piazza San Pancrazio

Piazza della Spada

Via Gino Capponi
Via Laura
Via della Colonna
Via degli Alfani
Via della Pergola
Via Cesare Battisti
Via Ricasoli
Via Cavour
Via San Gallo
Via Santa Reparata
Via Guelfa
Via San Zanobi
Via Nazionale
Via Panicale
Via Faenza
Via Fiume
Via Valfonda
Via dei Panzani
Largo Fratelli Alinari
Via dell'Ariento
Via Sant'Antonino
Via Taddea
Via delle Stuta
Borgo la Noce
Via de' Ginori
Via de' Gori
Via dei Martelli
Via de' Pucci
Via Ricasoli
Via de' Biffi
Via dei Servi
Via del Castellaccio
Via dei Pucci
Borgo San Lorenzo
Via de' Cerretani
Via de' Rondinelli
Via de' Banchi
Via del Trebbio
Via de' Panzani
Via del Giglio
Via dell'Alloro
Via degli Avelli
Via della Scala
Via del Fossi
Via de' Fossi
Via del Moro
Via del Sole
Via della Spada
Via del Palazzuolo
Via Palazzuolo
Via degli Agli
Via degli Strozzi
Via del Campidoglio
Via de' Corsi
Via dei Pecori
Via de' Tornabuoni
Via del Proconsolo
Via dello Studio
Via delle Oche
Via del Corso
Via del Calzaiuoli
Via Roma
Via dei Pecori
Via dell'Oriuolo
Via Sant'Egidio
Via Bufalini
Borgo degli Albizi
Borgo Pinti
Via F Zanetti
Via Valfonda
Via dell'Olio
Via del Campidoglio

1
2
3
4
6
7
8
11
12
13
14
17
21
23
24
30
31
32

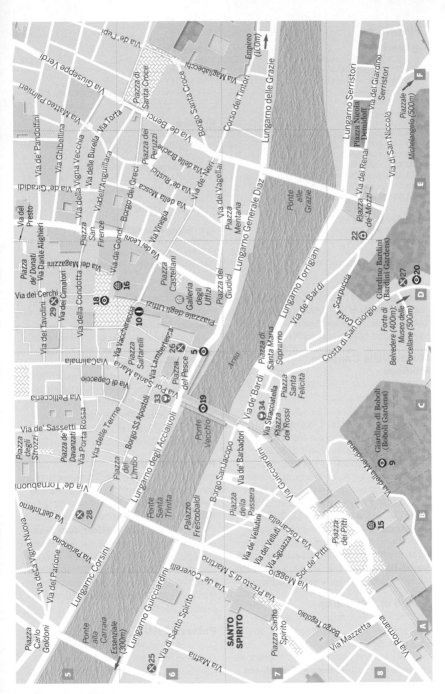

Florence

Jewish ghetto and slums, and the relocation of nearly 6000 residents. Vasari's lovely Loggia del Pesce (Fish Market) was saved and re-erected on Via Pietrapiana.

Museo delle Cappelle Medicee
Mausoleum

(Medici Chapels; ☑055 238 86 02; www.bargello musei.beniculturali.it/musei/2/medicee; Piazza Madonna degli Aldobrandini 6; adult/reduced €8/4; ⊗8.15am-2pm, closed 2nd & 4th Sun, 1st, 3rd & 5th Mon of month) Nowhere is Medici conceit expressed so explicitly as in the Medici Chapels. Adorned with granite, marble, semiprecious stones and some of Michelangelo's most beautiful sculptures, it is the burial place of 49 dynasty members. Francesco I lies in the dark, imposing **Cappella dei Principi** (Chapel of Princes) alongside Ferdinando I and II and Cosimo I, II and III. Lorenzo il Magnifico is buried in the graceful **Sagrestia Nuova** (New Sacristy), which was Michelangelo's first architectural work.

Museo di San Marco
Museum

(☑055 238 86 08; Piazza San Marco 3; adult/reduced €4/2; ⊗8.15am-1.50pm Mon-Fri, to 4.50pm Sat & Sun, closed 1st, 3rd & 5th Sun, 2nd & 4th Mon of month) At the heart of Florence's university area sits **Chiesa di San Marco** and an adjoining 15th-century Dominican monastery where both gifted painter Fra' Angelico (c 1395–1455) and the sharp-tongued Savonarola piously served God. Today the monastery, aka one of Florence's most spiritually uplifting museums, showcases the work of Fra' Angelico. After centuries of being known as 'Il Beato Angelico' (literally 'The Blessed Angelic One') or simply 'Il Beato' (The Blessed), the Renaissance's most blessed religious painter was made a saint by Pope John Paul II in 1984.

Ponte Vecchio
Bridge

Dating from 1345, iconic Ponte Vecchio was the only Florentine bridge to survive destruction at the hands of retreating German forces in 1944. Above jewellery shops on the eastern side, the **Corridoio Vasariano** (Vasari Corridor; guided visit by reservation Mar-Oct €45, Nov-Feb €20) is a 16th-century passageway between the Uffizi and Palazzo Pitti that runs around, rather than through, the medieval **Torre dei Mannelli** at the bridge's southern end.

Palazzo Pitti
Museum

(☑055 29 48 83; www.uffizi.it/en/pitti-palace; Piazza dei Pitti; adult/reduced Mar-Oct €16/8, Nov-Feb €10/5, combined ticket with Uffizi Mar-

Oct €38, Nov-Feb €18; ⊗8.15am-6.50pm Tue-Sun) Commissioned by banker Luca Pitta in 1458, this Renaissance palace was later bought by the Medici family. Over the centuries, it was a residence of the city's rulers until the Savoys donated it to the state in 1919. Nowadays it houses an impressive collection of silver and jewellery, a couple of art museums and a series of rooms re-creating life in the palace during House of Savoy times. Stop by at sunset when its entire facade is coloured a vibrant pink.

Giardino di Boboli   Gardens
(☑055 29 48 83; www.uffizi.it/en/boboli-garden; Piazza dei Pitti; adult/reduced incl Giardino Bardini & Museo delle Porcellane Mar-Oct €10/2, Nov-Feb €6/2; ⊗8.15am-6.50pm summer, reduced hours winter, closed 1st & last Mon of month) Behind Palazzo Pitti, the fountain- and sculpture-adorned Boboli Gardens – slowly but surely being restored to their former pristine glory thanks to a €2 million investment by Florence's homegrown fashion house Gucci – were laid out in the mid-16th century to a design by architect Niccolò Pericoli. At the upper, southern limit, beyond the box-hedged rose garden and **Museo delle Porcellane** (Porcelain Museum; ☑055 29 48 83; www.uffizi.it/giardino-boboli; Giardino di Boboli, Piazza dei Pitti; adult/reduced incl Giardino Bardini & Giardino di Boboli Mar-Oct €10/2, Nov-Feb €6/2; ⊗8.15am-6.50pm summer, reduced hours winter, closed 1st & last Mon of month), beautiful views over the Florentine countryside unfold.

Basilica di San Lorenzo   Basilica
(☑055 21 40 42; www.operamedicealaurenziana.org; Piazza San Lorenzo; €6, with Biblioteca Medicea Laurenziana €8.50; ⊗10am-5.30pm Mon-Sat) Considered one of Florence's most harmonious examples of Renaissance architecture, this unfinished basilica was the Medici parish church and mausoleum. It was designed by Brunelleschi in 1425 for Cosimo the Elder and built over a 4th-century church. In the solemn interior, look for Brunelleschi's austerely beautiful **Sagrestia Vecchia** (Old Sacristy) with its sculptural decoration by Donatello. Michelangelo was commissioned to design the facade in 1518, but his design in white

Carrara marble was never executed, hence the building's rough, unfinished appearance.

Basilica di Santa Maria Novella   Basilica
(☑055 21 92 57; www.smn.it; Piazza di Santa Maria Novella 18; adult/reduced €7.50/5; ⊗9am-7pm Mon-Thu, 11am-7pm Fri, 9am-6.30pm Sat, noon-6.30pm Sun Jul & Aug, shorter hours rest of year) The striking green-and-white marble facade of 13th- to 15th-century Basilica di Santa Maria Novella fronts an entire monastical complex, comprising romantic church cloisters and a frescoed chapel. The basilica itself is a treasure chest of artistic masterpieces, climaxing with frescoes by Domenico Ghirlandaio. The lower section of the basilica's striped marbled facade is transitional from Romanesque to Gothic; the upper section and the main doorway (1456–70) were designed by Leon Battista Alberti. Book in advance online to avoid queues.

Piazzale Michelangelo   Viewpoint
(☐13) Turn your back on the bevy of ticky-tacky souvenir stalls flogging *David* statues and boxer shorts and take in the spectacular city panorama from this vast square, pierced by one of Florence's two *David* copies. Sunset here is particularly dramatic. It's a 10-minute uphill walk along the serpentine road, paths and steps that scale the hillside from the Arno and Piazza Giuseppe Poggi; from Piazza San Niccolò walk uphill and bear left up the long flight of steps signposted Viale Michelangelo. Or take bus 13 from Stazione di Santa Maria Novella.

🅐 SHOPPING

Lorenzo Villoresi   Perfume
(☑055 234 11 87; www.lorenzovilloresi.it; Via de' Bardi 14; ⊗10am-7pm Mon-Sat) Artisan perfumes, bodycare products, scented candles and stones, essential oils and room fragrances crafted by Florentine perfumer Lorenzo Villoresi meld distinctively Tuscan elements such as laurel, olive, cypress and iris with essential oils and essences from around the world. His bespoke fragrances are highly sought after and visiting his

🍴 Florence's Best Panini

'Ino (☑055 21 45 14; www.inofirenze.com; Via dei Georgofili 3r-7r; panini €6-10; ☺noon-4.30pm) 🍴 Made-to-measure, gourmet panini by the Galleria degli Uffizi.

Semel (Piazza Ghiberti 44r; panini €3.50-5; ☺11.30am-2.30pm Mon-Sat) Irresistibly creative sandwiches to go in Sant'Ambrogio.

Mariano (☑055 21 40 67; Via del Parione 19r; panini €3.50-6; ☺8am-3pm & 5-7.30pm Mon-Fri, 8am-3pm Sat) Local neighbourhood cafe serving superfresh panini.

in the monastery garden. The shop, with an interior from 1848, sells fragrances, skincare products, ancient herbal remedies and preparations for everything from relief of heavy legs to improving skin elasticity, memory and mental energy.

Luisa Via Roma   Fashion & Accessories
(☑055 906 41 16; www.luisaviaroma.com; Via Roma 19-21r; ☺10.30am-7.30pm Mon-Sat, from 11am Sun) The flagship store of this historic boutique (think: small 1930s boutique selling straw hats) turned luxury online retailer is a must for the fashion-forward. Eye-catching window displays woo the digital generation with giant screens, while seasonal themes transform the interior maze of rooms into an exotic Garden of Eden, all sorts. Shop here for lesser-known designers as well as popular luxury fashion labels.

Pre- or post-shop, hob-nob with the city's fashionista set over fair-trade coffee, organic cuisine and creative cold-press juices in Luisa's chic 1st-floor cafe-bar **Floret** (☑055 29 59 24; www.floret-bar.com; salads & bowls €12-16; ☺10.30am-7.30pm Mon-Sat, from 11am Sun; 🛜) 🍴.

elegant boutique, at home in his family's 15th-century *palazzo,* is quite an experience.

Benheart   Fashion & Accessories
(www.benheart.it; Via dei Calzaivoli 78; ☺10am-7.30pm) This flagship store of local superstar Ben, a Florentine-based fashion designer who set up the business with schoolmate Matteo after undergoing a heart transplant, is irresistible. The pair swore that if Ben survived, they'd go it alone – which they did, with huge success. For real-McCoy handcrafted leather designs – casual shoes, jackets and belts for men and women – there is no finer address.

Officina Profumo-Farmaceutica di Santa Maria Novella   Gifts
(☑055 21 62 76; www.smnovella.it; Via della Scala 16; ☺9am-8pm) In business since 1612, this exquisite perfumery-pharmacy began life when Santa Maria Novella's Dominican friars began to concoct cures and sweet-smelling unguents using medicinal herbs cultivated

❌ EATING

Osteria Il Buongustai   Osteria €
(☑055 29 13 04; www.facebook.com/ibuongustai firenze; Via dei Cerchi 15r; meals €15-20; ☺9.30am-3.30pm Mon-Sat) Run with breathtaking speed and grace by Laura and Lucia, 'The Gourmand' is unmissable. Lunchtimes heave with locals and savvy students who flock here to fill up on tasty Tuscan home cooking at a snip of other restaurant prices. The place is brilliantly no-frills – watch women in hair caps at work in the kitchen, share a table and pay in cash.

Trattoria Mario   Tuscan €
(☑055 21 85 50; www.trattoria-mario.com; Via Rosina 2; meals €25; ☺noon-3.30pm Mon-Sat, closed 3 weeks Aug; ❄) Arrive by noon to ensure a spot at this noisy, busy, brilliant trattoria – a legend that retains its soul (and allure with locals) despite being in every guidebook. Charming Fabio, whose grand-

father opened the place in 1953, is front of house while big brother Romeo and nephew Francesco cook with speed in the kitchen. No advance reservations; cash only.

Pugi   Bakery €
(☏055 28 09 81; www.focacceria-pugi.it; Piazza San Marco 9b; per kilogram €15-25; ☺7.45am-8pm Mon-Sat, closed 2 weeks mid-Aug) The inevitable line outside the door says it all. This bakery is a Florentine favourite for pizza slices and chunks of *schiacciata* (Tuscan flatbread) baked up plain, spiked with salt and rosemary, or topped or stuffed with whatever delicious edible goodies are in season.

Il Teatro del Sale   Tuscan €€
(☏055 200 14 92; www.teatrodelsale.com; Via dei Macci 111r; brunch/dinner €20/30; ☺noon-2.30pm & 7-11pm Tue-Fri, noon-3pm & 7-11pm Sat, noon-3pm Sun, closed Aug) Florentine chef Fabio Picchi is one of Florence's living treasures. He steals the Sant' Ambrogio show with this eccentric, good-value, members-only club (everyone welcome, membership €7) inside an old theatre. He cooks up brunch and dinner, culminating

at 9.30pm in a live performance of drama, music or comedy arranged by his wife, artistic director and comic actress Maria Cassi.

Il Santo Bevitore   Tuscan €€
(☏055 21 12 64; www.ilsantobevitore.com; Via di Santo Spirito 64-66r; meals €40; ☺12.30-2.30pm & 7.30-11.30pm, closed Sun lunch & Aug) Reserve or arrive right at 7.30pm to snag the last table at this ever-popular address, an ode to stylish dining where gastronomes eat by candlelight in a vaulted, white-washed, bottle-lined interior. The menu is a creative reinvention of seasonal classics: pumpkin gnocchi with hazelnuts, coffee and green-veined blue di Capra (goats' cheese), *tagliatelle* with hare *ragù*, garlic cream and sweet Carmignano figs...

Essenziale   Tuscan €€€
(☏333 7491973 055 247 69 56; www.essenziale. me; Piazza di Cestello 3r; 6-/8-course tasting menu €65/80; ☺7-10pm Tue-Sat; ☎) There's no finer showcase for modern Tuscan cuisine than this loft-style restaurant in a 10th-century warehouse. Preparing dishes at the kitchen bar, in rolled-up shirt sleeves

Benheart

JOHN_SILVER / SHUTTERSTOCK ©

and navy butcher's apron, is dazzling young chef Simone Cipriani. Order one of his tasting menus to sample the full range of his inventive, thoroughly modern cuisine inspired by classic Tuscan dishes.

If you're lucky, it will be the chef himself who brings the dish to your table and treats you to a detailed explanation: don't miss the tale behind his remarkable Fior d'Evo dessert, notably with kale (another of his desserts includes artichokes). Reservations essential.

La Leggenda dei Frati   Tuscan €€€

(📞055 068 05 45; www.laleggendadeifrati.it; Villa Bardini, Costa di San Giorgio 6a; menus €105 & €130, meals €90; ⏱12.30-2pm & 7.30-10pm Tue-Sun; 🛜) Summertime's hottest address. At home in the grounds of historic **Villa Bardini** (📞055 2006 6233; www.villabardini.it; Costa San Giorgio 2, Via de' Bardi 1r; adult/reduced villa €10/5, gardens €6/3, gardens with Giardino di Boboli ticket free; ⏱villa 10am-7pm Tue-Sun, gardens 8.15am-7.30pm summer, shorter hours winter, closed 1st & last Mon of month), Michelin-starred Legend of Friars enjoys the most romantic terrace with a view in Florence. Veggies are plucked fresh from the vegetable patch,

tucked between waterfalls and ornamental beds in Giardino Bardini, and contemporary art jazzes up the classically chic interior. Cuisine is Tuscan, gastronomic and well worth the vital advance reservation.

🍷 DRINKING & NIGHTLIFE

Le Volpi e l'Uva   Wine Bar

(📞055 239 81 32; www.levolpieluva.com; Piazza dei Rossi 1; ⏱11am-9pm summer, 11am-9pm Mon-Sat winter) This humble wine bar remains as appealing as the day it opened in 1992. Its food and wine pairings are first class – taste and buy boutique wines by small Italian producers, matched perfectly with cheeses, cold meats and the finest crostini in town; the warm, melt-in-your-mouth *lardo di Cinta Sienese* (wafer-thin slices of aromatic of pork fat) is absolutely extraordinary.

La Terrazza Lounge Bar   Bar

(📞055 2726 5987, 342 1234710; www.lungarnocollection.com; Vicolo dell'Oro 6r; ⏱3.30-10.30pm Apr-Sep) This rooftop bar with a wood-decked terrace accessible from the 5th floor of the Hotel Continen-

tale is as chic as one would expect of a fashion-house hotel. Its *aperitivo* buffet is a modest affair (simple nuts and juicy olives), but who cares with that gorgeous panorama of Florence. Dress the part, or feel out of place. Count around €20 for a cocktail.

Empireo
Rooftop Bar

(☑055 262 35 00; www.hotelplazalucchesi.it; Lungarno della Zecca Vecchia 38; ⊗7.30am-midnight; 🛜) Many a Florentine's favourite cocktail bar, Empireo – located inside the historic Plaza Hotel Lucchesi – has been seducing cocktail lovers since 1860. Expertly mixed cocktails are de rigueur and the fashionable ground-floor bar frequently hosts cocktail masterclasses, live music etc. In summer, the drinking action moves to the rooftop – overlooking the rooftop pool.

🛈 INFORMATION

Tourist Office (☑055 21 22 45; www.firenze turismo.it; Piazza della Stazione 4; ⊗9am-7pm Mon-Sat, to 2pm Sun) Florence's main tourist office, handily located across from the Santa Maria Novella train station, sells the Firenze Card, has accommodation lists and helps with bookings for organised tours.

Other options include:

Airport Tourist Office (☑055 31 58 74; www. firenzeturismo.it; Via del Termine 11, Florence Airport; ⊗9am-7pm Mon-Sat, to 2pm Sun)

Infopoint Bigallo (☑055 28 84 96; www.firenze turismo.it; Piazza San Giovanni 1; ⊗9am-7pm Mon-Sat, to 2pm Sun)

🛈 GETTING THERE & AWAY

Most people arrive one of two ways: by air from international airports in Florence and Pisa, or by train to Stazione Campo di Marte or **Stazione di Santa Maria Novella** (www.firenzesantamaria novella.it; Piazza della Stazione), both in central Florence. Florence is on the Rome–Milan high-speed train line.

🛈 GETTING AROUND

Florence itself is small and best navigated on foot; most major sights are within easy walking distance.

> ★ **Top Five Florence Panoramas**
>
> Cupola del Brunelleschi (p402)
> Piazzale Michelangelo (p417)
> Campanile (p403)
> Palazzo Vecchio (p413)
> Ospedale degli Innocenti (p405)

From left: View of the Duomo (p400); Palazzo Vecchio (p413); Duomo's campanile (p403)

Bicycle Rent city bikes from in front of Stazione di Santa Maria Novella and elsewhere in the city.

Car & Motorcycle Nonresident traffic is banned from the historic centre; parking is an absolute headache and best avoided.

Public Transport There's an efficient network of buses and trams, most handy for visiting Fiesole and getting up the hill to Piazzale Michelangelo.

Taxi Cabs can't be hailed on the street; find ranks at the train and bus stations or call 055 42 42 or 055 43 90.

Siena

Siena is one of Italy's most enchanting medieval towns. Its walled centre is a beautifully preserved warren of dark lanes punctuated with Gothic *palazzi*, and at its heart, Piazza del Campo, the sloping square that is the venue for the city's famous annual horse race, Il Palio.

SIGHTS

Piazza del Campo Piazza

Popularly known as 'Il Campo', this sloping piazza has been Siena's social centre since being staked out by the ruling Consiglio dei Nove (Council of Nine) in the mid-12th century. Built on the site of a Roman marketplace, its paving is divided into nine sectors representing the number of members of the *consiglio* and these days acts as a carpet on which young locals meet and relax. The cafes around its perimeter are the most popular coffee and *aperitivi* spots in town.

Palazzo Pubblico Historic Building

(Palazzo Comunale; Piazza del Campo) Built to demonstrate the enormous wealth, proud independence and secular nature of Siena, this 14th-century Gothic masterpiece is the visual focal point of the Campo, itself the true heart of the city. Architecturally clever (notice how its concave facade mirrors the opposing convex curve), it has always housed the city's administration and been used as a cultural venue. Its distinctive bell tower, the **Torre del Mangia** (0577 29 26 15; ticket@comune.siena.it; adult/family €10/25; 10am-6.15pm Mar–mid-Oct, to 3.15pm mid-Oct–Feb), provides magnificent views to those who brave the steep climb to the top.

Museo Civico Museum

(Civic Museum; 0577 29 26 15; Palazzo Pubblico, Piazza del Campo 1; adult/reduced €10/9, with Torre del Mangia €15, with Torre del Mangia & Complesso Museale di Santa Maria della Scala €20; 10am-6.15pm mid-Mar–Oct, to 5.15pm Nov–mid-Mar) Entered via the Palazzo Pubblico's **Cortile del Podestà** (Courtyard of the Podestà), this wonderful museum showcases rooms richly frescoed by artists of the Sienese school. Commissioned by the city's governing body rather than by the Church, some of the frescoes depict secular subjects – highly unusual at the time. The highlights are two huge frescoes: Ambrogio Lorenzetti's *Allegories of Good and Bad Government* (c 1338–40) and Simone Martini's celebrated *Maestà* (*Virgin Mary in Majesty*; 1315).

Duomo Cathedral

(Cattedrale di Santa Maria Assunta; 0577 28 63 00; www.operaduomo.siena.it; Piazza Duomo; Mar-Oct/Nov-Feb €5/free, when floor displayed €8; 10.30am-6.30pm Mon-Sat & 1.30-5.30pm Sun Mar-Oct, 10.30am-5pm Mon-Sat & 1.30-5pm Sun Nov-Feb) Consecrated on the former site of a Roman temple in 1179 and constructed over the 13th and 14th centuries, Siena's majestic *duomo* (cathedral) showcases the talents of many great medieval and Renaissance architects and artists: Giovanni Pisano designed the intricate white, green and red marble facade; Nicola Pisano carved the elaborate pulpit; Pinturicchio painted the frescoes in the extraordinary **Libreria Piccolomini** (Piccolomini Library; 0577 28 63 00; www.operaduomo.siena.it; Piazza Duomo; €2; 10.30am-6.30pm Mon-Sat & 1.30-5.30pm Sun Mar-Oct, 10.30am-5pm Mon-Sat & 1.30-5pm Sun Nov-Feb); and Michelangelo, Donatello and Gian Lorenzo Bernini all produced sculptures.

Complesso Museale di Santa Maria della Scala Museum

(0577 28 63 00; www.santamariadellascala.com; Piazza Duomo 2; adult/reduced €9/7; 10am-7pm Fri-Wed, to 10pm Thu mid-Mar–mid-Oct, 10am-5pm Mon, Wed & Fri, to 8pm

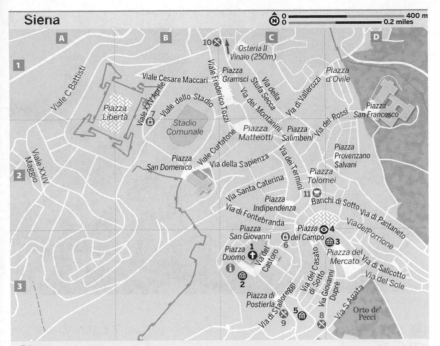

Siena

Thu, to 7pm Sat & Sun) Built as a hospice for pilgrims travelling the Via Francigena, this huge complex opposite the Duomo dates from the 13th century. Its highlight is the upstairs **Pellegrinaio** (Pilgrim's Hall), featuring vivid 15th-century frescoes by Lorenzo di Pietro (aka Vecchietta), Priamo della Quercia and Domenico di Bartolo. All laud the good works of the hospital and its patrons; the most evocative is di Bartolo's *Il governo degli infermi* (Caring for the Sick; 1440–41), which depicts many activities that occurred here.

Pinacoteca Nazionale   Gallery

(📞 0577 28 11 61; http://pinacotecanazionale. siena.it; Via San Pietro 29) Closed for a long-overdue renovation since December 2018, 4th-century **Palazzo Buonsignori** is home to an extraordinary collection of Gothic masterpieces from the Sienese school. These include works by Guido da Siena, Duccio (di Buoninsegna), Simone Martini, Niccolò di Segna, Lippo Memmi, Ambrogio and Pietro Lorenzetti, Bartolo di Fredi, Taddeo di Bartolo and Sano di Pietro. The museum's re-opening date is yet to be announced.

GIORGIO ROSSI / SHUTTERSTOCK ©

Cantuccini (almond biscuits)

🅰 SHOPPING

Il Magnifico   Food

(☎0577 28 11 06; www.ilmagnifico.siena.it; Via
dei Pellegrini 27; ⊙7.30am-7.30pm Mon-Sat)
Lorenzo Rossi is Siena's best baker, and
his *panforte* (spiced fruit-and-nut cake),
ricciarelli (sugar-dusted chewy almond
biscuits) and *cavallucci* (chewy biscuits flavoured with aniseed and other spices) are a
weekly purchase for most local households.
Try them at his bakery-shop behind the
Duomo, and you'll understand why.

Wednesday Market   Market

(⊙7.30am-2pm) FREE Spreading around
Fortezza Medicea and towards the Stadio
Comunale, this is one of Tuscany's largest
markets and is great for cheap clothing;
food is also sold.

🍴 EATING & DRINKING

La Vecchia Latteria   Gelato €

(☎0577 05 76 38; www.facebook.com/Gelateria
YogurteriaLaVecchiaLatteria/; Via San Pietro 10;
gelato €2-4.50; ⊙noon-11pm, to 8pm winter)

Sauntering through Siena's historic centre
is always more fun with a gelato in hand.
Just ask one of the many locals who
are regular customers at this *gelateria
artigianale* (maker of handmade gelato)
near the Pinacoteca Nazionale. Using quality produce, owners Fabio and Francesco
concoct and serve fruity-fresh or deca-
dently creamy iced treats – choose from
gelato or frozen yoghurt.

Osteria Il Vinaio   Tuscan €

(☎0577 4 96 15; Via Camollia 167; dishes €6.50-
13; ⊙10am-10pm Mon-Sat) Wine bars are thin
on the ground here in Siena, so it's not
surprising that Bobbe and Davide's neighbourhood *osteria* is so popular. Join the
multigenerational local regulars for a bowl
of pasta or your choice from the generous
antipasto display, washed down with a glass
or two of eminently quaffable house wine.

Ristorante Enzo   Tuscan €€€

(☎0577 28 12 77; www.daenzo.net; Via Camollia
49; meals €52; ⊙noon-2.30pm & 7.30-10pm Tue-
Sun) The epitome of refined Sienese dining,
Da Enzo, as it is popularly called, welcomes

guests with a complimentary glass of *prosecco* and follows up with Tuscan dishes made with skill and care. There's plenty of fish on the menu, as well as excellent handmade pasta and nonstandard meat dishes. The setting is equally impressive, with quality napery and glassware.

Osteria La Taverna di San Giuseppe
Tuscan €€€

(0577 4 22 86; www.tavernasangiuseppe.it; Via Dupré 132; meals €49; noon-2.30pm & 7-10pm Mon-Sat) Any restaurant specialising in beef, truffles and porcini mushrooms attracts our immediate attention, but not all deliver on their promise. Fortunately, this one does. A favoured venue for locals celebrating important occasions, it offers excellent food, an impressive wine list with plenty of local, regional and international choices, a convivial traditional atmosphere and efficient service.

Bar Pasticceria Nannini
Cafe

(0577 23 60 09; www.pasticcerienannini.it/en; Via Banchi di Sopra 24; 7.30am-10pm Mon-Thu, to 11pm Fri & Sat, to 10pm Sun) Established in 1886, Nannini's good coffee and location near the Campo ensure that it remains a local favourite. It's a great place to sample Sienese treats including *cantuccini* (crunchy, almond-studded biscuits), *cavallucci* (chewy biscuits flavoured with aniseed and other spices), *ricciarelli* (chewy, sugar-dusted almond biscuits), *panforte* (dense spiced cake with almonds and candied fruit) and *panpepato* (*panforte* with the addition of pepper and hazelnuts).

ⓘ INFORMATION

Tourist Office (0577 28 05 51; www.terresiena. it; Piazza Duomo 2, Santa Maria della Scala; 10am-6pm mid-Mar–Oct, to 4.30pm Nov–mid-Mar)

ⓘ GETTING THERE & AWAY

Bus service **Siena Mobilità** (800 922984; www. sienamobilita.it) links Siena with Florence (€7.80, 2¾ hours, at least hourly) and San Gimignano (€6, 2¾ hours, 10 daily Monday to Saturday). There's regular train service to Florence.

✶ Celebrating Il Palio

Dating from the Middle Ages, Il Palio is a spectacular annual event in July and August that includes a series of colourful pageants and a wild horse race in Piazza del Campo. Ten of Siena's 17 *contrade* (town districts) compete for the coveted *palio* (silk banner). Each *contrada* has its own traditions, symbol and colours, plus its own church and *palio* museum.

Festivities preceding Il Palio
LONGJON / SHUTTERSTOCK ©

Arezzo

Arezzo may not be a Tuscan centrefold, but those parts of its historic centre that survived merciless WWII bombings are as compelling as any destination in the region – the city's central square is as beautiful as it appears in Roberto Benigni's classic film *La vita è bella* (Life is Beautiful).

Today, the city is known for its churches, museums and fabulously sloping Piazza Grande, across which a huge antiques fair spills during the first weekend of each month. Come dusk, Arentini (locals of Arezzo) spill along the length of shop-clad Corso Italia for the ritual *passeggiata* (evening stroll).

◎ SIGHTS

Cappella Bacci
Church

(0575 35 27 27; www.pierodellafrancesca. it; Piazza San Francesco; adult/reduced €8/5; 9am-6pm Mon-Fri, to 5.30pm Sat, 1-5.30pm Sun, extended hours summer) This chapel, in the apse of 14th-century **Basilica di San**

Arezzo Money Saver

A combined ticket (adult/reduced €12/8) covers admission to Cappella Bacci (p425), Museo Archeologico Nazionale and **Museo di Casa Vasari** (Vasari House Museum; ☑0575 29 90 71; www.museistataliarezzo.it/museo-casa-vasari; Via XX Settembre 55; adult/reduced €4/2; ⊗8.30am-7.30pm Mon & Wed-Sat, to 1.30pm Sun). It's valid for two days and can be purchased at each museum.

Museo di Casa Vasari
V. ARCOMANO / ALAMY STOCK PHOTO ©

Francesco, safeguards one of Italian art's greatest works: Piero della Francesca's fresco cycle of the *Legend of the True Cross*. Painted between 1452 and 1466, it relates the story of the cross on which Christ was crucified. Only 30 people are allowed in every half hour, making advance booking (by telephone or email) essential in high season. The ticket office is down the stairs by the basilica's entrance.

Chiesa di Santa Maria della Pieve   Church
(Corso Italia 7; ⊗8am-12.30pm & 3-6.30pm) FREE This 12th-century church – Arezzo's oldest – has an exotic Romanesque arcaded facade adorned with carved columns, each uniquely decorated. Above the central doorway are 13th-century carved reliefs called *Cyclo dei Mesi* representing each month of the year. The plain interior's highlight – being restored at the **RICERCA Restoration Studio** (☑0575 2 86 70, 333 2851179; www.ricercarestauro.wordpress.com; Via G Mazzini 1; by donation; ⊗by appointment)

at the time of writing – is Pietro Lorenzetti's polyptych *Madonna and Saints* (1320–24). Below the altar is a 14th-century silver bust reliquary of the city's patron saint, San Donato.

Duomo di Arezzo   Cathedral
(Cattedrale di SS Donato e Pietro; Piazza del Duomo; ⊗7am-12.30pm & 3-6.30pm) FREE Construction of Arezzo's cathedral started in the 13th century but wasn't completed until 1511. In the northeast corner, next to the vestry door left of the intricately carved main altar, is Piero della Francesca's fresco of *Mary Magdalene* (c 1459). Also notable are five glazed terracottas by Andrea della Robbia and his studio in the **Cappella della Madonna del Conforto**.

Museo Archeologico Nazionale 'Gaio Cilnio Mecenate'   Museum
(Gaius Cilnius Maecenas Archeological Museum; ☑0575 2 08 82; www.facebook.com/archeologicoarezzo; Via Margaritone 10; adult/reduced €6/3; ⊗8.30am-7.30pm Mon-Sat) Overlooking the remains of a Roman amphitheatre that once seated up to 10,000 spectators, this museum – named after Gaius Maecenas (68–8 BC), a patron of the arts and trusted advisor to Roman Emperor Augustus – exhibits Etruscan and Roman artefacts in a 14th-century convent building. The highlight is the *Cratere di Euphronios*, a 6th-century-BC Etruscan vase decorated with vivid scenes showing Hercules in battle.

Also of note is an exquisite tiny portrait of a bearded man from the second half of the 3rd century AD that was executed in chrysography, a method in which a fine sheet of gold is engraved then encased between two glass panes.

The museum is open on occasional Sundays; call ahead to confirm dates and times.

🍴 EATING & DRINKING
Cremì   Gelato €
(www.facebook.com/gelateriaartigianalecremi; Corso Italia 100; cones & tubs €2-5; ⊗9am-8pm

Aerial view of Arezzo's Piazza Grande

Tue-Fri & Sun, to midnight Sun) Follow the locals to this bright, modern *gelateria artigianale* (artisan gelato shop) on Arezzo's main *passeggiata* (late afternoon–strolling) strip. Enticing seasonal flavours include pear and vanilla, strawberry cheesecake, peanut, and walnut and fig. Or opt for the luscious and wildly popular house speciality – *mousse di nutella* (a creamy, light-as-air chocolate- and hazelnut-flavoured mousse-like ice cream).

Crepes to take away too.

Antica Osterla Agania   Tuscan €

(☑0575 29 53 81; www.agania.com; Via G Mazzini 10; meals €20; ⊙noon-3pm & 6-10.30pm Tue-Sun) Operated by the Ludovichi family since 1905, Agania serves the type of die-hard traditional fare that remains the cornerstone of Tuscan dining. Specialities include sensational antipasti (with lots of vegetarian options), rustic soups, home-made pasta and *secondi* ranging from *lumache* (snails) to *grifi* (lambs' cheeks) with polenta, baccalà with chickpeas, and sausages with beans.

> *the city is known for its fabulously sloping Piazza Grande*

Caffè Vasari   Cafe

(☑0575 04 36 97; Piazza Grande 15; ⊙7.30am-9pm summer, 8.30am-6pm winter) Bathed in Tuscan sunrays from dawn to dusk, this cafe is the perfect spot for lapping up the ancient elegance and beauty of **Piazza Grande** over a coffee or *aperitivo*. Find it enviably squirrelled beneath the cinematic porticoes of **Palazzo delle Logge Vasariane**.

ℹ️ INFORMATION

Tourist Office (☑0575 40 33 19; www.centro guidearezzo.it)

ℹ️ GETTING THERE & AWAY

Arezzo is on the Florence–Rome train line. Service is frequent.

Montepulciano

Exploring this reclaimed narrow ridge of volcanic rock will push your quadriceps to failure point. When this happens, self-medicate with a generous pour of the highly reputed Vino Nobile while drinking in the spectacular views over the Val di Chiana and Val d'Orcia.

◎ SIGHTS

Il Corso   Street

Montepulciano's main street – called in stages Via di Gracciano, Via di Voltaia, Via dell'Opio and Via Poliziano – climbs up the eastern ridge of the town from Porta al Prato and loops to meet Via di Collazzi on the western ridge. To reach the centre of town (Piazza Grande) take a dog-leg turn into Via del Teatro.

In Piazza Savonarola, up from the Porta al Prato, is the **Colonna del Marzocca** (Piazza Savonarola), erected in 1511 to confirm Montepulciano's allegiance to Florence. The late-Renaissance **Palazzo Avignonesi** (Via di Gracciano nel Corso 91) is at No 91; other nota-

ble buildings include the **Palazzo di Bucelli** (Via di Gracciano nel Corso 73) at No 73 (look for the recycled Etruscan and Latin inscriptions and reliefs on the lower facade), and **Palazzo Cocconi** (Via di Gracciano nel Corso 70) at No 70.

Continuing uphill, you'll find Michelozzo's **Chiesa di Sant'Agostino** (Piazza Michelozzo; ☺9am-noon & 3-6pm), with its lunette above the entrance holding a terracotta Madonna and Child, John the Baptist and St Augustine. Opposite, the **Torre di Pulcinella** (Piazza Michelozzo), a medieval tower house, is topped by the town clock and the hunched figure of Pulcinella (Punch, of Punch and Judy fame), which strikes the hours. After passing historic **Caffè Poliziano** (☑0578 75 86 15; www.caffepoliziano.it; Via di Voltaia 27; ☺7am-9pm Mon-Fri, to 10.30pm Sat, to 9pm Sun; 🛜), the Corso continues straight ahead and Via del Teatro veers off to the right.

Museo Civico & Pinacoteca Crociani   Art Gallery, Museum

(☑0578 71 73 00; www.museocivicomonte pulciano.it; Via Ricci 10; adult/reduced €6/4; ☺10am-6.30pm Wed-Mon Apr-Oct, 10am-

Montepulciano's main square

KJSCHOEN / GETTY IMAGES ©

6pm Sat & Sun Nov-Mar) It was a curatorial dream come true: in 2011 a painting in the collection of this modest art gallery was attributed to Caravaggio. The work, *Portrait of a Man,* is thought to portray Cardinal Scipione Borghese, the artist's patron. It's now accompanied by a touch-screen interpretation that allows you to explore details of the painting, its restoration and diagnostic attribution. Other works here include two terracottas by Andrea Della Robbia, and Domenico Beccafumi's painting of the town's patron saint, Agnese.

Palazzo Comunale   Palace

(Piazza Grande; terrace & tower adult/reduced €5/2.50, terrace only €2.50; ⊙10am-6pm Apr-Christmas) Built in the 14th century in Gothic style and remodelled in the 15th century by Michelozzo, the Palazzo Comunale still functions as Montepulciano's town hall. Head up the 67 narrow stairs to the tower to enjoy extraordinary views – you'll see as far as Pienza, Montalcino and even, on a clear day, Siena.

⊗ EATING & DRINKING

Osteria Acquacheta   Tuscan €

(⌨0578 71 70 86; www.acquacheta.eu; Via del Teatro 22; meals €24; ⊙12.30-3pm & 7.30-10.30pm Wed-Mon mid-Apr–Dec) Hugely popular with locals and tourists alike, this bustling *osteria* specialises in *bistecca alla fiorentina* (chargrilled T-bone steak), which comes to the shared tables in huge, lightly seared and exceptionally flavoursome slabs (don't even *think* of asking for it to be served otherwise). Phone to book ahead.

E Lucevan Le Stelle   Wine Bar

(⌨0578 75 87 25; www.locandasanfrancesco.it; Piazza San Francesco 3; ⊙10am-midnight Easter-

Oct, 10am-11pm Sat & Sun Nov-Easter, closed 2 weeks Nov & 2 weeks Jan; 🛜) The decked terrace of this ultrafriendly *osteria* is the top spot in Montepulciano to watch the sun go down. Inside, squishy sofas, modern art and jazz on the sound system give the place a chilled-out vibe. Snacks include piandine (filled flat breads; €8), pastas (€9) and antipasto boards (€10-28).

ⓘ INFORMATION

Tourist Office (⌨0578 75 73 41; www. prolocomontepulciano.it; Piazza Don Minzoni 1; ⊙9.30am-1pm & 3-7pm Apr-Sep. 9.30am-1pm & 3-6pm Mon-Sat Oct-Mar; 🛜)

ⓘ GETTING THERE & AWAY

If driving from Florence, take the Valdichiana exit off the A1 (direction Bettolle-Sinalunga) and then follow the signs. From Siena, take the Siena–Bettolle–Perugia *superstrada*.

Siena Mobilità runs four buses daily between Siena and Montepulciano (€6.60, one hour) stopping at Pienza (€2.50) en route. There are three services per day to/from Florence (€11.20, 1½ hours).

BERLIN, GERMANY

Berlin, Germany

Berlin's combo of glamour and grit is bound to mesmerise anyone keen to explore its vibrant culture, cutting-edge architecture, fabulous food, intense parties and tangible history.

It's a city that staged a revolution, was headquartered by Nazis, bombed to bits, divided in two and finally reunited – and that was just in the 20th century! Berlin is a big multicultural metropolis, but deep down it maintains the unpretentious charm of an international village.

Two Days in Berlin

Start your first day at the **Reichstag** (p438), then stroll over to the iconic **Brandenburger Tor** (p444). Next, head west along Strasse des 17 Juli, passing the Soviet War memorial before you reach the **Siegessäule** (p450). Take the steps to the top to view the beautiful **Tiergarten** (p450), before getting lost in the park itself. Dedicate your second day to exploring the museums and galleries at **Museumsinsel** (p448).

Four Days in Berlin

Start your third day at the vast **Holocaust Memorial** (p444). Stroll through nearby **Potsdamer Platz** (p449) and then on to **Checkpoint Charlie** (p445). Use day four to visit the **Gedenkstätte Berliner Mauer** (p435) before heading to the **East Side Gallery** (p435), the longest surviving piece of the Wall. Do a day trip to **Schloss Neuschwanstein** (p462) before you move on.

Next stop: beautiful Prague (p535).

The map shows Berlin with labels including:

Tegel Airport, PRENZLAUER BERG, Volkspark Humboldthain, Mauerpark, Gedenkstätte Berliner Mauer, Fritz Schloss Park, Volkspark Friedrichshain, SCHEUNENVIERTEL, Schloss Charlottenburg, Hauptbahnhof, Museumsinsel, Karl-Marx-Allee, FRIEDRICHSHAIN, CHARLOTTEN-BURG, Siegessäule, Zentraler Omnibusbahnhof, Zoologischer Garten, Tiergarten, **Reichstag**, Ostbahnhof, Stasimuseum, Zoologischer Garten, POTSDAMER PLATZ, Checkpoint Charlie, Spree River, RAW Gelände, KREUZBERG, East Side Gallery, Story of Berlin, Deutsches Technikmuseum, Jüdisches Museum, Görlitzer Park, Treptower Park, WILMERSDORF, SCHÖNEBERG, NEUKÖLLN, Viktoriapark, Volkspark Hasenheide, Sowjetisches Ehrenmal Treptow, Former Tempelhof Airport, Schönefeld (12km), DAHLEM, TEMPELHOF

5 km
2.5 miles

Mitte Map (p446)
Kreuzberg & Potsdamer Platz (p450)
Charlottenburg Map (p452)

Arriving in Berlin

Tegel & Schönefeld Airports Handle domestic and international flights. Tegel is served directly only by bus and taxi. From Schönefeld, take the S-Bahn or a regional train to the city centre.

Hauptbahnhof Main train station in the city centre; served by S-Bahn, U-Bahn, tram, bus and taxi.

Zentraler Omnibus Bahnhof (ZOB) Point of arrival for most long-haul buses.

Where to Stay

Berlin has over 137,000 hotel rooms, but the most desirable properties book up quickly, especially in summer and around major holidays; prices soar and reservations are essential. Otherwise, rates are low by Western capital standards. Options range from chain hotels and Old Berlin–style B&Bs to happening hostels, handy self-catering apartments and trendy boutique hotels.

For information on what each Berlin neighbourhood has to offer, see the table on p461.

ALEXA CATALIN / SHUTTERSTOCK ©

The Berlin Wall

For 28 years the Berlin Wall was the most potent symbol of the Cold War. Surprisingly very few of its reinforced concrete slabs remain in today's reunited Berlin.

Construction

Shortly after midnight on 13 August 1961 East German soldiers and police began rolling out miles of barbed wire that would soon be replaced with prefab concrete slabs. The wall was a desperate measure taken by the German Democratic Republic (GDR) government to stop the sustained brain and brawn drain it had experienced since its 1949 founding. Around 3.6 million people had already left for the West, putting the GDR on the verge of economic and political collapse.

Demise

The Wall's demise in 1989 came as unexpectedly as its construction. Once again the GDR was losing its people in droves, this time via Hungary, which had opened its borders with Austria. Something had to give. It did on 9 November 1989 when a GDR

Great For...

☑ **Don't Miss**

The open-air mural collection of the East Side Gallery.

East Side Gallery

Hussitenstr
Bernauer Str

**Gedenkstätte
Berliner Mauer**

S Nordbahnhof

❶ Need to Know

A double row of cobblestones guides you along 5.7km of the Wall's course. Track down remaining fragments of the Wall using Memorial Landscape Berlin Wall (www.berlin-wall-map.com).

✕ Take a Break

Not far from the Gedenkstätte Berliner Mauer is the famous sausage kitchen **Konnopke's Imbiss** (☎030-442 7765; www.konnopke-imbiss.de; Schönhauser Allee 44a; sausages €1.60-2.90; ☉10am-8pm Mon-Fri, 11.30am-8pm Sat; ⓜM1, M10, M13, ⓤEberswalder Strasse).

★ Top Tip

There's a great view from the Documentation Centre's viewing platform.

spokesperson (mistakenly, it later turned out) announced during a press conference that all travel restrictions to the West would be lifted. When asked when, he said simply 'Immediately'. Amid scenes of wild partying, the two Berlins came together again.

During 1990 the Wall almost disappeared from Berlin, some bits smashed up and flogged to tourists, others carted off to museums, parks, embassies, exhibitions and even private gardens across the globe. The longest section still intact is the East Side Gallery.

Gedenkstätte Berliner Mauer

The outdoor **Berlin Wall Memorial** (Berlin Wall Memorial; ☎030-467 986 666; www.berliner-mauer-gedenkstaette.de; Bernauer Strasse btwn Schwedter Strasse & Gartenstrasse; ☉visitor & documentation centre 10am-6pm Tue-Sun, open-air exhibit 8am-10pm daily; ⓢNordbahnhof,

Bernauer Strasse, Eberswalder Strasse) **FREE** extends for 1.4km along Bernauer Strasse and integrates an original section of Wall, vestiges of the border installations and escape tunnels, a chapel and a monument. Multimedia stations, panels, excavations and a Documentation Centre provide context and explain what the border fortifications looked like and how they shaped the everyday lives of people on both sides of it.

East Side Gallery

When the Wall finally met its maker, most of it was quickly dismantled, but a 1.3km stretch became the **East Side Gallery** (www.eastsidegallery-berlin.de; Mühlenstrasse btwn Oberbaumbrücke & Ostbahnhof; ☉24hr; ⓤWarschauer Strasse, ⓢOstbahnhof, Warschauer Strasse) **FREE**, the world's largest open-air mural collection. More than 100 paintings portray the era's global euphoria and optimism.

The Berlin Wall

The construction of the Berlin Wall was a unique event in human history, not only for physically bisecting a city but for becoming a dividing line between competing ideologies and political systems. It's this global impact and universal legacy that continues to fascinate people decades after its triumphant tear-down. Fortunately, some of original Wall segments and other vestiges remain, along with museums and memorials, to help fathom the realities and challenges of daily life in Berlin during the Cold War.

Our illustration points out the top highlights you can visit to learn about different aspects of these often tense decades. The best place to start is the ❶ **Gedenkstätte Berliner Mauer**, for an excellent introduction to what the inner-city border looked liked and what it meant to live in its shadow. Reflect upon what you've learned while relaxing along the former death strip, now the ❷ **Mauerpark**, before heading to the emotionally charged exhibit at the ❸ **Tränenpalast**, an actual border-crossing pavilion. Relive the euphoria of the

Brandenburger Tor
People around the world cheered as East and West Berliners partied together atop the Berlin Wall in front of the iconic city gate, which today is a photogenic symbol of united Germany.

Potsdamer Platz
Nowhere was the death strip as wide as on the former no man's land around Potsdamer Platz, from which sprouted a new postmodern city quarter in the 1990s. A tiny section of the Berlin Wall serves as a reminder.

Checkpoint Charlie
Only diplomats and foreigners were allowed to use this border crossing. Weeks after the Wall was built, US and Soviet tanks faced off here in one of the hottest moments of the Cold War.

Tränenpalast
This modernist 1962 glass-and-steel border pavilion was dubbed 'Palace of Tears' because of the many tearful farewells that took place outside the building as East Germans and their Western visitors had to say goodbye.

Bernauer Strasse

Chausseestr

Unter den Linden

Leipziger Str

Wall's demise at the **④ Brandenburger Tor**, then marvel at the revival of **⑤ Potsdamer Platz**, which was nothing but death-strip wasteland until the 1990s. The Wall's geopolitical significance is the focus at **⑥ Checkpoint Charlie**, which saw some of the tensest moments of the Cold War. Wrap up by finding your favourite mural motif at the **⑦ East Side Gallery**.

It's possible to explore these sights by using a combination of walking and public transport, but a bike ride is the best method for gaining a sense of the former Wall's erratic flow through the central city.

FAST FACTS

Beginning of construction 13 August 1961

Fall of the Wall 9 November 1989

Total length 155km

Height 3.6m

Weight of each segment 2.6 tonnes

Number of watchtowers 300

② ···

Remnants of the Wall →

Mauerpark
Famous for its flea market and karaoke, this popular park actually occupies a converted section of the death strip. A 30m segment of surviving Wall is now an official practice ground for budding graffiti artists.

Gedenkstätte Berliner Mauer
Germany's central memorial to the Berlin Wall and its victims exposes the complexity and barbaric nature of the border installation, along a 1.4km stretch of the barrier's course.

Alexanderplatz

Alexanderstr

East Side Gallery
Paralleling the Spree for 1.3km, this is the longest Wall vestige. After its collapse, more than a hundred international artists expressed their feelings about this historic moment in a series of colourful murals.

⑦

HOLGS / GETTY IMAGES ©

The Reichstag

Reinstated as the home of the German parliament in 1999, the late 19th-century Reichstag is one of Berlin's most iconic buildings.

Great For...

☑ **Don't Miss**

Free auto-activated audioguides provide info on the building, landmarks and the workings of parliament.

The Reichstag's Beginnings

It's been burned, bombed, rebuilt, buttressed by the Wall, wrapped in plastic and finally brought back from the dead by Norman Foster: the expression 'turbulent history' just doesn't do justice to the life Berlin's most famous landmark has endured. This neobaroque edifice was finished in 1894 to house the German Imperial Diet and served its purpose until 1933 when it was badly damaged by fire in an arson attack carried out by Marinus van der Lubbe, a young Dutch communist. This shocking event conveniently gave Hitler a pretext to tighten his grip on the German state. In 1945 the building was a major target for the Red Army who raised the red flag from the Reichstag, an act that became a symbol of the Soviet victory over the Nazis.

The Reichstag's cupola

❶ Need to Know

Map p446; www.bundestag.de; Platz der Republik 1, Visitors Centre, Scheidemann-strasse; ⊘lift 8am-midnight, last entry 9.45pm, Visitors Centre 8am-8pm Apr-Oct, to 6pm Nov-Mar; ⛪; ☐100, ⑤Brandenburger Tor, Hauptbahnhof, Ⓤ Brandenburger Tor, Bundestag **FREE**

✕ Take a Break

For quick feeds, try tourist-geared, self-service **Berlin Pavillon** (Map p446; ⬩030-2065 4737; www.berlin-pavillon. de; Scheidemannstrasse 1; dishes €4.50-9; ⊘8am-9pm; ☐100, ⑤Brandenburger Tor, Ⓤ Brandenburger Tor, Bundestag).

★ Top Tip

For guaranteed access, make free reservations online before leaving home. All visitors must show ID to enter the building.

The Cold War Years

Although in West Berlin, the Reichstag found itself very near the dividing line between East and West Berlin and, from the early 1960s, the Berlin Wall. With the German government sitting safely in faraway Bonn, this grand facade lost its purpose and in the 1950s some in West Berlin thought it should be demolished. However, the wrecking balls never had their day and the Reichstag was restored, albeit without a lot of the decoration that had adorned the old building.

Reunification & Norman Foster

Almost a year after the Wall came down, the official reunification ceremony was symbolically held at the Reichstag, which, it was later decided, would become the seat of the German Bundestag (parliament) once again. Before Norman Foster began

his reconstruction work, the entire Reichstag was spectacularly wrapped in plastic sheeting by the Bulgarian-American artist Christo in the summer of 1995. The following four years saw the erection of Norman Foster's now famous glittering glass cupola, the centrepiece of the visitor experience today. It is the Reichstag's most distinctive feature, serviced by lift and providing fabulous 360-degree city views and the opportunity to peer down into the parliament chamber. To reach the top, follow the ramp spiralling up around the dome's mirror-clad central cone. The cupola was a spanking new feature, but Foster's brief also stipulated that some parts of the building were to be preserved. One example is the Cyrillic graffiti left by Soviet soldiers in 1945.

N+T • / GETTY IMAGES ©

Berlin Nightlife

With its well-deserved reputation as one of Europe's primo party capitals, Berlin offers a thousand-and-one scenarios for getting your cocktails and kicks (or wine or beer, for that matter).

Great For

☑ Don't Miss

Café am Neuen See (Map p452; ☎030-254 4930; www.cafeamneuensee.de; Lichtensteinallee 2; ⊘restaurant 9am-11pm, beer garden noon-late Mon-Fri, 11am-late Sat & Sun; 👪; ☐200, Ⓤ Zoologischer Garten, Ⓢ Zoologischer Garten, Tiergarten), generally regarded as Berlin's best beer garden.

Bars & Cafes

Berlin is a notoriously late-night city: bars stay packed from dusk to dawn and beyond, and some clubs don't hit their stride until 4am. The lack of a curfew never created a tradition of binge drinking.

Edgier, more underground venues cluster in Kreuzberg, Friedrichshain, Neukölln and up-and-coming outer boroughs like Wedding (north of Mitte) and Lichtenberg (past Friedrichshain). Places in Charlottenburg, Mitte and Prenzlauer Berg tend to be quieter and close earlier. Some proprietors have gone to extraordinary lengths to come up with special design concepts.

The line between cafe and bar is often blurred, with many changing stripes as the hands move around the clock. Alcohol, however, is served pretty much all day.

Bartender preparing mojitos in a Berlin bar

Cocktail bars are booming in Berlin and several new arrivals have measurably elevated the 'liquid art' scene. Dedicated drinking dens tend to be elegant cocoons with mellow lighting and low sound levels. A good cocktail will set you back between €10 and €15.

Beaches & Outdoor Drinking

Berliners are sun cravers and as soon as the first rays spray their way into spring, outdoor tables show up faster than you can pour a pint of beer. The most traditional places for outdoor chilling are of course the beer gardens with long wooden benches set up beneath leafy old chestnuts and with cold beer and bratwurst on the menu. In 2002, Berlin also jumped on the 'sandwagon' with the opening of its first beach bar, **Strandbar Mitte** (Map p446; ☎030-2838 5588; www.strandbar-mitte.de; Monbijoustrasse 3; dancing €4; ⏰10am-late May-Sep; 🚋M1, Ⓢ Oranienburger Strasse), in a prime location on the Spree River. Many that followed have since been displaced by development, which has partly fuelled the latest trend: rooftop bars.

Need to Know

Regular bars open around 6pm and close at 1am or 2am the next day. Trendy places and cocktail bars open at 8pm or 9pm and stay open until the last tippler leaves. Clubs open at 11pm or midnight, but don't fill up until 1am or 2am, peaking between 4am and 6am.

Take a Break

Check out the food offerings while you're chilling out in one of Berlin's beer gardens or enjoying the views from a rooftop bar.

★ Top Tip

There's generally no need to dress up at Berlin's clubs, and getting past bouncers is fairly easy.

Clubbing

Over the past 25 years, Berlin's club culture has put the city firmly on the map of hedonists. With more than 200 venues, finding one to match your mood isn't difficult. Electronic music in its infinite varieties continues to define Berlin's after-dark action but other sounds like hip-hop, dancehall, rock, swing and funk have also made inroads. The edgiest clubs have taken up residence in power plants, transformer stations, abandoned apartment buildings and other repurposed locations. The scene is in constant flux as experienced club owners look for new challenges and a younger generation of promoters enters the scene with new ideas and impetus.

Historical Highlights

This walk checks off Berlin's blockbuster landmarks as it cuts right through the historic city centre, Mitte (literally 'Middle'), the birthplace and glamorous heart of Berlin, a high-octane cocktail of culture, architecture and commerce.

Start Reichstag
Distance 3.5km
Duration Three hours

Classic Photo: The iconic Brandenburger Gate is now a cheery symbol of German reunification.

2 The **Brandenburg Gate** (p444) became an involuntary neighbour of the Berlin Wall during the Cold War.

Platz der Republik

START 1

Scheidemannstr

Dorotheenstr

Ebertstr

Brandenburger Tor

Unter den Linden

3

Friedrichstr

Tiergarten

Ebertstr

2

Behrenstr

3 Unter den Linden has been Berlin's showpiece road since the 18th century.

Take a Break... Stop in at **Augustiner am Gendarmenmarkt** (p453) for some German fare.

1 The sparkling glass dome of the **Reichstag** (p438) has become a shining beacon of unified Berlin.

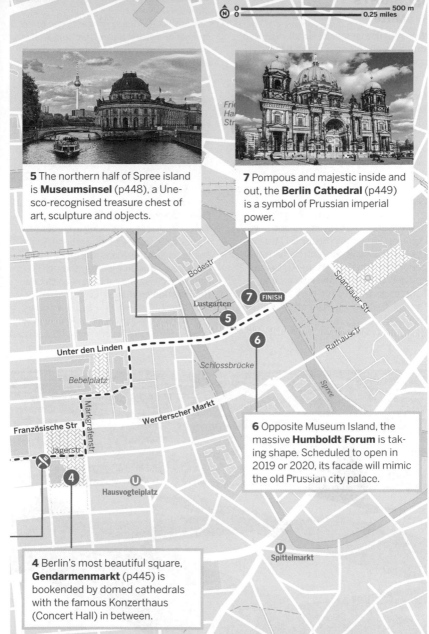

5 The northern half of Spree island is **Museumsinsel** (p448), a Unesco-recognised treasure chest of art, sculpture and objects.

7 Pompous and majestic inside and out, the **Berlin Cathedral** (p449) is a symbol of Prussian imperial power.

6 Opposite Museum Island, the massive **Humboldt Forum** is taking shape. Scheduled to open in 2019 or 2020, its facade will mimic the old Prussian city palace.

4 Berlin's most beautiful square, **Gendarmenmarkt** (p445) is bookended by domed cathedrals with the famous Konzerthaus (Concert Hall) in between.

◉ SIGHTS
◉ Mitte

With the mother lode of sights clustered within a walkable area, the most historic part of Berlin is a prime port of call for visitors.

Deutsches Historisches Museum   Museum

(German Historical Museum; Map p446; ☑030-203 040; www.dhm.de; Unter den Linden 2; adult/concession/child under 18yr incl IM Pei Bau €8/4/free; ☺10am-6pm; ☐100, 200, ⓊHausvogteiplatz, ⓈHackescher Markt) If you're wondering what the Germans have been up to for the past 1500 years, take a spin around the baroque Zeughaus, formerly the Prussian arsenal and now home of the German Historical Museum. Upstairs, displays concentrate on the period from the 6th century AD to the end of WWI in 1918, while the ground floor tracks the 20th century all the way through to the early years after German reunification.

Brandenburger Tor   Landmark

(Brandenburg Gate; Map p446; Pariser Platz; ⓈBrandenburger Tor, ⓊBrandenburger Tor) A symbol of division during the Cold War, the landmark Brandenburg Gate now epitomises German reunification. Carl Gotthard Langhans found inspiration in Athens' Acropolis for the elegant triumphal arch, completed in 1791 as the royal city gate.

Holocaust Memorial   Memorial

(Memorial to the Murdered Jews of Europe; Map p446; ☑030-2639 4336; www.stiftung-denkmal. de; Cora-Berliner-Strasse 1; audioguide €3; ☺24hr; ⓈBrandenburger Tor, ⓊBrandenburger Tor) **FREE** Inaugurated in 2005, this football-field-sized memorial by American architect Peter Eisenman consists of 2711 sarcophagi-like concrete columns rising in sombre silence from the undulating ground. You're free to access this maze at any point and make your individual journey through it. For context visit the subterranean **Ort der Information** (Information Centre; Map p446; ☑030-7407 2929; www.holocaust-mahnmal.de; ☺10am-8pm Tue-Sun Apr-Sep, to 7pm Oct-Mar, last admission 45min before closing) **FREE**, whose

Holocaust Memorial

ANTON HAVELAAR / SHUTTERSTOCK ©

exhibits will leave no one untouched. Audio-guides and audio translations of exhibit panels are available.

Gendarmenmarkt
Square

(Map p446; U Französische Strasse, Stadtmitte) This graceful square is bookended by the domed German and French cathedrals and punctuated by a grandly porticoed concert hall, the **Konzerthaus** (Map p446; ☑030-203 092 333; www.konzerthaus.de; Gendarmenmarkt 2; U Französische Strasse, Stadtmitte). It was named for the Gens d'Armes, an 18th-century Prussian regiment consisting of French Huguenot refugees.

Checkpoint Charlie
Historic Site

(Map p450; cnr Zimmerstrasse & Friedrichstrasse; ☺24hr; U Kochstrasse) FREE Checkpoint Charlie was the principal gateway for foreigners and diplomats between the two Berlins from 1961 to 1990. Unfortunately, this potent symbol of the Cold War has degenerated into a tacky tourist trap, though a free **open-air exhibit** that illustrates milestones in Cold War history is one redeeming aspect.

⊚ Scheunenviertel

Hackesche Höfe
Historic Site

(Hackesche Courtyards; Map p446; ☑030-2809 8010; www.hackesche hoefe.com; enter from Rosenthaler Strasse 40/41 or Sophienstrasse 6; ☒M1, S Hackescher Markt, U Weinmeisterstrasse) The Hackesche Höfe is the largest and most famous of the courtyard ensembles peppered throughout the Scheunenviertel. Built in 1907, the eight interlinked *Höfe* reopened in 1996 with a congenial mix of cafes, galleries, shops and entertainment venues. The main entrance on Rosenthaler Strasse leads to **Court I**, prettily festooned with art nouveau tiles, while Court VII segues to the romantic **Rosenhöfe** with a sunken rose garden and tendril-like balustrades.

Museum für Naturkunde
Museum

(Museum of Natural History; Map p446; ☑030-2093 8591; www.naturkundemuseum.berlin; Invalidenstrasse 43; adult/concession incl audioguide

📖 Sachsenhausen Concentration Camp

About 35km north of Berlin, **Sachsenhausen** (Memorial & Museum Sachsenhausen; ☑03301-200 200; www.stiftung-bg.de; Strasse der Nationen 22, Oranienburg; ☺8.30am-6pm mid-Mar–mid-Oct, to 4.30pm mid-Oct–mid-Mar, museums closed Mon mid-Oct–mid-Mar; P; S Oranienburg) FREE was built by prisoners and opened in 1936 as a prototype for other concentration camps. By 1945, some 200,000 people had passed through its sinister gates, most of them political opponents, Jews, Roma people and, after 1939, POWs. Tens of thousands died here from hunger, exhaustion, illness, exposure, medical experiments and executions. Thousands more succumbed during the death march of April 1945, when the Nazis evacuated the camp in advance of the Red Army.

A tour of the memorial site with its remaining buildings and exhibits will leave no one untouched.

The S1 makes the trip thrice hourly from central Berlin (eg Friedrichstrasse station) to Oranienburg (€3.40, 45 minutes). Hourly regional RE5 and RB12 trains leaving from Hauptbahnhof are faster (€3.40, 25 minutes). The camp is about 2km from the Oranienburg train station.

Guard tower at Sachsenhausen
ITZAVU / SHUTTERSTOCK ©

€8/5; ☺9.30am-6pm Tue-Fri, 10am-6pm Sat & Sun; 🚼; ☒M5, M8, M10, 12, U Naturkundemuseum) Fossils and minerals don't quicken your pulse? Well, how about Tristan the

Mitte

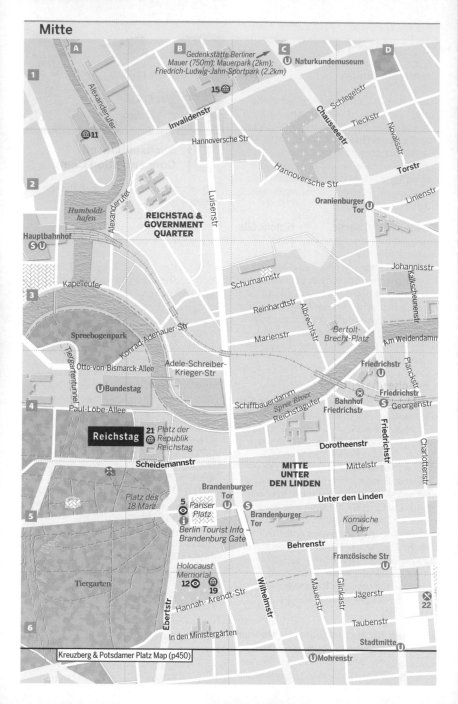

Gedenkstätte Berliner Mauer (750m); Mauerpark (2km); Friedrich-Ludwig-Jahn-Sportpark (2.2km)

Naturkundemuseum

15

11

Invalidenstr

Hannoversche Str

Alexanderufer

Schlegelstr

Chausseestr

Tieckstr

Novalisstr

Torstr

Hannoversche Str

Linienstr

Oranienburger Tor

Humboldt-hafen

Alexanderufer

Luisenstr

REICHSTAG & GOVERNMENT QUARTER

Hauptbahnhof

Johannisstr

Kalkscheunenstr

Kapelleufer

Schumannstr

Reinhardtstr

Albrechtstr

Marienstr

Bertolt-Brecht-Platz

Am Weidendamm

Spreebogenpark

Konrad-Adenauer-Str

Friedrichstr

Planckstr

Tiergartentunnel

Otto-von-Bismarck-Allee

Adele-Schreiber-Krieger-Str

Schiffbauerdamm

Spree River

Reichstagufer

Bahnhof Friedrichstr

Friedrichstr

Georgenstr

Bundestag

Paul-Löbe-Allee

Reichstag

21 Platz der Republik Reichstag

Dorotheenstr

Friedrichstr

Charlottenstr

Scheidemannstr

MITTE UNTER DEN LINDEN

Mittelstr

Platz des 18 März

Brandenburger Tor

5 Pariser Platz

Brandenburger Tor

Unter den Linden

Komische Oper

Berlin Tourist Info – Brandenburg Gate

Behrenstr

Französische Str

Holocaust Memorial

12

19

Tiergarten

Hannah-Arendt-Str

Ebertstr

Wilhelmstr

Mauerstr

Glinkastr

Jägerstr

22

Taubenstr

In den Ministergärten

Stadtmitte

Kreuzberg & Potsdamer Platz Map (p450)

Mohrenstr

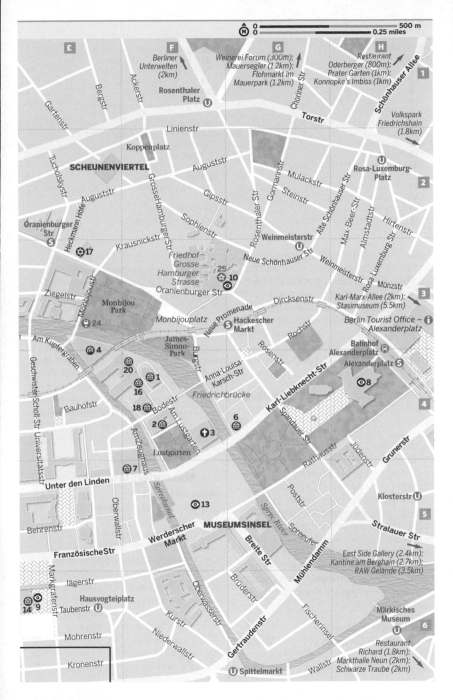

N 0 500 m
0 0.25 miles

E

F
Berliner
Unterwelten
(2km)
Rosenthaler
Platz ⓤ

G
Weinerei Forum (300m);
Mauersegler (1.2km);
Flohmarkt im
Mauerpark (1.2km)

H
Restaurant
Oderberger (800m);
Prater Garten (1km);
Konnopke's Imbiss (1km)

1

Schönhauser Allee

Torstr

Volkspark
Friedrichshain
(1.8km)

Linienstr

Gartenstr

Bergstr

Ackerstr

Choriner Str

Koppenplatz

SCHEUNENVIERTEL

Tucholskystr

Auguststr

Auguststr

Gipsstr

Gormannstr

Mulackstr

Steinstr

ⓤ Rosa-Luxemburg-
Platz

2

Oranienburger
Str Ⓢ

Heckmann Höfe

Grosse Hamburger Str

Sophienstr

Krausnickstr

Rosenthaler Str

Weinmeisterstr

Neue Schönhauser Str

Alte Schönhauser Str

Weinmeisterstr

Max-Beer-Str

Almstadtstr

Rosa-Luxemburg-Str

Hirtenstr

⊕17

Friedhof
Grosse
Hamburger
Strasse

25
☯ 10

Münzstr

3

Ziegelstr

Oranienburger Str

Dircksenstr

Karl-Marx-Allee (2km);
Stasimuseum (5.5km)

Monbijouplatz

Monbijou
Park

Neue Promenade

Ⓢ Hackescher
Markt

Rochstr

Berlin Tourist Office – ⓘ
Alexanderplatz

🏛24

🏛 4

Am Kupfergraben

Geschwister-Scholl-Str

Universitätsstr

James-
Simon-
Park

Burgstr

Anna-Louisa-
Karsch-Str

Rosenstr

Karl-Liebknecht-Str

Bahnhof
Alexanderplatz 🚆

Alexanderplatz Ⓢ

⊙8

4

🏛
20

🏛1

16

18🏛

Bauhofstr

Am Zeughaus

Bodestr

2🏛

Am Lustgarten

🏛3

Lustgarten

Friedrichbrücke

6
🏛

Spandauer Str

Rathausstr

Jüdenstr

Grunerstr

🏛7

Unter den Linden

Oberwallstr

Spreekanal

⊙13

Werderscher
Markt

MUSEUMSINSEL

Breite Str

Spree River

Spreeufer

Poststr

Mühlendamm

Klosterstr ⓤ

5

Stralauer Str

Behrenstr

FranzösischeStr

East Side Gallery (2.4km);
Kantine am Berghain (2.7km);
RAW Gelände (3.5km)

Jägerstr

Markgrafenstr

Hausvogteiplatz
Taubenstr ⓤ

Kurstr

Oderwasserstr

Bruderstr

Niederwallstr

Fischerinsel

⊙9

14

Mohrenstr

Gertraudenstr

Wallstr

Märkisches
Museum
ⓤ

6

Restaurant
Richard (1.8km);
Markthalle Neun (2km);
Schwarze Traube (2km)

Kronenstr

ⓤ Spittelmarkt

Mitte

T-Rex? His skeleton is among the best-preserved in the world and, along with the 12m-high *Brachiosaurus branchai,* is part of the Jurassic superstar line-up at this highly engaging museum. Elsewhere you can see the taxidermied Knut (once the world's most famous polar bear), marvel at the fragile bones of an ultrarare *Archaeopteryx* protobird, and find out why zebras are striped.

Neue Synagoge   Synagogue

(Map p446; ☎030-8802 8300; www.centrum judaicum.de; Oranienburger Strasse 28-30; adult/concession €5/4, audioguide €3; ◷10am-6pm Mon-Fri, to 7pm Sun, closes 3pm Fri & 6pm Sun Oct-Mar; ☒M1, Ⓤ Oranienburger Tor, ⓢ Oranienburger Strasse) The gleaming gold dome of the Neue Synagoge is the most visible symbol of Berlin's revitalised Jewish community. The 1866 original was Germany's largest synagogue but its modern incarnation is not so much a house of worship (although prayer services do take place) as a museum and place of remembrance called **Centrum Judaicum**. The dome can be climbed from April to September (adult/concession €3/2.50).

Hamburger Bahnhof –
Museum für Gegenwart   Museum

(Contemporary Art Museum; Map p446; ☎030-266 424 242; www.smb.museum; Invaliden-

strasse 50-51; adult/concession €10/5, free 4-8pm 1st Thu of the month; ◷10am-6pm Tue, Wed & Fri, to 8pm Thu, 11am-6pm Sat & Sun; ☒M5, M8, M10, ⓢ Hauptbahnhof, Ⓤ Hauptbahnhof) Berlin's contemporary art showcase opened in 1996 in an old railway station, whose grandeur is a great backdrop for this Aladdin's cave of paintings, installations, sculptures and video art. Changing exhibits span the arc of post-1950 artistic movements – from conceptual art and pop art to minimal art and Fluxus – and include seminal works by such major players as Andy Warhol, Cy Twombly, Joseph Beuys and Robert Rauschenberg.

⊙ Alexanderplatz

Museumsinsel   Museum

(Map p446; ☎030-266 424 242; www.smb.museum; day tickets for all 5 museums adult/concession/under 18 €18/9/free; ◷varies by museum; ☒100, 200, TXL, ⓢ Hackescher Markt, Friedrichstrasse, Ⓤ Friedrichstrasse) Walk through ancient Babylon, meet an Egyptian queen, clamber up a Greek altar or be mesmerised by Monet's ethereal landscapes. Welcome to Museumsinsel (Museum Island), Berlin's most important treasure trove, spanning 6000 years' worth of art, artefacts, sculpture and architecture from Europe and beyond. Spread across five grand museums built between 1830 and 1930, the complex takes up the entire northern half of the little Spree Island where Berlin's settlement began in the 13th century.

The first repository to open was the **Altes Museum** (Old Museum; Map p446; Am Lustgarten; adult/concession/under 18 €10/5/free; ⊙10am-6pm Tue, Wed & Fri-Sun, to 8pm Thu), which presents Greek, Etruscan and Roman antiquities. Behind it, the **Neues Museum** (New Museum; Map p446; Bodestrasse 1-3; adult/concession/under 18yr €12/6/free; ⊙10am-6pm Fri-Wed, to 8pm Thu) showcases the Egyptian collection, most famously the bust of Queen Nefertiti, and also houses the Museum of Pre- and Early History. The temple-like **Alte Nationalgalerie** (Old National Gallery; Map p446; Bodestrasse 1-3; adult/concession €10/5; ⊙10am-6pm Tue, Wed & Fri-Sun, to 8pm Thu) trains the focus on 19th-century European art. The island's top draw is the **Pergamonmuseum** (Map p446; Bodestrasse 1-3; adult/concession/under 18yr €12/6/free; ⊙10am-6pm Fri-Wed, to 8pm Thu), with its monumental architecture from ancient worlds, including the stunning Ishar Gate from Babylon. The **Bode-Museum** (Map p446; cnr Am Kupfergraben & Monbijoubrücke; adult/concession/under 18 €12/6/free; ⊙10am-6pm Tue, Wed & Fri-Sun, to 8pm Thu), at the island's northern tip, is famous for its medieval sculptures.

DDR Museum   Museum

(GDR (East Germany) Museum; Map p446; ☑030 847 123 731; www.ddr-museum.de; Karl-Liebknecht-Strasse 1; adult/concession €9.80/6; ⊙10am-8pm Sun-Fri, to 10pm Sat; ⬚100, 200, TXL, ⓢHackescher Markt) This touchy-feely museum does an insightful and entertaining job of pulling back the iron curtain on daily life in socialist East Germany. You'll learn how kids were put through collective potty training, engineers earned little more than farmers, and everyone, it seems, went on nudist holidays. A perennial crowd-pleaser among the historic objects on display is a Trabi, the tinny East German standard car – sit in it

to take a virtual spin around an East Berlin neighbourhood.

Fernsehturm   Landmark

(TV Tower; Map p446; ☑030-247 575 875; www.tv-turm.de; Panoramastrasse 1a; adult/child €15.50/9.50, fast track online ticket €19.50/12; ⊙9am-midnight Mar-Oct, 10am-midnight Nov-Feb, last ascent 11.30pm; ⬚100, 200, TXL, ⓤAlexanderplatz, ⓢAlexanderplatz) Germany's tallest structure, the TV Tower has been soaring 368m high since 1969 and is as iconic to Berlin as the Eiffel Tower is to Paris. On clear days, views are stunning from the observation deck (with bar) at 203m or from 207m at the upstairs **Sphere restaurant** (Map p446; ☑030-247 575 875; www.tv-turm.de/en/bar-restaurant; mains lunch €10.50-18, dinner €12.50-28; ⊙10am-11pm; ☎; ⬚100, 200, TXL, ⓤAlexanderplatz, ⓢAlexanderplatz), which makes one revolution per hour.

Berliner Dom   Church

(Berlin Cathedral; Map p446; ☑ticket office 030-2026 9136; www.berlinerdom.de; Am Lustgarten; adult/concession €7/5; ⊙9am-8pm Apr-Sep, to 7pm Oct-Mar; ⬚100, 200, TXL, ⓢHackescher Markt) Pompous yet majestic, the Italian Renaissance–style former royal court church (1905) does triple duty as house of worship, museum and concert hall. Inside it's gilt to the hilt and outfitted with a lavish marble-and-onyx altar, a 7269-pipe Sauer organ and elaborate royal sarcophagi. Climb up the 267 steps to the gallery for glorious city views.

◉ Potsdamer Platz & Tiergarten

Potsdamer Platz   Area

(Map p450; Alte Potsdamer Strasse; ⬚200, ⓢPotsdamer Platz, ⓤPotsdamer Platz) The rebirth of the historic Potsdamer Platz was Europe's biggest building project of the 1990s, a showcase of urban renewal masterminded by such top international architects as Renzo Piano and Helmut Jahn. An entire city quarter sprouted on terrain once bifurcated by the Berlin Wall

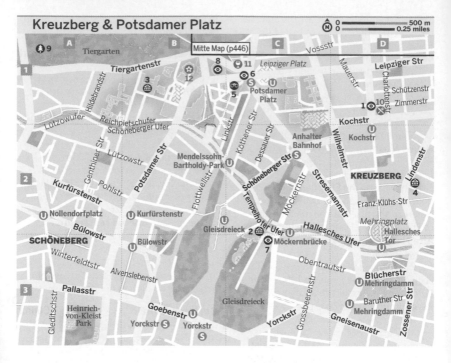

and today houses offices, theatres and cinemas, hotels, apartments and museums. Highlights include the glass-tented **Sony Center** (Map p450; www.potsdamer-platz.net; Potsdamer Strasse) and the **Panoramapunkt** (Map p450; ☑030-2593 7080; www.panoramapunkt.de; Potsdamer Platz 1; adult/concession €7.50/6, without wait €11.50/9; ☻10am-8pm Apr-Oct, to 6pm Nov-Mar) observation deck.

Tiergarten
Park

(Map p450; Strasse des 17 Juni; ☐100, 200, ⑤Potsdamer Platz, Brandenburger Tor, ⓤBrandenburger Tor) Berlin's rulers used to hunt boar and pheasants in the rambling Tiergarten until garden architect Peter Lenné landscaped the grounds in the 19th century. Today it's one of the world's largest urban parks, popular for strolling, jogging, picnicking, frisbee tossing and, yes, nude sunbathing and gay cruising (especially around the Löwenbrücke).

Gemäldegalerie
Gallery

(Gallery of Old Masters; Map p450; ☑030-266 424 242; www.smb.museum/gg; Matthäikirchplatz; adult/concession/under 18 €10/5/free; ☻10am-6pm Tue, Wed & Fri, to 8pm Thu, 11am-6pm Sat & Sun; ᵻ; ☐M29, M48, M85, 200, ⑤Potsdamer Platz, ⓤPotsdamer Platz) This museum ranks among the world's finest and most comprehensive collections of European art with about 1500 paintings spanning the arc of artistic vision from the 13th to the 18th century. Wear comfy shoes when exploring the 72 galleries: a walk past masterpieces by Titian, Dürer, Hals, Vermeer, Gainsborough and many more Old Masters covers almost 2km. Don't miss the Rembrandt Room (Room X).

Siegessäule
Monument

(Victory Column; Grosser Stern, Strasse des 17 Juni; adult/concession €3/2.50; ☻9.30am-6.30pm Mon-Fri, to 7pm Sat & Sun Apr-Oct,

Kreuzberg & Potsdamer Platz

10am-5pm Mon-Fri, to 5.30pm Sat & Sun Nov-Mar; 🚌100, ⓊHansaplatz, ⓈBellevue) Like arms of a starfish, five roads merge into the Grosser Stern roundabout at the heart of the huge Tiergarten (p450) park. The Victory Column at its centre celebrates 19th-century Prussian military triumphs and is crowned by a gilded statue of the goddess Victoria. Today it is also a symbol of Berlin's gay community. Climb 285 steps for sweeping views of the park.

⊙ Kreuzberg

Jüdisches Museum   Museum

(Jewish Museum; Map p450; 🖉030-2599 3300; www.jmberlin.de; Lindenstrasse 9-14; adult/concession €8/3, audioguide €3; ⊘10am-8pm; ⓊHallesches Tor, Kochstrasse) In a landmark building by American-Polish architect Daniel Libeskind, Berlin's Jewish Museum offers a chronicle of the trials and triumphs in 2000 years of Jewish life in Germany. The exhibit smoothly navigates all major periods, from the Middle Ages via the Enlightenment to the community's post-1990 renaissance. Find out about Jewish cultural contributions, holiday traditions, the difficult road to emancipation, outstanding individuals (eg Moses Mendelssohn and Levi Strauss) and the fates of ordinary people.

Deutsches Technikmuseum   Museum

(German Museum of Technology; Map p450; 🖉030-902 540; http://sdtb.de/technikmuseum; Trebbiner Strasse 9; adult/concession/child under 18 €8/4/after 3pm free; ⊘9am-

5.30pm Tue-Fri, 10am-6pm Sat & Sun; Ⓟ🚻; ⓊGleisdreieck, Möckernbrücke) A roof-mounted 'candy bomber' (the plane used in the 1948 Berlin Airlift) is merely the overture to this enormous and hugely engaging shrine to technology. Fantastic for kids, the giant museum includes the world's first computer, an entire hall of vintage locomotives and exhibits on aerospace and navigation in a modern annexe. At the adjacent **Science Center Spectrum** (Map p450; 🖉030-9025 4284; www.sdtb. de; Möckernstrasse 26; adult/concession/child under 18 €8/4/free after 3pm; ⊘9am-5.30pm Tue-Fri, 10am-6pm Sat & Sun; Ⓟ), entered on the same ticket, kids can participate in hands-on experiments.

⊙ Charlottenburg

Schloss Charlottenburg   Palace

(Charlottenburg Palace; Map p452; 🖉030-320 910; www.spsg.de; Spandauer Damm 10-22; day pass to all 4 bldgs adult/concession €17/13; ⊘hours vary by bldg; 🚌M45, 109, 309, ⓊRichard-Wagner-Platz, Sophie-Charlotte-Platz) Charlottenburg Palace is one of Berlin's few sites that still reflect the one-time grandeur of the Hohenzollern clan, which ruled the region from 1415 to 1918. Originally a petite summer retreat, it grew into an exquisite baroque pile with opulent private apartments, richly decorated festival halls, collections of precious porcelain and paintings by French 18th-century masters. It's lovely in fine weather, when you can fold a stroll in the palace park into a day of peeking at royal treasures.

Charlottenburg

🅖 TOURS

Berliner Unterwelten — Tours

(📞030-4991 0517; www.berliner-unterwelten.de; Brunnenstrasse 105; adult/concession €12/10; ⏱Dark Worlds tours in English 11am Wed-Sun, 11am & 1pm Mon year-round, 3pm Mon, Wed-Sun, 1pm & 3pm Wed-Sun Apr-Oct; ⑤Gesundbrunnen, ⓤGesundbrunnen) After you've checked off the Brandenburg Gate and the TV Tower, why not explore Berlin's dark and dank underbelly? Join Berliner Unterwelten on its 1½-hour 'Dark Worlds' tour of a WWII underground bunker and pick your way through a warren of claustrophobic rooms, past heavy steel doors, hospital beds, helmets, guns, boots and lots of other wartime artefacts.

Berlin on Bike — Cycling

(📞030-4373 9999; www.berlinonbike.de; Knaackstrasse 97, Kulturbrauerei, Court 4; tours incl bike adult/concession €24/20, bike rental per 24hr €10; ⏱8am-8pm mid-Mar–mid-Nov, 10am-4pm Mon-Sat mid-Nov–mid-Mar; 🚋M1, ⓤEberswalder Strasse) This well-established company has a busy schedule of insightful and fun bike tours led by locals. There are daily English-language city tours (Berlin's Best) and Berlin Wall tours, as well as an Alternative Berlin tour thrice weekly and a Street-Art tour on Fridays. Other tours (eg night tours) are available on request. Reservations recommended for all tours.

Original Berlin Walks
Walking

(☑030-301 9194; www.berlinwalks.de; adult/ concession from €14/12) Berlin's longest-running English-language walking tour company has a general city tour plus a roster of themed tours (eg Hitler's Germany, East Berlin, Queer Berlin), as well as a food crawl, a craft beer tour and trips out to Sachsenhausen concentration camp and Potsdam. The website has details on timings and meeting points.

🅐 SHOPPING

KaDeWe
Department Store

(Map p452; ☑030-212 10; www.kadewe.de; Tauentzienstrasse 21-24; ⊙10am-8pm Mon-Thu, to 9pm Fri, 9.30am-8pm Sat; ⓊWittenbergplatz) Continental Europe's largest department store has been going strong since 1907 and boasts an assortment so vast that a pirate-style campaign is the best way to plunder its bounty. If pushed for time, at least hurry up to the legendary 6th-floor gourmet food hall. The name, by the way, stands for *Kaufhaus des Westens* (department store of the West).

Bikini Berlin
Mall

(Map p452; ☑030-5549 6455; www.bikini berlin.de; Budapester Strasse 38-50; ⊙shops 10am-8pm Mon-Sat, Bldg 9am-8.30pm Mon-Sat, noon-6pm Sun; 🅟; 🚌100, 200, ⓊZoologischer Garten, ⓈZoologischer Garten) Germany's first concept mall opened in 2014 in a smoothly rehabilitated 1950s architectural icon nicknamed 'Bikini' because of its design: 200m-long upper and lower sections separated by an open floor, now chastely covered by a glass facade. Inside are three floors of urban indie boutiques, short-lease pop-up 'boxes'

for up-and-comers, and an international street-food court.

✖ EATING

🍽 Mitte

Augustiner am Gendarmenmarkt
German €€

(Map p446; ☑030-2045 4020; www.augustiner-braeu-berlin.de; Charlottenstrasse 55; mains €7.50-30, lunch special €5.90; ⊙10am-2am; ⓊFranzösische Strasse) Tourists, concertgoers and hearty-food lovers rub shoulders at rustic tables in this authentic Bavarian beer hall. Soak up the down-to-earth vibe right along with a mug of full-bodied Augustiner brew straight from Munich. Sausages, roast pork and pretzels provide rib-sticking sustenance with only a token salad offered for noncarnivores. Good-value weekday lunch specials.

Restaurant Tim Raue
Asian €€€

(Map p450; ☑030-2593 7930; www.tim-raue. com; Rudi-Dutschke-Strasse 26; 3-/4-course lunch €58/68, 8-course dinner €198, mains €48-66; ⊙noon-3pm & 7pm-midnight Wed-Sat; ⓊKochstrasse) Now here's a double-Michelin-starred restaurant we can get our mind around. Unstuffy ambience and a stylishly reduced design with walnut and Vitra chairs perfectly juxtapose with Berlin-born Tim Raue's brilliant Asian-inspired plates, which each shine the spotlight on a few choice ingredients. His interpretation of Peking duck is a perennial bestseller.

🍽 Prenzlauer Berg

Kanaan
Middle Eastern €

(☑0176 2258 6673; www.kanaan-berlin.de; Kopenhagener Strasse 17; dishes €4-10; ⊙5-10pm Wed, noon-10pm Thu & Fri, 10am-10pm Sat & Sun; 🅟🍴; 🚃M1, ⓊSchönhauser Allee, ⓈSchönhauser Allee) In this feel-good venture, an Israeli biz whiz and a Palestinian chef have teamed up to bring a progressive blend of vegan/vegetarian Middle Eastern fare to Berlin. Top menu

🗒️ East Berlin's Stasi Museum

East Berlin's **Stasi Museum** (☎030-553 6854; www.stasimuseum.de; Haus 1, Rus-chestrasse 103; adult/concession €6/4.50; ☺10am-6pm Mon-Fri, 11am-6pm Sat & Sun, English tour 3pm Sat-Mon; ⓤMagdalenen-strasse) provides an overview of the structure, methods and impact of the Ministry of State Security (Stasi), the secret police of former East Germany, inside the feared institution's fortress-like headquarters. At its peak, more than 8000 people worked in this compound alone; the scale model in the entrance foyer will help you grasp its vast dimensions. Other rooms introduce the ideology, rituals and institutions of East German society. You can marvel at cunningly low-tech surveillance devices (hidden in watering cans, rocks, even neckties), a prisoner transport van with tiny, lightless cells, and the stuffy offices of Stasi chief Erich Mielke. There's also background on the SED party and on the role of the youth organisation Junge Pioneere (Young Pioneers). Panelling is partly in English, and there are free English tours at 3pm Saturday and Sunday.

The museum is in the eastern district of Lichtenberg, just north of U-Bahn station Magdalenenstrasse.

picks include the Iraqi-style hummus, the *hummshuka* (hummus/shakshouka mash-up) and the chocolate-tahini mousse. Salads are also delish, especially the oven-roasted cauliflower. It's all served in a simple but stylish hut with a lovely garden.

Restaurant Oderberger   German €€€
(☎030-7800 8976 811; www.restaurant-oder berger.de; Oderberger Strasse 57; mains €18-28, 3-course menu €39; ☺6pm-midnight Tue-Sat; 🛜; 🚋M1, 12, ⓤEberswalder Strasse) 🍃 This exciting newcomer spreads across three open levels in an industrial-chic ex–boiler room of a public swimming pool. The chef's orchestrations are just as upbeat and tantalising as the decor. The 'Dit is Berlin' menu stars riffs on local classics like bacon-wrapped perch and veal dumplings in caper sauce while the seasonal menu comes alive with freshly gathered ingredients from regional farmers.

❌ Kreuzberg

Sironi   Bakery €
(www.facebook.com/sironi.de; Eisenbahnstrasse 42, Markthalle Neun; snacks from €2.50; ☺8am-8pm Mon-Wed, Fri & Sat, to 10pm Thu; ⓤGörlitzer Bahnhof) The focaccia and ciabatta are as good as they get without taking a flight to Italy, thanks to Alfredo Sironi, who hails from the Boot and now treats Berlin bread lovers to his habit-forming carb creations. Watch the flour magicians whip up the next batch in his glass bakery right in the iconic **Markthalle Neun** (☎030-6107 3473; www. markthalleneun.de; Eisenbahnstrasse 42-43; ☺noon-6pm Mon-Wed & Fri, noon-10pm Thu, 10am-6pm Sat), then order a piece to go.

Cafe Jacques   Mediterranean €€
(☎030-694 1048; http://cafejacques.de; Maybachufer 14; mains €12.50-19; ☺6pm-late; ⓤSchönleinstrasse) Like a fine wine, this darling French-Mediterranean lair keeps improving with age. Candlelit wooden tables and art-festooned brick walls feel as warm and welcoming as an old friend's embrace. And indeed, a welcoming embrace from charismatic owner-host Ahmad may well await you. The blackboard menu is a rotating festival of flavours, including mouth-watering meze, homemade pasta and fresh fish.

Restaurant Richard French €€€

(☑030-4920 7242; www.restaurant-richard.
de; Köpenicker Strasse 174; 4-/5-/6-/7-course
dinner €68/82/92/100; ☺7pm-midnight
Tue-Sat; ☑; ⓤSchlesisches Tor) This venue
where Nazis partied in the 1930s and left-
ists debated in the '70s has been reborn
as a fine-dining shrine, solidly rooted in
the French tradition and endowed with
a Michelin star. With its coffered ceiling,
bubble chandeliers and risqué canvases, the decor is as luscious as the fancy
food while the vibe remains charmingly
relaxed.

✖ Charlottenburg

Kuchenladen Cafe €

(Map p452; ☑030-3101 8424; www.derkuchen
laden.de; Kantstrasse 138; cakes €2.50-4.50;
☺10am-8pm; ⓢSavignyplatz) No-one can
resist the siren call of this classic cafe
whose homemade cakes are like works of
art wrought from flour, sugar and cream.
From cheesecake to carrot cake to the
ridiculously rich Sacher Torte, it's all delicious down to the last crumb.

Restaurant am Steinplatz German €€€

(Map p452; ☑030-554 444, ext 7053; www.
hotelsteinplatz.com; Steinplatz 4; 2-/3-course
lunch €19/23, dinner mains €23-30; ☺noon-
2.30pm & 6-10pm Mon-Fri, 6-10pm Sat & Sun;
℗; ▣M45, ⓤErnst-Reuter-Platz, Zoologischer
Garten, ⓢZoologischer Garten) The 1920s get
a 21st-century makeover at this stylish
outpost with an open kitchen, where chef
Nicholas Hahn and team create dishes with
technique and passion. The menu takes
diners on a culinary romp around Germany
with occasional touchdowns in other countries, resulting in intellectually ambitious
but super-satisfying dishes that often star
unusual or rare ingredients.

Mine Restaurant Italian €€€

(Map p452; ☑030-8892 6363; www.mine
restaurant.de; Meinekestrasse 10; mains €15-
29; ☺5.30pm-midnight; ⒷUhlandstrasse)
Italian restaurants may be a dime a dozen
but Mine's decor, menu and service all
blend together as perfectly as a Sicil-
ian stew. The Berlin outpost of Russian
TV celebrity chef Aram Mnatsakanov,

Café Jacques

From left: Restaurant am Steinplatz (p455); wine on display in a Berlin restaurant; Prater Garten

it presents feistily flavoured next-gen fare from around the Boot by riffing on traditional recipes in innovative ways. The wine list should make even demanding oenophiles swoon.

🍷 DRINKING & NIGHTLIFE

🍸 Potsdamer Platz & Tiergarten

Curtain Club   Bar

(Map p450; 📞030-337 775 403; www.ritz carlton.de; Potsdamer Platz 3, Ritz-Carlton Berlin; ⏰10am-late; 🚇200, 🚇Potsdamer Platz, 🚇Potsdamer Platz) Heavy drapes lead the way to this gentlemen's club–style bar with thick carpets, marble tables and leather armchairs. It's presided over by cocktail-meister Arnd Heissen who's not only an expert on classic drinks but also shakes things up with his own creations, each served in a distinctive vessel, be it a vase, a Viking's horn or a milk bottle.

Fragrances   Cocktail Bar

(Map p450; 📞030-337 775 403; www.ritz carlton.de; Potsdamer Platz 3, Ritz-Carlton Berlin; ⏰from 7pm Wed-Sat; 📶; 🚇200, 🚇Potsdamer Platz, 🚇Potsdamer Platz) Another baby by Berlin cocktail maven Arnd Heissen, Fragrances claims to be the world's first 'perfume bar', a libation station where Heissen mixes potable potions mimicking famous scents. The black-mirrored space in the Ritz-Carlton is like a 3D menu where adventurous drinkers sniff out their favourite from among a row of perfume bottles, then settle back into flocked couches for stylish imbibing.

🍸 Prenzlauer Berg

Prater Garten   Beer Garden

(📞030-448 5688; www.pratergarten.de; Kastanienallee 7-9; snacks €2.50-7.50; ⏰noon-late Apr-Sep, weather permitting; 🚼; 🚇M1, 12, 🚇Eberswalder Strasse) Berlin's oldest beer garden has seen beer-soaked days and nights since 1837 and is still a charismatic spot for guzzling a custom-brewed Prater pilsner (self-service) beneath the ancient chestnut trees. Kids can romp around the small play area.

EDEN BREITZ / ALAMY STOCK PHOTO ©

Weinerei Forum — Wine Bar

(☏030-440 6983; www.weinerei.com; Fehrbelliner Strasse 57; ⊘10am-midnight; 🛜; 🚋M1, ⓤRosenthaler Platz) After 8pm, this living-room-style cafe turns into a wine bar that works on the honour principle: you 'rent' a wine glass for €2, then help yourself to as much vino as you like and in the end decide what you want to pay. Please be fair to keep this fantastic concept going.

🥤 Kreuzberg

Schwarze Traube — Cocktail Bar

(☏030-2313 5569; www.schwarzetraube.de; Wrangelstrasse 24; ⊘7pm-2am Sun-Thu, to 5am Fri & Sat; ⓤGörlitzer Bahnhof) Mixologist Atalay Aktas was Germany's Best Bartender of 2013 and hasn't missed a step since. He and his staff still create their magic potions in this pint-sized drinking parlour with living-room looks. There's no menu, meaning each drink is calibrated to the taste and mood of each patron using premium spirits, expertise and a dash of psychology.

🥤 Friedrichshain

Berghain/Panorama Bar — Club

(www.berghain.de; Am Wriezener Bahnhof; ⊘Fri-Mon; ⓢOstbahnhof) Only world-class spin-masters heat up this hedonistic bass-junkie hellhole inside a labyrinthine ex-powerplant. Hard-edged minimal techno dominates the ex-turbine hall (Berghain), while house dominates at Panorama Bar, one floor up. Long lines, strict door, no cameras. Check the website for midweek concerts and record-release parties at the main venue and the adjacent **Kantine am Berghain** (admission varies; ⊘hours vary).

Briefmarken Weine — Wine Bar

(☏030-4202 5292; www.briefmarkenweine.de; Karl-Marx-Allee 99; ⊘7pm-midnight Mon-Sat; ⓤWeberwiese) For *dolce vita* right on socialist-era Karl-Marx-Allee, head to this charmingly nostalgic Italian wine bar ensconced in a former stamp shop. The original wooden cabinets cradle a hand-picked selection of Italian bottles that complement a snack menu of yummy cheeses,

Berliner Philharmonie

prosciutto and salami, plus a pasta dish of the day. Best to book ahead.

Hops & Barley
Microbrewery

(☏030-2936 7534; www.hopsandbarley-berlin.de; Wühlischstrasse 22/23; ☺5pm-late Mon-Fri, from 3pm Sat & Sun; ☐M13, ⓤWarschauer Strasse, ⓢWarschauer Strasse) Conversation flows as freely as the unfiltered pilsner, malty *Dunkel* (dark) and fruity *Weizen* (wheat) produced right here at one of Berlin's oldest craft breweries (since 2008). The pub is inside a former butcher's shop and still has the tiled walls to prove it. Two beamers project football (soccer) games.

Charlottenburg

Bar am Steinplatz
Cocktail Bar

(Map p452; ☏030-554 4440; www.hotelstein platz.com; Steinplatz 4; ☺4pm-late; ⓤErnst-Reuter-Platz) Christian Gentemann's liquid playground at the art deco Hotel am Steinplatz was crowned 'Hotel Bar of the Year' in 2016 and 2017, and for good reason. The drinks are simply sensational and the ambience a perfect blend of hip and grown-up. The illustrated cocktail menu teases the imagination by listing ingredients and tastes for each drink instead of just an abstract name.

Monkey Bar
Bar

(Map p452; ☏030-120 221 210; www.monkey barberlin.de; Budapester Strasse 40; ☺noon-2am; ☎; ☐100, 200, ⓢZoologischer Garten, ⓤZoologischer Garten) On the 10th floor of the 25hours Hotel Bikini Berlin, this mainstream-hip 'urban jungle' delivers fabulous views of the city and Zoo Berlin while the menu gives prominent nods to tiki concoctions (great Mai Tai!) and gin-based cocktail sorcery. Come early for chilled sundowners on the sweeping terrace. Different DJs spin nightly Friday to Sunday, from 4pm.

✪ ENTERTAINMENT

Berliner Philharmonie
Architecture, Concert Hall

(Map p450; ☏030-2548 8156; www.berliner-philharmoniker.de; Herbert-von-Karajan-Strasse 1; tours adult/concession €5/3; ☺tours 1.30pm Sep-Jun; ☐M29, M48, M85, 200, ⓢPotsdamer Platz, ⓤPotsdamer Platz) A masterpiece of or-

POSZTOS / SHUTTERSTOCK ©

ganic architecture, Hans Scharoun's 1963 iconic, honey-coloured concert venue is the home base of the prestigious **Berliner Philharmoniker** (⌨tickets 030-2548 8999; www.berliner-philharmoniker.de; tickets €21-290). The auditorium feels like the inside of a finely crafted instrument and boasts supreme acoustics and excellent sight lines from every seat.

Chamäleon Theatre   Cabaret

(Map p446; ⌨030-400 0590; www.chamaeleon berlin.com; Rosenthaler Strasse 40/41; tickets €37-59; ⌐M1, ⓈHackescher Markt) A marriage of art nouveau charms and high-tech theatre trappings, this intimate venue in a 1920s-style old ballroom hosts 'contemporary circus' shows that blend comedy, acrobatics, music, juggling and dance – often in sassy, sexy and unconventional fashion. Sit at the bar, at bistro tables or in comfy armchairs.

ⓘ INFORMATION

Visit Berlin (www.visitberlin.de), the Berlin tourist board, operates five walk-in offices, info desks at the airports, and a **call centre** (⌨030-2500 2333; ⊙9am-6pm Mon-Fri) whose multilingual staff field general questions and make hotel and ticket bookings.

Alexanderplatz (Map p446; lobby Park Inn, Alexanderplatz 7; ⊙7am-9pm Mon-Sat, 8am-6pm Sun; ⌐100, 200, TXL, ⓊAlexanderplatz, ⓈAlexanderplatz)

Brandenburger Tor (Map p446; Pariser Platz, Brandenburger Tor, south wing; ⊙9.30am-7pm Apr-Oct, to 6pm Nov-Mar; ⓈBrandenburger Tor, ⓊBrandenburger Tor)

Central Bus Station (ZOB; Masurenallee 4-6; ⊙8am-8pm Mon, Fri & Sat, to 4pm Tue-Thu & Sun; ⓈMesse Nord/ICC)

Europa-Center (Map p452; Tauentzienstrasse 9, Europa-Center, ground fl; ⊙10am-8pm Mon-Sat; ⌐100, 200, ⓊKurfürstendamm, Zoologischer Garten, ⓈZoologischer Garten)

Hauptbahnhof (Hauptbahnhof, Europaplatz entrance, ground fl; ⊙8am-10pm; ⓈHauptbahnhof, ⌐Hauptbahnhof)

🛍 Berlin's Flea Markets

Berlin's numerous flea markets set up on weekends (usually Sunday) year-round – rain or shine – and are also the purview of fledgling local fashion designers and jewellery makers.

Flohmarkt im Mauerpark (www.flohmarkt immauerpark.de; Bernauer Strasse 63-64; ⊙9am-6pm Sun; ⌐M1, M10, 12, ⓊEberswalder Strasse) Join the throngs of thrifty trinket hunters, bleary-eyed clubbers and excited tourists sifting for treasure at this always busy flea market with cult status, in a spot right where the Berlin Wall once ran. Source new favourites among retro threads, local-designer T-shirts, vintage vinyl and offbeat stuff. Street-food stands and beer gardens provide sustenance.

Nowkoelln Flowmarkt (www.nowkoelln. de; Maybachufer; ⊙10am-6pm 2nd & 4th Sun of month Mar-Oct or later; ⓊKottbusser Tor, Schönleinstrasse) This flea market sets up twice-monthly along the scenic Landwehrkanal and delivers secondhand bargains galore along with handmade threads and jewellery.

RAW Flohmarkt (www.raw-flohmarkt-berlin.de; Revaler Strasse 99; ⊙9am-5pm Sun; ⌐M10, M13, ⓈWarschauer Strasse, ⓊWarschauer Strasse) Bargains abound at this smallish flea market right on the grounds of **RAW Gelände**, a former train repair station-turned-party village. It's wonderfully free of professional sellers, meaning you'll find everything from the proverbial kitchen sink to 1970s go-go boots. Bargains are plentiful, and street food and a beer garden provide handy post-shopping pit stops.

Jam on display at Flohmarkt im Mauerpark
EAZN / SHUTTERSTOCK ©

✦ LGBT+ Berlin

Berlin's legendary liberalism has spawned one of the world's biggest, most divine and diverse LGBT+ playgrounds. Anything goes in 'Homopolis' (and we do mean anything!), from the highbrow to the hands-on, the bourgeois to the bizarre, the mainstream to the flamboyant. Except for the most hardcore places, gay spots get their share of opposite-sex and straight patrons.

Generally speaking, Berlin's gayscape runs the entire spectrum from mellow cafes, campy bars and cinemas to saunas, cruising areas, clubs with darkrooms and all-out sex venues. In fact, sex and sexuality are entirely everyday matters to the unshockable city folks and there are very few, if any, itches that can't be quite openly and legally scratched. As elsewhere, gay men have more options for having fun, but girls of all stripes won't feel left out either.

Rainbow flag being flown in Berlin
SERGEY KOHL / SHUTTERSTOCK ©

ⓘ GETTING THERE & AWAY

AIR

Most visitors arrive in Berlin by air. Berlin's new central airport, about 24km southeast of the city centre, is due for completion in 2020. Check www. berlin-airport.de for the latest. In the meantime, flights continue to land at the city's **Tegel** (TXL; ☏030-6091 1150; www.berlin-airport.de; 🚇Flughafen Tegel) and **Schönefeld** (SXF; ☏030-6091 1150; www.berlin-airport.de; 🚆Airport-Express, RE7 & RB14, ⑤S9, S45) airports.

BUS

Most long-haul buses arrive at the **Zentraler Omnibusbahnhof** (ZOB, Central Bus Station; ☏030-3010 0175; www.zob-berlin.de; Messedamm 8; ⑤Messe/ICC Nord, ⓤKaiserdamm) near the trade fairgrounds on the western city edge. Some stop at Alexanderplatz or other points in town. The closest U-Bahn station to ZOB is Kaiserdamm, about 400m north and served by the U2 line, which travels to Zoologischer Garten in about eight minutes and to Alexanderplatz in 28 minutes.

TRAIN

Berlin's **Hauptbahnhof** (Main Train Station; Europaplatz, Washingtonplatz; ⑤Hauptbahnhof, ⓤHauptbahnhof) is in the heart of the city, just north of the Government Quarter and within walking distance of major sights and hotels. From here, the U-Bahn, the S-Bahn, trams and buses provide links to all parts of town. Taxi ranks are located outside the north exit (Europaplatz) and the south exit (Washingtonplatz).

ⓘ GETTING AROUND

Berlin's extensive and efficient public transport system is operated by BVG (www.bvg.de) and consists of the U-Bahn (underground, or subway), the S-Bahn (light rail), buses and trams. For trip planning and general information, call the 24-hour hotline (☏030-194 49) or check the website.

U-Bahn Most efficient way to travel; operates 4am to 12.30am and all night Friday, Saturday and public holidays. From Sunday to Thursday, half-hourly night buses take over in the interim.

S-Bahn Less frequent than U-Bahn trains but with fewer stops, and thus useful for longer distances. Same operating hours as the U-Bahn.

Bus Slow but useful for sightseeing on the cheap. Run frequently 4.30am to 12.30am; half-hourly night buses in the interim. Metro-Buses (designated eg M1, M19) operate 24/7.

Tram Only in the eastern districts; MetroTrams (designated eg M1, M2) run 24/7.

Bicycle Bike lanes and rental stations abound; bikes allowed in specially marked U-Bahn and S-Bahn carriages.

Taxi Can be hailed, ordered by phone or picked up at ranks.

Where to Stay

Berlin offers the full gamut of places to unpack your suitcase – you can even sleep in a former bank, boat or factory, in the home of a silent-movie diva or in a 'flying bed'.

Neighbourhood	Atmosphere
Mitte	Close to major sights like Reichstag and Brandenburger Tor; great transport links; mostly high-end hotels; top restaurants; touristy, expensive, pretty dead at night.
Museumsinsel & Alexanderplatz	Supercentral sightseeing quarter; easy transport access; close to blockbuster sights and mainstream shopping; large and new hotels; noisy, busy and dusty thanks to major construction; hardly any nightlife.
Potsdamer Platz & Tiergarten	Urban flair in Berlin's only high-rise quarter; cutting-edge architecture; high-end hotels; top museums; limited eating options; pricey.
Scheunenviertel	Hipster quarter; trendy, historic, central; brims with boutique and designer hotels; strong cafe scene; top galleries and plenty of street art; pricey, busy in daytime, noisy, no parking, touristy.
City West & Charlottenburg	Great shopping; 'Old Berlin' bars and top restaurants; best range of good-value lodging; historic B&Bs; far from key sights and nightlife.
Kreuzberg & Neukölln	Best for bar-hopping and clubbing; high vibe; great foodie scene; excellent street art; gritty, noisy and busy.
Friedrichshain	Student and young family quarter; bubbling nightlife; limited sleeping options; not so central; transport difficult in some areas.
Prenzlauer Berg	Charming residential area; lively cafe and restaurant scene; indie boutiques and Mauerpark flea market; limited late-night action.

Castle exterior in autumn

Schloss Neuschwanstein, Germany

Appearing through the mountainous forest like a mirage, Schloss Neuschwanstein was the model for Disney's Sleeping Beauty castle. King Ludwig II drew the blueprints for this fairy-tale pile himself. He envisioned it as a giant stage on which to recreate the world of Germanic mythology, inspired by the operatic works of his friend Richard Wagner.

Great For...

❶ Need to Know

🎟tickets 08362-930 830; www.neuschwanstein.de; Neuschwansteinstrasse 20; adult/child €13/free, incl Hohenschwangau €25/free; ⊙9am-6pm Apr–mid-Oct, 10am-4pm mid-Oct–Mar

★ **Top Tip**

Arrive as early as 8am to make sure you bag a ticket for that day.

Ludwig II, the Fairy-Tale King

King Ludwig II's obsession with French culture and the Sun King, Louis XIV, further inspired the fantastical design.

Ludwig was an enthusiastic leader initially, but Bavaria's days as a sovereign state were numbered, and he became a puppet king after the creation of the German Reich in 1871. Ludwig withdrew completely to drink, draw up castle plans and view concerts and operas in private.

In January 1886, several ministers and relatives arranged a hasty psychiatric test that diagnosed Ludwig as mentally unfit to rule. That June, he was removed to Schloss Berg on Lake Starnberg. A few days later the dejected bachelor and his doctor took a Sunday-evening lakeside walk and were found several hours later, drowned in just a few feet of water. No one knows with certainty what happened that night, and conspiracy theories abound. That summer the authorities opened Neuschwanstein to the public to help pay off Ludwig's huge debts. King Ludwig II was dead, but the myth was just being born.

Construction

Built as a romantic medieval castle, the grey-white granite pile was begun in 1869 but was an anachronism from the start: at the time of Ludwig's death in 1886, the first high-rises had pierced New York's skyline. However, despite his love for the old-fashioned look, the palace had plenty of high-tech features, including a hot-air heating system and running water. Like so many of the king's grand schemes, Neuschwanstein was never finished. For all the coffer-depleting sums spent on

Interior

it, the king spent just over 170 days in residence.

The Interior

The most impressive room is the Sänger-saal (Minstrels' Hall), whose frescoes depict scenes from Wagner's opera *Tann-häuser*. Other completed sections include Ludwig's Tristan and Isolde–themed **bedroom**, dominated by a huge Gothic-style bed crowned with intricately carved cathedral-like spires; a gaudy artificial

---

☑ Don't Miss

The excellent **Museum der Bayer-ischen Könige** (Museum of the Bavarian Kings; www.museumderbayerischenkoenige. de; Alpseestrasse 27; adult/child €11/free; ⊙9am-5pm) is a short walk from the castle ticket office.

MIRONOV / SHUTTERSTOCK ©

grotto (another allusion to the *Tann-häuser*); and the Byzantine-style **Thron-saal** (Throne Room) with an incredible mosaic floor containing over two million stones. The painting opposite the (throne-less) throne platform depicts another castle dreamed up by Ludwig that was never built.

Schloss Hohenschwangau

King Ludwig II grew up at the sun-yellow **Schloss Hohenschwangau** (🖉08362-930 830; www.hohenschwangau.de; Alpseestrasse 30; adult/child €13/free, incl Neuschwanstein €25/free; ⊙8am-5pm Apr–mid-Oct, 9am-3pm mid-Oct–Mar) and later enjoyed sum-mers here until his death in 1886. His father, Maximilian II, built this palace in a neo-Gothic style atop 12th-century ruins left by Schwangau knights. Far less showy than Neuschwanstein, Hohenschwangau has a distinctly lived-in feel where every piece of furniture is a used original. After his father died, Ludwig's main alteration was having stars, illuminated with hidden oil lamps, painted on the ceiling of his bedroom.

Castle Tickets & Tours

Schloss Neuschwanstein and Hohen-schwangau can only be visited on guided tours (in German or English), which last about 35 minutes each (Hohenschwangau is first). Strictly timed tickets are available from the **Ticket Centre** (🖉08362-930 830; www.hohenschwangau.de; Alpenseestrasse 12; ⊙7.30am-5pm Apr–mid-Oct, 8.30am-3pm mid-Oct–Mar) at the foot of the castles.

Enough time is left between tours for the steep 30- to 40-minute walk between the castles. All Munich's tour companies run day excursions out to the castles.

★ Classic Image

For the postcard view of Neuschwan-stein, walk 10 minutes up to Marien-brücke (Mary's Bridge).

SWISS ALPS,
SWITZERLAND

Swiss Alps, Switzerland

You can sense the anticipation on the train from Täsch: couples gaze out of the window, kids fidget, folk rummage for their cameras. And then, as they arrive in Zermatt, all gasp at the pop-up-book effect of the Matterhorn, the hypnotically beautiful, one-of-a-kind peak that rises like a shark's fin above town.

Since the mid-19th century, Zermatt has starred among Switzerland's glitziest resorts. Today skiers cruise along well-kept pistes, spellbound by the scenery, while style-conscious visitors flit between the town's swish lounge bars.

Two Days in the Swiss Alps

Get up high with Europe's highest-altitude **cable car** (p471) or **cogwheel railway** (p471) and walk or ski down – never taking your eyes off the pyramid-perfect, bewitching Matterhorn. Dedicate day two to exploring Zermatt (p474) and gorging yourself on delicious raclette or fondue (p478).

Four Days in the Swiss Alps

Spend the morning hiking the Matterhorn Glacier Trail (p477) for more stunning Matterhorn views before taking to the slopes (p477) for the rest of the day. On the fourth day, hop aboard the **Glacier Express** (p472) in Zermatt, sit back and enjoy a spectacular train journey to St Moritz.

At the end of your trip, take a train to Florence (p397) or Provence (p289).

Previous page: Zermatt (p474) and Matterhorn (p470)

Zermatt Map (p476)

Arriving in the Swiss Alps

Train Direct trains to Zermatt depart hourly from Brig (Sfr38, 1½ hours), stopping at Visp en route. Zermatt is also the start/end point of the **Glacier Express** (p472) to/from St Moritz.

Car Zermatt is car-free. Motorists have to park in the Matterhorn Terminal Täsch (www.matterhornterminal.ch, per 24hr Sfr15.50) in Täsch and ride the Zermatt Shuttle train (return adult/child Sfr16.40/8.20, 12 minutes, every 20 minutes from 6am to 9.40pm) the last 5km up to Zermatt.

Where to Stay

Book well ahead in winter, and bear in mind that nearly everywhere closes from May to mid- or late June and mid-October to November or early December. With advanced warning, many places will pick you and your bags up at the station in an electro-shuttle. Check when you book.

Sleeping choices in Zermatt run from hostel beds to ultra-chic designer digs, with plenty of chalet-style midrange options in between.

JAKL LUBOS / SHUTTERSTOCK ©

Matterhorn

No mountain has so much pulling power and natural magnetism or is so easy to become obsessed with as this charismatic peak.

The beautiful Matterhorn demands to be admired, ogled and repeatedly photographed at sunrise and sunset, in different seasons, and from every last angle.

Climbing Matterhorn

Some 3000 alpinists summit Europe's most photographed, 4478m-high peak each year. You don't need to be superhuman to do it, but you do need to be a skilled climber (with crampons), be in tiptop physical shape (12-hours-endurance performance) and have a week in hand to acclimatise beforehand to make the iconic ascent up sheer rock and ice.

No one attempts the Matterhorn without local know-how: mountain guides at the Snow & Alpine Center (p477) charge Sfr1600 per person for the eight-hour

Great For...

☑ Don't Miss

Visiting the Matterhorn Museum (p474) to learn about the first successful ascent of the Matterhorn.

❶ Need to Know

Mid-July to mid-September is the best time of year to attempt the ascent.

✕ Take a Break

There are restaurants at Riffelalp (2211m) and Riffelberg (2582m) along the Gornergratbahn path.

★ Top Tip

For outstanding views of the Matterhorn, jump aboard the Sunnegga Express funicular (p477) to the top of Sunnegga.

return climb, including cable car from Zermatt to Schwarzee and half-board accommodation in a mountain hut. Client-to-guide ratios are 1:1. You'll probably be required to do training climbs first, just to prove you really are 100% up to it. The Matterhorn claims more than a few lives each year.

Matterhorn Glacier Paradise

Views from Zermatt's cable cars are all remarkable, but the **Matterhorn Glacier Paradise** (www.matterhornparadise.ch; Schluhmattstrasse; return adult/child aged 9-15/child under 9 Sfr100/50/free; ☉8.30am-4.50pm) is the icing on the cake. Ride Europe's highest-altitude cable car to 3883m and gawp at 14 glaciers and 38 mountain peaks over 4000m from the

Panoramic Platform (only open in good weather). Don't miss the **Glacier Palace**, an ice palace complete with glittering ice sculptures and an ice slide to swoosh down bum-first. End with some exhilarating **snow tubing** outside in the snowy surrounds.

Gornergratbahn

Europe's highest **cogwheel railway** (www.gornergrat.ch; Bahnhofplatz 7; return adult/child Sfr98/49; ☉7am-6.24pm) has climbed through picture-postcard scenery to **Gornergrat** (3089m) – a 30-minute journey – since 1898. On the way up, sit on the right-hand side of the little red train to goggle at the Matterhorn. Tickets allow you to get on and off en route at stops including Riffelalp (2211m) and Riffelberg (2582m). In summer an extra train runs once a week at sunrise and sunset – the most spectacular trips of all.

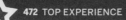

ALESSANDRO COLLE / SHUTTERSTOCK ©

Glacier Express

The Glacier Express is one of Europe's mythical train journeys. It starts and ends in two of Switzerland's oldest, glitziest mountain resorts – Zermatt and St Moritz – and the Alpine scenery is magnificent in parts.

Hop aboard the red train with floor-to-ceiling windows in St Moritz or Zermatt, and savour shot after cinematic shot of green peaks, glistening Alpine lakes, glacial ravines and other hallucinatory natural landscapes. Pulled by steam engine when it first puffed out of the station in 1930, the Glacier Express traverses 191 tunnels and 291 bridges on its famous 290km journey.

Highlights include the one-hour ride from Disentis to Andermatt, across the Oberalp Pass (2033m) – the highest point of the journey in every way; and the celebrity six-arch, 65m-high Landwasser Viaduct, pictured on almost every feature advertising the Glacier Express, that dazzles passengers during the 50km leg between Chur and Filisur.

Great For...

☑ **Don't Miss**

The ride from Disentis to Andermatt and the Landwasser Viaduct.

❶ Need to Know

www.glacierexpress.ch; adult/child aged 6-16/ child under 6s one way St Moritz-Zermatt Sfr152/76/free, obligatory seat reservation summer/winter Sfr43/23; ⏱3 trains daily May-Oct, 1 daily mid-Dec–Feb

✕ Take a Break

Have lunch in the vintage restaurant car or bring your own champagne picnic.

★ Top Tip

Check the weather forecast before committing: a blue sky is essential for the eight-hour train ride to be worthwhile.

A ticket is not cheap, and to avoid disappointment it pays to know the nuts and bolts of this 290km-long mountain train ride.

○ Don't asume it is amazing mountain views for the duration of the journey: the views in the tunnels the train passes through are not particularly wonderful, for starters.

○ The complete trip takes almost eight hours. If you're travelling with children or can't bear the thought of sitting all day watching mountain scenery that risks becoming monotonous, opt for just a section of the journey: the best bit is the one-hour ride from Disentis to Andermatt.

○ Windows in the stylish panoramic carriages are sealed and can't be opened, making it tricky to take good photographs or film. If photography/video is the reason you're aboard, ditch the direct glamour train for regional express SBB trains along the same route – cheaper, no reservations required, with windows that open and the chance to stretch your legs when changing trains.

○ The southern side of the train is said to have the best views.

○ Children aged under six years travel free (buy an extra seat reservation if you don't fancy a young child on your lap for eight hours), and children aged six to 16 years pay half-price plus seat reservation.

Zermatt

◉ SIGHTS

Meander main-strip **Bahnhofstrasse** with its flashy boutiques and the stream of horse-drawn sleds or carriages and electric taxis, then head downhill towards the noisy Vispa river along **Hinterdorfstrasse**. This old-world street is crammed with 16th-century pig stalls and archetypal Valaisian timber granaries propped up on stone discs and stilts to keep out pesky rats; look for the **fountain** commemorating Ulrich Inderbinen (1900–2004), a Zermatt-born mountaineer who climbed the Matterhorn 370 times, the last time at age 90. Nicknamed the King of the Alps, he was the oldest active mountain guide in the world when he retired at the ripe old age of 95.

Matterhorn Museum   Museum
(☏027 967 41 00; www.zermatt.ch/museum; Kirchplatz; adult/child aged 10-16/child under 10 Sfr10/5/free; ⊘11am-6pm Jul-Sep, 3-6pm Oct–mid-Nov, 3-6pm Fri-Sun mid-Nov–Mar, 2-6pm Apr-Jun) This crystalline, state-of-the-art museum provides fascinating insight into Valaisian village life, mountaineering, the dawn of tourism in Zermatt and the lives the Matterhorn has claimed. Short films portray the first successful ascent of the Matterhorn on 14 July 1865 led by Edward Whymper, a feat marred by tragedy on the descent when four team members crashed to their deaths in a 1200m fall. The infamous rope that broke is exhibited.

Gornerschlucht   Gorge
(☏027 967 20 96; www.gornergorge.ch; adult/child Sfr5/2.50; ⊘9.15am-5.45pm Jun–mid-Oct) It is a 1.5km walk from Zermatt along the river to this dramatic gorge, carved out of green serpentinite rock and accessed by a series of wooden staircases and walkways. Good fun for families.

Sunnegga   Viewpoint
(www.matterhornparadise.ch; adult/child aged 9-15/child under 9 one way Sfr16/8/free; ⚕) Take the *Sunnegga Express* 'tunnel funicular' up to Sunnegga (2288m) for amazing views of the Matterhorn. This is a top spot for families – take the Leisee Shuttle (free)

Matterhorn Museum entrance

NAVIN TAR / SHUTTERSTOCK ©

down to the lake for beginner ski slopes at Wolli's Park in winter, and for a children's playground and splashing around in the lake during summer. A marmot-watching station is a few minutes' walk from Sunnegga. It's a relatively easy downhill walk back to Zermatt (via Findeln) in about 1½ hours.

Ricola Herb Garden
Gardens

(www.ricola.com; Blatten; ⊘Jun-Sep) `FREE` Best known for its herby hard-boiled sweets, Ricola has a short herb-garden hike at Blatten where you can learn about the 13 herbs that go into every drop. Blatten is about halfway down the Matterhorn Express cable car between Füri and Zermatt, reached by walking track. The start of the herb-garden walk is next to the small chapel.

Mountaineers' Cemetery
Cemetery

(Kirchstrasse) A walk in Zermatt's pair of cemeteries – the Mountaineers' Cemetery in the garden of Zermatt's **St Mauritius Church** (Kirchplatz) and the main cemetery across the road – is a sobering experience. Numerous gravestones tell of untimely deaths on Monte Rosa, the Matterhorn and Breithorn.

🟢 ACTIVITIES

An essential stop in activity planning is the **Zermatters** (Snow & Alpine Center; ☑027 966 24 66; www.zermatters.ch; Bahnhofstrasse 58; ⊘8am-noon & 3-7pm Dec-Apr, 9am-noon & 3-7pm mid-Jun–Sep), home to Zermatt's ski school and mountain guides. In winter buy **lift passes** here (Sfr79/430 for a one-day/one-week pass excluding Cervinia, Sfr92/494 including Cervinia).

🟢 Skiing

Zermatt is cruising heaven, with mostly long, scenic red runs, plus a smattering of blues for ski virgins and knuckle-whitening blacks for experts. The main skiing areas in winter are **Rothorn**, **Stockhorn** and **Klein Matterhorn** – 52 lifts, 360km of ski runs in all, with a link from Klein Matterhorn to

🥾 Hiking with Kids

Try out these short-walk favourites for families with younger children:

⊙ Take the *Sunnegga Express* up to Sunnegga, then the Leisee Shuttle (or walk the 10 minutes) downhill to **Leisee**, a lake made for bracing summer dips with a bijou pebble beach and an old-fashioned wooden raft for children to tug themselves across the water pirate-style.

⊙ In town, embark on the 20-minute walk along the river to the Gornerschlucht, a dramatic gorge carved out of green serpentinite rock and accessed by a series of wooden staircases and walkways.

⊙ The easy circular walk around the Ricola Herb Garden (p477), in the pretty mountain hamlet of Blatten (signposted from Gornergratschlucht), bristles with aromatic herbs that end up in Ricola sweets, and there's a fun 'touch and smell' quiz to do.

⊙ The 1¼-hour circular walk (2.9km) in Füri takes in the **Gletschergarten Dossen** (Dossen Glacier Garden), with its bizarre glacial-rock formations, picnic area with stone-built barbecues to cook up lunch, and the dizzying 90m-high, 100m-long steel suspension bridge above the Gornerschlucht Gorge.

Child hiking at Gornerschlucht
ANNA NAHABED / SHUTTERSTOCK ©

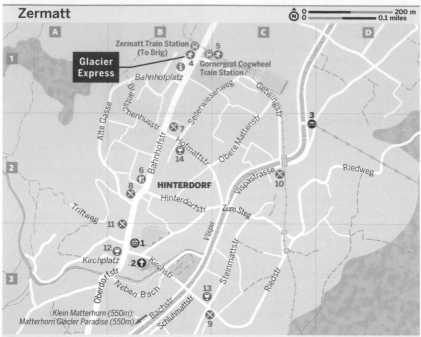

Zermatt

◎ Sights
1 Matterhorn Museum	....	B3
	Mountaineers' Cemetery	.... (see 2)
2 St Mauritius Church	....	B3
3 Sunnegga	....	C2

◎ Activities, Courses & Tours
4 Glacier Express	....	B1
5 Gornergratbahn	....	C1
6 Zermatters	....	B2

◎ Eating
7 Bayard Metzgerei	....	B2
8 Le Gitan – Zermatterstübli	....	B2
9 Schäferstube	....	B3
10 Snowboat	....	C2
11 Whymper Stube	....	B3

◎ Drinking & Nightlife
12 Elsie Bar	....	B3
13 Papperla Pub	....	B3
14 Vernissage Bar Club	....	B2

the Italian resort of **Cervinia** and a freestyle park with a half-pipe for snowboarders.

Summer skiing (20km of runs) and boarding (a gravity park at Plateau Rosa on the Theodul glacier) is Europe's most extensive. One-/two-day summer ski passes cost Sfr84/125.

🌀 Hiking

Zermatt is a hiker's paradise, with 400km of summer trails through some of the most incredible scenery in the Alps – the tourist office has trail maps. For Matterhorn close-ups, nothing beats the highly dramatic **Matterhorn Glacier Trail** (two hours, 6.5km) from Trockener Steg to Schwarzsee; 23 information panels en route tell you everything you could possibly need to know about glaciers and glacial life.

For those doing lots of walking, local excursion passes offer a convenient way to get into the high country. A **Peak Pass**, offering unlimited use of the Schwarzsee,

Rothorn and Matterhorn Glacier Paradise cable cars plus the Gornergratbahn cog railway, costs from Sfr188 for three days or from Sfr269 for a week. To find your perfect walk, search by duration, distance and difficulty on the hiking page of the excellent tourist-office website (www.zermatt.ch).

🍴 EATING

The entire Zermatt town centre is packed with restaurants, with the greatest concentration along busy Bahnhofstrasse.

Snowboat   International €

(☑027 967 43 33; www.zermattsnowboat.com; Vispastrasse 20; mains Sfr26.50-49.50; ☺2pm-midnight; ☑) This hybrid eating-drinking riverside address, with deckchairs sprawled across its rooftop sun terrace, is a blessing. When fondue tires, head here for barbecue-sizzled burgers (not just beef, but crab and veggie burgers, too), super-power creative salads (the Omega 3 buster is a favourite) and great cocktails. The vibe? Completely friendly, fun and funky.

Bayard Metzgerei   Swiss €

(☑027 967 22 66; www.metzgerei-bayard.ch; Bahnhofstrasse 9; sausage Sfr6; ☺8am-noon & 2-7pm Dec-Mar & Jul-Sep, to 6.30 Apr-Jun & Oct-Nov) Join the line for a street-grilled sausage (pork, veal or beef) and chunk of bread to down with a beer on the hop – or at a bar stool with the sparrows in the alley – of this first-class butcher's shop.

Klein Matterhorn   Pizza €

(☑027 967 01 42; www.kleinmatterhorn-zermatt.com; Schluhmattstrasse 50; pizza Sfr18-25; ☺8am-midnight, kitchen 11.30am-10pm) For first-rate Italian pizza in the sun with a Matterhorn view, this simple pizzeria and cafe-bar opposite the Matterhorn Glacier Express cable-car station is the address.

Chez Vrony   Swiss €€

(☑027 967 25 52; www.chezvrony.ch; Findeln; breakfast Sfr15-28, mains Sfr25-45; ☺9.15am-5pm Dec-Apr & mid-Jun–mid-Oct) Ride the

Sunnegga Express funicular to 2288m, then ski down or summer-hike 15 minutes to Zermatt's tastiest slope-side address in the Findeln hamlet. Delicious dried meats, homemade cheese and sausage come from Vrony's own cows, grazing away the summer on the high Alpine pastures (2100m) surrounding it, and the Vrony burger is legendary. Advance reservations essential in winter.

Schäferstube   Swiss €€

(☑027 966 76 05; www.julen.ch/en/schaeferstube; Riedstrasse 2; mains Sfr24-50; ☺6-11pm) Just the kind of warm, rustic, snugly lit hut where you'll pray for the flakes to fall in winter, the Schäferstube is as traditional as they come, with low timber ceilings, huge cowbells and hunting trophies galore. It's run by shepherd Paul Julen, so expect succulent cuts of lamb, cooked on a charcoal grill, alongside Valais raclette and cheese fondue.

Le Gitan – Zermatterstübli   Swiss €€

(☑027 968 19 40; www.legitan.ch; Bahnhofstrasse 64; mains from Sfr23; ☺11am-11pm) Le Gitan stands out for its elegant chalet-style interior and extra-tasty cuisine. Plump for a feisty pork or veal sausage with onion sauce and rösti, or dip into a cheese fondue – with Champagne (yes!), or, if you're feeling outrageously indulgent, Champagne and fresh truffles. End with coffee ice-cream doused in kirsch, or apricot sorbet with *abricotine* (local Valais apricot liqueur).

Whymper Stube   Swiss €€

(☑027 967 22 96; www.whymper-stube.ch; Bahnhofstrasse 80; raclette Sfr9, fondue from Sfr25; ☺11am-11pm Nov-Apr & Jun–mid-Oct) This cosy bistro, attached to the **Monte Rosa Hotel** that Whymper left from to climb the Matterhorn in 1865, is legendary for its excellent raclette and fondues. The icing on the cake is a segmented pot bubbling with three different cheese fondues. Service is relaxed and friendly, tables are packed tightly together, and the place – all inside – buzzes come dusk.

¡O¡ A Feast of a Meal: Fondue & Raclette

It is hard to leave Switzerland without dipping into a fondue. A pot of gooey melted cheese is placed in the centre of the table and kept on a slow burn while diners dip in cubes of crusty bread using slender two-pronged fondue forks. Traditionally a winter dish, the Swiss tend to eat it mostly if there's snow around or they're at a suitable altitude – unlike tourists who tuck in year-round and wherever they find it.

The classic fondue mix in Switzerland is equal amounts of emmental and gruyère cheese, grated and melted with white wine and a shot of kirsch (cherry-flavoured liquor), then thickened slightly with potato or corn flour. It is served with a basket of bread slices (which are soon torn into small morsels) and most people order a side platter of cold meats and tiny gherkins to accompany it.

Switzerland's other signature alpine cheese dish is raclette. Unlike fondue, raclette – both the name of the dish and the cheese at its gooey heart – is eaten year-round. A half-crescent slab of the cheese is screwed onto a specially designed 'rack oven' that melts the top flat side. As it melts, cheese is scraped onto plates for immediate consumption with boiled potatoes, cold meats and pickled onions or gherkins.

Croissant raclette
DMITRY_EVS / SHUTTERSTOCK ©

🍷 DRINKING & NIGHTLIFE

Still fizzing with energy after schussing down the slopes? Zermatt pulses in party-mad après-ski huts, suave lounge bars and Brit-style pubs. Most close (and some melt) in low season.

Elsie's Bar — Wine Bar

(📞027 967 24 31; www.elsiesbar.ch; Kirchplatz 16; ⊙4pm-1am) In a building originally erected in 1879, this elegant, old-world wine bar with wood-panelled walls, across from the church, has been known as Elsie's since 1961. Oysters, caviar and snails are on the winter menu, along with a top selection of wine and whisky.

Hennu Stall — Bar

(📞027 966 35 10; www.hennustall.ch; Klein Matterhorn; ⊙2-8pm Dec-Apr) Last one down to this snowbound 'chicken run' is a rotten egg. Hennu is the wildest après-ski shack on Klein Matterhorn, located below Furi on the way to Zermatt. Order a caramel vodka and take your ski boots grooving to live music on the terrace. A metre-long 'ski' of shots will make you cluck all the way down to Zermatt.

Vernissage Bar Club — Bar

(📞027 966 69 70; www.backstagehotel.ch; Hofmattstrasse 4; ⊙5pm-midnight Sun-Wed, to 2am Thu-Sat) The ultimate après-ski antithesis, Vernissage at the Backstage Hotel exudes grown-up sophistication. Local artist Heinz Julen has created a theatrical space with flowing velvet drapes, film-reel chandeliers and candlelit booths. Catch an exhibition, watch a movie, pose in the lounge bar.

Papperla Pub — Pub

(www.julen.ch; Steinmattstrasse 36; ⊙2pm-2am winter, 2pm-midnight Tue-Thu & Sun, to 2am Fri & Sat summer; 🛜) Rammed with sloshed skiers in winter and happy hikers in summer, this buzzing pub with red director chairs on its pavement terrace blends pulsating music with lethal Jägermeister bombs, good vibes and pub grub (from 5pm). Its downstairs **Schneewittli club** rocks until dawn in season.

A restaurant in Zermatt

ℹ️ INFORMATION

Make the Swiss tourist board, **Switzerland Tourism** (www.myswitzerland.com), your first port of call. For detailed information, contact the local **tourist office** (📞027 966 81 00; www.zermatt.ch; Bahnhofplatz 5; ⊗8am-8pm; 📶). Information and maps abound and somebody invariably speaks English. In German-speaking Switzerland tourist offices are called *Verkehrsbüro*, or *Kurverein* in some resorts.

ℹ️ GETTING THERE & AWAY

Switzerland's fully integrated public-transport system is among the world's most efficient. However, travel is expensive and visitors planning to use intercity routes should consider investing in a Swiss Travel Pass. Timetables often refer to *Werktags* (workdays), which means Mondays to Saturdays, unless there is the qualification

Zermatt pulses in party-mad après-ski huts, suave lounge bars and Brit-style pubs

ausser Samstag ('except Saturday'). For timetables and tickets, head to www.sbb.ch.

Drivers using Switzerland's motorways must purchase and display a special sticker (*vignette* in French and German, *contrassegno* in Italian), available for Sfr40 at major border crossings. For more details, see www.vignette.ch.

ℹ️ GETTING AROUND

Dinky electro-taxis zip around town transporting goods and the weary (and noiselessly taking pedestrians by surprise – watch out!). Pick one up at the main rank in front of the train station on Bahnhofstrasse.

DUBROVNIK,
CROATIA

Dubrovnik, Croatia

Whether you are visiting Croatia's Dubrovnik for the first time or the 100th, the sense of awe never fails to descend when you set eyes on the beautiful old town. Indeed it's hard to imagine anyone becoming jaded by the marble streets, the baroque buildings and the endless shimmer of the Adriatic, or not being inspired by a walk along the ancient city walls that protected a civilised, sophisticated republic for centuries.

Although the shelling of Dubrovnik in 1991 horrified the world, the city has bounced back with vigour to enchant visitors again.

Two Days in Dubrovnik

Start early with a walk along the **city walls** (p484), before it's too hot, then wander the marbled streets and call into whichever church, palace or museum takes your fancy.

On day two, take the cable car up Mt Srđ and visit the exhibition **Dubrovnik During the Homeland War** (p491). Afterwards, continue exploring the old town.

Four Days in Dubrovnik

With another couple of days up your sleeve you'll have the luxury of confining your old-town explorations to the evenings, when the cruise-ship hordes have returned to their boats. On day three, plan to spend the middle of the day on the island of **Lokrum** (p491). On your final day, jump on a boat to **Cavtat** (p489), allowing a couple of hours to stroll around the historic town.

Moving on from Dubrovnik? It's a short flight to Rome (p327) or Venice (p379).

Previous page: Cable car overlooking Dubrovnik
CANADASTOCK / SHUTTERSTOCK ©

Dubrovnik During the Homeland War

Srđ

SRĐ

Srd

Jadranska Cesta

Od Gaja

Gronji Kono

Jadranska Cesta

Petra Bakića

Jadranska Cesta

Gornji

Volantina

B Bogišića

Pera Budmani

Zagrebačka

Anice Bošković

Braniteja Dubrovnika

Srednji Kono

Cavtatska Obodska

PLOČE

Gradac Park

PILE

City Walls & Forts

Put od Bosanke

Petra Krešimira IV

DANČE

Frana Bulića

Od Tabakerije

Izmedu Vrta

Peline

Put Iza Grada

Frana Supila

Don F

Brsalje

Prijeko

Trg Oružja

Museum of Modern Art

Placa (Stradun)

Kovačka

Old Harbour

Za Rokom

Od Puča

Luža Square

Fort Lawrence

Od Rupa

Držićeva Poljana

Od Kaštela

Bunićeva Poljana

Adriatic Sea

Lokrum (4km); Cavtat (10km)

Dubrovnik Map (p490)

Arriving in Dubrovnik

Dubrovnik Airport In Čilipi, 19km southeast of Dubrovnik. Allow up to 280KN for a taxi, or Atlas runs the airport bus service (40KN, 30 minutes), which stops at the Pile Gate and the bus station.

Dubrovnik Bus Station Times are detailed at www.libertasdubrovnik.hr.

Where to Stay

There's limited accommodation in the compact old town itself. You should book well in advance, especially in summer.

Private accommodation can be a good, well-priced alternative; contact local travel agencies or the tourist office for options.

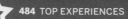

SCHNEPFDESIGN / SHUTTERSTOCK ©

City Walls & Forts

No visit to Dubrovnik would be complete without a walk around the spectacular city walls, the finest in the world and Dubrovnik's main claim to fame.

Great For...

☑ Don't Miss

The sublime view over the old town and the shimmering Adriatic from the top of the walls.

Walking the Walls

There are entrances to the walls from near the **Pile Gate** (Gradska vrata Pile), the **Ploče Gate** (Vrata od Ploča) and the **Maritime Museum** (Pomorski muzej; ☎020-323 904; www.dumus.hr; Tvrđava Sv Ivana; multimuseum pass adult/child 120/25KN; ⊘9am-6pm Tue-Sun Apr-Oct, to 4pm Nov-Mar). The Pile Gate entrance tends to be the busiest, and entering from the Ploče side has the added advantage of getting the steepest climbs out of the way first (you're required to walk in an anti-clockwise direction).

The round Fort Minčeta protects the landward edge of the city from attack, while Fort Revelin and Fort St John guard the eastern approach and the Old Harbour.

ⓘ Need to Know

Gradske zidine; ☑020-638 800; www. wallsofdubrovnik.com; adult/child 200/50KN; ⏰8am-6.30pm Apr-Oct, 9am-3pm Nov-Mar

✕ Take a Break

Bring your own snacks, and especially your own drinks: the few vendors selling water on the route tend to be overpriced.

★ Top Tip

Don't underestimate how strenuous the wall walk can be, particularly on a hot day.

the existing forts and add new ones, so that the entire old town was contained within a stone barrier 2km long and up to 25m high. The walls are thicker on the land side (up to 6m) and from 1.5m to 3m on the sea side.

Recent History

Caught in the cross-hairs of the war that ravaged the former Yugoslavia, Dubrovnik was pummelled with some 2000 shells in 1991 and 1992, suffering considerable damage. There were 111 strikes on the walls.

The walls themselves and all of the damaged buildings have since been restored, but you can get a good handle on the extent of the shelling damage by gazing over the rooftops as you walk the walls: those sporting bright new terra-cotta suffered damage and had to be replaced.

Fort Bokar and Fort Lawrence look west and out to sea. St Blaise gazes down from the walls of **Fort Lawrence** (Tvrđava Lovrjenac; www.citywallsdubrovnik.hr; Pile; 50KN, free with city walls ticket; ⏰8am-6.30pm Apr-Oct, 9am-3pm Nov-Mar), a large free-standing fortress. There's not a lot inside, but the battlements offer wonderful views over the old town and its large court-yard is often a venue for summer theatre and concerts.

History of the Walls

The first set of walls to enclose the city was built in the 9th century. In the middle of the 14th century the 1.5m-thick defences were fortified with 15 square forts. The threat of attacks from the Turks in the 15th century prompted the city to strengthen

Guided Tours

Dubrovnik Walks (☑095 80 64 526; www. dubrovnikwalks.com; Brsalje 8, Pile; ⏰Mar-Dec) runs excellent English-language guided walks departing from near the Pile Gate. The two-hour Walls & Wars tour is 130KN. No reservations necessary.

Rector's Palace

B·HIDE THE SCENE / SHUTTERSTOCK ©

Game of Thrones Locations

Dubrovnik is like a fantasy world for many, but fans of Game of Thrones have more reason to indulge in flights of fancy than most, as plenty of the immensely popular TV series was filmed here.

Great For...

☑ Don't Miss

The city walls, which have often featured in the TV series, particularly during the siege of King's Landing.

City Walls & Fort Lawrence

Tyrion Lannister commanded the defence of King's Landing from the seaward-facing walls (p484) during the Battle of the Blackwater. Fort Lawrence (p485) is King's Landing's famous Red Keep and both the interior and the exterior will be familiar. Cersei farewelled her daughter Myrcella from the little harbour beneath the fort.

Rector's Palace

The grand atrium of the **Rector's Palace** (Knežev dvor; ☎020-321 497; www.dumus. hr; Pred Dvorom 3; adult/child 80/25KN, incl in multimuseum pass adult/child 120/25KN; ⊙9am-6pm Apr-Oct, to 4pm Nov-Mar) featured as the palace of the Spice King of Qarth – they didn't even bother moving the statue! Built in the late 15th century for the elected rector who governed Dubrovnik, this

Fort Lawrence (p485)

LALS STOCK / SHUTTERSTOCK ©

Gothic-Renaissance palace contains the rector's office, his private chambers, public halls, administrative offices and a dungeon. Today the palace has been turned into the Cultural History Museum, with artfully restored rooms, portraits, coats of arms and coins, evoking the glorious history of Dubrovnik.

Trsteno Arboretum

The Red Keep gardens, where the Tyrells chatted and plotted endlessly during seasons three and four, are at the **Trsteno Arboretum** (☎020-751 019; adult/child 50/30KN; ⊗7am-7pm May-Oct, 8am-4pm Nov-Apr). These leafy gardens, 14km northwest of Dubrovnik, are the oldest of their kind in Croatia and well worth a visit. There is a Renaissance layout, with a set of geometric shapes made with plants and bushes, cit-

rus orchards, a maze, a fine palm collection and a gorgeous pond. To get to Trsteno, catch local bus 12, 15, 21, 22 or 35 from Dubrovnik's bus station.

Other Notable Spots

○ **Minčeta Tower** (Tvrđava Minčeta) The exterior of Qarth's House of Undying.

○ **Uz Jezuite** The stairs connecting the St Ignatius of Loyola Church to Gundulić Sq were the starting point for Cersei Lannister's memorable naked penitential walk. The walk continued down Stradun.

○ **Gradac Park** The site of the Purple Wedding feast, where King Joffrey finally got his comeuppance.

○ **Sv Dominika street** The street and staircase outside the **Dominican Monastery** (Dominikanski samostan i muzej; ☎020-321 423; www.dominicanmuseum.hr; Sv Dominika 4; adult/child 30/20KN; ⊗9am-5pm) were used for various King's Landing market scenes.

○ **Ethnographic Museum** (Etnografski muzej; ☎020-323 056; www.dumus.hr; Od Rupa 3; adult/child multimuseum pass 120/25KN; ⊗9am-4pm Wed-Mon) Littlefinger's brothel.

○ **Lokrum** (p491) The reception for Daenerys in Qarth was held in the monastery cloister.

◎ SIGHTS

Today Dubrovnik is the most prosperous, elegant and expensive city in Croatia. In many ways it still feels like a city state, isolated from the rest of the nation by geography and history. It's become such a tourism magnet that there's even talk of having to limit visitor numbers in the car-free old town – the main thoroughfares can get impossibly crowded, especially when multiple cruise ships disgorge passengers at the same time.

Cathedral of the Assumption
Cathedral

(Katedrala Marijina Uznesenja; Držićeva poljana; treasury 20KN; ⊘8am-5pm Mon-Sat, 11am-5pm Sun Easter-Oct, 9am-noon & 4-5pm Mon-Sat Nov-Easter) Built on the site of a 7th-century basilica, Dubrovnik's original cathedral was enlarged in the 12th century, supposedly funded by a gift from England's King

> *it still feels like a city state, isolated from the rest of the nation*

A golden reliquary in the Cathedral of the Assumption

Richard I, the Lionheart, who was saved from a shipwreck on the nearby island of Lokrum. Soon after the first cathedral was destroyed in the 1667 earthquake, work began on this, its baroque replacement, which was finished in 1713.

The cathedral is notable for its fine altars, especially the altar of St John of Nepomuk, made of violet marble. The most striking of its religious paintings is the polyptych of the *Assumption of the Virgin*, hanging behind the main altar, by 16th-century Venetian painter Titian.

To the left of the main altar is the cathedral's **treasury**. Dripping in gold and silver, it contains relics of St Blaise as well as over 150 other reliquaries largely made in the workshops of Dubrovnik's goldsmiths between the 11th and 17th centuries.

War Photo Limited
Gallery

(☑020-322 166; www.warphotoltd.com; Antuninska 6; adult/child 50/40KN; ⊘10am-10pm May-Sep, to 4pm Wed-Mon Apr & Oct) An immensely powerful experience, this gallery features compelling exhibitions curated by New Zealand photojournalist

PAUL PRESCOTT / SHUTTERSTOCK ©

Wade Goddard, who worked in the Balkans in the 1990s. Its intention is to expose the everyday, horrific and unjust realities of war. There's a permanent exhibition on the upper floor devoted to the wars in Yugoslavia; the changing exhibitions cover a multitude of conflicts.

Synagogue & Jewish Museum
Synagogue

(Sinagoga i Židovski muzej; Žudioska 5; 50KN; ⊙10am-5pm) With a religious practice that can be traced back to the 14th century, this is said to be the second-oldest still-functioning synagogue in Europe and the oldest Sephardic one. Sitting on a street that was once the Jewish ghetto, the synagogue also houses a small museum exhibiting religious relics and documentation on the local Jewish population, including records relating to their persecution during WWII.

Franciscan Monastery & Museum
Christian Monastery

(Franjevački samostan i muzej; ☑020-321 410; Placa 2; 30KN; ⊙9am-6pm Apr-Oct, to 2pm Nov-Mar) Within this monastery's solid stone walls are a gorgeous mid-14th-century **cloister**, a historic **pharmacy** and a small **museum** with a collection of relics and liturgical objects, including chalices, paintings and gold jewellery, and pharmacy items such as laboratory gear and medical books.

Museum of Modern Art
Gallery

(Umjetnička galerija; ☑020-426 590; www.ugdubrovnik.hr; Frana Supila 23, Ploče; with multi-museum pass adult/child 120/25KN; ⊙9am-8pm Tue-Sun) Spread over three floors of a significant modernist building east of the old town, this excellent gallery showcases Croatian artists, particularly painter Vlaho Bukovac from nearby Cavtat. Head up to the sculpture terrace for excellent views.

Sponza Palace
Palace

(Palača Sponza; ☑020-321 031; Placa bb; May-Oct free, Nov-Apr 25KN; ⊙archives display & cloister 10am-10pm May-Oct; cloister 10am-3pm Nov-Apr) One of the few buildings in

Day Trips from Dubrovnik

Dubrovnik is an excellent base for day trips to the surrounding region – and even in the surrounding countries of Montenegro and Bosnia.

A day trip to the **Elafiti Islands** northwest of Dubrovnik makes a perfect escape from the summer crowds. Out of 14 islands only the three largest – Koločep, Lopud and Šipan – are permanently inhabited. You can see all three in one day on a 'Three Islands & Picnic' tour, which is offered by various operators that have desks at Dubrovnik's Old Harbour (expect to pay between 250KN and 300KN, including drinks and lunch).

Set on a petite peninsula embraced by two harbours, the ancient town of **Cavtat** (pronounced tsav-tat) has a pretty waterfront promenade peppered with restaurants, pebbly beaches and an interesting assortment of artsy attractions.

Without Cavtat there would be no Dubrovnik, as it was refugees from Epidaurum (the Roman incarnation of Cavtat) who established the city in 614. The walls of its famous offshoot are visible in the distance and the two are well connected by both boat and bus, making Cavtat either an easy day-trip destination from Dubrovnik or a quieter (not to mention cheaper) alternative base.

Cavtat waterfront

the old town to survive the 1667 earthquake, the Sponza Palace was built from 1516 to 1522 as a customs house, and it has subsequently been used as a mint,

Dubrovnik

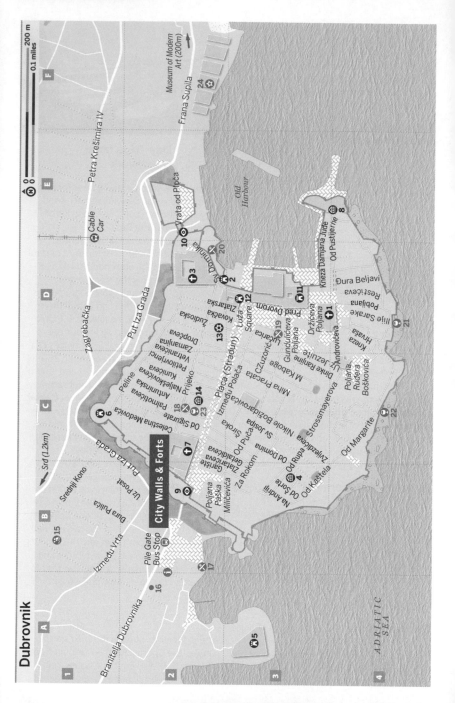

Museum of Modern Art (200m)

Frana Supila

Petra Krešimira IV

Cable Car

Zagrebačka

Put Iza Grada

Srđ (1.2km)

Srednji Kono

Uz Posat

Dura Pulića

Put Iza Grada

Braniteljia Dubrovnika

Između Vrta

Pile Gate Bus Stop

Vrata od Ploča

Sv Dominika

Old Harbour

Kneza Damjana Jude

Od Pustijerne

Đura Beljavi

Restićeva

Ilije Sarake

Poljana

Kneza Hrvaša

Poljana Ruđera Boškovića

Od Margarite

Androvićeva

Držićeva Poljana

Uz Jezuite

Dinke Ranjine

Gundulićeva Poljana

M Kaboge

Mina Pracata

Zvijezdićeva

Nikole Božidarevića

Od Puča

Od Domina

Sv Josipa

Za Rokom

Zlatarićeva

Garište

Poljana Paška Miličevića

Na Andriji

Od Sorte

Od Kaštela

Strossmayerova

Od Rupa

Između Polača

Placa (Stradun)

Lučarica

Za Rokom

Siroka

Lučarica

Luža Square

Zlatarska

Kovačka

Žudioska

Prijeko

Peline

Antuninska

Palmotićeva

Celeština Medovića

Od Sigurate

Naješković eva

Kunićeva

Petilovrijenci

Vetranićeva

Zamanjina

Dropčeva

Pred Dvorom

ADRIATIC SEA

City Walls & Forts

Map markers

- 1
- 2
- 3
- 4
- 5
- 6
- 7
- 8
- 9
- 10
- 11
- 12
- 13
- 14
- 15
- 16
- 17
- 18
- 19
- 20
- 21
- 22
- 23
- 24

200 m
0.1 miles

A B C D E F
1 2 3 4

Dubrovnik

treasury, armoury and bank. Architecturally it's a mixture of styles beginning with an exquisite Renaissance portico resting on six Corinthian columns. The 1st floor has late-Gothic windows and the 2nd-floor windows are in a Renaissance style, with an alcove containing a statue of St Blaise.

Srđ
Viewpoint

(Srđ bb) From the top of this 412m-high hill, Dubrovnik's old town looks even more surreal than usual – like a scale model of itself or an illustration on a page. The views take in all of Dubrovnik and Lokrum, with the Elafiti Islands filling the horizon. It's this extraordinary vantage point that made Srđ a key battleground during the 1990s war. That story is told in **Dubrovnik During the Homeland War** (Dubrovnik u Domovinskom ratu; ☑020-324 856; Fort Imperial, Srđ; adult/child 30/15KN; ☺8am-10pm; ℗), an exhibition housed in Fort Imperial at the summit.

The easiest and quickest way to get to the top is by cable car, or you can drive (follow the signs to Bosanka), walk via the **Way of the Cross** (Križni put; Jadranska cesta, Srđ), or catch bus 17 from the Pile stop to Bosanka and then walk the final 1.5km.

Lokrum
Island

(☑020-311 738; www.lokrum.hr; adult/child incl boat 150/25KN; ☺Apr-Nov) Lush Lokrum is a beautiful, forested island full of holm oaks, black ash, pines and olive trees, only a 10-minute ferry ride from Dubrovnik's Old Harbour. It's a popular swimming spot, although the beaches are rocky. Boats leave roughly hourly in summer (half-hourly in July and August). The public boat ticket price includes the entrance fee, but if you arrive with another boat, you're required to pay 120KN at the information centre on the island.

The island's main hub is its large medieval **Benedictine monastery**, which houses a restaurant and a display on the island's history and the TV show *Game of Thrones*, which was partly filmed on Lokrum. This is your chance to pose imperiously on a reproduction of the Iron Throne. The monastery has a pretty cloister garden and a significant botanical garden, featuring giant agaves and palms from South Africa and Brazil. Near the centre of the island is circular **Fort Royal**, commenced during the French occupation in the early 19th century but mainly used by the Austrians. Head up to the roof for views over the old town.

To reach the **nudist beach**, head left from the ferry and follow the signs marked FKK; the rocks at its far end are Dubrovnik's de facto gay beach. Another popular place for a swim is the small saltwater lake known as the **Dead Sea**.

Destruction & Reconstruction

From late 1991 to May 1992, images of the shelling of Dubrovnik dominated the news worldwide. While memories may have faded for those who watched it from afar, those who suffered through it will never forget – and the city of Dubrovnik is determined that visitors don't either.

Shells struck 68% of the 824 buildings in the old town, leaving holes in two out of three tiled roofs. Building facades and the paving stones of streets and squares suffered 314 direct hits and there were 111 strikes on the great wall. Nine historic palaces were completely gutted by fire, while the Sponza Palace, Rector's Palace, St Blaise's Church, Franciscan Monastery and the carved fountains Amerling and Onofrio all sustained serious damage. The reconstruction bill was estimated at some US$300 million. It was quickly decided that the repairs and rebuilding would be done with traditional techniques, using original materials whenever feasible.

Dubrovnik has since regained most of its original grandeur. The town walls are once again intact, the gleaming marble streets are smoothly paved and famous monuments have been lovingly restored, with the help of an international brigade of specially trained stonemasons.

Make sure you check what time the last boat to the mainland departs. Note that no one can stay overnight and smoking is not permitted anywhere on the island.

🟢 ACTIVITIES

Green Sea Safari   Volunteering

(📱095 55 20 190; https://greenseasafari.com; ⏰9.30am-5pm Jun-Sep) 🌿 These environmentally conscious excursions take volunteers out to help clean up remote shores around Dubrovnik, typically places inaccessible by public boats or tours. An hour is spent removing waste and the rest of the time enjoying beaches. Tours depart at 9.30am (weather permitting) from Gruž (across from the fish market) and pre-registration via the website is required.

Green Sea Safari tours are officially free, but donations are welcome.

Sveti Jakov Beach   Swimming

(Vlaha Bukovca bb, Viktorija) Head east from the Ploče Gate for 1.7km and you'll come to Sveti Jakov, a gorgeous little beach that doesn't get too rowdy and has showers, a bar and a restaurant.

Adriatic Kayak Tours   Kayaking, Cycling

(📱020-312 770; www.adriatickayaktours.com; Zrinsko Frankopanska 6, Pile; half-day from 280KN; ⏰Apr-Oct) Offers sea-kayak excursions (from a half-day paddle to a week-long trip), hiking and cycling tours, and Montenegro getaways (including rafting).

Outdoor Croatia   Kayaking

(📱020-418 282; www.outdoorcroatia.com; day trip 440KN) Rents kayaks and offers day trips around the Elafiti Islands, along with multiday excursions and kayaking-cycling combos.

Lapad Bay   Swimming

(Uvala Lapad; Lapad; 🚻) Bounded by the forested Petka hills on one side and the crest of Babin Kuk on the other, Lapad Bay is a busy string of pebble beaches, beachfront hotels and pedestrianised promenades. There are plenty of diversions here, both in and out of the water, including a kids playground and lots of cafes and bars.

Facing west, the main beach is particularly loved for the spectacular sunset views over the Grebeni rocks and Koločep Island.

✖ EATING

There are some very average restaurants in Dubrovnik, so choose carefully. Many places ride on the assumption that you're here just for a day (as many cruise-ship passengers are) and that you won't be coming back. Prices are also the highest in Croatia. That said, there are some great eateries scattered around the old town, Lapad and Gruž.

Nishta
Vegan €€

(☑020-322 088; www.nishtarestaurant.com; Prijeko bb; mains 98-108KN; ☺11.30am-11.30pm Mon-Sat; 🖋) The popularity of this tiny old-town restaurant is testament not just to the paucity of options for vegetarians and vegans in Croatia, but also to the imaginative and beautifully presented food produced within. Each day of the week has its own menu with a separate set of cooked and raw options.

Veranda
Croatian €€

(☑091 17 46 082; http://konobaveranda.com; Štikovica 24a; mains 95-140KN; ☺1-11pm Mar-Nov) Showcasing dishes from five different regions (Slavonia, Dalmatia, Istria, Southern Adriatic and neighbouring Hercegovina), the menu at Veranda is like a 'best of' Croatian and Hercegovinian foods. Seriously good home-style cooking (Istrian lamb ragout!) comes complete with a matching wine list and is served against the serene imagery of Zaton Bay. The 20-minute drive from Dubrovnik is best covered by cab.

Štikovica features a lovely pebble beach (a minute-long downhill stroll from Veranda), so consider making an afternoon of it.

Nautika
European €€€

(☑020-442 526; www.nautikarestaurants. com; Brsalje 3, Pile; mains 290-360KN; ☺6pm-midnight Apr-Oct) Nautika bills itself as 'Dubrovnik's finest restaurant' and it comes pretty close. The setting is sublime, overlooking the sea and the city walls, and the service is faultless: black-bow-tie formal but friendly. As for the food, it's sophisticated if not particularly adventurous, with classic techniques applied to the finest local produce. For maximum silver-service drama, order the salt-crusted fish.

Pantarul
Mediterranean €€€

(☑020-333 486; www.pantarul.com; Kralja Tomislava 1, Lapad; mains 108-180KN, 5-course lasting menus 390-410KN; ☺noon-4pm &

Kayaking in Dubrovnik

PAUL PRESCOTT / ALAMY SCOTT PHOTO ©

Restaurant 360°

> *Dubrovnik's glitziest restaurant offers fine dining at its best*

6pm-midnight Tue-Sun; P 🛜) This breezy bistro aligns its menu with the seasons and has a reputation for exceptional homemade bread, pasta and risotto, alongside the likes of steaks, ox cheeks, burgers and various fish dishes. There's a fresh, modern touch to most dishes.

Restaurant 360°   International €€€

(📞020-322 222; www.360dubrovnik.com; Sv Dominika bb; 2/3/5 courses 520/620/860KN; 🕙6.30-10.30pm Tue-Sun Apr-Sep; 🛜) Dubrovnik's glitziest restaurant offers fine dining at its best, with flavoursome, beautifully presented, creative cuisine, an impressive wine list and slick, professional service. The setting is unrivalled – on top of the city walls with tables positioned so you can peer through the battlements over the harbour.

🍷 DRINKING & NIGHTLIFE

You won't go thirsty in Dubrovnik – the city has swanky lounge bars, Irish pubs, bars clinging to cliffs, sophisticated wine bars and lots and lots of Croatian-style cafe-bars. And that's just the old town.

Bard Mala Buža   Bar

(Iza Mira 14; 🕙9am-3am May-Oct) The more upmarket and slick of two cliff bars pressed up against the seaward side of the city walls. This one is lower on the rocks and has a shaded terrace where you can lose a day quite happily, mesmerised by the Adriatic vistas.

D'vino   Wine Bar

(📞020-321 130; www.dvino.net; Palmotićeva 4a; 🕙9am-midnight Mar-Nov; 🛜) If you're interested in sampling top-notch Croatian wine, this convivial bar is the place to go. As well as a large and varied wine list, it offers tasting flights presented by cool and knowledgeable staff (three wines from 55KN) plus savoury breakfasts, snacks and platters. Sit outside for the authentic old-town-alley ambience, but check out the whimsical wall inscriptions inside.

Cave Bar More
Bar

(www.hotel-more.hr; Šetalište Nika i Meda Pucića bb, Babin Kuk; ⊙10am-midnight Jun-Aug, to 10pm Sep-May) This little beach bar serves coffee, snacks and cocktails to bathers reclining by the dazzlingly clear waters of Lapad Bay, but that's not the half of it – the main bar is set in an actual cave. Cool off beneath the stalactites in the side chamber, where a glass floor exposes a water-filled cavern.

Buža
Bar

(off Od Margarite; ⊙8am-2am Jun-Aug, to midnight Sep-May) Finding this ramshackle bar-on-a-cliff feels like a real discovery as you duck and dive around the city walls and finally see the entrance tunnel. However, Buža's no secret – it gets insanely busy, especially around sunset. Wait for a space on one of the concrete platforms, grab a cool drink in a plastic cup and enjoy the vibe and views.

⭐ ENTERTAINMENT

Summer sees classical concerts, theatre and dance performances popping up in historic fortresses and churches; look out for signs around town or enquire at any of the tourist offices. In the evening, various old-town bars host live music.

Lazareti
Arts Centre

(www.arl.hr; Frana Supila 8, Ploče) Housed in a former quarantine centre, Lazareti hosts cinema nights, club nights, live music, folk dancing, art exhibitions and pretty much all the best things in town.

ℹ INFORMATION

Dubrovnik's tourist board has offices in **Pile** (☑020-312 011; www.tzdubrovnik.hr; Brsalje

5; ⊙8am-8pm), **Gruž** (☑020-417 983; www. tzdubrovnik.hr; Obala Pape Ivana Pavla II 1; ⊙8am-8pm Jun-Oct, 8am-3pm Mon-Fri, to 1pm Sat Nov-Mar, 8am-8pm Mon-Fri, to 2pm Sat & Sun Apr & May) and **Lapad** (☑020-437 460; www.tzdubrovnik.hr; Dvori Lapad, Masarykov put 2; ⊙8am-8pm Jul & Aug, 8am-noon & 5-8pm Mon-Fri, 9am-2pm Sat Apr-Jun, Sep & Oct) that dispense maps, information and advice.

ℹ GETTING THERE & AWAY

Dubrovnik Airport (DBV, Zračna luka Dubrovnik; ☑020-773 100; www.airport-dubrovnik.hr; Čilipi) is in Čilipi, 19km southeast of Dubrovnik. Croatia Airlines, British Airways, Iberica, Turkish Airlines and Vueling fly to Dubrovnik year-round. In summer they're joined by dozens of other airlines flying seasonal routes and charter flights.

Buses from **Dubrovnik Bus Station** (Autobusni kolodvor; ☑060 305 070; www.libertas dubrovnik.hr; Obala Pape Ivana Pavla II 44a, Gruž; ⊙4.30am-10pm; 🛜) can be crowded, so purchase tickets online or book in advance in summer. The station has toilets and a *garderoba* for storing luggage. Departure times are detailed online.

ℹ GETTING AROUND

Dubrovnik has a superb bus service; buses run frequently and generally on time. The key tourist routes run until after 2am in summer, so if you're staying in Lapad, there's no need to rush home. The fare is 15KN if you buy from the driver and 12KN if you buy a ticket at a *tisak* (news stand). Timetables are available at www. libertasdubrovnik.hr.

To get to the old town from the bus station, take buses 1a, 1b, 3 or 8. To get to Lapad, take bus 7.

From the **bus stop** at Pile Gate, take bus 4, 5, 6 or 9 to get to Lapad.

ATHENS, GREECE

Athens, Greece

With equal measures of grunge and grace, Athens is a heady mix of history and edginess. The magnificent Acropolis and its crowning Parthenon are visible from almost every part of the city. It's the hub around which Athens still revolves. This temple city, built in the 5th century BC, serves as a daily reminder to Greeks of their heritage.

All over the urban basin, rooftops and balconies angle toward the landmark. Pull up your own chair, settle in and allow time to appreciate Athens' many moods, from veneration of the past to a manic embrace of today.

Two Days in Athens

Orient yourself by walking a loop around Athens' core. Climb to the glorious **Acropolis** (p500), then spend your day exploring its myriad sights, including the iconic **Parthenon** (p501) and the spectacular **Acropolis Museum** (p503) and its masterpieces. Wander around Plaka, either on back streets for photo ops, or along Adrianou for shopping. Explore the **Ancient Agora** (p506), the centre of ancient Athens' civic life.

Four Days in Athens

Move away from the Acropolis. Watch the changing of the guard at **Tomb of the Unknown Soldier** (p507) on Plateia Syntagmatos. Then see the **Benaki Museum of Greek Culture** (p506) for its extensive collections tracing Greek culture over millennia. See the **Temple of Olympian Zeus** (p506) and **Hadrian's Arch** (p507). Then hop on a trolleybus north to the **National Archaeological Museum** (p507).

Next stop: İstanbul (p517), perhaps via the Greek Islands (p512).

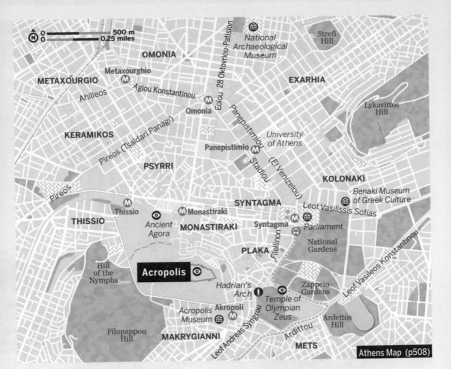

Arriving in Athens

Eleftherios Venizelos International Airport has service from cities worldwide. The Metro runs every 30 minutes to centre; taxis are available for a flat rate; an express bus offers a budget alternative.

The **Port of Piraeus** is Greece's ferry hub and is close to Athens. Ferries service dozens of Greek Islands as well as other countries around the Mediterranean. It's served by the Metro.

Where to Stay

Athens lodging covers the full range, from one to five stars, but it can all be a bit drab for the price. Most places are scattered in a loose ring around the Acropolis, especially in the Plaka. Athens gets very busy in the balmy months, so be sure to book a couple months ahead for your top choices.

Parthenon

SAMOT / SHUTTERSTOCK ©

Acropolis

The Acropolis is the most important ancient site in the Western world. Crowned by the Parthenon, it stands sentinel over Athens, visible from almost everywhere within the city. Its monuments and sanctuaries of white Pentelic marble gleam in the midday sun and gradually take on a honey hue as the sun sinks, while at night they stand brilliantly illuminated above the city.

Great For...

☑ Don't Miss

Performances of drama, music and dance are held at the Odeon of Herodes Atticus (p502) during the summer.

The Hill Through Time

Inspiring as the Acropolis monuments are, they are but faded remnants of the city of Pericles, who spared no expense – only the best materials, architects, sculptors and artists were good enough for a city dedicated to the cult of Athena.

The Acropolis was first inhabited in Neolithic times (4000–3000 BC). The earliest temples were built during the Mycenaean era, in homage to the goddess Athena.

Ravages inflicted during the years of foreign occupation, pilfering by foreign archaeologists, inept renovations, visitors' footsteps, earthquakes and, more recently, pollution have all taken their toll on the surviving monuments.

The Acropolis became a World Heritage–listed site in 1987. Major restoration pro-

Carved columns

ⓘ Need to Know

☎210 321 4172; http://odysseus.culture.
gr; adult/concession/child €20/10/free;
🕐8am-8pm May-Sep, reduced hours in
winter, last entry 30min before closing;
ⓂAkropoli

✕ Take a Break

The Acropolis Museum Restaurant
(p503) has superb views across the
way to the Acropolis and seats inside
and out.

★ Top Tip

The east entrance, near the Akropoli
metro, can be less crowded than the
main entrance.

grams are ongoing, and most of the original
sculptures and friezes have been moved to
the Acropolis Museum and replaced with
casts.

Parthenon

More than any other monument, the
Parthenon epitomises the glory of
Ancient Greece. The largest Doric temple
ever completed in Greece, and the only
one built completely of white Pentelic
marble (apart from its wooden roof), it
took 15 years to complete. It was designed
by Iktinos and Kallicrates and completed
in time for the Great Panathenaic Festival
of 438 BC.

Designed to be the pre-eminent
monument of the Acropolis and built on
its highest ground, the Parthenon had a
dual purpose: to house the great statue of

Athena commissioned by Pericles and to
serve as the new treasury. It was built on
the site of at least four earlier temples.

The temple consisted of eight fluted
Doric **columns** at either end and 17 on each
side. To achieve perfect form, its lines were
ingeniously curved to create an optical
illusion – the foundations are slightly concave and the columns are slightly convex
to make both look straight. The pediments
and friezes were brightly coloured and
gilded.

Desecrations

Much of the **frieze** depicting the Panathenaic Procession was damaged in a
devastating 1687 gunpowder explosion:
the Turks had been storing ammunition
here, which exploded when the Venetians
launched a mortar at it. Later, Christians
defaced some of the remaining pieces. But
the greatest existing part (over 75m long)

consists of the controversial Parthenon Marbles, taken by Lord Elgin and now housed in the British Museum in London.

Lost Parthenon

The metopes (the decorative panels on the frieze) were a great series of carved artworks depicting moments in Greek mythology and history. All are mostly lost.

The ceiling of the Parthenon, like that of the Propylaia, was painted blue and gilded with stars. At the eastern end was the holy cella (inner room of a temple), into which only a few privileged initiates could enter. Here stood the statue for which the temple was built (Parthenon means 'virgin's apartment'): the Athena Polias (Athena of the City), considered one of the wonders of the ancient world. The statue was gold plated over an inner wooden frame and stood almost 12m high on its pedestal. In AD 426 the statue was taken to Constantinople, where it disappeared.

Best Sights of the Acropolis

Temple of Athena Nike   Temple

The small but exquisitely proportioned Temple of Athena Nike sits at the southwest edge of the Acropolis, jutting in front and to the right of the Propylaia. Designed by Kallicrates, the temple was built of white Pentelic marble between 427 BC and 424 BC. The building is almost square, with four graceful Ionic columns at either end.

Odeon of Herodes Atticus   Theatre

(Herodeon; ☏210 324 1807;) This large amphitheatre was built in AD 161 by wealthy Roman Herodes Atticus in memory of his wife Regilla. It was excavated in

Odeon of Herodes Atticus

1857–58 and completely restored in the 1950s.

Acropolis Museum   Museum

(☎210 900 0900; www.theacropolismuseum.gr; Dionysiou Areopagitou 15, Makrygianni; adult/child €10/free; ☉8am-4pm Mon, to 8pm Tue-Thur & Sat-Sun, to 10pm Fri Apr-Oct, 9am-5pm Mon-Thu, to 10pm Fri, to 8pm Sat & Sun Nov-Mar) This dazzling museum at the foot of the Acropolis' southern slope showcases its surviving treasures. The

> ### ✖ Take a Break
>
> Close to the less-crowded east entrance to the Acropolis, **Duende** (☎210 924 7069; https://duende-bar-and-grill.business.site; Tzireon 2, Makrygianni; ☉8pm-3am;) is a perfect escape from the tourist mobs.

VIACHESLAV LOPATIN / SHUTTERSTOCK ©

collection covers the Archaic period to the Roman one, but the emphasis is on the Acropolis of the 5th century BC, considered the apotheosis of Greece's artistic achievement. The museum reveals layers of history – from ancient ruins beneath the building, to the Acropolis itself, always visible above through floor-to-ceiling windows. The good-value **restaurant** (☎210 900 0915; mains €8-34; ☉8am-4pm Mon, until 8pm Tue-Thu, Sat & Sun, until midnight Fri; 🛜) has superb views.

Propylaia   Architecture

The Propylaia formed the monumental entrance to the Acropolis. Built by Mnesicles between 437 BC and 432 BC, it ranks in architectural brilliance with the Parthenon (p501). It consists of a central hall with two wings on either side; each section had a gate, and in ancient times these five gates were the only entrances to the 'upper city'.

Theatre of Dionysos   Theatre

(Dionysiou Areopagitou) The tyrant Peisistratos introduced the annual Festival of the Great Dionysia during the 6th century BC, and held it in the world's first theatre, on the south slope of the Acropolis. The original theatre on this site was a timber structure and masses of people attended the contests, at which men clad in goatskins sang and danced, followed by feasting and revelry. Drama as we know it dates to these contests.

> ### ★ Top Tip
>
> Visit first thing in the morning or late in the day to avoid the greatest crowds and heat.

The Acropolis

A WALKING TOUR

Cast your imagination back in time, two and a half millennia ago, and envision the majesty of the Acropolis. Its famed and hallowed monument, the Parthenon, dedicated to the goddess Athena, stood proudly over a small city, dwarfing the population with its graceful grandeur. In the Acropolis' heyday in the 5th century BC, pilgrims and priests worshipped at the temples illustrated here (most of which still stand in varying states of restoration). Many were painted brilliant colours and were abundantly adorned with sculptural masterpieces crafted from ivory, gold and semiprecious stones.

As you enter the site today, elevated on the right perches one of the Acropolis' best-restored buildings: the diminutive ❶ **Temple of Athena Nike**. Follow the Panathenaic Way through the Propylaia and up the slope towards the Parthenon – icon of the Western world. Its ❷ **majestic columns** sweep up to some of what were the finest carvings of their time: wrap-around ❸ **pediments, metopes and a frieze**. Stroll around the temple's exterior and take in the spectacular views over Athens and Piraeus below.

As you circle back to the centre of the site, you will encounter those renowned lovely ladies, the ❹ **Caryatids** of the Erechtheion. On the Erechtheion's northern face, the oft-forgotten ❺ **Temple of Poseidon** sits alongside ingenious ❻ **Themistocles' Wall**. Wander to the Erechtheion's western side to find Athena's gift to the city: ❼ **the olive tree**.

Themistocles' Wall
Crafty general Themistocles (524–459 BC) hastened to build a protective wall around the Acropolis and in so doing incorporated elements from archaic temples on the site. Look for the column drums built into the wall.

Sanctuary of Pandion

Sanctuary of Zeus Polieus

Erechtheion

Temple of Poseidon
Though he didn't win patronage of the city, Poseidon was worshipped on the northern side of the Erechtheion, which still bears the mark of his trident-strike. Imagine the finely decorated coffered porch painted in rich colours, as it was in the past.

ALEXTRAVELERPHOTOGRAPHER/GETTY IMAGES ©

Porch of the Caryatids

Perhaps the most recognisable sculptural elements at the Acropolis are the majestic Caryatids (c 415 BC). Modelled on women from Karyai (modern-day Karyes, in Lakonia), the maidens are thought to have held a libation bowl in one hand, and to be drawing up their dresses with the other.

Parthenon Pediments, Metopes & Frieze

The Parthenon's pediments (the triangular elements topping the east and west facades) were filled with elaborately carved three-dimensional sculptures. The west side depicted Athena and Poseidon in their contest for the city's patronage, the east Athena's birth from Zeus' head. The metopes are square carved panels set between channelled triglyphs. They depicted battle scenes, including the sacking of Troy and the clash between the Lapiths and the Centaurs. The cella was topped by the Ionic frieze, a continuous sculptured band depicting the Panathenaic Procession.

Parthenon

3

Chalkotheke

Panathenaic Way

Sanctuary of Artemis Brauronia

2

Statue of Athena Promachos

Arrephorion

Propylaia

Pinakothiki

Entrance

1

Spring of Klepsydra

Temple of Athena Nike

Recently restored, this precious tiny Pentelic marble temple was designed by Kallicrates and built around 425 BC. The cella housed a wooden statue of Athena as Victory (Nike) and the exterior friezes illustrated Athenian battle triumphs.

Parthenon Columns

The Parthenon's fluted Doric columns achieve perfect form. Their lines were ingeniously curved to create an optical illusion: the foundations (like all the 'horizontal' surfaces of the temple) are slightly concave and the columns are slightly convex, making both appear straight.

Athena's Olive Tree

The flourishing olive tree next to the Erechtheion is meant to be the sacred tree that Athena produced to seize victory in the contest for Athens.

⊙ SIGHTS

Benaki Museum
of Greek Culture   Museum

(☑210 367 1000; www.benaki.gr; Koumbari 1,
cnr Leoforos Vasilissis Sofias, Kolonaki; adult/
student/child €9/7/free, 6pm-midnight Thu free;
⊙10am-6pm Mon, Wed, Fri & Sat, to midnight
Thu, to 4pm Sun; Ⓜ Syntagma, Evangelismos)
In 1930, Antonis Benakis – a politician's
son born in Alexandria, Egypt in the late
19th century – endowed what is perhaps
the finest museum in Greece. Its three
floors showcase impeccable treasures
from the Bronze Age up to WWII. Especially
gorgeous are the Byzantine icons and the
extensive collection of Greek regional costumes, as well as complete sitting rooms
from Macedonian mansions, intricately
carved and painted. Benakis had such a
good eye that even the agricultural tools
are beautiful.

Ancient Agora   Historic Site

(☑210 321 0185; http://odysseus.culture.gr;
Adrianou 24, Monastiraki; adult/student/child
€8/4/free; ⊙8am-8pm Apr-Oct, to 3pm Nov-
Mar; Ⓜ Monastiraki) The Agora was ancient
Athens' heart, the lively hub of administrative, commercial, political and social
activity. Socrates expounded his philosophy here; in AD 49 St Paul came here to win
converts to Christianity. The site today is
a lush respite, home to the grand **Temple
of Hephaistos**, a good **museum** (⊙10am-
3.30pm Mon, from 8.30pm Tue-Sun) and the
late-10th-century Byzantine **Church of the
Holy Apostles**, trimmed in brick patterns
that mimic Arabic calligraphy. The greenery
harbours birds and lizards. Allow about two
hours to see everything.

Temple of Olympian Zeus   Temple

(Olympieio; ☑210 922 6330; http://odysseus.
culture.gr; Leoforos Vasilissis Olgas, Plaka; adult/
student/child €6/3/free; ⊙8am-3pm Oct-Apr,
to 8pm May-Sep; Ⓜ Akropoli, Syntagma) A
can't-miss on two counts: it's a marvellous
temple, once the largest in Greece, and it's
smack in the centre of Athens. Of the temple's 104 original Corinthian columns (17m
high with a base diameter of 1.7m), only 15
remain – the fallen column was blown down
in a gale in 1852.

Ancient Agora

INU / SHUTTERSTOCK ©

Hadrian's Arch   Monument

(cnr Leoforos Vasilissis Olgas & Leoforos Vasilissis Amalias, Plaka; MAkropoli, Syntagma) **FREE**
The Roman emperor Hadrian had a great affection for Athens. Although he did his fair share of spiriting its Classical artwork to Rome, he also embellished the city with many temples and infrastructure improvements. As thanks, the people of Athens erected this lofty monument of Pentelic marble in 131 AD. It now stands on the edge of one of Athens' busiest avenues.

Tomb of the Unknown Soldier   Monument

(Plateia Syntagmatos, Syntagma; MSyntagma) **FREE** In front of **Parliament** (www.hellenicparliament.gr; ⊙tours 3pm Mon & Fri Jun, Jul & Sep) **FREE**, the traditionally costumed *evzones* (presidential guards) stand by the tomb and change every hour on the hour. On Sunday at 11am, a whole platoon marches down Vasilissis Sofias to the tomb, accompanied by a band. The *evzones* uniform of the *fustanella* (white skirt) and pom-pom shoes is based on the attire worn by the *klephts,* the mountain fighters of the War of Independence.

National Archaeological Museum   Museum

(⌨213 214 4800; www.namuseum.gr; Patision 44, Exarhia; adult/child €10/free mid Apr-Oct; €5/free Nov-mid Apr; ⊙8am-8pm Wed-Mon, 12.30am-8pm Tue mid Apr-Oct, reduced hours Nov-mid Apr; ⊒2, 3, 4, 5 or 11 to Polytechneio, MViktoria) Housing the world's finest collection of Greek antiquities in an enormous neoclassical building, this museum is one of Athens' top attractions. Treasures offering a view of Greek art and history – dating from the Neolithic era to Classical periods, including the Ptolemaic era in Egypt – include exquisite sculptures, pottery, jewellery, frescoes and artefacts found throughout Greece. The beautifully presented exhibits are displayed mainly thematically.

Kerameikos   Historic Site

(⌨210 346 3552; http://odysseus.culture.gr; Ermou 148, Kerameikos; adult/child incl museum €8/free; ⊙8am-8pm, reduced hours in low

📷 Athens Tours

Athens Walking Tours (⌨6945859662, 210 884 7269; www.athenswalkingtours.gr) Runs a full range of guided tours around and outside the city. It's especially notable for its cooking class (€77) in a Thisio taverna, which cuts no corners and even shows you how to roll out your own filo for *spanakopita* (spinach pie).

As the name promises, the well-run **Alternative Athens** (⌨211 012 6544; www.alternativeathens.com; tours from €40) offers walking tours with less-typical slants, covering various corners of the city. There's an excellent three-hour street-art tour and another visiting Athenian designers, as well as an LGBTQ bar and club crawl, food tours and even day trips out of town.

Spanakopita
IGOR DUTINA / SHUTTERSTOCK ©

season; MThissio) This lush, tranquil site is named for the potters who settled it around 3000 BC. It was used as a cemetery through the 6th century AD. The grave markers give a sense of ancient life; numerous marble *stelae* (grave markers) are carved with vivid portraits and familiar scenes.

🔒 SHOPPING

Korres   Cosmetics

(⌨210 321 0054; www.korres.com; Ermou 4, Syntagma; ⊙9am-9pm Mon-Fri, to 8pm Sat; MSyntagma) Many pharmacies stock some of this popular line of natural beauty products, but you can get the full range at the company's original location, where it grew out of a homeopathic pharmacy.

Athens

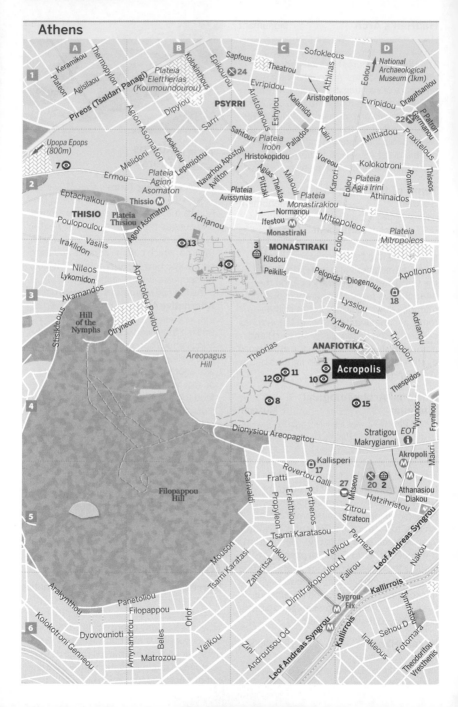

A1
B1
C1
D1
A2
B2
D2
A3
B3
C3
D3
A4
B4
C4
A5
D5
A6
B6

Keramikou
Thermopylion
Plateon
Agisilaou
Pireos (Tsaldari Panagi)
Plateia Eleftherias (Koumoundourou)
Kolokinthou
Epikourou
Sapfous
Sofokleous
Theatrou
Athinas
Eolou
National Archaeological Museum (1km)
Dipylou
Sarri
PSYRRI
Aristofanous
Evripidou
Eschylou
Kalamida
Aristogitonos
Evripidou
Dragatsaniou
Agion Asomaton
Leokoriou
Lepeniotou
Sahtouri
Navarhou Apostoli
Plateia Iroön
Hristokopidou
Pallados
Kalili
Voreou
P Patron
Germanou
22
Miltiadou
Praxitelous
Upopa Epops (800m)
7
Melidoni
Ermou
Eptachalkou
Plateia Agion Asomaton
Avliton
Agias Theklas
Pittaki
Miaouli
Karori
Eolou
Kolokotroni
Romvis
Thiseos
Plateia Agia Irini
Athinaidos
THISIO
Poulopoulou
Vasilis
Iraklidon
Plateia Thisiou
Agion Asomaton
Thissio M
Adrianou
Plateia Avissynias
Normanou
Ifestou
Plateia Monastirakiou
Mitropoleos
Plateia Mitropoleos
Nileos
Lykomidon
Akamandos
Stisikleous
Apostoliou Pavlou
Otryneon
13
4
Monastiraki M
Monastiraki
3
Kladou
Peikilis
MONASTIRAKI
Eolou
Pelopida
Diogenous
Apollonos
Hill of the Nymphs
Areopagus Hill
Theorias
Lyssiou
Prytaniou
ANAFIOTIKA
Tripodon
Adrianou
18
1
Acropolis
12
11
10
Thespidos
8
15
Filopappou Hill
Dionysiou Areopagitou
Stratigou Makrygianni
EOT
Vyronos
Fryniou
Makri
Akropoli M
Athanasiou Diakou
Garivaldi
Rovertou Galli
Fratti
Kallisperi
17
27
Mitseon
20
2
Propyleon
Erehthiou
Parthenos
Zitrou
Strateon
Hatzihristou
Mouson
Tsami Karatasi
Drakou
Zaharitsa
Tsami Karatasou
Veikou
Faliro
Petmeza
Leof Andreas Syngrou
Nakou
Arakynthou
Panetoliou
Filopappou
Orlof
Veikou
Dimitrakopoulou N
Sygrou-Fix M
Kallirrois
Kallirrois
Kolokotroni Genneou
Dyovounioti
Amynandrou
Beles
Matrozou
Zini
Androutsou Od
Leof Andreas Syngrou
Kallirrois
Irakleous
Tymfristou
Sehou D
Theodoritou
Vrestheni
Fotomara

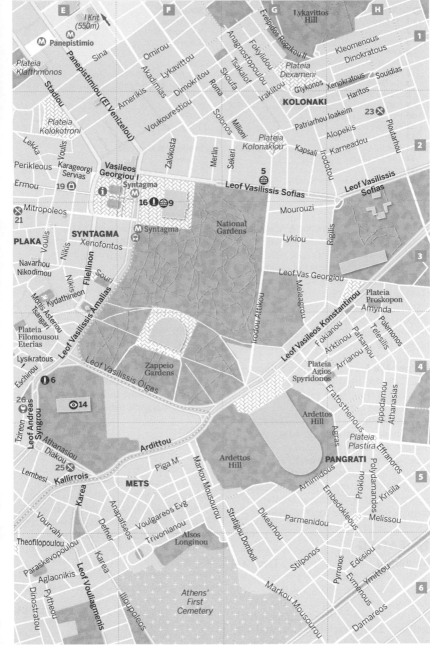

Athens

Athena Design Workshop   Fashion & Accessories

(☏210 924 5713; www.athenadesignworkshop.com; Parthenonos 30, Makrygianni; ◑11.30am-7pm Mon-Fri, until 5pm Sat; Ⓜ Akropoli) You can often find Krina Vronti busy woodblock printing her appealing graphic designs on T-shirts, cushion covers and paper at this combined studio and shop. The images are often inspired by ancient and classical themes but are given a contemporary twist.

Forget Me Not   Gifts & Souvenirs

(☏210 325 3740; www.forgetmenotathens.gr; Adrianou 100, Plaka; ◑10am-9pm Apr & May, until 10pm Jun, Sep & Oct, until 11pm Jul & Aug, until 8pm Nov-Mar; Ⓜ Syntagma, Monastiraki) This impeccable small store (two shops, one upstairs and one down around the corner) stocks super-cool gear, from fashion to housewares and gifts, all by contemporary Greek designers. Great for gift shopping – who doesn't want a set of cheerful 'evil eye' coasters or some Hermes-winged beach sandals?

✗ EATING

Kalderimi   Taverna €

(☏210 331 0049; Plateia Agion Theodoron, Panepistimio; mains €6-12; ◑11am-8pm Mon-Thu, to 10pm Fri & Sat; 🛜; Ⓜ Panepistimio) This downtown taverna offers Greek food at its most authentic. Everything is freshly cooked and delicious: you can't go wrong. Hand-painted tables edge a pedestrian street, providing for a feeling of peace in one of the busiest parts of the city. (It helps that it closes just before nearby bars get rolling.)

Veganaki   Vegan €

(☏210 924 4322; www.facebook.com/VeganakiGR; Athanasiou Diakou 38, Kynosargous; mains €3.50-6.50; ◑8.30am-11.30pm; ✔; Ⓜ) A fine addition to Athens' vegan dining options, this convivial spot may occupy a spot overlooking a busy road, but inside all is calm as customers enjoy falafel wraps and plates, sandwiches and traditional Greek pies, some of which are also gluten free. Also served here, a great cup of fair trade organic coffee.

Oikeio   Mediterranean €€

(☏210 725 9216; www.facebook.com/oikeio; Ploutarhou 15, Kolonaki; mains €10-12; ◑12.30pm-midnight Mon-Thu, to 1am Fri & Sat, to 6pm Sun; Ⓜ Evangelismos) With excellent homestyle cooking, this modern taverna lives up to its name (meaning 'homey'). It's decorated like a cosy bistro, and tables on the footpath allow people-watching without the usual Kolonaki bill. Pastas, salads and international fare are tasty, but try the daily *mayirefta* (ready-cooked meals), such as the excellent stuffed zucchini. Book ahead on weekends.

Telis   Taverna €€

(☏210 324 9582; Evripidou 86, Psyrri; meal with salad €13; ◑noon-midnight Mon-Sat;

M Thissio) A fluorescent-lit beacon of good food and kind service on a grimy block, Telis has been serving up simplicity since 1978. There's no menu, just a set meal: a small mountain of charcoal-grilled pork chops atop chips, plus a side vegetable. Greek salad is optional, as is beer or rough house wine.

I Kriti   Cretan €€

(☏210 382 6998; Veranzerou 5, Omonia; mains €6-12; ◷noon-midnight Mon-Sat; ☎; M Omonia) There is no shortage of Cretan restaurants in Athens, but this is the one that Cretans themselves recommend, especially for rare seasonal treats such as stewed snails, bittersweet pickled *volvi* (wild bulbs) and tender baby goat with nuts and garlic. It occupies several storefronts inside the arcade; on weekends it's a good idea to reserve.

Ergon House Agora   Greek €€

(☏210 010 9090; https://house.ergonfoods. com; Mitropoleos 23, Syntagma; mains €8-11.50; ◷7.30am-midnight; ☎; M Syntagma) A superb addition to Athens' culinary landscape is this deli, cafe and restaurant occupying a gorgeously designed atrium space flooded with light. There are separate areas for a greengrocer, fishmonger, butcher and bakery, plus shelves packed with top-quality Greek products sourced from small-scale producers around the country. You'll dine well here and, most likely, leave laden down with goodies.

🍷 DRINKING & NIGHTLIFE

Upopa Epops   Bar

(☏212 105 5214; www.facebook.com/upupa epopsthebar2016; Alkminis 7, Kato Petralona; ◷10am-2am, to 3am Fri & Sat; M Petralona) This lovely bar-restaurant is one of the reasons Petralona is considered a just-the-right-amount-of-cool neighbourhood. It has numerous rooms filled with vintage furniture and a pretty courtyard, the food and drinks are great and there's often a DJ, but there's always a place to have a conversation. And the name? Latin for the hoopoe bird.

Little Tree Book Cafe   Cafe

(☏210 924 3762; www.facebook.com/littletree booksandcoffee; Kavalloti 2, Makrygianni; ◷8am-11pm Tue-Thu, until 11.30pm Fri, 9am-11.30pm Sat & Sun; M Akropoli) This friendly social hub is much beloved by neighbourhood residents, who go for books (they stock a small selection of translated Greek authors here), but also excellent coffee, cocktails and snacks.

ℹ️ INFORMATION

EOT (Greek National Tourism Organisation; ☏210 331 0347, 210 331 0716; www.visitgreece.gr; Dionysiou Areopagitou 18-20, Makrygianni; ◷8am-8pm Mon-Fri, 10am-4pm Sat & Sun May-Sep, 9am-7pm Mon-Fri Oct-Apr; M Akropoli) Free Athens map, current site hours and bus and train information.

Athens City Information Kiosks Maps, transport information and all Athens info. Branches at the **Airport** (☏210 353 0390; www.athens conventionbureau.gr/en/content/info-kiosk-athens-international-airport; Eleftherios Venizelos International Airport; ◷8am-8pm; M Airport) and **Acropolis** (www.thisisathens.org; Plateia Syntagmatos, Syntagma; ◷9am-6pm; M Syntagma)

ℹ️ GETTING THERE & AWAY

Athens' **airport** (ATH; ☏210 353 0000; www.aia.gr), at Spata, 27km east of Athens, is a European hub.

Most ferry, hydrofoil and high-speed catamaran services to the islands leave from the massive port at **Piraeus**, southwest of Athens. Purchase tickets online at **Greek Ferries** (☏2810 529000; www.greekferries.gr), over the phone or at booths on the quay next to each ferry.

ℹ️ GETTING AROUND

The transit system uses the unified Ath.ena Ticket, a reloadable paper card available from ticket offices and machines in the metro. You can load it with a set amount of money or buy a number of rides (€1.40 each; discount when you buy five or 10) or a 24-hour/five-day travel pass for €4.50/9. Transport options include the following:

Buses There's a network that reaches everywhere.

Metro Fast and efficient; most useful for visitors.

Taxis Very affordable, and very much part of the 'public transport' system.

Fira, Santorini (p514)

Greek Islands, Greece

The Greek Islands ignite the imagination and satisfy the soul with a history laced in mythical tales and told through ancient, sun-bleached ruins. Modern tales centre on beaches and lazy days.

Great For...

ℹ Need to Know

Ferries link many islands with Pireaus, the port near Athens. Larger islands have flights to Athens.

★ **Top Tip**

In summer, book ferries and lodging early to get your top choices.

Greece's myriad islands dot the Ionian and Aegean Seas. No matter your tastes you'll find an island to match them. One of the world's great pleasures is an island-hopping adventure across these fabled lands surrounded by azure-blue water.

Santorini

The multicoloured cliffs, soaring above a sea-drowned caldera, are amazing indeed. The main towns of Fira and Oia – a snow-drift of white Cycladic houses that line the cliff tops and spill like icy cornices down the terraced rock – will take your breath away. And then there are the sunsets – the glorious sunsets – and the island's fascinating history, best revealed at the Minoan site of Akrotiri.

Rhodes

Rhodes (*ro*-dos) abounds in beaches, wooded valleys and ancient history. Whether you arrive in search of buzzing nightlife, languid sun worshipping, diving in crystal-clear waters or to embark on a culture-vulture journey through past civilisations, it's all here. The atmospheric Old Town of Rhodes is a maze of cobbled streets that will spirit you back to the days of the Byzantine Empire and beyond.

Crete

Greece's largest island, Crete is a tapestry of splendid beaches, ancient treasures, and landscapes encompassing vibrant cities and dreamy villages. The food is

Mykonos

superb – indulge in straight-from-the-ocean seafood, soft, tangy cheese, hand-spun filo and some of the world's best virgin olive oil.

Mykonos

Mykonos is the great glamour island of Greece and flaunts its sizzling St-Tropez-meets-Ibiza style and party-hard reputation. The high-season mix of hedonistic holidaymakers, cruise-ship crowds and posturing fashionistas throngs Mykonos Town, a traditional whitewashed Cycladic maze.

☑ **Don't Miss**

Summer nights at waterfront cafes listening boat chains clanking and people laughing.

AFINCCHIARO / GETTY IMAGES ©

Corfu

Corfu welcomes weary travellers with its lush scenery, bountiful produce and pristine beaches. Corfu is large enough to make it possible to escape the crowds. Venture across cypress-studded hills to find vertiginous villages in the fertile interior, and sandy coves lapped by cobalt-blue waters.

Lesvos

Greece's third-largest island, Lesvos is uncrowded and marked by long sweeps of rugged, desert-like western plains that give way to sandy beaches and salt marshes in the centre. To the east are thickly forested mountains and dense olive groves. Find your favorite flavour of serenity.

Tinos

Tinos is a wonderland of natural beauty, dotted with more than 40 marble-ornamented villages found in hidden bays, on terraced hillsides and atop misty mountains. Also scattered across the brindled countryside are countless ornate dovecotes, a legacy of the Venetians. The food, made from local produce (cheeses, sausage, tomatoes and wild artichokes), is some of the best you'll find in Greece.

Naxos

Naxos packs a lot of bang for its buck. Its main city of Hora (known also as Naxos) has a gorgeous waterfront and a web of steep cobbled alleys below its hilltop kastro, all filled with the hubbub of tourism and shopping. You needn't travel far, though, to find isolated beaches, atmospheric mountain villages and ancient sites.

✗ **Take a Break**

Wiggle your toes in the sand while enjoying a chilled beverage at a beachside cafe.

İSTANBUL, TURKEY

In This Chapter

İstanbul, Turkey

This magical meeting place of East and West has more top-drawer attractions than it has minarets (and that's a lot). İstanbul's strategic location has given it a rich history. The city straddles two continents and was the final stage on the legendary Silk Road linking Asia with Europe, giving the city a cultural diversity that it retains.

The Byzantines adorned their churches and palaces with mosaics and frescoes. Miraculously, many of these remain. Their successors, the Ottomans, contributed magnificently decorated imperial mosques. These architectural triumphs together form one of the world's great skylines.

Two Days in İstanbul

On your first day, don't miss **Aya Sofya** (p520), the **Blue Mosque** (p528) and the **Basilica Cistern** (p528). After your visits, wander through the **Hippodrome** (p528), where chariot races were held in ancient times. Afterwards, diverge from the tourist trail and head down to the Küçük Ayasofya neighbourhood.

On day two, investigate the lifestyles of the sultans at **Topkapı Palace** (p524) and explore the streets, cafes and boutiques of Galata, Tophane, Karaköy and Çukurcuma.

Four Days in İstanbul

Day three should see you explore the city's famous Bazaar District, visiting the most magnificent of all Ottoman mosques, the **Süleymaniye** (p529), and making your way to the world-famous **Grand Bazaar** (p528) to explore its labyrinthine lanes.

On day four, board the **Long Bosphorus Tour** for a one-way trip up the Bosphorus, then make your way back to town by bus, visiting museums and monuments along the way.

Moving on from İstanbul? It's a short hop to Athens (p497) or the Greek Islands (p512).

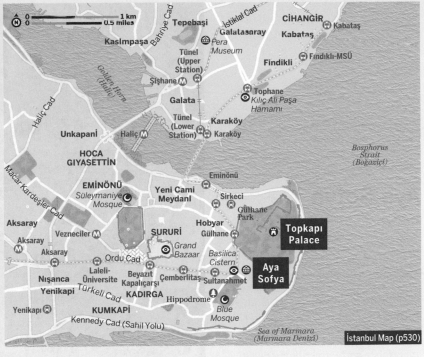

İstanbul Map (p530)

Arriving in İstanbul

İstanbul Airport This new airport is 52km northwest of central İstanbul. At time of writing, buses and taxis were the only form of transport into the city, though a metro link was scheduled to open in 2020.

Sabiha Gökçen International Airport Havabüs bus to Taksim Meydanı (₺18, 3.30am to 1am), from where a funicular (₺5) and tram (₺5) travel to Sultanahmet; Havabüs bus to Kadıköy (₺14, 4am to 1am); taxi ₺175 to Sultanahmet and ₺165 to Beyoğlu.

Where to Stay

Every accommodation style is available in İstanbul. You can live like a sultan in a world-class luxury hotel, bunk down in a dorm bed or settle into a stylish boutique establishment. The secret is to choose the neighbourhood that best suits your interests and then look for accommodation that will suit your style and budget – there are loads of options to choose from.

Aya Sofya

There are many important monuments in İstanbul, but this venerable structure – which was commissioned by the great Byzantine emperor Justinian, consecrated as a church in 537, converted to a mosque by Mehmet the Conqueror in 1453 and declared a museum by Atatürk in 1935 – surpasses the rest due to its innovative architectural form, rich history, religious importance and extraordinary beauty.

Great For...

❶ Need to Know

Hagia Sophia; ☏ 0212-522 1750, 0212-522 0989; www.ayasofyamuzesi.gov.tr/en; Aya Sofya Meydanı 1; adult/child under 8yr ₺60/free; ⊙9am-7pm Tue-Sun mid-Apr–Oct, to 5pm Nov–mid-Apr; ♿Sultanahmet

★ **Top Tip**

Go at lunchtime or late afternoon to beat the crowds.

Ground Floor

As you enter the building and walk into the inner narthex, look up to see a brilliant mosaic of *Christ as Pantocrator* (Ruler of All) above the third and largest door (the Imperial Door). Through this is the building's main space, famous for its dome, huge nave and gold mosaics.

The focal point at this level is the apse, with its magnificent 9th-century mosaic of the *Virgin and Christ Child*. The mosaics above the apse once depicted the archangels Gabriel and Michael; today only fragments remain.

The Byzantine emperors were crowned while seated on a throne placed within the omphalion, the section of inlaid marble in the main floor.

Ottoman additions to the building include a *mimber* (pulpit) and *mihrab* (prayer niche indicating the direction of Mecca); large 19th-century medallions inscribed with gilt Arabic letters; a curious elevated kiosk known as the *hünkar mahfili*; and an ornate library behind the omphalion.

Looking up towards the northeast (to your left if you are facing the apse), you should be able to see three mosaics at the base of the northern tympanum (semicircle) beneath the dome, although they have recently been obscured by a scaffolding tower used in restoration works. These are 9th-century portraits of St Ignatius the Younger, St John Chrysostom and St Ignatius Theodorus of Antioch. To their right, on one of the pendentives (concave triangular segments below the dome), is a 14th-century mosaic of the face of a seraph (six-winged angel charged with the caretaking of God's throne).

Mosaics

In the side aisle at the bottom of the ramp to the upstairs galleries is a column with a worn copper facing pierced by a hole. According to legend, the pillar, known as the Weeping Column, was blessed by St Gregory the Miracle Worker and putting one's finger into the hole is said to lead to ailments being healed if the finger emerges moist.

Upstairs Galleries

To access the galleries, walk up the switch-back ramp at the northern end of the inner narthex. In the south gallery (straight ahead and then left through the 6th-century marble door) are the remnants of a magnificent

☑ Don't Miss

The fabulous Byzantine mosaics that adorn the building.

Deesis (Last Judgement). This 13th-century mosaic depicts Christ with the Virgin Mary on his right and John the Baptist on his left.

Further on, at the eastern (apse) end of the gallery, an 11th-century mosaic depicts *Christ Enthroned with Empress Zoe and Constantine IX Monomachos*.

To the right of Zoe and Constantine is a 12th-century mosaic depicting *The Virgin Mary, Emperor John Comnenus II and Empress Eirene*. The emperor, who was known as 'John the Good', is on the Virgin's left and the empress, who was known for her charitable works, is to her right. Their son Alexius, who died soon after the portrait was made, is depicted next to Eirene.

Mosaics

In Justinian's day, the great dome, the semidomes, the north and south tympana and the vaults of the narthexes, aisles and galleries were all covered in gold mosaics. Remnants exist, but one can only imagine what the interior looked like.

Exiting the Building

As you leave the inner narthex, be sure to look back to admire the 10th-century mosaic of *Constantine the Great, the Virgin Mary and the Emperor Justinian* on the lunette of the inner doorway. Constantine (right) is offering the Virgin, who holds the Christ Child, the city of İstanbul; Justinian (left) is offering her Aya Sofya.

Just after you exit the building through the Beautiful Gate, a magnificent bronze gate dating from the 2nd century BC, there is a doorway on the left. This leads into a small courtyard that was once part of a 6th-century baptistry. In the 17th century the baptistry was converted into a tomb for Sultans Mustafa I and İbrahim I. The huge stone basin displayed in the courtyard is the original font.

✗ Take a Break

Head to Derviş Cafe & Restaurant (p533) for a tea and sandwich with Blue Mosque views.

MEMMETO / SHUTTERSTOCK ©

Topkapı Palace

Topkapı is the subject of more colourful stories than most of the world's museums put together. Libidinous sultans, ambitious courtiers, beautiful concubines and scheming eunuchs lived and worked here between the 15th and 19th centuries when it was the court of the Ottoman empire.

First & Second Courts

Pass through the Imperial Gate into the First Court, which is known as the Court of the Janissaries or the Parade Court. On your left is the Byzantine church of Aya İrini.

The Second Court has a beautiful park-like setting. Topkapı is a series of pavilions, kitchens, barracks, audience chambers, kiosks and sleeping quarters built around a central enclosure.

On the left (west) side of the Second Court is the ornate Imperial Council Chamber (Dîvân-ı Hümâyûn). The council met here to discuss matters of state, and the sultan sometimes eavesdropped through the gold grille high in the wall.

Harem

The sultans supported as many as 300 concubines in the Harem, although

---

Great For...

☑ **Don't Miss**

The ornate Imperial Council Chamber.

Harem

❶ Need to Know

Topkapı Sarayı; ☎0212-512 0480; www.topkapi sarayi.gov.tr; Babıhümayun Caddesi; palace adult/child under 8yr ₺60/free, Harem adult/ child under 6yr ₺35/free; ⊘9am-6.45pm Wed-Mon mid-Apr–Oct, to 4.45pm Nov–mid-Apr, last entry 45min before closing; ⓂSultanahmet

✕ Take a Break

Sample Ottoman dishes based on recipes perfected in the palace kitchens, over lunch at **Matbah** (☎0212-514 6151; www.matbahrestaurant.com; Ottoman Hotel Imperial, Caferiye Sokak 6/1; mezes ₺14-20, mains ₺29-65; ⊘noon-10.30pm; 🛜🖉; ⓂSultanahmet).

★ Top Tip

Buy the Museum Pass İstanbul or hire a private guide to jump the queue for admission.

numbers were usually lower than this. Upon entering the Harem, the girls would be schooled in Islam and in Turkish culture and language, as well as the arts of make-up, dress, comportment, music, reading, writing, embroidery and dancing. They then entered a meritocracy, first as ladies-in-waiting to the sultan's concubines and children, then to the *valide sultan* and finally – if they were particularly attractive and talented – to the sultan himself. The Harem complex has six floors, but only one of these can be visited. This is approached via the **Carriage Gate**.

Third Court & Imperial Treasury

The Third Court is entered through the Gate of Felicity. The sultan's private domain, it was staffed and guarded by white eunuchs. Inside is the Audience Cham-

ber, constructed in the 16th century but refurbished in the 18th century. Important officials and foreign ambassadors were brought to this little kiosk to conduct the high business of state. The sultan, seated on a huge divan, inspected the ambassadors' gifts and offerings as they were passed through the doorway on the left.

Located on the eastern edge of the Third Court, Topkapı's Treasury features an incredible collection of objects made from or decorated with gold, silver, rubies, emeralds, jade, pearls and diamonds. The building itself was constructed during Mehmet the Conqueror's reign in 1460 and was used originally as reception rooms. It was closed for a major restoration when we last visited.

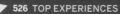

FIRATGOCMEN / GETTY IMAGES ©

Hamam Experience

Succumbing to a soapy scrub in a steamy hamam is one of İstanbul's quintessential experiences. Not everyone feels comfortable with baring all (or most) of their body in public, though. If you include yourself in this group, a number of the city's spas offer private hamam treatments.

Great For...

☑ Don't Miss

The real Turkish bath experience: to have an attendant wash, scrub and massage you.

Ayasofya Hürrem Sultan Hamamı

This meticulously restored twin **hamam** (☑0212-517 3535; www.ayasofyahamami.com; Aya Sofya Meydanı 2; bath treatments €55-160, massages €100-160; ⊘8am-10pm; 🚇Sultanahmet) dating to 1556 offers the most luxurious traditional bath experience in the Old City. Designed by Mimar Sinan, it was built just across the road from Aya Sofya by order of Süleyman the Magnificent and named in honour of his wife Hürrem Sultan, commonly known as Roxelana.

The building's three-year, US$13 million restoration, completed in 2011, was closely monitored by heritage authorities and the end result is wonderful: it retains Sinan's austere design but endows it with an understated modern luxury. There are separate baths for males and females, both with a handsome *soğukluk* (entrance

STEFANO SCATA / GETTY IMAGES ©

the result was well worth waiting for. The hamam's interior is simply stunning and the place is run with total professionalism, ensuring a clean and enjoyable Turkish bath experience. Services include a traditional hamam ritual (₺220) and massage (from ₺160).

Cağaloğlu Hamamı

Built in 1741 by order of Sultan Mahmut I, this gorgeous **hamam** (☑0212-522 2424; www.cagalogluhamami.com.tr; Prof Kazım İsmail Gürkan Caddesi 24; bath, scrub & massage packages €40-120, self-service €30; ☺9am-10pm; ⸚Sultanahmet) offers separate baths for men and women and a range of bath services that are, alas, overpriced considering how quick and rudimentary the wash, scrub and massage treatments are. Consider signing up for the self-service treatment (€30) only.

vestibule) surrounded by wooden change cubicles. Treatments are expert and the surrounds are exceptionally clean. The basic 45-minute bath treatment costs €80 and includes a scrub and soap massage, olive-oil soap and a personal *kese* (coarse cloth mitten used for exfoliation). Book ahead in high season. In warm weather, a cafe and restaurant operate on the outdoor terrace.

Kılıç Ali Paşa Hamamı

It took seven years to develop a conservation plan for this 1580 Mimar Sinan–designed **building** (☑0212-393 8010; http://kilicalipasahamami.com; Hamam Sokak 1, off Kemeraltı Caddesi, Tophane; traditional hamam ritual ₺270; ☺women 8am-4pm, men 4.30-11.30pm; ⸚Tophane) and to complete the meticulous restoration. Fortunately,

◎ SIGHTS

Basilica Cistern · Historic Site

(Yerebatan Sarnıçı; ☑0212-512 1570; www.
yerebatan.com; Yerebatan Caddesi; adult/child
under 8yr ₺20/free; ۞9am-5.30pm Nov–mid-
Apr, to 6.30pm mid-Apr–Oct; 🚇Sultanahmet)
This subterranean structure was commissioned by Emperor Justinian and built in
532. The largest surviving Byzantine cistern
in İstanbul, it was constructed using 336
columns, many of which were salvaged
from ruined temples and feature fine
carved capitals. Its symmetry and sheer
grandeur of conception are quite breathtaking, and its cavernous depths make a
great retreat on summer days.

Blue Mosque · Mosque

(Sultanahmet Camii; ☑0212-458 4468; Hippodrome; ۞closed to non-worshippers during 6 daily
prayer times; 🚇Sultanahmet) İstanbul's most
photogenic building was the grand project
of Sultan Ahmet I (r 1603–17), whose tomb
is located on the north side of the site facing
Sultanahmet Park. The mosque's wonderfully curvaceous exterior features a cascade
of domes and six slender minarets. Blue İznik
tiles adorn the interior and give the building
its unofficial but commonly used name.

Hippodrome · Park

(Atmeydanı; Atmeydanı Caddesi; 🚇Sultanahmet)
The Byzantine emperors loved nothing
more than an afternoon at the chariot
races, and this rectangular arena alongside Sultanahmet Park was their venue of
choice. In its heyday, it was decorated by
obelisks and statues, some of which remain
in place today. Re-landscaped in more
recent years, it is one of the city's most
popular meeting places and promenades.

Grand Bazaar · Market

(Kapalı Çarşı, Covered Market; www.kapalicarsi.
org.tr; ۞9am-7pm Mon-Sat, last entry 6pm;
🚇Beyazıt Kapalıçarşı) The colourful and chaotic Grand Bazaar is the heart of İstanbul's Old
City and has been so for centuries. Starting
as a small vaulted *bedesten* (warehouse)
built by order of Mehmet the Conqueror in
1461, it grew to cover a vast area as lanes
between the *bedesten,* neighbouring shops
and *hans* (caravanserais) were roofed and

Basilica Cistern

LUCIANO MORTULA - LGM / SHUTTERSTOCK ©

the market assumed the sprawling, labyrinthine form that it retains today.

Süleymaniye Mosque   Mosque

(Professor Sıddık Sami Onar Caddesi; ☺dawn-dusk; ⓂVezneciler) The Süleymaniye crowns one of İstanbul's seven hills and dominates the Golden Horn, providing a landmark for the entire city. Though it's not the largest of the Ottoman mosques, it is certainly one of the grandest and most beautiful. It's also unusual in that many of its original *külliye* (mosque complex) buildings have been retained and sympathetically adapted for reuse.

Pera Museum   Museum

(Pera Müzesi; ☑0212-334 9900; www.pera museum.org; Meşrutiyet Caddesi 65, Tepebaşı; adult/student/child under 12yr ₺20/10/free; ☺10am-7pm Tue-Thu & Sat, to 10pm Fri, noon-6pm Sun; ⓂŞişhane, 🚋Tünel) There's plenty to see at this impressive museum, but its major draw is undoubtedly the 2nd-floor exhibition of paintings featuring Turkish Orientalist themes. Drawn from Suna and İnan Kıraç's world-class private collection, the works provide fascinating glimpses into the Ottoman world from the 17th to 20th centuries and include the most beloved painting in the Turkish canon – Osman Hamdı Bey's *The Tortoise Trainer* (1906). Other floors host high-profile temporary exhibitions (past exhibitions have showcased Warhol, de Chirico, Picasso and Botero).

🅖 TOURS

İstanbul Walks   Walking

(☑0212-516 6300, 0554 335 6622; www. istanbulwalks.com; 1st fl, Şifa Hamamı Sokak 1; tours €60-130; 🚋Sultanahmet) Specialising in cultural tourism, this company is run by history buffs and offers a large range of guided walking tours conducted by knowledgeable English-speaking guides. Tours concentrate on İstanbul's various neighbourhoods, but there are also tours of major monuments, a Turkish coffee trail, and a Bosphorus and Golden Horn cruise by private boat. Significant discounts for children aged under seven.

💬 The Dying Art of Bargaining

The Grand Bazaar is perhaps the only place in the city where some stalls still take pride in practising the ancient art of bargaining. If you are keen to buy a carpet or rug, follow these tips:

○ The 'official' prices have almost always been artificially inflated, with 20% to 30% the rule of thumb.

○ Never feel pressured to buy something. Tea and conversation are gratis. If you accept them, you don't need to buy anything in exchange.

○ Do your research. Always shop around to compare quality and pricing.

○ Before starting to bargain, decide how much you like the carpet or rug and how much you are prepared to pay for it. It's important that you stick to this. The shopkeepers here are professional bargainers and have loads of practise in talking customers into purchases against their better judgement.

○ Your first offer should be around 60% of the initial asking price. The shopkeeper will laugh, look offended or profess to be puzzled, which is all part of the ritual.

○ They will then make a counter offer of 80% to 90%. You should look disappointed, explain that you have done your research and are not prepared to pay that amount, then offer around 70%.

○ By this stage you should have sized each other up. The shopkeeper will cite the price at which they are prepared to sell and, if you are happy to pay, you can agree to the deal. If not, you should smile, shake hands and walk away.

Grand Bazaar

İstanbul

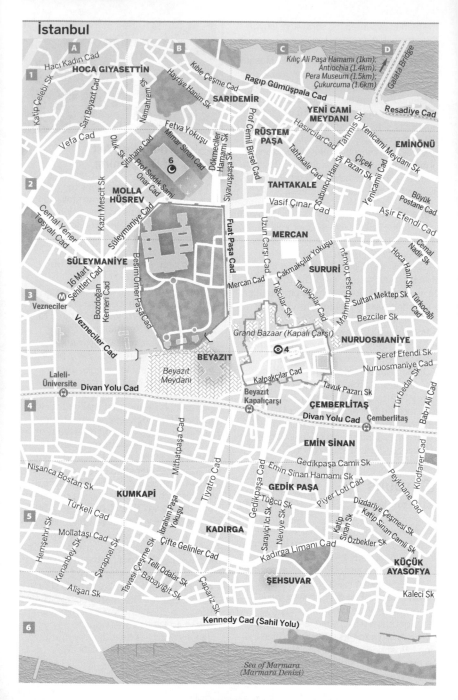

A · **B** · **C** · **D**

1 · **2** · **3** · **4** · **5** · **6**

Katip Çelebi Sk
Hacı Kadın Cad
HOCA GIYASETTİN
Vefa Cad
Sarı Beyazıt Cad
Namahrem Sk
Hayriye Hanım Sk
Kıble Çeşme Cad
Ragıp Gümüşpala Cad
Kılıç Ali Paşa Hamamı (1km);
Antiochia (1.4km);
Pera Museum (1.5km);
Çukurcuma (1.6km).
Galata Bridge
SARIDEMİR
Resadiye Cad
Fetva Yokuşu
Mimar Sinan Cad
Oluk Sk
Şifahane Cad
Prof Cemil Birsel Cad
RÜSTEM PAŞA
YENİ CAMİ MEYDANI
Hasırcılar Cad
Tahmis Sk
Yenicami Meydanı Sk
EMİNÖNÜ
Çiçek Pazarı Sk
Yenicamii Cad
Büyük Postane Cad
Dökmeciler Hamamı Sk
Şeyhşaşa Sk
Siyavuş
Onar Cad
Prof Sıddık Sami Onar Cad
MOLLA HÜSREV
Kazlı Mescit Sk
Süleymaniye Cad
6 🅖
Tahtakale Cad
Sabuncu Hanı Sk
TAHTAKALE
Vasif Çınar Cad
Aşir Efendi Cad
Cemal Yener Tosyalı Cad
SÜLEYMANİYE
16 Mart Şehitleri Cad
Bozdoğan Kemeri Cad
Besim Ömer Paşa Cad
Fuat Paşa Cad
Uzun Çarşı Cad
MERCAN
Çakmakçılar Yokuşu
SURURİ
Mahmutpaşa Yokuşu
Hoca Hanı Sk
Cemal Nadir Sk
🅜 **Vezneciler**
Vezneciler Cad
Mercan Cad
Tığcılar Sk
Tarakçılar Cad
Sultan Mektep Sk
Bezciler Sk
Türkocağı Cad
Grand Bazaar (Kapalı Çarşı) 🅸**4**
NURUOSMANİYE
Şeref Efendi Sk
Nuruosmaniye Cad
BEYAZIT
Beyazıt Meydanı
Kalpakçılar Cad
Tavuk Pazarı Sk
Türbedar Sk
Bab-ı Ali Cad
Laleli-Üniversite 🅜
Divan Yolu Cad
Beyazıt Kapalıçarşı
ÇEMBERLİTAŞ
Divan Yolu Cad Çemberlitaş 🅜
EMİN SİNAN
Nişanca Bostan Sk
Mithatpaşa Cad
Tiyatro Cad
Gedikpaşa Cad
Emin Sinan Hamamı Sk
Gedikpaşa Camii Sk
Piyer Loti Cad
Peykhane Cad
Klodfarer Cad
KUMKAPİ
Türkeli Cad
İbrahim Paşa Yokuşu
GEDİK PAŞA
Tuğcü Sk
Sarayiçi Sk
Neviye Sk
Dizdariye Çeşmesi Sk
Katip Sinan Camii Sk
Hemşehri Sk
Kenanbey Sk
Mollataşı Cad
Şarapnel Sk
Çifte Gelinler Cad
KADIRGA
Kadırga Limanı Cad
Katip Sinan Sk
Özbekler Sk
KÜÇÜK AYASOFYA
Alişan Sk
Tavası Çeşme Sk
Telli Odalar Sk
Babayiğit Sk
Çaparız Sk
ŞEHSUVAR
Kaleci Sk
Kennedy Cad (Sahil Yolu)

*Sea of Marmara
(Marmara Denizi)*

500 m
0.25 miles

Golden Horn
(Haliç)

Eminönü

Yalı Köşkü Cad

SİRKECİ

Sirkeci

Hamidiye Cad

Ankara Cad

Kennedy Cad (Sahil Yolu)

Sirkeci

İstasyon Arkası Sk

HOBYAR

Nöbethane Cad

Hüdavendigar Cad

Gülhane
Park

Ebussuud Cad

Ankara Cad

Gülhane

CAĞALOĞLU

Hükümet
Konağı Sk

Topkapı
Palace

7

Alayköşkü Cad

9

Molla Fenerı Sk

13

Çatal
Çeşme Sk

Yerebatan
Cad

Alemdar Cad

12

Soğukçeşme Sk

Topkapı Palace
Court of Janissaries
(First Court)

ALEMDAR

Sultanahmet

2

1 Aya Sofya

Aya Sofya
Meydanı

Ömran Cad

Oktem Cad

BİNBİRDİREK

Sultanahmet
Park

8

MEYDANI

14

İshakpaşa Cad

Kennedy Cad (Sahil Yolu)

5

Atmeydanı Cad

SULTANAHMET

Kutlugün Sk

3

11

Akbıyık Cad

Torun Sk

Tavukhane Sk

Cankurtaran Cad

Bosphorus Strait
(Boğaziçi)

Aksakal Cad

10

Küçük Ayasofya Cad

Oğul Sk

Akbıyık Değirmeni Sk

Ahırkapı Sk

Mustafa Paşa Sk

Oyuncu Sk

İstanbul

İstanbul Eats
Walking, Culinary

(http://istanbuleats.com; tours per person US$75-125) Full-day culinary walks around the Old City, Bazaar District, Beyoğlu, Kadıköy and the Bosphorus suburbs, as well as evenings spent sampling kebaps in Aksaray's 'Little Syria' district or visiting *meyhanes* (Turkish taverns) in Beyoğlu. All are conducted by the dedicated foodies who produce the excellent blog of the same name, and involve lots of eating.

🛍 SHOPPING

Özlem Tuna
Jewellery, Homewares

(☎0090-527 9285; www.ozlemtuna.com; Çukurcuma Caddesi 36, Çukurcuma; ☽9am-6pm Mon-Sat; 🚋Tophane) A leader in Turkey's contemporary-design movement, Özlem Tuna produces superstylish jewellery and homewares and sells them from her retail space near Orhan Pamuk's **Museum of Innocence** (Masumiyet Müzesi; ☎0212-252 9738; www.masumiyetmuzesi.org; Çukurcuma Caddesi, Dalgıç Çıkmazı 2; adult/student ₺40/30; ☽10am-6pm Tue-Sun, to 9pm Thu). Her pieces use forms and colours that reference İstanbul's history and culture (tulips, seagulls, Byzantine mosaics, *nazar boncuk* 'evil eye' charms) and include hamam bowls, coffee and tea sets, coasters, rings, earrings, cufflinks and necklaces.

Jennifer's Hamam
Homewares

(☎0212-516 3022; www.jennifershamam.com; Arasta Bazaar 135; ☽8.30am-9pm Apr-Oct, to 7pm Nov-Mar; 🚋Sultanahmet) Owned by Canadian Jennifer Gaudet, this shop stocks top-quality hamam items, including towels, robes and *peştemals* (bath wraps) produced using certified organic cotton and silk on old-style shuttled looms. It also sells natural soaps and *keses* (coarse cloth mittens used for exfoliation). Prices are set; no bargaining.

🍴 EATING & DRINKING

Sefa Restaurant
Turkish €

(☎0212-520 0670; www.sefarestaurant.com.tr; Nuruosmaniye Caddesi 11, Cağaloğlu; soups ₺6-12, portions ₺16-27; ☽7am-5pm; 🖥📶; 🚋Sultanahmet) Located between Sultanahmet and the Grand Bazaar, this clean and popular place offers *hazır yemek* (ready-made dishes) at reasonable prices. You can order from an English menu, but at busy times you may find it easier to just pick daily specials from the bain-marie. Try to arrive early-ish for lunch because many dishes run out by 1.30pm. No alcohol.

Antiochia
Anatolian €€

(☎0212-244 0820; www.antiochiaconcept.com; General Yazgan Sokak 3, Tünel; mezes & salads ₺15-20, pides ₺22, kebaps ₺33-62; ☽noon-midnight Mon-Fri, 3pm-midnight Sat; ❄🖥♿; 🚋Tünel) Dishes from the southeastern city of Antakya (Hatay) are the speciality here. Cold and hot mezes are equally delicious, pides are flavoursome and the kebaps are exceptional – try the succulent *şiş et* (grilled lamb). The set menus of mezes and a choice of main dish (₺39 to ₺66) offer excellent value and there's a good range of Suvla wines by glass and bottle.

Cuma   Modern Turkish €€€

(📞0212-293 2062; www.cuma.cc; Çukurcuma
Caddesi 53a, Çukurcuma; breakfast dishes ₺16-
27, lunch dishes ₺25-40, dinner mains ₺27-45;
🕑9am-midnight Mon-Sat, to 8pm Sun; 🛜🚲♿;
Ⓜ️Taksim) Banu Tiryakioğulları's laid-back
foodie oasis in the heart of Çukurcuma has
one of the most devoted customer bases in
the city. Tables are on the leafy terrace or
in the atmospheric upstairs dining space,
and the healthy, seasonally driven menu is
heavy on flavour and light on fuss – breakfast is particularly delicious (regulars tend
to share the *kahvaltı* – breakfast – plate).

Alancha   Modern Turkish €€€

(📞0212-261 3535; http://en.alancha.com; Maçka
Kempinski Residence, Şehit Mehmet Sokak
9, Maçka; menu ₺300; 🕑7pm-2am Mon-Sat;
Ⓜ️Osmanbey) Alancha's designer decor
is as striking as its colourful and artfully
arranged dinner dishes, which range from
servings of wild sea bass to filet mignon.
Go for the Anatolian tasting menu, which
features a dozen courses prepared with
artisan ingredients from the seven regions
of Anatolia, starting with stuffed mussels
and continuing through pistachio kebap to
baklava and *lokum* (Turkish Delight). Wine
pairing costs ₺160.

Asitane   Turkish €€€

(📞0212-635 7997; www.asitanerestaurant.com;
Kariye Oteli, Kariye Camii Sokak 6, Edirnekapı;
starters ₺18-28, mains ₺58; 🕑noon-11.30pm; 🚲;
🚌28 from Eminönü, 87 from Taksim, 🚢Ayvan-
saray) This elegant restaurant next to the
Kariye Museum (Chora Church) serves
Ottoman dishes devised for the palace
kitchens at Topkapı, Edirne and Dolma-
bahçe. Its chefs have been tracking down
historic recipes for years, and the menu is
full of versions that will tempt most modern
palates, including vegetarian.

Derviş Cafe & Restaurant   Tea Garden

(cnr Dalbastı Sokak & Kabasakal Caddesi;
🕑7am-midnight; 🚢Sultanahmet) Superbly
located directly opposite the Blue Mosque,
the Derviş beckons patrons with its comfortable cane chairs and shady trees. Efficient
service, reasonable prices and peerless
people-watching opportunities make it a
great place for a leisurely çay (₺4), nargile
(water pipe; ₺35), *tost* (toasted sandwich;
₺10) and a game of backgammon.

ℹ️ INFORMATION

Tourist offices operate in **Sultanahmet** (📞0212-
518 1802; Hippodrome, Sultanahmet; 🕑9am-
5.30pm; 🚢Sultanahmet) among other places.

ℹ️ GETTING THERE & AWAY

It's the national capital in all but name, so
getting to İstanbul is easy. There are two
international airports, one of which is the
shiny new Istanbul Airport. There is one
otogar (bus station) from which national
and international services arrive and
depart. At the time of writing there were
no international rail connections, but this
situation may change when upgrades to rail
lines throughout the country are completed
and when the security situation in Turkey's
east and in Syria improves.

ℹ️ GETTING AROUND

Public transport is cheap and efficient. Purchasing an İstanbulkart (transport card) is highly
recommended.

Tram Run from Bağcılar, in the city's west, to
Kabataş, in Beyoğlu, stopping at the Grand
Bazaar, Sultanahmet, Eminönü and Karaköy en
route. Connect with the metro at Zeytinburnu
and Sirkeci, with ferries at Eminönü and with
funiculars at Karaköy and Kabataş.

Metro The M1A connects Yenikapı with the
airport; the M2 connects Yenikapı with Hacıos-
man via Taksim; and the Marmaray connects
Kazlıçeşme, west of the Old City, with Sirkeci
before crossing under the Bosphorus to Üsküdar
and Ayrılık Çeşmesi.

Ferry Travel between the European and Asian
shores, along the Bosphorus and Golden Horn,
and to the Adalar (Princes' Islands).

Bus Along the Bosphorus and the Golden Horn
and between Üsküdar and Kadıköy.

PRAGUE, CZECH REPUBLIC

Prague, Czech Republic

Everyone who visits the Czech Republic starts with Prague, the cradle of Czech culture and one of Europe's most fascinating cities. Prague offers a near-intact medieval core of Gothic architecture that can transport you back 500 years – the 14th-century Charles Bridge, connecting two historic neighbourhoods across the Vltava River, with the castle ramparts and the spires of St Vitus Cathedral rising above, is one of the classic sights of world travel. But the city is not just about history, it's also a vital urban centre with a rich array of cultural offerings and a newly emerging foodie scene.

Two Days in Prague

Start the day wandering through the courtyards of **Prague Castle** (p538) before the main sights open, then spend the afternoon visiting the baroque beauty of **St Nicholas Church** (p544). End the day with a treat of a gourmet dinner at **Field** (p553) or **Kantýna** (p553). Spend the morning of day two in **Old Town Square** (p545), before visiting the half-dozen monuments that comprise the **Prague Jewish Museum** (p548).

Four Days in Prague

Explore the passages and arcades around **Wenceslas Square** (p549) on day three, then take in the historical and artistic treasures of the **Prague City Museum** (p549). On the final day take a metro ride out to Vyšehrad and explore Prague's other castle, the **Vyšehrad Citadel** (p551), with its gorgeous views along the Vltava, followed by lunch at **U Kroka** (p552). In the evening catch a performance at the **National Theatre** (p555) or the **Palác Akropolis** (p555).

After Prague travel to Budapest (p559) or Vienna (p577).

Previous page: Church of Our Lady Before Týn (p548) and Old Town Square (p545)
LUCIANO MORTULA - LGM / SHUTTERSTOCK ©

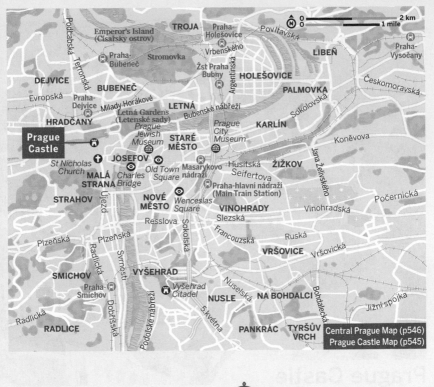

Central Prague Map (p546)
Prague Castle Map (p545)

Arriving in Prague

Václav Havel Airport Buses to metro stops Nádraží Veleslavín (service 119) and Zličín (100) depart every 10 minutes between 4am and midnight, from stops just outside the arrivals terminal (32Kč). A taxi to the centre costs 500Kč.

Praha hlavní nádraží Prague's main train station is in the city centre and is accessible by metro line C (red); all international rail connections arrive here.

Florenc bus station International buses arrive here, just east of Prague centre, with metro and tram links to the rest of the city.

Where to Stay

Gone are the days when Prague was a cheap destination. The Czech capital now ranks alongside most Western European cities when it comes to the quality, range and price of hotels.

Accommodation ranges from cosy, romantic hotels set in historic townhouses to the new generation of funky design hotels and hostels. Short-term-stay, self-catering apartments are an increasingly popular option.

Book as far in advance as possible (especially in May, at Easter and over Christmas/New Year).

V_E / SHUTTERSTOCK ©

Prague Castle

Prague Castle – Pražský hrad, or just hrad *to Czechs – is Prague's most popular attraction. Perched on a hill above the Vltava's left bank, its serried ranks of spires, towers and palaces dominate the city like a fairy-tale fortress. Within its walls lie historic buildings, museums and galleries showcasing some of the Czech Republic's greatest cultural treasures.*

Great For...

☑ Don't Miss

The tiny, colourful 16th-century cottages on Golden Lane, or the Princely Collections at Lobkowicz Palace.

First Courtyard

The First Courtyard lies within the castle's main gate on Hradčany Square (Hradčanské náměstí), flanked by huge, baroque statues of battling **Titans** (1767–70) that dwarf the castle guards standing beneath them. After the fall of communism in 1989, then-president Václav Havel hired his old pal Theodor Pistek, the costume designer on the film *Amadeus* (1984), to replace their communist-era khaki uniforms with the stylish pale-blue kit they now wear, which harks back to the army of the first Czechoslovak Republic of 1918 to 1938.

The **changing of the guard** takes place every hour on the hour, but the longest and most impressive display is at noon, when banners are exchanged while a brass band plays a fanfare from the windows of

Prague Castle surrounding St Vitus Cathedral (p544)

ⓘ Need to Know

Pražský hrad; Map p545; ☑224 372 423; www.hrad.cz; Hradčanské náměstí 1; adult/ concession from 250/125Kč; ☺grounds 6am-10pm, gardens 10am-6pm Apr-Oct, historic buildings 9am-5pm Apr-Oct, to 4pm Nov-Mar; MMalostranská, ☒22, 23

✕ Take a Break

Stop by Lobkowicz Palace Café (p552) for great goulash and superb city views.

★ Top Tip

To avoid the worst crowds, visit early or late – before 10.30am or after 3.30pm. Bring your passport or ID card to get through security at the entrance.

the Plečnik Hall, which overlooks the First Courtyard.

Second Courtyard

Beyond the Matthias Gate lies the Second Courtyard, centred on a baroque fountain and a 17th-century well with lovely Renaissance latticework.

On the right, the Chapel of the Holy Cross (1763) houses the **St Vitus Treasury** (Svatovítský poklad; Map p545; ☑224 372 423; www.hrad.cz; nádvoří II, Pražský hrad; adult/ child 250/150Kč, admission incl with Prague Castle Tour C ticket; ☺10am-6pm Apr-Oct, to 5pm Nov-Mar; ☒22), a spectacular collection of ecclesiastical bling that was founded by Charles IV in the 14th century. The oldest items include a reliquary arm of St Vitus dating from the early 10th century, while the most impressive treasures include a

gold coronation cross of Charles IV (1370) and a diamond-studded baroque monstrance from 1708.

The **Prague Castle Picture Gallery** (Map p545; adult/child 100/50Kč, admission incl with Prague Castle Tour C ticket; ☺9am-5pm Apr-Oct, to 4pm Nov-Mar; ☒22), in the castle's beautiful Renaissance stables, houses an exhibition of 16th- to 18th-century European art, based on the Habsburg collection that was begun in 1650 to replace stolen paintings; it includes works by Cranach, Holbein, Rubens, Tintoretto and Titian.

Third Courtyard

As you pass through the passage on the eastern side of the Second Courtyard, the huge western facade of St Vitus Cathedral (p544) soars directly above you; to its south (to the right as you enter) lies the

Third Courtyard. At its entrance you'll see a 16m-tall **granite monolith** (Map p545) dedicated to the victims of WWI, designed by Jože Plečnik in 1928, and a copy of a 14th-century bronze figure of **St George** (Map p545) slaying the dragon; the original is on display in the **Story of Prague Castle** (Map p545; www.hrad.cz; adult/child 140/70Kč; ⊙9am-5pm, to 4pm Nov-Mar; 🚊22, 23) exhibition.

The **Old Royal Palace** (Starý královský palác; Map p545; ⊙9am-5pm, to 4pm Nov-Mar; 🚊22, 23) at the courtyard's eastern end is one of the oldest parts of the castle, dating from 1135. It was originally used only by Czech princesses, but from the 13th to the 16th centuries it was the king's own palace.

The courtyard is dominated by the southern facade of St Vitus Cathedral (p544), one of the most richly endowed cathedrals in central Europe, and pivotal to the religious and cultural life of the Czech Republic. It houses treasures that range from the 14th-century mosaic of the Last Judgement and the tombs of St Wenceslas and Charles IV, to the baroque silver tomb of St John of Nepomuck, the ornate Chapel of St Wenceslas, and art nouveau stained glass by Alfons Mucha.

St George Square

St George Sq (Jiřské náměstí), the plaza to the east of St Vitus Cathedral, lies at the heart of the castle complex.

Basilica of St George

The striking, brick-red, early-baroque facade that dominates the square conceals the **Basilica of St George** (Bazilika sv Jiří; Map p545; www.hrad.cz; admission incl with Prague Castle tour A & B tickets; ⊙9am-5pm Apr-Oct, to 4pm Nov-Mar), the Czech Republic's best-preserved Romanesque basilica, established in the 10th century by Vratislav I (the father of St Wenceslas). What you see today is mostly the result of restorations made between 1887 and 1908.

★ Did You Know?

According to the *Guinness World Records*, Prague Castle is the largest ancient castle in the world – 570m long, an average of 128m wide and covering a total area bigger than seven football fields.

MILAN TOMAZIN / SHUTTERSTOCK ©

George Street

George Street (Jiřská) runs from the Basilica of St George to the castle's eastern gate.

The picturesque alley known as **Golden Lane** (Zlatá ulička; Map p545; ⊙9am-5pm, to 4pm Nov-Mar; ▣22, 23) runs along the northern wall of the castle. Its tiny, colourful cottages were built in the 16th century for the sharpshooters of the castle guard, but were later used by goldsmiths. In the 19th and early 20th centuries they were occupied by artists, including the writer Franz Kafka (who frequently visited his sister's house at No 22 from 1916 to 1917).

16th-century **Lobkowicz Palace** (Lobkovický palác; Map p545; ✆233 312 925; www.lobkowicz.com; Jiřská 3; adult/concession 295/220Kč; ⊙10am-6pm; ▣22, 23) houses a private museum known as the **Princely Collections**, which includes priceless paintings, furniture and musical memorabilia. Your tour includes an audio guide dictated by owner William Lobkowicz and his family – this personal connection really brings the displays to life and makes the palace one of the castle's most interesting attractions.

★ Top Tip

At the castle's eastern gate, you can take a sharp right and wander back to Hradčany Square through the **South Gardens** (Zahrada na valech; Map p545; ⊙10am-6pm Apr-Oct, closed Nov-Mar) **FREE**. The terrace garden offers superb views across the rooftops of Malá Strana.

Prague River Walk

The Vltava River runs through the heart of Prague and served as muse for composer Bedřich Smetana in writing his moving 'Vltava' (Moldau) symphony. But you don't need to be a musician to enjoy the river's breathtaking bridges and backdrops on this extended walk along the waterway.

Start Convent of St Agnes
Distance 8km
Duration 3 hours

2 Amble around **Letná Gardens** (p557) and take in the view of the Old Town and Malá Strana below.

Royal Garden
(Královská zahrada)

Brusnice

Old Castle Steps
(Staré Zámecké schody)

Malostranská Ⓜ

Valdštejnská

MALÁ STRANA

Wallenstein Garden
(Valdštejnská zahrada)

③

Thunovská

Vojan Gardens
(Vojanovy sady)

Nerudova

Malá Strana Square
(Malostranské náměstí)

Josefská

Tržiště

Mostecká

Na Kampě

Karmelitská

Čertovka

Classic Photo: Photogenic Prague Castle from any angle.

3 Enjoy views over the Vltava and the red roofs of Malá Strana from the ramparts of **Prague Castle** (p538) or from the beautifully manicured royal gardens.

6 The whimsical yet elegant **Dancing House**, by architects Vlado Milunić and Frank Gehry, surprisingly fits in with its ageing neighbours.

Janáčkovo nábřeží

Ⓝ 0 — 500 m
0 — 0.25 miles

SMÍCHOV

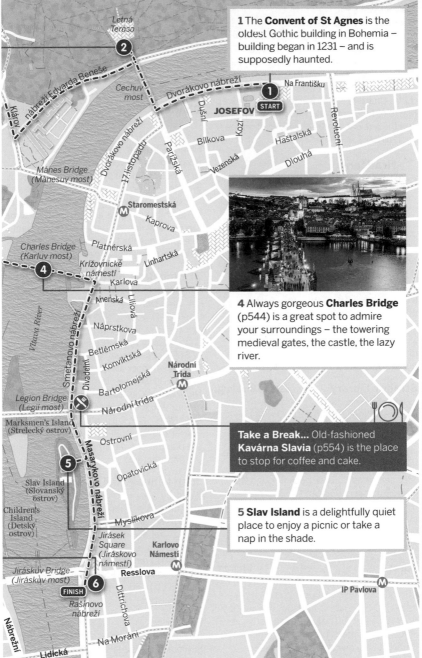

1 The **Convent of St Agnes** is the oldest Gothic building in Bohemia – building began in 1231 – and is supposedly haunted.

4 Always gorgeous **Charles Bridge** (p544) is a great spot to admire your surroundings – the towering medieval gates, the castle, the lazy river.

Take a Break... Old-fashioned **Kavárna Slavia** (p554) is the place to stop for coffee and cake.

5 Slav Island is a delightfully quiet place to enjoy a picnic or take a nap in the shade.

Map labels: Letná Teřasa; nábřeží Edvarda Beneše; Čechův most; Dvořákovo nábřeží; Na Františku; JOSEFOV; START; Dušní; Kozí; Haštalská; Revoluční; Bílkova; Vezeňská; Dlouhá; Pařížská; 17. listopadu; Dvořákovo nábřeží; Klárov; Mánes Bridge (Mánesův most); Staroměstská; Kaprova; Platnérská; Charles Bridge (Karlův most); Křižovnické náměstí; Linhartská; Karlova; Smetanovo nábřeží; Anenská; Liliová; Náprstkova; Betlémská; Konviktská; Národní Třída; Divadelní; Bartolomějská; Legion Bridge (Legií most); Národní třída; Marksmen's Island (Střelecký ostrov); Ostrovní; Vltava River; Masarykovo nábřeží; Slav Island (Slovanský ostrov); Opatovická; Children's Island (Dětský ostrov); Myslíkova; Jirásek Square (Jiráskovo náměstí); Karlovo Náměstí; Jiráskův Bridge (Jiráskův most); Resslova; FINISH; IP Pavlova; Dittrichova; Rašínovo nábřeží; Nábřežní; Na Moráni; Lidická

◉ SIGHTS

The Vltava River winds through the middle of Prague like a giant question mark, with the city centre straddling its lower half. The oldest parts of the city cluster tightly just south of the river bend – Hradčany, the medieval castle district, and Malá Strana (Little Quarter) on the western bank; Stáre Město (Old Town), Nové Město (New Town) and the ancient citadel of Vyšehrad on the eastern bank.

◉ Hradčany
St Vitus Cathedral   Church
(Katedrála sv Víta; Map p545; ☑257 531 622; www.katedralasvatehovita.cz; Prague Castle; ☺9am-5pm, from noon Sun, to 4pm Nov-Mar; 🚊22, 23) Built over a time span of almost 600 years, St Vitus is one of the most richly endowed cathedrals in central Europe. It is pivotal to the religious and cultural life of the Czech Republic, housing treasures that range from the 14th-century mosaic of the Last Judgment and the tombs of St Wenceslas and Charles IV, to the baroque silver tomb of St John of Nepomuk, the ornate Chapel of St Wenceslas and art nouveau stained glass by Alfons Mucha.

Strahov Library   Historic Building
(Strahovská knihovna; ☑233 107 718; www. strahovskyklaster.cz; Strahovské nádvoří 1; adult/ child 120/60Kč; ☺9am-noon & 1-5pm; 🚊22, 23) Strahov Library is the largest monastic library in the country, with two magnificent baroque halls dating from the 17th and 18th centuries. You can peek through the doors but, sadly, you can't go into the halls themselves – it was found that fluctuations in humidity caused by visitors' breath were endangering the frescoes. There's also a display of historical curiosities.

Loreta   Church
(☑220 516 740; www.loreta.cz; Loretánské náměstí 7; adult/child 150/80Kč, photography permit 100Kč; ☺9am-5pm Apr-Oct, 9.30am-4pm Nov-Mar; 🚊22, 23) The Loreta is a baroque place of pilgrimage founded by Benigna Kateřina Lobkowicz in 1626, designed as a replica of the supposed Santa Casa (Sacred House; the home of the Virgin Mary) in the Holy Land. Legend says that the original Santa Casa was carried by angels to the Italian town of Loreto as the Turks were advancing on Nazareth.

◉ Malá Strana
Charles Bridge   Bridge
(Karlův most; Map p546; ☺24hr; 🚊2, 17, 18 to Karlovy lázně, 12, 15, 20, 22 to Malostranské náměstí) Strolling across Charles Bridge is everybody's favourite Prague activity. However, by 9am it's a 500m-long fairground, with an army of tourists squeezing through a gauntlet of hawkers and buskers beneath the impassive gaze of the baroque statues that line the parapets. If you want to experience the bridge at its most atmospheric, try to visit it at dawn.

St Nicholas Church   Church
(Kostel sv Mikuláše; Map p545; ☑257 534 215; www.stnicholas.cz; Malostranské náměstí 38; adult/child 70/50Kč; ☺9am-5pm Mar-Oct, to 4pm rest of year; 🚊12, 15, 20, 22) Malá Strana is dominated by the huge green cupola of St Nicholas Church, one of Central Europe's finest baroque buildings. (Don't confuse it with the other Church of St Nicholas on Old Town Square.) On the ceiling, Johann Kracker's 1770 *Apotheosis of St Nicholas* is Europe's largest fresco (clever trompe l'oeil techniques have made the painting merge almost seamlessly with the architecture).

John Lennon Wall   Historic Site
(Velkopřevorské náměstí; 🚊12, 15, 20, 22) After his murder on 8 December 1980, John Lennon became a pacifist hero for many young Czechs. An image of Lennon was painted on a wall in a secluded square opposite the French embassy (there is a niche on the wall that looks like a tombstone), along with political graffiti and occasionally Beatles lyrics.

Petřín   Gardens
(☺24h; 🚊Nebozízek, Petřín) This 318m-high hill is one of Prague's largest green spaces.

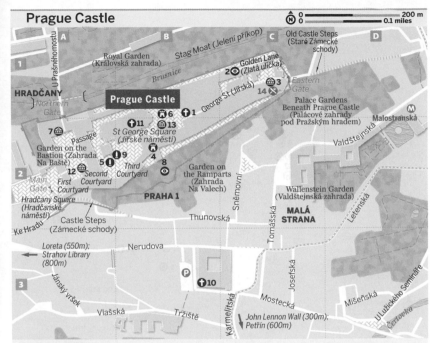

Prague Castle

⊙ **Sights**

1 Basilica of St George	B1
2 Golden Lane	C1
3 Lobkowicz Palace	C1
4 Old Royal Palace	B2
5 Plečník Monolith	A2
6 Prague Castle	B1
7 Prague Castle Picture Gallery	A2
8 South Gardens	B2
9 St George Slaying the Dragon	B2
10 St Nicholas Church	B3
11 St Vitus Cathedral	B2
12 St Vitus Treasury	A2
13 Story of Prague Castle	B2

✪ **Eating**

14 Lobkowicz Palace Café	C1

It's great for quiet, tree-shaded walks and fine views over the 'City of a Hundred Spires'. Most of the attractions atop the hill, including a lookout tower and mirror maze, were built in the late 19th to early 20th century, lending the place an old-fashioned, fun-fair atmosphere.

⊙ Staré Město

Old Town Square   Square

(Staroměstské náměstí; Map p546; Ⓜ Staroměstská) ⒻⓇⒺⒺ One of Europe's biggest and most beautiful urban spaces, Old Town Square (Staroměstské náměstí, or Staromák for

short) has been Prague's principal public square since the 10th century, and was its main marketplace until the beginning of the 20th century.

Astronomical Clock   Historic Site

(Map p546; ⊙ chimes on the hour 9am-9pm;) Every hour, on the hour, crowds gather beneath the **Old Town Hall Tower** (Věž radnice; Map p546; ☑ 236 002 629; www.staromestska radnicepraha.cz; Staroměstské náměstí 1; adult/ child 250/150Kč; ⊙ 11am-10pm Mon, 9am-10pm Tue-Sun; Ⓜ Staroměstská) to watch the Astronomical Clock in action. Despite a

Central Prague

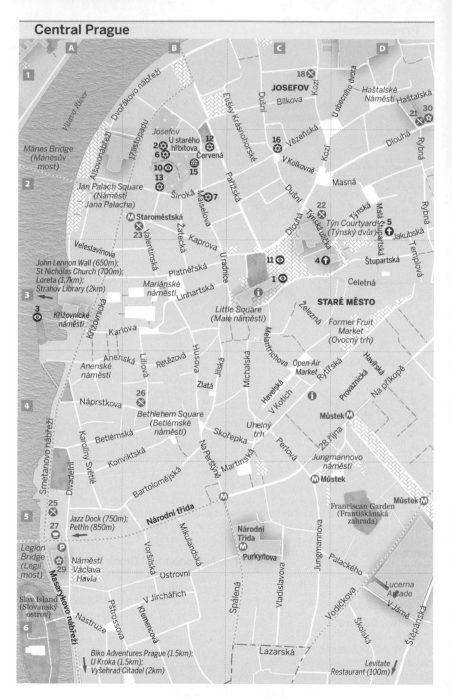

Vltava River

A | **B** | **C** | **D**

1

18

JOSEFOV

Haštalské
Náměstí Haštalská

Bílkova

Dušní

Kozí

U obecního dvora

21 30

Elišky Krásnohorské

Josefov

Vězeňská

Dlouhá

Rybná

U starého
hřbitova

16

2

6

Červená

Pařížská

V Kolkovně

Kozí

Masná

Mánes Bridge
(Mánesův
most)

2

10

13

15

Dušní

Dlouhá

Tynská

Malá
Rybná

Jan Palach Square
(Náměstí
Jana Palacha)

Široká

Maiselova

7

22

Týn Courtyard
(Týnský dvůr)

5

Jakubská

Temploví

Alšovo nábřeží

Dvořákovo nábřeží

17 listopadu

Veleslavínova

Staroměstská

23

Valentinská

Žatecká

Kaprova

U radnice

11

4

Štupartská

Štupartská

John Lennon Wall (650m);
St Nicholas Church (700m);
Loreta (1.7km);
Strahov Library (2km)

Platnéřská

1

Celetná

3

3

Križovnické
náměstí

Karlova

Mariánské
náměstí

Linhartská

Little Square
(Malé náměstí)

STARÉ MĚSTO

Former Fruit
Market
(Ovocný trh)

Križovnická

Anenská

Liliová

Řetězová

Husova

Jilská

Michalská

Melantrichova

Železná

Open-Air
Market

Rytířská

Havířská

Anenské
náměstí

Zlatá

Na příkopě

Náprstkova

26

Havelská

V Kotich

Provaznická

Betlémská

Bethlehem Square
(Betlémské
náměstí)

Uhelný
trh

Můstek

4

Konviktská

Skořepka

Perlová

28 října

Karolíny Světlé

Na Perštyně

Martinská

Jungmannovo
náměstí

Smetanovo nábřeží

Divadelní

Bartolomějská

Můstek

Franciscan Garden
(Františkánská
zahrada)

Můstek

5

25

27

Jazz Dock (750m);
Petřín (850m)

Národní třída

Mikulandská

Národní
Třída

Purkyňova

Jungmannova

Palackého

Legion
Bridge
(Legií
most)

29

Náměstí
Václava
Havla

Voršilská

Ostrovní

Spálená

Vladislavova

Vodičkova

Lucerna
Arcade

V Jámě

Masarykovo nábřeží

Slav Island
(Slovanský
ostrov)

6

Pštrossova

V Jirchářích

Křemencová

Nastruze

Lazarská

Školská

Štěpánská

Biko Adventures Prague (1.5km);
U Kroka (1.5km);
Vyšehrad Citadel (2km)

Levitate
Restaurant (100m)

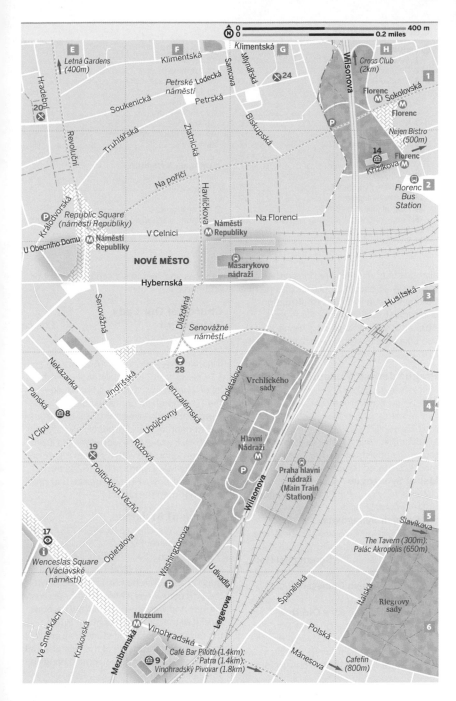

N 0 ____ 400 m
0 ____ 0.2 miles

Letná Gardens (400m)
Klimentská
Klimentská
Samcova
Mlynářská
⊗24
Cross Club (2km)
Wilsonova
Petrské Lodecká náměstí
Petrská
Soukenická
Biskupská
Florenc Ⓜ Sokolovská
Ⓜ Florenc
20 ⊗
Hradební
Revoluční
Truhlářská
Zlatnická
Na poříčí
Havlíčkova
Na Florenci
Nejen Bistro (500m)
14 🏛
Florenc Ⓜ
Křižíkova
Florenc Bus Station
Králodvorská
Republic Square (náměstí Republiky)
V Celnici
Náměstí Ⓜ Republiky
Husitská
U Obecního Domu Ⓜ Náměstí Republiky
NOVÉ MĚSTO
🏛 Masarykovo nádraží
Hybernská
Senovážná
Dlážděná
Senovážné náměstí
Nekázanka
Jindřišská
🍴 28
Panská
V Cípu
🏛8
Jeruzalémská
Opletalova
Vrchlického sady
Upujčovny
19 ⊗
Růžová
Hlavní Nádraží Ⓜ
Politických Vězňů
Wilsonova
Ⓟ
Praha hlavní nádraží (Main Train Station)
Slavíkova
17 ◉
The Tavern (300m); Palác Akropolis (650m)
ⓘ
Wenceslas Square (Václavské náměstí)
Opletalova
Washingtonova
U divadla
Legerova
Španělská
Italská
Riegrovy sady
Ve Smečkách
Krakovská
Mezibranská
Muzeum Ⓜ
Vinohradská
Polská
Mánesova
🏛9
Café Bar Pilotů (1.4km); Patra (1.4km); Vinohradský Pivovar (1.8km)
Cafefin (800m)

E F G H
1 2 3 4 5 6

Central Prague

slightly underwhelming performance that takes only 45 seconds, the clock is one of Europe's best-known tourist attractions, and a 'must-see' for visitors to Prague. After all, it's historic, photogenic and – if you take time to study it – rich in intriguing symbolism.

Prague Jewish Museum   Museum
(Židovské muzeum Praha; Map p546; ☑222 749 211; www.jewishmuseum.cz; Reservation Centre, Maiselova 15; combined-entry ticket adult/child 350/250Kč; ☺9am-6pm Sun-Fri, to 4.30pm Nov-Mar; ⓂStaroměstská) This museum consists of six Jewish monuments clustered together in Josefov: the **Maisel Synagogue** (Maiselova synagóga; Map p546; Maiselova 10); the **Pinkas Synagogue** (Pinkasova synagóga; Map p546; Široká 3); the **Spanish Synagogue** (Španělská synagóga; Map p546; Vězeňská 1); the **Klaus Synagogue** (Klauzová synagóga; Map p546; U starého hřbitova 1); the **Ceremonial Hall** (Obřadní síň; Map p546; Old Jewish Cemetery); and the **Old Jewish Cemetery** (Starý židovský hřbitov; Map p546; Pinkas Synagogue, Široká 3). There is also the **Old-New Synagogue** (Staronová synagóga; Map p546; ☑222 749 211; Červená 2; adult/child 220/150Kč; ☺9am-6pm Sun-Fri, to 4.30pm Nov-Mar; 🚇17), which is still used for religious

services and requires a separate ticket or additional fee.

Church of Our Lady Before Týn   Church
(Kostel Panny Marie před Týnem; Map p546; ☑222 318 186; www.tyn.cz; Staroměstské náměstí; suggested donation 50Kč; ☺10am-1pm & 3-5pm, to noon Sun Mar-Dec; ⓂStaroměstská) Its distinctive twin Gothic spires make the Týn Church an unmistakable Old Town landmark. Like something out of a 15th-century – and probably slightly cruel – fairy tale, they loom over Old Town Square, decorated with a golden image of the Virgin Mary made in the 1620s from the melted-down Hussite chalice that previously adorned the church.

Church of St James   Church
(Kostel sv Jakuba; Map p546; ☑224 828 814; http://praha.minorite.cz; Malá Štupartská 6; ☺9.30am-noon & 2-4pm Tue-Sat, 2-4pm Sun; ⓂNáměstí Republiky) **FREE** The great Gothic mass of the Church of St James began in the 14th century as a Minorite monastery church, and was given a beautiful baroque facelift in the early 18th century. But in the midst of the gilt and stucco is a grisly memento: on the inside of the western wall (look up to the right as you enter) hangs a shrivelled human arm.

◎ Nové Město

Wenceslas Square   Square

(Václavské náměstí; Map p546; MMůstek,
Muzeum) More a broad boulevard than a
typical city square, Wenceslas Square has
witnessed a great deal of Czech history – a
giant Mass was held here during the revolu-
tionary upheavals of 1848; in 1918 the creation of the new Czechoslovak Republic was
celebrated here; and it was here in 1989
where many anticommunist protests took
place. Originally a medieval horse market,
the square was named after Bohemia's
patron saint during the nationalist revival of
the mid-19th century.

National Museum   Museum

(Národní muzeum; Map p546; ☑224 497 111;
www.nm.cz; Václavské náměstí 68; adult/child
250/170Kč; ☉10am-6pm; MMuzeum) Looming
above Wenceslas Square is the neo-
Renaissance bulk of the National Museum,
designed in the 1880s by Josef Schulz
as an architectural symbol of the Czech
National Revival. Its magnificent interior
is a shrine to the cultural, intellectual and
scientific history of the Czech Republic. The
museum's main building reopened in 2018
after several years of renovation work.

Prague City Museum   Museum

(Muzeum hlavního města Prahy; Map p546; ☑221
709 674; www.muzeumprahy.cz; Na Poříčí 52;
adult/child 150/60Kč; ☉9am-6pm Tue-Sun;
MFlorenc) This excellent museum, opened
in 1898, is devoted to the history of Prague
from prehistoric times to the 20th century
(labels are in English as well as Czech).
Among the many intriguing exhibits are
an astonishing scale model of Prague, and
the Astronomical Clock's original 1866
calendar wheel with Josef Mánes' beautiful
painted panels representing the months –
that's January at the top, toasting his toes
by the fire, and August near the bottom,
sickle in hand, harvesting the corn.

Mucha Museum   Gallery

(Muchovo muzeum; Map p546; ☑224 216 415;
www.mucha.cz; Panská 7; adult/child 240/160Kč;
☉10am-6pm; ☐3, 5, 6, 9, 14, 24) This fascinating (and busy) museum features the
sensuous art nouveau posters, paintings
and decorative panels of Alfons Mucha
(1860–1939), as well as many sketches,
photographs and other memorabilia. The
exhibits include countless artworks showing Mucha's trademark Slavic maidens with
flowing hair and piercing blue eyes, bearing
symbolic garlands and linden boughs.

⊙ TOURS

Prague offers so much intriguing history
and culture that it's easy to feel over-
whelmed. A guided tour can ease you into
an aspect of the city that reflects your
interests. The **Prague City Tourism** (Prague
Welcome; Map p546; ☑221 714 714; www.prague.
eu; Staroměstské náměstí 1, Old Town Hall;
☉9am-7pm, to 6pm Jan & Feb; MStaroměstská)
office in the Old Town Hall provides details
of tours.

Biko Adventures Prague   Cycling

(☑733 750 990; www.bikoadventures.com;
Vratislavova 3, Vyšehrad; bike hire per day 490Kč,
tours per person from 1300Kč; ☉9am-6pm Apr-
Oct; ☐2, 3, 7, 17, 21) Italian owner Fillippo Mari
loves to cycle, ski and hike and has created
this small outfit dedicated to outdoor
pursuits of all kinds. From April to October
Biko rents bikes and offers day-long guided
cycling trips for riders of all levels. Rental
bikes include standard mountain bikes and
high-end hardtails from Giant.

⊗ EATING

Mistral Café   Bistro €

(Map p546; ☑222 317 737; www.mistralcafe.cz;
Valentinská 11; mains 150-260Kč; ☉8am-11pm,
from 9am Sat & Sun; ☎♨; MStaroměstská)
Is this the coolest bistro in the Old Town?
Pale stone, bleached birchwood and potted
shrubs make for a clean, crisp, modern
look, and the clientele of local students and
office workers clearly appreciate the com-
petitively priced, well-prepared food. Fish
and chips in crumpled brown paper with
lemon and black-pepper mayo – yum!

Lokál
Czech €

(Map p546; 734 283 874; www.lokal-dlouha. ambi.cz; Dlouhá 33; mains 155-265Kč; 11am-1am, to midnight Sun; ; 6, 8, 15, 26) Who'd have thought it possible? A classic Czech beer hall (albeit with slick modern styling); excellent *tankové pivo* (tanked Pilsner Urquell); a daily-changing menu of traditional Bohemian dishes; and smiling, efficient, friendly service! Top restaurant chain Ambiente has turned its hand to Czech cuisine, and the result has been so successful that the place is always busy.

Cafefin
Cafe €

(www.cafefinvpraze.com; náměstí Jiřího z Poděbrad 4; mains 120-180Kč; 8am-9pm Mon-Sat, 10am-7:30pm Sun; Jiřího z Poděbrad) A pioneer in Vietnamese coffee in Prague, since its opening in 2017, Cafefin is clearly leading the trend of modern Vietnamese gastronomy. You'll find rich noodle bowls, colourful salads, all things avocado, coffee with latté art, artisan cakes and delicacies for vegans, vegetarians and general food lovers. It's essentially a fusion of Vietnamese and modern European cuisine.

The Tavern
Burgers €

(www.thetavern.cz; Chopinova 26, Vinohrady; burgers 190-230Kč; 11.30am-10pm; ; Jiřího z Poděbrad, 11, 13) This cosy sit-down burger joint is the dream of a husband-and-wife team of American expats who wanted to create the perfect burger using organic products and free-range, grass-fed beef. Great pulled-pork sandwiches, fries and bourbon-based cocktails too. Reservations are taken via the website.

Levitate Restaurant
Gastronomy €€

(724 516 996; www.levitaterestaurant.cz; Štěpánská 611/14; mains 250-590Kč; noon-3pm Thu-Sun, 6pm-midnight Tue-Sun; ; Štěpánská) One of Prague's hidden treats, this gastronomy restaurant combines Asian traditions with Nordic flavours, using local ingredients. You simply can't come here 'just to eat'. This calm oasis near the bustling heart of Prague is aiming for the stars. Make sure to reserve your table.

Czech goulash and *karlovarský knedlíky* (dumplings)

STEPANEK PHOTOGRAPHY / SHUTTERSTOCK ©

SmetanaQ Café & Bistro   Bistro €€

(Map p546; ✆722 409 757; http://smetanaq.
cz/#cafe-bistro; Smetanovo nábřeží 334/4;
breakfast 105-279Kč, salads 149-239Kč; ⏰8am-
9pm Mon-Sat, 9am-8pm Sun; 🛜; 🚋3, 6, 9, 13,
17, 18, 22, 23) Opened in 2017, SmetanaQ
features a spacious interior with large
windows overlooking the Vltava River and,
in winter, offers a view of Prague Castle.
Coffee (49Kč to 70Kč) comes from a local
roaster, and the plentiful cakes, pies and
bread are all made in-house.

Sansho   Asian, Fusion €€

(Map p546; ✆222 317 425; www.sansho.cz;
Petrská 25; mains 200-250Kč, 6-course dinner
900-1200Kč; ⏰11.30am-2pm & 6-11pm Tue-Fri,
6-11pm Sat, last orders 10pm; 🖋; 🚋3, 8, 14, 24)
🍃 'Friendly and informal' best describes
the atmosphere at this groundbreaking
restaurant where British chef Paul Day
champions Czech farmers by sourcing all
his meat and vegetables locally. There's no
menu as such – the waiter will explain what
dishes are available, depending on market
produce. Typical dishes include curried rabbit, pork belly with watermelon and hoisin,
and 12-hour beef rendang. Reservations
recommended.

La Bottega Bistroteka   Italian €€

(Map p546; ✆222 311 372; www.bistroteka.cz;
Dlouhá 39; mains 265-465Kč; ⏰9am-10.30pm,
to 9pm Sun; 🛜; 🚋6, 8, 15, 26) You'll find
smart and snappy service at this stylish
deli-cum-bistro, where the menu makes the
most of all that delicious Italian produce
artfully arranged on the counter; the beef-
cheek cannelloni with parmesan sauce and
fava beans, for example, is just exquisite.
It's best to book, but you can often get a
walk-in table at lunchtime.

Nejen Bistro   Bistro €€

(✆721 249 494; www.nejenbistro.cz; Křižíkova
24, Karlín; mains 220-390Kč; ⏰11am-11pm; 🛜;
🚋3, 8, 24) 🍃 Nejen (Not Only) is emblem-
atic of the new breed of restaurant that is
transforming Karlín into one of Prague's
hottest neighbourhoods. Its quirky interior
has been nominated for a slew of design

Prague's Spiritual Heart

Towering Vyšehrad fortress, topped
by its trademark twin-spired church,
claims a place as the spiritual heart of
Prague. It's a leafy oasis, with pretty
views over the river, and an art-
nouveau-inspired cemetery that's a
work of art in itself.

Vyšehrad Citadel (✆261 225
304; www.praha-vysehrad.cz; ⏰24hr;
Ⓜ Vyšehrad) 🆓 refers to the complex of buildings and structures atop
Vyšehrad Hill that have played an
important role in Czech history for
over 1000 years – as a royal residence,
religious centre and military fortress.
Most of the surviving structures actually date from the 18th century and
are spread out over a wide area, with
commanding views out over the Vltava
and surrounding city. Don't miss the
cemetery, final resting place for dozens
of Czech luminaries, including Antonín
Dvořák, Bedřich Smetana and Alfons
Mucha, with magnificent tombs and
headstones.

Vyšehrad Citadel
RHOMBUR / GETTY IMAGES ©

awards, but just as much attention is
lavished on the food: it makes the most
of the kitchen's fancy Josper grill, turning
out superb steaks, beef ribs and Nejen's
signature Black Angus burger.

U Kroka   Czech €€

(✆775 905 022; www.ukroka.cz; Vratislavova
12, Vyšehrad; mains 170-295Kč; ⏰11am-11pm;
🛜; 🚋2, 3, 7, 17, 21) Cap a visit to historic

From left: Traditional Czech desserts; Letná Beer Garden; vegetarian dish at Maitrea

Vyšehrad Citadel with a hearty meal at this traditional pub that delivers not just excellent beer but very good food as well. Classic dishes like goulash, boiled beef, rabbit and duck confit are served in a festive setting. Daily lunch specials (around 140Kč) are available from 11am to 3pm. Reservations (advisable) are only possible after 3pm.

Lobkowicz Palace Café
Cafe €€

(Map p545; ☑602 332 086; www.lobkowicz.com; Jiřská 3; mains 225-310Kč; ☉10am-6pm; 🛜👶; 🚊22, 23) This cafe, housed in the 16th-century Lobkowicz Palace, is the best eatery in the castle complex by an imperial mile. Try to grab one of the tables on the balconies at the back – the view over the city is superb, as are the soups, sandwiches and goulash. The coffee is good too, and service is fast and friendly.

Maitrea
Vegetarian €€

(Map p546; ☑221 711 631; www.restaurace-maitrea.cz; Týnská ulička 6; weekday lunch 145Kč, mains 200-250Kč; ☉11.30am-11.30pm, from noon Sat & Sun; 🥢👶; Ⓜ Staroměstská)

Maitrea (a Buddhist term meaning 'the future Buddha') is a beautifully designed space full of flowing curves and organic shapes, from the sensuous polished-oak furniture and fittings to the blossom-like lampshades. The menu is inventive and wholly vegetarian, with dishes such as Tex-Mex quesadillas, spicy goulash with wholemeal dumplings, and spaghetti with spinach, crispy shredded tofu and rosemary pesto.

Field
Czech €€€

(Map p546; ☑222 316 999; www.fieldrestaurant. cz; U Milosrdných 12; mains 590-620Kč, 6-course tasting menu 2800Kč; ☉11am-2.30pm & 6-10.30pm Mon-Fri, noon-3pm & 6-10pm Sat & Sun; 🛜; 🚊17) 🍃 This Michelin-starred restaurant is unfussy and fun. The decor is an amusing art-meets-agriculture blend of farmyard implements and minimalist chic, while the chef creates painterly presentations from the finest local produce along with freshly foraged herbs and edible flowers. You'll have to book at least a couple of weeks in advance to have a chance of a table.

Kantýna   Czech €€€

(Map p546; www.kantyna.ambi.cz; Politických vězňů 5; soup 58-75Kč, meat 98-188Kč per 100g; ⊘11.30am-11pm; ⓂMůstek) Kantýna is both a meat-heavy restaurant and a butcher's specialising in locally sourced meat. It has a unique interior set in a former bank. It's not a place to linger: walk to the counter, pick your meat dish and enjoy it in the buzzing atmosphere. Table service available for drinks and items on the menu but not for counter food.

V Zátiší   Czech, Indian €€€

(Map p546; ☑222 221155; www.vzatisi.cz; Liliová 1; multi-course tasting menu from 1190Kč; ⊘noon-3pm & 5.30-11pm; 🛜; 🚋2, 17, 18) 'Still Life' is one of Prague's top restaurants, famed for the quality of its cuisine. The decor is bold and modern, with quirky glassware, boldly patterned wallpapers and cappuccino-coloured crushed-velvet chairs. The menu ranges from high-end Indian cuisine to gourmet versions of tradi-tional Czech dishes – the South Bohemian duck with white cabbage and herb dump-lings is superb.

🍷 DRINKING & NIGHTLIFE

Vinograf   Wine Bar

(Map p546; ☑214 214 681; www.vinograf.cz; Senovážné náměstí 23; ⊘11.30am-midnight, from 5pm Sat & Sun; 🛜; 🚋3, 5, 6, 9, 14, 24) With knowledgeable staff, a relaxed atmosphere and an off-the-beaten-track feel, this appealingly modern wine bar is a great place to discover Moravian wines. There's good finger food (mostly cheese and charcuterie) to accompany your wine, with food and wine menus (in Czech and English) on big blackboards behind the bar. Very busy at weekends, when it's worth booking a table.

Letná Beer Garden   Beer Garden

(☑233 378 200; www.letenskyzamecek.cz; Letenské sady 341; ⊘11am-11pm May-Sep; 🚋1, 8, 12, 25, 26) No accounting of watering holes in the neighbourhood would be complete without a nod towards the city's best beer garden, with an amazing panorama, situated at the eastern end of the Letná Gardens (p557). Buy a takeaway beer from a small kiosk and grab a picnic table. Kiosks

Czech Beer

There are two main varieties of beer: *světlé* (light) and *tmavy* or *černé* (dark). The *světlé* is a pale amber or golden lager-style beer with a crisp, refreshing, hoppy flavour. Dark beers are sweeter and more full-bodied, with a rich, malty or fruity flavour.

Czechs like their beer served at cellar temperature (around 6°C to 10°C) with a tall, creamy head (known as *pěna*, meaning 'foam'). Americans and Australians may find it a bit warm, but this improves the flavour. Most draught beer is sold in *půl-litr* (0.5L) glasses; if you prefer a small beer, ask for a *malé pivo* (0.3L). Some bars confuse the issue by using 0.4L glasses, while others offer a German-style 1L mug known as a *tuplák*.

Prague pubs traditionally offered just three beers on tap, all from one large brewery such as Pilsner Urquell; some pioneering bar owners added a *čtvrtá pípa* ('fourth pipe') to allow them to offer a rotating range of guest beers from various independent regional breweries. Many have five, six or even more pipes.

Beer tasting at a Prague pub
ARIEH / SHUTTERSTOCK ©

also sell small food items like chips and sandwiches.

Vinohradský Pivovar — Pub
(☏222 760 080; www.vinohradskypivovar. cz; Korunní 106, Vinohrady; ⊘11am-midnight; 🛜; 🚃10, 16) This popular and highly

recommended neighbourhood pub and restaurant offers its own home-brewed lagers as well as a well-regarded IPA. There's seating on two levels and a large events room at the back for concerts and happenings. The restaurant features classic Czech pub dishes at reasonable prices (180Kč to 230Kč). Book in advance for an evening meal.

Café Bar Pilotů — Cocktail Bar
(☏739 765 694; www.facebook.com/cafebar pilotu; Dónská 19, Vršovice; drinks 160-180Kč; ⊘7pm-1am Mon-Thu, to 2am Fri & Sat; 🛜; 🚃4, 13, 22) This old-fashioned cocktail bar, with a big wooden serving bar and walls of books behind, features inventive cocktails based on favourite locales around the neighbourhood. There are plenty of tables or you can hang out on the street until 10pm. Friendly and professional service.

Patra — Bar
(☏226 886 622; www.patrakrymska.cz; Krymská 17; ⊘3pm-midnight; 🚃4, 13, 22) It's hard to pigeon-hole Patra. Let's say it's a popular, trendy, gay-friendly bar and cafe that on any given evening might screen a film or host a music act or piece of performance art. If you're in the neighbourhood, drop by to see what's on. The crowd is inclusive, the service friendly and the cocktail and coffee prices very good value.

Cross Club — Club
(☏775 541 430; www.crossclub.cz; Plynární 23; live shows 100-200Kč; ⊘6pm-5am Sun-Thu, to 7am Fri & Sat; 🛜; Ⓜ Nádraží Holešovice) An industrial club in every sense of the word: the setting in an industrial zone; the thumping music (both DJs and live acts); and the interior, an absolute must-see jumble of gadgets, shafts, cranks and pipes, many of which move and pulsate with light to the music. The program includes occasional live music, theatre performances and art happenings.

Kavárna Slavia — Cafe
(Map p546; ☏224 218 493; www.cafeslavia.cz; Smetanovo nábřeží 1012/2; ⊘8am-midnight Mon-Fri, 9am-midnight Sat & Sun; 🛜; 🚃2, 9,

18, 22) The Slavia is the most famous of Prague's old cafes, a cherrywood-and-onyx shrine to art-deco elegance, with polished limestone-topped tables and big windows overlooking the river. It has been a celebrated literary meeting place since the early 20th century – Rainer Maria Rilke and Franz Kafka hung out here, and it was frequented by Václav Havel and other dissidents in the 1970s and '80s.

⭐ ENTERTAINMENT

From ballet to blues, jazz to rock, theatre to film, eclectic Prague promises a bewildering range of entertainment. The city is now as much a European centre for jazz, rock and hip-hop as it is for classical music, although its biggest draw remains Maytime's **Prague Spring** (Pražské jaro; ✆box office 227 059 234, program 257 310 414; www.festival.cz; ✹May) international festival of classical music and opera.

Palác Akropolis   Live Music
(✆296 330 913; www.palacakropolis.cz; Kubelíkova 27, Žižkov; ticket prices vary; ✹7pm-5am;

📶; 🚋5, 9, 15, 26) The Akropolis is a Prague institution, a labyrinthine, sticky-floored shrine to alternative music and drama. Its various performance spaces host a smorgasbord of musical and cultural events, from DJs and string quartets to Macedonian Roma bands, local rock gods and visiting talent – Marianne Faithfull, the Flaming Lips and the Strokes have all played here.

National Theatre   Opera, Ballet
(Národní divadlo; Map p546; ✆224 901 448; www.narodni-divadlo.cz; Národní třída 2; tickets 100-1290Kč; ✹box office 9am-6pm, from 10am Sat & Sun; 🚋2, 9, 18, 22) The much-loved National Theatre provides a stage for traditional opera, drama and ballet by the likes of Smetana, Shakespeare and Tchaikovsky, sharing the program alongside more modern works by composers and playwrights such as Philip Glass and John Osborne. The box offices are in the Nový síň building

> *Prague promises a bewildering range of entertainment*

Hurra Torpedo performing at Palác Akropolis

J MORC / ALAMY STOCK PHOTO ©

Roxy

next door, in the Kolowrat Palace (opposite the Estates Theatre) and at the State Opera.

Roxy   Live Music
(Map p546; ☑608 060 745; www.roxy.cz; Dlouhá 33; tickets 100-700Kč; ☺7pm-5am; ☒6, 8, 15, 26) Set in the ramshackle shell of an art deco cinema, the legendary Roxy has nurtured the more independent end of Prague's club spectrum for more than two decades. This is the place to see the Czech Republic's top DJs. On the 1st floor is NoD, an 'experimental space' that stages drama, dance, cinema and live music.

Jazz Dock   Jazz
(☑774 058 838; www.jazzdock.cz; Janáčkovo nábřeží 2, Smíchov; tickets 170-400Kč; ☺3pm-4am Mon-Thu, from 1pm Fri-Sun Apr-Sep, 5pm-4am Mon-Thu, from 3pm Fri-Sun Oct-Mar; ☜; ⓂAnděl, ☒9, 12, 15, 20) Most of Prague's jazz clubs are cellar affairs, but this riverside club is a definite step up, with clean, modern decor and a decidedly romantic view out over the Vltava. It draws some of the best local talent and occasional

international acts. Go early or book to get a good table. Shows normally begin at 7pm and 10pm.

❶ INFORMATION

Prague City Tourism branches are scattered around town, including at both airport arrivals terminals. Offices also sell **Prague Card** (www.praguecard.com) discount cards and arrange guides and tours.

Prague City Tourism – Old Town Hall (p549)

Prague City Tourism – Rytířská (Prague Welcome; Map p546; ☑221 714 714; www.prague.eu; Rytířská 12; ☺9am-7pm; ⓂMůstek)

Prague City Tourism – Wenceslas Square (Map p546; ☑221 714 714; Václavské náměstí 42; ☺10am-6pm; ⓂMůstek, Muzeum)

❶ GETTING THERE & AWAY

AIR

Václav Havel Airport Prague (Prague Ruzyně International Airport; ☑220 111 888; www.prg.aero; K letišti 6, Ruzyně; ☜; ☒100, 119), **17km**

west of the city centre, is the main international gateway to the Czech Republic and hub for the national carrier Czech Airlines.

BUS

Several bus companies offer long-distance coach services connecting Prague to cities around Europe. International buses (and most domestic services) use the user-friendly **Florenc bus station** (ÚAN Praha Florenc; Map p546; ✆900 144 444; www.florenc.cz; Pod výtopnou 13/10, Karlín; ⊙5am-midnight; ☎; ⓂFlorenc).

TRAIN

Prague is well integrated into European rail networks. Train travel makes the most sense if travelling to/from Berlin and Dresden to the north or Vienna, Kraków, Bratislava and Budapest to the east and south. Most domestic and all international trains arrive at **Praha hlavní nádraží** (Prague Main Train Station; ☑information 221 111 122; www.cd.cz; Wilsonova 8, Nové Město; ⊙3.30am-12.30am; ⓂHlavní nádraží), Prague's main station, a short walk from Wenceslas Square.

Most services are operated by the Czech state rail operator, **České dráhy** (ČD, Czech Rail; ☑national hotline 221 111 122; www.cd.cz), though two private rail companies, **Leo Express** (www.le.cz; Wilsonova 8, Praha hlavní nádraží; ⊙ticket office 7.10am-8.10pm; ⓂHlavní Nádraží) and **RegioJet** (Student Agency; www.regiojet.cz; Wilsonova 8, Praha Hlavní Nádraží; ⊙8am-8pm; ⓂHlavní nádraží), compete with České dráhy on some popular lines.

❶ GETTING AROUND

Central Prague is easily managed on foot (though be sure to wear comfortable shoes). For longer trips, the city has a reliable public-transport system of metros, trams and buses. The system is integrated, meaning that the same

🔭 A Walk in the Park

Lovely **Letná Gardens** (Letenské sady; ⊙24hr; 👹; 🚋1, 8, 12, 25, 26 to Letenské náměstí) occupies a bluff over the Vltava River, north of the Old Town, and has postcard-perfect views out over the city, river and bridges. It's ideal for walking, jogging and beer-drinking at a popular beer garden (p554) at the eastern end of the park. From the Old Town, find the entrance up a steep staircase at the northern end of Pařížská ulice (across the bridge). Alternatively, take the tram to Letenské náměstí and walk south for about 10 minutes.

Letná Gardens at sunset
PETR PAVLICA / SHUTTERSTOCK ©

tickets are valid on all types of transport, and for transfers between them.

Walking Central Prague is compact, and individual neighbourhoods are easily explored on foot.

Tram Extensive network; best way to get around shorter distances between neighbourhoods.

Metro Fast and frequent, good for visiting outlying areas or covering longer distances.

Bus Not much use in the city centre, except when travelling to/from the airport; operates in areas not covered by tram or metro.

Taxi Relatively cheap but prone to rip-off drivers.

BUDAPEST, HUNGARY

Budapest, Hungary

Budapest is paradise for explorers. Architecturally, the city is a treasure trove, with enough baroque, neoclassical and art nouveau buildings to satisfy everyone. Amid these splendid edifices, history waits around every corner, with bullet holes and shrapnel pockmarks serving as poignant reminders of past conflicts. And to buoy the traveller on their explorations, the city generously supplies delicious Magyar cuisine (among an array of other top eats), excellent wines, rip-roaring nightlife and an abundance of hot springs to soak the day's aches away.

Two Days in Budapest

Spend most of the first day on **Castle Hill** (p571), taking in the views and visiting the **Royal Palace** (p562) and a museum or two. In the afternoon, make your way to the **Gellért Baths** (p565) via **Clark Ádám tér**. In the evening, head to Erzsébetváros and the Jewish Quarter. On the second day take a walk up **Andrássy út**, stopping off at the **House of Terror** (p566). In the afternoon, take the waters at the **Széchenyi Baths** (p565).

Four Days in Budapest

The next day, concentrate on the two icons of Hungarian nationhood and the places that house them: the Crown of St Stephen in **Parliament** (p570) and the saint-king's mortal remains in the **Basilica of St Stephen** (p567). In the evening, go for drinks at a **ruin pub** (p575). On day four visit the **Great Synagogue** (p566) and in the afternoon cross over to idyllic **Margaret Island** (p567). Spend the rest of the afternoon at **Veli Bej Bath** (p565).

Waltz on to Vienna (p577) next, 2½ hours by train or 5½ to 6½ hours by boat.

Budapest Map (p568)

Map labels:
Aquincum
Vác (30 km)
Óbuda Island (Óbudai-sziget)
ISTVÁNTELEK
ÓBUDA
REMETEHEGY
Duna
Váci út
Béke u
ANGYALFÖLD
MÁTYÁSHEGY
Hűvösvölgyi út
ÚJLAK
FELHÉVÍZ
Margaret Island (Margit-sziget)
Budakeszi út
RÓZSADOMB
Nyugati Train Station
City Park (Városliget)
HERMINAMEZŐ
RÉZMÁL
Dózsa György út
Parliament
ORBÁNHEGY
Bem rkp
Keleti Train Station
Déli Train Station
Great Synagogue
Kerepesi út
FARKASRÉT
Royal Palace
Fiumei út
Kerepesi Cemetery
József krt
Farkasréti temető
Citadella
JÓZSEFVÁROS
SASHEGY
Budaörsi út
Üllői út
Népliget
SASAD
Egyetemisták parkja
FERENCVÁROS
KELENFÖLD
LÁGYMÁNYOS
Soroksári út

Scale: 0 — 2 km / 0 — 1 mile

Arriving in Budapest

Ferenc Liszt International Airport
Minibuses, buses and trains to central Budapest run from 4am to midnight. A taxi will cost between 6000Ft and 7000Ft.

Keleti, Nyugati & Déli Train Stations
All three are connected to metro lines of the same name; night buses call when the metro is closed.

Stadion & Népliget Bus Stations Both
are on metro lines and are served by trams.

Where to Stay

Accommodation in Budapest runs the gamut from hostels in converted flats and private rooms in far-flung housing estates to luxury guesthouses in the Buda Hills and five-star properties charging upwards of €350 a night.

Because of the changing value of the forint, many midrange and top-end hotels quote their rates in euros.

IAKOV FILIMONOV / SHUTTERSTOCK ©

Royal Palace

The enormous Royal Palace (Királyi Palota) has been razed and rebuilt six times over the past seven centuries. Today the palace contains two important museums, the national library and an abundance of statues and monuments. It is the focal point of Buda's Castle Hill and the city's most visited sight.

Great For...

☑ Don't Miss

Late Gothic altarpieces, Gothic statues and heads, and the Renaissance door frame.

Hungarian National Gallery

The **Hungarian National Gallery** (Magyar Nemzeti Galéria; ☎1-201 9082; www.mng.hu; I Szent György tér 2, Bldgs A-D; adult/concession 1800/900Ft, audio guide 800Ft; ⊙10am-6pm Tue-Sun; 🚌16, 16A, 116) boasts an overwhelming collection that traces Hungarian art from the 11th century to the present day. The largest collections include medieval and Renaissance stonework, Gothic wooden sculptures and panel paintings, late Gothic winged altars and late Renaissance and baroque art. The museum also has an important collection of Hungarian paintings and sculptures from the 19th and 20th centuries. Much of the gallery was closed for renovations at the time of writing, and by 2019 the collection is due to move to a purpose-built gallery in City Park.

Hungarian National Gallery

Royal Palace ⊙

❶ Need to Know

Királyi Palota; I Szent György tér; 🚌16, 16A, 116

✕ Take a Break

If you need something hot and/or sweet after your visit, head for **Ruszwurm Cukrászda** (📞1-375 5284; www.ruszwurm. hu; I Szentháromság utca 7; ⊙10am-7pm Mon-Fri, to 6pm Sat & Sun; 🚌16, 16A, 116).

★ Top Tip

Exiting through the museum's back courtyard door will take you straight down to I Szarvas tér in the Tabán.

heads and fragments of courtiers, squires and saints, discovered during excavations in 1974.

A wonderful exhibit on the 1st floor called '1000 Years of a Capital' traces the history of Budapest from the arrival of the Magyars and the Turkish occupation to modern times, taking an interesting look at housing, ethnic diversity, religion and other such issues over the centuries. The excellent audioguide is 1200Ft.

National Széchenyi Library

The **National Széchenyi Library** (Országos Széchenyi Könyvtár, OSZK; 📞1-224 3700; www. oszk.hu; I Szent György tér 4-6, Bldg F; ⊙9am-8pm Tue-Sat, stacks to 7pm Tue-Fri, to 5pm Sat; 🚌16, 16A, 116) contains codices and manuscripts, a large collection of foreign newspapers and a copy of everything published in Hungary or the Hungarian language. It was founded in 1802 by Count Ferenc Széchenyi, father of the heroic István, who endowed it with 15,000 books and 2000 manuscripts.

Castle Museum

The **Castle Museum** (Vármúzeum; 📞1-487 8800; www.btm.hu; I Szent György tér 2, Bldg E; adult/concession 2400/1200Ft; ⊙10am-6pm Tue-Sun Mar-Oct, to 4pm Tue-Sun Nov-Feb; 🚌16, 16A, 116, 🚋19, 41), part of the multi-branched Budapest History Museum, explores the city's 2000-year history over three floors. Restored palace rooms dating from the 15th century can be entered from the basement, where there are three vaulted halls. One of the halls features a magnificent **Renaissance door frame** in red marble, leading to the Gothic and Renaissance halls, the Royal Cellar and the vaulted Tower Chapel (1320) dedicated to St Stephen.

On the ground floor, exhibits showcase Budapest during the Middle Ages, with dozens of important **Gothic statues**,

UNGVARI ATTILA / SHUTTERSTOCK ©

Thermal Baths & Spas

Budapest sits on a crazy quilt of almost 125 thermal springs, and 'taking the waters' is very much a part of everyday life here. Some baths date from Turkish times, others are art nouveau marvels and still others are chic modern spas boasting all the mod cons.

Great For...

☑ Don't Miss

The sight of locals playing chess on floating boards (regardless of the weather) at Széchenyi Baths.

History of a Spa City

The remains of two sets of baths found at Aquincum – both for the public and the garrisons – indicate that the Romans took advantage of Budapest's thermal waters almost two millennia ago. But it wasn't until the Turkish occupation of the 16th and 17th centuries that bathing became an integral part of everyday Budapest life. In the late 18th century, Habsburg Empress Maria Theresa ordered that Budapest's mineral waters be analysed/recorded in a list at the Treasury's expense. By the 1930s Budapest had become a fashionable spa resort.

Healing Waters

Of course, not everyone goes to the baths for fun and relaxation. The warm, mineral-rich waters are also meant to relieve a

Széchenyi Baths

the most Turkish of all in Budapest, built in 1566, with an octagonal pool, domed cupola and eight massive pillars. It's mostly men only during the week, but turns into a real zoo on mixed weekend nights.

Gellért Baths (Gellért Gyógyfürdő; ☏06 30 849 9514, 1-466 6166; www.gellertbath.hu; XI Kelenhegyi út 4, Danubius Hotel Gellért; incl locker/cabin Mon-Fri 5600/6000Ft, Sat & Sun 5800/6200Ft; ⏰6am-8pm; ☐7, 86, Ⓜ M4 Szent Gellért tér, ☐18, 19, 47, 49) Soaking in these art nouveau baths, now open to both men and women at all times, has been likened to taking a bath in a cathedral.

Széchenyi Baths (Széchenyi Gyógyfürdő; ☏1-363 3210, 06 30 462 8236; www.szechenyibath. hu; XIV Állatkerti körút 9-11; tickets incl locker/cabin Mon-Fri 5200/5700Ft, Sat & Sun 5400/5900Ft; ⏰6am-10pm; Ⓜ M1 Széchenyi fürdő) The gigantic 'wedding-cake' building in City Park houses these baths, which are unusual for three reasons: their immensity (a dozen thermal baths and three outdoor swimming pools); the bright, clean atmosphere; and the high temperature of the water (up to 40°C).

Veli Bej Baths (Veli Bej Fürdője; ☏1-438 8587; www.irgalmasrend.hu/site/velibej/sprachen/ en; II Árpád fejedelem útja 7; 6am-noon 2240Ft, 3-7pm 2800Ft, after 7pm 2240Ft; ⏰6am-noon & 3-9pm; ☐9, 109, ☐4, 6, 17, 19) This venerable (1575) Turkish bath in Buda has got a new lease of life after having been forgotten for centuries.

number of specific complaints, ranging from arthritis and muscle pain to poor blood circulation and post-traumatic stress. They are also a miracle cure for that most unpleasant of afflictions, the dreaded hangover.

Choosing a Bath

The choice of bathhouses today is legion, and which one you choose is a matter of taste and what exactly you're looking for – be it fun, a hangover cure, or relief for something more serious.

Rudas Baths (Rudas Gyógyfürdő; ☏1-356 1322; http://en.rudasfurdo.hu; I Döbrentei tér 9; incl cabin Mon-Fri/Sat & Sun 3500/4000Ft, morning/ night ticket 2800/5100Ft; ⏰men 6am-8pm Mon & Wed-Fri, women 6am-8pm Tue, mixed 10pm-4am Fri, 6am-8pm & 10pm-4am Sat, 6am-8pm Sun; ☐7, 86, ☐18, 19) These renovated baths are

⊙ SIGHTS

Budapest's most important museums are found on Castle Hill, in City Park, along Andrássy út in Erzsébetváros and in Southern Pest. The area surrounding the Parliament is home to the splendid Parliament building, as well as Budapest's most iconic church, the Basilica of St Stephen. Both Parliament and its surrounds and Belváros feature some of the city's best art nouveau architecture. Margaret Island and City Park are the city's most appealing green spaces, while the Buda Hills is a veritable playground for hikers, cavers and bikers. Óbuda is home to extensive Roman ruins and quirky museums, and Gellért Hill gives you some of the best views of the city.

Great Synagogue Synagogue

(Nagy Zsinagóga; ☏1-413 5584, 1-413 1515; www.greatsynagogue.hu/gallery_syn.html; VII Dohány utca 2; adult/concession/family incl museum 4000/3000/9000Ft; ⊙10am-7.30pm Sun-Thu, to 3.30pm Fri May-Sep, 10am-5.30pm Sun-Thu, to 3.30pm Fri Mar, Apr & Oct, 10am-3.30pm Sun-Thu, to 1.30pm Fri Nov-Feb; Ⓜ︎M2 Astoria, ⊞47, 49) Budapest's stunning Great Synagogue is the world's largest Jewish house of worship outside New York City. Built in 1859, the synagogue has both Romantic and Moorish architectural elements. Inside, the **Hungarian Jewish Museum & Archives** (Magyar Zsidó Múzeum és Levéltár; ☏1-413 5500; www.milev.hu;) contains objects relating to both religious and everyday life. On the synagogue's north side, the **Holocaust Tree of Life Memorial** (Raoul Wallenberg Memorial Park, opp VII Wesselényi utca 6) presides over the mass graves of those murdered by the Nazis.

House of Terror Museum

(Terror Háza; ☏1-374 2600; www.terrorhaza.hu; VI Andrássy út 60; adult/concession 3000/1500Ft, audio guide 1500Ft; ⊙10am-6pm Tue-Sun; Ⓜ︎M1 Vörösmarty utca, ⊞4, 6) The headquarters of the dreaded ÁVH secret police houses the disturbing House of Terror, focusing on the crimes and atrocities of Hungary's fascist and Stalinist regimes in a permanent exhibition called Double Occupation. The years after WWII leading

Great Synagogue

up to the 1956 Uprising get the lion's share of the exhibition space (almost three-dozen spaces on three levels). The reconstructed prison cells in the basement and the Perpetrators' Gallery on the staircase, featuring photographs of the turncoats, spies and torturers, are chilling.

Liberty Monument   Monument

(Szabadság-szobor; 🚌27) The Liberty Monument, the lovely lady with the palm frond in her outstretched arms, proclaiming freedom throughout the city, is southeast of the Citadella. Standing 14m high, she was raised in 1947 in tribute to the Soviet soldiers who died liberating Budapest in 1945. The victims' names in Cyrillic letters on the plinth and the soldiers' statues were removed in 1992 and sent to Memento Park. The inscription reads: 'To those who gave up their lives for Hungary's independence, freedom and prosperity.'

Memento Park   Historic Site

(🖉1-424 7500; www.mementopark.hu; XXII Balatoni út & Szabadkai utca; adult/student 1500/1200Ft; ⊘10am-dusk; 🚌101B, 101E, 150) Home to more than 40 statues, busts and plaques of Lenin, Marx, Béla Kun and others whose likenesses have ended up on trash heaps elsewhere, Memento Park, 10km southwest of the city centre, is truly a mind-blowing place to visit. Ogle the socialist realism and try to imagine that some of these relics were erected as recently as the late 1980s.

Basilica of St Stephen   Cathedral

(Szent István Bazilika; 🖉1-338 2151, 06 30 703 6599; www.basilica.hu; V Szent István tér; requested donation 200Ft; ⊘9am-7pm Mon-Sat, 7.45am-7pm Sun; Ⓜ M3 Arany János utca) **FREE** Budapest's neoclassical cathedral is the most sacred Catholic church in all of Hungary and contains its most revered relic: the mummified right hand of the church's patron, King St Stephen. It was built over half a century to 1905. Much of the interruption during construction had to do with a fiasco in 1868 when the dome

🐦 Margaret Island

Situated in the middle of the Danube, leafy Margaret Island is neither Buda nor Pest, but its shaded walkways, large swimming complexes, thermal spa and gardens offer refuge to the denizens of both sides of the river. The island was always the domain of one religious order or another until the Turks turned it into a harem, and it remains studded with picturesque ruins.

The island is bigger than you think, so rent a bicycle or other wheeled equipment from **Bringóhintó** (🖉1-329 2073; www.bringohinto.hu; XIII Margit-sziget; per 30/60min/day mountain bikes 720/990/ 2800Ft, pedal coaches for 4 people 2680/ 3980Ft; ⊘8am-dusk; 🚌26, 226) at the refreshment stand near the Japanese Garden in the northern part of the island, then work your way south.

collapsed during a storm, and the structure had to be demolished and then rebuilt from the ground up. The view from the **dome** (Panoráma kilátó; 🖉1-269 1849; adult/child 600/400Ft; ⊘10am-6pm Jun-Sep, to 5.30pm Apr, May & Oct, to 4.30pm Nov-Mar; Ⓜ M3 Arany János utca) is phenomenal.

Hungarian State Opera House   Notable Building

(Magyar Állami Operaház; 🖉06 30 279 5677, 1-332 8197; www.operavisit.hu; VI Andrássy út 22; adult/concession 2490/2200Ft; ⊘tours in English 2pm, 3pm & 4pm; Ⓜ M1 Opera) The neo-Renaissance Hungarian State Opera

Budapest

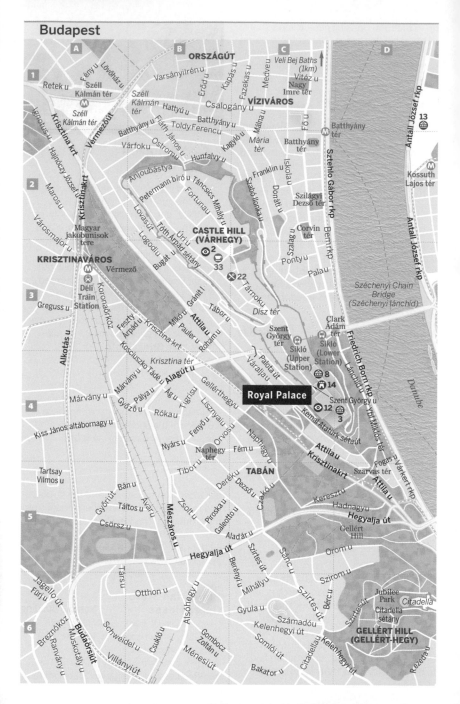

Budapest

House was designed by Miklós Ybl in 1884 and is among the most beautiful buildings in Budapest. Its facade is decorated with statues of muses and opera greats such as Puccini, Mozart, Liszt and Verdi, while its interior dazzles with marble columns, gilded vaulted ceilings, chandeliers and near-perfect acoustics. If you cannot attend a performance, join one of the three 45-minute daily tours. Tickets are available from a desk in the lobby.

Parliament   Historic Building

(Országház; ☎1-441 4904, 1-441 4415; http://latogatokozpont.parlament.hu/en; V Kossuth Lajos tér 1-3; adult/student EU citizen 2400/1200Ft, non-EU citizen 6000/3100Ft; ⊙8am-6pm Apr-Oct, to 4pm Nov-Mar; Ⓜ M2 Kossuth Lajos tér, 🚊2) The Eclectic-style Parliament, designed by Imre Steindl and completed in 1902, has 691 sumptuously decorated rooms. You'll get to see several of these and other features on a guided tour of the North Wing: the Golden Staircase; the Dome Hall, where the **Crown of St Stephen**, the nation's most important national icon, is on display; the **Grand**

Staircase and its wonderful landing; **Loge Hall**; and **Congress Hall**, where the House of Lords of the one-time bicameral assembly sat until 1944.

Royal Postal Savings Bank   Notable Building

(V Hold utca 4; 🚊15) East of Szabadság tér, the former Royal Postal Savings Bank is a Secessionist extravaganza of colourful tiles and folk motifs, built by Ödön Lechner in 1901. One of the most beautiful buildings in Pest, it is now part of the National Bank of Hungary.

Hungarian National Museum   Museum

(Magyar Nemzeti Múzeum; ☎1-327 7773, 1-338 2122; www.hnm.hu; VIII Múzeum körút 14-16; adult/concession/family 1600/800/3600Ft; ⊙10am-6pm Tue-Sun; Ⓜ M3/4 Kálvin tér, 🚊47, 49) The Hungarian National Museum houses the nation's most important collection of historical relics in an impressive neoclassical building, purpose built in 1847. Exhibits on the 1st floor trace the history of the Carpathian Basin from earliest times to the arrival of the Magyars in the 9th century; the ongoing story of the Magyar people resumes on the 2nd floor, from the conquest of the basin to the end of communism.

Castle Hill   Hill

(Várhegy; 🚌16, 16A, 116, Ⓜ M2 Batthyány tér, Széll Kálmán tér;, 🚋19, 41;) Castle Hill is a kilometre-long limestone plateau towering 170m above the Danube. It contains some of Budapest's most important medieval monuments and museums and is a Unesco World Heritage Site. Below it is a 28km-long network of caves formed by thermal springs.

The walled area consists of two distinct parts: the **Old Town** to the north, where commoners once lived, and the Royal Palace (p562) to the south, the original site of the castle built by Béla IV in the 13th century and reserved for the nobility.

Aquincum   Archaeological Site

(🖉1-430 1081; www.aquincum.hu; III Szentendrei út 135; adult/concession museum & archaeological park Apr-Oct 1600/800Ft, Nov-Mar 1000/500Ft, archaeological park only Apr-Oct 1000/500Ft; ⊙museum 10am-6pm Tue-Sun Apr-Oct, to 4pm Nov-Mar, archaeological park 9am-6pm Tue-Sun Apr-Oct; 🚋34, 106, 🚈(HÉV) H5 Aquincum) The most complete Roman civilian town in Hungary was built around 100 AD and became the seat of the Roman province of Pannonia Inferior in AD 106. Visitors can explore its houses, baths, courtyards, fountains and sophisticated underfloor heating systems, as well as a recreation of a Roman painter's dwelling and Symphorus Mithraeum.

The purpose-built Aquincum Museum, just inside the entrance, puts the ruins in perspective, with a vast collection of Roman daily life objects and wall paintings.

🔒 SHOPPING

Nagycsarnok   Market

(Great Market Hall; 🖉1-366 3300; www.piac online.hu; IX Vámház körút 1-3; ⊙6am-5pm Mon, to 6pm Tue-Fri, to 3pm Sat; Ⓜ M4 Fővám tér, 🚋47, 49) Completed in 1897, this is Budapest's

biggest market, though it has become a tourist magnet since its renovation for the millecentenary celebrations in 1996. Still, plenty of locals come here for fruit, vegetables, deli items, fish and meat. Head up to the 1st floor for Hungarian folk costumes, dolls, painted eggs, embroidered tablecloths, carved hunting knives and other souvenirs.

Madison Perfumery   Perfume

(🖉06 30 386 9973, 06 30 971 0933; www. madisonperfumery.com; VI Andrássy út 26; ⊙10am-8pm Mon-Fri, to 7pm Sat, noon-6pm Sun; 🚋105, Ⓜ M1 Opera) There are three reasons why you should visit this shop: (1) it is Budapest's finest perfumery and even does a Tokaji Aszú scent; (2) it is housed in an early 20th-century pharmacy that is museum quality; (3) it serves the best roasted coffee in town made with a coveted Kees van der Westen espresso machine.

Rózsavölgyi Csokoládé   Chocolate

(🖉06 30 504 4294; www.rozsavolgyi.com; V Királyi Pál utca 6; ⊙10.30am-1pm & 1.30-6.30pm Mon-Fri, noon-6pm Sat; Ⓜ M3/4 Kálvin tér) Tiny, low-lit boutique selling delicious and artfully packaged, award-winning bean-to-bar chocolate made in nearby Budafok. The range of handmade chocolates includes such interesting flavours as coffee and balsamic vinegar, and star anise with red peppercorn.

✴ EATING

Budavári Rétesvár   Hungarian €

(Strudel Castle; 🖉06 70 408 8696; www. budavariretesvar.hu; I Balta köz 4; strudel 350Ft; ⊙8am-8pm; 🚋16, 16A, 116) Strudel in all its permutations – from poppyseed with sour cherry to dill with cheese and cabbage – is available at this hole-in-the wall dispensary in a narrow alley of the Castle District.

Olimpia   Hungarian €€

(🖉1-321 0680; www.olimpiavendeglo. com; VII Alpár utca 5; 2-/3-course lunches 3050/3190Ft, 4-/5-/6-/7-course dinners

Budapest's Best Flea Markets

Jostling with locals shopping for bargains at **Ecseri Piac** (Ecseri Market; www.piaconline.hu; XIX Nagykőrösi út 156; ⊗8am-4pm Mon-Fri, 5am-3pm Sat, 8am-1pm Sun; 🚌54, 84E, 89E 94E), one of Central Europe's largest flea markets, is a fabulous way to spend a Saturday morning. Lose yourself amid a cornucopia of gramophones, rocking horses, uniforms, violins and even suits of armour.

Old electronics for sale at Ecseri Piac
WESTEND61 PREMIUM / SHUTTERSTOCK ©

8500/9600/10,500/10,990Ft; ⊗noon-3pm Tue-Fri, 7-10pm Tue-Sat; 📶; 🚌20E, 30, Ⓜ M2 Keleti pályaudvar, 🚌trolleybus 75, 79) Traditional Hungarian with a twist is on offer at this brilliant restaurant that offers a *table d'hôte* set-lunch menu of two or three courses and a dinner menu of up to seven; the set lunches are a steal. Book ahead.

Kőleves
Jewish €€

(📱1-322 1011, 06 20 213 5999; www.koleves vendeglo.hu; VII Kazinczy utca 41; mains 2180-5080Ft; ⊗8am-midnight Mon-Thu, 8am-1am Fri, 9am-1am Sat, 9am-midnight Sun; 📶📱; Ⓜ M1/2/3 Deák Ferenc tér) Always buzzy and lots of fun, the 'Stone Soup' attracts a young crowd with its Jewish-inspired (but not kosher) menu, lively decor, great service and reasonable prices. Good vegetarian choices. Breakfast (760Ft to 920Ft) is served from 8 to 11am (11.30am on the weekend). The daily lunch is just 1350Ft (1200Ft for the vegetarian version).

ESCA Studio
Hungarian €€

(📱06 30 752 1509; http://escastudiorestaurant. hu; VII Dohány utca 29; 2-/3-/6-course menu 4500/8500/12,000Ft, with wine pairing 7500/13,500/19,000Ft; ⊗noon-3pm & 6-11pm; 🚌trolleybus 74, Ⓜ M2 Blaha Lujza tér, 🚌4, 6) One of the best new modern Hungarian bistros, this place offers both excellent cooking and superb value. With internationally trained chef/owner Gábor Fehér at the helm, expect such 'oddities that work' as tomato soup with blueberry and red currants and seared calves' feet with smoked mayonnaise. The place is small so be sure you book ahead – lunch is only available if you have a reservation.

Pesti Disznó Bisztró
Hungarian €€

(📱1-951 4061; www.pestidiszno.hu; VI Nagymező utca 19; mains 2790-6690Ft; ⊗9am-midnight; Ⓜ M1 Oktogon) Punters would be forgiven for thinking that the 'Pest Pig' was all about pork. In fact, of the 10 or so main courses more than half are beef, poultry, fish or vegetarian. It's a wonderful space, loft-like almost, with high tables and charming, informed service. The wine card is very, very good and most wines are available by the glass, too.

Kispiac
Hungarian €€

(📱1-269 4231, 06 30 430 0142; www.kispiac.eu; V Hold utca 13; mains 2450-4450Ft; ⊗noon-10pm Mon-Sat; Ⓜ M3 Arany János utca) This small retro-style restaurant – an absolute favourite – serves seriously Hungarian things like stuffed *csülök* (pig's trotter – and way better than it sounds, 2950Ft), roast *malac* (piglet, 3250Ft) and the ever-popular wild-boar spare ribs (3950Ft), as well as an infinite variety of *savanyúság* (pickled vegetables). Perfectly selected wine list and a warm welcome.

Borkonyha
Hungarian €€€

(Wine Kitchen; 📱1-266 0835; www.borkonyha. hu; V Sas utca 3; mains 3450-7950Ft; ⊗noon-4pm & 6pm-midnight Mon-Sat; 🚌15, 115, Ⓜ M1 Bajcsy-Zsilinszky út) Chef Ákos Sárközi's approach to Hungarian cuisine at this Michelin-starred restaurant is contemporary, and the menu changes every week or two. Go for the signature foie gras appetiser with apple and celeriac and a glass of sweet Tokaji Aszú wine. If *mangalica* (a special type of Hungarian pork) is on the menu, try it with a glass of dry Furmint.

🍷 DRINKING & NIGHTLIFE

Doblo   Wine Bar
(☑06 20 398 8863; www.budapestwine.com; VII Dob utca 20; ☺2pm-2am Sun-Wed, to 4am Thu-Sat; Ⓜ M1/2/3 Deák Ferenc tér) Brick-lined and candlelit, Doblo is where you go to taste Hungarian wines, with scores available by the 1.5cL (15mL) glass for 900Ft to 2150Ft. There's food such as meat and cheese platters and live music nightly at 9pm.

Boutiq' Bar   Cocktail Bar
(☑06 30 554 2323; www.boutiqbar.hu; V Paulay Ede utca 5; ☺6pm-1am Tue-Thu, to 2am Fri & Sat; Ⓜ M1 Bajcsy-Zsilinszky utca) A low-lit 'speak-easy' serving expertly mixed cocktails (1950Ft to 5950Ft) using fresh juices and an educated selection of craft spirits. For something specifically Hungarian, try a

creation that includes Unicum like Die Kaiser, or plum *pálinka* (fruit brandy) such as Positive Drinking. The gin-based Budapest BBQ is something else. Informed, charming service; reservations are advised.

Léhűtő   Bar
(Loafer; ☑06 30 731 0430; www.facebook.com/lehuto.kezmuvessorozo; VII Holló utca 12-14; ☺4pm-midnight Sun-Tue, to 2am Wed & Thu, to 4am Fri & Sat; 🛜; Ⓜ M1/2/3 Deák Ferenc tér) Drop into this basement bar if you fancy a craft beer, of which it stocks a large range of Hungarian and international labels. Friendly staff are on hand to advise and let you taste before you buy. There's also above-ground seating amid an often-buzzing crowd that gathers at this cross-roads on warm nights. Tapas (690Ft to 1690Ft) available as blotter.

High Note Roof Bar   Rooftop Bar
(☑06 20 438 8648; www.highnoteskybar.hu/en; V Hercegprímás utca 5; ☺noon-midnight; 🚌15, 115, Ⓜ M1 Bajcsy-Zsilinszky út) If you need to impress someone – even yourself – lead them up to this rooftop bar above the Aria

Doblo

Hungarian State Opera House

Hotel . With your noses stuck into the dome of the basilica and virtually every landmark in Budapest within your grasp, you'll only be able to utter 'Wow!'. Great cocktails and friendly staff. What's not to love? Book ahead.

Instant   Club

(☑06 70 638 5040; www.instant.co.hu; VII Akácfa utca 51; ☺4pm-6am; ☐trolleybus 70, 74, 78, ☐4, 6) Many still love this 'ruin bar' even in its new location as part of the **Fogas** (☑06 70 638 5040; www.fogashaz.hu; VII Akácfa utca 49; ☺4pm-6am; ☎; ☐trolleybus 70, 74, 78, ☐4, 6) stable, and so do all our friends. It has a couple of dozen rooms to get lost in, seven bars, seven stages and two gardens with underground DJs and dance parties. It's always heaving.

Szatyor Bár és Galéria   Bar

(Carrier Bag Bar & Gallery; ☑1-279 0290; www. szatyorbar.com; XIII Bartók Béla út 36-38; ☺noon-1am; Ⓜ️M4 Móricz Zsigmond körtér, ☐18, 19, 47, 49) Sharing the same building as the **Hadik Kávéház** (☑1-279 0290; www.hadikkavehaz. com; XIII Bartók Béla út 36; ☺noon-midnight;

Ⓜ️M4 Móricz Zsigmond körtér, ☐18, 19, 47, 49) and separated by just a door, the Szatyor is the funkier of the twins, with cocktails, street art on the walls and a Lada driven by the poet Endre Ady. Cool or what? There's food here, too (mains 1990Ft to 2990Ft).

⭐ ENTERTAINMENT

Hungarian State Opera House   Opera

(Magyar Állami Operaház; ☑1-814 7100, box office 1-332 7914; www.opera.hu; VI Andrássy út 22; ☺box office 10am-5pm Mon-Fri; Ⓜ️M1 Opera) The gorgeous neo-Renaissance opera house is worth a visit as much to admire the incredibly rich decoration inside as to view a performance and hear the perfect acoustics. Tours (p567) are still departing while the opera house undergoes massive renovations (due to be completed in 2020) but most of the operas and musicals are being staged in the **Erkel Theatre** (Erkel Színház; ☑1-332 6150; www.opera.hu; VIII II János Pál pápa tér 30; ☺box office 10am-8pm; ☐7, Ⓜ️M2 Keleti pályaudvar), Budapest's 'other' opera house.

Liszt Music Academy   Classical Music
(Liszt Zeneakadémia; ☑1-462 4600, box office
1-321 0690; www.zeneakademia.hu; VI Liszt
Ferenc tér 8; 1400-19,800Ft; ⊘box office 10am-
6pm; ⓂM1 Oktogon, ☑4, 6) Performances at
Budapest's most important concert hall
are usually booked up at least a week in advance, but more expensive (though still affordable) last-minute ones can sometimes
be available. It's always worth checking.

ℹ INFORMATION

Budapest Info (☑1-576 1401; www.budapestinfo.
hu; V Sütő utca 2; ⊘8am-8pm; ⓂM1/2/3 Deák
Ferenc tér, ☑47, 49) is the main tourist office;
there is another **branch** (☑1-576 1404; www.
budapestinfo.hu; XIV Olof Palme sétány 5;
⊘9am-7pm; ⓂM1 Hősök tere) in City Park and
info desks in the arrivals sections of Ferenc Liszt
International Airport's Terminals 2A and 2B.

ℹ GETTING THERE & AWAY

AIR

Budapest's **Ferenc Liszt International Airport**
(BUD; ☑1-296 7000; www.bud.hu/en) has two
modern terminals side by side 24km southeast
of the city centre.

TRAIN

Keleti Train Station (Keleti pályaudvar; ☑06
40 494 949; www.mavcsoport.hu; VIII Kerepesi
út 2-6; ⓂM2/M4 Keleti pályaudvar) Most international trains (and domestic traffic to/from the
north and northeast) arrive here.

MÁV (Magyar Államvasutak, Hungarian State
Railways; ☑1-349 4949; www.mavcsoport.hu)
links up with the European rail network in all
directions.

Nyugati Train Station (Western Train Station;
☑1-349 4949; VI Nyugati tér) Trains from some
international destinations (eg Romania) and
from the Danube Bend and Great Plain.

Déli Train Station (Déli pályaudvar; ☑1-349
4949; I Krisztina körút 37; ⓂM2 Déli pályaudvar)
Trains from some destinations in the south, eg
Osijek in Croatia and Sarajevo in Bosnia, as well
as some trains from Vienna.

🍷 Ruin Pubs

Romkocsmák (ruin pubs) began to
appear in the city from the early 2000s,
when entrepreneurial free thinkers took
over abandoned buildings and turned
them into pop-up bars. At first a very
word-of-mouth scene, the ruin bars'
popularity grew exponentially and many
have transformed from ramshackle, temporary sites full of flea-market furniture
to more slick, year-round fixtures with
covered areas to protect patrons from
the winter elements. Budapest's first
romkocsmá, **Szimpla Kert** (☑06 20 261
8669; http://en.szimpla.hu/szimpla-garden;
VII Kazinczy utca 14; ⊘noon-4am Mon-Fri,
9am-4am Sat & Sun; ⓂM2 Astoria) is firmly
on the drinking tourists' trail, but remains
a landmark place for a beverage.

Szimpla Kert

ℹ GETTING AROUND

Travel passes valid for one day to one month are
valid on all trams, buses, trolleybuses, HÉV suburban trains (within the city limits) and metro lines.

Metro The quickest but least scenic way to get
around. Runs 4.30am to about 11.50pm.

Bus Extensive network of regular buses runs
from around 4.30am to between 9pm and
11.50pm; from 11.50pm to 4.30am a network of
40 night buses (three digits beginning with '9' –
901 to 999) kicks in.

Tram Faster and more pleasant for sightseeing
than buses. Tram 6 on the Big Ring Road runs
overnight.

Trolleybus Mostly useful for getting to and
around City Park in Pest.

VIENNA, AUSTRIA

Vienna, Austria

Few cities in the world waltz so effortlessly between the present and the past like Vienna. Its splendid historical face is easily recognised: grand imperial palaces and bombastic baroque interiors, revered opera houses and magnificent squares. But Vienna is also one of Europe's most dynamic urban spaces. A stone's throw from the Hofburg (Imperial Palace), the MuseumsQuartier houses provocative and high-profile contemporary art behind a striking basalt facade. In the Innere Stadt (Inner City), up-to-the-minute design stores sidle up to old-world confectioners, and Austro-Asian fusion restaurants stand alongside traditional Beisl (small taverns).

Two Days in Vienna

Start your day at Vienna's heart, the **Stephansdom** (p589), and be awed by the cathedral's cavernous interior. Soak up the grandeur of the **Hofburg** (p584), a Habsburg architectural masterpiece, then end the day with a craft beer at **Brickmakers Pub & Kitchen** (p596). Spend the morning of the second day in the **Kunsthistorisches Museum** (p582) and the afternoon in at least one of the museums in the **Museums-Quartier** (p585).

Four Days in Vienna

Divide your morning between **Schloss Belvedere** (p590) and its magnifi-cently landscaped French-style formal gardens. Make your way to the **Prater** (p585), Vienna's playground of woods, meadows and sideshow attractions. Dedicate your final day to **Schloss Schönbrunn** (p580). If there's any time left, check out **Karlskirche** (p590) or **Secession** (p589).

Looking for more castles? Take a train to Schloss Neuschwanstein (p462) or fly to Dubrovnik (p481).

Vienna Map (p586)

Arriving in Vienna

Vienna International Airport The frequent City Airport Train (CAT; €11, 16 minutes) leaves the airport every 30 minutes from 6.09am to 11.39pm. There's also a cheaper but slower S7 suburban train (€4.20, 37 minutes) from the airport to Wien-Mitte. A taxi costs €25 to €50.

Wien Hauptbahnhof Situated 3km south of Stephansdom, Vienna's main train station handles all international trains. It's linked to the centre by U-Bahn line 1, trams D and O, and buses 13A and 69A. A taxi to the centre costs about €10.

Where to Stay

Vienna's lodgings cover it all, from inexpensive youth hostels to luxury establishments with chandeliers, antique furniture and original 19th-century oil paintings. In between are homey, often family-run *Pensionen* (guesthouses, many of which are traditional), and less ostentatious hotels, plus a smart range of apartments. It's wise to book ahead at all times; for the best value, especially in the centre, at least a few weeks in advance is advisable.

Schloss Schönbrunn

The Habsburg Empire is revealed in all its frescoed, gilded, chandelier-lit glory in the wondrously ornate apartments of Schloss Schönbrunn, which are among Europe's best-preserved baroque interiors.

Great For...

☑ Don't Miss

The Great Gallery, Neptunbrunnen and panoramic Gloriette.

State Apartments

The frescoed **Blue Staircase** makes a regal ascent to the palace's upper level. First up are the 19th-century apartments of Emperor Franz Josef I and his beloved wife Elisabeth. The tour whisks you through lavishly stuccoed, chandelier-lit apartments such as the **Billiard Room**, where army officials would pot a few balls while waiting to attend an audience, and Franz Josef's **study**, where the emperor worked tirelessly from 5am.

In the exquisite white-and-gold **Mirror Room**, a six-year-old Mozart performed for a rapturous Maria Theresia in 1762. Fairest of all, however, is the 40m-long **Great Gallery**, where the Habsburgs threw balls and banquets, a frothy vision of stucco and chandeliers, topped with a fresco by Italian artist Gregorio Guglielmi showing the glorification of Maria Theresia's reign. Decor aside, this was where the historic meeting

❶ Need to Know

☑01-811 13-0; www.schoenbrunn.at; 13, Schönbrunner Schlossstrasse 47; adult/child Imperial Tour €16/11.50, Grand Tour €20/13, Grand Tour with guide €24/15; ⊘8am-6.30pm Jul & Aug, to 5.30pm Apr-Jun, Sep & Oct, to 5pm Nov-Mar; ⓤSchönbrunn, Hietzing

✕ Take a Break

Head to **Waldemar** (☑0664 361 61 27; www.waldemar-tagesbar.at; 13, Altgasse 6; dishes €6-11.50; ⊘8am-8pm Mon-Fri, 9am-3pm Sat & Sun; ☎; ⓤHietzing) for bolstering coffee and cake or a superhealthy lunch.

★ Top Tip

If you plan to see several sights at Schönbrunn, it's worth buying one of the combined tickets, which can be purchased in advance online.

between John F Kennedy and Soviet leader Nikita Khrushchev took place in 1961.

If you have a Grand Tour ticket, you can continue through to the palace's **east wing**. Franz Stephan's apartments begin in the sublime **Blue Chinese Salon**, where the intricate floral wall paintings are done on Chinese rice paper. The negotiations that led to the collapse of the Austro-Hungarian Empire in 1918 were held here.

Schloss Schönbrunn Gardens

The beautifully tended formal **gardens** (⊘6.30am-dusk) [FREE] of the palace, arranged in the French style, are appealing whatever the season: they are a symphony of colour in the summer and a wash of greys and browns in winter.

The grounds, which were opened to the public by Joseph II in 1779, hide a number of attractions in the tree-lined avenues (arranged according to a grid and star-shaped

system between 1750 and 1755), including the 1781 **Neptunbrunnen** (Neptune Fountain; ⊘10am-4pm mid-Apr–Sep), a riotous ensemble from Greek mythology. The crowning glory is the 1775 **Gloriette** (adult/child €4.50/3.20; ⊘9am-7pm Jul & Aug, to 6pm Apr-Jun & Sep, to 5pm Oct-early Nov; ☒8A, 63A Gassmannstrasse, ⓤSchönbrunn). Its view, looking back towards the palace with Vienna shimmering in the distance, ranks among the best in the city. It's also possible to venture onto the roof.

Wagenburg

The **Wagenburg** (Imperial Coach Collection; www.kaiserliche-wagenburg.at; adult/child €9.50/free; ⊘9am-5pm mid-Mar–Nov, 10am-4pm Dec–mid-Mar) is *Pimp My Ride* imperial style. On display is a vast array of carriages, including Emperor Franz Stephan's coronation carriage, with its ornate gold plating, Venetian glass panes and painted cherubs. The whole thing weighs an astonishing 4000kg.

ANTON_IVANOC / SHUTTERSTOCK ©

Kunsthistorisches Museum Vienna

Occupying a neoclassical building as sumptuous as the art it contains, this museum takes you on a time-travel treasure hunt – from classical Rome to Egypt and the Renaissance.

Great For...

☑ Don't Miss

Dutch Golden Age paintings, the Kunstkammer and the Offering Chapel of Ka-ni-nisut.

Picture Gallery

The vast Picture Gallery is by far and away the most impressive of the museum's collections. First up is the German Renaissance, where the key focus is the prized Dürer collection, followed by the Flemish baroque, epitomised by Rubens, Van Dyck and Pieter Bruegel the Elder.

In the 16th- and 17th-century Dutch Golden Age paintings, the desire to faithfully represent reality is captured in works by Rembrandt, Ruisdael and Vermeer.

High on your artistic agenda in the 16th-century Venetian rooms should be Titian's *Nymph and Shepherd* (1570), Veronese's dramatic *Lucretia* (1583) and Tintoretto's *Susanna at her Bath* (1556).

Devotion is central to Raphael's *Madonna of the Meadow* (1506), one of the true masterpieces of the High Renaissance, just as

❶ Need to Know

KHM, Museum of Art History; www.khm.at; 01, Maria-Theresien-Platz; adult/child incl Neue Burg museums €16/free; ⊙10am-6pm Fri-Wed, to 9pm Thu Jun-Aug, closed Mon Sep-May; ⓊMuseumsquartier, Volkstheater

✗ Take a Break

Head to hip **Said the Butcher to the Cow** (☏01-535 69 69; www.butcher-cow.at; 01, Opernring 11; burgers €12-20.50, steaks €28.50-39; ⊙kitchen 2pm-10pm Tue & Wed, to 11pm Thu-Sat, bar 5pm-1am Tue & Wed, to 2am Thu-Sat; ☏; ⓍD, 1, 2, 71 Kärntner Ring/Oper, ⓊKarlsplatz) for a post-museum burger.

★ Top Tip

If your time's limited, skip straight to the Old Master paintings in the Picture Gallery.

It is to the *Madonna of the Rosary* (1601), a stirring Counter-Reformation altarpiece by Italian baroque artist Caravaggio.

Of the artists represented in the final rooms dedicated to Spanish, French and English painting, the undoubted star is Spanish court painter Velázquez.

Kunstkammer

The Habsburgs filled their *Kunstkammer* (cabinet of art and curiosities) with an encyclopaedic collection of the rare and the precious, from narwhal-tusk cups to table holders encrusted with fossilised shark teeth.

Egyptian & Near Eastern Collection

Decipher the mysteries of Egyptian civili-sations with a chronological romp through this miniature Giza of a collection. Here the **Offering Chapel of Ka-ni-nisut** spells out the life of the high-ranking 5th-dynasty official in reliefs and hieroglyphs.

In the Near Eastern collection, the representation of a prowling lion from Babylon's triumphal Ishtar Gate (604–562 BC) is the big attraction.

Greek & Roman Antiquities

This rich Greek and Roman repository reveals the imperial scope for collecting classical antiquities, with 2500 objects traversing three millennia from the Cypriot Bronze Age to early medieval times.

Among the Greek Art is a fragment from the Parthenon's northern frieze, while the sizeable Roman stash includes the 4th-century-AD *Theseus Mosaic* from Salzburg and the captivating 3rd-century-AD *Lion Hunt* relief.

◉ SIGHTS

◎ The Hofburg & Around

Hofburg   Palace

(Imperial Palace; ☑01-533 75 70; www.hofburg-wien.at; 01, Michaelerkuppel; ⬜D, 1, 2, 71 Burgring, ⓊHerrengasse) Nothing symbolises Austria's resplendent cultural heritage more than its Hofburg, home base of the Habsburgs from 1273 to 1918. The oldest section is the 13th-century **Schweizerhof** (Swiss Courtyard), named after the Swiss guards who protected its precincts. The Renaissance **Swiss gate** dates from 1553. The courtyard adjoins a larger courtyard, **In der Burg**, with a monument to Emperor Franz II adorning its centre. The palace now houses the Austrian president's offices, the preserved Kaiserappartements and a raft of museums.

Kaiserappartements   Palace

(Imperial Apartments; ☑01-533 7570; www.hofburg-wien.at; 01, Michaelerplatz; adult/child €15/9, incl guided tour €18/10.50; ◷9am-6pm Jul & Aug, to 5.30pm Sep-Jun; ⬜D, 1, 2, 71 Burgring, ⓊHerrengasse) The Kaiserappartements, once the official living quarters of Franz Josef I and Empress Elisabeth, are dazzling in their chandelier-lit opulence. The **Sisi Museum** is devoted to Austria's most beloved empress, with a strong focus on the clothing and jewellery of Austria's monarch. Multilingual audioguides are included in the admission price. Guided tours (English available) take in the Kaiser-appartements, the Sisi Museum and the **Silberkammer** (Silver Depot, Imperial Silver Collection), whose largest silver service caters for 140 dinner guests.

Kaiserliche Schatzkammer   Museum

(Imperial Treasury; ☑01-525 24-0; www.kaiserliche-schatzkammer.at; 01, Schweizerhof; adult/child €12/free; ◷9am-5.30pm Wed-Mon; ⓊHerrengasse) The Hofburg's Kaiserliche Schatzkammer contains secular and ecclesiastical treasures (including devotional images and altars, particularly from the baroque era) of priceless value and splendour – the sheer wealth of this collection of crown jewels is staggering. As you walk through the rooms you'll see magnificent treasures such as a golden rose, diamond-studded Turkish sabres, a 2680-carat Colombian emerald and, the highlight of the treasury, the imperial crown.

MuseumsQuartier

TASFOTONL / GETTY IMAGES ©

Albertina Gallery

(01-534 830; www.albertina.at; 01, Albertinaplatz 1; adult/child €16/free; 10am-6pm
Sat-Tue & Thu, to 9pm Wed & Fri; D, 1, 2, 71
Kärntner Ring/Oper, Karlsplatz, Stephansplatz)
Once used as the Habsburgs' imperial
apartments for guests, the Albertina is now
a repository for an exceptional collection
of graphic art. The permanent Batliner Collection – with over 100 paintings covering
the period from Monet to Picasso – and the
high quality of changing exhibitions make
the Albertina highly worthwhile.

Multilingual audioguides (€4) cover all
exhibition sections and tell the story behind
the apartments and the works on display.

Neue Burg Museums Museum

(01-525 24-0; www.khm.at; 01, Heldenplatz,
Hofburg; adult/child €16/free; 10am-6pm
Fri-Wed, to 9pm Thu Jun-Aug, closed Wed Sep-May;
 D, 1, 2, 71 Burgring, Herrengasse, Museums-
quartier) Three Neue Burg museums can be
visited on one ticket. The **Sammlung Alter
Musik Instrumente** (Collection of Ancient
Musical Instruments) contains a wonderfully
diverse array of instruments. The **Ephesos
Museum** features artefacts unearthed dur-
ing Austrian archaeologists' excavations at
Ephesus in Turkey between 1895 and 1906.
The **Hofjägd und Rüstkammer** (Arms and
Armour) museum contains armour dating
mainly from the 15th and 16th centuries.
Admission includes the Kunsthistorisches
Museum Vienna (p582) and all three Neue
Burg museums. Audioguides cost €5.

The Museum District & Neubau

MuseumsQuartier Museum

(Museum Quarter; MQ; 01-523 58 81; www.
mqw.at; 07, Museumsplatz; information & ticket
centre 10am-7pm; 49 Volkstheater, Museumsquartier, Volkstheater) The MuseumsQuartier is
a remarkable ensemble of museums, cafes,
restaurants and bars inside former imperial
stables designed by Fischer von Erlach. This
breeding ground of Viennese cultural life
is the perfect place to hang out and watch
people on warm evenings. With over 90,000
sq metres of exhibition space, the complex
is one of the world's most ambitious cultural
hubs. It includes the Leopold Museum,

Prater & the Riesenrad

Spread across 60 sq km, central
Vienna's largest park, **Prater** (www.
wiener-prater.at; ; Praterstern) FREE
comprises woodlands of poplar and
chestnut, meadows, and tree-lined
boulevards, as well as children's playgrounds, a swimming pool, a golf course
and a racetrack. Fringed by statuesque
chestnut trees that are ablaze with
russet and gold in autumn and frilly with
white blossom in spring, the central
Hauptallee avenue is the main vein.
It runs straight as an arrow from the
Praterstern to the **Lusthaus** (01-728
95 65; 02, Freudenau 254; mains €13-20;
 noon-10pm Mon-Tue & Thu-Fri, to 6pm Sat
& Sun; ; 77A), a former 16th-century
Habsburg hunting lodge that today shelters a chandelier-lit cafe and restaurant
serving classic Viennese fare.

Twirling above the Würstelprater
amusement park is one of the city's most
visible icons, the **Riesenrad** (www.wiener
riesenrad.com; 02, Prater 90; adult/child
€12/5; 9am-midnight, shorter hours winter;
 ; Praterstern). It's top of every Prater
wish list, at least for anyone who's seen
Orson Welles' cuckoo clock speech in
British film noir *The Third Man* (1949),
set in a shadowy postwar Vienna. Built
in 1897 by Englishman Walter B Basset,
the Ferris wheel rises to 65m and takes
about 20 minutes to rotate its 430-tonne
weight one complete circle – giving you
ample time to snap some fantastic shots
of the city spread out below.

Prater
MRGB / SHUTTERSTOCK ©

Vienna

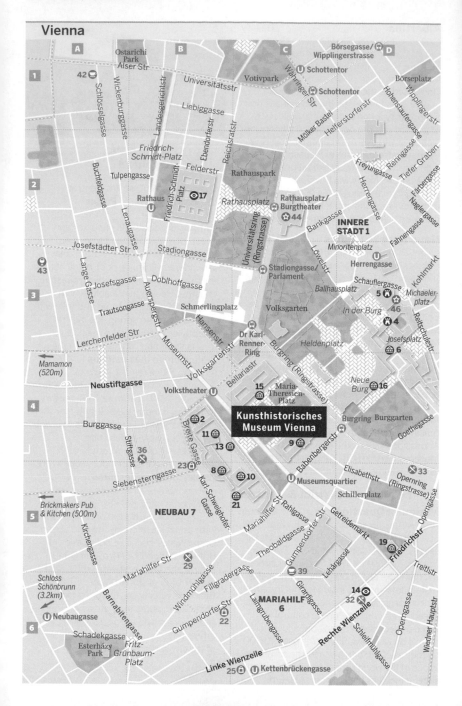

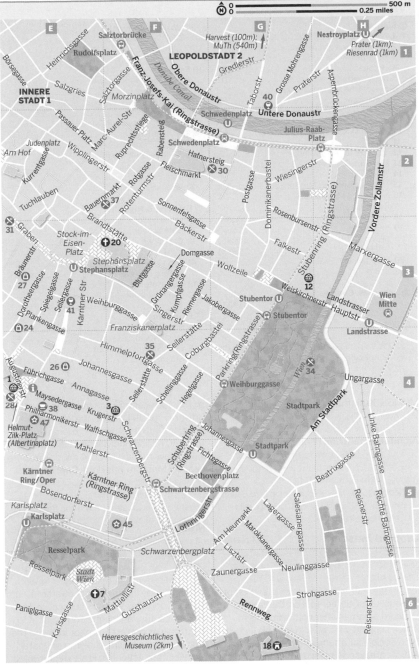

Harvest (100m);
MuTh (540m)

Prater (1km);
Riesenrad (1km)

Heeresgeschichtliches
Museum (2km)

Vienna

MUMOK, **Kunsthalle** (Arts Hall; ☑01-521 890; www.kunsthallewien.at; adult/child €8/free; ⊙11am-7pm Tue, Wed & Fri-Sun, to 9pm Thu), **Architekturzentrum** (Vienna Architecture Centre; ☑01-522 31 15; www.azw.at; adult/child €9/2.50; ⊙architecture centre 10am-7pm, library 10am-5.30pm Mon, Wed & Fri, to 7pm Sat & Sun) and **Zoom** (☑01-524 79 08; www.kindermuseum. at; exhibition adult/child €6/free, activities child €5-7, accompanying adult €6; ⊙Tue-Sun).

Leopold Museum   Museum
(www.leopoldmuseum.org; 07, Museumsplatz 1; adult/child €14/10; ⊙10am-6pm Fri-Wed, to 9pm Thu Jun-Aug, closed Mon Sep-May; ☐49 Volkstheater, Ⓤ Volkstheater, Museumsquartier) Part of the MuseumsQuartier (p585), the Leopold Museum is named after ophthalmologist Rudolf Leopold, who, after buying his first Egon Schiele for a song as a young student in 1950, amassed a huge private collection of mainly 19th-century and modernist Austrian artworks. In 1994 he sold the lot – 5266 paintings – to the Austrian government for €160 million (individually, the paintings would have made him €574 million), and the Leopold Museum was born. **Café Leopold** (www.cafeleopold.wien; 07, Museumsplatz 1; ⊙9.30am-midnight; ☎; Ⓤ Museumsquartier, Volkstheater) is located on the top floor.

MUMOK   Gallery
(Museum Moderner Kunst; Museum of Modern Art; www.mumok.at; 07, Museumsplatz 1; adult/child €12/free; ⊙2-7pm Mon, 10am-7pm Tue, Wed & Fri-Sun, 10am-9pm Thu; ☐49 Volkstheater, Ⓤ Volkstheater, Museumsquartier) Modern-art museum MUMOK contains Vienna's finest collection of 20th-century art, centred on fluxus, nouveau realism, pop art and photorealism. The best of expressionism, cubism, minimal art and Viennese Actionism is also represented

in a collection of 9000 works that are rotated and exhibited by theme – but note that sometimes all this Actionism is packed away to make room for temporary exhibitions. The dark basalt edifice and sharp corners provide a complete contrast to the historic MuseumsQuartier (p585) buildings.

Naturhistorisches Museum   Museum

(Museum of Natural History; www.nhm-wien. ac.at; 01, Maria-Theresien-Platz; adult/child €12/ free, planetarium extra €5/3, rooftop tours €8; ☺9am-6.30pm Thu-Mon, to 9pm Wed, rooftop tours in English 3pm Fri, Sat & Sun Apr-Dec, 3pm Sun Jan-Mar; ⓊVolkstheater) Four billion years of natural history are covered in a blink at Vienna's Naturhistorisches Museum. Among its minerals, fossils and dinosaur bones are one-of-a-kind finds like the minuscule 25,000-year-old Venus von Willendorf and a peerless 1100-piece meteorite collection. Audioguides cost €5.

The late-19th-century building, with its exquisitely stuccoed, frescoed halls and cupola, is the identical twin of the Kunsthistorisches Museum Vienna opposite. Tours take you onto the building's rooftop to view the ornate architecture up-close; children under 12 aren't allowed.

Rathaus   Historic Building

(City Hall; ☏01-502 55; www.wien.gv.at; 01, Rathausplatz 1; ☺tours 1pm Mon, Wed & Fri Sep-Jun, 1pm Mon-Fri Jul & Aug; ⓆD, 1, 2, 71 Rathausplatz/Burgtheater, ⓊRathaus) 𝗙𝗥𝗘𝗘 Vienna's neo-Gothic City Hall, completed in 1883 by Friedrich von Schmidt of Cologne Cathedral fame and modelled on Flemish city halls, is the highlight of the Ringstrasse boulevard's 19th century architectural ensemble. From the fountain-filled **Rathauspark**, where Josef Lanner and Johann Strauss I, fathers of the Viennese waltz, are immortalised in bronze, you get the full effect of its facade of lacy stonework, pointed-arch windows and spindly turrets. Free one-hour guided tours are in German; multilingual audioguides are also free.

⊚ Stephansdom & the Historic Centre

Stephansdom   Cathedral

(St Stephen's Cathedral; www.stephanskirche. at; 01, Stephansplatz; adult/child including audio-guide or guided tour €6/2.50, all-inclusive ticket €14.90/3.90; ☺9-11.30am & 1-4.30pm Mon-Sat, 1-4.30pm Sun, English tours 10.30am Mon-Sat; ⓊStephansplatz) Vienna's Gothic masterpiece Stephansdom – or Steffl (Little Stephan), as it's ironically nicknamed – is Vienna's pride and joy. A church has stood here since the 12th century, and reminders of this are the Romanesque **Riesentor** (Giant Gate) and **Heidentürme** (Towers of the Heathens). From the exterior, the first thing that will strike you is the glorious tiled roof, with its dazzling row of chevrons and Austrian eagle. Inside, the magnificent Gothic stone pulpit presides over the main nave, fashioned in 1515 by Anton Pilgrim.

Haus der Musik   Museum

(www.hausdermusik.com; 01, Seilerstätte 30; adult/child €13/6, incl Mozarthaus Vienna €18/8; ☺10am-10pm; Ⓠ2, 71 Schwarzenbergplatz, ⓊKarlsplatz) The Haus der Musik explains the world of sound and music to adults and children alike (in English and German) in an amusing and interactive way. Exhibits are spread over four floors and cover everything about how sound is created, from Vienna's Philharmonic Orchestra to street noises. The staircase between floors acts as a piano; its glassed-in ground-floor courtyard hosts musical events. After 8pm, adult admission drops to €6.50.

⊚ Karlsplatz & Around Naschmarkt

Secession   Museum

(www.secession.at; 01, Friedrichstrasse 12; adult/ child €9.50/6; ☺10am-6pm Tue-Sun; ⓊKarlsplatz) In 1897, 19 progressive artists swam away from the mainstream Künstlerhaus artistic establishment to form the Wiener Secession (Vienna Secession). Among their number were Gustav Klimt, Josef Hoffman, Kolo Moser and Joseph M Olbrich. Olbrich designed the new exhibition centre of the Secessionists, which combined sparse functionality with stylistic motifs. Its biggest draw is Klimt's exquisitely gilded Beethoven Frieze. One-hour guided tours in English (€3) take place at 11am Saturday. An audioguide costs €3.

Naschmarkt & Flohmarkt

Vienna's famous **market** (www.wien.gv.at; 06, Linke & Rechte Wienzeile; ⊘6am-7.30pm Mon-Fri, to 5pm Sat; ⓊKettenbrückengasse) and eating strip began life as a farmers market in the 18th century, when the fruit market on Freyung was moved here.

The fruits of the Orient poured in, the predecessors of the modern-day sausage stand were erected, and sections were set aside for coal, wood and farming tools and machines. Officially, it became known as *Naschmarkt* ('munch market') in 1905, a few years after Otto Wagner bedded the Wien River down in its open-topped stone-and-concrete sarcophagus. This Otto Wagnerian horror was a blessing for Naschmarkt, because it created space to expand. Today the Naschmarkt is not only the place to shop for food, but also has the weekly Flohmarkt antique market.

One of the best flea markets in Europe, and a Vienna institution, **Flohmarkt** (Flea Market; 05, Linke Wienzeile; ⊘6.30am-2pm Sat; ⓊKettenbrückengasse) brims with antiques and *Altwaren* (old wares). Stalls hawking books, clothes, records, ancient electrical goods, old postcards, ornaments and carpets stretch for several blocks. Arrive early, as it gets increasingly crammed as the morning wears on, and be prepared to haggle.

Wares for sale at Flohmarkt
ARTUR BORISOV / SHUTTERSTOCK ©

Karlskirche — Church
(St Charles Church; www.karlskirche.at; 04, Karlsplatz; adult/child €8/4; ⊘9am-6pm Mon-Sat, noon-7pm Sun; ⓊKarlsplatz) Built between 1716 and 1739, after a vow by Karl VI at the end

of the 1713 plague, Vienna's finest baroque church rises at the southeast corner of Resselpark. It was designed and commenced by Johann Bernhard Fischer von Erlach and completed by his son Joseph. The huge elliptical copper **dome** reaches 72m; the highlight is the lift to the cupola (included in admission) for a close-up view of the intricate frescoes by Johann Michael Rottmayr.

⊙ Schloss Belvedere to the Canal

Schloss Belvedere — Palace
(www.belvedere.at; Prinz-Eugen-Strasse 27; adult/child Oberes Belvedere €16/free, Unteres Belvedere €14/free, combined ticket €22/free; ⊘9am-6pm Sat-Thu, to 9pm Fri; 🚊D, 71 Schwarzenbergplatz, ⓊTaubstummengasse, Südtiroler Platz) A masterpiece of total art, Schloss Belvedere is one of the world's finest baroque palaces. Designed by Johann Lukas von Hildebrandt (1668–1745), it was built for the brilliant military strategist Prince Eugene of Savoy, who defeated the Turks in 1718. What giddy romance is evoked in its sumptuously frescoed halls, replete with artworks by Klimt, Schiele and Kokoschka; what stories are conjured in its landscaped gardens, which drop like the fall of a theatre curtain to reveal Vienna's skyline.

Heeresgeschichtliches Museum — Museum
(Museum of Military History; www.hgm.at; 03, Arsenal; adult/under 19yr €7/free, 1st Sun of month free; ⊘9am-5pm; ⓊSüdtiroler Platz) The superb Heeresgeschichtliches Museum is housed in the Arsenal, a large neo-Byzantine barracks and munitions depot. Spread over two floors, the museum works its way from the Thirty Years' War (1618–48) to WWII, taking in the Hungarian Uprising and the Austro-Prussian War (ending in 1866), the Napoleonic and Turkish Wars, and WWI. Highlights on the 1st floor include the Great Seal of Mustafa Pasha, which fell to Prince Eugene of Savoy in the Battle of Zenta in 1697.

Museum für Angewandte Kunst — Museum
(MAK, Museum of Applied Arts; www.mak.at; 01, Stubenring 5; adult/under 19yr €12/free, 6-10pm Tue €5, tours €3.50; ⊘10am-6pm Wed-Sun, to 10pm Tue, English tours noon Sun; 🚊2 Stubentor,

U Stubentor) MAK is devoted to craftsmanship and art forms in everyday life. Each exhibition room showcases a different style, which includes Renaissance, baroque, orientalism, historicism, empire, art deco and the distinctive metalwork of the Wiener Werkstätte. Contemporary artists were invited to present the rooms in ways they felt were appropriate, resulting in eye-catching and unique displays. The 20th-century design and architecture room is one of the most fascinating, and Frank Gehry's cardboard chair is a gem.

ACTIVITIES

Wrenkh Cookery School   Cooking
(01-533 15 26; www.wrenkh-wien.at; 01, Bauernmarkt 10; per person from €48; U Stephansplatz) Wrenkh's cookery school in its **restaurant** (mains €11.50-30; 11am-10pm Mon-Sat;) has classes in English and German covering Austrian classics such as schnitzels, *Tafelspitz* (boiled beef), freshwater fish and apple strudel, along with international cuisines (Indian, Thai etc) and vegetarian and vegan cooking. Look out for foraging expeditions, too. Courses range

from €48 for 2½ hours to €130 for 6 hours. Check programs online.

Donauinsel   Outdoors
(Danube Island; U Donauinsel) The svelte Danube Island stretches some 21.5km from opposite Klosterneuburg in the north to the Nationalpark Donau-Auen in the south and splits the Danube in two, creating a separate arm known as the Neue Donau (New Danube). Created in 1970, it is Vienna's aquatic playground, with sections of beach (don't expect much sand) for swimming, boating and a little waterskiing.

SHOPPING

Beer Lovers   Drinks
(www.beerlovers.at; 06, Gumpendorfer Strasse 35; 11am-8pm Mon-Fri, 10am-5pm Sat; U Kettenbrückengasse) A wonderland of craft beers, this emporium stocks over 1000 labels from over 125 different breweries in over 70 styles, with more being sourced every day. Tastings are offered regularly, and cold beers are available in the walk-in glass fridge and in refillable growlers. It also stocks craft ciders, small-batch liqueurs and boutique nonalcoholic drinks such as ginger beers.

Karlskirche

CÉSAR ASENSIO / 500PX©

★ Top Five Cafes

POC Café (p595)

Café Sperl (p595)

Café Sacher (p595)

Waldemar (p581)

Café Leopold (p588)

From left: Sacher torte at Café Sacher (p595); Café Leopold (p588); Café Sperl (p595)

Julius Meinl am Graben   Food & Drinks

(www.meinlamgraben.at; 01, Graben 19; ⏱8am-7.30pm Mon-Fri, 9am-6pm Sat; Ⓤ Stephansplatz) Vienna's most prestigious providore brims with quality foodstuffs from around the world (over 17,000 products in all). Chocolate and confectionery dominate the ground floor, and impressive cheeses (some 400 varieties) and cold meats are tantalisingly displayed upstairs. The basement stocks European and Austrian wine and fruit liqueurs and has a classy on-site **wine bar** (⏱11am-midnight Mon-Sat); there's also an exceptional on-site **restaurant** (☏01-532 33 34 6000; mains €27-39, 4-course menus €79; ⏱8am-11pm Mon-Fri, 9am-11pm Sat; 📶).

J&L Lobmeyr Vienna   Homewares

(www.lobmeyr.at; 01, Kärntner Strasse 26; ⏱10am-7pm Mon-Fri, to 6pm Sat; Ⓤ Stephansplatz) Reached by a beautifully ornate wrought-iron staircase, this is one of Vienna's most lavish retail experiences. The collection of Biedermeier pieces, Loos-designed sets, fine/arty glassware and porcelain on display here glitters from the lights of the chandelier-festooned atrium. Lobmeyr has been in business since 1823, when it exclusively supplied the imperial court.

Steiff   Toys

(www.steiff-galerie-wien.at; 01, Bräunerstrasse 3; ⏱10am-12.30pm & 1.30-6pm Mon-Fri, 10am-12.30pm & 1.30-5pm Sat; Ⓤ Stephansplatz) Founded in Germany in 1880, Steiff is widely regarded as the original creator of the teddy bear, which it presented at the 1902 Leipzig Toy Fair: an American businessman bought 3000, selling them under the name 'teddy bear' after US president Theodore ('Teddy') Roosevelt. Today its flagship Austrian shop is filled with adorable bears and other premium quality cuddly toys.

Die Werkbank   Design

(www.werkbank.cc; 07, Breite Gasse 1; ⏱1-6.30pm Tue-Fri, 11am-5pm Sat; 🚌49 Volkstheater) Furniture, lamps, rugs, vases, jewellery, watches, graphic art, bags, even bicycles are among the creations you might find on display at 'The Workbench', an all-white space that operates as a design collective, where some of Vienna's most innovative designers showcase their works.

Dorotheum   Antiques

(www.dorotheum.com; 01, Dorotheergasse 17; ⏱10am-6pm Mon-Fri, 9am-5pm Sat; Ⓤ Stephansplatz) The Dorotheum is among the largest

MOJMIR FOTOGRAFIE / SHUTTERSTOCK ©

auction houses in Europe, and for the casual visitor it's more like a museum, housing everything from antique toys and tableware to autographs, antique guns and, above all, lots of quality paintings. You can bid at the regular auctions held here; otherwise just drop by and enjoy browsing.

🍴 EATING

Mamamon   Thai €
(🖉01-942 31 55; www.mamamonthaikitchen.com; 08, Albertgasse 15; mains €7.50-10.90; ⊙11.30am-9.30pm Mon-Fri, noon-9.30pm Sat; Ⓤ Josefstädter Strasse, Rathaus) Owner Piano, who named her restaurant for her mum Mon, has spiced up Vienna's burgeoning Southeast Asian food scene with a menu of southern Thai flavours, street-style decor and an indie soundtrack. On mild nights, a young, happy crowd spills out into the courtyard, while single diners pull up a stool at the large communal table or window seats within.

Bitzinger Würstelstand
am Albertinaplatz   Street Food €
(www.bitzinger-wien.at; 01, Albertinaplatz; sausages €3.50-4.70; ⊙8am-4am; 🚊D, 1, 2, 71 Kärntner Ring/Oper, Ⓤ Karlsplatz, Stephansplatz) Behind

the Staatsoper, Vienna's best sausage stand has cult status. Bitzinger offers the contrasting spectacle of ladies and gents dressed to the nines, sipping beer, wine or Joseph Perrier Champagne while tucking into sausages at outdoor tables or the heated counter after performances. Mustard comes in *süss* (sweet, ie mild) or *scharf* (fiercely hot).

Eis Greissler   Ice Cream €
(www.eis-greissler.at; 06, Mariahilfer Strasse 33; 1/2/3/4/5 scoops €1.60/3/4.30/5.30/6; ⊙11am-8pm; Ⓤ Museumsquartier) 🌿 The inevitable queue makes Eis Greissler easy to spot. Locals flock here whatever the weather for ice cream made from organic milk, yoghurt and cream from its own farm in Lower Austria, and vegans are well catered for with soy and oat-milk varieties. All-natural flavours vary seasonally but might include goat's cheese, pumpkin-seed oil, cinnamon, pear or marzipan.

Harvest   Vegan €
(🖉0676 492 77 90; www.harvest-bistrot.at; 02, Karmeliterplatz 1; mains €4.50-11, brunch €16.60, lunch €8.80; ⊙2pm-midnight Mon-Fri, 10am-midnight Sat-Sun; 🖋; 🚊2 Karmeliterplatz, Ⓤ Nestroyplatz) A bubble of bohemian

Griechenbeisl, decorated for Christmas

warmth, Harvest swears by seasonality in its superhealthy vegetarian and vegan dishes, swinging from lentil, pear, walnut and smoked tofu salad to coconutty vegetable curries. Candles, soft lamp light and mismatched vintage furniture set the scene, and there's a terrace for summer dining. Alt Wien–roasted coffee, homemade cakes and weekend brunches round out the picture.

Griechenbeisl   Austrian €€

(☏01-533 19 77; www.griechenbeisl.at; 01, Fleischmarkt 11; mains €17-29; ⏱11.30am-11.30pm; 🖾; 🚋1, 2 Schwedenplatz, Ⓤ Schwedenplatz) Dating from 1447 and frequented by Beethoven, Brahms, Schubert and Strauss among other luminaries, Vienna's oldest restaurant has vaulted rooms, wood panelling and a figure of Augustin trapped at the bottom of a well inside the front door. Every classic Viennese dish is on the menu, along with three daily vegetarian options. In summer, head to the plant-fringed front garden.

Tian Bistro   Vegetarian €€

(☏01-890 466 532; www.tian-bistro.com; 07, Schrankgasse 4; mains €9-18; ⏱5.30-10pm Mon, noon-10pm Tue-Fri, 10am-10pm Sat & Sun; 🖾; 🚋49 Siebensterngasse) Colourful tables set up on the cobbled laneway outside Tian Bistro in summer, while indoors, a glass roof floods the atrium-style, greenery-filled dining room in light. It's the cheaper, more relaxed offspring of Michelin-starred vegetarian restaurant **Tian** (☏01-890 46 65; www.tian-restaurant.com; 01, Himmelpfortgasse 23; 4-/6-/8-course lunch menus €89/109/127, 8-course dinner menu €127; ⏱6-9pm Tue, noon-2pm & 6-9pm Wed-Sat; 🖾; 🚋2 Weihburggasse, Ⓤ Stephansplatz) 🌿. It serves sensational vegetarian and vegan dishes such as black truffle risotto with Piedmont hazelnuts, as well as brunch until 1pm on weekends.

Steirereck im Stadtpark   Gastronomy €€€

(☏01-713 31 68; http://steirereck.at; 03, Am Heumarkt 2a; mains €38-58, 6-/7-course menus €149/165; ⏱11.30am-2.30pm & 6.30pm-midnight Mon-Fri; Ⓤ Stadtpark) Heinz Reitbauer is at the culinary helm of this two-starred Michelin restaurant, beautifully lodged in a 20th-century former dairy building in the leafy Stadtpark. His tasting menus are an exuberant feast, fizzing with natural, integral flavours that speak of a chef with exacting standards. Wine pairing is an additional €79/89 (six/seven courses).

DRINKING & NIGHTLIFE

POC Cafe Coffee

(www.facebook.com/pg/poccafe; 08, Schlösselgasse 21; 8am-5pm Mon-Fri; 5, 43, 44, U Schottentor) Friendly Robert Gruber is one of Vienna's coffee legends and his infectious passion ripples through this beautifully rambling, lab-like space. POC stands for 'People on Caffeine'; while filter, espresso-style or a summertime iced cold brew are definitely this place's raison d'etre, it's also known for moreish sweets like killer poppyseed cake, cheesecake or seasonal fruit tarts.

Café Sperl Coffee

(www.cafesperl.at; 06, Gumpendorfer Strasse 11; 7am-10pm Mon-Sat, 10am-8pm Sun, closed Sun Jul & Aug; ; U Museumsquartier, Kettenbrückengasse) With its gorgeous *Jugendstil* fittings, grand dimensions, cosy booths and unhurried air, Sperl (c 1880) is one of the finest coffee houses in Vienna. The must-try is *Sperl Torte,* an almond-and-chocolate-cream dream. Grab a slice and a newspaper, order a coffee (from some three dozen kinds) and join the people-watching patrons. A live pianist plays from 3.30pm to 5.30pm on Sundays.

Weinstube Josefstadt Wine Bar

(www.facebook.com/WeinstubeJosefstadt; 08, Piaristengasse 27; 4pm-midnight Apr-Dec; U Rathaus) Weinstube Josefstadt is one of Vienna's loveliest *Stadtheurigen* (city wine taverns), a leafy green oasis spliced between towering residential blocks. Its tables of friendly, well-liquored locals are squeezed in between the trees and shrubs looking onto a pretty, painted *Salettl,* or wooden summerhouse. Wine is local and cheap, food is typical, with a buffet-style meat and fritter selection. Cash only.

Das Loft Bar

(www.dasloftwien.at; 02, Praterstrasse 1; noon-2am Mon-Sat, 12:30pm-2am Sun; 2 Gredlerstrasse, U Schwedenplatz) What a view! Take the lift to Das Loft on the Sofitel's 18th floor to reduce Vienna to toy-town scale. From this slinky, glass-walled lounge, you can pick out landmarks such as the Stephansdom and the Hofburg over a tonka bean sour or mojito. By night, the backlit ceiling swirls with an impressionist painter's palette of colours.

Viennese Specialities

Vienna has a strong repertoire of traditional dishes. One or two are variations on dishes from other regions. Classics include the following:

Schnitzel Wiener *Schnitzel* should always be crumbed veal, but pork is gaining ground in some places.

Goulash *Rindsgulasch* (beef goulash) is everywhere in Vienna. Originating in Hungary, the Austrian version is often served with *Semmelknoedel* (bread dumplings).

Tafelspitz Traditionally this boiled prime beef swims in the juices of locally produced *Suppengrün* (fresh soup vegetables), before being served with *Kren* (horseradish) sauce.

Beuschel Offal, usually sliced lung and heart, with a slightly creamy sauce.

Backhendl Fried, breaded chicken, often called *steirischer Backhendl.*

Zwiebelrostbraten Slices of roast beef smothered in gravy and fried onions.

Schinkenfleckerln Oven-baked ham-and-noodle casserole.

Bauernschmaus Platter of cold meats.

The undeniable monarchs of all desserts are *Kaiserschmarrn* (sweet pancake with raisins) and *Apfelstrudel* (apple strudel), but also look out for *Marillenknödel* (apricot dumplings) in summer.

Schnitzel Wiener

STEPANEK PHOTOGRAPHY / SHUTTERSTOCK ©

Café Sacher Coffee

(www.sacher.com; 01, Philharmonikerstrasse 4; 8am-midnight; D, 1, 2, 71 Kärntner Ring/Oper, U Karlsplatz) With a battalion of waiters and air of nobility, this grand cafe is

Opera & Classical Music

The glorious **Staatsoper** (☎01-514 44 7880; www.wiener-staatsoper.at; 01, Opernring 2; tickets €14-287, standing room €4-10; U Karlsplatz) is Vienna's premier opera and classical-music venue. Productions are lavish, formal affairs, where people dress up accordingly. In the interval, wander the foyer and refreshment rooms to fully appreciate the gold-and-crystal interior. Opera is not performed here in July and August (tours still take place). Tickets can be purchased up to two months prior.

POSZTOS / SHUTTERSTOCK ©

celebrated for its *Sacher Torte*, a wonderfully rich iced-chocolate cake with apricot jam once favoured by Emperor Franz Josef. For the full-blown experience, head to the opulent chandelier-lit interior. There's also a covered pavement terrace, and a 1920s-styled tearoom, Sacher Eck, next door serving the same menu.

Loos American Bar Cocktail Bar
(www.loosbar.at; 01, Kärntner Durchgang 10; ⌚noon-4am; U Stephansplatz) Loos is *the* spot in the Innere Stadt for a classic cocktail such as its signature dry martini, expertly whipped up by talented mixologists. Designed by Austrian architect Adolf Loos in 1908, this tiny 27-sq-m box (seating just 20 or so patrons) is bedecked from head to toe in onyx, marble, mahogany and polished brass, with space-enhancing mirrored walls.

Brickmakers Pub & Kitchen Craft Beer
(☎01-997 44 14; www.brickmakers.at; 07, Zieglergasse 42; ⌚4pm-1am Mon-Wed, to 2am Thu & Fri, 10am-2am Sat, to 1am Sun; 🚋49 Westbahnstrasse/Zieglergasse) Racing-green metro tiles, a mosaic floor and a soundtrack of disco, hip hop, funk and soul set the scene for brilliant craft beers and ciders: there are 30 on tap and over 150 by the bottle. American BBQ food includes smoked-beef brisket and bourbon-marinated sticky ribs. Happy hour runs from 5pm to 7pm Monday to Friday.

✪ ENTERTAINMENT

Spanish Riding School Performing Arts
(Spanische Hofreitschule; ☎01-533 90 31-0; www.srs.at; 01, Michaelerplatz 1; tickets €27-225, standing room €13; ⌚hours vary; U Herrengasse) The world-famous Spanish Riding School is a Viennese institution truly reminiscent of the imperial Habsburg era. This unequalled equestrian show is performed by Lipizzaner stallions formerly kept at an imperial stud established at Lipizza (hence the name). These graceful stallions perform an equine ballet to a program of classical music while the audience watches from pillared balconies – or from a cheaper standing-room area – and the chandeliers shimmer above.

Burgtheater Theatre
(National Theatre; ☎01-514 44 4140; www.burgtheater.at; 01, Universitätsring 2; seats €7-61, standing room €3.50; ⌚box office 9am-5pm Mon-Fri, closed Jul & Aug; 🚋D, 1, 71 Rathausplatz/Burgtheater) The Burgtheater hasn't lost its touch over the years – this is one of the foremost theatres in the German-speaking world, staging some 800 performances a year, from Shakespeare to Woody Allen. The theatre also runs the 500-seater Akademietheater, which was built between 1911 and 1913.

Musikverein Concert Venue
(☎01-505 81 90; www.musikverein.at; 01, Musikvereinsplatz 1; tickets €15-105, standing room €7-15; ⌚box office 9am-8pm Mon-Fri, to 1pm Sat Sep-Jun, 9am-noon Mon-Fri Jul & Aug; U Karlsplatz) The opulent Musikverein holds the proud title of the best acoustics of any concert hall in Austria, which the Vienna Philharmonic Orchestra embraces. The lavish interior can be visited by 45-minute guided tour (in English; adult/child €8.50/5) at 1pm Tuesday to Saturday.

Spanish Riding School

Smaller-scale performances are held in the Brahms Saal. There are no student tickets.

MuTh   Concert Venue

(☎01-347 80 80; www.muth.at; 02, Obere Augartenstrasse 1e; Vienna Boys' Choir Fri performance €39-89; ◷4-6pm Mon-Fri & 1 hour before performances; Ⓤ Taborstrasse) This striking baroque meets contemporary concert hall is the home of the Wiener Sängerknaben, or Vienna Boys' Choir, who previously only performed at the Hofburg. Besides Friday afternoon choral sessions at 5pm with the angelic-voiced lads, the venue stages a top-drawer roster of dance, drama, opera, classical, rock and jazz performances.

ⓘ INFORMATION

Tourist Info Wien (☎01-245 55; www.wien.info; 01, Albertinaplatz; ◷9am-7pm; ☎; 🚋D, 1, 2, 71 Kärntner Ring/Oper, Ⓤ Stephansplatz) Vienna's main tourist office has free maps and racks of brochures.

ⓘ GETTING THERE & AWAY

If you're bringing your own vehicle, you'll need a Motorway Vignette (toll sticker). For 10 days/two months it costs €9/26.20 per car, €5.20/13.10 per motorcycle. Buy it at petrol stations in neighbouring countries before entering Austria. More information is available at www.austria.info.

ⓘ GETTING AROUND

Transport maps are posted in all U-Bahn stations and at many bus and tram stops. Free maps are available from **Wiener Linien** (☎01-7909-100; www.wienerlinien.at), located in U-Bahn stations.

U-Bahn Fast, comfortable and safe. Trains run from 5am to midnight Monday to Thursday and continuously from 5am Friday through to midnight Sunday. Tickets are sold at machines or windows at stations. Validate tickets prior to boarding.

Tram Slower but more enjoyable. Depending on the route, trams run from around 5.15am to about 11.45pm. Buy tickets at kiosks or from the driver (more expensive). Validate tickets when boarding.

Bus Reliable, punctual, with several very useful routes for visitors. Most run from 5am to midnight; services can be sporadic or nonexistent on weekends. Buy tickets from the driver or a *Tabakladen* (tobacconist). Validate tickets on boarding.

Night Bus Especially useful for outer areas; runs every 30 minutes from 12.30am to 5am. Main stops are located at Schwedenplatz, Schottentor and Kärntner Ring/Oper.

In Focus

Performers at Eurovision 2019

Europe Today

These are challenging times for Europe. Economically, many countries are still struggling, while politically, pro- and anti-European Union (EU) forces are engaged in a titanic struggle for the soul of the continent. The UK public narrowly voted for 'Brexit' – leaving the EU – and that process has proved more complicated than many people imagined.

State of the Union

Where Europe should be headed as a political entity remains a burning question for EU nations, especially those hostile to relinquishing further powers to the EU parliament. In 2016, a referendum in the UK over the issue saw voters opt, by a slim majority, for 'Brexit'. The Conservative government went on to trigger Article 50 of the Treaty of Lisbon at the end of March 2017, setting the UK on course to leave the EU by 2019, if British politicians can finally agree to a deal.

EU membership also raises questions about democratic representation: in exchange for their financial bailouts, financially strapped countries have been forced to follow the political will of Brussels, often in direct contradiction to the wishes of their own constituents, causing considerable unease across the union.

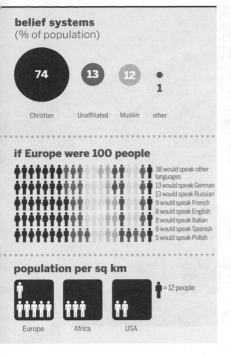

belief systems
(% of population)

74 — Christian
13 — Unaffiliated
12 — Muslim
1 — other

if Europe were 100 people

38 would speak other languages
13 would speak German
13 would speak Russian
9 would speak French
8 would speak English
8 would speak Italian
6 would speak Spanish
5 would speak Polish

population per sq km

≈ 12 people

Europe   Africa   USA

Refugee Crisis

Hostility to Muslims has been on the rise in the wake of the worst refugee crisis to hit Europe since the end of WWII. Since 2015, over 1 million refugees and migrants have arrived in the EU, the majority of them fleeing from war and terror in Syria and other troubled countries. The response has varied: some countries in the EU's Schengen Area have closed previously open borders, while at the other extreme Germany has implemented an open-arms policy of accepting refugees.

Despite the unease over this, the French presidential election in 2017 saw a decisive victory for the pro-EU centrist candidate Emmanuel Macron, over the far-right National Rally leader Marine Le Pen. It was a similar story in the Netherlands. In the March 2017 general election the centre-right Volkspartij voor Vrijheid en Democratie (VVD) party prevailed over the right-wing Partij voor de Vrijheid (PVV) led by Geert Wilders, an anti-EU politician advocating a ban on immigration from Muslim countries and the closing down of mosques. But far-right, anti-EU forces are on the rise elsewhere, including in Hungary and Italy.

Greener Europe

On a brighter note, many European countries are stepping up efforts to combat climate change. Increasingly, high-speed rail services provide an ecofriendly alternative to short-haul flights, green spaces flourish in urban areas, share-bicycle schemes are becoming prevalent in cities and towns, and vehicle emissions are being reduced with more electric and hybrid engines and biofuels. Mayor Sadiq Khan has added a £10 charge for motorists driving older, more polluting vehicles on top of the congestion charge that already exists for central London. The mayors of Paris, Madrid and Athens also plan to take diesel cars and vans off their roads by 2025.

The Eurovision Issue

On a lighter note, every May Europe plops down on the sofa to enjoy the Eurovision Song Contest. This one-of-a-kind musical marathon has been screened every year since 1956, making it the longest-running television show of its kind.

Created to symbolise Euro harmony, the contest has also developed into a reflection of Euro discord. Is the voting system rigged? Should acts sing in English or in their own language? Is that kitschy pop song some kind of coded political statement?

Each country enters one song, and then votes for their favourites among the competitors'. Inevitably this leads to accusations of 'bloc voting' (neighbouring countries voting for each other). Confusingly, too, several non-European countries are allowed to enter. The host city, with a few exceptions, is in the winner country of the previous year, with cities competing domestically for the honour and associated tourism boost.

Dubrovnik

DREAMER4787 / SHUTTERSTOCK ©

History

Understanding Europe's long and often troubled history is a crucial part of figuring out what makes this continent tick. Fragments of that history can be encountered in the tumbledown remains of Roman ampitheatres and bathhouses, in the fabulously ostentatious architecture of French chateaux and German castles, and in the winding streets, broad boulevards and governing institutions of its many stately cities.

4500–2500 BC
Neolithic tribes build burial tombs, barrows, stone circles and alignments across Europe.

1st century BC – 4 AD
The Romans conquer much of Europe. The Roman Empire flourishes under Augustus and his successors.

410
The sacking of Rome by the Goths brings an end to Roman dominance.

Prehistory

The first settlers arrived in Europe around two million years ago, but it wasn't until the end of the last major ice age between 12,000 BC and 8000 BC that humans really took hold. As the glaciers and ice sheets retreated, hunter-gatherer tribes extended their reach northwards in search of new land. Some of Europe's earliest human settlements were left behind by Neolithic tribes.

Greeks & Romans

The civilisation of ancient Greece emerged around 2000 BC and made huge leaps forward in science, technology, architecture, philosophy and democratic principles. Many of the writers, thinkers and mathematicians of ancient Greece, from Pythagoras to Plato, still exert a profound influence to this day. Then came the Romans, who set about conquering most of Europe and devised the world's first republic. At its height, Roman power extended

1066
William the Conqueror defeats the English King Harold at the Battle of Hastings.

1340s–1350s
The Black Death reaches its peak in Europe, killing between 30% and 60% of Europe's population.

15th Century
The Italian Renaissance brings about a revolution in art, architecture and science.

★ Best Historical Buildings

Colosseum (p369), Rome
Pompeii (p370), Italy
City Walls & Forts (p489), Dubrovnik
Tower of London (p66), London
Prague Castle (p538), Prague
Trinity College (p125), Dublin
Holocaust Memorial (p444), Berlin

Prague Castle (p538)

VLADA ZH / SHUTTERSTOCK ©

all the way from Celtic Britain to ancient Persia (Iran). The Romans' myriad achievements are almost too numerous to mention: they founded cities, raised aqueducts, constructed roads, laid sewers and built baths all over the continent, and produced a string of brilliant writers, orators, politicians, philosophers and military leaders.

Dark Ages to Middle Ages

Rome's empire-building ambitions eventually proved too much, and a series of political troubles and military disasters resulted in the sacking of Rome (in 410) by the Goths. Although Roman emperors clung onto their eastern Byzantine empire for another thousand years, founding a new capital at Constantinople (modern-day İstanbul), Rome's dominance over Western Europe was over. A new era, the Dark Ages, had begun.

The next few centuries were marked by a series of conflicts in which the various kingdoms of the European mainland sought to gain political and strategic control. In 711 AD, the Moors – Arabs and Berbers who had converted to the Islamic religion prevailing throughout northern Africa – crossed the Straits of Gibraltar, defeating the Visigothic army. They went on to rule the Iberian Peninsula for almost 800 years, until the fall of Granada in 1492, leaving behind a flourishing architectural, scientific and academic legacy.

Meanwhile, in the late 8th century Charlemagne, King of the Franks, would bring together much of Western Europe under what would become known as the Holy Roman Empire. This alliance of Christian nations sent troops to wrest the Holy Land from Islamic control in a series of campaigns known as the Crusades.

The Renaissance

Europe's troubles rumbled on into the 14th and 15th centuries. In the wake of further conflicts and political upheavals, as well as the devastating outbreak of the Black Death (estimated to have wiped out somewhere between one-third and two-thirds of Europe's population), control over the Holy Roman Empire passed into the hands of the Austrian Habsburgs,

1517
Martin Luther nails his demands to the church door in Wittenburg, sparking the Reformation.

1789
France becomes a republic following the French Revolution. Numerous aristocrats are executed by guillotine.

1815
France's defeat at the Battle of Waterloo ends the First French Empire and military career of Napoleon Bonaparte.

a political dynasty that was to become one of the continent's dominant powers.

The Italian city states of Genoa, Venice, Pisa and Amalfi consolidated their control over the Mediterranean, establishing trading links with much of the rest of Europe and the Far East, and embarking on some of the first journeys in search of the New World.

In the mid-15th century, a new age of artistic and philosophical development broke out across the continent. The Renaissance encouraged writers, artists and thinkers to challenge the accepted doctrines of theology, philosophy, architecture and art. The centre of this artistic tsunami was Florence, Italy, where such inspirational figures as Michelangelo and Leonardo da Vinci made great strides in art and architecture. Another epoch-changing development was under way in Germany: the invention of the printing press by Johannes Gutenburg in around 1440. The advent of 'movable type' made printed books available to the masses for the first time.

The Reformation

While the Renaissance challenged artistic ideas, the Reformation dealt with questions of religion. Challenging Catholic 'corruption' and the divine authority of the Pope, the German theologian Martin Luther established his own breakaway branch of the Church, to which he gave the name 'Protestantism', in 1517. Luther's stance was soon echoed by the English monarch Henry VIII, who cut ties with Rome in 1534 and went on to found his own (Protestant) Church of England, sowing the seeds for centuries of conflict between Catholics and Protestants.

The New World

The schisms of the Church weren't the only source of tension. The discovery of the 'New World' in the mid-16th century led to a colonial arms race between the major European nations, in which each country battled to lay claim to the newly discovered lands – often enslaving or killing the local populace in the process.

More trouble followed during the Thirty Years' War (1618–48), which began as a conflict between Catholics and Protestants and eventually sucked in most of Europe's principal powers. The war was ended by the Peace of Westphalia in 1648, and Europe entered a period of comparative stability.

The Enlightenment

The Enlightenment (sometimes known as 'The Age of Reason') is the name given to a philosophical movement that spread throughout European society during the mid- to late-17th century. It emphasised the importance of logic, reason and science over the doctrines of religion. Key figures included the philosophers Baruch Spinoza, John Locke, Immanuel Kant and Voltaire, as well as scientists such as Isaac Newton.

19th century	**1914**	**1939–45**
The Industrial Revolution transforms European society, with railways and factories bringing in the modern age.	The assassination of Archduke Franz Ferdinand leads to the outbreak of WWI (1914–18).	WWII rages across Europe, devastating many cities. After peace is declared, much of Eastern Europe falls under communist rule.

The Enlightenment also questioned the political status quo. Since the Middle Ages, the majority of Europe's wealth and power had been concentrated in the hands of an all-powerful elite, largely made up of monarchs and aristocrats. This stood in direct contradiction to one of the core values of the Enlightenment – equality. Many thinkers believed it was an impasse that could only be solved by revolution.

Revolution

Things came to a head in 1789 when armed mobs stormed the Bastille prison in Paris, thus kick-starting the French Revolution. The Revolution began with high ideals, inspired by its iconic slogan of *liberté, egalité, fraternité* (liberty, equality, brotherhood). Before long things turned sour and heads began to roll. Hardline republicans seized control and demanded retribution for centuries of oppression. Scores of aristocrats met their end under the guillotine's blade, including the French monarch Louis XVI, who was publicly executed in January 1793 in Paris' Place de la Concorde, and his queen, Marie-Antoinette, killed in October that year.

The Reign of Terror between September 1793 and July 1794 saw religious freedoms revoked, churches closed, cathedrals turned into 'Temples of Reason' and thousands beheaded. In the chaos, a dashing young Corsican general named Napoleon Bonaparte (1769– 1821) seized his chance.

Napoleon assumed power in 1799 and in 1804 was crowned Emperor. He fought a series of campaigns across Europe and conquered vast swathes of territory for the French empire but, following a disastrous campaign to conquer Russia in 1812, his grip on power faltered and he was defeated by a coalition of British and Prussian forces at the Battle of Waterloo in 1815.

Industry, Empire & WWI

Having vanquished Napoleon, Britain emerged as Europe's predominant power. With such innovations as the steam engine, the railway and the factory, Britain unleashed the Industrial Revolution and, like many of Europe's major powers (including France, Spain, Belgium and the Austro-Hungarian empire), set about developing its colonies across much of Africa, Australasia and the Middle and Far East.

Before long these competing empires clashed again, with predictably catastrophic consequences. The assassination of the heir to the Austro-Hungarian Empire Franz Ferdinand in 1914 led to the outbreak of the Great War, or WWI, as it came to be known. By the end of hostilities in 1918, huge tracts of northern France and Belgium had been razed and over 16 million people across Europe had been killed.

In the Treaty of Versailles, the defeated powers of Austro-Hungary and Germany lost large areas of territory and found themselves crippled with a massive bill for reparations, sowing seeds of discontent that would be exploited a decade later by a fanatical Austrian painter by the name of Adolf Hitler.

1957	**1989**	**1993**
The European Economic Community (EEC) is formed by a collection of Western European countries.	The fall of the Berlin Wall heralds the downfall of oppressive regimes across much of Eastern Europe.	The Maastricht Treaty leads to the formation of the European Union (EU).

Rise of Fascism

Hitler's rise to power was astonishingly swift. By 1933 he had become Chancellor and, as the head of the Nazi Party, assumed total control of Germany. Having spent much of the 1930s building up a formidable war machine, assisting General Franco's nationalist forces during the Spanish Civil War, Hitler annexed former German territories in Austria and parts of Czechoslovakia, before extending his reach onwards into Poland in 1939.

The occupation of Poland proved the final straw. Britain, France and its Commonwealth allies declared war on Germany, which had formed its own alliance of convenience with the Axis powers of Italy (led by the fascist dictator Mussolini) and Japan.

WWII

Having done a secret deal with Stalin over the Soviet Union's spheres of influence to the east, Hitler unleashed his blitzkrieg on an unsuspecting western Europe and within a few short months conquered huge areas of territory, forcing the French into submission and driving the British forces to a humiliating retreat at Dunkirk. Europe was to remain under Nazi occupation for the next six years.

The Axis retained the upper hand until the Japanese attack on Pearl Harbor forced a reluctant USA into the war in 1941. Hitler's subsequent decision to invade the Soviet Union in 1941 proved to be a catastrophic error, resulting in devastating German losses that opened the door for the Allied invasion of Normandy in June 1944.

After several months of bitter fighting, Hitler's remaining forces were pushed back towards Berlin. Hitler committed suicide on 30 April 1945 and the Russians took the city, crushing the last pockets of German resistance. By 8 May Germany and Italy had unconditionally surrendered to the Allied powers, bringing the war in Europe to an end.

The Iron Curtain

Differences of opinion between the Western powers and the communist Soviet Union soon led to a stand-off. The USSR closed off its assigned sectors, including East Berlin, East Germany and much of Eastern Europe, which heralded the descent of the Iron Curtain and the beginning of the Cold War. This period of political tension and social division in Europe lasted for 40 years and saw popular uprisings in Prague and Budapest put down by communist forces.

By the late 1980s the Soviet Union's grip on Eastern Europe was weakening as the former superpower's economic feet of clay crumbled. The Cold War era came to an end in 1989 with the fall of the Berlin Wall. Germany was reunified in 1990; a year later the USSR was dissolved. Shortly afterwards Romania, Bulgaria, Poland, Hungary and Albania had implemented multiparty democracy. In Czechoslovakia (now the Czech Republic and Slovakia), the so-called Velvet Revolution brought about the downfall of the communist government through mass demonstrations and other nonviolent means.

2002

Twelve member states of the EU ditch their national currencies in favour of the euro.

2009

Europe is rocked by a series of financial crises, leading to costly bailouts for Ireland, Greece, Portugal and Spain.

2014

Scotland votes on and rejects becoming a fully independent nation and so remains part of the United Kingdom.

Europe United

The process of political and economic integration across Europe has continued apace since the end of WWII. The formation of the European Economic Community (EEC) in 1957 began as a loose trade alliance between six nations. By 1992, this alliance had evolved into the European Union (EU) and since the Treaty of Maastricht came into effect in 1993 its core membership has expanded to 28 countries. Even though the UK is in the process of leaving the EU, five other candidates – Turkey, Macedonia, Montenegro, Albania and Serbia – are on the books for future membership. All except Albania and Macedonia have started negotiations for entry.

Another key development was the implementation of the Schengen Agreement in 1995, which abolished border checks across much of mainland Europe and allowed EU citizens to travel freely throughout member states (with the notable exceptions of the UK and Ireland).

Even more momentous was the adoption of the single currency of the euro on 1 January 1999 as a cashless accounting currency; euro banknotes and coins have been used since 1 January 2002. To date, 19 countries have joined the Eurozone, while the UK, Denmark and Sweden have chosen to retain their national currencies. In future any new states joining the EU will be required to adopt the euro as a condition of entry. It's a hot topic, especially since the financial crash in countries including Greece and Spain, which has required richer nations (principally France and Germany) to bail out several of their more indebted European neighbours.

Economic Challenges

Since the 2009 European debt crisis, growth throughout the EU has been sluggish, with many countries dipping in and out of recession. Unemployment figures across many European nations remain high, especially in Spain and Greece.

Although the euro stabilised after a series of multi-billion-euro rescue packages for Greece, Ireland, Portugal and Spain, the currency is still subject to uncertainty. In 2015, an extension of Greece's bailout was granted in the hope of keeping the country within the eurozone, to avoid a Greek exit (aka 'Grexit'), and to avoid other debt-saddled countries following suit. And the European Central Bank launched massive quantitative easing (QE) measures involving money printing and bond buying, pumping over €1 trillion into the economy in an effort to resuscitate it.

By 2019, most eurozone economies were well on the way to recovery, but the uncertainty surrounding the UK's decision to leave the EU posed unprecedented political and economic questions for the future of Europe.

2015

Greece defaults on loan payments. Bailout proposals with tough conditions trigger riots and Greek banks close.

2016

Some EU borders are shut as millions of refugees and other unofficial migrants attempt to reach safe European havens.

2017

Following a referendum in favour of quitting the EU, the UK triggers Article 50 setting in motion 'Brexit'.

Arts & Architecture

For millennia great art and architecture has sprung forth from Europe. The continent's museums and galleries are repositories of all kinds of creative treasures. Caesars, royal families and wealthy elites served as patrons to artists of the stature of Michelangelo, Rembrandt and Monet. Modern and contemporary architects such as Antonio Gaudí and Richard Rogers have designed buildings that are mammoth works of art in their own right.

Arts

Medieval Art

During the Middle Ages, the power of the Church and its importance as an artistic patron meant that the majority of medieval art dealt with religious subjects. The Old Testament, the crucifixion, the apostles and the Last Judgment were common topics. Some of the finest medieval artworks are actually woven into the fabric of Europe's churches in the form of frescoes painted onto panels or walls.

Centre Georges Pompidou (p272)
designed by Renzo Piano and Richard Rogers

PICS FACTORY / SHUTTERSTOCK ©

★ **Best Modern Art Galleries**

Tate Modern (p77), London

Museu Picasso (p204), Barcelona

Centre Pompidou (p272), Paris

Designmuseum Danmark (p136),
Copenhagen

Flemish and German painting produced several important figures during the period, including Jan van Eyck (c1390–1441) and Hans Memling (c1430–94), known for their lifelike oils, and Hieronymus Bosch (1450–1516), known for his use of fantastic imagery and allegorical concepts.

The Renaissance

The Renaissance marked Europe's golden age of art. Artists such as Leonardo da Vinci (1452–1519), Michelangelo (1475–1564), Raphael (1483–1520), Titian (c1488/90–1576) and Botticelli (1445–1510) introduced new techniques, colours and forms into the artistic lexicon, drawing inspiration from the sculptors and artists of the classical world.

Landscape and the human form gained increasing importance during the Renaissance. Michelangelo's masterpiece, David, is often cited as the perfect representation of the human figure (despite the fact that the artist deliberately distorted its proportions to make it more pleasing to the eye). The sculpture is now displayed at the Galleria dell'Accademia in Florence. Florence's Galleria degli Uffizi contains the greatest collection of Italian Renaissance art.

In the wake of the Renaissance came the great names of the baroque period, epitomised by the Italian artist Caravaggio (1571–1610) and the Dutch artists Rembrandt (1606–69), Rubens (1577–1640) and Johannes Vermeer (1632–75). The baroque artists employed light and shadow (*chiaroscuro*) to heighten the drama of a scene and give their work a photographic intensity.

Romanticism & Impressionism

During the 18th century, Romantic artists such as Caspar David Friedrich (1774–1840) and JMW Turner (1775–1851) explored the drama of the natural landscape – cloud-capped mountains, lonely hilltops, peaceful meadows and moody sunsets. Other artists, such as Théodore Géricault (1791–1824) and Eugène Délacroix (1798–1863), drew inspiration from French history and prominent people of the day. One of Spain's most important artists, Francisco Goya (1746–1828), covered everything from royal portraits to war scenes, bull-fight etchings and tapestry designs.

During the late 19th century, artists such as Claude Monet (1840–1926), Edgar Degas (1834–1917), Camille Pissarro (1830–1903), Edouard Manet (1832–83) and Pierre-Auguste Renoir (1841–1919) aimed to capture the general 'impression' of a scene rather than its naturalistic representation (hence the name of their movement, 'Impressionism').

Their bold experiments with light, colour and form segued into that of their successors, the post-Impressionists such as Paul Cézanne (1839–1906), Vincent van Gogh (1853–90) and Paul Gauguin (1848–1903).

From Fauvism to Conceptual Art

The upheavals of the 20th century inspired many new artistic movements. The fauvists were fascinated by colour, typified by Henri Matisse (1869–1954), while the cubists, such as Georges Braque (1882–1963) and Pablo Picasso (1881–1973), broke their work down into abstract forms, taking inspiration from everything from primitive art to psychoanalysis.

The dadaists and surrealists took these ideas to their illogical extreme, exploring dreams and the subconscious: key figures include René Magritte (1898– 1967) from Belgium, Max Ernst (1891–1976) from Germany, and Joan Miró (1893–1983) and Salvador Dalí (1904–89) from Spain.

Modern & Contemporary Art

The late 20th century and 21st century to date have introduced many more artistic movements: abstract expressionism, neoplasticism, minimalism, formalism and pop art, to name a few.

Britain has a particularly vibrant contemporary art scene: key names such as Tracy Emin (1963–), Dinos (1962–) and Jake (1966–) Chapman (known as the Chapman Brothers), Rachel Whiteread (1963–), Mark Wallinger (1959–) and Damien Hirst (1965–), famous for his pickled shark and diamond-encrusted skull, continue to provoke controversy.

Top Musical Destinations

Vienna The Staatsoper is the premier venue in a city synonymous with opera and classical music.

Berlin Everything from the world's most acclaimed techno venue to the Berlin Philharmonic can be seen in Germany's music-obsessed capital.

Dublin The Irish have music in their blood and it takes little to get them singing, particularly down the pub.

Lisbon Portuguese love the melancholic and nostalgic songs of fado; hear it in the city's Alfama district.

Reykjavík Iceland's capital has a vibrant live-music scene producing famous pop talents such as Björk and Sigur Rós.

Architecture

Greek & Roman Architecture

Athens is the best place to appreciate Greece's golden age: the dramatic monuments of the Acropolis illustrate the ancient Greeks' sophisticated understanding of geometry, shape and form, and set the blueprint for many of the architectural principles that have endured to the present day.

The Romans were even more ambitious, and built a host of monumental structures designed to project the might and majesty of the Roman Empire. Roman architecture was driven by a combination of form and function – structures such as the Pont du Gard in southern France show how the Romans valued architecture that looked beautiful but also served a practical purpose. Rome has the greatest concentration of architectural treasures, including the famous Colosseum, but remains of Roman buildings are scattered all over the continent.

Romanesque & Gothic Architecture

The solidity and elegance of ancient Roman architecture echoed through the 10th and 11th centuries in buildings constructed during the Romanesque period. Many of Europe's

Reichstag (p438)

★ **Best Modern Buildings**

Reichstag (p438), Berlin

Centre Pompidou (p272), Paris

La Sagrada Família (p184), Barcelona

earliest churches are classic examples of Romanesque construction, using rounded arches, vaulted roofs, and massive columns and walls.

Even more influential was the development of Gothic architecture, which gave rise to many of Europe's most spectacular cathedrals. Telltale characteristics include the use of pointed arches, ribbed vaulting, great showpiece windows and flying buttresses.

Renaissance & Baroque Architecture

The Renaissance led to a huge range of architectural experiments. Pioneering Italian architects such as Brunelleschi, Michelangelo and Palladio shifted the emphasis away from Gothic austerity towards a more human approach. They combined elements of classical architecture with new building materials, and specially commissioned sculptures and decorative artworks. Florence and Venice are particularly rich in Renaissance buildings, but the movement's influence can be felt right across Europe.

Architectural showiness reached its zenith during the baroque period, when architects pulled out all the stops to show off the wealth and prestige of their clients. Baroque buildings are all about creating drama, and architects often employed swathes of craftsmen and used the most expensive materials available to create the desired effect. Paris' Hôtel des Invalides is a good example of the ostentation and expense that underpinned baroque architecture.

The Industrial Age

The 19th century was the great age of urban planning, when the chaotic streets and squalid slums of many of Europe's cities were swept away in favour of grand squares and ruler-straight boulevards. One of the most obvious examples of urban remodelling was Baron Haussmann's reinvention of Paris during the late 19th century, which resulted in the construction of the city's great boulevards and many of its landmark buildings.

Nineteenth-century architects began to move away from the showiness of the baroque and rococo periods in favour of new materials such as brick, iron and glass. Neo-Gothic architecture was designed to emphasise permanence, solidity and power, reflecting the confidence of the industrial age. It was an era that gave rise to many of Europe's great public buildings, including many landmark museums, libraries, city halls and train stations.

The 20th Century

By the turn of the 20th century, the worlds of art and architecture had both begun to experiment with new approaches to shape and form. The flowing shapes and natural forms of art nouveau had a profound influence on the work of Charles Rennie

Mackintosh in Glasgow, the Belgian architect Victor Horta and the Modernista buildings of Spanish visionary Antonio Gaudí. Meanwhile, other architects stripped their buildings back to the bare essentials, emphasising strict function over form: Le Corbusier, Ludwig Mies van der Rohe and Walter Gropius are among the most influential figures of the period.

Functional architecture continued to dominate much of the mid 20th century, especially in the rush to reconstruct Europe's shattered cities in the wake of two world wars, although the 'concrete box' style of architecture has largely fallen out of fashion over recent decades. Europeans may have something of a love-hate relationship with modern architecture, but the best buildings eventually find their place – a good example is the inside-out Centre Pompidou in Paris (designed by the architectural team of Richard Rogers, Renzo Piano and Gianfranco Franchini), which initially drew howls of protest but is now considered one of the icons of 20th-century architecture.

Contemporary Architecture

The fashion for sky-high skyscrapers seems to have caught on in several European cities, especially London, where a rash of multistorey buildings have recently been completed, all with their own nickname (the Walkie Talkie, the Cheesegrater and so on). The official name for the Norman Foster–designed 'Gherkin' buildling is 30 St Mary Axe. Topping them all is the Shard, which became the EU's highest building at 309.6m when it was completed in 2013.

A quirky peacock among Rome's classical architecture is the Maxxi, a contemporary art museum designed by the late Zaha Hadid. Norman Foster's Reichstag is an icon of modern, unified Germany, while Frank Gehry's Museo Guggenheim is a silvery masterpiece that is perhaps Europe's most dazzling piece of modern architecture.

Italian cheese, cured meats and flatbread

KABVISIO / GETTY IMAGES ©

Food & Drink

Europe is united by its passion for eating and drinking with gusto. Every country has its own flavours, incorporating olive oils and sun-ripened vegetables in the hot south, rich cream and butter in cooler areas, fresh-off-the-boat seafood along the coast, delicate river and lake fish, and meat from fertile mountains and pastures. Each country has its own tipples, too, spanning renowned wines, beers, stouts and ciders, and feistier firewater.

Britain & Ireland

Britain might not have a distinctive cuisine, but it does have a thriving food culture, with a host of celebrity chefs and big-name restaurants. Britain's colonial legacy has also left it with a taste for curry – a recent poll suggested the nation's favourite food was chicken tikka masala.

The Brits love a good roast, traditionally eaten on a Sunday and accompanied by roast potatoes, vegetables and gravy. The classic is roast beef with Yorkshire pudding (a crisp batter puff), but lamb, pork and chicken are equally popular. 'Bangers and mash' (sausages and mashed potato) and fish and chips (battered cod or haddock served with thick-cut fried potatoes) are also old favourites.

Specialities in Scotland include haggis served with 'tatties and neeps' (potato and turnip). Ireland's traditional dishes reflect the country's rustic past: look out for colcannon (mashed potato with cabbage), coddle (sliced sausages with bacon, potato and onion) and boxty (potato pancake), plus classic Irish stew (usually made with lamb or mutton).

The traditional British brew is ale, served at room temperature and flat, in order to bring out the hoppy flavours. It's an acquired taste, especially if you're used to cold, fizzy lagers. Ireland's trademark ale is stout – usually Guinness, but you can also sample those produced by Murphy's or Beamish.

Scotland and Ireland are both known for whisky-making, with many distilleries open for tours and tasting sessions.

Denmark & Iceland

In Copenhagen you can sample creations inspired by the New Nordic culinary movement that has got foodies the world over talking. Simpler but no less tasty are smørrebrød, slices of rye bread topped with anything from beef tartar to egg and prawns.

The caraway-spiced schnapps *akvavit* is Denmark's best loved spirit – drink it as a shot followed by a chaser of *øl* (beer). Denmark is also the home of Carlsberg as well as a battalion of microbreweries including Mikkeller and Grauballe.

Fish, seafood, lamb, bread and simple vegetables still form the typical Icelandic diet. A popular snack is Harðfiskur – dried strips of haddock eaten with butter. More challenging dishes include *svið* (singed sheep's head, complete with eyes, sawn in two, boiled and eaten fresh or pickled); and the famous stomach churner, *hákarl* – Greenland shark, an animal so inedible it has to rot away underground for six months before humans can even digest it.

Wash it all down with the traditional alcoholic brew *brennivín* (schnapps made from potatoes and caraway seeds), a drink fondly known as 'black death'. If that's not to your taste, there are plenty of craft beers.

Spain

Spain's cuisine is typical of the flavours of Mediterranean cooking, making extensive use of tomatoes, onions, garlic and lashings of olive oil. The nation's signature dish is *paella*, consisting of rice and chicken, meat or seafood, simmered with saffron in a large pan. Valencia is considered the spiritual home of *paella*.

Spain also prides itself on its ham and spicy sausages (including *chorizo*, *lomo* and *salchichón*). These are often used in making the bite-size Spanish dishes known as tapas (or *pintxos* in the Basque region). Tapas is usually a snack, but it can also be a main meal – three or four dishes are generally enough for one person.

Spain boasts the largest area (1.2 million hectares) of wine cultivation in the world. La Rioja and Ribera del Duero are the principal wine-growing regions.

Portugal

The Portuguese take pride in simple but flavourful dishes honed to perfection over the centuries. Bread remains integral to every meal, and it even turns up in some main courses. Be on the lookout for *açorda* (bread stew, often served with shellfish), *migas* (bread pieces prepared as a side dish) and *ensopados* (stews with toasted or deep-fried bread).

Europe's Favourite Cheeses

Britain Cheddar is tops but also try Wensleydale, Red Leicester and Stilton.

Spain Manchego, a semihard sheep's cheese with a buttery flavour, is often used in tapas.

France The big names are camembert, brie, Livarot, Pont l'Évêque and Époisses (all soft cheeses); Roquefort and Bleu d'Auvergne (blue cheeses); and Comté, cantal and gruyère (hard cheeses).

Netherlands Edam and gouda, sometimes served as bar snacks with mustard.

Italy Prestigious varieties include Parmesan, ricotta and mozzarella.

Switzerland Emmental and gruyère are the best-known Swiss cheeses.

British Sunday roast

★ **Best Foodie Experiences**

Sunday roast in a British pub (p84)

A light-as-air macaron in Paris (p280)

Crispy pizza in a real Roman pizzeria (p361)

Coffee and cake in a Vienna cafe (p593)

Seafood stews are superb, particularly *caldeirada*, which is a mix of fish and shellfish in a rich broth, not unlike a bouillabaisse. *Bacalhau* (dried salt-cod) is bound up in myth, history and tradition, and is excellent in baked dishes. Classic meat dishes include *porco preto* (sweet 'black' pork), *cabrito assado* (roast kid) and *arroz de pato* (duck risotto).

Portuguese wines are also well worth sampling, including the fortified port and reds from the Douro valley, and *alvarinho* and *vinho verde* (crisp, semisparkling wine) from the Minho.

France

Each French region has its distinctive dishes. Broadly, the hot south favours dishes based around olive oil, garlic and tomatoes, while the cooler north tends towards root vegetables, earthy flavours and creamy or buttery sauces.

Bouillabaisse, a saffron-scented fish stew, is a signature southern dish. It's served with spicy rouille sauce, gruyère cheese and croutons. The Alps are the place to try fondue, hunks of toasted bread dipped into cheese sauces. Brittany and Normandy are big on seafood, especially mussels and oysters. Central France prides itself on its hearty cuisine, including *foie gras* (goose liver), *boeuf bourgignon* (beef cooked in red wine), *confit de canard* (duck cooked in preserved fat) and black truffles.

France is Europe's biggest wine producer. The principal regions are Alsace, Bordeaux, Burgundy, Languedoc, the Loire and the Rhône, all of which produce reds, whites and rosés. Then, of course, there's Champagne – home to the world's favourite bubbly, aged in centuries-old cellars beneath Reims and Épernay.

The Netherlands

The Netherlands' colonial legacy has given the Dutch a taste for Indonesian and Surinamese-inspired meals like *rijsttafel* (rice table): an array of spicy dishes such as braised beef, pork satay and ribs, all served with white rice. Other Dutch dishes to look out for are *erwertensoep* (pea soup with onions, carrots, sausage and bacon), *krokotten* (filled dough balls that are crumbed and deep-fried) and, of course, *friet* (fries).

Beer is the tipple of choice. Small Dutch brewers like Gulpen, Haarlem's Jopen, Bavaria, Drie Ringen and Leeuw are all excellent. Jenever (gin) is also a favourite in the Netherlands.

Italy

Italian cuisine is dominated by the twin staples of pizza and pasta, which have been eaten in Italy since Roman times. A full meal comprises an *antipasto* (starter), *primo* (pasta or rice dish), *secondo* (usually meat or fish), *contorno* (vegetable side dish or salad), *dolce* (dessert) and coffee.

Italian pasta comes in numerous shapes, from bow-shaped *farfalle* to twisty *fusilli*, ribbed *rigatoni* and long *pappardelle*. Italian pasta is made with durum flour, which gives it a distinctive *al dente* bite; the type of pasta used is usually dictated by the type of dish being served (ribbed or shaped pastas hold sauce better, for example).

Italian pizza comes in two varieties: the Roman pizza with a thin crispy base, and the Neapolitan pizza, which has a higher, doughier base. The best are always prepared in a *forno a legna* (wood-fired oven).

Italy's wines run the gamut from big-bodied reds such as Piedmont's Barolo, to light white wines from Sardinia and sparkling prosecco from the Veneto.

Germany, Austria & Switzerland

The Germanic nations are all about big flavours and big portions. *Wurst* (sausage) comes in hundreds of forms, and is often served with *sauerkraut* (fermented cabbage).

The most common types of *Wurst* include *Bratwurst* (roast sausage), *Weisswurst* (veal sausage) and *Currywurst* (sliced sausage topped with ketchup and curry powder). Austria's signature dish is *Wiener Schnitzel* (breaded veal cutlet) but schnitzel in general (usually featuring pork) is also popular in Germany.

Sweet Treats

From pralines to puddings, Europe specialises in foods that are sweet, sticky and sinful. Germans and Austrians have a particularly sweet tooth – treats include *Salzburger nockerl* (a fluffy soufflé) and *Schwarzwälder kirschtorte* (Black Forest cherry cake), plus many types of *apfeltasche* (apple pastry) and *strudel* (filled filo pastry).

The Italians are famous for their *gelaterie* (ice-cream stalls; the best will be labelled *produzione propria*, indicating that it's handmade on the premises). In Lisbon, don't miss out on the deliciously creamy egg custard tarts known as *pastel de nata*.

But it's the French who have really turned dessert into a fine art. Stroll past the window of any *boulangerie* (bakery) or patisserie and you'll be assaulted by temptations, from creamy *éclairs* (filled choux buns) and crunchy *macarons* (macaroons) to fluffy *madeleines* (shell-shaped sponge cakes) and wicked *gâteaux* (cakes).

The Swiss are known for their love of fondue and the similar dish raclette (melted cheese with potatoes).

Beer is the national beverage in Germany. *Pils* is the crisp pilsner Germany is famous for, often slightly bitter. Weizenbier is made with wheat instead of barley malt and served in a tall, 500mL glass. Helles bier is light beer, while Dunkles bier is dark.

Germany is principally known for white wines – inexpensive, light and intensely fruity. The Rhine and Moselle Valleys are the largest wine-growing regions.

Croatia

Croatian food echoes the varied cultures that have influenced the country over its history. There's a sharp divide between the Italian-style cuisine along the coast and the flavours of Hungary, Austria and Turkey in the continental parts. From grilled sea bass smothered in olive oil in Dalmatia to robust, paprika-heavy meat stews in Slavonia, each region proudly touts its own speciality, but everywhere you'll find tasty food made from fresh, seasonal ingredients.

Croatia is famous for its *rakija* (grappa), which comes in different flavours. The most commonly drunk are *loza* (made from grapes, like the Italian grappa), *šljivovica* (plum brandy) and *travarica* (herbal brandy).

Greece & Turkey

The essence of traditional Greek cuisine lies in seasonal homegrown produce. Dishes are simply seasoned. Lemon juice, garlic, pungent Greek oregano and extra virgin olive oil

Vegetarians & Vegans

Vegetarians will have a tough time in many areas of Europe – eating meat is still the norm, and fish is often seen as a vegetarian option. However, you'll usually find something meat-free on most menus, though don't expect much choice. Vegans will have an even tougher time – cheese, cream and milk are integral ingredients of most European cuisines.

Vegetable-based antipasti (starters), tapas, meze, pastas, side dishes and salads are good options for a meat-free meal. Shopping for yourself in markets is an ideal way of trying local flavours without having to compromise your principles.

are the quintessential flavours, along with tomato, parsley, dill, cinnamon and cloves.

Greeks are masterful with grilled and spit-roasted meats. Souvlaki – arguably the national dish – comes in many forms, from cubes of grilled meat on a skewer to pitta-wrapped snacks with pork or chicken gyros done kebab-style on a rotisserie. Fish is often grilled whole and drizzled with *lad-holemono* (lemon-and-oil dressing). Other favourite dishes include mayirefta (home-style, one-pot, baked or casserole dishes), mezedhes (small shared dishes) and the ubiquitous Greek salad (*horiatiki* or 'village salad'), made of tomatoes, cucumber, onions, feta and olives.

Ouzo – Greece's famous liquor – is made from distilled grapes with residuals from fruit, grains and potatoes, and flavoured with spices, primarily aniseed, giving it that liquorice flavour. Beyond ouzo, the Greek wine renaissance has been gaining international attention and awards.

Turks love to eat out, particularly in restaurants serving their beloved national cuisine. In İstanbul, the Syrian-influenced dishes of Turkey's southeast are particularly fashionable at the moment, but the number one choice when it comes to dining out is almost inevitably a Black Sea–style fish restaurant or meyhane. The only dishes that can be said to be unique to İstanbul are those served at Ottoman restaurants where the rich concoctions enjoyed by the sultans and their courtiers are recreated.

Czech Republic

Like many nations in Eastern Europe, Czech cuisine revolves around meat, potatoes and root vegetables, dished up in stews, goulashes and casseroles. *Pečená kachna* (roast duck) is the quintessential Czech restaurant dish, while *klobása* (sausage) is a common beer snack. A common side dish is *knedliky*, boiled dumplings made from wheat or potato flour.

The Czechs have a big beer culture, with some of Europe's best *pivo* (beer), usually lager style. The Moravian region is the up-and-coming area for Czech wines.

Hungary

Hungary has an ever-increasing range of eating options, particularly in Budapest. For most places, it's fine to book on the day or not at all; for fine dining in Budapest, book a week or so ahead if possible.

Restaurants Range from cheap Hungarian to refined sushi and Michelin-starred fine-dining establishments.

Vendéglő Regional restaurants typically serving inexpensive, homestyle cooking.

Cafes Open during the day, these are great for coffee, cake and light (or sometimes substantial) meals.

Csárda Typically rustic places serving large portions of Hungarian cuisine, often accompanied by Gypsy music.

Hungary has a half-dozen main wine regions, and these wines tend to be relatively inexpensive and of excellent quality; they can be sampled in bars and restaurants all over the country.

Trams in Lisbon (p234)

BENNY MARTY / SHUTTERSTOCK ©

Survival Guide

Directory A–Z

Accessible Travel

Cobbled medieval streets, 'classic' hotels, congested inner cities and underground subway systems make Europe a tricky destination for people with mobility issues. However, the train facilities are good and some destinations boast new tram services or lifts to platforms.

Download Lonely Planet's free Accessible Travel guide from http://lptravel.to/AccessibleTravel. The following websites can help with specific details.

Accessible Europe (www.accessibleurope.com) Specialist European tours with van transport.

Book Your Stay Online

For more accommodation reviews by Lonely Planet authors, check out http://hotels.lonelyplanet.com/europe. You'll find independent reviews, as well as recommendations on the best places to stay. Best of all, you can book online.

DisabledGo.com (www.disabledgo.com) Detailed access information for thousands of venues across the UK and Ireland.

Mobility International Schweiz (www.mis-ch.ch) Good site (only partly in English) listing 'barrier-free' destinations in Switzerland and abroad, plus wheelchair-accessible hotels in Switzerland.

Mobility International USA (www.miusa.org) Publishes guides and advises travellers with disabilities on mobility issues.

Society for Accessible Travel & Hospitality (SATH; www.sath.org) Reams of information for travellers with disabilities.

Accommodation

Reservations

During peak holiday periods, particularly Easter, summer and Christmas – and any time of year in popular destinations such as London, Paris and Rome – it's wise to book ahead. Most places can be reserved online. Always try to book directly with the establishment; this means you're paying just for your room, with no surcharge going to a hostel- or hotel-booking website.

B&Bs & Guesthouses

Guesthouses (pension, Gasthaus, chambre d'hôte etc) and B&Bs offer greater comfort than hostels for a marginally higher price.

Most are simple affairs, normally with shared bathrooms.

In some destinations, particularly in Eastern Europe, locals wait in train stations, touting rented rooms. Just be sure such accommodation isn't in a far-flung suburb that requires an expensive taxi ride to and from town. Confirm the price before agreeing to rent a room and remember that it's unwise to leave valuables in your room when you go out.

B&Bs in the UK and Ireland often aren't really budget accommodation – even the lowliest tend to have midrange prices and there is a new generation of 'designer' B&Bs, which are positively top end.

Camping

Most camping grounds are some distance from city centres. National tourist offices provide lists of camping grounds and camping organisations. Also see www.coolcamping.co.uk for details on prime campsites across Europe.

Homestays & Farmstays

You needn't volunteer on a farm to sleep on it. In Switzerland and Germany, there's the opportunity to sleep in barns or 'hay hotels'. Farmers provide cotton undersheets (to avoid straw pricks) and woolly blankets for extra warmth, but guests need their own sleeping bag and torch. For further details, visit Abenteuer im

Stroh (www.schlaf-im-stroh.ch).

Italy has a similar and increasingly popular network of farmstays called *agriturismi*. Participating farms must grow at least one of their own crops. Otherwise, accommodation runs the gamut from small rustic hideaways to grand country estates. See www.agriturismo.it for more details.

Hostels

You can organise a lengthy excursion in Europe based purely in cheap hostels – as any nostalgic InterRailer will happily relate.

HI hostels (those affiliated to Hostelling International; www.hihostels.com) usually offer the cheapest (secure) roof over your head in Europe and you don't have to be particularly young to use them. That said, if you're over 26 you'll frequently pay a small surcharge (usually about €3) to stay in an official hostel.

Hostel rules vary per facility and country, but some ask that guests vacate the rooms for cleaning purposes or impose a curfew. Most offer a complimentary breakfast, although the quality varies.

You need to be a YHA or HI member to use HI-affiliated hostels, but nonmembers can stay by paying a few extra euros, which will be set against future membership. After sufficient nights (usually six), you automatically become a member. To join,

ask at any hostel or contact your national hostelling office, which you'll find on the HI website – where you can also make online bookings.

Europe has many private hostelling organisations and hundreds of unaffiliated backpacker hostels. These have fewer rules, more self-catering kitchens and fewer large, noisy school groups. Dorms in many private hostels can be mixed sex. If you aren't happy to share mixed dorms, be sure to ask when you book.

Price Ranges

Rates in our reviews are for high season and often drop outside high season by as much as 50%. High season in ski resorts is usually between Christmas and New Year and around the February to March winter holidays.

Hotels

Hotels are usually the most expensive accommodation option, though at their lower end there is little to differentiate them

Climate

London

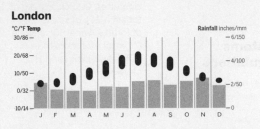

Paris

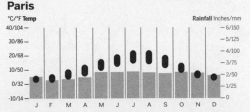

Rome

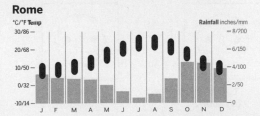

from guesthouses or even hostels.

Cheap hotels around bus and train stations can be convenient for late-night or early-morning arrivals and departures, but some are also unofficial brothels or just downright sleazy. Check the room beforehand and make sure you're clear on the price and what it covers.

Discounts for longer stays are usually possible and hotel owners in southern Europe might be open to a little bargaining if times are slack. In many countries it's common for business hotels (usually more than two stars) to slash their rates by up to 40% on Friday and Saturday nights.

Customs Regulations

The EU has a two-tier customs system: one for goods bought duty-free to import to or export from the EU, and one for goods bought in another EU country where taxes and duties have already been paid.

• When entering or leaving the EU, you are allowed to carry duty-free 200 cigarettes, 50 cigars or 250g of tobacco; 2L of still wine plus 1L of spirits over 22% alcohol or another 4L of wine (sparkling or otherwise); for other goods (eg, coffee, perfume, electronics) up to €430 (air/sea entry) or €300 (land entry).

• When travelling from one EU country to another, the duty-paid limits are 800 cigarettes, 200 cigars, 1kg of tobacco, 10L of spirits, 20L of fortified wine, 90L of wine (of which not more than 60L is sparkling) and 110L of beer.

Electricity

Europe generally runs on 220V, 50Hz AC, but there are exceptions. The UK runs on 230/240V AC, and some old buildings in Italy and Spain have 125V (or even 110V in Spain). The continent is moving towards a 230V standard. If your home country has a vastly different voltage you will need a transformer for delicate and important appliances.

The UK and Ireland use three-pin square plugs. Most of Europe uses the 'europlug' with two round pins. Greece, Italy and Switzerland use a third round pin in a way that the two-pin plug usually – but not always in Italy and Switzerland – fits. Buy an adapter before leaving home; those on sale in Europe generally

Type C
220V/50Hz

Type F
230V/50Hz

Type G
230V/50Hz

go the other way, but ones for visitors to Europe are also available – airports are always a good place to buy them.

Food

Rates in our reviews are based on the price of a main meal.

Health

Before You Go

Recommended Vaccinations

No jabs are necessary for Europe. However, the World Health Organization (WHO) recommends that all travellers be covered for diphtheria, tetanus, measles, mumps, rubella and polio, regardless of their destination. Since most vaccines don't produce immunity until at least two weeks after they're given, visit a physician at least six weeks before departure.

Health Insurance

It is unwise to travel anywhere in the world without travel insurance. A good policy should include comprehensive health insurance including medical care and emergency evacuation. If you are engaging in hazardous sports, you may need to pay for extra cover.

If you're an EU citizen, the free EHIC (European Health Insurance Card) covers you for most medical care in the 28 EU member states, including maternity care and care for chronic illnesses such as diabetes (though not for emergency repatriation). However, you will normally have to pay for medicine bought from pharmacies, even if prescribed, and perhaps for some tests and procedures. The EHIC does not cover private medical consultations and treatment out of your home country; this includes nearly all dentists, and some of the better clinics and surgeries. In the UK, you can apply for an EHIC online, by telephone, or by filling out a form available at post offices.

Non-EU citizens should find out if there is a reciprocal arrangement for free medical care between their country and the EU country they are visiting.

Websites

The World Health Organization (www.who.int) publishes the free online book *International Travel and Health,* which is revised annually. MD Travel Health (www.mdtravelhealth.com) provides up-to-date travel-health recommendations for every country.

It's usually a good idea to consult your government's website before departure, if one is available:

○ **Australia** (www.smartraveller.gov.au)

Tap Water

Tap water is generally safe to drink in Western Europe. However, bottled water is recommended in most of Eastern Europe and is a must in some countries, including Russia and Ukraine, where the giardia parasite can be a problem. Do not drink water from rivers or lakes as it may contain bacteria or viruses.

○ **Canada** (www.phac-aspc.gc.ca)

○ **UK** (www.gov.uk/foreign-travel-advice)

○ **USA** (www.cdc.gov/travel)

In Europe

Good healthcare is readily available in Western Europe, and for minor illnesses, pharmacists can give valuable advice and sell over-the-counter medication. They can also advise if you need specialised help and point you in the right direction. The standard of dental care is usually good.

While the situation in Eastern Europe is improving since the EU accession of many countries, quality medical care is not always readily available outside major cities. Embassies, consulates and five-star hotels can usually recommend doctors or clinics.

Condoms are widely available in Europe, however emergency contraception may not be, so take the necessary precautions.

With Brexit negotiations ongoing as of early 2019, it is unclear how the EHIC health card will be affected for British citizens. Check www.nhs.uk for updates.

Insurance

It's foolhardy to travel without insurance to cover theft, loss and medical problems. There is a wide variety of policies, so check the small print.

Some policies specifically exclude 'dangerous activities', which can include scuba diving, motorcycling, winter sports, adventure sports or even hiking.

Check that the policy covers ambulances or an emergency flight home.

Worldwide travel insurance is available online at www.lonelyplanet.com/travel-insurance. You can buy, extend and claim online anytime – even if you're already on the road.

Internet Access

Internet access varies enormously across Europe. In most places, you'll be able to find wireless (wi-fi, also called WLAN in some countries), although whether it's free varies greatly.

Where the wi-fi icon appears, it means that the establishment offers free wi-fi that you can access immediately, or by asking for the access code from staff.

Access is generally straightforward, although a few tips are in order. If you can't find the @ symbol on a keyboard, try Alt Gr + 2, or Alt Gr + Q. Watch out for German keyboards, which reverse the Z and the Y positions. Using a French keyboard is an art unto itself.

Where necessary in relevant countries, click on the language prompt in the bottom right-hand corner of the screen or hit Ctrl + Shift to switch between the Cyrillic and Latin alphabets.

Legal Matters

You can generally purchase alcohol (beer and wine) from between the age of 16 and 18 (usually 18 years for spirits), but if in doubt, ask. Although you can drive at 17 or 18 years, you might not be able to hire a car until you're 25.

Drugs are often quite openly available in Europe, but that doesn't mean they're legal. The Netherlands is most famed for its liberal attitudes, with coffee shops openly selling cannabis even though the drug is not technically legal. However, a blind eye is generally turned to the trade as the possession and purchase of small amounts (5g) of 'soft drugs' (ie marijuana and hashish) is allowed and users won't be prosecuted for smoking or carrying this amount. Don't take this relaxed attitude as an invitation to buy harder drugs; if you get caught, you'll be punished. Since 2008 magic mushrooms have been banned in the Netherlands.

Spain also has pretty liberal laws regarding marijuana, although its use is usually reserved for private places.

In Belgium the possession of up to 3g of cannabis is legal, but selling the drug isn't, so if you get caught at the point of sale, you could be in trouble. Switzerland, Italy, Moldova, Russia, Ukraine, Malta, Luxembourg, Estonia, Croatia, Austria, Slovenia and the Czech Republic have also decriminalised possession of marijuana, but selling remains illegal. Portugal was the first country to decriminalise the use of all drugs in 2001.

Getting caught with drugs in some parts of Europe can lead to imprisonment. If in any doubt, err on the side of caution, and don't even think about taking drugs across international borders.

LGBT+ Travellers

Across Western Europe you'll find very liberal attitudes towards homosexuality. The Netherlands, Belgium and Spain were the first three countries in the world to legalise same-sex marriage in 2001, 2003 and 2005, respectively. Further east, while there is no legislation against it, homosexuality is frowned upon by many locals – especially outside major cities – and it pays to be discreet.

London, Paris, Berlin, Munich, Amsterdam, Madrid, Lisbon and İstanbul have thriving gay communities and pride events. There's a small gay scene in Budapest and Dubrovnik has a gay beach. The Greek islands of Mykonos and Lesvos are popular gay beach destinations, while Gran Canaria and Ibiza in Spain are big centres for both gay clubbing and beach holidays.

Maps

Tourist offices usually provide free but fairly basic maps.

Road atlases are essential if you're driving or cycling. Leading brands are Freytag & Berndt, Hallwag, Kümmerly + Frey, and Michelin.

Maps published by European automobile associations, such as Britain's AA (www.theaa. co.uk) and Germany's ADAC (www.adac.de), are usually excellent and sometimes free if membership of your local association gives you reciprocal rights.

Money

ATMs

Across major European towns and cities international ATMs are common, but you should always have a back-up option, as there can be glitches. In some remote areas, ATMs might be scarce.

Much of Western Europe now uses a chip-and-pin system for added security. You will have problems if you don't have a four-digit PIN number and might have difficulties if your card doesn't have a metallic chip. Check with your bank.

Always cover the keypad when entering your PIN and make sure there are no unusual devices attached to the machine, which can copy your card's details or cause it to get stuck in the machine. If your card disappears and the screen goes blank before you've even entered your PIN, don't enter it – especially if a 'helpful' bystander tells you to do so. If you can't retrieve your card, call your bank's emergency number, if you can, before leaving the ATM.

Cash

It's a good idea to bring some local currency in cash, if only to cover yourself until you get to an exchange facility or find an ATM. The equivalent of €150 should usually be enough. Some extra cash in an easily exchanged currency is also a good idea, especially in Eastern Europe.

Credit Cards

Visa and MasterCard/ Eurocard are more widely accepted in Europe than Amex and Diners Club; Visa (sometimes called Carte Bleue) is particularly strong in France and Spain.

There are, however, regional differences in the general acceptability of credit cards; in Germany, for example, it's rare for restaurants to take credit cards. Cards are not widely accepted once you're off the beaten track.

To reduce the risk of fraud, always keep your card in view when making transactions; for example, in restaurants that do accept cards, pay as you leave, following your card to the till. Keep transaction records and either check your statements when you return home, or check your account online while still on the road.

Letting your credit-card company know roughly where you're going lessens the chance of fraud – or of your bank cutting off the card when it sees (your) unusual spending.

Currency

Croatia, Czech Republic, Denmark, Hungary, Iceland, Norway, Switzerland, Turkey and the UK have their own currencies, but all other countries covered in this guide use the euro, which is made up of 100 cents. Notes come in denominations of €5, €10, €20, €50, €100, €200 and €500 euros, though any notes above 50 are rarely used on a daily basis. Coins come in 1c, 2c, 5c, 10c, 20c, 50c, €1 and €2.

Debit Cards

It's always worthwhile having a Maestro-compatible debit card, which differs from a credit card in deducting money straight from your bank account. Check with your bank or Master-Card (Maestro's parent) for compatibility.

Exchanging Money

Euros, US dollars and UK pounds are the easiest currencies to exchange. You may have trouble exchanging some lesser-known ones at small banks.

Importing or exporting some currencies is restricted or banned, so try to get rid of any local currency before you leave. Get rid of Scottish pounds before leaving the UK; nobody outside Britain will touch them.

Most airports, central train stations, big hotels and many border posts have banking facilities outside regular business hours, at times on a 24-hour basis. Post offices in Europe often perform banking tasks, tend to be open longer hours and outnumber banks in remote places. While they always exchange cash, they might balk at handling travellers cheques not in the local currency.

The best exchange rates are usually at banks. *Bureaux de change* usually – but not always – offer worse rates or charge higher commissions. Hotels and airports are almost always the worst places to change money.

International Transfers

International bank transfers are good for secure one-off movements of large amounts of money, but they might take three to five days and there will be a fee (about £25 in the UK, for example). Be sure to specify the name of the bank, plus the sort code and address of the branch where you'd like to pick up your money. To avoid bank charges consider using an online transfer service such as TransferWise.

In an emergency it's quicker but more costly to have money wired via an Amex office or Western Union.

Taxes & Refunds

When non-EU residents spend more than a certain amount (around €75, but amounts vary from country to country), they can usually reclaim any sales tax when leaving the country.

Making a tax-back claim is straightforward. First, make sure the shop offers duty-free sales (often a sign will be displayed reading 'Tax-Free Shopping'). When making your purchase, ask the shop attendant for a tax-refund voucher, filled in

with the correct amount and the date. This can be used to claim a refund directly at international airports, or stamped at ferry ports or border crossings and mailed back for a refund.

Tipping

○ 'Service charges' are increasingly added to bills. In theory this means you're not obliged to tip. In practice that money often doesn't go to the server. Don't pay twice. If the service charge is optional, remove it and pay a tip. If it's not optional, don't tip.

○ Tipping isn't such a big deal in Europe as it is in North America. If you tip, 5% to 10% will usually suffice.

Opening Hours

Opening times vary significantly between countries. The following is a general overview.

Shops & businesses 9am to 6pm Monday to Friday, to 1pm or 5pm Saturday. In smaller towns there may be a one- to two-hour closure for lunch. Some shops close on Sunday. Businesses also close on national holidays and local feast days.

Banks 9am to between 3pm and 5pm Monday to Friday. Occasionally shut for lunch.

Restaurants noon to midnight

Bars 6pm to midnight or later

Museums closed Monday or (less commonly) Tuesday

Public Holidays

There are large variations in statutory holidays in Europe. The following are the most common across the board.

New Year's Day 1 January
Good Friday March/April
Easter Sunday March/April
May Day 1 May
Pentecost/Whitsun May/June
Christmas Day 25 December

Safe Travel

Travelling in Europe is usually very safe.

Discrimination

In some parts of Europe travellers of African, Arab or Asian descent might encounter unpleasant attitudes that are unrelated to them personally. In rural areas travellers whose skin colour marks them out as foreigners might experience unwanted attention.

Attitudes vary from country to country. People tend to be more accepting in cities than in the country. Race is also less of an issue in Western Europe than in parts of the former Eastern Bloc.

Druggings

Although rare, some drugging of travellers does occur in Europe. Travellers are especially vulnerable on trains

and buses where a new 'friend' may offer you food or a drink that will knock you out, giving them time to steal your belongings.

Gassings have also been reported on a handful of overnight international trains. The best protection is to lock the door of your compartment (use your own lock if there isn't one) and to lock your bags to luggage racks, preferably with a sturdy combination cable.

If you can help it, never sleep alone in a train compartment.

Pickpockets & Thieves

Theft is definitely a problem in parts of Europe and you have to be aware of unscrupulous fellow travellers. The key is to be sensible with your possessions.

○ Don't store valuables in train-station lockers or luggage-storage counters and be careful about people who offer to help you operate a locker. Also be vigilant if someone offers to carry your luggage: they might carry it away altogether.

○ Don't leave valuables in your car, on train seats or in your room. When going out, don't flaunt cameras, laptops and other expensive electronic goods.

○ Carry a small day pack, as shoulder bags are an open invitation for snatch-thieves. Consider using small zipper locks on your packs.

○ Pickpockets are most active in dense crowds,

especially in busy train stations and on public transport during peak hours. Be careful in these situations.

○ Spread valuables, cash and cards around your body or in different bags.

○ A money belt with your essentials (passport, cash, credit cards, airline tickets) is usually a good idea. However, so you needn't delve into it in public, carry a wallet with a day's worth of cash.

○ Having your passport stolen is less of a disaster if you've recorded the number and issue date or, even better, photocopied the relevant data pages. You can also scan them and email them to yourself. If you lose your passport, notify the police immediately to get a statement and contact your nearest consulate.

○ Carry photocopies of your credit cards, airline tickets and other travel documents.

Unrest & Terrorism

Civil unrest and terrorist bombings are relatively rare in Europe, all things considered, but they do

Emergency Numbers

The phone number 112 can be dialled free for emergencies in all EU states. See individual countries for country-specific emergency numbers.

occur. A spike in attacks by extremists in the UK, France, Germany, Belgium and Spain occurred in the mid-2010s – seven of them between 2015 and 2017 – although things seemed to have quietened down somewhat since. Keep an eye on the news and avoid areas where any flare-up seems likely.

Although Turkey is by no means a dangerous country to visit, particular care should be taken anywhere close to Turkey's borders with Syria and Iraq, while the country's south-east experiences periodic outbreaks of unrest.

Telephone

Mobile Phones

If your mobile phone is European, it's often perfectly feasible to use it on roaming throughout the continent.

If you're coming from outside Europe, it's usually worth buying a prepaid local SIM in one European country. Even if you're not staying there long, calls across Europe will still be cheaper if they're not routed via your home country and the prepaid card will enable you to keep a limit on your spending. In several countries you need your passport to buy a SIM card.

In order to use other SIM cards in your phone, you'll need to have your handset unlocked by your home provider. Even if your phone is locked, you can use apps such as WhatsApp to send free text messages internationally wherever you have wi-fi access, or Skype to make free international calls whenever you're online.

Europe uses the GSM 900 network, which also covers Australia and New Zealand, but is not compatible with the North American GSM 1900 or the totally different system in Japan and South Korea. If you have a GSM phone, check with your service provider about using it in Europe. You'll need international roaming, but this is usually free to enable.

You can call abroad from almost any phone box in Europe. Public telephones accepting phonecards (available from post offices, telephone centres, news stands or retail outlets) are virtually the norm now; coin-operated phones are rare if not impossible to find.

Without a phonecard, you can ring from a telephone booth inside a post office or telephone centre and settle your bill at the counter. Reverse-charge (collect) calls are often possible. From many countries the Country Direct system lets you phone home by billing the long-distance carrier you use at home. These numbers can often be dialled from public phones without even inserting a phonecard.

Time

Europe is divided into four time zones. The countries covered in this guide fall into the following zones:
UTC (Britain, Ireland, Portugal) GMT (GMT+1 in summer)
CET (the majority of European countries) GMT+1 (GMT+2 in summer)

At 9am in Britain it's 1am (GMT/UTC minus eight hours) on the US west coast, 4am (GMT/UTC minus five hours) on the US east coast, 10am in Paris and Prague, 11am in Athens, midday in Moscow and 7pm (GMT/UTC plus 10 hours) in Sydney.

Nearly all of Europe, with several exceptions (including Iceland), observes daylight saving time on synchronised dates in late March (clocks go forward an hour) and late October (clocks go back an hour).

● Britain, Ireland and Portugal (GMT)

● Central Europe (GMT plus one hour)

● Greece, Turkey and Eastern Europe (GMT plus two hours)

Toilets

Many public toilets require a small fee either deposited in a box or given to the attendant. Public-toilet provision is changeable from city to city. If you can't find one, simply drop into a hotel or restaurant and ask to use theirs.

Tourist Information

Unless otherwise indicated, tourist offices are common and widespread, although their usefulness varies enormously.

Visas

◦ Citizens of the USA, Canada, Australia, New Zealand and the UK need only a valid passport to enter nearly all countries in Europe, including the entire EU.

◦ Transit visas are usually cheaper than tourist or business visas but they allow only a very short stay (one to five days) and can be difficult to extend.

◦ All visas have a 'use-by' date and you'll be refused entry afterwards. In some cases it's easier to get visas as you go along, rather than arranging them all beforehand. Carry spare passport photos (you may need from one to four every time you apply for a visa).

◦ Visas to neighbouring countries are usually issued immediately by consulates in Eastern Europe, although some may levy a hefty surcharge for 'express service'.

◦ Consulates are generally open weekday mornings (if there's both an embassy and a consulate, you want the consulate).

Women Travellers

◦ Women might attract unwanted attention in Turkey, rural Spain and southern Italy, especially Sicily, where many men view whistling and catcalling as flattery. Conservative dress can help deter this.

◦ Hitchhiking alone is not recommended anywhere.

◦ Female readers have reported assaults at Turkish hotels with shared bathrooms, so women travelling to Turkey might want to consider a more expensive room with private bathroom.

◦ Journeywoman (www.journeywoman.com) maintains an online newsletter about solo female travels all over the world.

Transport

Getting There & Away

Europe is one of the world's major destinations, whose busiest airports have routes fanning out to the far corners of the globe. More adventurous travellers can enter from Asia on some epic long-distance train routes. Numerous ferries jockey across the Mediterranean between Europe and Africa.

Flights, cars and tours can be booked online at lonelyplanet.com/bookings.

Air

To save money, it's best to travel off-season. This means, if possible, avoid mid-June to early September, Easter, Christmas and school holidays.

Regardless of your ultimate destination, it's sometimes better to pick a recognised transport 'hub' as your initial port of entry, where high traffic volumes help keep prices down. Long-haul airfares to Eastern Europe are rarely a bargain; you're usually better off flying to a Western European hub and taking an onward budget-airline flight or train. The main hubs in Eastern Europe are Budapest and Prague.

Gateway cities such as London and Paris are also well serviced by low-cost carriers that fly to other parts of Europe.

Land

It's possible to reach Europe by various different train routes from Asia. Most common is the Trans-Siberian Railway, connecting Moscow to Siberia, the

Russian Far East, Mongolia and China. See www.seat61.com for more information about these adventurous routes.

Border Crossings

Border formalities have been relaxed in most of the EU, but still exist in all their original bureaucratic glory in the more far-flung parts of Eastern Europe.

In line with the Schengen Agreement, there are officially no passport controls at the borders between 26 European states. Sometimes, however, there are spot checks on trains crossing borders, so always have your passport. The UK maintains border controls

over traffic from other EU countries (except Ireland, with which it shares an open border), although there is no customs control. The same goes for Ireland. For up-to-date details see www.schengenvisainfo.com.

Sea

There are numerous ferry routes between Europe and Africa, including links from Spain to Morocco, Italy to Tunisia, France to Morocco and France to Tunisia. Check out www.traghettiweb.it for comprehensive information on all Mediterranean ferries. Ferries are often filled to capacity in summer, especially to and from Tunisia, so book

well in advance if you're taking a vehicle across.

Getting Around

Air

Airlines

Low-cost carriers have revolutionised European transport. Most airlines, budget or otherwise, have a similar pricing system – namely that ticket prices rise with the number of seats sold on each flight, so book as early as possible to get a decent fare.

Some low-cost carriers – Ryanair being the prime

The Schengen Area

Twenty-six European countries are signatories to the Schengen Agreement, which has effectively dismantled internal border controls between them. They are Austria, Belgium, Czech Republic, Denmark, Estonia, Finland, France, Germany, Greece, Iceland, Italy, Hungary, Latvia, Liechtenstein, Lithuania, Luxembourg, Malta, the Netherlands, Norway, Poland, Portugal, Slovenia, Slovakia, Spain, Sweden and Switzerland.

The UK and Ireland, as well as much of Eastern Europe, are not part of the Schengen Agreement. Visitors from non-EU countries will have to apply for visas to these countries separately.

Citizens of the USA, Australia, New Zealand, Canada and the UK only need a valid passport to enter Schengen countries (as well as the UK and Ireland). However, other nationals, including South Africans, can apply for a single visa – a Schengen visa – when travelling throughout this region.

Non-EU visitors (with or without a Schengen visa) should expect to be questioned, however perfunctorily, when first entering the region. However, later travel within the zone is much like a domestic trip, with no border controls.

If you need a Schengen visa, you must apply at the consulate or embassy of the country that's your main destination, or your point of entry. You may then stay up to a maximum of 90 days in the entire Schengen area within a six-month period. Once your visa has expired, you must leave the zone and may only reenter after three months abroad. Shop around when choosing your point of entry, as visa prices may differ from country to country.

If you're a citizen of the USA, Australia, New Zealand or Canada, you may stay visa-free a total of 90 days, during six months, within the entire Schengen region.

For up-to-date details see www.schengenvisainfo.com.

example – have made a habit of flying to smaller, less convenient airports on the outskirts of their destination city, or even to the airports of nearby cities, so check the exact location of the departure and arrival airports before you book. Many flights also leave at the crack of dawn or arrive inconveniently late at night.

Departure and other taxes (including booking fees, checked-baggage fees and other surcharges) soon add up and are included in the final price by the end of the online booking process – usually a lot more than you were hoping to pay – but with careful choosing and advance booking you can get excellent deals.

For a comprehensive overview of which low-cost carriers fly to or from which European cities, check out the excellent www. flycheapo.com.

Air Passes

Various travel agencies and airlines offer air passes including the three main airline alliances: **Oneworld** (www.oneworld.com), **Star Alliance** (www.staralliance. com) and **SkyTeam** (www. skyteam.com). Check with your travel agent for current promotions.

Bicycle

Much of Europe is ideally suited to cycling. It's easy to hire bikes throughout most of Europe but, for major cycling trips, it's best to have a bike you're familiar

---

Climate Change & Travel

Every form of transport that relies on carbon-based fuel generates CO_2, the main cause of human-induced climate change. Modern travel is dependent on aeroplanes, which might use less fuel per kilometre per person than most cars but travel much greater distances. The altitude at which aircraft emit gases (including CO_2) and particles also contributes to their climate change impact. Many websites offer 'carbon calculators' that allow people to estimate the carbon emissions generated by their journey and, for those who wish to do so, to offset the impact of the greenhouse gases emitted with contributions to portfolios of climate-friendly initiatives throughout the world. Lonely Planet offsets the carbon footprint of all staff and author travel.

---

with, so consider bringing your own rather than buying on arrival. If coming from outside Europe, ask about the airline's policy on transporting bikes before buying your ticket.

A primary consideration on a cycling trip is to travel light, but you should take a few tools and spare parts, including a puncture-repair kit and an extra inner tube. Panniers are essential to balance your possessions on either side of the bike frame. Wearing a helmet is not compulsory in most countries, but is certainly sensible.

Seasoned cyclists can average 80km a day, but it depends on what you're carrying and your level of fitness.

Cyclists' Touring Club (CTC; www.ctc.org.uk) The national cycling association of the UK runs organised trips to continental Europe.

European Cyclists' Federation (www.ecf.com) Has details of

'EuroVelo', the European cycle network of 12 pan-European cycle routes, plus tips for other tours.

SwitzerlandMobility (www. veloland.ch/en/cycling-in-switzerland.html) Details of Swiss national routes and more.

Boat

Several different ferry companies compete on the main ferry routes, resulting in a comprehensive but complicated service. The same ferry company can have a host of different prices for the same route, depending on the time of day or year, validity of the ticket and length of your vehicle. Vehicle tickets usually include the driver and often up to five passengers free of charge.

It's worth booking ahead where possible as there may be special reductions on off-peak crossings and advance-purchase tickets. On English Channel routes, apart from one-day or short-term excursion returns, there is little price advantage in buying a return ticket versus two singles.

Rail-pass holders are entitled to discounts or free travel on some lines. Food on ferries is often expensive (and lousy), so it is worth bringing your own. Also be aware that if you take your vehicle on board, you are usually denied access to it during the voyage.

Lake and river ferry services operate in many countries, Austria and Switzerland being just two. Some of these are very scenic.

Bus

International Buses

Europe's biggest organisation of international buses operates under the name Eurolines (www.eurolines. com), comprised of various national companies. A Eurolines Pass (www.eurolines. com/en/eurolines-pass) is offered for extensive travel, allowing passengers to visit a choice of 53 cities across Europe over 15 or 30 days. In the high season (mid-June to mid-September) the pass costs €315/405 for those aged under 26, or €375/490 for those 26 and over. It's cheaper in other periods.

Busabout (www. busabout.com) offers a 'hop-on, hop-off' service around Europe, stopping at major cities. Buses are often oversubscribed, so book each sector to avoid being stranded. It departs every two days from May to the end of October.

National Buses

Domestic buses provide a viable alternative to trains in most countries. Again, they are usually slightly cheaper and somewhat slower. Buses are generally best for short hops, such as getting around cities and reaching remote villages, and they are often the only option in mountainous regions.

Car & Motorcycle

Travelling with your own vehicle gives flexibility and is the best way to reach remote places. However, the independence does sometimes isolate you from local life. Also, cars can be a target for theft and are often impractical in city centres, where traffic jams, parking problems and getting thoroughly lost can make it well worth ditching your vehicle and using public transport. Various car-carrying trains can help you avoid long, tiring drives.

Campervan

One popular way to tour Europe is for a group of three or four people to band together and buy or rent a campervan. London is the usual embarkation point. Look at the ads in London's free magazine *TNT* (www. tntmagazine.com) if you wish to form or join a group. *TNT* is also a good source for purchasing a van, as is Loot (www.loot.com).

Some secondhand dealers offer a 'buy-back' scheme for when you return from the continent,

but check the small print before signing anything and remember that if an offer is too good to be true, it probably is. Buying and reselling privately should be more advantageous if you have time. In the UK, DUInsure (www.duinsure.com) offers a campervan policy.

Motorcycle Touring

Europe is made for motorcycle touring, with quality winding roads, stunning scenery and an active motorcycling scene. Just make sure your wet-weather motorcycling gear is up to scratch.

○ Rider and passenger crash helmets are compulsory everywhere in Europe.

○ Austria, France, Germany, Portugal and Spain require that motorcyclists use headlights during the day; in other countries it is recommended.

○ On ferries, motorcyclists rarely have to book ahead as they can generally be squeezed on board.

○ Take note of the local custom about parking motorcycles on pavements (sidewalks). Though this is illegal in some countries, the police often turn a blind eye provided the vehicle doesn't obstruct pedestrians.

Fuel

○ Fuel prices can vary enormously (though fuel is always more expensive than in North America or Australia).

o Unleaded petrol only is available throughout Europe. Diesel is usually cheaper, though the difference is marginal in Britain, Ireland and Switzerland.

o Ireland's Automobile Association maintains a webpage of European fuel prices at www.theaa.ie/aa/motoring-advice/petrol-prices.aspx.

Insurance

o Third-party motor insurance is compulsory. Most UK policies automatically provide this for EU countries. Get your insurer to issue a Green Card (which may cost extra), an internationally recognised proof of insurance, and check that it lists every country you intend to visit. You'll need this in the event of an accident outside the country where the vehicle is insured.

o Ask your insurer for a European Accident Statement form, which can simplify things if worst comes to worst. Never sign statements that you can't read or understand – insist on a translation and sign that only if it's acceptable.

o For non-EU countries, check the requirements with your insurer. Travellers from the UK can obtain additional advice and information from the Association of British Insurers (www.abi.org.uk).

o Take out a European motoring assistance policy. Non-Europeans might find it cheaper to arrange

international coverage with their national motoring organisation before leaving home. Ask your motoring organisation for details about the free services offered by affiliated organisations around Europe.

o Residents of the UK should contact the RAC (www.rac.co.uk) or the AA (www.theaa.co.uk) for more information. Residents of the US, contact AAA (www.aaa.com).

Rental

o Renting a car is ideal for people who will need cars for 16 days or fewer. Anything longer, it's better to lease.

o Big international rental firms will give you reliable service and good vehicles. National or local firms can often undercut the big companies by up to 40%.

o Usually you will have the option of returning the car to a different outlet at the end of the rental period, but there's normally a charge for this and it can be very steep if it's a long way from your point of origin.

o Book early for the lowest rates and make sure you compare rates in different cities. Taxes range from 15% to 20% and surcharges apply if rented from an airport.

o If you rent a car in the EU you might not be able to take it outside the EU, and if you rent the car outside the EU, you will only be able

to drive within the EU for eight days. Ask at the rental agencies for other such regulations.

o Make sure you understand what is included in the price (unlimited or paid kilometres, tax, injury insurance, collision damage waiver etc) and what your liabilities are. We recommend taking the collision damage waiver, though you can probably skip the injury insurance if you and your passengers have decent travel insurance.

o The minimum rental age is usually 21 years and sometimes 25. You'll need a credit card and to have held your licence for at least a year.

o Motorcycle and moped rental is common in some countries, such as Italy, Spain, Greece and southern France.

Road Conditions & Road Rules

o Conditions and types of roads vary across Europe. The fastest routes are generally four- or six-lane highways known locally as motorways, autoroutes, autostrade, autobahnen etc. These tend to skirt cities and plough through the countryside in straight lines, often avoiding the most scenic bits.

o Some highways incur tolls, which are often quite hefty (especially in Italy, France and Spain), but there will always be an alternative route. Motorways and other primary routes are generally in good condition.

○ Road surfaces on minor routes are unreliable in some countries (eg parts of eastern Europe and Ireland), although normally they will be more than adequate.

○ Except in Britain and Ireland, you should drive on the right. Vehicles brought to the continent from any of these locales should have their headlights adjusted to avoid blinding oncoming traffic (a simple solution on older headlight lenses is to cover up a triangular section of the lens with tape). Priority is often given to traffic approaching from the right in countries that drive on the right-hand side.

○ Speed limits vary from country to country. You may be surprised at the apparent disregard for traffic regulations in some places (particularly in Italy and Greece), but as a visitor it is always best to be cautious. Many driving infringements are subject to an on-the-spot fine. Always ask for a receipt.

○ European drink-driving laws are particularly strict. The blood-alcohol concentration (BAC) limit when driving is usually between 0.05% and 0.08%, but in certain areas it can be zero.

○ Always carry proof of ownership of your vehicle (Vehicle Registration Document for British-registered cars). An EU driving licence is acceptable for those driving through Europe. If you have any other type of licence, you should obtain an International Driving Permit (IDP) from your motoring organisation. Check what type of licence is required in your destination prior to departure.

○ Every vehicle that travels across an international border should display a sticker indicating its country of registration. A warning triangle, to be used in the event of breakdown, is compulsory almost everywhere.

○ Some recommended accessories include a first-aid kit (compulsory in Austria and Croatia), a spare bulb kit (compulsory in Spain), a reflective jacket for every person in the car (compulsory in France, Italy and Spain) and a fire extinguisher.

Taxis

Taxis in Europe are metered and rates are usually high. There might also be surcharges for things such as luggage, time of day, pick-up location and extra passengers.

Good bus, rail and underground-railway networks often render taxis unnecessary, but if you need one in a hurry, they can be found idling near train stations or outside big hotels. Lower fares make taxis more viable in some countries such as Spain, Greece, Portugal and Turkey.

Uber operates in most of Europe's large cities, although you won't find it in Bulgaria, Denmark or Hungary, where it is currently banned.

Train

Comfortable, frequent and reliable, trains are the way to get around Europe.

○ Many state railways have interactive websites publishing their timetables and fares, including www.bahn. de (Germany) and www.sbb. ch (Switzerland), which both have pages in English. Eurail (www.eurail.com) links to 28 European train companies.

○ The Man in Seat 61 (www. seat61.com) is very comprehensive and a gem; the US-based Budget Europe Travel Service (www.budge-teuropetravel.com) can also help with tips.

○ European trains sometimes split en route to service two destinations, so even if you're on the right train, make sure you're also in the correct carriage.

○ A train journey to almost every station in Europe can be booked via Voyages-sncf. com (http://uk.voyages-sncf.com/en), which also sells InterRail and other passes.

Language

Don't let the language barrier get in the way of your travel experience. This section offers basic phrases and pronunciation guides to help you negotiate your way around Europe. Note that in our pronunciation guides, the stressed syllables in words are indicated with italics.

To enhance your trip with a phrasebook (covering all of these languages in much greater detail), visit **lonelyplanet.com**.

Czech

Hello.	*Ahoj.*	*uh*·hoy
Goodbye.		
Na shledanou.	*nuh*·skhle·duh·noh	
Yes./No.	*Ano./Ne.*	*uh*·no/ne
Please.	*Prosím.*	*pro*·seem
Thank you.	*Děkuji.*	*dye*·ku·yi
Excuse me.	*Promiňte.*	*pro*·min'·te
Help!	*Pomoc!*	*po*·mots

Do you speak English?
Mluvíte anglicky? mlu·vee·te *uhn*·glits·ki
I don't understand.
Nerozumím. ne·ro·zu·meem
How much is this?
Kolik to stojí? *ko*·lik to *sto*·yee
I'd like ..., please.
Chtěl/Chtěla bych ..., khtyel/*khtye*·luh bikh ...
prosím. (m/f) *pro*·seem
Where's (the toilet)?
Kde je (záchod)? gde ye (*za*·khod)
I'm lost.
Zabloudil/ zuh·bloh·dyil/
Zabloudila jsem. (m/f) zuh·bloh·dyi·luh ysem

Dutch

Hello.	*Dag.*	dakh
Goodbye.	*Dag.*	dakh
Yes.	*Ja.*	yaa
No.	*Nee.*	ney
Please.	*Alstublieft.*	al·stew·*bleeft*
Thank you.	*Dank u.*	dangk ew
Excuse me.	*Excuseer mij.*	eks·kew·*zeyr* mey
Help!	*Help!*	help

Do you speak English?
Spreekt u Engels? spreykt ew *eng*·uhls
I don't understand.
Ik begrijp het niet. ik buh·*khreyp* huht neet
How much is this?
Hoeveel kost het? hoo·*veyl* kost huht
I'd like ..., please.
Ik wil graag ... ik wil khraakh ...
Where's (the toilet)?
Waar zijn waar zeyn
(de toiletten)? (duh twa·*le*·tuhn)
I'm lost.
Ik ben verdwaald. ik ben vuhr·*dwaalt*

French

Hello.	*Bonjour.*	bon·zhoor
Goodbye.	*Au revoir.*	o·rer·vwa
Yes.	*Oui.*	wee
No.	*Non.*	noh
Please.	*S'il vous plaît.*	seel voo play
Thank you.	*Merci.*	mair·see
Excuse me.	*Excusez-moi.*	ek·skew·zay·mwa
Help!	*Au secours!*	o skoor

Do you speak English?
Parlez-vous anglais? par·lay·voo ong·glay
I don't understand.
Je ne comprends pas. zher ner kom·pron pa
How much is this?
C'est combien? say kom·byun
I'd like ..., please.
Je voudrais ..., zher voo·dray ...
s'il vous plaît. seel voo play
Where's (the toilet)?
Où sont oo son
(les toilettes)? (lay twa·let)
I'm lost.
Je suis perdu(e). (m/f) zhe swee·pair·dew

German

Hello.	Guten Tag.	goo·ten taak
Goodbye.	Auf Wiedersehen.	owf vee·der·zey·en
Yes.	Ja.	yaa
No.	Nein.	nain
Please.	Bitte.	bi·te
Thank you.	Danke.	dang·ke
Excuse me.	Entschuldigung.	ent·shul·di·gung
Help!	Hilfe!	hil·fe

Do you speak English?
Sprechen Sie Englisch? shpre·khen zee eng·lish
I don't understand.
Ich verstehe nicht. ikh fer·shtey·e nikht
How much is this?
Was kostet das? vas kos·tet das
I'd like ..., please.
Ich hätte gern ..., bitte. ikh he·te gern ... bi·te
Where's (the toilet)?
Wo ist (die Toilette)? vaw ist (dee to·a·le·te)
I'm lost.
Ich habe mich verirrt. ikh haa·be mikh fer·irt

Icelandic

Hello.	Halló.	ha·loh
Goodbye.	Bless.	bles
Yes.	Já.	yow
No.	Nei.	nay
Thank you.	Takk./ Takk fyrir.	tak/ tak fi·rir
Excuse me.	Afsakið.	af·sa·kidh
Help!	Hjálp!	hyowlp

Do you speak English?
Talar þú ensku? ta·lar thoo ens·ku
I don't understand.
Ég skil ekki. yekh skil e·ki
How much is this?
Hvað kostar þetta? kvadh kos·tar the·ta
I'd like a/the..., please.
Get ég fengið..., takk get yekh fen·gidh..., tak
Where's (the toilet)?
Hvar er snyrtingin? kvar er snir·tin·gin
I'm lost.
Ég er villtur/villt. (m/f) yekh er vil·tur/vilt

Italian

Hello.	Buongiorno.	bwon·jor·no
Goodbye.	Arrivederci.	a·ree·ve·der·chee
Yes.	Sì.	see
No.	No.	no
Please.	Per favore.	per fa·vo·re
Thank you.	Grazie.	gra·tsye
Excuse me.	Mi scusi.	mee skoo·zee
Help!	Aiuto!	a·yoo·to

Do you speak English?
Parla inglese? par·la een·gle·ze
I don't understand.
Non capisco. non ka·pee·sko
How much is this?
Quanto costa? kwan·to ko·sta
I'd like ..., please.
Vorrei ..., per favore. vo·ray ... per fa·vo·re
Where's (the toilet)?
Dove sono (i gabinetti)? do·ve so·no (ee ga·bee·ne·ti)
I'm lost.
Mi sono perso/a. (m/f) mee so·no per·so/a

Spanish

Hello.	Hola.	o·la
Goodbye.	Adiós.	a·dyos
Yes.	Sí.	see
No.	No.	no
Please.	Por favor.	por fa·vor
Thank you.	Gracias.	gra·thyas
Excuse me.	Disculpe.	dees·kool·pe
Help!	¡Socorro!	so·ko·ro

Do you speak English?
¿Habla inglés? a·bla een·gles
I don't understand.
No entiendo. no en·tyen·do
How much is this?
¿Cuánto cuesta? kwan·to kwes·ta
I'd like ..., please.
Quisiera ..., por favor. kee·sye·ra ... por fa·vor
Where's (the toilet)?
¿Dónde están (los servicios)? don·de es·tan (los ser·vee·thyos)
I'm lost.
Estoy perdido/a. (m/f) es·toy per·dee·do/a

Index

Behind the Scenes

Acknowledgements

Climate map data adapted from Peel MC, Finlayson BL & McMahon TA (2007) 'Updated World Map of the Köppen-Geiger Climate Classification', *Hydrology and Earth System Sciences*, 11, 1633–44.

Illustrations pp190–1, pp260–1, pp278–9, pp376–7, pp504–5 by Javier Zarracina

Cover photograph: Lavender field in France, Linhking/Getty Images ©

Send Us Your Feedback

We love to hear from travellers – your comments keep us on our toes and help make our books better. Our well-travelled team reads every word on what you loved or loathed about this book. Although we cannot reply individually to postal submissions, we always guarantee that your feedback goes straight to the appropriate authors, in time for the next edition. Each person who sends us information is thanked in the next edition, the most useful submissions are rewarded with a selection of digital PDF chapters.

Visit lonelyplanet.com/contact to submit your updates and suggestions or to ask for help. Our award-winning website also features inspirational travel stories, news and discussions.

Note: We may edit, reproduce and incorporate your comments in Lonely Planet products such as guidebooks, websites and digital products, so let us know if you don't want your comments reproduced or your name acknowledged. For a copy of our privacy policy visit lonelyplanet. com/privacy.

This Book

This 2nd edition of Lonely Planet's *Best of Europe* guidebook was curated by Alexis Averbuck, Anthony Ham, Catherine Le Nevez, Andy Symington and Nicola Williams, who also researched and wrote it along with Mark Baker, Oliver Berry, Cristian Bonetto, Kerry Christiani, Belinda Dixon, Peter Dragicevich, Steve Fallon, Emilie Filou, Damian Harper, Virginia Maxwell, Christopher Pitts, Kevin Raub, Brendan Sainsbury, Andrea Schulte-Peevers and Neil Wilson. This guidebook was produced by the following:

Destination Editors Daniel Fahey, Gemma Graham, Niamh O'Brien, Tom Stainer, Anna Tyler, Brana Vladislavljevic, Clifton Wilkinson

Senior Product Editor Sandie Kestell

Regional Senior Cartographers Mark Griffiths, Anthony Phelan

Product Editor Will Allen

Book Designer Wibowo Rusli

Assisting Editors Sarah Bailey, Judith Bamber, Michelle Bennett, Nigel Chin, Katie Connolly, Joel Cotterell, Melanie Dankel, Andrea Dobbin, Victoria Harrison, Gabrielle Innes, Kellie Langdon, Lou McGregor, Kate Morgan, Rosie Nicholson, Lorna Parkes, Susan Paterson, Monique Perrin, Sarah Reid, Fionnuala Twomey, Maja Vatrić, Sam Wheeler, Simon Williamson

Assisting Cartographers Anita Banh, Mick Garrett, Corey Hutchison

Cover Researcher Naomi Parker

Thanks to Jennifer Carey, Vesna Čelebić, Fiona Flores Watson, Esme Fox, Evan Godt, Jennifer Hattam, Sandra Henriques Gajjar, Amy Lysen, Anne Mason, Emily Matarczyk, Catherine Naghten, Claire Naylor, Karyn Noble, Zora O'Neill, Genna Patterson, Joseph Q, Antonia Roberts, Kathryn Rowan, James Smart, Angela Tinson, Donna Wheeler

Symbols & Map Key

Look for these symbols to quickly identify listings:

- ◉ Sights
- ✦ Activities
- ⊖ Courses
- ⊘ Tours
- ✱ Festivals & Events
- ✷ Eating
- ◷ Drinking
- ✪ Entertainment
- ⊙ Shopping
- ❶ Information & Transport

These symbols and abbreviations give vital information for each listing:

🌿 Sustainable or green recommendation

FREE No payment required

- ☏ Telephone number
- ◷ Opening hours
- P Parking
- ⊖ Nonsmoking
- ✳ Air-conditioning
- @ Internet access
- ⊚ Wi-fi access
- ⊠ Swimming pool
- 🚌 Bus
- 🚢 Ferry
- 🚊 Tram
- 🚆 Train
- 🍴 English-language menu
- 🌱 Vegetarian selection
- 🚼 Family-friendly

Find your best experiences with these Great For... icons.

- Art & Culture
- Beaches
- Budget
- Cafe/Coffee
- Cycling
- Detour
- Drinking
- Entertainment
- Events
- Family Travel
- Food & Drink
- History
- Local Life
- Nature & Wildlife
- Photo Op
- Scenery
- Shopping
- Short Trip
- Sport
- Walking
- Winter Travel

Sights

- ◉ Beach
- ◉ Bird Sanctuary
- ◉ Buddhist
- ◉ Castle/Palace
- ◉ Christian
- ◉ Confucian
- ◉ Hindu
- ◉ Islamic
- ◉ Jain
- ◉ Jewish
- ◉ Monument
- ◉ Museum/Gallery/ Historic Building
- ◉ Ruin
- ◉ Shinto
- ◉ Sikh
- ◉ Taoist
- ◉ Winery/Vineyard
- ◉ Zoo/Wildlife Sanctuary
- ◉ Other Sight

Points of Interest

- ◎ Bodysurfing
- ◎ Camping
- ◎ Cafe
- ◎ Canoeing/Kayaking
- • Course/Tour
- ◎ Diving
- ◎ Drinking & Nightlife
- ◎ Eating
- ◎ Entertainment
- ◎ Sento Hot Baths/ Onsen
- ◎ Shopping
- ◎ Skiing
- ◎ Sleeping
- ◎ Snorkelling
- ◎ Surfing
- ◎ Swimming/Pool
- ◎ Walking
- ◎ Windsurfing
- ◎ Other Activity

Information

- $ Bank
- ◎ Embassy/Consulate
- ✚ Hospital/Medical
- ◎ Internet
- ◎ Police
- ◎ Post Office
- ◎ Telephone
- ◎ Toilet
- ❶ Tourist Information
- • Other Information

Geographic

- ◎ Beach
- ◄ Gate
- ◎ Hut/Shelter
- ◎ Lighthouse
- ◎ Lookout
- ▲ Mountain/Volcano
- ◎ Oasis
- ◎ Park
-)(Pass
- ◎ Picnic Area
- ◎ Waterfall

Transport

- ◎ Airport
- Ⓑ BART station
- ◎ Border crossing
- Ⓣ Boston T station
- ◎ Bus
- ╬◎╬ Cable car/Funicular
- ◎ Cycling
- ◎ Ferry
- Ⓜ Metro/MRT station
- ╬◎ Monorail
- P Parking
- ◎ Petrol station
- Ⓢ Subway/S-Bahn/ Skytrain station
- ◎ Taxi
- ◎ Train station/Railway
- ⌇⌇⌇ Tram
- Ⓤ Underground/ U-Bahn station
- • Other Transport

Brendan Sainsbury

Born and raised in the UK in a town that never merits a mention in any guidebook (Andover, Hampshire), Brendan spent the holidays of his youth caravanning in the English Lake District and didn't leave Blighty until he was 19. Making up for lost time, he's since squeezed 70 countries into a sometimes precarious existence as a writer and professional vagabond. In the last 11 years, he has written over 40 books for Lonely Planet. When not scribbling research notes, Brendan likes partaking in ridiculous 'endurance' races, strumming old Clash songs on the guitar, and experiencing the pain and occasional pleasures of following Southampton Football Club.

Andrea Schulte-Peevers

Born and raised in Germany and educated in London and at UCLA, Andrea has travelled the distance to the moon and back in her visits to some 75 countries. She has earned her living as a professional travel writer for over two decades and authored or contributed to nearly 100 Lonely Planet titles as well as to newspapers, magazines and websites around the world. She also works as a travel consultant, translator and editor. Andrea's destination expertise is especially strong when it comes to Germany, the UAE, Crete and the Caribbean Islands. She makes her home in Berlin.

Neil Wilson

Neil was born in Scotland and has lived there most of his life. Based in Perthshire, he has been a full-time writer since 1988, working on more than 80 guidebooks for various publishers, including the Lonely Planet guides to Scotland, England, Ireland and Prague. An outdoors enthusiast since childhood, Neil is an active hill-walker, mountain-biker, sailor, snowboarder and rock-climber, and a qualified fly-fishing guide and instructor. He has climbed and tramped in four continents, including ascents of Jebel Toubkal in Morocco, Mount Kinabalu in Borneo, the Old Man of Hoy in Scotland's Orkney Islands and the northwest face of Half Dome in California's Yosemite Valley.

Contributing Writers

Kate Armstrong, James Bainbridge, Jade Bremner, Fionn Davenport, Marc Di Duca, Duncan Garwood, Gemma Graham, Paula Hardy, Craig McLachlan, Isabella Noble, John Noble, Simon Richmond

Belinda Dixon

Only happy when her feet are suitably sandy, Belinda has been (gleefully) travelling, researching and writing for Lonely Planet since 2006. This has seen her navigating mountain passes and soaking in hot-pots in Iceland's Westfjords, marvelling at Stonehenge at sunrise, scrambling up Italian mountain paths, horse riding across Donegal's golden sands, gazing at Verona's frescoes and fossil hunting on Dorset's Jurassic Coast. Belinda is also a podcaster and adventure writer and helps lead wilderness expeditions. See her blog posts at https://belindadixon.com

Peter Dragicevich

After a successful career in niche newspaper and magazine publishing, both in his native New Zealand and in Australia, Peter finally gave into Kiwi wanderlust, giving up staff jobs to chase his diverse roots around much of Europe. Over the last decade he's written literally dozens of guidebooks for Lonely Planet on an oddly disparate collection of countries, all of which he's come to love. He once again calls Auckland, New Zealand his home – although his current nomadic existence means he's often elsewhere.

Steve Fallon

A native of Boston, Massachusetts, Steve graduated from Georgetown University with a Bachelor of Science in modern languages. After working for several years for an American daily newspaper and earning a master's degree in journalism, his fascination with the 'new' Asia led him to Hong Kong, where he lived for over a dozen years, working for a variety of media and running his own travel bookshop. Steve lived in Budapest for three years before moving to London in 1994. He has written or contributed to more than 100 Lonely Planet titles. Steve is a qualified London Blue Badge Tourist Guide. Visit his website at www.steveslondon.com.

Emilie Filou

Emilie is a freelance journalist specialising in business and development issues, with a particular interest in Africa. Born in France, Emilie is now based in London, UK, from where she makes regular trips to Africa. Her work has appeared in publications such as the Economist, the Guardian, the BBC, the Africa Report and the Christian Science Monitor. She has contributed to some 20 Lonely Planet guides, including France, Provence, London, West Africa, Madagascar and Tunisia. You can find out more at www.emiliefilou.com.

Damian Harper

Damian has been writing for Lonely Planet for over two decades, contributing to titles for destinations as diverse as China, Vietnam, Thailand, Ireland, Mallorca, Malaysia, Hong Kong and the UK. A seasoned guidebook writer, Damian has penned articles for numerous newspapers and magazines, including the Guardian and the Daily Telegraph, and currently makes Surrey, England, his home. A self-taught trumpet novice, his other hobbies include photography, taekwondo and collecting modern first editions. Follow Damian on Instagram @damian.harper.

Virginia Maxwell

Although based in Australia, Virginia spends at least half of her year updating Lonely Planet destination coverage across the globe. The Mediterranean is her major area of interest – she has covered Spain, Italy, Turkey, Syria, Lebanon, Israel, Egypt, Morocco and Tunisia – but she also covers Finland, Bali, Armenia, the Netherlands, the US and Australia. Follow her @maxwellvirginia on Instagram and Twitter.

Christopher Pitts

Born in the year of the Tiger, Chris' first expedition in life ended in failure when he tried to dig from Pennsylvania to China at the age of six. Hardened by reality but still infinitely curious about the other side of the world, he went on to study Chinese in university, living for several years in Kunming, Taiwan and Shanghai. A chance encounter in an elevator led to a Paris relocation, where he lived with his wife and two children for over a decade before the lure of Colorado's sunny skies and outdoor adventure proved too great to resist.

Kevin Raub

Atlanta native Kevin Raub started his career as a music journalist in New York, working for Men's Journal and Rolling Stone magazines. He ditched the rock 'n' roll lifestyle for travel writing and has written for over 95 Lonely Planet guides, focused mainly on Brazil, Chile, Colombia, the USA, India, the Caribbean and Portugal. Raub also contributes to a variety of travel magazines in both the USA and the UK. Along the way, the self-confessed hophead is in constant search of wildly high IBUs in local beers. Follow him on Twitter and Instagram @ RaubOnTheRoad.

Catherine Le Nevez

Catherine's wanderlust kicked in when she roadtripped across Europe from her Parisian base aged four, and she's been hitting the road at every opportunity since, travelling to some 60 countries and completing her Doctorate of Creative Arts in Writing, Masters in Professional Writing, and postgrad qualifications in Editing and Publishing along the way. Over the past decade-and-a-half she's written scores of Lonely Planet guides and articles covering Paris, France, Europe and far beyond. Her work has also appeared in numerous online and print publications. Topping Catherine's list of travel tips is to travel without any expectations.

Andy Symington

Andy has written or worked on over a hundred books and other updates for Lonely Planet (especially in Europe and Latin America) and other publishing companies, and has published articles on numerous subjects for a variety of newspapers, magazines, and websites. He part-owns and operates a rock bar, has written a novel and is currently working on several fiction and non-fiction writing projects. Andy, from Australia, moved to northern Spain many years ago. When he's not off with a backpack in some far-flung corner of the world, he can probably be found watching the tragically poor local football side or tasting local wines after a long walk in the nearby mountains.

Nicola Williams

Border-hopping is way of life for British writer, runner, foodie, art aficionado and mum-of-three Nicola Williams who has lived in a French village on the southern side of Lake Geneva for more than a decade. Nicola has authored more than 50 guidebooks on Paris, Provence, Rome, Tuscany, France, Italy and Switzerland for Lonely Planet and covers France as a destination expert for the *Telegraph*. She also writes for the *Independent*, *Guardian*, lonelyplanet.com, *Lonely Planet Magazine*, *French Magazine*, *Cool Camping France* and others. Catch her on the road on Twitter and Instagram @tripalong.

Mark Baker

Mark Baker is a freelance travel writer with a penchant for offbeat stories and forgotten places. He's originally from the United States, but now makes his home in the Czech capital, Prague. He writes mainly on eastern and central Europe for Lonely Planet as well as other leading travel publishers, but finds real satisfaction in digging up stories in places that are too remote or quirky for the guides. Prior to becoming an author, he worked as a journalist for the *Economist*, Bloomberg News and Radio Free Europe, among other organisations. Follow Mark on Instagram and Twitter @markbakerprague, and at his blog: www.markbakerprague.com.

Oliver Berry

Oliver Berry is a writer and photographer from Cornwall. He has worked for Lonely Planet for more than a decade, covering destinations from Cornwall to the Cook Islands, and has worked on more than 30 guidebooks. He is also a regular contributor to many newspapers and magazines, including *Lonely Planet Traveller*. His writing has won several awards, including The Guardian Young Travel Writer of the Year and the TNT Magazine People's

Choice Award. His latest work is published at www.oliverberry.com.

Cristian Bonetto

Cristian has contributed to over 30 Lonely Planet guides to date, including *New York City*, *Italy*, *Venice & the Veneto*, *Naples & the Amalfi Coast*, *Denmark*, *Copenhagen*, *Sweden* and *Singapore*. Lonely Planet work aside, his musings on travel, food, culture and design appear in numerous publications around the world, including the *Telegraph* (UK) and *Corriere del Mezzogiorno* (Italy). When not on the road, you'll find the reformed playwright and TV scriptwriter slurping espresso in his beloved hometown, Melbourne. Instagram: @rexcat75

Kerry Christiani

Kerry is an award-winning travel writer, photographer and Lonely Planet author, specialising in central and southern Europe. Based in Wales, she has authored and co-authored more than a dozen Lonely Planet titles. An adventure addict, she loves mountains, cold places and true wilderness. She features her latest work at https://its-a-small-world.com and tweets @kerrychristiani.

Our Story

A beat-up old car, a few dollars in the pocket and a sense of adventure. In 1972 that's all Tony and Maureen Wheeler needed for the trip of a lifetime – across Europe and Asia overland to Australia. It took several months, and at the end – broke but inspired – they sat at their kitchen table writing and stapling together their first travel guide, *Across Asia on the Cheap*. Within a week they'd sold 1500 copies. Lonely Planet was born.

Today, Lonely Planet has offices in Franklin, London, Melbourne, Oakland, Dublin, Beijing, and Delhi, with more than 600 staff and writers. We share Tony's belief that 'a great guidebook should do three things: inform, educate and amuse'.

Our Writers

Alexis Averbuck

Alexis Averbuck has travelled and lived all over the world, from Sri Lanka to Ecuador, Zanzibar and Antarctica. In recent years she's lived on the Greek island of Hydra, in the wilds of NYC, and on the California coast. For Lonely Planet she explores the cobbled lanes of Rome and the azure seas of Sardinia, samples oysters in Brittany and careens through hill-top villages in Provence; and adventures along Iceland's surreal lava fields, sparkling fjords and glacier tongues. A travel writer for over two decades, Alexis has lived in Antarctica for a year, crossed the Pacific by sailboat and written books on her journeys through Asia, Europe and the Americas. She's also a painter – visit www.alexisaverbuck.com – and promotes travel and adventure on video and television.

Anthony Ham

Anthony is a freelance writer and photographer who specialises in Spain, East and Southern Africa, the Arctic and the Middle East. When he's not writing for Lonely Planet, Anthony writes about and photographs Spain, Africa and the Middle East for newspapers and magazines in Australia, the UK and US. In 2001, after years of wandering the world, Anthony finally found his spiritual home when he fell irretrievably in love with Madrid on his first visit to the city. Less than a year later, he arrived there on a one-way ticket, with not a word of Spanish and not knowing a single person in the city. When he finally left Madrid ten years later, Anthony spoke Spanish with a Madrid accent, was married to a local and Madrid had become his second home. Now back in Australia, Anthony continues to travel the world in search of stories.

More Writers

STAY IN TOUCH LONELYPLANET.COM/CONTACT

AUSTRALIA The Malt Store, Level 3, 551 Swanston St, Carlton, Victoria 3053 ☏03 8379 8000, fax 03 8379 8111

IRELAND Digital Depot, Roe Lane (off Thomas St), Digital Hub, Dublin 8, D08 TCV4, Ireland

USA 155 Filbert St, Suite 208, Oakland, CA 94607 ☏510 250 6400, toll free 800 275 8555, fax 510 893 8572

UK 240 Blackfriars Road, London SE1 8NW ☏020 3771 5100, fax 020 3771 5101

 twitter.com/ lonelyplanet

facebook.com/ lonelyplanet

 instagram.com/ lonelyplanet

 youtube.com/ lonelyplanet

 lonelyplanet.com/ newsletter